Selected Papers on Fun & Games

CSLI Lecture Notes Number 192

Selected Papers on Fun & Games

Donald E. Knuth

CSLI Publications
Stanford, California

Copyright ©2011
Center for the Study of Language and Information
Leland Stanford Junior University
22 21 20 19 18 17 16   8 7 6 5 4

Library of Congress Cataloging-in-Publication Data

Knuth, Donald Ervin, 1938–
    Selected papers on fun and games / Donald E. Knuth.
    xvii,742 p. 23 cm. -- (CSLI lecture notes ; no. 192)
    Includes bibliographical references and index.
    ISBN 978-1-57586-585-0 (cloth : alk. paper) --
    ISBN 978-1-57586-584-3 (pbk. : alk. paper)
1. Mathematics--Miscellanea. 2. Computer science--Miscellanea.
I. Title. II. Series.
 QA99.K58 2010
    510--dc22   2010032404
                                                    CIP
    ISBN 978-1-57586-677-2 (electronic)

Internet page
    http://www-cs-faculty.stanford.edu/~knuth/fg.html
contains further information and links to related books.

to Martin Gardner (1914–2010)
who inspired most of these words

Contents

Preface

Mathematics and computer science can be both playful and serious at the same time. That's why research in those fields is so much fun. But recreational aspects are often played down, because of a popular notion that the pursuit of pleasure is somehow just a minor goal, of little importance. College professors like me are mainly expected to keep our noses to the grindstone so that we produce works of "real value."

This book takes the opposite approach. It brings together dozens of things that I've written during the past 50-plus years in which the primary focus has simply been to enjoy the ride and to develop new patterns that add to life's pleasures.

Maybe I'm just a cockeyed optimist. I do know that life is full of significant challenges, that billions of people are forced to lead a hard-scrabble existence, and that, hey, "All work and no play makes jack." But for me, the pursuit of money has always played second fiddle to the pursuit of beauty. Thank goodness for mathematics and computer science, whose methods offer many ways by which our left brains and our right brains can both be happy, simultaneously.

I'm dedicating this book to Martin Gardner, the grand master of mathematical recreations, who has inspired much of what appears inside. He gave a nice characterization of the subject matter in his book *A Gardner's Workout* [Natick, Massachusetts: A K Peters, 2001, page 192]:

> Obviously no sharp line separates entertaining math from serious math. One reason is that creative mathematicians regard their work as much a form of play as golf is to a professional golfer. In general, math is considered recreational if it has a strong aspect of play that can be appreciated by any layman interested in mathematics.

Indeed, I've never been able to see any boundary between scientific research and game-playing. Over the years, I've used many of the topics in this book as the basis for entertaining and instructive talks given to advanced high-school students or to undergraduate math clubs, and the audiences were enthusiastic about the ideas.

The topics treated here were often inspired by patterns that are visually compelling, or by paradoxical truths that are logically compelling, or by combinations of numbers and/or symbols that fit together just right. These were papers that I couldn't not write.

I believe that the creation of a great puzzle or a great pattern is a scholarly achievement of great merit, an important contribution to world culture, even though the author of such a breakthrough is often an amateur who has no academic credentials. Therefore I've devoted considerable time to tracing the history of the often unsung pioneers who have come up with significant new "mind-benders" as civilization developed, and I'm proud to follow in their footsteps.

Many years ago I wrote an essay that asked "Are toy problems useful?" [reprinted as Chapter 10 in *Selected Papers on Computer Science*] in which I discussed at some length my view that students are best served by teachers who present them with well-chosen recreational problems. And I've carried on in the same vein ever since, most recently on pages 7–9 of *The Art of Computer Programming*, Volume 4A, in a subsection entitled "Puzzles versus the real world."

Thus it's not surprising that many of the chapters in the present book have resulted from my attempts to answer puzzling questions that have no immediately obvious relation to any practical applications of mathematics or of computer science. Or that sometimes I had an urge to embellish or extend the answers to classical enigmas that had previously been resolved. And of course I've also come up with a few new puzzles in the process, several of which I don't yet know how to tackle.

In other words, I believe that diversions are useful, and I've tried in this book to provide useful diversions that meet high standards of quality. Of all the papers that I've written, the ones included here have given me the most personal pleasure — in fact, sheer joy at times! The various chapters include my earliest work as well as my latest. Many of them have an autobiographical flavor, because they're associated with some of the most memorable moments of my life.

Actually I've had great fun with these papers not only when writing them but also when revisiting them, as I was preparing this collection. Now, as I write this preface, I can't help but celebrate the fact that I've finally been able to put together the book that I've always dreamed of writing, a book that best expresses the quirky things that I enjoy. I'm quite sure that this book isn't for everybody; but if you're anything like me, you will enjoy it too, at least in part.

Chapter 1 reprints the article that has always headed my list of technical publications, in spite of the fact that it did not appear in a scientific journal. One has to start somewhere, and for me the natural starting place was *MAD* magazine. Chapter 2 presents the (much longer) original manuscript from which the *MAD* editors selected a digestible subset. And Chapter 3 is my own attempt at boiling down the details, in this case for the engineering magazine that had just been launched at my undergraduate college. These three chapters contain everything that you'll ever want to know, and more, about the Potrzebie System of Weights and Measures. Then, to round out the story, Chapter 4 presents my first *rejected* paper: *MAD* didn't want this one.

Now let's fast forward a few years. Chapter 5 is a short spoof of a formal math paper, privately circulated when my wife and I announced the birth of our son John in 1965. That served as a model for the more elaborate spoof in Chapter 6, "The complexity of songs," inspired by a road trip with 11-year-old John and his 9-year-old sister Jenny.

Chapter 7 is zany in yet a different way. Science and mathematics are fun, but so is programming; this chapter completes my earlier study of the world's first 20 programming languages by discussing the world's canonically *worst* programming language. There's hacker hilarity here, if you're ready for it; people who are sufficiently weird may enjoy decoding some of the purest ultrarefined geekology that I've ever come up with.

Recreational mathematics comes next. Chapter 8 contains two short notes about graph plotting that I wrote as an undergraduate; then Chapter 9 discusses a problem about billiard balls that launched my many years of correspondence with Martin Gardner. In Chapter 10 I explore what can happen if we start with the number 4 and repeatedly take factorials and/or square roots. Square arrays of numbers that are "magic" in almost all conceivable directions are investigated in Chapter 11. Then Chapter 12 deals with a probability paradox, related to elevators that move at random.

Fibonacci numbers, which are capable of endless surprises, now come into play. Chapter 13 uses them to define a new kind of multiplication with noteworthy properties; Chapter 14 uses them to construct a remarkable linear recurrence of integers that includes no prime numbers; and Chapter 15 uses them to define fundamental constants that satisfy no polynomial equation with integer coefficients.

Some readers who get to page 100 might ask, "Are we having fun yet?" Well, surely Fibonacci numbers are fun. But perhaps even more so are the huge, "supernatural" numbers considered in Chapter 16, which features a guessing game that is equivalent to efficient coding schemes.

Then comes a change of pace and a change of place, from my desk to my automobile: Chapters 17 and 18 are devoted to curious things that have caught my attention during a lifetime of driving, related to creativity in local folk culture. First I analyze personalized license plates, especially those that have a mathematical flavor; then I exhibit favorite specimens of the diamond-shaped warning signs that traffic engineers have erected on highways.

Another avocation, music, takes over in Chapter 19, where I present a short piece that I orchestrated for concert band when I was in high school. Fragments from a brief musical comedy skit that I composed in college appear in Chapter 20, and a pre-Christmas song that I wrote with my wife is the subject of Chapter 21. Chapter 22 discusses a remarkable algorithm due to David Kraehenbuehl that harmonizes an arbitrary melody in exponentially many ways. (I had great fun coaxing METAPOST to typeset the music in those four chapters.)

Some readers who get to page 200 might ask, "Are we having games yet?" Competitive games come to center stage in Chapter 23, which tells the story of my undergraduate adventures with college basketball: I introduced math and computing into the gymnasium, and our team actually did well! Then Chapter 24 develops a controversial theory of three-person shootouts; and Chapter 25 turns to Master Mind, a game of logic for two players or for one player against a machine. An experimental variant of chess is the subject of Chapter 26.

Then we get to a real computer game. Chapter 27, which is my all-time favorite example of a literate program, is a faithful translation into English and C of the original Adventure game by Crowther and Woods, the famous (or infamous?) time-sink that was destined to beget a huge gaming industry. If you want to have fun and improve your programming skills by reading code, this book gives you two choices, both of which happen to stem from some of the hilarious innovations devised by Don Woods in the 1970s: You can read either the illiterate program in Chapter 7 or the literate one in Chapter 27.

Word play comes next. Chapter 28 recounts my first extracurricular escapade, which took place when I was 13 years old and entered a contest to find as many words as possible that could be made from a certain collection of letters. (Was I thinking algorithmically, and taking on big projects, already in those early days?) A few years later, when learning chemistry, I composed a short story entirely from words that made sense as chemical formulas at that time (see Chapter 29). Some experiments with typesetting during the 1980s, which in fact were featured later on the cover of the book *Digital Typography*, led to the curious cryptograms in Chapter 30. And Chapter 31 is a short poem that can be read in two ways, paradoxically losing a line in the process.

Lewis Carroll's popular pastime of changing one word to another, by modifying one letter at a time (think `word-ford-form-foam-flam-flay-play`), is the topic of Chapters 32–34. Other amusing arrangements of words into rectangles, squares, and cubes are considered in Chapters 35–37.

Many of my favorite mechanical puzzles are special cases of a combinatorial challenge that's known technically as the *exact cover problem*. Chapter 38 introduces the notion of "dancing links," a simple-yet-important technique for dealing with such problems and with exhaustive searches in general. Several put-together puzzles are solved there. Appealing constraints of another kind are considered briefly in Chapter 39.

The most famous combinatorial pastime of all, with a continuous history that goes back to the 9th century, is to investigate what Martin Gardner has called "knights of the square table": In what ways can a single knight make a tour of the entire chessboard, encountering each square just once? I've naturally been unable to withstand an impulse to contribute some new ideas to the vast literature that this intriguing question has spawned. Chapters 40–43, two of which are published here for the first time, contain the results of those explorations.

Perhaps the nicest thing about knight's tours is that they often yield pretty pictures. Even more beautiful, however, and mathematically more elegant, are the "dragon curve" designs that are discussed in Chapters 44 and 45. Those chapters were published several years before Benoît Mandelbrot coined the word *fractal* to denote what is now recognized as a significant family of patterns and natural phenomena.

My wife and I have often collaborated on projects that try to tie together the æsthetics of art with the æsthetics of mathematics and computer science. Several of these projects, usually made just for ourselves or as gifts for friends, are surveyed in Chapters 46 and 47.

Chapter 48 is a brief tribute to Martin Gardner, written shortly after his recent death. Oh, how I wish I could have presented him with a copy of this book — but without such a chapter — a few months earlier! Surely his spirit lives on, here and throughout the world.

This book closes, indeed, on an upbeat note, by completing a round baker's MAD of chapters. Chapter 49 is, I think, a fitting way to conclude the sequence of publications that began with Chapter 1.

As in previous books of selected papers, I've taken the liberty here to correct errors of fact and of style that had appeared in the original publications, so that each chapter now appears in the form that I hope it will be remembered. Nearly every chapter also ends with an Addendum, which attempts to bring the material up to date with reports on subsequent developments.

Now that this book is complete, I can't help but be overwhelmed by an enormous feeling of gratitude. I'm truly at a loss for words to describe the transcendental glow that fills me at this moment. What a miracle it has been, to have been able to live my life at a time and place in which it was possible to write a book such as this!

I'm grateful for having been able to work jointly with coauthor Chandler Davis on Chapter 44. My wife, Jill, was coauthor of Chapters 21 and 45, and she contributed substantially to the material in several of the other chapters. Some of my research was supported by the National Science Foundation, the Office of Naval Research, and/or Norges Almenvitenskapelige Forskningsråd. Max Etchemendy helped to prepare the electronic form of some of the older journal articles; then I applied spit and polish and handed the text to the incredible proofreading team of Dan Eilers, Ashutosh Mehra, Mark Ward, and Udo Wermuth. I've used John Hobby's marvelous METAPOST to redraw all of the illustrations. Emma Pease facilitated many aspects of the production.

This book is the eighth and final volume of my collected papers, published by Stanford's Center for the Study of Language and Information (CSLI); I've been saving it up for "dessert." It joins *Literate Programming* (1992); *Selected Papers on Computer Science* (1996); *Digital Typography* (1999); *Selected Papers on Analysis of Algorithms* (2000); *Selected Papers on Computer Languages* (2003); *Selected Papers on Discrete Mathematics* (2003); and *Selected Papers on Design of Algorithms* (2010). The entire series was conceived, shepherded, and masterminded by Dikran Karagueuzian. We plan to issue a comprehensive index to all eight volumes in the near future.

In conclusion, let me close this preface by warmly thanking the KTG society and its fictitious leader, whose existence is sort of an enigma that can be deciphered only by carefully pondering the index at the rear of this book. Readers who are able to solve this weird puzzle will find that my eccentric muse was not at all able to resist the temptation to finish off the final preface of this eight-book series by adding some symbolic "book-ends," so that the fun and games would last longer.

Donald E. Knuth
Stanford, California
21114 C.D.

Acknowledgments

"The potrzebie system of weights and measures" originally appeared in *MAD* **1**, number 33 (June 1957), pp. 36–37. Copyright ©1957 by E.C. Publications, Inc. Reprinted by permission.

"The revolutionary potrzebie" originally appeared in *Engineering and Science Review: Case Institute of Technology* **2**, number 1 (November 1958), pp. 18–20. Copyright by the author.

"The complexity of songs" originally appeared in *SIGACT News* **9**, number 2 (Summer 1977), pp. 17–24. (New York: Association for Computing Machinery, Inc.) Copyright presently held by the author.

"Math ace: The plot thickens" originally appeared in *Engineering and Science Review: Case Institute of Technology* **3**, number 1 (November 1959), p. 45; **3**, number 4 (May 1960), p. 24. Copyright by the author.

"Billiard balls in an equilateral triangle" originally appeared in *Recreational Mathematics Magazine*, issue number 14 (January–February 1964), pp. 20–23. (Kent, Ohio: Joseph S. Madachy, publisher.) Copyright ©1964 by Recreational Mathematics Magazine. Reprinted by permission of Joseph S. Madachy.

"Representing numbers using only one 4" originally appeared in *Mathematics Magazine* **37** (1964), pp. 308–310. Copyright ©1964 by The Mathematical Association of America (Incorporated). Reprinted by permission.

"Very magic squares" originally appeared in *American Mathematical Monthly* **75** (1968), pp. 260–264. Copyright ©1968 by The Mathematical Association of America (Incorporated). Reprinted by permission.

"The Gamow–Stern elevator problem" originally appeared in *Journal of Recreational Mathematics* **2** (1969), pp. 131–137. Copyright ©1969 by Greenwood Periodicals, Inc. Reprinted by permission of Baywood Publishing Company, Inc.

"Fibonacci multiplication" originally appeared in *Applied Mathematics Letters* **1** (1988), pp. 57–60. Copyright ©1988 by Pergamon Journals Limited. Reprinted by permission of Elsevier Science.

"A Fibonacci-like sequence of composite numbers" originally appeared in *Mathematics Magazine* **63** (1990), pp. 21–25. Copyright ©1990 by The Mathematical Association of America (Incorporated). Reprinted by permission.

"Transcendental numbers based on the Fibonacci sequence" originally appeared in *The Fibonacci Quarterly* **2** (February 1964), pp. 43–44, 52. Copyright ©1964 The Fibonacci Quarterly. Reprinted by permission.

"Supernatural numbers" originally appeared in *The Mathematical Gardner*, edited by D. A. Klarner, pp. 310–325. Copyright ©1981 by Wadsworth International. Reprinted by permission of Dover Publications, Inc.

"The triel: A new solution" originally appeared in *Journal of Recreational Mathematics* **6** (1973), pp. 1–7. Copyright ©1973 by Baywood Publishing Company, Inc. Reprinted by permission.

"The computer as Master Mind" originally appeared in *Journal of Recreational Mathematics* **9** (1976), pp. 1–6. Copyright ©1976 by Baywood Publishing Company, Inc. Reprinted by permission.

"Move It Or Lose It" originally appeared in *Variant Chess* **8**, issue 60 (April 2009), p. 96. (Coulsdon, Surrey: British Chess Variants Society.) Copyright ©2009 by John Beasley and Donald E. Knuth. Reprinted by permission.

"Th_5E_4 $CH_3EmIC_2Al_2$ Ca_3P_4Er" originally appeared in *Engineering and Science Review: Case Institute of Technology* **2**, number 3 (March 1959), p. 32. Copyright by the author.

"N-ciphered texts" originally appeared in *Word Ways* **20** (1987), pp. 173–174, 191–192. Copyright ©1987 by A. Ross Eckler. Reprinted by permission.

"Disappearances" originally appeared in *The Mathematical Gardner*, edited by D. A. Klarner, p. 264. Copyright ©1981 by Wadsworth International. Reprinted by permission of Dover Publications, Inc.

"Lewis Carroll's `word–ward–ware–dare–dame–game`" originally appeared in *GAMES* **2**, issue 4 (July–August 1978), pp. 22–23. Copyright ©1978 by Games Publications, Inc. Reprinted by permission.

"Blood, sweat, and tears" originally appeared in *GAMES* **2**, issue 4 (July–August 1978), p. 49. Copyright ©1978 by Games Publications, Inc. Reprinted by permission.

"Biblical ladders" originally appeared in *The Mathemagician and Pied Puzzler*, a collection in tribute to Martin Gardner, edited by Elwyn Berlekamp and Tom Rodgers (Wellesley, Massachusetts: A K Peters, 1999), pp. 29–34. Copyright ©1999 by A K Peters, Ltd. Reprinted by permission.

"ETAOIN SHRDLU non-crashing sets" originally appeared in *Word Ways* **27** (1994), p. 138. Copyright ©1994 by A. Ross Eckler. Reprinted by permission.

"Quadrata obscura" originally appeared in *Word Ways* **42** (2009), p. 248, under the title "Latin square word puzzles," with solutions in *Word Ways* **43** (2010), p. 14. Copyright ©2009, 2010 by Jeremiah Farrell. Reprinted by permission.

"$5 \times 5 \times 5$ word cubes by computer" originally appeared in *Word Ways* **26** (1993), pp. 95–97. Copyright ©1993 by A. Ross Eckler. Reprinted by permission.

"Dancing links" originally appeared in *Millennial Perspectives in Computer Science*, proceedings of the 1999 Oxford–Microsoft Symposium in honour of Professor Sir Antony Hoare, edited by Jim Davies, Bill Roscoe, and Jim Woodcock (Houndmills, Basingstoke, Hampshire: Palgrave, 2000), pp. 187–214. Copyright ©2000 Donald E. Knuth. Reprinted by permission.

"Uncrossed knight's tours" originally appeared in *Journal of Recreational Mathematics* **2** (1969), pp. 155–157, as a letter to the editor. Copyright ©1969 by Greenwood Periodicals, Inc. Reprinted by permission of Baywood Publishing Company, Inc.

Chapter 1

The Potrzebie System of Weights and Measures

[Pictures by Wallace Wood. Originally published in MAD 1, 33 (June 1957), 36–37. Reprinted in William M. Gaines's Like, MAD, edited by Albert B. Feldstein, Signet Pocket Books S1838 (New York: New American Library, 1960), 139–145. Page 36 reprinted in Completely MAD by Maria Reidelbach (Boston, Mass.: Little, Brown, 1991), 191. "The author's first technical paper."]

When Milwaukee's Donald Knuth first presented his revolutionary system of weights and measures to the members of the Wisconsin Academy of Sciences, Arts and Letters, *they were astounded... mainly because Donald also has two heads. All kidding aside, Donald's system won first prize as the "most original presentation." So far, the system has been adopted in Tierra del Fuego, Afghanistan, and Southern Rhodesia. The U.N. is considering it for world adoption.*

The Potrzebie System

This new system of measuring, which is destined to become the measuring system of the future, has decided improvements over the other systems now in use. It is based upon measurements taken on 6-9-12 at the Physics Lab. of Milwaukee Lutheran High School, in Milwaukee, Wis., when the thickness of MAD Magazine #26 was determined to be 2.263348451743817321473 mm. This unit is the basis for the entire system, and is called one potrzebie of length.

The potrzebie has also been standardized at 3515.3516 wave lengths of the red line in the spectrum of cadmium. A partial table of the Potrzebie System, the measuring system of the future, is given below.

1

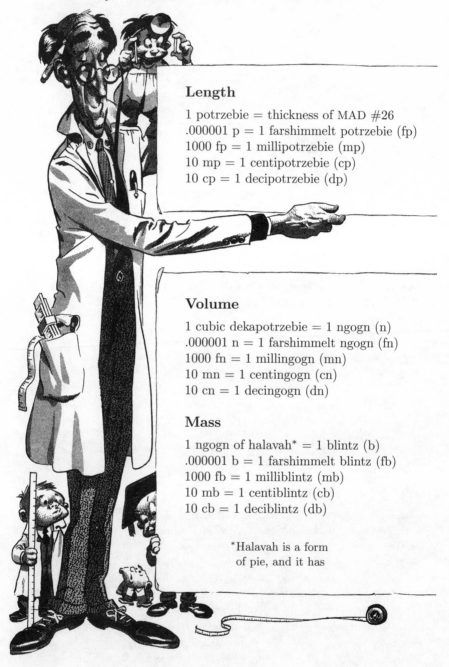

Length

1 potrzebie = thickness of MAD #26
.000001 p = 1 farshimmelt potrzebie (fp)
1000 fp = 1 millipotrzebie (mp)
10 mp = 1 centipotrzebie (cp)
10 cp = 1 decipotrzebie (dp)

Volume

1 cubic dekapotrzebie = 1 ngogn (n)
.000001 n = 1 farshimmelt ngogn (fn)
1000 fn = 1 millingogn (mn)
10 mn = 1 centingogn (cn)
10 cn = 1 decingogn (dn)

Mass

1 ngogn of halavah* = 1 blintz (b)
.000001 b = 1 farshimmelt blintz (fb)
1000 fb = 1 milliblintz (mb)
10 mb = 1 centiblintz (cb)
10 cb = 1 deciblintz (db)

*Halavah is a form
of pie, and it has

10 dp = 1 potrzebie (p)
10 p = 1 dekapotrzebie (Dp)
10 Dp = 1 hectopotrzebie (Hp)
10 Hp = 1 kilopotrzebie (Kp)
1000 Kp = 1 furshlugginer potrzebie (Fp)

10 dn = 1 ngogn (n)
10 n = 1 dekangogn (Dn)
10 Dn = 1 hectongogn (Hn)
10 Hn = 1 kilongogn (Kn)
1000 Kn = 1 furshlugginer ngogn (Fn)

10 db = 1 blintz (b)
10 b = 1 dekablintz (Db)
10 Db = 1 hectoblintz (Hb)
10 Hb = 1 kiloblintz (Kb)
1000 Kb = 1 furshlugginer blintz (Fb)

a specific gravity of 3.1416
and a specific heat of .31416.

Time

1 average rotation of the
  earth = 1 clarke (cl)
.00000001 cl = 1 wolverton (wl)
1000 wl = 1 kovac (kov)
100 kov = 1 martin (mtn)
100 mtn = 1 wood (wd)
10 wd = 1 clarke (cl)
10 cl = 1 mingo (mi)
10 mi = 1 cowznofski (cow)

Date

October 1, 1952 is the day MAD
was first published according to
the old calendar. On the new calendar, this is clarke 1 of cowznofski 1. Cowznofskis before this date
are referred to as "Before MAD
(B.M.)" and cowznofskis following
this date are referred to as "Cowznofsko Madi (C.M.)." The calendar for each cowznofski contains 10
mingos named as follows: 1. Tales
(Tal.) 2. Calculated (Cal.) 3. To
(To) 4. Drive (Dri.) 5. You (You)
6. Humor (Hum.) 7. In (In) 8. A (A)
9. Jugular (Jug.) 10. Vein (Vei.)

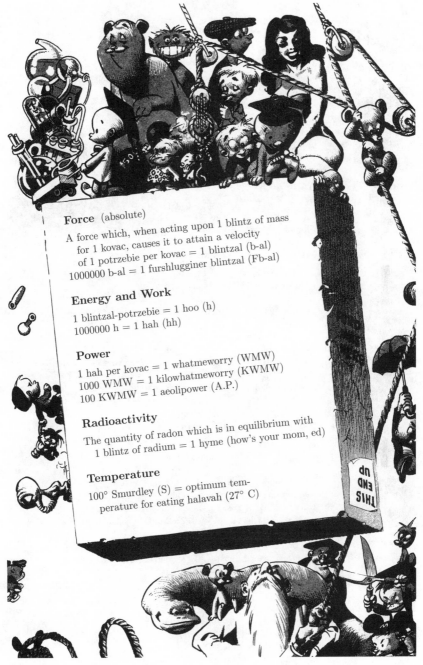

Force (absolute)

A force which, when acting upon 1 blintz of mass for 1 kovac, causes it to attain a velocity of 1 potrzebie per kovac = 1 blintzal (b-al)
1000000 b-al = 1 furshlugginer blintzal (Fb-al)

Energy and Work

1 blintzal-potrzebie = 1 hoo (h)
1000000 h = 1 hah (hh)

Power

1 hah per kovac = 1 whatmeworry (WMW)
1000 WMW = 1 kilowhatmeworry (KWMW)
100 KWMW = 1 aeolipower (A.P.)

Radioactivity

The quantity of radon which is in equilibrium with 1 blintz of radium = 1 hyme (how's your mom, ed)

Temperature

100° Smurdley (S) = optimum temperature for eating halavah (27° C)

THIS END UP

Heat Energy

The amount of heat necessary to raise 1
  blintz of halavah 1° S = 1 vreeble (v)
1000 v = 1 large vreeble (V)

Counting

48 things = 1 MAD
49 things = 1 baker's MAD

Angular Measure

100 quircits ($''''$) = 1 zorch ($'''$)
100 zorch ($'''$) = 1 zygo (§)
100 zygo (§) = 1 circle or circumference

Miscellaneous Measurements

speed of light = 114441 Fp/kov
1 light cowznofski = 1.14441×10^{12} Fp
1 vreeble = 574.8 hah
1 cosmo per square potrzebie = 3.1416 bumbles
1 faraday = 122400 blobs/blintz equivalent weight
1 electron-ech = 5.580×10^{-15} hoo
1 blintz molecular weight of a gas = 70.4 Kn
density of H_2O = .3183 blintzes per ngogn (distilled water)
1 atmosphere pressure = 1.4531 b/p^2 = 335.79 p of Hg
gravity = 3234.4 p per kov per kov
downward force of 1 b = 3234.4 b-al

Basic Conversion Factors   (abbreviated table)

1 inch = 11.222 potrzebies
1 mile = .71105 furshlugginer potrzebies
1 potrzebie = 2.2633 millimeters = .089108 inches
1 furshlugginer potrzebie = 2.2633 kilometers = 1.4064 miles
1 centimeter = 4.4182 potrzebies
1 kilometer = .44182 furshlugginer potrzebies
1 ngogn = 11.59455 cc = .012252 quarts = 2.3523 teaspoons
1 blintz = 36.42538361 grams
1 kiloblintz = 80.3042 pounds
1 furshlugginer blintz = 36.425 metric tons
1 wood = 144 minutes
1 kovac = .864 seconds
1 year = 3.6524 cowznofskis
1 watt = 3.456482 whatmeworries
1 horsepower = 2.58 kilowhatmeworries
1 aeolipower = 38.797 horsepower
1 vreeble = 34.330 calories

wood

225 LAFAYETTE STREET · NEW YORK 12, NEW YORK · CANAL 6-1994

February 18, 1957

Mr. Don Knuth
7436 W. Caldwell Ave.
Milwaukee 16, Wisc.

Dear Don,

Surprise.

Bet you thought we forgot all about you.

Actually, we held off "Potrzebie System" for two issues
pending the realignment of our talent. We then made the
changes necessary, and...

It's coming out in MAD #33.

Illustrated by Wood.

Credited to you.

So, enclosed is a check for $25.00 for the rights to
print it in MAD, with the slight changes.

Also, enclosed is a copy of No. 4, which you said you
didn't have. No.5 we don't even have!

Thanks again for letting us use your revolutionary
measuring system. We're sure its inclusion in MAD
will mean absolutely nothing to the world of science.

Al Feldstein
Editor

Addendum

When I devised this system in 1955 I had absolutely no idea what the word 'potrzebie' signified, if anything. I knew it only as a strange-looking jumble of letters that had been appearing regularly in *MAD* as a staple element of random weirdness.* Shortly afterwards, in college, I learned that it is a not-uncommon word in Polish. Friends later sent me a clipping from page 1A of *The Milwaukee Journal* dated Sunday, 19 November 1989, which began with the following banner headline:

'Nasza ziemia znów w potrzebie'
(*Our homeland is again in need*— Lech Walesa)

The *MAD* typesetters accidentally dropped out a digit from the true number of millimeters per potrzebie; they printed it incorrectly as '2.26348517438173216473'. In a letter to the editor of the *Case Tech* in 1959, I pointed out that the correct number is easily memorized:

> Just remember the poem "If by doubts you are much dismayed, this rhyme, a helping hand, was purveyed." Then, assuming you can spell "purveyed," just count the letters in each word and you get 2.2633484517438, correct to 14 places.

I'm pleased to have this opportunity to set the record straight, after more than 50 years. Readers who wonder where this fundamental constant arose should try to calculate the exact number of potrzebies in 9 inches, using the United States standard inch that was in force when I made the crucial initial measurements.†

---

* 'Potrzebie' made its debut on the letters page of *MAD* #10 (April 1954), when a reader wrote "Please tell me what in the world 'Furshlugginer' means." Editor Kurtzman replied, "It means the same as **Potrzebie**." One month later, Jack Davis included the word in his contribution to *MAD* #11; Will Elder, Bernard Krigstein, and Wallace Wood followed suit in #12. Then #13 printed letters from four different readers, asking respectively for definitions of 'furshlugginer', 'potrzebie', 'blintzes', and 'halavah'. Answer: *Perhaps it might be all explained by illustrating the usage of the words in question, such as, "Who stuffed the furshlugginer blintzes with halavah? They taste like potrzebie!"*

† Between 1893 and 1959, the famous Mendenhall rule stipulated that 1 meter equals 39.37 US inches, exactly. A simpler standard, the international inch — which is precisely 2.54 cm — was adopted in America on 1 July 1959.

Chapter 2

Official Tables of the Potrzebie System

[The notes below, dated "Jugular 2, 13" (4 April 1956), were privately distributed in mimeographed form to members of the Wisconsin Junior Academy of Science in 1956. They served as the source from which MAD editors subsequently extracted the article in the previous chapter.]

The Potrzebie System of Weights and Measures

This new system of measuring, which is destined to become the measuring system of the future, has decided improvements over the other systems now in common use. It is based upon measurements taken on 6-9-12 at the Physics Lab of Milwaukee Lutheran High School, Milwaukee, Wis., when the thickness of *MAD* Magazine #26 was determined to be 2.26334 84517 43817 32164 73780 74941 60547 91419 5114 mm. This unit is the basis for the entire system, and is called one potrzebie of length. The potrzebie has also been standardized at 3515.3516 wave lengths of the red line in the spectrum of cadmium. A complete table of the Potrzebie System is given below.

Length (see ruler at right)

    1 potrzebie = thickness of *MAD* #26
    .000001 p = 1 farshimmelt potrzebie (fp)
    1000 fp = 1 millipotrzebie (mp)
    10 mp = 1 centipotrzebie (cp)
    10 cp = 1 decipotrzebie (dp)
    10 dp = 1 potrzebie (p)
    10 p = 1 dekapotrzebie (Dp)
    10 Dp = 1 hectopotrzebie (Hp)
    10 Hp = 1 kilopotrzebie (Kp)
    1000 Kp = 1 furshlugginer potrzebie (Fp)

9

Volume

1 cubic dekapotrzebie = 1 ngogn (n)
.000001 n = 1 farshimmelt ngogn (fn)
1000 fn = 1 millingogn (mn)
10 mn = 1 centingogn (cn)
10 cn = 1 decingogn (dn)
10 dn = 1 ngogn (n)
10 n = 1 dekangogn (Dn)
10 Dn = 1 hectongogn (Hn)
10 Hn = 1 kilongogn (Kn)
1000 Kn = 1 furshlugginer ngogn (Fn)

Mass

1 ngogn of halavah* = 1 blintz (b)
.000001 b = 1 farshimmelt blintz (fb)
1000 fb = 1 milliblintz (mb)
10 mb = 1 centiblintz (cb)
10 cb = 1 deciblintz (db)
10 db = 1 blintz (b)
10 b = 1 dekablintz (Db)
10 Db = 1 hectoblintz (Hb)
10 Hb = 1 kiloblintz (Kb)
1000 Kb = 1 furshlugginer blintz (Fb)

Time

1 average rotation of the earth on its axis = 1 price (pr)
.00000001 pr = 1 wolverton (wl)
1000 wl = 1 severin (sev)
100 sev = 1 davis (dv)
100 dv = 1 wood (wd)
10 wd = 1 price (pr)
10 pr = 1 elder (el)
10 el = 1 kurtzman (k♩)

Date

October 1, 1952 is the day *MAD* was first published according to the old calendar. On the new calendar this is price 1 of kurtzman 1. Kurtzmans

---

*Halavah is a form of pie, and it has a specific gravity of 3.1416 and a specific heat of .31416.

before this date are referred to as "Before *MAD* (B.M.)" and kurtzmans after this date are referred to as "*Kurtzmano Madi* (K.M.)." The calendar for each kurtzman contains 10 elders named as follows:

1 Tales (Tal.)	6 Humor (Hum.)
2 Calculated (Cal.)	7 In (In)
3 To (To)	8 A (A)
4 Drive (Dri.)	9 Jugular (Jug.)
5 You (You)	10 Vein (Vei.)

Force (absolute)

A force which, when acting upon 1 blintz of mass for 1 severin, causes it to attain a velocity of 1 potrzebie per severin
= 1 blintzal (b-al)
1000000 b-al = 1 furshlugginer blintzal (Fb-al)

Energy and Work

1 blintzal-potrzebie = 1 hoo (h)
1000000 h = 1 hah (hh)

Power

1 hah per severin = 1 whatmeworry (WMW)
1000 WMW = 1 kilowhatmeworry (KWMW)
100 KWMW = 1 aeolipower (A.P.)

Temperature

100° Smurdley (S) = optimum temperature for eating halavah (27° C)
0° S = absolute zero

Heat Energy

The amount of heat necessary to raise one blintz of halavah 1° S
= 1 vreeble (v)
1000 v = 1 large vreeble (V)

Light Energy

The intensity in a given direction of one square potrzebie of surface of a black body radiator at the temperature of freezing platinum (about 681° S), the surface being normal to the given direction,
= 1 cosmo (cos)

The luminous flux produced in a solid angle of one steradian by
a uniform point source of one cosmo at the vertex of the angle
= 1 shermlock (shr)

The quantity of light that passes a cross section of a beam of light
in one severin when the flux is one shermlock
= 1 shermlock-severin (shr-sev)

The illumination on a surface all points of which are at a distance
of 1 kilopotrzebie from a uniform point source of one cosmo
= 1 kilopotrzebie-cosmo, or potcosmo (pc)

The average brightness of a surface emitting or reflecting light at the
rate of one shermlock per square dekapotrzebie of actual surface
= 1 bumble (bum)

(The prefixes used in mass, volume, and length units are applied to all
these units and those following to show larger or smaller quantities.)

Magnetism and Electricity

a. *Magnetic Pole Strength.*   The strength of a pole that will repel
an equal like pole at a distance of one potrzebie in a vacuum
with a force of one blintzal
= 1 klek

b. *Magnetic Field Intensity.*   The intensity of a magnetic field
at a point when a pole of one klek placed at the point is
acted upon by a force of one blintzal
= 1 hester (hes)

c. *Magnetic Flux Density.*   The flux density of a magnetic field
at a point in a vacuum when the field intensity at that
point is one hester
= 1 schvester (sch), also called 1 bentney per square potrzebie

d. *Magnetic Flux.*   The amount of magnetic flux in a square
potrzebie of area when the flux density is one schvester
= 1 bentney (ben)
10^9 bentneys = 1 kilofurshlugginer bentney (KFB)

e. *Magnetomotive Force.*   The magnetomotive force producing the
flux when one hoo of work is required to move a pole of one klek
completely around a magnetic circuit against the field intensity
= 1 gookum (gk)*

f. *Magnetic Reluctance.*   The reluctance of a magnetic path one
potrzebie in length with a cross-sectional area of one square

---

* Also measured in ganef-turns, where 1 ganef-turn = 12.566 gk.

potrzebie and the permeability of a vacuum
= 1 hex

g. *Electric Current.* The electric current that, in a wire
one potrzebie long at right angles to a magnetic field of
one schvester, is acted upon by a force of one blintzal
at right angles to the current and the flux
= 1 ganef (gan)

h. *Electric Quantity.* The quantity of electricity that passes
the cross-section of a conductor when a current of one ganef
is maintained for one severin
= 1 blob

i. *Electric Potential and Electromotive Force.* The electromotive
force induced in a coil of one turn when the flux changes
through it at the rate of one bentney per severin
= 1 farshimmelt ech (f-ech)
One ech (secondary definition) is the potential difference
between two points when one hah of work is required to
carry a charge of one blob from the first point to the second

j. *Electric Resistance.* The resistance of a conductor in which
a current of one ganef is maintained by a potential difference
of one ech
= 1 heap

k. *Electric Resistivity.* The resistivity of a material when the
resistance between the opposite faces of a cubic potrzebie
of the material is one heap
= 1 heap-potrzebie

l. *Electric Conductance.* The conductance of a conductor that
has a resistance of one heap
= 1 paeh

m. *Electric Conductivity.* The conductivity of a material that
has a resistivity of one heap-potrzebie
= 1 paeh per potrzebie

n. *Electric Inductance.* The self-inductance of a coil in which a
back electromotive force of one ech is induced when the current
in the coil changes at the rate of one ganef per severin
= 1 schmetnik (smn)

o. *Electric Capacitance.* The capacitance of a condenser that,
when charged with one blob of electricity, has a potential
difference of one furshlugginer ech between its plates
= 1 flip

p. *Electrostatic Quantity.* The quantity of electricity that will repel an equal like quantity at a distance of one potrzebie in a vacuum with a force of one blintzal
= 1 glob*

q. *Electric Kinetic Energy.* The kinetic energy of an electron that has fallen freely through a potential difference of one ech
= 1 electron-ech

Radioactivity

The quantity of radon in equilibrium with one blintz of radium
= 1 hyme (how's your mom, ed)

Angular Measure

100 quircits ($''''$) = 1 zorch ($'''$)
$100''' = 1$ zygo ($\circledcirc$)
$100^{\circledcirc} = 1$ circle or circumference

Counting

64 things = 1 MAD
65 things = 1 baker's MAD

Lens Strength

The power of a lens whose focal length is one kilopotrzebie
= 1 glarf

Miscellaneous Measurements

density of H_2O = .31831 blintzes per ngogn
1 atmosphere pressure = 1.4531 b/p^2 = 335.79 p of Hg
1 b downward force = 3234.4 b-al
gravity = 3234.42243 p per sev per sev
speed of light = 114441 Fp/sev
1 light k⚡ = 1.14441×10^{12} Fp
1 year = 3.6524 k⚡
1 faraday = 122400 blobs/blintz equivalent weight
1 blob = 1.14441×10^{11} globs
1 glob = 1.5660×10^9 electrons
1 blob = 1.792×10^{20} electrons
1 electron-ech = 5.580×10^{-15} hoo

---

* The other units of current electricity are used in electrostatics also.

Basic Conversion Factors

1 p = 2.2633 mm = .089108 in

1 Fp = 2.2633 km = 1.4064 mi

1 cm = 4.4182 p;   1 km = .44182 Fp

1 in = 11.222 p;   1 mi = .71105 Fp

1 acre = 789.9779 square Kp

1 n = 11.59455971 cc = 11.59424 ml = .012252 qt = 2.3523 teaspoons

1 b = 36.42538361 g = 1.28487 oz

1 Kb = 80.3042 lb;   1 cb = 5.6213 grains

1 Fb = 36.425 metric tons = 40.152 T

1 g = 27.453 mb;   1 lb = 12.4526 b

1 wd = 144.000 min;   1 sev = .864000 sec

1 b-al = 11.04404251 dynes

1 poundal = 1251.85 b-al

1 erg = .400055743 h;   1 joule = 4.00056 hh

1 h = 2.4996516525 erg

1 watt = 3.456481623 WMW

1 H.P. = 2.5775 KWMW

1 A.P. = 38.797 H.P.

$S = \frac{1}{3}(C + 273.15) = \frac{5}{27}(F + 459.67)$

$F = 5.4S - 459.67$; $C = 3S - 273.15$

1 v = 34.330 calories;   1 B.T.U. = 7.35 v

1 vreeble = 574.8 hah

25☉ = right angle;   1☉ = 3.6°

$1''' = 2.16' = .64$ mil; $1'''' = 1.296''$

1 radian = 15☉91'''55'''' or 15:9155

1 candle = .32535 cosmo;   1 cosmo = 3.0736 candle

1 shermlock = 3.0736 lumen

1 pc = .055742 footcandle;   1 footcandle = 17.94 pc

1 pc = .60000 lux;   1 Fpc = 60 phot

1 bumble = .60000 lambert

1 cosmo per square potrzebie = 3.1416 bum

1 klek = .75217 unit pole

1 hester = 14.683 oersteds

1 schvester = 14.683 gauss or line/cm^2

1 ben = .75217 maxwell;   1 KFB = 7.5217 webers

1 gk = 3.3233 gilberts

1 hex = 4.4182 rowlands

1 ganef = 33.23257816 amperes

1 blob = 28.71294753 coulombs

1 kiloech = 8.705660224 volts
1 kiloheap = .2619616264 ohm
1 heap-potrzebie = .000059291 ohm-cm = 356.65 ohm/mil ft
1 paeh = 3817.4 mhos
1 paeh per potrzebie = 16866 mho/cm
1 smn = .00022633 henry
1 flip = .003298193 farad
1 glob = .7521690433 statcoulomb
1 hyme = 36.425 curies
1 glarf = .44182 diopter

Date Conversion

A.D.	=	New Kurtzman's Day of K.M.
10-1-1952		1
11-5-1953		5
3-20-1955		10
8-1-1956		15
12-14-1957		20
11-9-1979		100

Official presentation of the system on 5 May 1956
(photo by Ervin Knuth)

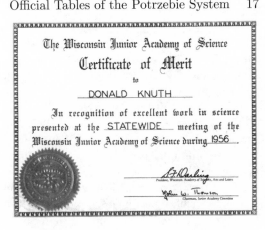

The Wisconsin Junior Academy of Science
Certificate of Merit
to
DONALD KNUTH

In recognition of excellent work in science
presented at the STATEWIDE meeting of the
Wisconsin Junior Academy of Science during 1956.

Addendum

A well-written article entitled " 'Science' Has Odd Tongues: 'Ngogns' Take Over" appeared in *The Milwaukee Journal* on Sunday, 6 May 1956, part 2, column 1 of page 15. The anonymous reporter did an exceptionally good job of explaining all of the Potrzebie System's key features, especially considering the fact that my presentation had been given late in the afternoon on the previous day. [See also John W. Thomson, Jr., "Junior Academy news," *Wisconsin Academy Review* **3** (1956), 129.]

Notice that my 1955 names for the units of time were severin (sev), davis (dv), wood (wd), price (pr), elder (el), and kurtzman (k⚢), honoring many of the major contributors to *MAD*'s early issues.* Those units later became respectively kovac (kov), martin (mtn), wood (wd), clarke (cl), mingo (mi), and cowznofski (cow), because of personnel changes at *MAD* headquarters during 1956.

Modern readers may be surprised by the distinction between milliliters and cubic centimeters in the conversion table, because international standards have changed. Between 1901 and 1964, a "liter" was defined to be the volume of one kilogram of pure water under standard atmospheric pressure, at the temperature where water becomes most dense; this meant that a liter was approximately 1000.028 cc. [See the definition of "litre" in the *Oxford English Dictionary* for several relevant quotations.]

---

* Students of the very first issues of *MAD* will wonder why I passed up the opportunity to measure temperature in "degrees Melvin" instead of degrees Smurdley. The reason is simple: I had friends named Melvin.

Thus a liter of halavah weighed exactly π kilograms in 1955, and I wish to maintain this exact relation with respect to the new standard in which one liter equals exactly 1000 cc. Accordingly, I now define the blintz in such a way that 1 cc of halavah weighs precisely π grams.

Similarly, I now define time units in such a way that 1 day equals precisely 86400 international standard seconds.

With these conventions, essentially all of the conversion factors in the basic table above can in principle be computed to arbitrary precision, using the infinitely precise value of $\theta = 2.2633\ldots$ suggested in the addendum to the previous chapter. For example, $\theta^3 = 11.59\ldots$ is the number of cc per ngogn; $\theta^3\pi = 36.425\ldots$ is the number of grams per blintz. The number of dynes per blintzal is $\chi = 10^5\theta^4\pi/864^2 = 11.044\ldots$, and there are $100/(\theta\chi) = 4.000557\ldots$ hah per joule. Electromagnetic conversion factors like $10\sqrt{\chi} = 33.23\ldots$, the number of amperes per ganef, and $\theta\sqrt{\chi}/10 = .752169\ldots$, the number of maxwells per bentney, are trickier but still doable.

I made a dozen or so rounding errors in my original computations, most notably when I took absolute zero to be Lord Kelvin's original approximation $-273°\text{C}$ instead of the standard value $-273.15°\text{C}$. More serious were my erroneous calculations of poundals, mils per quircit, and ohms per mil-foot. All of those mistakes have been corrected in the tables presented above, which should be regarded as completely definitive for the Potrzebie System except with respect to the units of counting and time, and the conventions of the new calendar. Revised definitions of the latter quantities appear in the next chapter.

Chapter 3

The Revolutionary Potrzebie

[Originally published in Engineering and Science Review, Case Institute of Technology, 2, 1 (November 1958), 18–20.]

The units for measuring mass, time, and many other quantities are basic tools of every engineer and scientist. Unfortunately, the hodgepodge of units in existence today is so inconvenient and confusing that thousands of man-woods, that is, man-hours, are wasted in converting one unit into another.

Engineers must first spend their time learning the screwball English system — where there are 12 inches to a foot, 16 ounces in a pound, and absolute zero is approximately −459.67 degrees. Then they learn the metric system, which contains different units for the same quantities already measured in the English system. They discover that the metric system has a definite advantage because it is based on powers of 10, for easy calculation; yet even in this system there are 60 minutes in an hour, 24 hours in a day, and 365.2422 days in a year. A cubic centimeter does not equal a milliliter. And in electricity the metric system is split into three separate systems, electrostatic, electromagnetic, and "MKS." In summary, they find that the whole situation is a furshlugginer mess.

How do we solve the difficulty? The Potrzebie System comes to our rescue. Once it has been adopted, the world will at last have one good, consistent, and practical system of units. (Until then, however, it just adds to the general confusion.) Great strides are being made by enterprising governments around the globe: The Potrzebie System has already been adopted in Lichtenburg; Perdido County, Texas; Tierra del Fuego; and both Northern and Southern Rhodesia. In fact, the United Nations is soon to consider it for world adoption.

Humble Beginnings

At the very beginning, let us decide to pronounce the name right: potter-zee-bee. A **potrzebie** (p) is the basic unit of length for the system; this measurement was absolutely determined on day 1158 in Milwaukee, Wisconsin, when the thickness of MAD Magazine number 26 was found to be 2.26334 84517 43817 32164 73780 74941 60547 91419 5114 mm. This length is defined to be one potrzebie (which is also standardized as 3515.3516 wave lengths of the red line in the cadmium spectrum). The total height of the page you are reading is approximately 100 p, and the right edge of the previous page contains a ruler for other measurements.

When larger units are desirable, the **dekapotrzebie** (Dp) is equal to ten potrzebies; a **hectopotrzebie** (Hp) equals 100 p; a **kilopotrzebie** (Kp), 1000 p; and a **furshlugginer potrzebie** (Fp) is 1,000,000 p. For smaller units we have the **decipotrzebie** (dp) equal to one-tenth of a potrzebie; a **centipotrzebie** (cp), which is .01 p; a **millipotrzebie** (mp) equal to .001 p; and a **farshimmelt potrzebie** (fp), .000001 p. Similar prefixes are applied to any other units of the system when larger or smaller units are desired. For very small measurements of distance, the **Neuman Unit** (Ň), equal to one millionth of a farshimmelt potrzebie, is used. The distance from Cleveland to Sandusky is about 42 furshlugginer potrzebies. In Russia, one verst equals 471.34 kilopotrzebies; in ancient Greece, one "stadium" was equal to 81.88 Kp.

Next come the units of volume. One **ngogn** (n) is defined to be a cubic dekapotrzebie. As a result, one ngogn equals .012252 quarts, 11.59455971 cc, or 11.594235 ml. In the kitchen, an ngogn is approximately 2.3523 teaspoons (and in Japanese kitchens, one koku equals 16 Kn). One bushel is 3.0393 kilongogns.

The potrzebie unit of mass is defined in terms of volume units and the theoretical substance, halavah. Halavah is a form of pie, so it has a specific gravity of approximately 3.1415927. One ngogn of halavah has, by definition, a mass of one **blintz** (b). Thus a blintz is 1.28487 ounces or 36.42538361 grams.

Let's take a breather for a minute and consider the new units of counting:

48 things = 1 **MAD**

49 things = 1 **baker's MAD**

Already we have enough units defined to see that the density of water is .31831 blintzes per ngogn, and that one atmosphere of pressure is 1.4531 blintzes per square potrzebie (or 335.79 potrzebies of mercury).

One "blintz molecular weight" of a gas is 70.4 kilongogn; Avogadro's number becomes 2.19×10^{25} molecules per blintz-mole.

Time and New Calendar

The Potrzebie System features a revolutionary new improvement in the units of time. Each day is broken into ten periods called "woods"; each **wood** (wd) contains 100 **martins** (mtn); and a hundredth of a martin is a **kovac** (kov). One wood is 144 minutes; a second is 1.1574 kovacs. The new, decimal clock is pictured at the time corresponding to 2:15 p.m.

A logical, decimal chronometer shown at .59375 o'clock.

Longer periods of time are reckoned using a new calendar. It is absurd to attempt to make the year of days coincide with the year of seasons, for the two are incommensurable. Our present calendar, for example, becomes another day out of step with the seasons every 3,323 years. For this reason, the potrzebie "year" is taken to be exactly 100 days long. No leap years, no "thirty days hath September" rhymes, no muss, no fuss; and birthdays come almost four times as often.

The potrzebie year is called a **cowznofski** (cow), and it is divided into ten 10-day periods called **mingos**. The mingos in every cowznofski are numbered from 0 to 9, and the days in each mingo are also numbered from 0 to 9 rather than from 1 to 10. In this manner, each day can be represented by a two-digit number from 00 to 99. The new calendar is illustrated on the next page with the names of each mingo. Date 00 cowznofski 0 was October 1, 1952, in the Gregorian calendar; cowznofskis preceding this date are referred to as **Before MAD** (B.M.) and those after this date are designated by the Latin phrase **Cowznofsko Dimentii** (C.D.), "in the cowznofski of MAD." December 1, 1958, is therefore Humor 2, 22 C.D. by the new calendar.

The next New Cowznofski's Day will be celebrated on January 18, 1959 when we burst into cowznofski number 23 (after a big party on New Cowznofski's Eve). Christmas is celebrated every 100 days as the date Jugular 1, since Christ was born on Jugular 1, 7144 B.M. Other holidays in the United States are Washington's Birthday (To 5, 806 B.M.); Independence Day (To 9, 644 B.M.); Columbus Day (Tales 9, 1680 B.M.); and Armistice Day (To 2, 124 B.M.).

The Cowznofski Calendar

0 : TALES

0	1	2	3	4
5	6	7	8	9

1 : CALCULATED

0	1	2	3	4
5	6	7	8	9

2 : TO

0	1	2	3	4
5	6	7	8	9

3 : DRIVE

0	1	2	3	4
5	6	7	8	9

4 : YOU

0	1	2	3	4
5	6	7	8	9

5 : HUMOR

0	1	2	3	4
5	6	7	8	9

6 : IN

0	1	2	3	4
5	6	7	8	9

7 : A

0	1	2	3	4
5	6	7	8	9

8 : JUGULAR

0	1	2	3	4
5	6	7	8	9

9 : VEIN

0	1	2	3	4
5	6	7	8	9

Since the entire scheme of time reckoning is at last completely decimal, we can specify a moment of history with a single decimal number. For example, 2271.65498 would mean "54 martins and 98 kovacs past 6 woods on day 71 of cowznofski 22" — which corresponds to 43 minutes and 10.272 seconds past 3 p.m. on December 20, 1958. The opening words of Lincoln's Gettysburg address can be rewritten as "Six MAD and thirty-one cowznofskis ago, our fathers brought forth . . . ."

The acceleration of gravity is 3234.4 potrzebies per kovac squared in the new system and the speed of light is 114,441 furshlugginer potrzebies per kovac. Astronomical distances can now be measured in **light cowznofskis**, where one light cowznofski equals 1.14441×10^{12} Fp.

Force, Work, Energy, Power

Units of force, work, and power are derived in the usual way from units of mass, length, and time: One **blintzal** is the amount of force that, when acting upon one blintz of mass for one kovac, causes it to attain a velocity of one potrzebie per kovac. A blintzal-potrzebie is one **hoo** (h), the unit of work and energy; one million hoo equals one **hah** (hh). We also define one hah of work per kovac to be one **whatmeworry** (WMW) of power. A **kilowhatmeworry** is, of course, 1000 WMW; a special unit of power, the **aeolipower** (A.P.), is equal to 100 KWMW. From these definitions we see that a blintzal is 11.04404251 dynes, a joule is 4.00055743 hah, and one aeolipower is 38.797 horsepower.

Heat energy has units of its own. The potrzebie temperature scale is an absolute scale measured in **degrees Smurdley** (° S). Zero degrees Smurdley is absolute zero; 100° S is the "optimum temperature for eating halavah" — which comes to exactly 26.85 degrees Centigrade. From this definition we obtain the fact that temperature in degrees Smurdley is the Centigrade temperature plus 273.15 divided by three. Thus, water freezes at 91.05° S and boils at 124.38° S, and the "normal" human temperature, 98.6° F, is 103.4° S. Heat energy then is measured in Potrzebie Thermal Units (P.T.U.) or **vreebles** (v), where a vreeble is the amount of heat that raises the temperature of one blintz of halavah by one degree Smurdley. Halavah is known to have a specific heat of .31415927 independent of its temperature. Diet-watchers no longer have to count calories; they can count vreebles instead: One large calorie is 29.13 vreebles, and one B.T.U. is 7.35 v. For the mechanical equivalent of heat we find that one vreeble equals 574.8 hah.

The new unit of light intensity is the **cosmo**, named after the brilliant Cosmo McMoon. One cosmo is the intensity of a square potrzebie of surface of a black body radiator at the temperature of freezing platinum (681° S), in a direction normal to the surface. An **axolotl** is the illumination on a surface that is one kilopotrzebie away from a point source of one cosmo. (One cosmo equals 3.0736 candles; one footcandle is 17.94 axolotl; one axolotl is .60 lux.) One **glarf** is the focal power of a lens that has a focal length of one kilopotrzebie (namely .44182 diopters).

Magnetism and Electricity Get Theirs

Yes, there are new units of electricity also. Unfortunately the definitions of these units are even more tedious than the ones that have already been given; non-electrical engineers may do well to skip this section completely! Here are the gory details; we start with magnetism: A theoretical magnetic pole of one **klek** will repel an equal like pole, which is one potrzebie away in a vacuum, with a force of one blintzal. The **bentney** is the magnetic flux in a square potrzebie of area when the flux density is such as to cause a one klek pole to be acted upon by one blintzal of force. Now we get to electric current: A current of one **ganef** is the current that is acted upon by a force of one blintzal per potrzebie of wire length when normal to a magnetic field of one bentney per square potrzebie. The quantity of charge that passes through a conductor when a current of one ganef is maintained for one kovac is a **blob**. One **ech** is the potential difference between two points when one hah of work is required to carry a charge of one blob from the first point to the second. With these definitions in hand, we stop to observe a byproduct of our choices of definitions so far: The electromotive force induced in a coil of one turn when the flux changes through it at the rate of bentney per kovac is one farshimmelt ech. (Proof of this is left to the reader.)

Resistance is calculated in "heaps," where one **heap** is the resistance of a conductor when a ganef of current is maintained by a potential of one ech. Conductance is therefore measured in **paeh**s. The self-inductance of a unit coil, in which a back electromotive force of one ech is induced when the current in the coil changes at the rate of one ganef per kovac, is one **schmetnik**. The capacitance of a unit condenser, which has a potential difference of one furshlugginer ech between its plates when charged with one blob of electricity, is one **flip**. Finally we have the **glob** for static electricity: The force between two globs of charge, when they are one potrzebie apart in a vacuum, is one blintzal.

As a consequence of these definitions we find the following conversion factors:

$$
\begin{aligned}
1 \text{ bentney} &= .7521690433 \text{ maxwells} \\
1 \text{ ganef} &= 33.23257816 \text{ amperes} \\
1 \text{ blob} &= 28.71294753 \text{ coulombs} \\
1 \text{ kiloech} &= 8.705660224 \text{ volts} \\
1 \text{ kiloheap} &= .2619616264 \text{ ohm} \\
1 \text{ heap-potrzebie} &= 356.65 \text{ ohms per mil foot} \\
1 \text{ paeh} &= 3817.352999 \text{ mhos} \\
1 \text{ schmetnik} &= .0002263348 \text{ henry} \\
1 \text{ flip} &= .0032981930 \text{ farad} \\
1 \text{ glob} &= .7521690433 \text{ statcoulomb} \\
1 \text{ blob} &= 1.14441 \times 10^{11} \text{ globs} \\
1 \text{ electron-ech} &= 5.580 \times 10^{-15} \text{ hoo} \\
\text{Faraday's constant} &= 122{,}400 \text{ blobs per blintz-equivalent-weight}
\end{aligned}
$$

More Still

Many more units, of the obscure variety, round out the Potrzebie System so that actually all existing units are wiped out. They are too numerous to be catalogued here, but examples are the **furd** (unit of viscosity), the **egr** (ech-ganef-reactance, to replace the "var"), and the **hyme** ("how's your mom, ed" — the unit of radioactivity).

As soon as our computer has figured out Planck's constant in the new units, the system will be finished. Meanwhile we suggest that everyone either throw away all of the old textbooks in sight, or write new units in place of the old wherever they appear, in preparation for future years when the Potrzebie System will make all the present measures obsolete. All kidding aside, I am sure that the reader will find it very instructive to actually take all of the data from a given problem and convert it into potrzebie units, work the problem in the new system, and then transfer the answer back into the original units again.

Addendum

My original article contained a few instances of incorrect rounding; as in the previous chapters, they have been silently corrected here. I also was slow to appreciate the full beauty of 0-origin indexing at the time I wrote this exposition, because I still had a residual blind spot: I referred to October 1, 1952 as "date 00 cowznofski 1" instead of 00 cowznofski 0. Thus all of my newfangled dates were off by one.

I didn't learn until later that Chinese people had long ago divided each day into 100 equal parts called *ke* (刻), before being influenced by European missionaries. Nor was I aware that the 18th-century French revolutionaries had used a decimal clock, with each day divided into ten equal *heures*, each of which was divided into 100 *minutes décimales*, each of which was divided into 100 *secondes décimales* — a failed experiment that ran from 22 September 1794 to 7 April 1795. (Incidentally, decimal clocks of that era said '10' at the top, not '0'.)

The need for a cowznofski calendar has been mitigated by what astronomers call "Julian date," which is obtained by adding 2434286.5 to the cowznofski time. For example, 2271.65498 C.D. is JD 2436558.15498. (Note that the UNIX epoch began at 6301.00000 C.D.; hence I propose the celebration of a hacker holiday every 100 days on "Tales 1.")

In addition to adopting *MAD*'s new names for the units of time, this article introduced the "axolotl" for what was previously called a potcosmo. It also cited "furd" and "egr" units, whose definitions I have totally forgotten.

Many of the basic potrzebie units have been acceptable for some time to the Google Calculator as well as to Wolfram|Alpha™, so it is natural to wonder how many other software systems will adopt them in the future. Although my own system, TEX, does not accommodate potrzebies directly, an excellent approximation (good to within .09 nanometers) is obtainable in TEX documents by saying, for example,

```
\newdimen\pz \pz=2.2633484517438mm
```

and then giving commands like '`\vskip 2\pz`'. (Indeed, I did precisely that, just now.)

Chapter 4

A MAD Crossword

[The puzzle on the following two pages was submitted to MAD magazine on 28 April 1960 and promptly returned by their Ideas Editor. "The author's first rejected paper."]

Notes by the author, July 2009: Flushed with success after my first contribution to *MAD*-had appeared in print, near the end of my freshman year at Case Institute of Technology, I advertised my publication record in campaign posters when I ran for a position in the student senate.

And of course I lost miserably.

My friends tried to cheer me up. They said, "C'mon, Don, hey, write an article that we can understand."

I didn't get another inspiration, however, until a couple years later, when I noticed that Alfred E. Neuman's teeth looked rather like part of a crossword puzzle. "Yes, that's it," I thought: "If I add a bunch of white and black squares in Alfred's hair, and maybe some more in place of his nose, I could design just the sort of puzzle that *MAD* needs to round out its contents."

Indeed, crossword puzzles were one of the few things that *MAD* had not yet subjected to its special brand of satire. Will Elder had prepared a great spoof on other kinds of puzzles in issue number 19 (January 1955), with rebuses, mazes, and visual riddles like connect-the-dots, matching, or "What's wrong with this picture?" A nice take-off on multiple-choice questionnaires had also appeared in Jack Davis's "Pictoquiz" at the end of issue 24 (July 1955). But a real crossword puzzle? Not yet.

Thus it happened that I decided to devote part of spring break, during my senior year, to the design of a Neuman-based crossword puzzle.

Well, it turned out that my ideas didn't find favor on Lafayette Street in New York; not this time. The editors, displaying possibly uncharacteristic wisdom, declined my submission, and my potential career as a writer of humor in a jugular vein was nipped in the bud.

But now, after 50 years of writing and with the opportunity to select whatever I want for publication, I get the last laugh ...

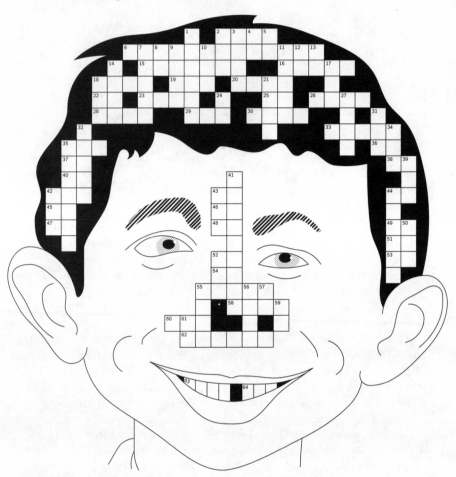

Across

2 Name of kid pictured
6 This puzzle is a _____ mess
15 Larval salamander
16 Bootlegger-shaped country
18 Opposite of "not over"
19 Human limb
20 MAD pencil and paper game
22 Radioactive material
23 Sailors' booze
25 Ionium

26 Educational Comics (abbr.)
28 Munny
29 _____ и дружба (тост)
30 Roe ate a new pie
33 Comedian (singular)
35 Ammonia
36 Alcoholics Anonymous
37 Chemical element 31
38 Beginning of the English
   alphabet

40 Opposite of "to" (Russian)
42 Second sound of man being strangled
43 XXX
44 Maverick film studio
45 Opposite of "out"
46 Pronoun
47 No good
48 Conjunction
49 Blood factor

Down

1 Old physiological humor
2 Author of puzzle
3 Ugly
4 Foreign car weighing many milligrams
5 Nickel
7 First sound of man being strangled
8 Prescription
9 Unaided performance
10 Power of 10; or, record book
11 Former California senator
12 Past of "eat"
13 Egyptian god of crossword puzzles
14 Meaningless expression
17 Pound (abbr.)
18 Marvin _____, inventor of the wheel
21 Buckeye state
24 Opposite of opposite of "across"
27 Typical Maddict

51 48 across backwards
52 "What, _____ worry?"
53 Half a yoyo
54 Beginning of Greek alphabet
55 Auf Wiedersehen
58 Repeated cry
60 Anterior omentum
62 Mr. Z' Beard
63 Pull out a gun
64 Most important person

31 American Automobile Association
32 "_____ me worry?"
34 Civil Aeronautics Authority
35 Sound of ecstasy
39 Ray's sidekick
41 "Być w _____" (Polish, to suffer want)
42 What opponent says when playing gin
43 Train to Yuma (see MAD #41)
44 "What, me _____ "
50 _____ Hah
52 Name of this magazine (no fair looking at cover)
55 Unisymmetrical poly-saccharide
56 Repeated cry
57 Word used when searching for better word
59 Oxygen
61 To finish

Solution

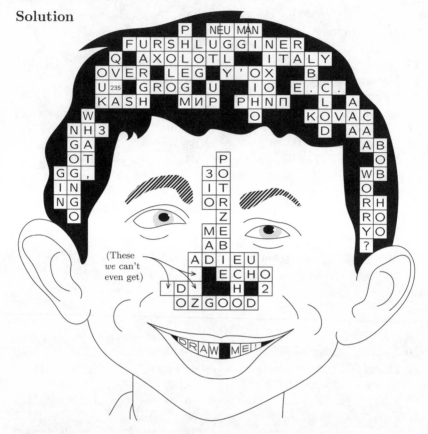

(These *we* can't even get)

References

[1] W. S. Appleton, "Veritas," in the seal of Harvard University (1885).

[2] Jack Davis, "Hoohah!" *MAD* **1**, 1 (October 1952), 1–8.

[3] Will Elder, "Are you *ever* lovely to love?" *MAD* **1**, 24 (July 1955), 5.

[4] Bob Elliott and Ray Goulding, "House to house," *MAD* **1**, 35 (October 1957), 36–38.

[5] A. B. Feldstein, "MAD rejection slip," *MAD* **1**, 38 (March 1958), 5.

[6] Marginal Marvin, "MAD Y'OX," *MAD* **1**, 54 (April 1960), 2, 3, 4, 5, 6, 8, 9, 12, 13, 14, 16, 17, 19, 21, 22, 23, 25, 26, 27, 28, 29, 40, 41, 42, 48.

[7] Roger Price, *In One Head and Out the Other* (New York: Simon and Schuster, 1951), 12–17.

[8] George Woodbridge (illustrator), "Go west, old format; go east, old western," *MAD* **1**, 41 (September 1958), 16–19.

Chapter 5

Counterexample to a Statement of Peano

[A research announcement that was privately circulated in 1965.]

In 1896, G. Peano [1] claimed that

$$1 + 1 = 2. \tag{1}$$

However, consider the following result:

Theorem. *Under special circumstances,*

$$1 + 1 = 3. \tag{2}$$

Proof. Consider the appearance of John Martin Knuth, who exhibits the following characteristics:

Weight	8 lb. 10 oz.	(3912.23419125 grams)	(3)
Height	21.5 inches	(0.5461 meters)	(4)
Voice	loud	(60 decibels)	(5)
Hair	dark brown	(Munsell 5.0Y2.0/11.8)	(6)

Q.E.D. ☐

Remarks

Peano's error, Eq. (1), has been repeated in the Principia Mathematica [2] and possibly elsewhere. It is not known to what extent the theorem above will cause the foundations of mathematics to crumble.

It is conjectured that the stronger result

$$1 + 1 = 4 \tag{7}$$

may also be true. Further research on this problem is contemplated, and results will be reported in a future paper.

Acknowledgments

I wish to thank my wife Jill, who worked continuously on this project for nine months. We also thank Dr. James Caillouette, who helped to deliver the final result.

This research was not supported by the National Science Foundation.

References

[1] Giuseppe Peano, *Formulario Mathematico* (Rome: Edizioni cremonese, 1960), 29; Df 2 and prop. 3.3.

[2] Alfred North Whitehead and Bertrand Russell, *Principia Mathematica* **2** (Cambridge University Press, 1910), 83; prop. 110.643.

CALIFORNIA INSTITUTE OF TECHNOLOGY
PASADENA, CALIFORNIA

Received July 21, 1965

Chapter 6

The Complexity of Songs

*[Originally published in SIGACT News **9**, 2 (Summer 1977), 17–24.]*

Every day brings new evidence that the concepts of computer science are applicable to areas of life that have little or nothing to do with computers. The purpose of this survey paper is to demonstrate that important aspects of *popular songs* are best understood in terms of modern complexity theory.

It is known [3] that almost all songs of length n require a text of length $\sim n$. But this puts a considerable space requirement on one's memory, if many songs are to be learned; hence our ancient ancestors invented the concept of a refrain [14]. When the song has a refrain, its space complexity can be reduced to cn, where $c < 1$, as shown by the following lemma:

Lemma 1. *Let S be a song of length n containing m verses of length V and a refrain of length R, where the refrain is to be sung first, last, and between adjacent verses. Then the space complexity of S is*

$$\frac{V}{V+R}n + O(1)$$

for fixed V and R as $m \to \infty$.

Proof. The length of S when sung is

$$n = R + (V+R)m, \tag{1}$$

while its space complexity is

$$c = R + Vm. \tag{2}$$

By the Distributive Law and the Commutative Law [4] we have

$$\begin{aligned}
c &= n - (V+R)m + mV \\
&= n - Vm - Rm + Vm \\
&= n - Rm.
\end{aligned} \tag{3}$$

33

The lemma follows.   □

(It is possible to generalize this lemma to the case of verses of differing lengths $V_1, V_2, \ldots, V_m$, provided that the sequence $\langle V_k \rangle$ satisfies a certain smoothness condition. Details will appear in a future paper.)

A significant improvement on Lemma 1 was discovered in medieval European Jewish communities, where an anonymous composer was able to reduce the complexity to $O(\sqrt{n})$. His song, "Eḥad Mi Yode'a" or "Who Knows One?", is still traditionally sung near the end of the Passover ritual, reportedly in order to keep the children awake [6]. It consists of a refrain and thirteen verses $v_1, \ldots, v_{13}$, where v_k is followed by $v_{k-1} \ldots v_2 v_1$ before the refrain is repeated; hence m verses of text lead to $m^2/2 + O(m)$ verses of singing. A similar song called "Green Grow the Rushes O" or "The Dilly Song" is often sung in western Britain at Easter time, but it has only ten verses; see [1]. Breton, Flemish, German, Greek, Medieval Latin, Moravian, and Scottish versions are known.

The coefficient of $\sqrt{n}$ was improved further by a Scottish farmer named O. MacDonald, whose construction* appears in Lemma 2.

Lemma 2. *Given positive integers α and λ, there exists a song whose complexity is $(20 + \lambda + \alpha)\sqrt{n/(30 + 2\lambda)} + O(1)$.*

Proof. Consider the following schema [9]:

$V_0 = $ 'Old MacDonald had a farm, ' R_1

$R_1 = $ 'Ee-igh, '² 'oh! '

$R_2(x) = V_0$ 'And on this farm he had some ' x ', ' R_1 'With a '

$U_1(x, x') = x$ ', ' x' ' here and a ' x ', ' x' ' there; '

$U_2(x, x') = x$ 'here a ' x' ', '

$U_3(x, x') = U_1(x, x')\, U_2(\epsilon, x)\, U_2(\text{'t'}, x')\, U_2(\text{'everyw'}, x\text{ ', '}x')$

$$V_k = U_3(W_k, W_k')\, V_{k-1} \quad \text{for } k \geq 1 \tag{4}$$

where

$$W_1 = \text{'chick'}, \quad W_2 = \text{'quack'}, \quad W_3 = \text{'gobble'},$$
$$W_4 = \text{'oink'}, \quad W_5 = \text{'moo'}, \quad W_6 = \text{'hee'}, \tag{5}$$

and

$$W_k' = W_k \quad \text{for } k \neq 6; \qquad W_6' = \text{'haw'}. \tag{6}$$

---

* Actually MacDonald's priority has been disputed by some scholars; Peter Kennedy [8, p. 676] claims that "I Bought Myself a Cock" and similar farmyard songs are actually much older.

The song of order m is defined by

$$\mathcal{S}_0 = \epsilon,$$
$$\mathcal{S}_m = R_2(W_m'') \, V_m \, \mathcal{S}_{m-1} \qquad \text{for } m \geq 1, \tag{7}$$

where

$$W_1'' = \text{'chicks'}, \ W_2'' = \text{'ducks'}, \ W_3'' = \text{'turkeys'},$$
$$W_4'' = \text{'pigs'}, \ W_5'' = \text{'cows'}, \ W_6'' = \text{'donkeys'}. \tag{8}$$

The length of $\mathcal{S}_m$ is

$$n = 30m^2 + 180m + 4\big(ml_1 + (m{-}1)l_2 + \cdots + l_m\big) + (a_1 + \cdots + a_m) \tag{9}$$

while the length of the corresponding schema is

$$c = 20m + 211 + (l_1 + \cdots + l_m) + (a_1 + \cdots + a_m). \tag{10}$$

Here $l_k = |W_k| + |W_k'|$ and $a_k = |W_k''|$, where $|x|$ denotes the length of string x. The result follows at once, if we assume that $l_k = \lambda$ and $a_k = \alpha$ for all large k. $\quad\square$

Note that the coefficient $(20 + \lambda + \alpha)/\sqrt{30 + 2\lambda}$ assumes its minimum value at

$$\lambda = \max(1, \alpha - 10) \tag{11}$$

when α is fixed. Therefore if MacDonald's farm animals ultimately have long names they should make slightly shorter noises.

Similar results were achieved by a French Canadian ornithologist, who named his song schema "Alouette" [2, 15], and at about the same time by a Tyrolean butcher whose schema [5] is popularly called "Ist das nicht ein Schnitzelbank?". Several other cumulative songs have been collected by Peter Kennedy [8], including "The Mallard" with seventeen verses and "The Barley Mow" with eighteen. More recent compositions, like "There's a Hole in the Bottom of the Sea" and "I Know an Old Lady Who Swallowed a Fly," unfortunately have comparatively large coefficients.

A fundamental improvement was claimed in England in 1824, when the true love of U. Jack gave to him a total of 12 ladies dancing, 22 lords a-leaping, 30 drummers drumming, 36 pipers piping, 40 maids a-milking, 42 swans a-swimming, 42 geese a-laying, 40 golden rings, 36 collie birds, 30 french hens, 22 turtle doves, and 12 partridges in pear trees during the twelve days of Christmas [11, 12, 13]. This amounted to $m^3/6 + m^2/2 + m/3$ gifts in m days, when summed, so the complexity appeared to be $O(\sqrt[3]{n})$; however, another researcher soon pointed out [10] that his computation was based on n *gifts* rather than on n units of singing. The correct complexity of order $\sqrt{n/\log n}$ was finally established (see [7]).

Thus the partridge in the pear tree gave an improvement of only $1/\sqrt{\log n}$; but the importance of this discovery should not be underestimated, since it showed that the $n^{.5}$ barrier could be broken. The next big breakthrough was in fact obtained by generalizing the partridge schema in a remarkably simple way. It was J. W. Blatz of Milwaukee, Wisconsin, who first discovered a class of songs known as "m Bottles of Beer on the Wall"; her elegant construction* appears in the following proof of the first major result in the theory.

Theorem 1. *There exist songs of complexity $O(\log n)$.*

Proof.   Consider the schema

$$V_k = T_k \; B \; W \; ',\,'$$
$$T_k \; B \; ';\,'$$
$$\text{'If one of those bottles should happen to fall, '}$$
$$T_{k-1} \; B \; W'.\,' \tag{12}$$

where

$$B = \text{' bottles of beer'},$$
$$W = \text{' on the wall'}, \tag{13}$$

and where T_k is a translation of the integer k into English. Only $O(m)$ space is required to define T_k for all $k < 10^m$, since we can let

$$T_{q\cdot 10^m + r} \;=\; T_q \text{ ' times 10 to the ' } T_m \text{ ' plus ' } T_r \tag{14}$$

for $1 \le q \le 9$ and $0 \le r < 10^{m-1}$.

Therefore the songs S_k defined by

$$S_0 = \epsilon, \qquad S_k = V_k \, S_{k-1} \quad \text{for } k \ge 1 \tag{15}$$

have length $n \asymp k \log k$, but the schema that defines them has length $O(\log k)$; the result follows.   □

---

* Again Kennedy [8] claims priority for the English, in this case because of the song "I'll drink m if you'll drink $m+1$." However, the English start at $m = 1$ and get no higher than $m = 9$, possibly because they actually drink the beer instead of allowing the bottles to fall.

Theorem 1 was the best result known until recently,* perhaps because it satisfied all practical requirements for song generation with limited memory space. In fact, 99 bottles of beer usually seemed to be more than sufficient in most cases.

However, the advent of modern drugs has led to demands for still less memory, and the ultimate improvement of Theorem 1 has consequently just been announced:

Theorem 2. *There exist arbitrarily long songs of complexity $O(1)$.*

Proof (due to KC and the Sunshine Band).   Consider the songs S_k defined by (15), but with

$$V_k = \text{'That's the way, '} U \text{ '(I like it), '} U$$
$$U = \text{'uh huh, '}^2 \tag{16}$$

for all k.   □

It remains an open problem to study the complexity of nondeterministic songs.

Acknowledgment

I wish to thank J. M. Knuth and J. S. Knuth for suggesting the topic of this paper, on a trip to Pinnacles National Monument in October 1976.

The research reported here was supported in part by the National Institute of Wealth under grant $262,144.

References

[1] S. Baring-Gould, H. Fleetwood Sheppard, and F. W. Bussell, edited by Cecil J. Sharp, *Songs of the West: Folk Songs of Devon & Cornwall* (London: Methuen, 1905), 160–161.

[2] Oscar Brand, *Singing Holidays: The Calendar in Folk Song* (New York: Alfred Knopf, 1957), 68–69.

[3] Gregory J. Chaitin, "On the length of programs for computing finite binary sequences: Statistical considerations," *Journal of the Association for Computing Machinery* **16** (1969), 145–159.

[4] G. Chrystal, *Algebra, an Elementary Textbook for the Higher Classes of Secondary Schools and for Colleges* (Edinburgh: Adam and Charles Black, 1886), Chapter 1.

---

* The chief rival for this honor was "This old man, he played m, he played knick-knack ...".

[5] Anton Dörrer, *Tiroler Fasnacht innerhalb der alpenländischen Win-
ter- und Vorfrühlingsbräuche* (Vienna: Österreichischer Bundes-
verlag für Unterricht, Wissenschaft und Kunst, 1949), 480 pages.

[6] *Encyclopædia Judaica* **6** (New York: Macmillan, 1971), 503; *The
Jewish Encyclopedia* (New York: Funk and Wagnalls, 1903), articles
on Eḥad Mi Yode'a.

[7] U. Jack, "Logarithmic growth of verses," *Acta Perdix* **15** (1826),
1–65535.

[8] Peter Kennedy, editor, *Folksongs of Britain and Ireland* (New York:
Schirmer, 1975), 824 pages.

[9] Norman Lloyd, *The New Golden Song Book* (New York: Golden
Press, 1955), 20–21.

[10] N. Picker, "Once señores brincando al mismo tiempo," *Acta Perdix*
12 (1825), 1009.

[11] ben shahn, *a partridge in a pear tree* (new york: the museum of
modern art, 1949), 28 pages (unnumbered).

[12] Cecil J. Sharp, editor, *One Hundred English Folksongs* (Boston:
Oliver Ditson, 1916), xlii, 224–225 (song number 96).

[13] Christopher J. Shaw, "That old favorite, *Apiapt* / a Christmastime
algorithm," with illustrations by Gene Holtan, *Datamation* **10,** 12
(December 1964), 48–49. Reprinted in *Faith, Hope and Parity*,
edited by Jack Moshman (Washington, D.C.: Thompson, 1966),
37, 48–51.

[14] Gustav Thurau, *Beiträge zur Geschichte und Charakteristik des
Refrains in der französischen Chanson* (Weimar: Felber, 1899),
47 pages.

[15] Marcel Vigneras, editor, *Chansons de France* (Boston: D. C. Heath,
1941), 52 pages.

Addendum

I wrote this paper for the April 1977 issue of *SIGACT News*, not knowing that no such issue would exist; the editor had meanwhile decided
that the successor to the January–March 1977 issue should be dated
"Summer 1977" in order to correspond better with the time when people actually received their copies. My original goal was finally achieved
when the paper was reprinted in the April 1984 issue of ACM's *Communications*. [More formally, the reference is: Donald E. Knuth, "The

complexity of songs," *Communications of the ACM* **27** (April 1984), 344–346; errata (June 1984), 593.]

Guy Steele Jr. wrote me in June 1977 to mention tradeoffs between time complexity and space complexity. He observed that successive verses of Jacques Brel's song *Carousel* are sung with increasing tempo. "This latter property is of importance to songwriters: While refrains increase the efficiency of writing the song, the nonconstant tempo decreases it, given that royalties on recordings are based on song-minutes (with some per-song quantization) under both the old and new copyright laws."

Guy later published "The TELNET song ('Control-Uparrow Q')," *Communications of the ACM* **27** (April 1984), 347–348, a brilliant composition whose complexity is $O(\log \log n)$.

Extensions of the theory have also been developed by Charles Crowley, "A finite state machine for western swing," SIGPLAN *Notices* **16**, 4 (April 1981), 33–35; and by Kurt Eisemann, "Further results on the complexity of songs," *Communications of the ACM* **28** (1985), 235.

Chapter 7

TPK in INTERCAL

[Based on an unpublished manuscript written in 2003.]

Sooner or later every "real" programmer discovers INTERCAL, the mind-boggling Compiler Language With No Pronounceable Acronym [7]. The successful completion of a nontrivial INTERCAL program is, to a programmer, a thrill that's rather like the successful ascent of Mount Everest is to a climber.

On the other hand, one should be aware of the formidable dangers that lurk therein, because INTERCAL is full of "twisted technical yuks and an inexorable descent into brain-sucking obsession ... for ... übergeeks .... Expressions that look like line noise. Control constructs that will make you gasp, make you laugh, and possibly make you hurl. ... INTERCAL. Designed very early one May morning in 1972 by two hackers who are still trying to live it down." [4]

Luis Trabb Pardo and I once wrote a paper [3] in which we discussed the details of about two dozen programming languages that were developed before 1958. We introduced a simple procedure called the "TPK algorithm," and gave the flavor of each language by expressing TPK in each particular style. Since then, TPK has been programmed for just about every other language [6] — except one. The purpose of this note is to remove that much-needed gap from the computer-language literature.

The TPK algorithm inputs eleven numbers a_0, a_1, ..., a_{10}; then it outputs a sequence of eleven pairs $(10, b_{10})$, $(9, b_9)$, ..., $(0, b_0)$, where

$$b_i = \begin{cases} f(a_i), & \text{if } f(a_i) \leq 400; \\ 999, & \text{if } f(a_i) > 400; \end{cases} \qquad f(x) = \sqrt{|x|} + 5x^3.$$

This simple task is obviously not much of a challenge, in any decent computer language. But Don Woods and Jimbo Lyon intended INTERCAL to have nothing at all in common with any of the languages they'd ever seen before; so they left out little things like addition, multiplication,

41

conditional statements, loops, etc. "INTERCAL's main advantage over other programming languages is its strict simplicity. It has few capabilities, and thus there are few restrictions to be kept in mind. Since it is an exceedingly easy language to learn, one might expect it would be a good language for initiating novice programmers. Perhaps surprising, then, is the fact that it would be more likely to initiate a novice into a search for another line of work." [7]

Although INTERCAL has no intrinsic arithmetic operations, it does perform input and output, which it calls "writing in" and "reading out." And it does work with sequences of 0s and 1s that might be regarded as numbers, so we may as well say that its bit strings are numbers. But it has only two ways to combine two numbers, namely *mingling* and *selecting*. If $x = (\ldots x_2 x_1 x_0)_2$ and $y = (\ldots y_2 y_1 y_0)_2$ are bit strings that represent binary numbers, they can be mingled to form

$$x \mathbin{\cancel{c}} y \;=\; (\ldots x_2 y_2 x_1 y_1 x_0 y_0)_2.$$

(Nowadays this operation is more commonly called a "perfect shuffle" or the "zipper function," $x \mathbin{\ddagger} y$; see Eq. 7.1.3–(76) in [1].) The selection operation $x \sim y$ is more difficult to describe via formulas, but it too is intuitively simple: If exactly s of the bits of y are equal to 1, namely bits y_{j_i} for $s > i \geq 0$ where $j_{s-1} > \cdots > j_1 > j_0$, then

$$x \sim y \;=\; (x_{j_{s-1}} \ldots x_{j_1} x_{j_0})_2.$$

Of course $x \sim 0 = 0$. Notice that $y \sim y = 2^s - 1$.

All numbers in INTERCAL are either short (16 bits) or long (32 bits), and they're always nonnegative. Thus short numbers are always integers that are less than 65536; long numbers are always integers that are less than 4294967296. INTERCAL allows you to specify any short number directly, by providing 65536 constants written respectively as #0, #1, ..., #65535. It also allows you to use up to 65535 short variables, called respectively .1, .2, ..., .65535, which can take on any short number as a value; similarly it permits up to 65535 long variables, called :1, :2, ..., :65535. There are 65535 short array variables (,1 through ,65535) and 65535 long array variables (;1 through ;65535) too. Lotsa variables.

We're ready now to look at a short (and very trivial) example of INTERCAL code. Line *01* of the program excerpt in Table 1 says that ,16080 is an array with 15 elements. The remaining lines set the last seven of those elements respectively to $(0, 6, 41, 136, 322, 999, 999, 999)$. Notice that each statement in Table 1 begins either with PLEASE, DO, or PLEASE DO. These three possibilities are interchangeable, except that the

TABLE 1. Initializing part of a small array of short numbers

```
01        PLEASE DO ,16080 <- #15
02        DO ,16080 SUB #8 <- #0
03        DO ,16080 SUB #9 <- #6
04        DO ,16080 SUB #10 <- #41
05        PLEASE ,16080 SUB #11 <- #136
06        DO ,16080 SUB #12 <- #322
07        DO ,16080 SUB #13 <- #999
08        PLEASE DO ,16080 SUB #14 <- ,16080 SUB #13
09        DO ,16080 SUB #15 <- #29 ¢ #27
```

ratio of polite statements must be between 1/5 and 1/3 in any program
that has more than two statements.*

Besides the binary operators $x \notin y$ and $x \sim y$, INTERCAL has
three *unary* operators that transform one number into another, namely
and (&), *or* (V), and *xor* (∀). When applied to a number x, a unary
operator yields the result that's obtained by first (i) rotating x cyclically one place to the right, yielding y, then (ii) applying the specified bitwise operation to x and y. For example, suppose x equals
2009, namely $(\ldots 011111011001)_2$. Then the *and* operation will yield
$(\ldots 001111001000)_2$. The *xor* operation will yield $(1000010000110101)_2$
if x is short, but $(10000000000000000000010000110101)_2$ if x is long.

Let's look now at some algebraic expressions that use several operations at once. Subexpressions that are to be evaluated first are grouped
by enclosing them within a pair of either single quotes or double quotes:

TABLE 2. One way to use the short numbers installed by Table 1

```
10        PLEASE DO :2 <- :1~'#65534¢#65532'
11        DO .1 <- ':2~:2'~#1
12        DO .1 <- !1¢.1'¢#4
13        DO READ OUT ,16080 SUB '"V':1~#7'¢.V1"~#85'
```

Suppose variable :1 contains the value x. Statement *10* sets :2 to $\lfloor x/8 \rfloor$,
by shifting x right three places, because '#65534¢#65532' is the 32-bit constant $(1 \ldots 11000)_2$. The statement in line *11* then sets .1 to 0 if :2 is
zero, otherwise to 1; in other words, it sets .1 to 1 if and only if $x \geq 8$.
Statement *12* uses ! as a convenient abbreviation for the two symbols '.
(which would otherwise make the expression look more complex); you
can check that .1 is now 16 if $x < 8$, 26 otherwise. Finally, the pile of
hair following SUB in line *13* illustrates the fact that the unary operator
symbols of INTERCAL are always placed one character to the right of

---

* Please do remember that Don Woods wrote Adventure (Chapter 27) in 1977.

where their operands actually begin: The value of .V1 is the *or* of .1 (which of course is either 24 or 31); and the other V computes the *or* of the stuff in double quotes, namely ':1¯#7'¢.V1. (Similarly, #&11 equals #1, etc.) Thus it turns out that the subscript evaluates to $x + 8$ if $x < 8$, while it evaluates to 15 whenever $x \geq 8$.

Line *13* therefore outputs the respective values 0, 6, 41, 136, 322, 999, 999, ..., if x is respectively equal to 0, 1, 2, 3, 4, 5, 6, 7, ...

Wow! What a coincidence! Those are exactly the values b_i that the TPK algorithm is supposed to output, when $a_i = x$!

Indeed, the TPK algorithm is a no-brainer on a machine that deals only with nonnegative integers, because b_i can take at most six different values. I should have realized that fact when discussing Böhm's compiler of 1951 in [3], rather than laboriously writing a subroutine to calculate square roots that would never contribute to the program output.

But hmmm: I really want to illustrate INTERCAL, most of whose features have yet to be mentioned. In the words of Randy Bachman and Ronald Reagan, "You ain't seen nothin' yet." Let us therefore change the problem and work with fixed-point, *scaled* numbers, represented as integers within an INTERCAL program: Let's assume that the values a_i and b_i are nonnegative real numbers with at most six digits to the right of the decimal point. In other words, we'll suppose that $10^6 a_i$ and $10^6 b_i$ are nonnegative integers. The revised problem will give us a chance to stop, think, learn, and smile.

I don't have space enough here to provide a full INTERCAL tutorial. Instead, I'm exhibiting the complete TPK program in Table 3, which extends over the next several pages; and I shall explain its general principles in the remainder of these notes.

All of INTERCAL's idiosyncrasies are detailed in the reference manual [7], which is available online. If you truly are one of my soul-mates, programmingwise — which you probably are, if you've read this far — I believe you'll enjoy unlocking the manifold mysteries of this puzzling code, by consulting [7] whenever the program uses a feature that's not fully explained in the hints that follow Table 3.

TABLE 3. My favorite illiterate program

```
001          PLEASE ABSTAIN FROM (29733)
002  (29733) DON KNUTH'S IMPLEMENTATION OF TPK IN INTERCAL
003                  (C) MARCH 2003, NOVEMBER 2010
004          REFERENCE --- THE EARLY HISTORY OF PROGRAMMING
005          LANGUAGES, BY D E KNUTH AND L TRABB PARDO
006
```

```
007          NOTA BENE: THE INPUT AND OUTPUT DATA ARE SCALED
008          DECIMAL NUMBERS WITH SIX DIGITS TO THE RIGHT OF
009          THE DECIMAL POINT; THUS AN INPUT OF
010              THREE ONE FOUR ONE FIVE NINE THREE
011          DENOTES 3.141593, AND THAT VALUE WOULD BE OUTPUT AS
012
013              ------
             MMMCXLMDXCIII
014
015          PLEASE NOTICE THAT VARIABLE NAMES AND SUBROUTINE NAMES USE
016          THE 5-BIT TELEPRINTER CODE IN LETTER-SHIFT MODE, NAMELY
017    / E @ A : S I U 1/4 D R J N F C K T Z L W H Y P Q O B G " M X V $
018          (WHICH ALAN TURING ADVISED EVERY PROGRAMMER TO LEARN)
019
020          PLEASE (6534) NEXT
021          DO ;29 <- #2
022          DO ;3 <- #11 BY #2
023          PLEASE DO .6 <- #0
024          DO (1) NEXT
025   (1)    PLEASE DO FORGET #1
026          DO WRITE IN :1
027          DO (22919) NEXT
028          PLEASE .1 <- .6
029          PLEASE DO (1020) NEXT
030          DO .11 <- .1
031          DO ;3 SUB .11 #1 <- ;1 SUB #1
032          DO ;3 SUB .11 #2 <- ;1 SUB #2
033          DO .1 <- #10
034          DO (29904) NEXT
035          DO (1) NEXT
036          DO REINSTATE NEXTING
037          PLEASE DO (2) NEXT
038   (2)    DO FORGET #1
039          DO .984 <- #0
040          PLEASE .1 <- .6
041          PLEASE DO (1020) NEXT
042          DO .11 <- .1
043          DO ;29 SUB #1 <- ;3 SUB .11 #1
044          DO ;29 SUB #2 <- ;3 SUB .11 #2
045          PLEASE DO (13) NEXT
046          DO (15478) NEXT
047          DO (15320) NEXT
048          DO :2 <- #6528¢#32544
049          PLEASE DO (23438) NEXT
050          DO :1 <- #31640¢#20792
051          DO REMEMBER :1
052          DO READ OUT .6 + :1
053          DO .1 <- #0
054          DO ABSTAIN FROM (711)
055          PLEASE DO (29904) NEXT
```

```
056        DO (2) NEXT
057        DO GIVE UP
058
059        PLEASE USE THE FOLLOWING FUNCTION, WHICH SETS ;1 <- F(;X)
060        WHERE ;29 AND ;1 ARE EXTENDED FIXED-POINT NUMBERS
061        (THAT IS, THEY ARE VECTORS WITH TWO COMPONENTS,
062            #1=INTEGER PART, #2=FRACTION PART)
063  (13)  DO STASH ;2
064        DO ;1 SUB #1 <- ;29 SUB #1
065        DO ;1 SUB #2 <- ;29 SUB #2
066        PLEASE STASH ;1
067        PLEASE DO ;2 SUB #1 <- ;29 SUB #1
068        DO ;2 SUB #2 <- ;29 SUB #2
069        DO (30300) NEXT
070        DO (30300) NEXT
071        DO ;2 SUB #1 <- #5
072        DO ;2 SUB #2 <- #0
073        PLEASE DO (30300) NEXT
074        PLEASE DO ;2 SUB #1 <- ;1 SUB #1
075        DO ;2 SUB #2 <- ;1 SUB #2
076        PLEASE RETRIEVE ;1
077        DO (30499) NEXT
078        PLEASE DO (30218) NEXT
079        DO (29987) NEXT
080        DO RETRIEVE ;2
081        PLEASE RESUME #1
082
083        DO NOTHING BUT BASIC SUBROUTINES FROM HERE ON
084        --------------
085        FIRST THERE ARE ROUTINES FOR EXTENDED ARITHMETIC
086        (DOUBLE-DOUBLE PRECISION), WHICH CONSISTS OF
087        TWO 32-BIT NUMBERS WITH A BINARY POINT BETWEEN THEM
088
089        TO GET STARTED, DO (INI) FIRST; IT DEFINES BASIC ARRAYS
090  (6534) DO ;1 <- #3
091        DO ;2 <- #2
092        PLEASE RESUME #1
093
094        DON'T FORGET TO TEST FOR OVERFLOW AFTER A SERIES OF
095        EXTENDED ARITHMETIC OPERATIONS:
096        THE (OVC) ROUTINE SETS :1 TO THE MAX VALUE IF .OV IS 1
097        ... SO YOU'D BETTER SET .OV TO 0 PERIODICALLY
098 (15320) PLEASE DO (2000) NEXT
099        DO :1 <- #65535¢#65535
100        PLEASE RESUME #1
101  (2000) PLEASE DO (2001) NEXT
102        PLEASE RESUME #2
103  (2001) DO RESUME '∀.984¢#1'~#3
104
```

```
105          DOING (ADY) NEXT SETS ;1 <- ;1+;2+.C~2 AND .C <- CARRY+1
106          DOING (ADZ) NEXT SETS ;1 <- ;1+;2 AND .C <- CARRY+1
107  (17699) PLEASE .14 <- #1
108  (21795) DO STASH :1 + :2 + :3 + :4
109          DO :1 <- ;1 SUB #2
110          PLEASE DO :2 <- .14~#2
111          PLEASE DO (1509) NEXT
112          DO .14 <- :4~#2
113          DO :1 <- :3
114          PLEASE DO :2 <- ;2 SUB #2
115          DO (1509) NEXT
116          DO ;1 SUB #2 <- :3
117          DO :1 <- ;1 SUB #1
118          DO :2 <- "V.14¢':4~#2'"~#1
119          DO (1509) NEXT
120          DO .14 <- :4
121          DO :1 <- :3
122          DO :2 <- ;2 SUB #1
123          DO (1509) NEXT
124          DO ;1 SUB #1 <- :3
125          DO .14 <- 'V:4¢.14'~#6
126          PLEASE RETRIEVE :1 + :2 + :3 + :4
127          PLEASE RESUME #1
128
129          DOING (ADX) NEXT SETS ;1 <- ;1+;2 AND TRACKS OVERFLOW
130          DOING (ABX) NEXT SETS ;1 <- ABS(;1)
131  (29987) PLEASE STASH .14
132          DO (17699) NEXT
133          DO .984 <- "V.984¢!14~#2'"~#1
134          PLEASE RETRIEVE .14
135  (30499) DO RESUME #1
136
137          DOING (SUX) NEXT SETS ;1 <- ;1-;2 AND TRACKS OVERFLOW
138  (29925) PLEASE STASH ;2 + .14
139          DO ;2 SUB #1 <- '"V'";2 SUB #1"~"#65535¢#0"'¢#65535"~"#0¢#65535"'¢
140                        '"V'";2 SUB #1"~"#0¢#65535"'¢#65535"~"#0¢#65535"'
141          DO ;2 SUB #2 <- '"V'";2 SUB #2"~"#65535¢#0"'¢#65535"~"#0¢#65535"'¢
142                        '"V'";2 SUB #2"~"#0¢#65535"'¢#65535"~"#0¢#65535"'
143          DO .14 <- #2
144          DO (21795) NEXT
145          PLEASE DO .984 <- "V.984¢!14~#1'"~#1
146          PLEASE RETRIEVE ;2 + .14
147          DO RESUME #1
148
149          DOING (SHY) NEXT SETS ;2 <- :3 * 2^16 AND CLOBBERS :3
150  (22149) DO ;2 SUB #1 <- :3 ~ '#65280¢#65280'
151          DO :3 <- '"':3~#43690'¢#0"~"#65535¢#1"' ¢
152               '"':3~#21845'¢#0"~"#65535¢#1"'
153          PLEASE :3 <- ":3~'#511¢#1'" ¢ ":3~'#1¢#511'"
```

```
154           PLEASE :3 <- ":3~'#1023¢#3'" ¢ ":3~'#3¢#1023'"
155           DO ;2 SUB #2 <- ":3~'#4095¢#15'" ¢ ":3~'#15¢#4095'"
156           PLEASE RESUME #1
157
158           DOING (MLY) NEXT SETS ;1 <- :1 * :2 / 2^32
159  (22108) PLEASE STASH :1 + :2 + :3 + ;2 + .14
160           DO :1 <- :1 ~ #65535
161           DO :2 <- :2 ~ #65535
162           DO (1540) NEXT
163           DO ;1 SUB #2 <- :3
164           DO ;1 SUB #1 <- #0
165           PLEASE RETRIEVE :1
166           PLEASE STASH :1
167           DO :1 <- :1 ~ '#65280¢#65280'
168           DO (1540) NEXT
169           DO (22149) NEXT
170           DO (17699) NEXT
171           PLEASE RETRIEVE :1 + :2
172           PLEASE STASH :1 + :2
173           DO :1 <- :1 ~ #65535
174           DO :2 <- :2 ~ '#65280¢#65280'
175           DO (1540) NEXT
176           DO (22149) NEXT
177           DO (17699) NEXT
178           PLEASE RETRIEVE :1
179           PLEASE STASH :1
180           DO :1 <- :1 ~ '#65280¢#65280'
181           DO (1540) NEXT
182           DO ;2 SUB #2 <- #0
183           DO ;2 SUB #1 <- :3
184           DO (17699) NEXT
185           PLEASE RETRIEVE :1 + :2 + :3 + ;2 + .14
186           PLEASE RESUME #1
187
188           DOING (MLZ) NEXT SETS ;1 <- ;1 + (:1 * :2 / 2^32), TRACKING OVERFLOW
189  (18012) PLEASE STASH ;1 + ;2
190           DO (22108) NEXT
191           PLEASE ;2 SUB #1 <- ;1 SUB #1
192           PLEASE ;2 SUB #2 <- ;1 SUB #2
193           PLEASE RETRIEVE ;1
194           DO (29987) NEXT
195           PLEASE RETRIEVE ;2
196           PLEASE RESUME #1
197
198           DOING (MLX) NEXT SETS ;1 <- ;1*;2 AND TRACKS OVERFLOW
199  (30300) PLEASE STASH :1 + :2 + :3 + :4 + ;1 + ;2
200           DO :1 <- ;1 SUB #2
201           DO :2 <- ;2 SUB #2
202           DO (22108) NEXT
```

```
203          DO :1 <- ;1 SUB #1
204          DO :2 <- ';1 SUB #2' ~ '#32768¢#0'
205          DO (1500) NEXT
206          PLEASE RETRIEVE ;1
207          DO :4 <- ;1 SUB #2
208          DO :1 <- ;1 SUB #1
209          DO :2 <- ;2 SUB #1
210          DO (22108) NEXT
211          PLEASE DO .984 <- "V.984¢' "';1 SUB #1'~';1 SUB #1'" ~#1'" ~ #1
212          DO ;1 SUB #1 <- ;1 SUB #2
213          DO ;1 SUB #2 <- :3
214          DO :2 <- ;2 SUB #2
215          DO (18012) NEXT
216          DO :1 <- :4
217          DO :2 <- ;2 SUB #1
218          DO (18012) NEXT
219          PLEASE RETRIEVE :1 + :2 + :3 + :4 + ;2
220          PLEASE RESUME #1
221
222          DOING (RTX) NEXT SETS ;1 <- SQRT(;1)
223 (30218) PLEASE STASH .6 + ;2 + ;3 + ;4 + :1 + :2 + .1 + .2 + .3 + .14 + .984
224          DO ;4 <- #2
225          DO ;3 <- #2
226          DO .6 <- #1
227          DO ;3 SUB #1 <- #0
228          DO ;3 SUB #2 <- #0
229          DO ;4 SUB #1 <- #65535¢#65535
230          DO ;4 SUB #2 <- ;4 SUB #1
231          DO :1 <- ;1 SUB #1
232          DO :2 <- ;1 SUB #2
233          PLEASE (2003) NEXT
234 (2002)  DO ;2 SUB #1 <- ;1 SUB #1
235          DO ;2 SUB #2 <- ;1 SUB #2
236          DO (17699) NEXT
237          DO ;2 SUB #1 <- ;1 SUB #1
238          DO ;2 SUB #2 <- ;1 SUB #2
239          DO (17699) NEXT
240          PLEASE DO ;2 SUB #1 <- #0
241          PLEASE DO ;2 SUB #2 <- .2
242          DO (17699) NEXT
243          PLEASE DO ;2 SUB #2 <- .3
244          DO (29925) NEXT
245          PLEASE DO ;3 SUB #1 <- ;1 SUB #1
246          PLEASE DO ;3 SUB #2 <- ;1 SUB #2
247          PLEASE DO ;1 SUB #1 <- ;4 SUB #1
248          PLEASE DO ;1 SUB #2 <- ;4 SUB #2
249          DO ;2 SUB #1 <- ;1 SUB #1
250          DO ;2 SUB #2 <- ;1 SUB #2
251          DO (17699) NEXT
```

```
252          DO ;2 SUB #1 <- #0
253          PLEASE DO ;2 SUB #2 <- "∀#1¢.3"~#1
254          DO (17699) NEXT
255          PLEASE DO ;4 SUB #1 <- ;1 SUB #1
256          PLEASE DO ;4 SUB #2 <- ;1 SUB #2
257          DO .1 <- ":1 ~ '#21845¢#0'" ¢
258              '"∀':1~"#10922¢#1"' ¢ '"∀':1~#1'¢':2~"#32768¢#0"'"~#1'" ~#21845'
259          DO .2 <- ":1 ~ '#0¢#21845'" ¢
260              '"∀':1~"#0¢#10923"' ¢ '"∀':1~#1'¢':2~"#0¢#32768"'"~#1'" ~#21845'
261          DO :1 <- .1 ¢ .2
262          DO .1 <- ":2 ~ '#21845¢#0'" ¢
263              '"&':2~"#10922¢#1"' ¢ #65534" ~ #21845'
264          DO .2 <- ":2 ~ '#0¢#21845'" ¢
265              '"&':2~"#0¢#10923"' ¢ #65534" ~ #21845'
266          DO :2 <- .1 ¢ .2
267 (2003)   DO .2 <- :1 ~ '#32768¢#32768'
268          DO ;1 SUB #1 <- ;3 SUB #1
269          DO ;1 SUB #2 <- ;3 SUB #2
270          DO ;2 SUB #1 <- ;4 SUB #1
271          DO ;2 SUB #2 <- ;4 SUB #2
272          DO .14 <- #2
273          DO (21795) NEXT
274          DO .3 <- ' " '"';1 SUB #1'~';1 SUB #1'"~#1' ¢
275                      '"';1 SUB #2'~';1 SUB #2'"~#1' " ¢ .2' ~ #15
276          DO .3 <- '&"!3~.3'~#1" ¢ .14' ~ #2
277          PLEASE DO (2004) NEXT
278          DO ;1 SUB #1 <- ;3 SUB #1
279          DO ;1 SUB #2 <- ;3 SUB #2
280          DO (2005) NEXT
281 (2004)   DO (2006) NEXT
282 (2005)   PLEASE FORGET #1
283          PLEASE DO .1 <- #49
284          DO (29904) NEXT
285          DO (2002) NEXT
286          PLEASE REINSTATE NEXTING
287          DO ;2 SUB #1 <- ;4 SUB #1
288          DO ;2 SUB #2 <- ;4 SUB #2
289          DO ;1 SUB #1 <- #0
290          DO ;1 SUB #2 <- #0
291          DO (29925) NEXT
292          DO ;2 SUB #1 <- #0
293          DO ;2 SUB #2 <- "∀.3¢#1"~#1
294          DO (29925) NEXT
295          PLEASE RETRIEVE .6 + ;2 + ;3 + ;4 + :1 + :2 + .1 + .2 + .3 + .14 + .984
296          PLEASE RESUME #50
297 (2006)   PLEASE RESUME "∀.3¢#2"~#3
298
299          DOING (UNP) NEXT SETS ;1 <- :1 / 1000000
300          (WHICH IS ESSENTIALLY DECIMAL TO BINARY CONVERSION)
```

```
301  (22919) PLEASE STASH :1 + :2 + :3 + :4 + .3
302          DO :2 <- #784 ¢ #904
303          PLEASE DO (1550) NEXT
304          PLEASE DO ;1 SUB #1 <- :3
305          DO :1 <- :3
306          DO (1540) NEXT
307          DO RETRIEVE :1
308          PLEASE STASH :1
309          DO :2 <- :3
310          PLEASE DO (1510) NEXT
311          PLEASE DO :4 <- #32768 ¢ #0
312          DO ;2 SUB #1 <- #0
313          DO ;2 SUB #2 <- #0
314          DO :1 <- :3
315          PLEASE DO (2008) NEXT
316  (2007)  DON'T RESUME #1
317          DO :1 <- ;1 SUB #2
318          DO .3 <- :4~#1
319          DO (2009) NEXT
320          DO :4 <- :4~'#65535¢#65534'
321  (2008)  DO :2 <- :1
322          PLEASE DO (1500) NEXT
323          DO :1 <- :3
324          DO ;1 SUB #2 <- :3
325          DO :2 <- #48576
326          PLEASE DO (1500) NEXT
327          DO .3 <- :3~'#0¢#1024'
328          DO ;1 SUB '"∀.3¢#2"~#6' <- ':3~'#65535¢#0"' ¢
329              '"&'":3~'#0¢#65535'"¢#64511'" ~ "#0¢#65535"'
330          DO :2 <- ;2 SUB '"∀.3¢#1"~#3'
331          DO :2 <- "'V":2~'#65535¢#0'"¢":4~'#65535¢#0'"' ~ '#0¢#65535'" ¢
332              "'V":2~'#0¢#65535'"¢":4~'#0¢#65535'"' ~ '#0¢#65535'"
333          PLEASE DO ;2 SUB '"∀.3¢#1"~#3' <- :2
334          PLEASE DO (2007) NEXT
335          DO ;1 SUB #2 <- ;2 SUB #2
336          PLEASE ABSTAIN FROM (2007)
337          PLEASE RETRIEVE :1 + :2 + :3 + :4 + .3
338          PLEASE RESUME #34
339  (2009)  PLEASE DO (2006) NEXT
340          DO REINSTATE (2007)
341          PLEASE FORGET #2
342          DO (2008) NEXT
343
344          DOING (PAK) NEXT SETS :1 <- 1000000 * ;1, TRACKING OVERFLOW
345          (WHICH IS ESSENTIALLY BINARY TO DECIMAL CONVERSION)
346  (15478) PLEASE STASH ;1 + ;2 + :2 + :3 + :4
347          DO ;2 SUB #1 <- #784 ¢ #904
348          DO ;2 SUB #2 <- #0
349          DO (30300) NEXT
```

```
350        DO :1 <- ;1 SUB #1
351        DO :2 <- ';1 SUB #2' ~ '#32768¢#0'
352        DO (1509) NEXT
353        DO .984 <- "V.984¢':4~#2'"~#1
354        PLEASE RETRIEVE ;1 + ;2 + :2 + :3 + :4
355        PLEASE RESUME #1
356
357        DON'T STOP READING YET: TWO IMPORTANT UTILITY ROUTINES REMAIN
358
359        ---------- UTILITIES -----------------------------------
360
361        DOING (CMP) NEXT IMMOBILIZES :1 IF :1 < :2
362        HERE I USE A SLICK TRICK FROM THE ORIGINAL INTERCAL DIVISION ROUTINE
363 (23438) PLEASE STASH .3 + :1
364        DO :1 <- ' "∀ ':1~"#65535¢#0"' ¢ ':2~"#65535¢#0"' " ~ "#0¢#65535"' ¢
365            ' "∀ ':1~"#0¢#65535"' ¢ ':2~"#0¢#65535"' " ~ "#0¢#65535"'
366        DO .3 <- ':2~:1' ~
367         " ' "∀ '"∀:1~:1"~"#65535¢#0"' ¢ #32768"~"#0¢#65535" ' ¢
368            '"∀:1~:1"~"#0¢#65535"' "
369        PLEASE RETRIEVE :1
370        DO (2010) NEXT
371        DO (2011) NEXT
372 (2010) DO (2006) NEXT
373        PLEASE IGNORE :1
374 (2011) DO RETRIEVE .3
375        DO RESUME #2
376
377        DOING (TIX) NEXT IS INTENDED TO SIMPLIFY LOOPS ON THE VARIABLE .I
378        IF .I = .1, NEXTING IS TURNED OFF
379        OTHERWISE .I IS INCREASED BY +1 OR -1, WHERE THE
380        INCREMENT IS -1 IF (UP) HAS JUST BEEN ABSTAINED FROM
381 (29904) PLEASE STASH .1 + .2 + .3 + .4
382        DO .3 <- "'"∀.6¢.1"~#21845' ~ '"∀.6¢.1"~#21845'" ~ #1
383        DO (2012) NEXT
384        PLEASE ABSTAIN FROM NEXTING
385        PLEASE RETRIEVE .1 + .2 + .3 + .4
386        PLEASE RESUME #1
387 (2012) DO (2006) NEXT
388        DO .1 <- .6
389 (711)  DO (2013) NEXT
390        PLEASE REINSTATE (711)
391        DO .2 <- #1
392        DO (1010) NEXT
393        DO .6 <- .3
394        DO (2014) NEXT
395 (2013) DO (1020) NEXT
396        DO .6 <- .1
397 (2014) PLEASE RETRIEVE .1 + .2 + .3 + .4
398        DO RESUME #3
```

399
400   PLEASE NOTIFY THE AUTHOR IF YOU'VE BEEN ABLE TO
401   UNDERSTAND ALL OF THIS; BUT PLEASE DON'T SEND EMAIL
402
403   FINAL PUZZLE: WHAT IS SO INTERESTING ABOUT 885205232?

Hints For Understanding Table 3

Let's pretend that we're the computer that performs this program. Line *001* tells us to "abstain from" line *002*, the statement whose label is 29733. That means we should ignore it, if we get to it (and of course we immediately do). It's good to ignore that statement, because it doesn't conform to INTERCAL's syntax; an erroneous statement would otherwise abort the run, with the rude message CORRECT SOURCE AND RESUBNIT [sic]. Error-filled statements have been sprinkled liberally through this program, in places where the program shouldn't ever go, because INTERCAL provides no other way to give helpful comments.

A much more drastic type of abstention is specified on line *384*, which says that we must abstain from *every* statement that uses the NEXT command (namely the statements on lines *020*, *024*, *027*, *029*, ..., *395*). Every statement has an "abstention flag," either on or off; an ABSTAIN command turns one or more of these flags on. Conversely, a REINSTATE command, as on line *036* or *390*, can be used to turn them back off.

Spaces and line breaks are ignored throughout an INTERCAL program, except within the keywords PLEASE and DO. They appear in Table 3 only to enhance readability.

If NOT or N'T immediately follows PLEASE or DO or PLEASE DO, as on lines *007*, *015*, *083*, *094*, ..., *401*, the statement's abstention flag is *initially* on. Thus we actually begin to perform the TPK program by skipping past many lines of opening comments, until reaching line *020*. There we are told to invoke the subroutine whose label is (6534).

The teleprinter code on line *017* is important, because it explains why subroutine (6534) was given that label: 6534 is the number that Alan Turing knew as INI, using the notation that he advised everyone to learn when working with the early Manchester computers. Indeed, the subroutine in question begins on line *090*; line *089* refers to it by the symbolic equivalent (INI), because its purpose is to do a bit of initialization. Similarly, (22919) on line *027* calls the (UNP) subroutine of line *301*, in order to unpack data. Notice that Turing's notation was little-endian (right-to-left): He denoted 22919 by UNP, not PNU.

How do subroutines work in INTERCAL? Easy: The NEXT command on line *020* places the location of the following statement (line *021*) onto a stack, and jumps to line *090*, the statement labeled (6534). Lines *090* and *091* set up a three-element array ;1 and a two-element array ;2; then the RESUME command on line *092* pops one (i.e., #1) element off the stack, and transfers control there. We're back from the subroutine, at line *021*.

Line *021* initializes the array x (which is ;29, teleprinterwise), declaring it to be a pair (x_1, x_2) of 32-bit numbers. This implementation of TPK works with "double-double precision" values, meaning that x represents the number $x_1 + x_2/2^{32}$.

Line *022*, similarly, declares a to be a two-dimensional array, 11×2. It has entries (a_{i1}, a_{i2}) for $1 \le i \le 11$; in other words, it's an array of eleven double-doubles.

Lines *023* through *036* are TPK's first loop on i (aka .6 or .I), an index variable that runs from 0 up to 10. First we set $i \leftarrow 0$ in *023*; then we "call subroutine (1)" in *024*. But that instruction turns out to be "go to (1)" in reality, because the FORGET command in *025* discards the top element of the stack.

Incrementation and testing of the loop variable are handled by the (TIX) subroutine that's called in lines *033* through *036*. Those lines essentially mean "if $i = 10$, exit the loop [by disabling the go-to statement on line *035*]; otherwise set $i \leftarrow i + 1$ and return to (1)."

When you're ready to see how the (TIX) routine on lines *377–398* actually accomplishes this magic, you should appreciate the fact that the command REINSTATE NEXTING also reinstates (UP), the statement on line *389*. Now, however, we will stick to high-level programming constructions instead of delving into minutiæ of the low-level utilities.

The body of the first loop on i runs from *026* to *032*. Line *026* inputs a 32-bit number, which is unpacked to the double-double ;1 by the (UNP) routine invoked by line *027*. In other words, each execution of the loop begins by setting ;1 to the next input value.

Then the loop proceeds to set $j \leftarrow i+1$ in lines *028*, *029*, *030*. Here's how: All statements with labels (1000)–(1999) are part of INTERCAL's standard System Library [7], which the compiler appends to the code of any program that refers to such a label. Thus line *029* invokes the standard subroutine (1020), which increases .1 by one.

Lines *031* and *032* complete the body of the loop by setting $a_j \leftarrow$;1.

The next loop, in lines *037–056*, is similar, but it causes i to vary from 10 down to 0. The ABSTAIN command on line *054* causes (TIX) to decrease i instead of increasing it.

Line *039* sets $ov \leftarrow 0$; this variable will be set to 1 if an overflow occurs during the subsequent calculation. The next few lines set $x \leftarrow a_j$, where again $j = i + 1$. Then line *045* calls subroutine (F), which sets variable ;1 equal to $f(x)$ as defined by the TPK formula. The (PAK) subroutine, invoked on line 046, then computes the scaled-decimal integer :1 that corresponds to ;1; and (OVC) on line 047 changes :1 to $2^{32} - 1$ if overflow had occurred.

Lines 048–051 present an interesting high-level way to achieve the effect of "if :1 is 400 or more, change :1 to 999."* First we set :2 to 400 (line 048); then we call (CMP) (line 049); then we set :1 to 999 (line 050). Subroutine (CMP) amazingly causes the latter instruction to be ignored if :1 was less than :2, by invoking the command IGNORE :1 (line 373) in such a case. Line 051 undoes any ignoring that (CMP) might have done.

After the second loop, the program reaches its normal end (line 057).

So we turn now to subroutine (F). The STASH commands on lines 063 and 066 place two arrays onto an auxiliary stack, independent of the nexting stack, without changing their values, so that ;1 and ;2 can be temporarily modified. These arrays are restored to their former states by using RETRIEVE commands (076, 080).

Thus (F) basically follows the standard TPK pattern: First we set ;1 and ;2 to x. Then in 069 we use subroutine (MLX), which replaces ;1 by ;1 × ;2, to form x^2; and we invoke it again to form x^3. After multiplying by 5 we put $5x^3$ in ;2. Then (line 076) we put x back into ;1. The next three lines invoke (ABX) to replace ;1 by its absolute value, then (RTX) to replace ;1 by its square root, and (ADX) to increase ;1 by ;2. That gives us $f(x)$, so (F) is done.

The classic TPK algorithm has therefore been entirely specified by almost-palatable "high level" INTERCAL code, on lines 020–081 of Table 3. The remaining lines are my extensions to the standard library, namely the routines for double-double precision arithmetic (including square root), together with the (CMP) and (TIX) utilities.

I heartily encourage the reader to study these extensions, as stated earlier, because they represent the soul of INTERCAL's machine. But I shall confine myself in the rest of these notes to rather sparse hints about the shenanigans that I pulled when writing them.

It's best to start small, and to figure out why line 103 of (OVC) exits by 2 levels if $ov = 1$, but by 1 level if $ov = 0$.

Addition and subtraction in double-double precision are, of course, quite straightforward because they reduce to addition and subtraction of 32-bit numbers. But before you can totally understand (ADX) and (SUX) you need to know the specs of several standard library routines:

---

* The TPK algorithm actually says that 999 should not be used if the value is exactly 400. Fortunately this boundary case can never arise.

(1010) sets $.3 \leftarrow (.1 - .2) \bmod 2^{16}$. (1509) sets $:3 \leftarrow :1 + :2$ and $:4 \leftarrow 1 + \text{carry}$; (1500) is similar, but it aborts if there is a carry. (1510) sets $:3 \leftarrow (:1 - :2) \bmod 2^{32}$. (1540) sets $:3 \leftarrow :1 \times :2$, but aborts if the product exceeds $2^{32} - 1$. And (1550) sets $:3 \leftarrow \lfloor :1/:2 \rfloor$ if $:2 \neq 0$, otherwise $:3 \leftarrow 0$.

The mess on lines *139–142* looks horrible at first glance, but in reality it simply complements the double-double number in ;2.

Double-double multiplication is basically reduced to a series of multiplications of short numbers by short numbers.

The double-double square root routine, (RTX), consists primarily of a loop on i from 1 to 49, using (TIX) in line *284*. Variable ;3 holds the remainder-so-far and ;4 holds the complement of the sqrt-so-far; variables :1 and :2 hold the bits that haven't yet been examined. We begin by jumping into the middle of the loop, where lines *267–276* compute the next bit .3 of the square root (left to right) by essentially setting

$$;1 \leftarrow ;3 + ;4 + 1, \quad \text{and} \quad .3 \leftarrow [;1 \neq 0 \text{ or } .2 \neq 0] \times [\text{carry occurred}],$$

where .2 holds the two leading bits of :1. Then lines *277–282* set $;1 \leftarrow ;3$ if $.3 = 0$. In the earlier portion of the loop, lines *234–256* set

$$;3 \leftarrow 4 \times ;1 + (.2 - .3)/2^{32} \quad \text{and} \quad ;4 \leftarrow 2 \times ;4 + (1 - .3)/2^{32},$$

then lines *257–266* shift (:1, :2) two bits to the left.

Regarding line *296*, I admit that it isn't great programming practice to let 50 items accumulate on the nexting stack. But hey, I saved a line of code by doing so.

The climax of this program is (UNP), the unpacking subroutine, which is primarily concerned with computing the 32 leading bits of the fraction $(:1 \bmod 1000000)/1000000$ and rounding them properly. Variable :4 runs through the values $2^{31}, 2^{30}, \ldots, 2^0$, while the two components of an auxiliary array ;2 accumulate the answer and its complement. The basic idea is simply to double the fraction repeatedly, modulo 1, and to remember where carries occurred.

Let x and y denote :1 and ;1, respectively. Lines *321–329* essentially put $2x$ into y_2 and then $z \bmod 2^{20}$ into $y_{3-\lfloor z/2^{20} \rfloor}$, where $z = 2^{20} + 2x - 1000000$; therefore y_2 has been set to $2x \bmod 1000000$. This value replaces x in line *317*.

Line *316* launches a sneaky trick that can be perpetrated only in INTERCAL. A close inspection shows that line *340* temporarily changes it from DON'T RESUME #1 to DO RESUME #1, so that we can go through the loop one more time, finally delivering a properly rounded result in line *335*.

Another noteworthy trick, which can be found in Woods and Lyon's original standard library [7], appears in lines *364–368*. The gist is that one can compute $t \leftarrow [x > y]$ by doing just a few xor, shift, and selection operations: $z \leftarrow x \oplus y$, $t \leftarrow x \sim z$, $z \leftarrow z \sim z$, $z \leftarrow z \oplus (z \gg 1)$, $t \leftarrow t \sim z$.

Using the Compiler

If your computer doesn't already have an INTERCAL compiler, you can readily install the one developed by Eric Raymond [4], assuming that you have a UNIX-inspired operating system. The program tpk.i in Table 3 can be downloaded from my website [2], together with sample input data tpk.in and the corresponding output tpk.out, so that you can watch it in action and do your own experiments.

I tested Table 3 on the following eleven values: 0.000000, 0.000001, 0.015625, and 4.000000 (when the square root is exact); 5.000000, 3.141592, 3.141593, and 0.768033 ("random" data); 4294.967295 (the maximum possible input); 4.301409 and 4.301410 (near the root of $f(x) = 400$). To input a value like 0.015625, say, INTERCAL wants you to type ONE FIVE SIX TWO FIVE; so that's what actually appears in the sample file tpk.in mentioned above.

The corresponding outputs — which appear in tpk.out using INTERCAL's version of Roman numerals, but converted here to scaled decimal — are 0.000000, 0.001000, 0.125019, and 322.000000; 999.000000, 156.803740, 156.803888, and 3.141591; 999.000000; 399.999898 and 999.000000. These results are perfectly rounded, except for the fact that 156.803889 would have been slightly better than 156.803888. (We can't expect perfect accuracy when fixed-point scaled arithmetic is used on a problem like this; an error of ϵ in x leads to an error of roughly $(1/(2\sqrt{x}) + 15x^2)\epsilon$ in $f(x)$.)

The total computation in this example amounted to the dynamic execution of 3,903,231 INTERCAL statements (including 3,760,185 in the standard library), plus 6,179 abstentions (5,801 of which were within the library).

By the way, many other esoteric programming languages [5] now exist, inspired by INTERCAL as their canonical example yet wildly different. I don't think TPK has yet reached them all. Go hack.

References

[1] Donald E. Knuth, *Combinatorial Algorithms*, Part 1, Volume 4A of *The Art of Computer Programming* (Upper Saddle River, New Jersey: Addison–Wesley, 2010).

[2] Donald E. Knuth, tpk.i in "Programs to read," online at http:
//www-cs-faculty.stanford.edu/~knuth/programs.html [ac-
cessed July 2010].

[3] Donald E. Knuth and Luis Trabb Pardo, "The early development
of programming languages," in *Encyclopedia of Computer Science
and Technology*, edited by Jack Belzer, Albert G. Holzman, and
Allen Kent, Volume 7 (New York: Marcel Dekker, 1977), 419–493.
Reprinted in *A History of Computing in the Twentieth Century*,
edited by N. Metropolis, J. Howlett, and G.-C. Rota (New York:
Academic Press, 1980), 197–273. Reprinted with revisions and extensions as Chapter 1 of *Selected Papers on Computer Languages*,
CSLI Lecture Notes 139 (Stanford, California: Center for the Study
of Language and Information, 2003), 1–94.

[4] Eric S. Raymond, *The INTERCAL Resources Page* (5 July 2008),
http://www.catb.org/~esr/intercal [accessed July 2010].

[5] Wikipedia, "Esoteric programming language," online at http://en.
wikipedia.org/wiki/Esoteric_programming_language [accessed
July 2010].

[6] Wikipedia, "Trabb Pardo–Knuth algorithm," online at http://en.
wikipedia.org/wiki/Trabb_Pardo-Knuth_algorithm [accessed
July 2010].

[7] Donald R. Woods and James M. Lyon, *The INTERCAL Programming Language Reference Manual* (privately published in 1973),
38 pages. A revised version is available on the Internet [4].

*I like to think of C-INTERCAL as being much in the spirit of the
Potrzebie System of Weights and Measures.*

— ERIC S. RAYMOND, in an email to the author (18416.29075 C.D.)

Chapter 8

Math Ace: The Plot Thickens

*[Originally published in Engineering and Science Review, Case Institute of Technology, **3**, 1 (November 1959), 45; **3**, 4 (May 1960), 24.]*

The classical formulas shown to analytic geometry students always have familiar shapes when graphed: circles, ellipses, parabolas, lemniscates, and so on. The graphs of textbook equations invariably lead to lines or curves. But there are many relatively simple equations that are satisfied by whole areas of the plane, not just by points that lie on paths. For example, the equation "$|x| = x$" is satisfied by all points that lie in the first and fourth quadrants (all points with $x \geq 0$, regardless of y).

After playing around with equations like this during odd moments of my freshman year, I began to notice that interesting shapes could be produced by a variety of techniques. In fact, the discovery of such "shady equations" might well lead to a new and highly impractical branch of analytic geometry. One of the unusual formulas derived was the equation

$$
\begin{aligned}
&\bigl|20 - |x+y| - |x-y|\bigr| - 20 + |x+y| + |x-y| \\
&\quad + \bigl|18 - |x+y| - |x-y|\bigr| + \bigl|16 - |x+y| - |x-y|\bigr| \\
&\quad - 2\bigl|17 - |x+y| - |x-y|\bigr| \\
&\quad + \sum_{j=-3}^{3} \sum_{k=|j|-4}^{3-|j|} \Bigl(\bigl|2 - |x+y+4j| - |x-y+4k+2|\bigr| \\
&\qquad\qquad\qquad + 2 - |x+y+4j| - |x-y+4k+2| \Bigr) = 0,
\end{aligned}
$$

which happens to be satisfied by precisely the points (x, y) that are plotted in Figure 1 on the next page.

Calculus pros are encouraged to guess the shape, before turning the page to see the answer. Take a sheet of graph paper and systematically pick values for x and y, putting a black dot wherever the equation holds. For example, you'll find that the values $x = 0$ and $y = 0$ nicely satisfy the equation, while $x = -1$ and $y = +1$ do not.

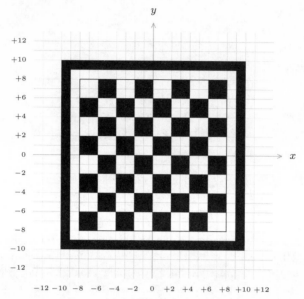

FIGURE 1. The points that satisfy the mysterious equation.

Right, you guessed it: A chessboard.

Or maybe you thought it was something else? To squelch any objections by skeptics, I fed the formula into the 650 computer for verification. The machine tried 6400 points on the plane, at intervals of one half for the values of x and y, and punched 80 cards to illustrate the graph that it found. (This process took approximately an hour.) The result was perfect agreement with the predicted graph; the computer's version is reproduced in Fig. 2, but omitting the 39 cards that were blank. A rigorous analytic proof could also be given.

One added note: It is theoretically possible to put chessmen into any position of this diagram. But the resulting equation would take several pages to reproduce.

A Sequel

To prove yet again that mathematicians are able to make simple things complex, I went back to the drawing board and wrote down another equation for intrepid plotters.

The pile of hair below Figure 2 is mystery formula number two. Can you psych this one out, now that you totally understand Figure 1?

Some of my former friends have been anticipating my burial plot.

FIGURE 2. The 650 has a habit of using 8's for points that satisfy an equation.

$$\left(\left| \left| 3 - |x| \right| - 3 + |x| \right| + \left| \left| \sqrt{|9 - x^2|} - \left| y - \tfrac{2}{3}|x| \right| \right| - \sqrt{|9 - x^2|} + \left| y - \tfrac{2}{3}|x| \right| \right| \right)$$

$$\left(\left| |xy| + xy \right| + \left(\left| \left| 2 - |33 - 3|x|| \right| - 2 + |33 - 3|x|| \right| + |14 - |y|| \right) \right)$$

$$\left(\left| 16 - |y| - 3|11 - |x|| \right| \left| \left| \sqrt{\left| 1 - (11 - |x|)^2 \right|} - \left| 11 - |y| + \tfrac{2}{3}|11 - |x|| \right| \right| \right. \right.$$

$$\left. - \sqrt{\left| 1 - (11 - |x|)^2 \right|} + \left| 11 - |y| + \tfrac{2}{3}|11 - |x|| \right| \right|$$

$$\left. + \left| \left| 1 - |11 - |x|| \right| - 1 + |11 - |x|| \right| \right) \right)$$

$$\left(|13 - |x|| + \left| |15 - |y|| - 15 + |y| \right| \right) \left(|18 - |y|| + \left| |10 - |x|| - 10 + |x| \right| \right)$$

$$\left(\left| 9 - (10 - |x|)^2 - (15 - |y|)^2 \right| + \left| |10 - |x|| + 10 - |x| \right| + \left| |15 - |y|| + 15 - |y| \right| \right)$$

$$= 0.$$

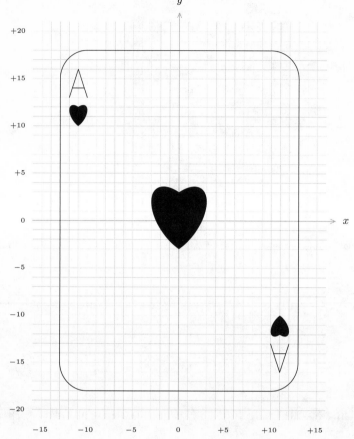

FIGURE 3. Solution to the second mysterious equation.

Addendum

I noticed some years later that the simple equation $\lfloor x \rfloor + \lfloor y \rfloor = 2\lfloor x/2 \rfloor + 2\lfloor y/2 \rfloor + 1$ defines an infinite chessboard, although it includes only two of the four boundary edges of each filled square.

Chapter 9

Billiard Balls in an Equilateral Triangle

[Originally published in Recreational Mathematics Magazine #14 (January–February 1964), 20–23.]

This note investigates the infinite cyclic paths that can be traced by a billiard ball as it ricochets inside an equilateral-triangular table. We are given the equilateral triangle ABC and a point X on the side AB. We want to determine all paths that start at X and bounce off the sides of the triangle according to the law of reflection, in such a way that the ball will eventually return to X and start the same pattern once again.

We let x be the ratio of the lengths AX/AB; thus $0 < x < 1$. Taking AB to be of length 1, then AX has length x, and the altitude of the triangle is $\sqrt{3}/2$. Figure 1 shows an example of such a triangle, together with a closed path (in gray) that is a particular solution to our problem. The path starts and ends at X by making some angle θ with the bottom edge. Since this angle determines the path completely, the problem becomes one of determining exactly which angles θ will lead to cyclic paths. In Figure 1 we have $\theta = 60°$, which defines an inter-

FIGURE 1.

esting six-bounce cycle. Two other cases of interest are $\theta = 90°$ and $\theta = 30°$, which yield unusual cycles in which one half of the path retraces the other half but in the opposite direction. (Those cases are illustrated in Figures 5 and 7 below.) All of the values of θ mentioned so far will give solutions regardless of the position of X; in fact, we will see that the permissible values of θ are actually independent of X in general.

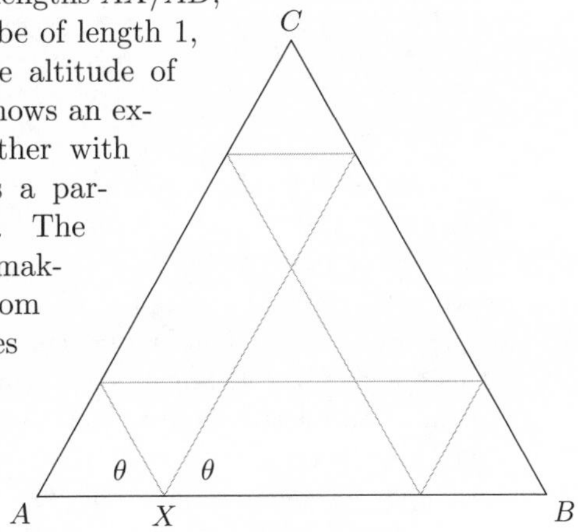

The law of reflection used here is the familiar one that the "angle of incidence equals the angle of reflection." There is a particular case that merits special study, however: What do we do when the path leads directly into a corner of the triangle? Figure 2 shows the situation when the path comes very close to a corner as the ball bounces three times; the limiting behavior of this case leads us to the reflection law shown in Figure 3 when the path hits the corner exactly.

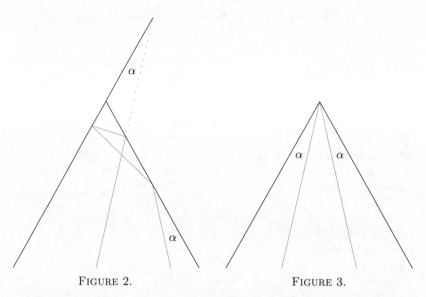

FIGURE 2.   FIGURE 3.

Our problem can be solved by expanding the diagram in such a way that the ball's path is a straight line; this can be done by repeating the triangle ABC infinitely many times, as indicated in Figure 4. In this diagram the triangle ABC appears in six different orientations. Straight lines on this figure, such as the gray lines shown, give paths in the original triangle that satisfy the reflection law if the diagram is folded appropriately. Conversely, any path that satisfies the reflection law corresponds to a straight line in this diagram. Path L corresponds to Figure 5, path N corresponds to Figure 6, and path P corresponds to Figure 7; path M corresponds to Figure 1.

To solve our problem, we observe that each of our paths begins to repeat at some point in time when it passes through one of the copies of the point X. We may assume, by the law of reflection, that the path begins by traveling upward and to the right, unless $\theta = 90°$. Now the point X where the path begins to repeat might conceivably appear on

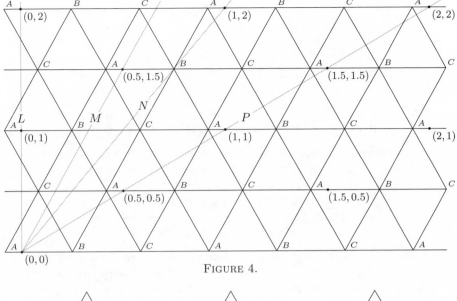

FIGURE 4.

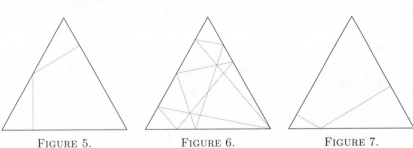

FIGURE 5.   FIGURE 6.   FIGURE 7.

a line with the "/" slope; but the path makes an angle of $\theta + 120°$ with that line, not θ. A second possibility is that the cycle point X occurs on a line with the "\" slope. But we see from Figure 8 that this situation can occur only when $\theta = 60°$, and indeed only in this case when $x = \frac{1}{2}$.

The path corresponding to $\theta = 60°$ and $x = \frac{1}{2}$ is a very special case that occasionally behaves quite differently from the less symmetrical cases, and we will have to treat it specially.

We are now left with the case where the repetition starts at a point X on a line of horizontal "＿" slope. Not only is such a case possible, it is easy to see conversely that every line that connects two X points on different horizontal lines is a cyclic path. These X points therefore play an important role in

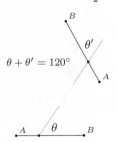

$\theta + \theta' = 120°$

FIGURE 8.

our investigation, and they are labeled in Figure 4 with coordinates of two types, either (m, n) or $(m + \frac{1}{2}, n + \frac{1}{2})$, where m and n are integers.

We conclude that all possible cyclic paths are obtained by connecting point $(0,0)$ to one of the points labeled (p, q) in Figure 4, and that all paths of this type are cyclic. The tangent of the angle θ for such a path is easily determined; it is equal to $q/(p\sqrt{3})$. These observations prove

Theorem 1. *If $0 < \theta < 90°$, the path corresponding to θ is cyclic if and only if $\tan\theta = r/\sqrt{3}$, where r is a positive rational number.* □

Let us now investigate the cyclic paths a little more closely. Suppose we are given θ with $\tan\theta = r/\sqrt{3}$ and $r > 0$. Then the path passes through all points (p, q) where $r = q/p$. The first such point may be determined as follows: Suppose that the fraction q/p is in lowest terms. If p and q are both odd, the path passes first through the point $(p/2, q/2)$; otherwise it passes first through (p, q). This reasoning leads to

Theorem 2. *The length of the path traveled in each cycle may be determined as follows: Let $\tan\theta = q/(p\sqrt{3})$ where p and q are integers with no common factor, and where $p \geq 0$, $q > 0$. Then the length is $\sqrt{9p^2 + 3q^2}/2$ when p and q are both odd, and $\sqrt{9p^2 + 3q^2}$ otherwise — except that the length is only $3/2$ when $\theta = 60°$ and $x = 1/2$.* □

Corollary. *If $x \neq 1/2$, the shortest path length is $\sqrt{3}$; it occurs when $\theta = 30°$ and when $\theta = 90°$.* □

We now turn to the number of "bounces" in each path. To account for the degenerate cases when the path heads directly into a corner, we will count that event as three bounces (motivated again by Figure 2). It is not hard to see that the path from $(0,0)$ to (p, q) in Figure 4 passes $2q$ lines with slope "__", $|3p - q|$ lines with slope "$/$", and $3p + q$ lines with slope "$\backslash$". This calculation yields our next theorem:

Theorem 3. *The number of bounces occurring in each cycle may be determined as follows: Let p and q be as in Theorem 2. Then the number is $q + \max(3p, q)$ when p and q are odd, otherwise it is $2q + \max(6p, 2q)$ — except when $\theta = 60°$ and $x = 1/2$, when the number is 3.* □

Corollary. *If $x \neq 1/2$, the least number of bounces per cycle is 4; it occurs when $\theta = 30°$ and when $\theta = 90°$. The number of bounces for $x \neq 1/2$ is always even.* □

Finally, we consider the following fallacious argument (see Martin Gardner's "Mathematical Games" in *Scientific American* **209**, 3 (September 1963), page 252), which motivated this entire study: A line is drawn between two corresponding X's as shown in Figure 9. Moving from the lower X to the upper X corresponds to the path of a billiard ball that is driven "against side B-C so that it rebounds, hits side A-C, then returns to its original position on side A-B"; and we might think at first glance that the same path will then recur. But the path doesn't really begin to recycle immediately unless X bisects AB, as we have seen above. We now inquire under what circumstances the path of Figure 9 is even *cyclical* if we continue to extend it. Thus we compute

$$\tan\theta \;=\; \left(\frac{\sqrt{3}}{2}(1+x)\right)\Big/\left(\frac{3}{2}(1-x)\right) \;=\; \frac{1}{\sqrt{3}}\left(\frac{1+x}{1-x}\right)$$

where $x = AX/AB$, and we see that $(1+x)/(1-x) = r$ must be rational. This equation implies $x = (r-1)/(r+1)$, so we get our final result:

Theorem 4. *The line in Figure 9 leads to a cyclic path if and only if* AX/AB *is rational.*   □

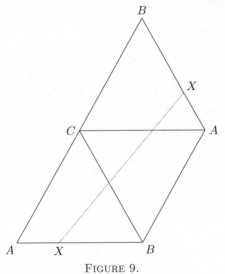

FIGURE 9.

Addendum

These billiard-ball paths have been independently investigated from a somewhat different point of view by Andrew M. Baxter and Ronald Umble, "Periodic orbits for billiards on an equilateral triangle," *American Mathematical Monthly* **115** (2008), 479–491.

I wrote to Martin Gardner on 5 September 1963, saying "Dear Mr. Gardner: I suppose you'll be getting much more mail this month than usual, because at last you goofed! ... If I hadn't noticed this error, I'd have put the magazine down and forgotten all about it, but as it was I spent the greater part of the afternoon working on this topic! It's easy to prove that there is only one cyclic path which has only three bounces per cycle, i.e., only one solution to the problem you stated. For if we denote the incidence angles by a, b, c we find from the diagram

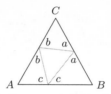

that $a + b + c = 180°$ [since, e.g., the sum of the interior angles of the middle triangle is $180° = (180° - 2a) + (180° - 2b) + (180° - 2c)$]; and this shows further that $a = b = c = 60°$. The enclosed note discusses these things in a little more detail, and they are interesting because they are so completely elementary. ... Well, it has been fun to catch you once."

Martin responded almost immediately, on 15 September. Neither of us knew it at the time, but this — our first exchange — was destined to become the beginning of a long correspondence, writing back and forth every few weeks. He said "I think your note deserves full publication somewhere," and he recommended *Recreational Mathematics Magazine* because he knew that an article about ball-bouncing in an ellipse was already scheduled to appear there.

Many mathematicians have similarly benefited from Martin's kindness and good counsel at early stages of their careers.

Chapter 10

Representing Numbers Using Only One 4

*[Originally published in Mathematics Magazine **37** (1964), 308–310.]*

In the Mathematical Games section of *Scientific American*, January 1964, Martin Gardner asks his readers to try their hand at the well-known problem of representing the number 64 using precisely four, three, and two 4's, respectively, combined with arithmetic operations. The "two-4" problem was first posed by J. A. Tierney (see [1]), and some of the answers given were

$$64 = \sqrt{\sqrt{\sqrt{(4^{4!})}}} = \sqrt{(4^{\Gamma(4)})} = 4^{\lfloor \ln 4! \rfloor} = \varphi(\varphi(4^4)) = \varphi(4!)^{\sqrt 4} = 4^{\sqrt{(\pi(4!))}}.$$

It is the purpose of this note to show that the number 64 can be represented with only *one* 4, and indeed this may be true of all positive integers.

Using only the three operations $\sqrt{\ }$, $\lfloor\ \rfloor$, and !, and the single digit 4, we have

$$64 = \lfloor \sqrt{\sqrt{\sqrt{\sqrt{\sqrt{\sqrt{\sqrt{\sqrt{\sqrt{\sqrt{}}}}}}}}} \lfloor \sqrt{\sqrt{\sqrt{\sqrt{\sqrt{\sqrt{\sqrt{\sqrt{\sqrt{\sqrt{}}}}}}}}} \lfloor \sqrt{\sqrt{\sqrt{\sqrt{\sqrt{\sqrt{\sqrt{\sqrt{\sqrt{\sqrt{\sqrt{\sqrt{}}}}}}}}}}}$$
$$\lfloor \sqrt{\sqrt{\sqrt{\sqrt{\sqrt{\sqrt{\sqrt{\sqrt{}}}}}}} \lfloor \sqrt{\sqrt{\sqrt{\sqrt{\sqrt{\sqrt{\sqrt{\sqrt{\sqrt{\sqrt{}}}}}}}}}$$
$$\lfloor \sqrt{ \lfloor \sqrt{ \lfloor \sqrt{\sqrt{\sqrt{\sqrt{\sqrt{(4!)!}}}}} \rfloor ! \rfloor ! \rfloor ! \rfloor ! \rfloor ! \rfloor ! \rfloor ! \rfloor !.$$

(In this representation, the notation $\sqrt{x}!$ stands for $\sqrt{(x!)}$, not $(\sqrt x)!$. Parentheses have been placed in the subformula '(4!)!' because the unparenthesized expression '4!!' traditionally means $4 \cdot 2$.)

To verify this formula we will compute successively the quantities inside each of the nested brackets. The innermost floor brackets represent the number 5, since

$$5^{32} = \quad 232\ 83064\ 36538\ 69628\ 90625$$
$$24! = \quad 6204\ 48401\ 73323\ 94393\ 60000$$
$$6^{32} = 79586\ 61109\ 94640\ 08843\ 91936$$

and hence $\lfloor\sqrt{}\sqrt{}\sqrt{}\sqrt{}\sqrt{24!}\rfloor = 5$. The next level of brackets obviously gives 10, since $10 = \lfloor\sqrt{5!}\rfloor$. Proceeding similarly, we can evaluate the kth brackets to obtain the integer a_k, where

$$a_k^{2^t} < a_{k-1}! < (a_k + 1)^{2^t}$$

for some appropriate integer t. The details are:

k	a_k	t	$a_k^{2^t}$	$a_{k-1}!$	$(a_k + 1)^{2^t}$
3	1904	1	36 25216	36 28800	36 29025
4	442	11	6.7×10^{5417}	4.2×10^{5419}	6.8×10^{5419}
5	6673	8	1.062×10^{979}	1.097×10^{979}	1.104×10^{979}
6	577	13	3.6×10^{22619}	9.1×10^{22623}	5.2×10^{22625}
7	422	9	1.4×10^{1344}	2.5×10^{1344}	4.9×10^{1344}
8	64	9	5.8×10^{924}	2.1×10^{926}	1.6×10^{928}

With such large numbers, of course, logarithms are used for the calculations. Logarithms of factorials up to 1200! are given to 18 places in J. Peters, *Ten Place Logarithm Table* **1** (New York: Ungar, 1957). The logarithms of larger factorials are easily computed by means of Stirling's approximation.

Notice that $\lfloor\sqrt{\lfloor x\rfloor}\rfloor = \lfloor\sqrt{x}\rfloor$, so the floor operation is needed only around the final result and before factorials are taken. Since $3 = \lfloor\sqrt{10}\rfloor$, we can represent 3 with one four, hence also $3! = 6$, and so on. It seems a plausible conjecture that all positive integers possess such a representation, but this fact (if true) seems to be tied up with very deep properties of the integers.

The referee has suggested a stronger conjecture, that a representation may be found in which all factorial operations precede all square root operations; and moreover, if the greatest integer function is not used, an arbitrary positive real number can probably be approximated as closely as desired in this manner. If N_k is the number $(\cdots((4!)!)!\cdots)!$ with k factorial operations, this conjecture is equivalent to the statement that the values of

$$\log_2(N_k/2^{\lfloor\log_2(\log_2 N_k)\rfloor}), \qquad k = 1, 2, 3, \ldots,$$

are dense in the interval $(1 .. 2)$.

A computer program was written to see what small numbers can be represented in a fashion similar to our formula for 64. For all x and y less than 1000, the machine determined whether or not

$$x = \lfloor\sqrt[2^u]{\lfloor\sqrt[2^v]{y!}\rfloor!}\rfloor$$

for some integers u and v, provided that the calculations could all be carried out without numbers becoming too large, and provided that round-off error could be shown to have absolutely no effect. If we write $y \to x$ when this relationship holds, we can also write $y \to\hspace{-0.5em}\to x$ to mean that $y \to y_1 \to y_2 \to \cdots \to y_k = x$, for some $y_1, y_2, \ldots, y_k$. Then the number n can be represented with just one 4 whenever $4 \to\hspace{-0.5em}\to n$. The results of this computer run were that $4 \to\hspace{-0.5em}\to n$ for all $n < 208$. The fact that 208 was not obtained is probably due to the limited search that was carried out; however, it is interesting that all numbers $n \leq 200$ can be written as $4 \to n_1 \to n_2 \to \cdots \to n$ where each n_i is at most 999.

A further improvement can be made by using negation in connection with the other operations, since $-\lfloor -x \rfloor$ is the least integer greater than or equal to x. This possibility has not been fully explored. It can be used, for example, to extend the list of numbers represented in a simple way by four 1's to at least 37, using

$$35 = -\lfloor \sqrt{(11 + 1)/(-.1)} \rfloor,$$
$$36 = (\sqrt{(1/.\dot{1})})! \, (\sqrt{(1/.\dot{1})})!,$$
$$37 = 1 - \lfloor -\sqrt{11} \rfloor /.\dot{1},$$

and the list of representations of 1 through 34 in [2]. (Here '$.\dot{1}$' stands for '$.1111\ldots$'.) The latter article contains an excellent bibliography.

References

[1] J. A. Tierney, Elementary problem E 631, "Two fours," *American Mathematical Monthly* **51** (1944), 405; **52** (1945), 219.

[2] Marjorie Bicknell and Verner E. Hoggatt, "64 ways to write 64 using four 4's," *Recreational Mathematics Magazine* #14 (1964), 13–15.

Addendum

I've modernized the notation that was used in 1964, when the "floor brackets" $\lfloor x \rfloor$ had not yet been invented. At that time $\lfloor x \rfloor$ was called the "greatest integer function of x" and written $[x]$.

Martin Gardner's original column from January 1964, which instigated my work, has been thrice reprinted (with significant alterations) as Chapter 5 of a series of ever-longer books: *The Numerology of Dr. Matrix* (New York: Simon and Schuster, 1967); *The Incredible Dr. Matrix* (New York: Charles Scribner's Sons, 1976); *The Magic Numbers of Dr. Matrix* (Buffalo, New York: Prometheus, 1985). His discussion sketches the history of similar recreations and refers to many related publications.

The referee's conjecture, about the numbers obtainable by repeated factorialing followed by repeated square-rooting, had previously been stated at the close of an elegant note by J. H. Conway and M. J. T. Guy, "π in four 4's," *Eureka: The Archimedeans' Journal* **25** (1962), 18–19. Although this conjecture is eminently plausible, it seems to be well beyond any conceivable explicit proof.

Suppose we define the sequence N_k by letting $N_0 = 4$ and $N_{k+1} = N_k!$; surely there's no way to calculate an integer k for which the 2^vth root of N_k lies between 64 and 65 for some v. (This would mean that the binary representation of $\log_2 N_k$ begins with 11 and is less than the leading digits 11000000101101110011110... of the binary representation of $\log_2 65$.) A little analysis shows, for example, that

$$2^{85} < \log_2 N_3 < 2^{85} + 2^{83} \qquad \text{and} \qquad 2^{2^{85}} < \log_2 N_4 < 2^{2^{85}+2^{83}}.$$

Furthermore, it isn't extremely difficult to determine the leading bits 11111000000011010001110... of $\log_2 N_4$. With a century or so of computation, one might also determine the leading bits of $\log_2 N_5$, which is approximately $N_4 \log_2 N_4$. But it's a safe bet that nobody will ever know whether the most significant binary digits of $\log_2 N_6$ are 10 or 11.

Thanks to 21st-century software, I can now redo the calculations at the end of my original note, by letting $y \rightarrowtail x$ when $3 \leq x, y < 1000$ and

$$x = \lfloor \sqrt[2^v]{y!} \rfloor \qquad \text{or} \qquad x = \lfloor \sqrt[2^u]{\lfloor \sqrt[2^v]{y!} \rfloor!} \rfloor;$$

no precautions about numbers becoming too large are now necessary. This directed graph on 997 vertices has a strongly connected component of size 963 that includes all vertices < 418. In particular we have $4 \rightarrowtail n$ for $3 \leq n \leq 417$; all such n have a one-4 representation of length 765 or less, except for $n = 337$. The 85-symbol representation of 64 that I found in 1964 remains the shortest known, if we restrict ourselves to factorial, square root, and floor functions. The shortest such representation that I know for 337 has length 5175:

$$337 = \lfloor \sqrt[2^{3676}]{\lfloor \sqrt{\lfloor \sqrt[2^{1422}]{\lfloor \sqrt{\sqrt{\lfloor \sqrt[2^6]{\lfloor \sqrt[2^{42}]{\lfloor \sqrt{(4!)!} \rfloor!} \rfloor!} \rfloor!} \rfloor!} \rfloor}} \rfloor} \rfloor.$$

With the ceiling function we can of course do better. The best representation that I currently know for "64 with one 4," eschewing exotic unary operations such as !! and ¡, is

$$64 = \lceil \sqrt{\sqrt{\sqrt{\sqrt{\sqrt{\sqrt{\lceil \sqrt{\lfloor \sqrt{\sqrt{\lfloor \sqrt{\lceil \sqrt{\sqrt{\sqrt{\sqrt{(4!)!} \rceil!} \rfloor!} \rfloor!} \rceil!} \rceil}}}}}}}}}}}}}}}}}}}}}}}}}}}} \rceil.$$

Chapter 11

Very Magic Squares

*[Originally published in American Mathematical Monthly **75** (1968), 260–264.]*

A square matrix A is "magic" in the weakest sense when it has a generalized "doubly stochastic" property, namely when all of its row sums and column sums have the same value s. The matrix is even more "magic" when the sums of its elements along certain diagonals are also equal to s.

If A is an $m \times m$ matrix whose elements are denoted by A_{xy} for $1 \le x, y \le m$, let us say that a *generalized diagonal* of A is the set of all A_{xy} such that $ax + by \equiv c$ (modulo m), for some given integers a, b, c with a and b relatively prime to each other. For example, a 5×5 matrix has 30 distinct generalized diagonals, namely the sets of elements of the same value c in the following squares:

11111	23451	35241	42531	54321	12345
22222	34512	41352	53142	15432	12345
33333	45123	52413	14253	21543	12345
44444	51234	13524	25314	32154	12345
55555	12345	24135	31425	43215	12345
$x \equiv c$	$x+y \equiv c$	$x+2y \equiv c$	$x+3y \equiv c$	$x+4y \equiv c$	$y \equiv c$

When m is not prime, further types of generalized diagonals appear; if, for example, $m = 6$ we have the following 6×12 cases:

111111	234561	351351	414141	531531	654321
222222	345612	462462	525252	642642	165432
333333	456123	513513	636363	153153	216543
444444	561234	624624	141414	264264	321654
555555	612345	135135	252525	315315	432165
666666	123456	246246	363636	426426	543216
$x \equiv c$	$x+y \equiv c$	$x+2y \equiv c$	$x+3y \equiv c$	$x+4y \equiv c$	$x+5y \equiv c$

73

345612	525252	165432	456123	513513	123456
561234	141414	321654	123456	246246	123456
123456	363636	543216	456123	513513	123456
345612	525252	165432	123456	246246	123456
561234	141414	321654	456123	513513	123456
123456	363636	543216	123456	246246	123456
$2x + y \equiv c$	$2x + 3y \equiv c$	$2x + 5y \equiv c$	$3x + y \equiv c$	$3x + 2y \equiv c$	$y \equiv c$

Clearly each row of a matrix is a special case of a generalized diagonal, with $a = 1$ and $b = 0$; each column has $a = 0$, $b = 1$; and the principal diagonals have $a = 1$, $b = 1$, $c = 1$ and $a = 1$, $b = -1$, $c = m$.

The object of this note is to give a short proof of the fact that *a square matrix has equal sums along all of its generalized diagonals if and only if all of its elements are equal.* In other words, only trivial squares can be "magic" with respect to all possible generalized diagonals. A proof was given by Rosser and Walker [1] when m is prime; they also stated that "This theorem is true for squares of any order. The proof is very complicated, so it is not included here. A typewritten copy of the proof has been deposited in the Cornell University library ...."

More generally we have the following result for n-dimensional arrays of numbers:

Theorem 1. *The m^n complex numbers $A(x_1, \ldots, x_n)$, for integers $1 \leq x_1, \ldots, x_n \leq m$, satisfy the conditions*

$$\sum \{A(x_1, \ldots, x_n) \mid a_1 x_1 + \cdots + a_n x_n \equiv c \ (\text{modulo } m)\} = s, \quad (1)$$

for all integers $a_1, \ldots, a_n, c$ with $\gcd(a_1, \ldots, a_n) = 1$, if and only if

$$A(x_1, \ldots, x_n) = sm^{1-n} \qquad \text{for all } x_1, \ldots, x_n. \quad (2)$$

Proof.   A proof that (1) implies (2) can be based on the idea of a "finite Fourier transform." Let $\omega = e^{2\pi i/m}$, and define

$$a(t_1, \ldots, t_n) = \sum_{1 \leq x_1, \ldots, x_n \leq m} \omega^{-t \cdot x} A(x_1, \ldots, x_n), \quad (3)$$

where $t \cdot x = t_1 x_1 + \cdots + t_n x_n$. (We consider $x = (x_1, \ldots, x_n)$ and $t = (t_1, \ldots, t_n)$ to be n-dimensional vectors of integers.) It follows that, when $1 \leq x_1, \ldots, x_n \leq m$,

$$A(x_1, \ldots, x_n) = \frac{1}{m^n} \sum_{1 \leq t_1, \ldots, t_n \leq m} \omega^{t \cdot x} a(t_1, \ldots, t_n), \quad (4)$$

since the latter sum is

$$\sum_{1 \leq t_1, \ldots, t_n \leq m} \ \sum_{1 \leq y_1, \ldots, y_n \leq m} \omega^{t \cdot (x-y)} A(y_1, \ldots, y_n)$$

and since the sum over t_j is a multiple of $\sum_{t_j=1}^{m} \omega^{t_j(x_j-y_j)}$, a geometric series whose value is 0 unless $x_j \equiv y_j$ (modulo m).

Now if $(t_1, \ldots, t_n) = (t'_1 d, \ldots, t'_n d)$ and $\gcd(t'_1, \ldots, t'_n) = 1$, equation (1) implies that

$$a(t_1, \ldots, t_n) = \sum_{c=1}^{m} \sum \{ \omega^{-cd} A(x_1, \ldots, x_n) \mid$$
$$1 \leq x_1, \ldots, x_n \leq m \text{ and } t' \cdot x \equiv c \text{ (modulo } m) \}$$
$$= s \sum_{c=1}^{m} \omega^{-cd} = \begin{cases} ms, & \text{if } d \equiv 0 \text{ (modulo } m); \\ 0, & \text{if } d \not\equiv 0 \text{ (modulo } m). \end{cases}$$

In other words, $a(t_1, \ldots, t_n)$ is zero except when $t_1 \equiv \cdots \equiv t_n \equiv 0$ (modulo m). Therefore the sum in (4) reduces to the single term with $t_1 = \cdots = t_n = m$, and (2) is immediate.

To prove that (2) implies (1), we must show that the congruence

$$a_1 x_1 + \cdots + a_n x_n \equiv c \text{ (modulo } m), \quad 1 \leq x_1, \ldots, x_n \leq m \quad (5)$$

has precisely m^{n-1} solutions when $\gcd(a_1, \ldots, a_n) = 1$, regardless of the choice of c. Since there are integers $a'_1, \ldots, a'_n$ such that $a_1 a'_1 + \cdots + a_n a'_n = 1$, we may take $x_1 \equiv ca'_1, \ldots, x_n \equiv ca'_n$ to obtain one solution of (5); then all solutions are obtained by adding solutions of (5) with $c = 0$ to this particular solution. Therefore there are the same number of solutions for $c = 0$, $c = 1$, $\ldots$, $c = m - 1$; and this number must be m^{n-1}, since m^n combinations of $x_1, \ldots, x_n$ are possible. This analysis completes the proof of the theorem. $\square$

Theorem 1 is the discrete analog of results on continuous functions discussed by Rényi (see [2, 3]).

Let us now consider whether Theorem 1 has hypotheses that are too strong. Is it perhaps possible to show that the array has constant values if we insist only that it has constant sums along a few of the generalized diagonals? The next result gives further information that follows from a slightly deeper analysis of the relevant structure:

Theorem 2. Let $\omega = e^{2\pi i/m}$, and for $1 \leq x_1, \ldots, x_n \leq m$ let

$$A(x_1, \ldots, x_n) = \omega^{t \cdot x}, \quad (6)$$

where $t = (t_1, \ldots, t_n)$ is an integer vector with $\gcd(t_1, \ldots, t_n) = 1$. Then

$$\sum \{ A(x_1, \ldots, x_n) \mid a \cdot x \equiv c \text{ (modulo } m) \} = 0 \quad (7)$$

for all integers $a_1, \ldots, a_n$, c *with* $\gcd(a_1, \ldots, a_n) = 1$, *except when*

$$(a_1, \ldots, a_n) \equiv (\xi t_1, \ldots, \xi t_n) \quad (\text{modulo } m) \qquad (8)$$

for some integer ξ *relatively prime to* m.

Proof. Consider first the case when $m = p^e$ is the power of a prime number. Then some a_k, say a_1, is not a multiple of p, and we can find b so that $a_1 b \equiv 1$ (modulo m). The sum (7) is therefore

$$\sum_{1 \le x_2, \ldots, x_n \le m} \omega^{\eta(x)}, \qquad \eta(x) = t_1 bc + (t_2 - bt_1 a_2) x_2 + \cdots + (t_n - bt_1 a_n) x_n.$$

Since ω is a primitive mth root of unity, this sum vanishes unless

$$t_2 \equiv bt_1 a_2, \quad \ldots, \quad t_n \equiv bt_1 a_n \quad (\text{modulo } m).$$

And in that case t_1 cannot be a multiple of p, since $t_1 \equiv bt_1 a_1$ and $\gcd(t_1, \ldots, t_n) = 1$. So (8) holds if $\xi b t_1 \equiv 1$ (modulo m).

Now if m is not a prime power, let the canonical factorization of m into primes be

$$m = p_1^{e_1} p_2^{e_2} \ldots p_r^{e_r}, \qquad (9)$$

and for $1 \le j \le r$ determine constants b_j by the Chinese remainder theorem such that

$$b_j \equiv 1 \ (\text{modulo } p_j^{e_j}); \qquad b_j \equiv 0 \ (\text{modulo } p_k^{e_k}), \quad k \ne j. \qquad (10)$$

Then for any integers $y_1, y_2, \ldots, y_r$, and y,

$$y \equiv y_j \ (\text{modulo } p_j^{e_j}), \ 1 \le j \le r, \ \text{implies } y \equiv b \cdot y \ (\text{modulo } m). \qquad (11)$$

It follows that we can write the sum in (7) as

$$\sum \omega_1^{t_1 x_{11} + \cdots + t_n x_{n1}} \omega_2^{t_1 x_{12} + \cdots + t_n x_{n2}} \ldots \omega_r^{t_1 x_{1r} + \cdots + t_n x_{nr}}, \qquad (12)$$

where $\omega_j = \omega^{b_j}$ and where the sum is over all sequences of integers x_{ij} such that $1 \le x_{ij} \le p_j^{e_j}$ and $a_1 x_{1j} + a_2 x_{2j} + \cdots + a_n x_{nj} \equiv c$ (modulo $p_j^{e_j}$). Consequently the sum (12) is $S_1 S_2 \ldots S_r$, where each S_j is a sum like (7) for the case $m = p_j^{e_j}$ with ω_j substituted for ω. By (10), ω_j is a primitive $p_j^{e_j}$th root of unity; so if none of the S_j are zero, we know by the previous argument that there exist integers $\xi_1, \xi_2, \ldots, \xi_r$ such that

$$(a_1, \ldots, a_n) \equiv (\xi_j t_1, \ldots, \xi_j t_n) \ (\text{modulo } p_j^{e_j}), \quad 1 \le j \le r.$$

Finally, let $\xi = b_1 \xi_1 + b_2 \xi_2 + \cdots + b_r \xi_r$ to obtain (8), as desired. $\quad \square$

Theorem 2 can be interpreted in the following way: Let us say that any sequence of integers a_1, a_2, ..., a_n with $\gcd(a_1, a_2, \ldots, a_n) = 1$ determines a *family* of generalized diagonals, namely the diagonals $a_1 x_1 + a_2 x_2 + \cdots + a_n x_n \equiv c$ (modulo m) for various values of c. The families determined by $(a_1, \ldots, a_n)$ and $(t_1, \ldots, t_n)$ are *equivalent* if (8) holds for some ξ prime to m; equivalent families are in fact essentially equal. Our matrix example above shows the six possible families when $m = 5$ and the twelve possible families when $m = 6$. (The number of families is $m(1 + p_1^{-1})(1 + p_2^{-1}) \ldots (1 + p_r^{-1})$ when m has the form (9) and $n = 2$.)

The content of Theorem 2 is that nonconstant arrays $A(x_1, \ldots, x_n)$ might have constant sums on all generalized diagonals except for those in one family. Therefore Theorem 1 is "best possible" in the sense that we cannot prove (2) if we leave any particular family of diagonals out of condition (1).

Since (7) is a system of linear equations in the $A(x_1, \ldots, x_n)$ with integer coefficients, and since (6) is a nonzero solution in terms of complex values, there must exist integer-valued solutions of (7). For example, the 6×6 square

$$
\begin{matrix}
1 & 2 & 3 & 3 & 2 & 1 \\
2 & 1 & 1 & 2 & 3 & 3 \\
3 & 3 & 2 & 1 & 1 & 2 \\
1 & 2 & 3 & 3 & 2 & 1 \\
2 & 1 & 1 & 2 & 3 & 3 \\
3 & 3 & 2 & 1 & 1 & 2
\end{matrix}
\tag{13}
$$

is "magic" with respect to each of the 72 possible generalized diagonals, except for 4 of the diagonals that belong to the family $2x + 5y \equiv c$ (modulo 6).

The preparation of this paper has been supported in part by the National Science Foundation.

References

[1] Barkley Rosser and R. J. Walker, "The algebraic theory of diabolic magic squares," *Duke Mathematical Journal* **5** (1939), 705–728.

[2] A. Rényi, "On projections of probability distributions," *Acta Mathematica Academiæ Scientiarum Hungaricæ* **3** (1952), 131–142.

[3] John W. Green, "On the determination of a function in the plane by its integrals over straight lines," *Proceedings of the American Mathematical Society* **9** (1958), 758–762.

Chapter 12

The Gamow–Stern Elevator Problem

[Originally published in the Journal of Recreational Mathematics **2** *(1969), 131–137.]*

An amusing mathematical problem was devised by George Gamow and Marvin Stern, after they had been somewhat frustrated by the elevator service in their office building. Gamow's office was on the second floor and Stern's on the sixth floor of a seven-story building. Gamow notes that, whenever he wished to visit Stern, the first elevator to arrive at the second floor was almost always "going down," not up. It seemed as though new elevators were being created at the top floor and destroyed at the ground floor, since no elevator ever would bypass the second floor intentionally on its way up. But when waiting for a descending elevator on the sixth floor, precisely the opposite effect was observed: The first elevator to pass was almost always "going up"!

Gamow and Stern account for this phenomenon in their enjoyable book *Puzzle-Math* [1, pages 9–10, 59–63], but their explanation is not completely valid. It may therefore be of interest to give a correct solution to the problem here.

Preliminary Considerations

In order to analyze the situation, let us assume that we have an "ideal" elevator system, which everyone knows does not exist, but which makes it possible to give a reasonable analysis. We will assume that each elevator goes continually up and down from the bottom floor to the top floor of the building and back again, in a cyclic fashion (independent of other elevators). At the moment we begin to wait for an elevator on some given floor of the building, we may assume that each elevator in the system is at a random point in its cycle, and that each will proceed at the same rate of speed until one reaches our floor. Let

$$p = \frac{distance\ from\ our\ floor\ to\ bottom\ floor}{distance\ from\ top\ floor\ to\ bottom\ floor}$$

be the ratio expressing our percentage distance from the bottom floor.

The one-elevator problem is easy to solve: If there is only one elevator and if we approach it at a random time, there is probability p that it is below us (and it will therefore be going up when it next encounters our floor), and there is probability $1 - p$ that is above us (and consequently will be going down when we next see it). So if $p = 1/6$, as in Gamow's case, the next elevator stopping at the second floor will be going down five times out of every six.

The Two-Elevator Problem

When there is more than one elevator, Gamow and Stern say that "the situation will, of course, remain the same." But that's not true! Many a mathematician has fallen into a similar trap, being misled by something that seems self-evident; and nearly every example of faulty reasoning that has been published is accompanied by the phrase "of course" or its equivalent.

Let us consider, for example, the two-elevator problem. We may assume that $p \leq 1/2$; for if p were greater than $1/2$ we could consider the analogous problem where p is replaced by $1 - p$ and the directions are reversed. Our goal is to compute the probability that the first elevator arriving at our floor will be on its way down.

To solve this problem, we may break it into three cases:

Case 1, both elevators are above our floor. Then surely the next elevator we see will be going down. This case occurs with probability $(1 - p)^2$.

Case 2, both elevators are below our floor. Then the next elevator we see will be going up. This case occurs with probability p^2.

Case 3, one elevator is above us, the other is below. This case occurs with probability $p(1-p) + (1-p)p = 2p(1-p)$. Here we might see either elevator first, depending on their relative positions. If the upper elevator is within distance pD of us, where D is the distance traveled by the elevator in each cycle (that is, D is twice the distance from the bottom floor to the top floor), we have a 50–50 chance of getting the upper or the lower one first; this subcase occurs with probability $2p^2$. Otherwise the lower elevator will arrive first, going up; that subcase occurs with probability $2p(1 - 2p)$.

Summing up, the probability that the first elevator to arrive at our floor will be descending is

$$(1 - p)^2 \cdot 1 \; + \; p^2 \cdot 0 \; + \; 2p^2 \cdot \frac{1}{2} \; + \; 2p(1 - 2p) \cdot 0 \;\; = \;\; 1 - 2p + 2p^2.$$

If $p = 1/6$, for example, the first elevator will be going downward with probability $13/18$, about 72%. This is somewhat better than the 83% we had in the one-elevator case, if we want to go up; but it is still sufficiently biased against us to make us suspect that some sort of conspiracy is causing the elevators to go the wrong way.

Why is the two-elevator problem different from the one-elevator problem? Suppose, for example, that we call the two elevators A and B. If we restrict consideration to elevator A, we will find it going down five out of every six times when it first arrives; and the same happens if we restrict our consideration to elevator B. Furthermore, elevator A will be the first to arrive, half of the time, and elevator B will be the first to arrive during the other half of the time. So why don't we get the same five-to-six ratio when *both* elevators are considered?

The fallacy in this argument is due to a rather subtle failure to consider conditional probabilities. (Indeed, Gamow and Stern correctly describe several similar fallacies in their book.) The choice of which elevator is first to arrive is partly contingent on whether it was above us or below us, since an elevator that is below us when we begin to wait is more likely to arrive before an elevator that is above us (all other things being equal), when $p < 1/2$.

The n-Elevator Problem

Let us now turn to the general situation where there are n independent elevators. In this section we will discuss a "brute force" attack on the problem. Our solution will involve some interesting elementary interplay between discrete mathematics and the infinitesimal calculus; but readers who are not especially concerned with such topics may safely ignore the following material and skip directly to the "elegant" solution in the next section below.

One way to compute the probability that the next elevator is going down is to compute n times the probability that a certain *designated* elevator will be the first to arrive and that it will be going down. If the designated elevator reaches our floor, going downward, at time t_0, the desired probability is equal to t_0 minus the time of the previous elevator arrival at our floor, measured in units of "elevator cycles." Since

$p \leq 1/2$, one of the *undesignated* elevators must be the last to arrive before time t_0.

Let

$$f(t) = \begin{cases} t, & \text{if } 0 \leq t < p; \\ t - p, & \text{if } p \leq t \leq 1. \end{cases}$$

If an undesignated elevator reaches our floor going downwards at time $t_0 - t$, where $0 < t < 1$, it will reach our floor going upwards at time $t_0 - t + p$; therefore at time t_0 we will have last seen that elevator $f(t)$ units of time ago. Consequently, if the $n - 1$ undesignated elevators reach our floor going downwards at the respective times $t_0 - t_1$, $t_0 - t_2$, ..., $t_0 - t_{n-1}$, the amount of time that has elapsed between t_0 and the previous elevator arrival is

$$\min\big(f(t_1), f(t_2), \ldots, f(t_{n-1})\big).$$

To obtain the probability that the *designated* elevator arrives first on our floor at t_0, if we enter at a random point in time, we now multiply this quantity by $dt_1 \, dt_2 \ldots dt_{n-1}$ (the differential probability that the undesignated elevators arrive at our floor going downwards at respective times $t_0 - t_1$, $t_0 - t_2$, ..., $t_0 - t_{n-1}$), and integrate over $0 \leq t_1 \leq 1$, $0 \leq t_2 \leq 1$, ..., $0 \leq t_{n-1} \leq 1$, obtaining the formula

$$\int_0^1 \int_0^1 \cdots \int_0^1 \min\big(f(t_1), f(t_2), \ldots, f(t_{n-1})\big) \, dt_{n-1} \ldots dt_2 \, dt_1.$$

We can evaluate this integral by breaking it into 2^{n-1} integrals of the form

$$\int_{a_1}^{b_1} \int_{a_2}^{b_2} \cdots \int_{a_{n-1}}^{b_{n-1}} \min\big(f(t_1), f(t_2), \ldots, f(t_{n-1})\big) \, dt_{n-1} \ldots dt_2 \, dt_1,$$

where each pair (a_i, b_i) is either $(0, p)$ or $(p, 1)$. For example, when $n = 3$ we have

$$\int_0^1 \int_0^1 = \int_0^p \int_0^p + \int_0^p \int_p^1 + \int_p^1 \int_0^p + \int_p^1 \int_p^1.$$

Each of the latter integrals is simpler to deal with than the original, because we may replace $f(t_i)$ by t_i when $(a_i, b_i) = (0, p)$, and by $t_i - p$ when $(a_i, b_i) = (p, 1)$. By symmetry, we may also permute the pairs (a_i, b_i) without changing the value of the integral; and there are $\binom{n-1}{k}$ integrals having k of the (a_i, b_i) equal to $(p, 1)$ and having $n - 1 - k$ of them equal to $(0, p)$. Hence the original integral reduces to

$$\sum_k \binom{n-1}{k} A_{n-1,k}, \qquad (*)$$

where

$$A_{m,k} = \overbrace{\int_0^p \cdots \int_0^p}^{m-k} \overbrace{\int_p^1 \cdots \int_p^1}^{k} \min(t_1, \ldots, t_{m-k},$$
$$t_{m+1-k}-p, \ldots, t_m-p)\, dt_m \ldots dt_1.$$

Replacing t_j by $t_j + p$ for $m - k < j \le m$, we have to evaluate

$$A_{m,k} = \overbrace{\int_0^p \cdots \int_0^p}^{m-k} \overbrace{\int_0^{1-p} \cdots \int_0^{1-p}}^{k} \min(t_1, \ldots, t_m)\, dt_m \ldots dt_1.$$

If $0 < k < m$ we can break the integration over t_m into two parts: Over the range 0 to p we get $A_{m,k-1}$, and over the range p to $1 - p$ we get $(1 - 2p)A_{m-1,k-1}$, since t_m will never be $\min(t_1, \ldots, t_m)$ when $t_m > p$ and $k < m$. Therefore we have the recurrence

$$A_{m,k} = A_{m,k-1} + (1 - 2p)A_{m-1,k-1}, \qquad \text{for } 0 < k < m.$$

If $k = 0$ we have, by definition,

$$A_{m,0} = \int_0^p \cdots \int_0^p \min(t_1, \ldots, t_m)\, dt_m \ldots dt_1,$$

which (by symmetry) is $m!$ times the same integral over the region $0 \le t_m \le \cdots \le t_2 \le t_1 \le p$; hence

$$A_{m,0} = m! \int_0^p \int_0^{t_1} \cdots \int_0^{t_{m-1}} t_m \, dt_m \ldots dt_1.$$

The latter integral is readily evaluated by induction on m, and we obtain

$$A_{m,0} = p^{m+1}/(m+1).$$

Similarly,

$$A_{m,m} = (1 - p)^{m+1}/(m+1).$$

By induction on k we can now use the recurrence above to find that

$$A_{m,k} = \binom{k}{0}\frac{p^{m+1}}{m+1} + \binom{k}{1}\frac{p^m}{m}(1-2p)$$
$$+ \binom{k}{2}\frac{p^{m-1}}{m-1}(1-2p)^2 + \cdots, \quad \text{for } 0 \le k < m.$$

The solution to the n-elevator problem can finally be obtained by multiplying $(*)$ by n and carrying out the necessary sums:

$$n\sum_k \binom{n-1}{k} A_{n-1,k}$$

$$= nA_{n-1,n-1} + n\sum_{k<n-1} \binom{n-1}{k}\sum_j \binom{k}{j}\frac{p^{n-j}}{n-j}(1-2p)^j$$

$$= (1-p)^n + n\sum_{k<n-1}\sum_j \binom{n-1}{j}\binom{n-1-j}{k-j}\frac{p^{n-j}}{n-j}(1-2p)^j$$

$$= (1-p)^n + n\sum_{j<n} \binom{n-1}{j}\frac{p^{n-j}}{n-j}(1-2p)^j(2^{n-1-j}-1)$$

$$= (1-p)^n + \frac{1}{2}\sum_{j<n}\binom{n}{j}(2p)^{n-j}(1-2p)^j - \sum_{j<n}\binom{n}{j}p^{n-j}(1-2p)^j$$

$$= (1-p)^n + \left(\frac{1}{2} - \frac{1}{2}(1-2p)^n\right) - \left((1-p)^n - (1-2p)^n\right)$$

$$= \frac{1}{2} + \frac{1}{2}(1-2p)^n.$$

This formula agrees with our earlier calculations when $n=1$ or $n=2$. The simple manipulations of binomial coefficients that are used in this derivation are explained, for example, in [2, Section 1.2.6].

An "Elegant" Solution

After all of the involved calculations just made, we have come up with a very simple formula, $(1+(1-2p)^n)/2$, for the "going down" probability. In fact, our formula is so simple it suggests that there must be a much simpler way to reach the same result. Let us therefore try to see why the quantity $(1-2p)^n$ is meaningful in this problem.

After some reflection, we can make the following observations: Each elevator's cycle can be represented as a circle of unit circumference, with two points separated by an arc of length p to represent the two stops on our floor. (See Figure 1.) Our problem consists of choosing n points at random on the circle, then rotating them synchronously until one point hits either the "Going down" or the "Going up" mark. What is the probability that we first hit "Going down"?

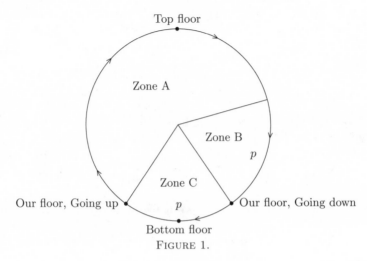

Top floor

Zone A

Zone B

Zone C

Our floor, Going up

Our floor, Going down

Bottom floor
FIGURE 1.

For an "elegant" solution to this problem, we can mark off another arc of length p and divide the circle into three zones, as shown in the illustration. If all of the n points fall into Zone A (an event that occurs with probability $(1-2p)^n$), then the next elevator to reach our floor will obviously be going down. But if one or more of the points fall into Zones B or C (an event that occurs with probability $1 - (1-2p)^n$), the symmetry of the situation shows that there will be a 50–50 chance for the next elevator to be going down. Thus the probability is

$$(1-2p)^n + \frac{1}{2}\left(1 - (1-2p)^n\right) \;=\; \frac{1}{2} + \frac{1}{2}(1-2p)^n,$$

just as we derived the hard way.

Although our calculations so far are valid only when $p \le 1/2$, it is not difficult to modify the final formulas so that they are valid for all p between 0 and 1: The probability that the first elevator arriving at our floor will be going down is, in general,

$$\frac{1}{2} + \frac{1}{2}(1-2p)\,|1-2p|^{n-1}.$$

Notice that this quantity approaches $1/2$ as n approaches infinity.

Happiness

In accordance with this result, let us calculate how many elevators a building needs to keep its occupants happy. For convenience, we will assume that a person who waits for a descending elevator on the next-to-top floor of the building will not be unduly annoyed if the first elevator to arrive is going down at least 40% of the time. If the building has m floors above its bottom floor, we want to have enough elevators, n, that

$$\frac{1}{2} + \frac{1}{2}(1-2p)\,|1-2p|^{n-1} \geq 0.4,$$

where $p = (m-1)/m$ and $m \geq 3$. By simple manipulation this relation is equivalent to

$$n \geq (\log 5)/(\log(1 + 2/(m-2))) = \frac{\ln 5}{2}(m-1) + O(1/m);$$

so the number of elevators must be roughly proportional to the number of floors!

The following table shows the dependence of n on m:

m	3	4	5	10	20	100	1000
n	2	3	4	8	16	80	804

Acknowledgments

I wish to thank Peter Weiner for some stimulating discussions of this problem, and I also wish to thank the referee for several suggestions that improved the presentation in this paper.

References

[1] George Gamow and Marvin Stern, *Puzzle-Math* (New York: Viking Press, 1958).

[2] Donald E. Knuth, *Fundamental Algorithms*, Volume 1 of *The Art of Computer Programming* (Reading, Massachusetts: Addison–Wesley, 1968).

Chapter 13

Fibonacci Multiplication

*[Originally published in Applied Mathematics Letters **1** (1988), 57–60.]*

A curious binary operation on the nonnegative integers is shown to be associative.

A well-known theorem of Zeckendorf [1, 3, 4] states that every nonnegative integer has a unique representation as a sum of Fibonacci numbers, if we stipulate that no two consecutive Fibonacci numbers occur in the sum. In other words we can uniquely write

$$n = F_{k_r} + \cdots + F_{k_2} + F_{k_1}, \quad k_r \gg \cdots \gg k_2 \gg k_1 \gg 0, \quad r \geq 0, \quad (1)$$

where the relation "$k \gg j$" means that $k \geq j + 2$. The Fibonacci numbers are defined as usual by the recurrence

$$F_0 = 0, \qquad F_1 = 1, \qquad F_k = F_{k-1} + F_{k-2} \quad \text{for } k \geq 2. \qquad (2)$$

Given the Zeckendorf representations

$$m = F_{j_q} + \cdots + F_{j_1}, \qquad n = F_{k_r} + \cdots + F_{k_1}, \qquad (3)$$

let us define "circle multiplication" to be the following binary operation:

$$m \circ n = \sum_{b=1}^{q} \sum_{c=1}^{r} F_{j_b + k_c}. \qquad (4)$$

In particular, $F_j \circ F_k = F_{j+k}$, if $j \geq 2$ and $k \geq 2$.

The purpose of this note is to prove that circle multiplication satisfies the associative law:

$$(l \circ m) \circ n = l \circ (m \circ n). \qquad (5)$$

87

The proof is based on a variant of ordinary radix notation that uses Fibonacci numbers instead of powers. Let us write

$$(d_s \ldots d_1 d_0)_F = d_s F_s + \cdots + d_1 F_1 + d_0 F_0 . \tag{6}$$

Then $(d_s \ldots d_1 d_0)_F$ is a Zeckendorf representation if and only if the following three conditions hold:

Z1. Each digit d_i is 0 or 1.

Z2. Each pair of adjacent digits satisfies $d_{i+1} d_i = 0$.

Z3. $d_1 = d_0 = 0$.

For example, here are the Zeckendorf representations for the numbers 1 to 16:

$$
\begin{aligned}
1 &= \quad (100)_F & 9 &= \quad (1000100)_F \\
2 &= \quad (1000)_F & 10 &= \quad (1001000)_F \\
3 &= \quad (10000)_F & 11 &= \quad (1010000)_F \\
4 &= \quad (10100)_F & 12 &= \quad (1010100)_F \\
5 &= \quad (100000)_F & 13 &= (10000000)_F \\
6 &= \quad (100100)_F & 14 &= (10000100)_F \\
7 &= \quad (101000)_F & 15 &= (10001000)_F \\
8 &= (1000000)_F & 16 &= (10010000)_F
\end{aligned}
$$

Addition of 1 is easy in radix-F: We simply set $d_1 \leftarrow 1$ and $d_0 \leftarrow 1$ (thereby adding 1 to the value) and then use the "carry" rule

$$0\,1\,1 \rightarrow 1\,0\,0 \tag{7}$$

as often as possible until there are no two 1s remaining in a row. Finally, we set $d_0 \leftarrow 0$. This procedure makes $d_1 = 0$ after the first carry, so conditions (Z1, Z2, Z3) continue to hold.

In fact, if we begin with any digits $(d_s \ldots d_1 d_0)_F$ that satisfy Z1, we can systematically apply (7) until both Z1 and Z2 are valid. This is obvious because the *binary value* $(d_s \ldots d_1 d_0)_2 = 2^s d_s + \cdots + 2 d_1 + d_0$ increases whenever a carry is performed; therefore the process cannot get into a cycle. A given integer has only finitely many representations as a sum of positive Fibonacci numbers, so the process must terminate.

We can also try to add two numbers in radix-F notation, using a variant of ordinary binary addition. First we simply add the digits without carrying; this gives us digits that are 0, 1, or 2. Then we can use the two carry rules

$$0\,(d{+}1)\,(e{+}1) \rightarrow 1\,d\,e \tag{8}$$
$$0\,(d{+}2)\,0\,e \rightarrow 1\,d\,0\,(e{+}1) \tag{9}$$

to restore the conditions Z1 and Z2.

In fact, we can start with an arbitrary sequence of nonnegative digits $(d_s \ldots d_1 d_0)_F$ and systematically propagate carries by using (8) and (9), always working as far to the left as possible. Each carry increases the binary value, so the process must terminate with a final configuration $(d'_t \ldots d'_1 d'_0)_F$. Since rule (8) is no longer applicable, we must have $d'_{i+1} d'_i = 0$ for all $i \geq 0$. Since rule (9) is no longer applicable, we must also have $d'_i \leq 1$ for all $i \geq 2$.

Lemma 1. *If $d_1 = d_0 = 0$ and $d_i \leq 2$ for all $i \geq 2$, the carrying process just described transforms $(d_s \ldots d_1 d_0)_F$ into a sequence $(d'_t \ldots d'_1 d'_0)_F$ that satisfies Z1 and Z2.*

Proof. The result is vacuously true when $s \leq 1$. If $s > 1$, the carrying process applied to $(d_s \ldots d_3 \, 0 \, 0)_F$ inductively produces $(d'_t \ldots d'_3 d'_2 d'_1)_F$ with all $d'_i \leq 1$; hence the sequence $(d_s \ldots d_3 d_2 d_1 d_0)_F$ is transformed into $(d'_t \ldots d'_3 (d_2 + d'_2) d'_1 d_0)_F$. If $d_2 + d'_2 \leq 1$ or if $d'_3 = 1$, further carries with (8) will lead to termination without changing d'_1. Otherwise we have $d'_3 = 0$ and $2 \leq d_2 + d'_2 \leq 3$. If $d'_1 = 1$, rule (8) clears d'_1; otherwise rule (9) sets $d_0 \leftarrow 1$ and only 0s and 1s remain. $\quad\square$

The addition procedure just described is not complete, however, since condition Z3 might not be satisfied. If we can add two numbers without "carrying down" into positions d_1 and d_0, we say that the addition is *clean*. An unclean addition can be finished up by setting $d'_0 \leftarrow d'_1$ and then carrying if necessary.

Let $\overline{n}$ be the smallest subscript, k_1, in the Zeckendorf representation of n, when $n > 0$. Thus we have $n = (\ldots 1 \, 0 \ldots 0)_F$, with $\overline{n}$ zeros after the rightmost 1. We also define $\overline{0} = \infty$.

Lemma 2. *If $\overline{m} \geq 4$ and $\overline{n} \geq 4$, the radix-F addition $m + n$ is clean. Moreover, $\overline{m + n} \geq \min(\overline{m}, \overline{n}) - 2$.*

Proof. Lemma 1 shows that radix-F addition never reduces the number of trailing zeros by more than 2. $\quad\square$

Circle multiplication $m \circ n$ has a natural radix-F interpretation, because it is completely analogous to ordinary binary multiplication. Thus, for example,

$$
\begin{aligned}
6 \circ 12 = (100100)_F &\circ (1010100)_F \\
= \quad & (10010000)_F \\
+ \, & (1001000000)_F \\
+ \, & (100100000000)_F
\end{aligned}
\tag{10}
$$

because we have $j_2 = 5$, $j_1 = 2$, $k_3 = 6$, $k_2 = 4$, and $k_1 = 2$ in the notation of (3); the three lines of (10) represent the sums $\sum_{b=1}^{2} F_{j_b+k_c}$ for $c = 1, 2, 3$. These are "partial products" $m \circ F_{k_c}$.

Radix-F representation makes it easy to see that circle multiplication is monotonic:

$$l < m \quad \Longrightarrow \quad l \circ n < m \circ n, \qquad \text{for } n > 0. \tag{11}$$

For if we increase the left factor by 1, every partial product increases.

Lemma 3. *Radix-F addition of the partial products of $m \circ n$ is clean.*

Proof. The partial product $m \circ F_k$ has $\overline{m \circ F_k} = \overline{m} + k \geq k + 2$. Since $k_r \gg k_{r-1} \gg \cdots \gg k_1$, we have, successively,

$$\overline{m \circ F_{k_r} + m \circ F_{k_{r-1}}} \geq k_{r-1},$$

$$\overline{m \circ F_{k_r} + m \circ F_{k_{r-1}} + m \circ F_{k_{r-2}}} \geq k_{r-2},$$

$$\cdots \quad \overline{m \circ F_{k_r} + \cdots + m \circ F_{k_1}} \geq k_1,$$

by Lemma 2; all of these additions are spanking clean. □

Theorem. *Let the Zeckendorf representations of l, m, and n be*

$$l = F_{i_p} + \cdots + F_{i_2} + F_{i_1},$$
$$m = F_{j_q} + \cdots + F_{j_2} + F_{j_1},$$
$$n = F_{k_r} + \cdots + F_{k_2} + F_{k_1}.$$

Then the three-fold circle product is the three-fold sum

$$(l \circ m) \circ n = \sum_{a=1}^{p} \sum_{b=1}^{q} \sum_{c=1}^{r} F_{i_a+j_b+k_c}. \tag{12}$$

Proof. By Lemma 3, each partial product $(l \circ m) \circ F_k$ can be obtained by a clean addition of the partial products $(l \circ F_j) \circ F_k$ of $l \circ m$, shifted left k. Hence $(l \circ m) \circ F_k = \sum_{a=1}^{p} \sum_{b=1}^{q} F_{i_a+j_b+k}$, and the result follows by summing over $k = k_1, \ldots, k_r$. □

Since the sum in (12) is symmetric in l, m, and n, the circle product must be associative as claimed in (5).

We can extend the proof of Lemma 3 without difficulty to show that the three-fold addition in (12) is clean. Hence we obtain a similar t-fold sum for the t-fold circle product of any t numbers.

The Fibonacci number F_k is asymptotically $\phi^k/\sqrt{5}$, where ϕ is the "golden ratio" $(1 + \sqrt{5})/2$; hence we have

$$F_j \circ F_k \sim \sqrt{5}\, F_j F_k \,, \qquad \text{as } j, k \to \infty. \tag{13}$$

It follows that the circle product $m \circ n$ is approximately $\sqrt{5}\, mn \approx 2.24mn$ when m and n are large. But $1 \circ n$ is closer to $\phi^2 n \approx 2.62n$; and $2 \circ n$ is approximately $\phi^3 n \approx 2.12(2n)$.

This paper was inspired by recent work of Porta and Stolarsky [2], who made the remarkable discovery that the more complicated operation

$$m * n = mn + \lfloor \phi m \rfloor \lfloor \phi n \rfloor$$

is associative. Their "star product" satisfies $m * n \approx 3.62mn$.

This research was supported in part by National Science Foundation grant CCR-86-10181, and in part by Office of Naval Research contract N00014-87-K-0502.

References

[1] C. G. Lekkerkerker, "Voorstelling van natuurlijke getallen door een som van getallen van Fibonacci," *Simon Stevin* **29** (1952), 190–195.

[2] A. S. Fraenkel, H. Porta, and K. B. Stolarsky, "Some arithmetical semigroups," *Progress in Mathematics* **85** (1990), 255–264.

[3] E. Zeckendorf, "Représentation des nombres naturels par une somme de nombres de Fibonacci ou de nombres de Lucas," *Bulletin de la Société Royale des Sciences de Liège* **41** (1972), 179–182.

[4] E. Zeckendorf, "A generalized Fibonacci numeration," *Fibonacci Quarterly* **10** (1972), 365–372.

Addendum

Zeckendorf's representation can actually be traced back hundreds of years to medieval India, where the anonymous author of Prākṛta Paiṅgala (c. 1320) presented algorithms for the equivalent problem of finding the nth possible rhythm in Sanskrit poetry. Using '0' for a short syllable and '10' for a long syllable, the possibilities are 0, 10, 100, 1000, 1010, 10000, 10010, etc., preceded by as many 0s as needed to make a given total number of beats.

Yuri Matiyasevich wrote to me on 1 May 1990 to point out that he had devised the operation $m \circ n$ already in 1967. He called it the *indirect product* in his paper "Two reductions of Hilbert's tenth problem" [*Seminars in Mathematics, V. A. Steklov Mathematical Institute* **8** (1970), 68–74, which is a translation of his original Russian article in Записки Научных Семинаров Ленинградского Отделения Математического Института имени В. А. Стеклова **8** (1968), 145–158].

Matiyasevich had not known that his multiplication is associative; he sent me the following elegant algebraic proof of associativity, to complement the algorithmic proof that I had found: If n has the Zeckendorf representation (1), let $\overline{n} = F_{k_r+1} + \cdots + F_{k_2+1} + F_{k_1+1}$ be the number obtained from n by shifting the bits $d_s \ldots d_0$ of (6) left one place. Then the well-known identity $F_{k+l} = F_{k+1}F_l + F_k F_{l-1} = F_{k+1}F_l + F_k F_{l+1} - F_k F_l$ implies that

$$m \circ n = \overline{m}n + m\overline{n} - mn.$$

Hence $(l \circ m) \circ n = (\overline{l \circ m})n + (l \circ m)\overline{n} - (l \circ m)n = (l \circ \overline{m})n + (l \circ m)(\overline{n} - n) = \overline{\overline{m}}ln + \overline{m}(\overline{l}n + l\overline{n} - 2ln) + m(\overline{l}\overline{n} - \overline{l}n - l\overline{n} + ln)$ is symmetric in l and n, so it must be equal to $l \circ (m \circ n)$.

Indeed, if we also let $\underline{n} = \overline{n} - n$ denote the operation of shifting n's Zeckendorf representation one place to the *right*, we discover that

$$m \circ n = \overline{m}\overline{n} - \underline{m}\underline{n} = \underline{m}n + m\underline{n} + mn;$$
$$l \circ m \circ n = \overline{l}\overline{m}\overline{n} + lmn - \underline{l}\underline{m}\underline{n}.$$

Moreover, $\overline{n} = \lfloor (n+1)\phi \rfloor - 1$ and $\underline{n} = \lfloor (n+1)/\phi \rfloor$. (These Fibonacci-shift operations yield surprisingly good ways to convert from miles to kilometers or vice versa; see *Concrete Mathematics*, Section 6.6.)

Pierre Arnoux ["Some remarks about Fibonacci multiplication," *Applied Mathematics Letters* **2** (1989), 319–320] observed that, assuming Z1–Z3, $(d_s \ldots d_1 d_0)_F$ is the Zeckendorf representation of n if and only if $(d_s \ldots d_1 d_0)_{\widehat{\phi}} = n\widehat{\phi} + \underline{n}$, where $(d_s \ldots d_1 d_0)_{\widehat{\phi}}$ denotes $d_s \widehat{\phi}^s + \cdots + d_1 \widehat{\phi} + d_0$ (as usual) and $\widehat{\phi} = (1 - \sqrt{5})/2 = -1/\phi$ is the other root of the equation $x^2 = x + 1$ satisfied by ϕ. These numbers α_n all lie in the interval $1/\phi - 1 < \alpha_n < 1/\phi$; hence the set $\{\alpha_0, \alpha_1, \alpha_2, \ldots\}$ is closed under multiplication. Thus the rule $\alpha_m \alpha_n = \alpha_{m \circ n}$ gives a very nice way to understand the circle product and why it is associative; that is,

$$(m\widehat{\phi} + \underline{m})(n\widehat{\phi} + \underline{n}) = (m \circ n)\widehat{\phi} + \underline{m \circ n}.$$

Generalizations of his results to other numbers θ instead of ϕ, where θ is any so-called "Pisot number" (an algebraic integer > 1 whose conjugates all lie inside the unit circle) have been found by P. J. Grabner, A. Pethő, R. F. Tichy, and G. J. Woeginger, "Associativity of recurrence multiplication," *Applied Mathematics Letters* **7** (1994), 85–90.

Note to hackers: If $x = (d_s \ldots d_1 d_0)_2$ corresponds to the Zeckendorf representation of n, the following bitwise operations will cleverly convert it to the representation of $n + 1$:

$$y \leftarrow x \mid (x \gg 1), \quad z \leftarrow y \mathbin{\&} \sim(y + 4), \quad x \leftarrow (x \mid z) + 4.$$

Chapter 14

A Fibonacci-Like Sequence of Composite Numbers

*[Originally published in Mathematics Magazine **63** (1990), 21–25.]*

Ronald L. Graham [1] found relatively prime integers a and b such that the sequence $\langle A_0, A_1, A_2, \ldots \rangle$ defined by

$$A_0 = a, \qquad A_1 = b, \qquad A_n = A_{n-1} + A_{n-2} \tag{1}$$

contains no prime numbers. His original method proved that the integers

$$\begin{aligned} a &= \ \ 331635635998274737472200656430763 \\ b &= 1510028911088401971189590305498785 \end{aligned} \tag{2}$$

have this property. The purpose of the present note is to show that the smaller pair of integers

$$\begin{aligned} a &= 62638280004239857 \\ b &= 49463435743205655 \end{aligned} \tag{3}$$

also defines such a sequence.

Let $\langle F_0, F_1, F_2, \ldots \rangle$ be the Fibonacci sequence, defined by (1) with $a = 0$ and $b = 1$; and let $F_{-1} = 1$. Then

$$A_n = F_{n-1}a + F_n b. \tag{4}$$

Graham's idea was to find eighteen triples of numbers (p_k, m_k, r_k) with the properties that

- p_k is prime;
- F_n is divisible by p_k if and only if n is divisible by m_k.
- Every integer n is congruent to r_k modulo m_k for some k.

He chose a and b so that

$$a \equiv F_{m_k - r_k}, \qquad b \equiv F_{m_k - r_k + 1} \quad (\text{modulo } p_k) \qquad (5)$$

for $1 \le k \le 18$. It followed that

$$A_n \equiv 0 \quad (\text{modulo } p_k) \qquad \Longleftrightarrow \qquad n \equiv r_k \quad (\text{modulo } m_k) \qquad (6)$$

for all n and k. Each A_n was consequently divisible by some p_k; it could not be prime.

The eighteen triples in Graham's construction were

$$
\begin{array}{lll}
(3, 4, 1), & (2, 3, 2), & (5, 5, 1), \\
(7, 8, 3), & (17, 9, 4), & (11, 10, 2), \\
(47, 16, 7), & (19, 18, 10), & (61, 15, 3), \\
(2207, 32, 15), & (53, 27, 16), & (31, 30, 24), \\
(1087, 64, 31), & (109, 27, 7), & (41, 20, 10), \\
(4481, 64, 63), & (5779, 54, 52), & (2521, 60, 60).
\end{array} \qquad (7)
$$

(It is easy to check that the second property above holds, because m_k is the first subscript such that F_{m_k} is divisible by p_k. The third property holds because the first column nicely "covers" all odd values of n; the middle column covers all even n that are not divisible by 6; the third column covers all multiples of 6.) It is not difficult to verify by computer that the values of a and b in (2) satisfy (5) for all eighteen triples (7); therefore, by the Chinese remainder theorem, these values are the smallest nonnegative integers that satisfy (5) for $1 \le k \le 18$. Moreover, these huge numbers are relatively prime, so they produce a sequence of the required type.

Incidentally, the values of a and b in (2) are not the same as the 34-digit values in Graham's original paper [1]. A minor slip caused his original numbers to be respectively congruent to F_{32} and F_{33} (mod 1087), not to F_{33} and F_{34}, although all the other conditions were satisfied. Therefore the sequences defined by his published starting values may contain a prime number A_{64n+31}. We are fortunate that calculations with large integers are now much simpler than they were in the early 60s when Graham originally investigated this problem.

But we need not use the full strength of (5) to deduce (6). For example, if we want

$$A_n \equiv 0 \quad (\text{modulo } 3) \qquad \Longleftrightarrow \qquad n \equiv 1 \quad (\text{modulo } 4),$$

it is necessary and sufficient to choose $a \not\equiv 0$ and $b \equiv 0$ (modulo 3); we need not stipulate that $a \equiv 2$ as required by (5). Similarly if we want

$$A_n \equiv 0 \quad \text{(modulo 17)} \qquad \Longleftrightarrow \qquad n \equiv 4 \quad \text{(modulo 9)}$$

it is necessary and sufficient to have

$$A_4 \equiv 0 \quad \text{(modulo 17)} \qquad \text{and} \qquad A_5 \not\equiv 0 \quad \text{(modulo 17)};$$

the sequence $\langle A_4, A_5, A_6, \dots \rangle$ will then be, modulo 17, a nonzero multiple of the Fibonacci sequence $\langle F_0, F_1, F_2, \dots \rangle$. The latter condition can also be rewritten in terms of a and b,

$$b \equiv 5a \quad \text{(modulo 17)} \qquad \text{and} \qquad a \not\equiv 0 \quad \text{(modulo 17)},$$

because $A_4 = 2a + 3b$ and $A_5 = 3a + 5b$. This pair of congruences has 16 times as many solutions as the corresponding relations $a \equiv 5$ and $b \equiv 8$ in (5).

Proceeding in this way, we can recast the desired congruence conditions (6) in an equivalent form

$$b \equiv d_k a \quad \text{(modulo } p_k) \qquad \text{and} \qquad a \not\equiv 0 \quad \text{(modulo } p_k), \qquad (8)$$

for each of the first seventeen values of k. We choose d_k so that

$$F_{r_k - 1} + d_k F_{r_k} \equiv 0 \quad \text{(modulo } p_k);$$

this can be done since $0 < r_k < m_k$, hence F_{r_k} is not a multiple of p_k. The following pairs (p_k, d_k) are obtained:

$$
\begin{array}{lll}
(3, 0), & (2, 1), & (5, 0), \\
(7, 3), & (17, 5), & (11, 10), \\
(47, 3), & (19, 17), & (61, 30), \\
(2207, 3), & (53, 4), & (31, 21), \\
(1087, 3), & (109, 100), & (41, 21), \\
(4481, 1), & (5779, 2), & (2521, *).
\end{array}
$$

In each case except the last we have

$$F_{r_k} + d_k F_{r_k + 1} \not\equiv 0 \quad \text{(modulo } p_k).$$

(Otherwise it would follow that $F_n + d_k F_{n+1} \equiv 0$ for all n and we would have a contradiction when $n = 0$.)

The final case is different, because $r_{18} = m_{18}$. We want

$$a \equiv 0 \quad \text{(modulo 2521)} \qquad \text{and} \qquad b \not\equiv 0 \quad \text{(modulo 2521)} \qquad (9)$$

in order to ensure that (6) holds in this case.

Let us therefore try to find "small" integers a and b that satisfy conditions (8) and (9). The first step is to find an integer D such that

$$D \equiv d_k \quad \text{(modulo } p_k) \qquad (10)$$

for $1 \le k \le 17$. Then (8) is equivalent to

$$b \equiv aD \quad \text{(modulo } P) \qquad \text{and} \qquad \gcd(a, P) = 1 \,, \qquad (11)$$

where

$$P = p_1 p_2 \ldots p_{17} = 9757748694274371001434366645870 \,. \qquad (12)$$

Such an integer D can be found by using the Chinese remainder algorithm (see, for example, Knuth [2, Section 4.3.2]); it is

$$D = -2548019807824558291186669488975 \,, \qquad (13)$$

uniquely determined modulo P.

Our goal is now to find reasonably small positive integers a and b such that

$$a = 2521n \,, \qquad b = aD \bmod P \,, \qquad (14)$$

for some integer n. If a and b are also relatively prime, we will be done, because (8) and (9) will hold.

Let $C = 2521D \bmod P$. We can solve (14) in principle by trying the successive values $n = 1, 2, 3, \ldots$, looking for small remainders $b = nC \bmod P$ that occur before the value of $a = 2521n$ gets too large. In practice, we can go faster by using the fact that the smallest values of $nC \bmod P$ can be computed from the continued fraction for C/P (or equivalently from the quotients that arise when Euclid's algorithm is used to find the greatest common divisor of C and P).

Namely, suppose that Euclid's algorithm produces the quotients and remainders

$$\begin{aligned}
P_0 &= q_1 P_1 + P_2 \,, \\
P_1 &= q_2 P_2 + P_3 \,, \\
P_2 &= q_3 P_3 + P_4 \,, \quad \ldots
\end{aligned} \qquad (15)$$

when $P_0 = P$ and $P_1 = C$. Let us construct the sequence

$$n_0 = 1, \quad n_1 = q_1, \quad n_j = q_j n_{j-1} + n_{j-2}. \tag{16}$$

Then it is well known (and not difficult to prove from scratch, see Knuth [3, exercise 6.4–8]) that the "record-breaking" smallest values of $nC \bmod P$ as n increases, starting at $n = 1$, are the following:

n	$nC \bmod P$	
$kn_1 + n_0$	$P_1 - kP_2$	for $0 \le k \le q_2$
$kn_3 + n_2$	$P_3 - kP_4$	for $0 \le k \le q_4$
$kn_5 + n_4$	$P_5 - kP_6$	for $0 \le k \le q_6$

and so on. (Notice that when, say, $k = q_4$, we have $kn_3 + n_2 = n_4$ and $P_3 - kP_4 = P_5$; so the second row of this table overlaps with the case $k = 0$ of the third row. The same overlap occurs between every pair of adjacent rows.) In our case we have

$$\langle q_1, q_2, q_3, \ldots \rangle = \langle 1, 2, 3, 2, 1, 3, 28, 1, 4,$$
$$1, 1, 1, 6, 12626, 1, 195, 4, 7, 1, 1, 2, \ldots \rangle \tag{17}$$

and it follows that

$$\langle n_1, n_2, n_3, \ldots \rangle = \langle 1, 3, 10, 23, 33, 122, 3449, 3571, 17733, \ldots \rangle.$$

The record-breaking values of $nC \bmod P$ begin with

n	$nC \bmod P$
1	6798454001099037863589679223555
2	3839159307923704725744991988840
3	8798646147483715879003047532555
13	5601637658181532137565317778555
23	2404629168879348396127588024555
56	1612249848456513050817446295055
89	8198705280336777055073045655555
122	2749120761084236019716283605555

These special values of n increase exponentially as the corresponding values of $nC \bmod P$ decrease exponentially.

The "best" choice of $a = 2521n$ and $b = nC \bmod P$, if we try to minimize $\max(a, b)$, is obtained when a and b are approximately equal. This crossing point occurs among the values $n = kn_{17} + n_{16}$, for $0 \le k \le q_{18} = 7$, when we have

$a = 2521n$	$b = nC \bmod P$	$\gcd(a, b)$
2502466953682069	237607917830996295	11
12525102462108367	206250504149697855	1
22547737970534665	174893090468399415	35
32570373478960963	143535676787100975	1
42593008987387261	112178263105802535	17
52615644495813559	80820849424504095	1
62638280004239857	49463435743205655	1
72660915512666155	18106022061907215	5

We must throw out cases with $\gcd(a, b) \ne 1$, but (luckily) this condition doesn't affect the two values that come nearest each other. The winning numbers are the 17-digit values quoted above in (3).

Slight changes in (7) will probably lead to starting pairs (a, b) that are slightly smaller than the 17-digit numbers in (3). But a proof applicable to substantially smaller starting values, with say fewer than ten digits each, would be quite remarkable.

This research was supported in part by the National Science Foundation under grant CCR-86-10181, and by the Office of Naval Research contract N00014-87-K-0502.

References

[1] Ronald L. Graham, "A Fibonacci-like sequence of composite numbers," *Mathematics Magazine* **37** (1964), 322–324.

[2] Donald E. Knuth, *Seminumerical Algorithms*, Volume 2 of *The Art of Computer Programming* (Reading, Massachusetts: Addison–Wesley, 1969).

[3] Donald E. Knuth, *Sorting and Searching*, Volume 3 of *The Art of Computer Programming* (Reading, Massachusetts: Addison–Wesley, 1973).

Addendum

Smaller values of a and b have been found by Herbert S. Wilf [Letter to the editor, *Mathematics Magazine* **63** (1990), 284]; John W. Nicol ["A Fibonacci-like sequence of composite numbers," *Electronic Journal of Combinatorics* **6** (1999), #R44]; and M. Vsemirnov ["A new Fibonacci-like sequence of composite numbers," *Journal of Integer Sequences* **7** (2004), article 04.3.7]. The latter article has the currently smallest known starting pair: $a = 106276436867$, $b = 35256392432$.

Chapter 15

Transcendental Numbers Based on the Fibonacci Sequence

*[Originally published in Fibonacci Quarterly **2** (1964), 43–44, 52.]*

A well-known theorem due to Liouville [1] states that if ξ is an irrational algebraic number of degree n, then the inequality

$$\left| \xi - \frac{p}{q} \right| < \frac{1}{q^{n+\epsilon}} \tag{1}$$

has only finitely many solutions for integers p and q, given any $\epsilon > 0$. Therefore, an irrational number ξ for which

$$\left| \xi - \frac{p}{q} \right| < \frac{1}{q^t} \tag{2}$$

has solutions for arbitrarily large t must be transcendental. Numbers of this type have been called Liouville numbers.

In 1955, Roth [2] published his celebrated improvement of Liouville's theorem, replacing "n" by "2" in (1). Let us say that an irrational number ξ is a *Roth number* if the inequality

$$\left| \xi - \frac{p}{q} \right| < \frac{1}{q^{2+\epsilon}} \tag{3}$$

has infinitely many solutions for some $\epsilon > 0$. Roth numbers include not only the Liouville numbers but also many more; Roth's theorem proves that all such numbers are transcendental.

Let b be an integer greater than 1. Then we define ξ_b to be the continued fraction

$$\xi_b = \cfrac{1}{b^{F_0} + \cfrac{1}{b^{F_1} + \cfrac{1}{b^{F_2} + \cfrac{1}{b^{F_3} + \cdots}}}}. \tag{4}$$

Theorem. *The constant ξ_b is a Roth number, so it is transcendental.*

99

Proof. From the elementary theory of continued fractions, it is well known that if p_n/q_n is the nth convergent to ξ_b, then

$$\left| \xi_b - \frac{p_n}{q_n} \right| < \frac{1}{q_n q_{n+1}}. \tag{5}$$

In the present case, $q_0 = 1$, $q_1 = b^{F_0}$, and $q_{n+1} = b^{F_n} q_n + q_{n-1}$. We can therefore easily verify by induction that

$$q_n = \frac{b^{F_{n+1}} - 1}{b - 1}. \tag{6}$$

In particular, as $n \to \infty$ we have $q_{n+1}/q_n \to b^{F_{n+2}}/b^{F_{n+1}} = b^{F_n} \approx ((b-1)q_n)^{\phi-1}$, where $\phi = (1 + \sqrt{5})/2 \approx 1.618\ldots$ is the golden ratio. Therefore for large n we have approximately

$$\left| \xi_b - \frac{p_n}{q_n} \right| < \frac{1}{q_n^{1+\phi}} \tag{7}$$

and this completes the proof of the theorem.   □

Remarks

It can be easily shown that the set of Roth numbers has measure zero, but it is uncountable. For example, the number $\sum_{n=1}^{\infty} b^{-c_n}$, where $\langle c_n \rangle$ is a strictly increasing sequence of positive integers, is a Roth number if $\limsup_{n\to\infty}(c_{n+1}/c_n) > 2$, and it is a Liouville number if this $\limsup$ is infinite. In terms of continued fractions, the number

$$\cfrac{1}{a_1 + \cfrac{1}{a_2 + \cfrac{1}{a_3 + \cdots}}}$$

is a Roth number if and only if

$$\limsup_{n\to\infty} \frac{\log a_n}{\log q_n} > 0,$$

where q_n denotes the nth denominator as in the proof of the theorem above.

The rapid convergence of (4) allows us to evaluate ξ_b easily with high precision. For example,

$$\xi_2 = .70980\ 34428\ 61291\ 31464\ 17873\ 99444\ 57559\ 70125 \ldots;$$
$$\xi_3 = .76859\ 75605\ 93155\ 19850\ 83724\ 86230\ 63473\ 93713 \ldots.$$

References

[1] J. Liouville, "Des classes très-étendues de quantités dont la valeur n'est ni rationnelle ni même réductible à des irrationnelles algébriques," *Compte Rendu des séances de l'Académie des sciences* **18**, 20 (15 May 1844), 883–885; "Nouvelle démonstration d'un théorème sur les irrationnelles algébriques," *Compte Rendu des séances de l'Académie des sciences* **18**, 21 (20 May 1844), 910–911; "Sur des classes très-étendues de quantités dont la valeur n'est ni algébrique, ni même réductible à des irrationnelles algébriques," *Journal de mathématiques pures et appliquées* (1) **16** (1851), 133–142.

[2] K. F. Roth, "Rational approximations to algebraic numbers," *Mathematika* **2** (1955), 1–20, 168.

Addendum

P. E. Böhmer ["Über die Transzendenz gewisser dyadischer Brüche," *Mathematische Annalen* **96** (1927), 367–377, 735] published a general theorem that implies the surprising identity

$$\xi_b = (b-1) \sum_{n=1}^{\infty} \frac{1}{b^{\lfloor \phi n \rfloor}},$$

although he did not mention this simple case explicitly. In particular, we have the binary and ternary representations

$$\xi_2 = (.1011010110110101101011011010110110101101\ldots)_2,$$
$$\xi_3 = (.2022020220220202202020220220202202202202\ldots)_3,$$

a pattern of zeros and nonzeros known as the *infinite Fibonacci word* or the *Fibonacci string* S_∞, which arises in several other contexts. I would surely have discovered this property in 1964 if I had had time to compute the value of ξ_{10}! [See E. Hecke, "Über analytische Funktionen und die Verteilung von Zahlen mod. eins," *Abhandlungen aus dem Mathematischen Seminar der Hamburgischen Universität* **1** (1921), 54–76; William W. Adams and J. L. Davison, "A remarkable class of continued fractions," *Proceedings of the American Mathematical Society* **65** (1977), 194–198; Jean-Paul Allouche and Jeffrey Shallit, *Automatic Sequences* (Cambridge University Press, 2003), §7.1, §9.1, §9.3, §13.6.]

Notice that $\xi_b/(b-1)$ is a number of the special form $\sum_{n=1}^{\infty} b^{-c_n}$ that I mentioned in the remarks at the close of my short paper, with $c_n = \lfloor n\phi \rfloor$. It is a Roth number even though $\lim_{n\to\infty}(c_{n+1}/c_n) = 1$.

Steven R. Finch calls ξ_2 the "rabbit constant" in his book *Mathematical Constants* (Cambridge University Press, 2003), §6.8.4.

At the time I wrote this paper, I was especially interested in knowing whether or not the constant

$$\xi = 0.101001000100001\ldots = \sum_{n=1}^{\infty} 10^{-n(n+1)/2}$$

is transcendental. (Indeed, I had secretly defined the fundamental potrzebie constant

$$2.26334\,84517\,43817\,32164\,73780\,74941\,60547\,91419\,51140\ldots$$

by laboriously computing the number $900/(3937\xi)$; see Chapter 1.)

My question was finally resolved by Daniel Duverney, Keiji Nishioka, Kumiko Nishioka, and Iekata Shiokawa ["Transcendence of Jacobi's theta series," *Proceedings of the Japan Academy* **A72** (1996), 202–203] and independently at about the same time by Daniel Bertrand ["Theta functions and transcendence," *Ramanujan Journal* **1** (1997), 339–350], who used results of Yu. V. Nesterenko [«Модулярные функции и вопросы трансцендентности», *Математический Сборник* **187** № 9 (1996), 65–96; "Modular functions and transcendence questions," *Sbornik: Mathematics* **187** (1996), 1319–1348] to prove in fact that the number $\sum_{n=1}^{\infty} \alpha^{n(n+1)}$ is transcendental whenever α is an algebraic number between 0 and 1.

Chapter 16

Supernatural Numbers

[Originally published in The Mathematical Gardner, edited by David A. Klarner, a festschrift for Martin Gardner on his 65th birthday (Belmont, California: Wadsworth, 1981), 310–325.]

"God," said Leopold Kronecker [11], "made the integers; everything else is the work of man." If Kronecker was right, it would be heresy to claim that any noninteger numbers are *supernatural* in the sense that they have miraculous powers. On the other hand, mathematicians generally refer to the nonnegative integers $\{0, 1, 2, \ldots\}$ as the set of *natural* numbers; therefore if any numbers are supernatural, they are also natural. The purpose of this essay is to discuss the representation of natural numbers that are "super" in the sense that they are extremely large: Many superscripts are needed to express them in conventional notation.

It doesn't take a very big number to transcend the size of the known universe. For example, if we consider a cube that's 40 billion light years long on each edge, and if we pack that cube with tiny little 10^{-13} cm $\times$ 10^{-13} cm $\times 10^{-13}$ cm cubes (so that each tiny cube is much smaller than a proton or neutron), the total number of little cubes is less than 10^{125}. This quantity isn't really humongous; it has only 125 digits.

The great Archimedes seems to have been the first person to discuss the existence of extremely large numbers. His famous essay "The sand reckoner" [1] concludes by demonstrating that fewer than 10^{63} grains of sand would be enough to fill the universe as defined in his day. Furthermore he introduced a system of nomenclature by which he could speak of numbers up to $10^{80,000,000,000,000,000}$.

The English language doesn't have names for such large quantities, and it is instructive to consider how we could provide them systematically. In these inflationary days, we may soon need new words to express prices; during 1923, for example, Germany issued postage stamps worth 50 billion marks each, but those stamps were almost valueless.

When we stop to examine our conventional names for numbers, it is immediately apparent that these names are "Menschenwerk"; they could have been designed much better. For example, it would be better to forget about thousands entirely, and to make a *myriad* (10^4) the next unit after hundreds. After all, numbers like 1984 are conventionally read as "nineteen hundred eighty-four," not as "one thousand nine hundred eighty-four."* The use of myriads would provide us with decent names for everything up to 10^8. For instance, the prime number 9999,9989 would be called "ninety-nine hundred ninety-nine myriad ninety-nine hundred eighty-nine."

The next unit we need after myriads is 10^8. Let's agree to call this a myllion (pronounced mile-yun); similar words like myllionaire will, of course, also be of use. After myllions come byllions; one byllion equals 10^{16}, the square of a myllion. The unambiguous word byllion for this next step is clearly an improvement over present practice, since people have never been able to agree about what a "billion" is. (German people and some old Englishmen think it is a million million, while Americans and some old Frenchmen think it is a thousand million.) Notice also the comforting fact that our national debt is only a small fraction of a byllion dollars. The nomenclature should now continue as follows:

10^{32}	tryllion	10^{2048}	nonyllion	10^{131072}	quindecyllion
10^{64}	quadryllion	10^{4096}	decyllion	10^{262144}	sexdecyllion
10^{128}	quintyllion	10^{8192}	undecyllion	10^{524288}	septendecyllion
10^{256}	sextyllion	10^{16384}	duodecyllion	$10^{1048576}$	octodecyllion
10^{512}	septyllion	10^{32768}	tredecyllion	$10^{2097152}$	novemdecyllion
10^{1024}	octyllion	10^{65536}	quattuor-decyllion	$10^{4194304}$	vigintyllion

For example, the total number of ways to shuffle a pack of cards, 52!, is the number '8065::8175,1709;4387,8571:6606,3685;6403,7669;;7528,9505;4408,8327:7824,0000;0000,0000', if we use punctuation marks to group the digits by fours, eights, sixteens, and so on. The English name for this number under the proposed system would be "eighty hundred sixty-five quadryllion eighty-one hundred seventy-five myriad seventeen hundred nine myllion forty-three hundred eighty-seven myriad eighty-five hundred seventy-one byllion sixty-six hundred six myriad thirty-six hundred eighty-five myllion sixty-four hundred three myriad seventy-six hundred sixty-nine tryllion seventy-five hundred twenty-eight myriad

---

* We might also consider changing "nineteen" to "onety-nine," etc.; but that might make our nomenclature *too* logical.

ninety-five hundred five myllion forty-four hundred eight myriad eighty-three hundred twenty-seven byllion seventy-eight hundred twenty-four myriad myllion." This number is inexpressible in our present American language, unless one resorts to something like "eighty thousand six hundred fifty-eight vigintillion one hundred seventy-five nonillion ... eight hundred twenty-four trillion," since unabridged dictionaries don't give names for any units bigger than one vigintillion ($= 10^{63}$) except one centillion ($= 10^{303}$).

Of course we need to go past vigintyllions and even centyllions if we are to have names in our language for all of God's creation. The next unit after vigintyllion presumably should be called "unvigintyllion," if we extrapolate the pattern above and go further in Latin-like nomenclature. Thus, from the formula

$$80{,}000{,}000{,}000{,}000{,}000 = 2^{56} + 2^{52} + 2^{51} + 2^{50} + 2^{45} + 2^{44} + 2^{42} + 2^{41}$$
$$+ 2^{40} + 2^{39} + 2^{36} + 2^{33} + 2^{32} + 2^{30} + 2^{29} + 2^{28} + 2^{27} + 2^{26} + 2^{25} + 2^{19},$$

a reader who understands the proposed system will know the new name of Archimedes's last number $10^{80{,}000{,}000{,}000{,}000{,}000}$. (The answer appears at the end of this chapter.)

Sooner or later we will run out of Latin names to give to the units, since Romans never did count very high. Even if Roman scholars had adopted Archimedes's scheme, we would have trouble naming a unit like

$$10^{2^{10^{80{,}000{,}000{,}000{,}000{,}000}}+3}.$$

But we can get around this problem by simply giving each basic unit $10^{2^{n+2}}$ the name "latin{the name of n with spaces deleted}yllion" for all large n. For example, $10^{2^{10000000000000002}}$ would be "latinbyllionyllion." In this way we obtain English names for all the natural numbers, no matter how super they are. For example, one of the names would be "latinlatinlatinbyllionyllionyllionyllion"; can the reader deduce its magnitude? (See the end of this chapter for the answer.)

At this point the reader may be thinking, "So what? Who cares about names for gigantic numbers, when ordinary decimal or binary notation gives a simpler representation that is much more suited to calculations?" Well, it's quite true that number names are more interesting to the linguistic parts of our brains than to the little gray cells that we use for calculation; the mere fact that a great man like Archimedes wrote about some topic doesn't necessarily prove that it has any scientific interest. Our discussion has not been completely pointless, however, because it has prepared us to talk about a more important problem whose solution involves somewhat similar concepts.

The problem we shall discuss in the remainder of this chapter is this: How can arbitrarily large natural numbers be represented as sequences of 0s and 1s so that the following two properties hold?

1 The representation of each number is never a "prefix" of the representation of any other number.

2 The representation of each number should be "lexicographically smaller" than the representation of every larger number.

Condition 1 means that if some number is represented by the sequence 01101, say, then no other number will have a representation that *begins* with 01101. The notion of "lexicographically smaller" in condition 2 means "to occur earlier in a dictionary"; thus, for example, 01101 is lexicographically smaller than all sequences that begin with 1 or with 0111 or with 011010 or 011011.

The importance of this representation problem is that we often want to communicate a *sequence* of numbers to a computer, without putting spaces or other separators between consecutive values. Such a sequence might, for example, stand for instructions that tell the computer what to do. The critical problem is that the computer must know where one number stops and the next one begins; condition 1 ensures that this will be the case, since the computer can read the sequence from left to right and there will be no ambiguity. Condition 2 isn't quite so critical, but it is a nice property to have: It implies that the representation is *order-preserving* in the sense that, whenever one sequence of numbers is lexicographically smaller than another, the representation of the first sequence will also be lexicographically smaller than the representation of the second.

Conditions 1 and 2 are easy to achieve if we need to represent only a few numbers. For example, if we happen to know that only a few small numbers will ever be needed, say 0 through 7, we can make all the representations of the same length: 000, 001, 010, 011, 100, 101, 110, 111. But we want to be able to encode *all* of the natural numbers, not just the small ones.

Perhaps the first correct solution that comes to mind is a "unary" scheme, where we represent 0 as '0', 1 as '10', 2 as '110', and so forth; the representation of n is '$1^n 0$', that is, n ones followed by a single zero. The zero acts as an end-marker or "comma" between successive numbers that the computer must read. This representation clearly satisfies 1 and 2;

but it is hardly a practical way to represent numbers that are moderately large, and it's horrible in the really big cases, because it requires $n + 1$ bits to represent n. We really want to have a representation that is as concise as possible, subject to conditions **1** and **2**.

Perhaps the next simplest solution is based on the ordinary binary notation for integers, namely $\{0, 1, 10, 11, 100, 101, \dots\}$. This representation as it stands doesn't satisfy either **1** or **2**; but we can beef it up by prefixing the binary notation by a suitable sequence to indicate the length, as follows:

$0 \mapsto 00$	$8 \mapsto 1110000$	$64 \mapsto 1111110000000$
$1 \mapsto 01$	$9 \mapsto 1110001$	$127 \mapsto 1111110111111$
$2 \mapsto 100$	$10 \mapsto 1110010$	$128 \mapsto 111111100000000$
$3 \mapsto 101$	$15 \mapsto 1110111$	$255 \mapsto 111111101111111$
$4 \mapsto 11000$	$16 \mapsto 111100000$	$256 \mapsto 11111111000000000$
$5 \mapsto 11001$	$31 \mapsto 111101111$	$511 \mapsto 11111111011111111$
$6 \mapsto 11010$	$32 \mapsto 11111000000$	$512 \mapsto 1111111110000000000$
$7 \mapsto 11011$	$63 \mapsto 11111011111$	$1000 \mapsto 1111111110111101000$

In general for $n \geq 2$, if the binary representation of n is $(1\alpha)_2$ where α is any sequence of 0s and 1s, the new representation of n is

$$1^{|\alpha|}0\alpha$$

where $|\alpha|$ denotes the *length* of α. If m bits are needed to write n in binary notation, where $m > 1$, the new representation has $2m - 1$ bits. We have roughly doubled the number of bits needed to represent n, in order to indicate unambiguously where each representation ends.

This solution can be improved, but before we pursue the investigation any further it is interesting to point out that our problem is essentially equivalent to a *guessing game*, where one person has thought of an arbitrary natural number and the other person tries to guess it. The rules of this game are something like Twenty Questions: The one who guesses is only allowed to ask "Is your number less than g?" for nonnegative integers g, and the opponent answers "yes" or "no." The game might last longer than twenty questions, because infinitely many secret numbers are allowed; there's no way to distinguish between more than 2^{20} numbers based on the answers to only 20 yes-no questions. But the general idea is to guess the number as quickly as possible.

The relation between this guessing game and the sequence representation problem is not difficult to see. Any fixed strategy that can be used by the guesser to deduce all natural numbers leads to a solution to

1 and **2**: We simply let the representation of n be the sequence of answers that would be given when the secret number is n, with 0 standing for "yes" and 1 for "no." Conversely, given a solution to **1** and **2**, we can construct a guessing strategy that corresponds to it under this rule, if we also allow the guesser to ask the stupid question "Is your number less than infinity?" (The answer to that question will always be "yes"; some solutions to **1** and **2** have every representation beginning with 0.)

The unary solution that we discussed first corresponds to the strategy under which the guesser simply asks

> Is your number less than 1?
> Is your number less than 2?
> Is your number less than 3?

and so on, until receiving the first "yes." Our second solution is more clever: It begins with the questions

> Is your number less than 2?
> Is your number less than 4?
> Is your number less than 8?

and so on; then it uses a "binary search" to pinpoint the secret number once the first "yes" answer has revealed its order of magnitude.

Under this equivalence between the guessing game and the representation problem, a good strategy for the guesser corresponds to a concise representation for numbers. So our search for good representations boils down to the same thing as the search for a good number-guessing scheme.

Incidentally, the number-guessing game isn't just frivolous; it has important practical applications. For example, if a continuous function $f(x)$ is known to have exactly one positive root, where $f(0)$ is negative and $f(x)$ is positive for all sufficiently large x, the root is less than g if and only if $f(g)$ is positive. Thus a good strategy for number guessing leads to an efficient procedure for root location without evaluating derivatives of f.

We can improve on the second solution above by realizing that it is essentially using the unary strategy to represent the length of n's binary representation; the binary strategy can be substituted instead! In other words, the sequence $1^{|\alpha|}0$ used to encode the length of α can be replaced by a more concise representation of $|\alpha|$. By using this idea repeatedly, we obtain progressively shorter and shorter representations for large numbers. And we are eventually led to what might be called a *recursive* strategy, of the following form: "First guess the number of

binary digits of n, then use binary search to determine the exact value."
To guess the number of digits of n, the same strategy is to be used,
recursively; thus we first guess the number of digits in the number of
digits of n, by guessing the number of digits in the number of digits in
the number of digits of n, et cetera. The first questions in the recursive
strategy are:

> Is your number less than 1?
> Is your number less than 2?
> Is your number less than 4?
> Is your number less than 16?
> Is your number less than 65536?

and so on, until the answer is "yes." (Notice that $2 = 2^1$, $4 = 2^2$, $16 = 2^4$,
and $65536 = 2^{16}$; the next question would refer to 2^{65536}, and the next
would refer to 2^{that}.) Eventually this recursive strategy finds an upper
bound on the secret number; then it proceeds to unwind the recursion.
If the secret number is really enormous, the guesser will soon be guessing
really enormous values.

The recursive representation corresponding to this recursive guessing
scheme can be defined very simply: Let $R(n)$ be the sequence of 0s and
1s that represents n. Then

$$R(0) = 0; \quad \text{and} \quad R((1\alpha)_2) = 1R(|\alpha|)\alpha.$$

Small integers are represented as follows:

$0 \mapsto 0$	$8 \mapsto 11101000$	$64 \mapsto 11110010000000$
$1 \mapsto 10$	$9 \mapsto 11101001$	$127 \mapsto 11110010111111$
$2 \mapsto 1100$	$10 \mapsto 11101010$	$128 \mapsto 111100110000000$
$3 \mapsto 1101$	$15 \mapsto 11101111$	$255 \mapsto 111100111111111$
$4 \mapsto 1110000$	$16 \mapsto 111100000000$	$256 \mapsto 11110100000000000$
$5 \mapsto 1110001$	$31 \mapsto 111100001111$	$511 \mapsto 11110100011111111$
$6 \mapsto 1110010$	$32 \mapsto 1111000100000$	$512 \mapsto 111101001000000000$
$7 \mapsto 1110011$	$63 \mapsto 1111000111111$	$1000 \mapsto 111101001111101000$

It's easy to see that this representation satisfies **1** and **2**. Computer
scientists interested in the transformation of recursive methods to iterative methods will enjoy finding a simple nonrecursive procedure that
evaluates n, given its representation; a solution appears at the end of
this chapter.

The recursive representation of a large number n will be about half
as long as its representation under the binary scheme. For example, the
representation of $2^{65536} - 1$ in the binary scheme is the sequence

$$1^{65535}01^{65535}$$

of length 131071, while its representation in the recursive scheme is

$$1^5 01^{65554},$$

only 65560 bits long. On the other hand, the recursive scheme takes quite awhile to show any payoff when we examine its encodings of small numbers; the binary scheme produces a representation that is shorter than the recursive one for all values of n between 2 and 127 inclusive! (The recursive scheme wins out only when $n = 0$ or when n is 512 or more.) Thus the binary scheme will be preferable in many applications.

We can improve the recursive scheme's performance for small n by observing that all sequences except for the sequence representing 0 begin with 1; if we only want to represent strictly positive numbers, we can safely drop the initial '1'. Furthermore the natural numbers are in one-to-one correspondence with the strictly positive integers, so there is a representation $Q(n)$ such that

$$1Q(n) = R(n+1).$$

Under this modified recursive scheme we have

$$0 \mapsto 0$$
$$1 \mapsto 100$$
$$2 \mapsto 101$$
$$3 \mapsto 110000$$
$$4 \mapsto 110001$$

and so on; the binary scheme beats this one only for $n = 1$, 3, 4, 5, 6, 7, and for $15 \le n \le 63$. The same transformation can be applied to the Q scheme, for the same reasons, yielding a P scheme where

$$1P(n) = Q(n+1),$$

so that we have

$$0 \mapsto 00$$
$$1 \mapsto 01$$
$$2 \mapsto 10000$$
$$3 \mapsto 10001$$
$$4 \mapsto 10010$$

etc.; now the binary scheme wins only for 24 values of n.

In some sense we would like to find the *best possible* strategy, but it is hard to say exactly what that means. The binary strategy looks a lot better than the unary one, but even the unary strategy beats the binary scheme when $n = 0$. We will see below that this situation is inevitable: No strategy for the guessing game can completely dominate another — in the sense that the first needs no more questions than the second does to determine n, for all n, and the first sometimes even gets by with fewer questions — unless, of course, the dominated strategy asks stupid questions whose answer "yes" or "no" is already deducible from the previous answers. If one nonstupid strategy is better than another, for some n, it will necessarily be worse for others. You win some, you lose some.

In order to analyze just how good these schemes are, we ought to be more quantitative. (Let the reader beware: The rest of this chapter involves mathematical technicalities that are elementary but sometimes a bit subtle.) If $n \geq 1$, let us write λn for the unique natural number such that $2^{\lambda n} \leq n < 2^{1+\lambda n}$. Thus if $n = (1\alpha)_2$ in binary notation, the number λn is $|\alpha|$, the length of α. It is convenient to define $\lambda 0 = 0$, so that λn is a natural number whenever n is a natural number. We shall write $\lambda\lambda n$ for $\lambda(\lambda n)$, and so on; furthermore $\lambda^m n$ will stand for the m-fold repetition of the λ function, so that $\lambda^0 n = n$ and $\lambda^3 n = \lambda\lambda\lambda n$, etc. Finally, we also write $\lambda^* n$, to denote the least integer m such that $\lambda^m n = 0$.

It is easy to express the length of various representations of n in terms of such functions. Let $c(n)$ be this length, that is, the "cost" of representing n. In the guessing game, $c(n)$ is the number of questions needed to determine a given secret number. The unary guessing strategy has a rather large cost,

$$c_U(n) = n + 1,$$

while the binary strategy reduces this to

$$c_B(n) = \begin{cases} 2, & \text{if } n = 0 \text{ or } n = 1; \\ 2\lambda n + 1, & \text{if } n > 1. \end{cases}$$

The cost of the recursive strategy is

$$c_R(n) = \lambda n + \lambda\lambda n + \lambda\lambda\lambda n + \cdots + \lambda^* n + 1,$$

where the infinite series implied by the $\cdots$ is really finite, since $\lambda^m n = 0$ whenever $m \geq \lambda^* n$. Finally, the modified recursive strategies have costs

$$c_Q(n) = c_R(n+1) - 1, \qquad c_P(n) = c_R(n+2) - 2.$$

These formulas verify our remark that the recursive strategies cost about half as much as the binary scheme when n is large.

Let us say that a representation scheme is *irredundant* if the corresponding guessing game never asks any questions that are "stupid" as discussed earlier. Irredundant schemes have the following property: If α is any sequence of 0s and 1s such that α occurs as a prefix of some representation of an integer, but α is not itself the entire representation of any n, then both $\alpha 0$ and $\alpha 1$ occur as prefixes of representations.

All reasonable schemes are irredundant. For if, say, $\alpha 0$ occurs as a prefix but $\alpha 1$ doesn't, we can shorten the representation of some integers without violating **1** or **2** merely by deleting the 0 following α whenever α appears as a prefix.

The cost functions of irredundant representations satisfy an important arithmetical relation:

Fact 1. *Let $c(n)$ be the cost of representing n in an irredundant representation scheme. Then*

$$\frac{1}{2^{c(0)}} + \frac{1}{2^{c(1)}} + \frac{1}{2^{c(2)}} + \cdots = 1.$$

Proof. In fact, if α is the representation of n, we have

$$\frac{1}{2^{c(0)}} + \frac{1}{2^{c(1)}} + \cdots + \frac{1}{2^{c(n-1)}} = (.\alpha)_2 \qquad (*)$$

in binary notation, for all n. This formula clearly holds when $n = 0$, since there can be no 1s in an irredundant representation of 0. Let β be the representation of $n + 1$; we need to show that

$$(.\alpha)_2 + \frac{1}{2^{|\alpha|}} = (.\beta)_2.$$

No number is represented by a sequence of 1s only, since the sequence 1^m is followed in lexicographic order only by sequences of which it is a prefix. Thus $(.\alpha)_2 + 2^{-|\alpha|} = (.a_1 a_2 a_3 \ldots)_2$ is the smallest binary fraction greater than $(.\alpha)_2$ that doesn't have α as a prefix. If $(.\beta)_2 = (.b_1 b_2 b_3 \ldots)_2$ is unequal to $(.a_1 a_2 a_3 \ldots)_2$, let j be minimal such that $b_j \neq a_j$ and let k be maximal such that $a_k = 1$. Notice that k is the position of the rightmost 0 in α.

We have $(.b_1 b_2 b_3 \ldots)_2 > (.a_1 a_2 a_3 \ldots)_2$; hence $b_j = 1$ and $a_j = 0$. If $k < j$, the sequence $b_1 \ldots b_{j-1}$ is a redundant prefix, because $b_1 \ldots b_{j-1} 1$ occurs as a prefix of the representation of $n + 1$ but $b_1 \ldots b_{j-1} 0$ never occurs as a prefix. If $k > j$, the sequence $a_1 \ldots a_{k-1}$ is a redundant prefix, because $a_1 \ldots a_{k-1} 0$ occurs as a prefix of the representation of n

but $a_1 \ldots a_{k-1}1$ never occurs as a prefix. But k cannot equal j, since $a_k = 1$. This contradiction proves $(*)$, by induction on n.

The irredundancy condition implies that 1^m occurs as a prefix for all m. Now if 1^m is a prefix of the representation of n, the sum $2^{-c(0)} + 2^{-c(1)} + \cdots + 2^{-c(n-1)}$ lies between $(.1^m)_2 = 1 - 2^{-m}$ and 1; hence the infinite sum as $n \to \infty$ converges to 1.   □

(This proof uses both properties **1** and **2**, and indeed the result would be false if only property **1** were assumed. For example, the following procedure generates representations of length $n + k$ for each integer $n \geq 0$ in an irredundant fashion, for any fixed $k \geq 2$: Represent 0 by 0^k. Then for $n = 1, 2, 3, \ldots$, find a sequence α such that (a) α has occurred as a prefix of a representation for some number less than n but not as a representation; (b) $\alpha 0$ and $\alpha 1$ have not both occurred as prefixes; and (c) α is as short as possible satisfying (a) and (b). The representation of n can be any sequence of length $n + k$ that contains $\alpha 0$ or $\alpha 1$ as a prefix, whichever hasn't previously occurred. One such representation scheme for $k = 2$ begins

$$
\begin{array}{lll}
0 \mapsto 00 & 3 \mapsto 11000 & 6 \mapsto 11100000 \\
1 \mapsto 100 & 4 \mapsto 011000 & 7 \mapsto 010100000 \\
2 \mapsto 0100 & 5 \mapsto 1010000 & 8 \mapsto 0111000000.
\end{array}
$$

On the other hand, it is not difficult to prove the inequality

$$
\frac{1}{2^{c(0)}} + \frac{1}{2^{c(1)}} + \frac{1}{2^{c(2)}} + \cdots \leq 1
$$

for all representations that satisfy property **1**; this relation is known as "Kraft's inequality" [10].)

There is also a converse to Fact 1:

Fact 2. *Let $c(0), c(1), c(2), \ldots$ be a nondecreasing sequence of positive integers such that*

$$
\frac{1}{2^{c(0)}} + \frac{1}{2^{c(1)}} + \frac{1}{2^{c(2)}} + \cdots = 1.
$$

Then there is an irredundant representation scheme with cost function $c(n)$.

Proof. We obtain a scheme with the desired properties by letting the representation α of n be defined by $(*)$ and $|\alpha| = c(n)$.   □

If X is an irredundant representation scheme whose cost function c_X is not monotonic, we can permute the integers to obtain another representation with the same costs sorted into nondecreasing order. Facts 1 and 2 now show that there exists an irredundant scheme having these sorted costs. Representation schemes with monotonic cost functions can be called *standard*, since most applications prefer to have $c_X(n) \leq c_X(n+1)$ for all n.

Let us conclude our investigations by trying to find the best possible scheme, putting an emphasis on asymptotic questions (that is, on the efficient representation of very very large integers). Clearly the binary method is more efficient than the unary method, and we also prefer the recursive method to the binary method because of its superior performance when n is large. These examples suggest the following definition: "A representation scheme Y with cost function $c_Y(n)$ *dominates* another scheme X with cost function $c_X(n)$ if we have $c_Y(n) \leq c_X(n)$ for all large n and $c_Y(n) < c_X(n)$ for infinitely many n." If Y dominates X and Z dominates Y by this definition, then Z dominates X.

Clearly the recursive methods P, Q, R all dominate the binary method B, and B dominates the unary method U. When we try to compare the three recursive schemes with each other, however, it turns out that none of them is dominant. Method P is best nearly all the time; in particular, whenever $\lambda n = \lambda(n+2)$ we have $c_P(n) = c_Q(n) - 1 = c_R(n) - 2$. But there are infinitely many n where Q is better than both P and R (namely when $n = 2^{2^k} - 2$ and $k \geq 1$); and there are infinitely many n where R is better than both P and Q (namely when $n = 2^{2^{2^k}} - 1$). These facts suggest that it might be impossible to dominate method R, and in that sense we might conclude that method R is "optimal." However, any such hopes are quashed by

Fact 3. *If X is any standard representation scheme, there is another standard representation scheme Y that dominates X and satisfies $c_Y(n) \leq c_X(n)$ for all but one value of n.*

Proof. The general idea of the proof is to choose a binary sequence α of length c and replace it by infinitely many sequences, of respective lengths $c+1$, $c+2$, $c+3$, etc., because $2^{-c} = 2^{-c-1} + 2^{-c-2} + 2^{-c-3} + \cdots$.

Proceeding more formally, we may assume that X is irredundant. For $k \geq 1$ let a_k be the number of n's such that $c_X(n) = k$, and let $j = c_X(0)$. Let $b_k = 0$ for $1 \leq k < j$, $b_j = a_j - 1$, and $b_k = a_k + 1$ for $k > j$. Then there is a unique nondecreasing function $c_Y(n)$ having exactly b_k values of n with $c_Y(n) = k$; and this function satisfies $2^{-c_Y(0)} + 2^{-c_Y(1)} + \cdots = 2^{-c_X(0)} + 2^{-c_X(1)} + \cdots$. By Fact 1 and Fact 2, there is an irredundant standard representation scheme with cost function c_Y. Furthermore we easily see that $c_Y(n) \le c_X(n)$ except for the single value of n such that $c_X(n) = j$ and $c_X(n+1) > j$; and we have $c_Y(n) < c_X(n)$ whenever $j + 1 < c_X(n-1) < c_X(n)$.   □

It is hopeless to find a strictly optimum scheme, because repeated application of the construction in the proof of Fact 3 will give an infinite family of better and better schemes, each dominating its predecessors. However, no scheme can actually be much better than our recursive scheme R, in spite of all the apparent improvement guaranteed by Fact 3.

Fact 4. *Let Λn be the function defined by*

$$\Lambda n = \lambda n + \lambda\lambda n + \lambda\lambda\lambda n + \cdots.$$

Every cost function $c(n)$ that corresponds to a representation scheme satisfies

$$c(n) > \Lambda n + \lambda\lambda^* n$$

for infinitely many n.

Proof. Let $d(n) = \Lambda n + \lambda\lambda^* n$; we shall show that the sum $\sum_{n=0}^{\infty} 2^{-d(n)}$ diverges. This will suffice to complete the proof, for if the cost function could satisfy $c(n) \le d(n)$ for all $n \ge m$ we would have the impossible inequality

$$1 = \sum_{n=0}^{\infty} 2^{-c(n)} \ge \sum_{n=0}^{m-1} \left(2^{-c(n)} - 2^{-d(n)}\right) + \sum_{n=0}^{\infty} 2^{-d(n)}.$$

In general if $f(n) = \Lambda n + g(\lambda^* n)$ for any function g, we have the (rather amazing) identity

$$\sum_{n=0}^{\infty} \frac{1}{2^{f(n)}} = \sum_{n=0}^{\infty} \frac{1}{2^{g(n)}}, \qquad (**)$$

since the left-hand side can be written

$$\sum_{m=0}^{\infty} \frac{1}{2^{g(m)}} \sum_{\lambda^* n = m} \frac{1}{2^{\Lambda n}}$$

and for $m \ge 1$ we have

$$\sum_{\lambda^* n = m} \frac{1}{2^{\Lambda n}} = \sum_{\lambda^* \lambda n = m-1} \frac{1}{2^{\lambda n + \Lambda\lambda n}} = \sum_{\lambda^* k = m-1} \frac{1}{2^{k + \Lambda k}} \sum_{\lambda n = k} 1$$

$$= \sum_{\lambda^* k = m-1} \frac{1}{2^{\Lambda k}}.$$

Thus the sum $\sum_{n \ge 0} 2^{-d(n)}$ diverges if and only if the sum $\sum_{n \ge 0} 2^{-\Lambda n}$ diverges. And it does.   □

Using the same proof technique, we can show in fact that

$$c(n) > \Lambda n + \Lambda\lambda^* n + \Lambda\lambda^*\lambda^* n + \cdots + \Lambda(\lambda^*)^m n + \lambda(\lambda^*)^{m+1} n$$

infinitely often, for any fixed representation scheme and any fixed m.

Let us close by showing how to improve scheme R so that we obtain "ultimate" schemes that come very close to this lower bound. The sequence $R(n)$ begins with $1^{\lambda^* n} 0$, a sequence of length $\lambda^* n + 1$ that serves to identify $\lambda^* n$, followed by a sequence of length Λn that characterizes n once $\lambda^* n$ is known. In this sense, the R method starts by using a unary approach to guess $\lambda^* n$; and we know that we can do better. Let us therefore use the R method to determine $\lambda^* n$, then continue to determine n as before, calling this the RR method. The new cost function will be

$$c_{RR}(n) = \Lambda n + c_R(\lambda^* n) = \Lambda n + \Lambda\lambda^* n + \lambda^*\lambda^* n + 1,$$

and the RR representation of n will begin with the sequence $1^{\lambda^*\lambda^* n} 0$.

But wait; let's start by guessing $\lambda^*\lambda^* n$. Then we obtain an RRR method whose cost function is

$$\begin{aligned} c_{RRR}(n) &= \Lambda n + \Lambda\lambda^* n + c_R(\lambda^*\lambda^* n) \\ &= \Lambda n + \Lambda\lambda^* n + \Lambda\lambda^*\lambda^* n + \lambda^*\lambda^*\lambda^* n + 1. \end{aligned}$$

The R^{m+1} method has a cost function equal to

$$c(n) = \Lambda n + \Lambda\lambda^* n + \cdots + \Lambda(\lambda^*)^m n + (\lambda^*)^{m+1} n + 1,$$

and this upper bound is almost the same as our lower bound.

Related Work

Philip Davis [5] has written a delightful introduction to the elementary facts about large numbers.

An ancient Chinese mathematician named Hsü Yo, about A.D. 200, discussed a nomenclature for large numbers containing the units *wan* = 10^4, $i = 10^8$, *chao* = 10^{16}, and *ching* = 10^{32}, in his interesting book *Shu Shu Chi I*; see [13, page 87]. I am indebted to Tung Yun-Mei for this reference.

The representation scheme B with $c(n) \approx 2\lambda n$ was published by Stig Comét in [4]. The problem of representation schemes in general was introduced by Levenshteĭn [12], who presented method R and proved that $c(n) > \Lambda n - \lambda^* n$ for infinitely many n; he also discussed representations with more than two symbols. The representation problem has also been studied independently by Elias [6] and by Even and Rodeh [7]. The guessing game for unbounded search was suggested by Bentley and Yao [2]. Methods P and Q were proposed by Jim Boyce and David Fuchs during a recent conversation with the author.

Numbers much larger than those considered here are discussed in [9]. Using the notation of that article, we have $\lambda^*(2 \uparrow\uparrow m) = m + 1$ and $\lambda^*(2 \uparrow\uparrow\uparrow m) = (2 \uparrow\uparrow\uparrow (m - 1)) + 1$, suggesting that the upper and lower bounds we have derived are really not so close together after all. Perhaps the introduction of functions $\lambda^{**}n$ and $\lambda^{***}n$, etc., will lead to further clarification of "optimum" representation schemes when we imagine ourselves dealing with supersupernatural numbers.

There is a beautiful connection between the concepts we've discussed and the information-theoretic concept of algorithmic complexity, originated independently by L. A. Levin in Russia and G. J. Chaitin in Argentina. A certain function $l(n)$, called $KP(n)$ by Levin (see [8]) and $H(n)$ by Chaitin [3], has the following two properties: (a) There is a representation scheme for natural numbers that satisfies condition **1** and has cost $l(n)$. (b) For every representation scheme satisfying condition **1** and having cost $c(n)$, there is a constant C such that $l(n) \leq c(n) + C$. Intuitively, $l(n)$ represents the length of the "simplest" description of an algorithm to compute n. This function $l(n)$ is not computable, but it is semicomputable from above, in the sense that, if $l(n)$ is actually less than a given number m, we can prove this fact in a finite amount of time. If $c(n)$ is the cost function for any representation scheme that satisfies conditions **1** and **2**, there is a constant C such that $\lambda n + l(\lambda n) \leq c(n) + C$. Furthermore there is a constant C_0 such that $\left| \lambda n + l(\lambda n) - \max_{1 \leq k \leq n} l(k) \right| \leq C_0$. Thus the constructions we have given provide bounds on $\max_{1 \leq k \leq n} l(k)$. I am indebted to Péter Gács for these references.

References

[1] Archimedes, "The sand reckoner," in *The World of Mathematics* **1**, edited by James R. Newman (New York: Simon and Schuster, 1956), 420–429.

[2] Jon Louis Bentley and Andrew Chi-Chih Yao, "An almost optimal algorithm for unbounded searching," *Information Processing Letters* **5** (1976), 82–87.

[3] Gregory J. Chaitin, "A theory of program size formally identical to information theory," *Journal of the Association for Computing Machinery* **22** (1975), 329–340.

[4] Stig Comét, "Notations for partitions," *Mathematical Tables and Other Aids to Computation* **9** (1955), 143–146.

[5] Philip J. Davis, *The Lore of Large Numbers* (New York: Random House, 1961). [Volume 6 of the *New Mathematical Library*.]

[6] Peter Elias, "Universal codeword sets and representations of the integers," *IEEE Transactions on Information Theory* **IT-21** (1975), 194–203.

[7] S. Even and M. Rodeh, "Economical encoding of commas between strings," *Communications of the ACM* **21** (1978), 315–317.

[8] Péter Gács, "On the symmetry of algorithmic information," *Soviet Mathematics Doklady* **15**, 5 (1974), 1477–1480; **15**, 6 (1974), v. [Translation of П. Гач, «О симметрпии алгоритмической информации», *Докады Академии Наук СССР* **218** (1974), 1265–1267.]

[9] Donald E. Knuth, "Mathematics and computer science: Coping with finiteness," *Science* **194** (1976), 1235–1242. [Reprinted as Chapter 2 of *Selected Papers on Computer Science*, CSLI Lecture Notes 59 (Stanford, California: Center for the Study of Language and Information, 1996), 31–58.]

[10] Leon G. Kraft, Jr., "A device for quantizing, grouping, and coding amplitude-modulated pulses," M.S. thesis in Electrical Engineering (Cambridge, Massachusetts: Massachusetts Institute of Technology, 1949), 62 pages.

[11] L. Kronecker, remark in a lecture at the Berlin scientific congress (1886): "Die ganzen Zahlen hat der liebe Gott gemacht, alles andere ist Menschenwerk." Quoted by H. Weber, *Mathematische Annalen* **43** (1893), 15.

[12] V. I. Levenshtein, "On the redundancy and delay of decodable coding of natural numbers," *Systems Theory Research* **20** (1968), 149–155. [Translation of В. И. Левенштейн, «Об избыточности и замедлении разделимого кодирования натуральных чисел», *Проблемы Кибернетики* **20** (1968), 173–179.]

[13] Joseph Needham, *Science and Civilization in China* **3** (Cambridge: Cambridge University Press, 1959).

Solutions

1 Archimedes's last number: One septendecyllion trevigintyllion quattuorvigintyllion quinvigintyllion sexvigintyllion septenvigintyllion octovigintyllion trigintyllion untrigintyllion quattuortrigintyllion septentrigintyllion octotrigintyllion novemtrigintyllion quadragintyllion duoquadragintyllion trequadragintyllion octoquadragintyllion novemquadragintyllion quinquagintyllion quattuorquinquagintyllion. (His own name for this number was much shorter, but the new system beats his in lots of other cases.)

Incidentally, American names for large numbers are not based on good Latin (sexdecillion should be "sedecillion" and novemdecillion should be "undevigintillion"); so it isn't clear how much further the American system can be extrapolated. See Dmitri A. Borgmann, "Naming the numbers" and "Renaming the numbers," *Word Ways* **1** (1968), 28–31, 89–93, for proposals by Rudolf Ondrejka; see also John Candelaria, "Extending the number names," *Word Ways* **8** (1975), 141–142; "Renaming the extended numbers," *Word Ways* **9** (1976), 39; "A new number nomenclature," *Word Ways* **16** (1983), 125–127; A. Ross Eckler, "The only man infinity fears," *Word Ways* **19** (1986), 252–254. More recent proposals have been made by John H. Conway, Richard K. Guy, and Allan Wechsler, on pages 13–16 of Conway and Guy's *The Book of Numbers* (New York: Copernicus, 1996).

2 One latinlatinlatinbyllionyllionyllionyllion is

$$10^{2^{(10^{2^{(10^{2^{10000000000000002}}+2)}}+2)}}.$$

We might call this one umptyllion, for short.

3 An iterative decoding procedure for method R: Let the input sequence be $s_1 s_2 s_3 \ldots$, where each s_i is 0 or 1. Let k be the number of input bits already read; let l be the length of a number to be input; let m be the stack depth in a recursive implementation; and let n be the answer returned. The following recursive method corresponds directly to the definition, with k initially zero, using only global variables:

PROCEDURE R.
Set $k \leftarrow k + 1$.
If $s_k = 0$, set $n \leftarrow 0$ and exit from R.
Otherwise call R (recursively).
Then set $l \leftarrow n$ and $n \leftarrow 1$.
While $l > 0$, repeatedly set $k \leftarrow k + 1$, $n \leftarrow 2n + s_k$, $l \leftarrow l - 1$.
Exit from R.

The recursive program above can be transformed mechanically into the following purely iterative procedure:

Set $k \leftarrow 1$ and $m \leftarrow 0$.
While $s_k = 1$, repeatedly set $m \leftarrow m + 1$ and $k \leftarrow k + 1$.
Set $n \leftarrow 0$.
While $m > 0$, repeatedly do the following operations:

Set $m \leftarrow m - 1$, $l \leftarrow n$, $n \leftarrow 1$.

While $l > 0$, repeatedly set $k \leftarrow k + 1$, $n \leftarrow 2n + s_k$, $l \leftarrow l - 1$.

The corresponding encoding procedure can be treated similarly.

Addendum

When I was asked in 1978 to write something for Martin Gardner's 65th birthday, I chose the title "Supernatural numbers" as a sort of counterpoint to my novelette about *Surreal Numbers* (Reading, Massachusetts: Addison–Wesley, 1974), with which Martin was quite familiar. I had no idea that many mathematicians were already using the term 'supernatural numbers' in a serious way, to stand for the multiplicative extension of positive integers that consists of all possible products — finite or countably infinite — of prime numbers. [See, for example, Stephen S. Shatz, *Profinite Groups, Arithmetic, and Geometry*, Annals of Mathematics Studies 67 (Princeton, New Jersey: Princeton University Press, 1972), 12.] That concept had been introduced by Ernst Steinitz in section 16 of his classic paper "Algebraische Theorie der Körper," *Journal für die reine und angewandte Mathematik* **137** (1910), 167–309, under the name *G*-Zahlen (Gradzahlen). Jean-Pierre Serre called them the 'nombres surnaturels' in section I.1.3 of his book *Cohomologie Galoisienne* [*Lecture Notes in Mathematics* **5** (1964)], and his name for them has become standard terminology. Such numbers, the "real" supernatural numbers, continue to find more and more uses as mathematics advances.

Chapter 17

Mathematical Vanity Plates

*[An abridgment of this chapter was published in The Mathematical Intelligencer **33**, 1 (Spring 2011), 33–45.]*

Introduction

This story began in the spring of 1967 when I made a visit to Madison, Wisconsin, in order to give a lecture at the university. I was driving near the campus on a fine, sunny day. There was moderate traffic, and when a red light stopped me I happened to glance at the license plate of the car ahead. My jaw dropped—wow! It said "H65·536". I can still picture that plate in my mind, as plain as day (see Figure 1), although more than forty years have passed.

FIGURE 1. A historic license plate, recreated in 2009 via the magic of Adobe Photoshop®.

I started to jump out of my car, thinking that I might approach the driver to ask him if he knew what a fantastic license number he owned. But the light turned green; he drove away and I was unable to follow. I'll never know if he was aware that the state had assigned one of the most important numbers in mathematics to his car. How I envied him!

Indeed, 65536 is not just an ordinary power of 2, and not simply the order of the multiplicative group in the Galois field of the largest known

121

Fermat prime. It is

$$2^{2^{2^2}} = 2^{2^{2^{2^{2^0}}}},$$

a number of huge importance in computer algorithms. Already in 1967 I had become a big fan of this number, and my appreciation has continued to grow as I continue to learn more.

The Old Rules

In those days each state of the USA required its drivers to purchase new license plates with new license numbers every few years, assigning the values in sequence. Thus your chance of getting any particular number n was at most $1/n$. People began to covet the small numbers— not because small numbers are mathematically interesting (which they are), but because small numbers are easy to remember. Small numbers also connote rank: The governor was number 1. The *New York Times* reported in 1959 [87] that

> [a state commission] is recommending the elimination of thousands of "distinctive number plates"—unofficially called "vanity" plates. Low-numbered "vanity" plates have had a long and distinguished history in the automobile business. They have traditionally been obtained by politicians for their friends and campaign contributors. They have long been doggedly sought after by celebrities, egomaniacs and men who have everything. Last year about 69,000 New Yorkers paid $5 extra for special low-numbered plates.

About 5 million automobiles were registered in New York state at that time; New York plates contained one or two letters to encode a county, together with a serial number. The $5 fee for distinctive plates with fewer than six letters and/or digits had been inaugurated in 1954 [1].

Clever people didn't actually have to settle for a random number on their licenses, however. It was perfectly legal in many states, including New York and California, to get your plates in a remote county, far from where you lived. During a vacation to a sparsely populated area, you could drop in to the local office and obtain decent numbers without much competition. Furthermore, your initials might well be available in some rural county.

My father-in-law, who lived at 525 Summit Street in the medium-sized city of Fostoria, Ohio, was able to drive Ohio plates reading 525 S (his address) ever since the 1950s, because he was a friend of the local people who were in charge of auto registration.

Beginning in 1967, Wisconsin motorists could obtain plates of the forms A9, A99, A999, A9999, or AA999 by paying a surcharge, where A denotes any letter and 9 denotes any digit. Thus a person could pay to have G256, say, but not H65536.

I like to imagine that the man who acquired the plate in Figure 1 had obtained it on a day when he knew that the 65,500s were being distributed. By carefully trading places with people behind him in line, he could then have seized the opportunity to get the license number of his dreams. Wisconsinites are friendly folks who would have been quite willing to accommodate such a whim — unless of course two mathematicians had been in the same line.

Every state in the USA has its own esoteric rules about license tags, except in one respect: All plates made since 1956 or so have the same size, $6'' \times 12''$, so that automobile manufacturers know how much space to allocate for plate display on their cars.

When California adopted the standard size, it had to rethink the format of license numbers because the existing plates were somewhat larger. The old 'digit-letter-digit-digit-digit-digit-digit' style was capable of distinguishing 26,000,000 vehicles (see Fig. 2); but a maximum of

FIGURE 2. A typical California license plate of the early 1950s, faked by Photoshop®.

six characters was desirable on the new plates, and California had more than 5.5 million registered cars [2]. So the authorities introduced a new tagging scheme in which all passenger cars were identified by three black letters followed by three black digits, on a yellow base, potentially allowing $230^3 = 12,167,000$ combinations. (The letters I, O, and Q were excluded.) These plates were distributed in batches of 1000 to district offices; thus you could easily identify where any given license had been obtained, by knowing the local letter codes. As before, the plates were designed to last for several years. Drivers were annually expected to purchase little stickers to paste in the upper right corner, as proof that they had renewed their registration.

By 1963 it was time for new plates, and all Californians got new numbers again. The new scheme featured three *yellow* letters followed by three *yellow* digits, on a *black* base; my wife and I received WHZ 065.

FIGURE 3. What
I drove to Caltech
(another re-creation).

(Mnemonic: "Whiz by at 65 miles per hour" — the legal speed limit.)
I didn't realize until later that, with this plate, we already owned three of
the six characters in Figure 1. Notice that if I had been just 66 places earlier in the queue, my car would have been repeatedly asking, "WHY 999"?

Late in 1962, a determined 30-year-old man named Bill Sherinyan
had driven from Los Angeles to the small town of Alturas in the rugged
northeastern corner of California, where he stood in line for 42 hours,
braving both cold and rain to win the ultimate prize: California license
AAA 000, the first of the new series [3]. I remember seeing him inter-
viewed on television when he substituted this trophy for his former plate
(which incidentally was WWW 333).

"There is a motorist in Marysville who has a plate reading ACH 000.
Gesundheit." [60]

Three-Letter Words

The 1963 licenses began to allow the letter Q as well as the vowels I
and O, in the first and second positions, thus forming many new three-
letter combinations with familiar connotations. Back in those days LOL
didn't make anybody laugh; but the license ONE 234 was quickly spotted
on a black Corvette [80]. Staunch Democrats refused to accept GOP, but
HIS and HER plates became popular with two-car families [40].

More serious, however, were three-letter combinations that were
patently offensive, like (censored), (censored), (censored), and (censored). California's license czars had foreseen this problem already in
1955, when they asked Prof. Emeneau of the linguistics department at
UC Berkeley to find all of the unsuitable words in the set

$$\{A, B, C, D, E, F, G, H, J, K, L, M, N, P, R, S, T, U, V, W, X, Y, Z\}^3.$$

He and his helpers "came up with 152 no-nos" [60], including the word
YES — because they feared that a woman might be uncomfortable with
such a plate.

I was told many years ago that Stanford Research Institute was asked to revise the UC list of banned words after I, O, and Q became permissible, but I haven't been able to confirm this rumor. And the revised list continued to grow; I do know that LSD and PIG became proscribed in the late 1960s [60]. George Reasons, a reporter for the *Los Angeles Times*, was evidently allowed to peek at the list in 1962, because he wrote an amusing essay that incorporated 34 of the excluded triples:

> They've DUN it again. Some BUM at the Department of Motor Vehicles ordered all the FUN out of license-plate watching. It's a GYP. ... They HAD some SAD SAK at the University of California CUL out all of the GAG words. ... DUM if you ask me. We lost some pretty good watching words, SOB, SOB. ... GEE, nobody argues about taking out references to GOD and minority groups. They get RAW. And everybody knows SEX is BAD. ... BRA I can see. BUT BVD? ... BAH. [79]

By 1979 the BAD list had grown to 215 items, which are now posted online [49]. But state authorities began to relent in 1993, and 75 of those 215 now do occur on ordinary plates — including YES, as well as the words BUM, GYP, HAD, SAD, GAG, and BAH in the quotation above. On the other hand, four new combinations (including HIV) are now DOA [49].

California's Department of Motor Vehicles has always disallowed CHP (California Highway Patrol) and CIA (Central Intelligence Agency) on license plates; but DMV is OK. Perhaps they don't know that DMV stands for Deutsche Mathematiker-Vereinigung.

Four-Letter Words

American license plates rarely contained more than two letters during the first half of the 20th century. The reason may have been that license numbers were regarded as, well, numbers. Or perhaps officials realized that the possibilities for mischief grow exponentially as the number of letters increases. At any rate, motorists continued to want more and more varieties of personalized license tags, until finally the concept of vanity plates became much broader than before: Instead of simply having small numbers and/or our own initials, we're now essentially free to express ourselves in any tasteful way.

Seeds of this revolution were planted in 1937, when Connecticut motorists with a good driving record were allowed to get plates containing just their three initials. Four-letter combinations appeared in Connecticut during the 1940s [9]. New Hampshire issued vanity plates of up to five letters in 1957; and Vermont followed soon after, allowing letters and numbers to be mixed. (See [48, 65, 90].)

After a few years, the idea of decorating automobiles with personal names gradually began to evolve into the display of personal *statements*. For example, when vanity plates of up to five letters became available in the District of Columbia in 1964, people's first choices were the one-letter plates from A to Z; numbers 1, 2, 3 were pre-reserved for the mayor, deputy mayor, and city council chair. (I don't think 0 was permitted.) Five years later, Colman McCarthy [71] surveyed the 6000 choices that DC drivers had reserved during their first years of plate-naming freedom. He found that most motorists chose their initials or their first names, in order to make their cars look swanky. A second group, reacting against "faceless numbers sent by a faceless computer," wanted to be identified in a more personal way using nicknames; the B-names in this category were BABS, BABY, BALDY, BEBE (*not* owned by Mr. Rebozo), BIRDY, BOBO, BOOFY, BUBI, BUNNY, BUTCH, and BUZZ.

But the new folk art of devising witty licenses was also beginning to develop in DC: A man named Carl Levin got C-11 for himself and S-11 for his wife Sonia. A man named Ware had two cars, respectively AWARE and BWARE. A retired Navy captain's Buick sported the license AWOL, received as a gift when he stepped down as head of the Citizen's Association of Georgetown. Uplifting messages like FAITH, HOPE, LOVE, JOY, MERCY, PEACE (and PAX) were also in evidence. Although YES was forbidden in California, the District of Columbia had both YES and NO as well as OUI; also OH NO, SORRY, and OOPS. Somebody in the nation's capital had MONEY, and I imagine somebody else had POWER — but McCarthy didn't speak to that.

California Vanities

A definitive history of vanity plates has yet to be written, and I'm certainly not qualified to write it. But I can perhaps shed some light on the California side of the story, because I've lived in that state for nearly fifty years.

All-letter licenses in California had an eccentric debut: One of the first of the 1963 plates to be printed was discovered to read YOUBUM. (It was smuggled into a DMV office by the clever convict or convicts at Folsom prison who had manufactured it for the state [4]. This plate, and a later one that said HELP, unfortunately had to be destroyed.) The tale took yet another twist in 1967, when dozens of souvenir plates reading THANKS were given out as Republican Party favors at the inauguration dinner for Governor Ronald Reagan [50]. Later that year, a resident of

Pomona was spotted with a POMONA plate from Massachusetts; it was legal for him to use the license he had obtained for a car leased in that state [5]. (Massachusetts had introduced vanity plates containing two to six characters in 1966 [69].)

Finally the lid came off in 1970. Page 1 of the *San Francisco Chronicle* proclaimed, on 22 August 1970, that "Senator Milton Marks finally won his 10-year fight yesterday to allow Californians to order car license plates carrying letters or numbers they desire." Motorists were to pay $25 for this privilege, and $10 per year afterwards, all earmarked for a special fund to fight pollution; thus the plates became officially known as *environmental plates*. When Governor Reagan signed the bill authorizing this new policy, sitting next to a giant replica of a license emblazoned CLEAN, he predicted that the plates "will serve as a symbol of the motorist's personal concern for preserving and enhancing the beauty of California's environment." Application forms were available at DMV branches statewide, allowing people to list three choices, and giving four examples of the new possibilities: CLEAN, ZAP, WOW, and I KNOW [6]. Up to six letters and/or numbers were permissible, plus an optional space.

Hundreds of motorists responded almost immediately. Among the first requests were PAID 4, OREGON, TURTLE, WHY WAR, GRANNY, and 32 FORD [31, 46, 91]. Initial applications were collected for 30 days so that the most popular choices could be awarded by lot; but afterwards the rule was to be strictly first-come, first-served. The most wanted words, among about 10,000 applications received by September 22, were PEACE, SMILE, JAGUAR, GEORGE, TBIRD, BOB, LAWYER, MARGIE, MORGAN, LARRY, SNOOPY, LOVE, in decreasing order of popularity. A drawing was held in San Francisco on October 26 to select the winner among 38 applicants who sought PEACE; another, in San Diego, determined which of 20 Californians would SMILE. The first California vanity plate actually delivered, however, was presented in Sacramento by the governor on that day to Mr. and Mrs. Robert E. Klees, who had submitted the only request for AMIGO. Then Reagan drew from a hat to decide which of four candidates should have NO SMOG. (See [7, 35, 61, 84].) By December, the number one Christmas gift in southern California was a new license plate with a message like HOHOHO or XMAS 70 [29].

Californians purchased more than 65 thousand personalized plates during the first 1.5 years, thereby raising more than $1.5 million for the environmental fund; about 1500 new requests were being processed each week. The fund had received $18 million by 1977, and a total of 423,213 plates had been issued before April 1979, although 55,523 of them had not been renewed. California began to use narrower letters and numbers in 1979 so that the licenses could contain up to seven characters; thus many more choices became possible, and about 600 new applications began to be filed every day. The millionth environmental plate was produced in 1982, at which time about 750,000 were actually in circulation. (See [8, 21, 62].)

A Complete List

One of my cherished possessions is the official list [20] of all California environmental plates that were current on 21 July 1981, obtained from a friendly administrator in 1982 when I explained that I was a computer science professor interested in database research. Altogether 665,571 entries appear in this list, and I estimate via random sampling that about 40% of them have length 7.

What a wealth of ingenuity exudes from almost every page! For example, I wondered if anybody had wanted to put BONFIRE on their vanity plate; sure enough, there it was — together with BONFYR and BONFYRE, as well as FALO, FALO1, and FALO2.

To get an inkling of this 836-page list, let's consider page 316, which contains 798 entries from HOWZEIT to HRNDEZ. Among them are

HOWZIT	HP	HPNOSIS	HRCULES	HRD2GIT	HRIZON
HOW2WIN	HPBMW	HPOWER	HRDCORE	HRD2PAS	HRLEQIN
HOXIE	HPBOOKS	HPTYHOP	HRDROCK	HRD2PLZ	HRMIONE
HOY	HPBOSS	HPYTRLS	HRDRSR	HRD24GT	HRMMPH
HOYLES	HPBRDAY	HRBLOCK	HRDTOP	HRGOD	HRMNIZE
HOZWIFE	HPENNY	HRBONUS	HRDWARE	HRH	HRNBLWR

and another word that I'll mention later. (Spaces have been suppressed because they don't count, in the DMV's test for equality of names.)

One thing that's immediately clear is that people with the same idea have been forced to spell it in different ways. We find plates like PLEYBOY, JIGOLO, FORSAIL, STOLIN, JILLOPY, LAEMON, NOWHEY, and POETIQ; of course this is just poetic license.

All 24 letters of the Greek alphabet are present in [20] — except for ZETA and XI, which are represented by ZETA7 and XICHI. And they often occur with "subscripts": ALPHA0, ALPHA1, ..., ALPHA8, as well as ALPHA01 and ALPHA99 (which I guess were chosen by statisticians or social scientists). Latin scholars have contributed ERGOSUM, ERGOIAM, and ERGOIGO. We find both PUBLISH and PERISH, as well as HANSEL and GRETEL, PEARL and OYSTER, GOLD and SILVER, DONNER and BLITZEN, etc.

Yet there also are surprising gaps: The English numerals ONE, THREE, FOUR, FIVE, SIX, SEVEN, EIGHT, NINE, TEN, ELEVEN are present and accounted for, but TWO and TWELVE are lacking. Nobody in 1981 had even thought of VEHICLE. There was neither YIN nor YANG. Music lovers had named their plates after HAYDN, MOZART, B8HOVEN, BRAHMS, and MAHLER; also BACH, BACHJS, JSBACH, JSBACH1, and PDQBACH. But not (yet) BERLIOZ, DVORAK, or MILHAUD. Somebody had OPUS 132. ADAGIO, ALLEGRO, ANDANTE, LARGO, and PRESTO? Yes. LENTO and VIVACE? No.

Other States

I've already mentioned early appearances of vanity plates in Connecticut, New Hampshire, Vermont, Massachusetts, and the District of Columbia. Many other states, like New Jersey, New York, and Pennsylvania, allowed motorists to pay extra for plates that were especially desirable, provided that they would stick to letters and numbers that conform to the ordinary license number syntax.

I ran across a few other facts while researching the California story, such as the following front-page item in the *Wall Street Journal* for 7 May 1969:

> To glean extra revenue from auto licenses, New Mexico began offering "prestige plates" — auto tags with any letters a car owner asked for — for a $25 premium. The executive secretary of the New Mexico Cattle Growers Association ordered BEEF and a Volkswagen owner asked for BUG. But last year, the state sold only 155 vanity plates. Now the legislature has marked down the price to $15 (as of June 20), in hopes that car owners will go for cut-rate status.

A brief note on page 15 of the Baltimore *Afro-American*, 8 July 1967, reported that "The North Carolina Department of Motor Vehicles is accepting applications for personalized 1968 license plates." And a filler item from Texas on page 21 of *The New York Times*, 6 February 1969, stated that

> Personalized license plates are the thing in Fort Worth despite the $10 extra cost. One motorist got big red-lettered plates reading SMILE. ... The most exuberant ordered YIPEEE. More than 1,000 persons have ordered special plates.

Thus the phenomenon was certainly becoming contagious. A survey by Robert E. Dallos in 1977 [27] reported that

> A dozen years ago, fewer than 15 states offered special plates. Now, only Mississippi doesn't have them. ... South Dakota's

plate law went into effect July 1. Although it had passed the Legislature a number of times, it had always been vetoed by the governor. This time it was allowed to take effect because, according to a spokesman, the state could use the $50 initial fee and $35 annual charge.

The revolution still wasn't complete in the 1970s, however, because several states were still severely limiting the amount of allowable personalization as Wisconsin had done in 1967. Wisconsin began to allow genuine "own choice" plates in 1979, followed by Illinois in 1980, Mississippi in 1981, and West Virginia in 1982 [85]. Even today, Massachusetts requires all numbers to be preceded by letters; you can say MITPHD or MIT69 but not MY69MG. Furthermore there must be at least two letters. Illinois is similar, but there must be a space separating letters from numbers. (The pure numbers 1 to 999 are said to be legal in Illinois, but they were all snapped up long ago.)

Stefan Lonce, working with the American Association of Motor Vehicle Administrators, collected statistics from all 50 states and the District of Columbia, determining the total number of registered motor vehicles in 2005 as well as the total number that were "vanitized" as of 2006 or 2007. The results [66] showed that the current fraction of vanity plates in the USA was $9292843/242991747 \approx 3.8\%$ at that time, with greatest penetration in Virginia ($1065217/6578773 \approx 16.2\%$) and least in Texas ($97315/17347615 \approx 0.6\%$). California ranked 22nd, with a ratio of $1136772/32592000 \approx 3.5\%$.

These statistics make it clear that vanity plates have now become thoroughly integrated into American pop culture. Several books have been written on the subject [25, 30, 44]; see also the nice survey of vintage 1986 plates by Faith W. Eckler [34].

A complete list of current South Dakota vanity plates, containing 15,483 entries from 001 to ZZZZOOM, was posted on the Internet on 25 October 2009 [67], and it's interesting to compare it to the California list of 1981. The interval from page 316 of [20], discussed above, intersects the South Dakota data in only three cases: HPYDAYS, HPYTRLS, HRDROCK. There are 22 other South Dakota plates in the corresponding interval, including HPBD2ME, HPYGIRL, HRDLUCK, HRDLY, HRHOTRD, and HRMSWAY.

Choices with inappropriate connotations, as discussed above for 3-letter words, must of course be weeded out by committees in each state. Sometimes the prisoners who manufacture the plates are able to help by catching obscure obscenities at the last minute [8]. An interesting game remains, however, to get past the censors with "dirty words" that still are sufficiently highbrow to be acceptable in polite company. The best I've seen in this category so far are SWIVE (a Chaucerian verb) and HRAKA (a Lapine noun from Richard Adams's *Watership Down*).

The Challenge

So how do mathematicians fit into this trend? Dentists can advertise their specialty with "dental plates" such as DENTIST, 2TH DR, DRILLER, SMILE, MOLARS, CUSPID, GUMSAVR, NO DK, FLOSSEM, CROWNS. Physicists now sport licenses like PHYSICS, NUCLEON, DELTA S, GLAST, XRAY BMR, CY N TIST, E PLUS, and E MINUS [26]. And of course E COLI [20] belongs to a biologist.

If you, like me, don't already own a vanity plate, what would be your first choice? What's the briefest and best way to represent yourself to the world? If there's something that's uniquely you, there's a greater chance that it won't already be reserved.

Ideally your choice should bring a smile to people who see it. They'll think, "Aha! A person who loves mathematics!" Alternatively, you might choose something that will please and amaze specialists, although the masses won't get the point; that can still lead to teachable moments.

Many of the things we deal with as mathematicians involve words that are much too long: MATHEMATICS, ARITHMETIC, DETERMINANT, CONJUGATE, DIFFERENTIAL, INTEGRATION, COMPUTATION, PERMUTATION, LOGARITHM, ALGORITHM, COUNTEREXAMPLE, etc., etc. There are some shorter terms like MATHS, ALGEBRA, SINE, COSINE, TANGENT, MATRIX, GROUP; but they're in [20], already claimed ages ago. What's left?

I remember discussing this question with my son, long ago when he was in elementary school and vanity plates were fairly new. I told him that, ha ha, our car should say VANITY. (I naïvely believed that this was an original thought.)

But he had a much better idea: How about letting the plate be entirely blank? At that very moment I realized that he was a budding mathematician, wise beyond his years. For indeed, what could be more vain, yet more rich in mathematical properties, than the empty set? This idea trumps even the governor's number 1.

Unfortunately, though, the empty string is too *short* a word for state bureaucrats to understand. And even if they did issue a blank plate when you left the form blank, what do you think highway patrolmen would do when you drove by? Not everybody understands nullity, alas.

On the other hand — surprise — I happened to spot 7 SPACES, on 8 August 2004. Aha, I learned, the empty plate *does* exist! (Moreover, 7 BLANKS is still available in California, as of 5 November 2009.)

The Character Set

Before we investigate the possibilities further, we need to know the ground rules, which differ from state to state.

The most important limitation is the total number of characters. Wyoming residents are expected to be most creative: They must express themselves in four symbols or less, in order to leave room for a county code and the famous bronco-buster logo. (Unfortunately, this state and some others have recently switched to "digital plate technology," produced by laser printing instead of embossing, with an atrocious font. It looks cheap, perhaps because it is. If I lived there I'm afraid I would choose the word UGLY until they reverted to the beautiful style of 2002.)

The maximum message length in Alaska, Connecticut, Hawaii, Kentucky, Maine, Massachusetts, Missouri, Oregon, Rhode Island, and Texas is 6. All other states have a limit of 7, except for New York, North Carolina, and West Virginia, where you can (gasp) go up to 8. Only in the latter three states can you claim GEOMETRY or TOPOLOGY.

What can those 4 or 6 or 7 or 8 characters be? All 26 uppercase letters from A to Z are legal, and New Mexico allows also Ñ. The digits 2 through 9 are obviously all OK too. But 1 is equivalent to I in Louisiana and Minnesota; and O presents a really sticky problem.

Consider the following nineteen entries from [20]:

```
        OOO                                      OOOOOOO OOOOOOO
OO      OOO    OOOO    OOOOO OOOOO    OOOOOO      OOOOOOO OOOOOOO
OO      OOO    OOOO    OOOOO OOOOO    OOOOOO      OOOOOOO OOOOOOO
        OOO                                      OOOOOOO OOOOOOO
```

There are 240 or 241 combinations* of O and 0 that don't conflict with plates in the ordinary sequential series; by July of 1981, Californians had reserved those 19. These plates must have caused nightmares for police officers because they're so hard to distinguish. Therefore O and 0 have now become identical in California; also in Colorado, Louisiana, Minnesota, Nevada, North Carolina, Vermont, and Wisconsin. I don't know when this change was made, or if cars with visually ambiguous licenses are still on the road in California.

South Dakota still considers O and 0 to be distinct; I know this because [67] lists both 0000000 and 0000000 but no other combinations of length 7. Massachusetts does too, because AUTO is taken but AUT0 is not.

---

*I don't know if 0000000 would have been legal. California plate 999ZZZ in the ordinary series was followed by 1AAA000 in April of 1981; plates numbered 2AAA000, 3AAA000, 4AAA000, 5AAA000, and 6AAA000 came out in 1984, 1992, 1999, 2003, and 2007, respectively. When the present series runs out, 9ZZZ999 probably won't be followed by 0AAA000. But who knows?

The most interesting variation between states, vanity-wise, is the set of allowable delimiters or punctuation marks that can appear. My eyes popped in 1985 when I first saw New Hampshire plates containing + signs as well as - signs, opening up a whole new world of mathematical vanities. Complex analysts in the Granite State can adorn their cars with X+IY. (California now has + signs too; see below.) New Hampshire had used heavier, red-cross-like symbols on their license plates for ambulances since 1939 or earlier. In 1974 they reserved AMB for ambulances, and eventually they made vanity pluses available for use by anybody [47].

Furthermore, New Hampshire drivers are able to use *ampersands*. Hence they can construct the wonderful formula -X&X, which yields the least significant 1-bit, if any, in the binary representation of X (see [58, Eq. 7.1.3–(37)]). I checked both X+IY and -X&X on New Hampshire's website in November 2009, and both of them were available. But X&-X was illegal, because consecutive punctuation marks are forbidden.

Most states allow only letters and digits. But a minus sign (hyphen) is permissible in Alabama, Colorado, Delaware, Florida, Kentucky, Louisiana, Minnesota, Missouri, New Mexico, North Carolina, Oklahoma, Oregon, Pennsylvania, Virginia, and Washington, as well as New Hampshire. An ampersand is legal in Delaware, New Hampshire, North Carolina, North Dakota, South Carolina, and Virginia. You can use a dot in Colorado, Connecticut, Louisiana, and North Carolina. Apostrophes are OK in Missouri, New Mexico, and (again) North Carolina.

North Carolina, in fact, is Vanity Plate Heaven. We've seen that tarheels are able to enjoy up to 8 characters that include pluses (+), minuses (-), dots (.), and apostrophes (’); and in fact they can also have number signs (#), question marks (?), dollar signs ($), asterisks (*), slashes (/), equals signs (=), at signs (@), colons (:), double quotes ("), commas (,), and exclamation points (!)! Unfortunately for mathematicians, the list stops there; parentheses, and the relational signs < and >, aren't permitted. Unfortunately for TeX users, backslashes and curly braces are lacking too.

But hey, $720=6!$ in this state. Calculus and physics teachers can have dx/dt, etc. (All special characters are ignored when comparing two plates; thus 7206 and dxdt would be indistinguishable from those examples, and so would #7+2/0-6 and dx/dt?, both of which happen to be presently available—subject to approval by the authorities.)

I wonder if a fallacious proposition like $120=6!$ would also be acceptable to the North Carolina censors. Probably it would, thereby setting back education in the Southeast. Even worse, I fear that somebody will ask for BAD@MATH and be proud to display it. But let's not be pessimistic; North Carolina deserves applause for leaping way ahead of everybody else.

Besides ordinary punctuation, a few special characters are also available. New Mexico has an enchanting Zia Sun symbol, which their website illustrates with the example VAN✹ITY. New York offers a blob in the shape of its empire, which I won't illustrate here.

Since 1994, California has allowed a single delimiter to appear on vanity plates, taking the place of a letter or digit. There are four choices: Drivers can use either a plus sign or one of the unique symbols $\{ \maltese, \star, \heartsuit \}$. The senior co-editor-in-chief of this journal could be C♥LER D if he moved to California; Steve Smale could be ♥LE BODY. Both of these are currently up for grabs, as are X+IY, I♥MATHS, and L★SPACE.

The rules for spaces (I mean blank spaces, not L^*-spaces) are too complicated to explain here. Suffice it to say that most states allow you to insert them in order to improve readability.

Examples on the Road

Let's look now at how some mathematicians and/or their friends have risen to the occasion by meeting these constraints.

Cathy Seeley, who was president of the National Council of Teachers of Mathematics (NCTM) from 2004 to 2006, likes her license plate so much that she included it in an illustrated lecture that I found on the Internet:

FIGURE 4. An exhortation.

Her plate sits in a holder that was in fact produced by the NCTM, saying "Do math and you can do anything!" (I'd amend that to "Do math and learn to write, and you can do anything" — but my version wouldn't fit.)

She told me about two other nice examples: Ed Rathmell, a math professor at the University of Northern Iowa who does a lot of work with education, is MATH ED. And Gail Englert, a middle-school math teacher in Norfolk, Virginia, has IEDUK8M, with a nice play on 'K–8' in education.

David Eisenbud, who was president of the American Mathematical Society (AMS) during 2003 and 2004, received an appropriate plate from his wife shortly after he became director of the Mathematical Sciences Research Institute in 1997:

FIGURE 5. An institution.

Incidentally, when I spotted the California plate I AM PAMS on 2 January 2001, I realized that it did not refer to *Proceedings of the American Mathematical Society* — because Clifford J. Earle, Jr. was at Cornell.

Vanity plates that name the basic words of our discipline are more difficult to come by, because more people try to reserve them. Victor Miller has been doubly successful in this regard, because he not only owned New York ALGEBRA in 1978, he purchased New Jersey ALGEBRA in 1993! He still drives it:

FIGURE 6. An acquisition.

Dave Bayer is another lucky mathematician who obtained the plate of his dreams, perfectly suited to his work on geometric invariants [14]:

FIGURE 7. A celebration.

He is evidently not alone, because the California list from 1981 [20] already contained SYZYGY, SYZYGY1, SYZYGY2, SYZYGY3, SYZYGYS, and SYZYGYX, as well as SYZ WIZ.

The key words NUMBER, THEORY, and THEOREM were also unavailable to Californians who sought new vanity plates in 1981. But eventually two of them came back into play: Fan Chung and her husband Ron Graham (the AMS president in 1993 and 1994) now have personal plates, acquired in 1999, that are amazingly appropriate when parked side by side:

FIGURE 8. A perfect matching.

The existence of Ron's plate implies that THEOREM is once again unavailable; so I used the DMV website to try for LEMMA. It, too, is currently taken, and so is DILEMMA. So are MATRIX and VECTOR; but not TENSOR. (According to [67], NUMBER, THEORY, THEOREM, LEMMA, DILEMMA, MATRIX, VECTOR, and TENSOR are all presently available in South Dakota, as are DO MATH, MATH SCI, ALGEBRA, and SYZYGY. This observation doesn't prove that South Dakotans are anti-mathematics; indeed, [67] does list MATH ROX, NUMBERS, and NUMB3RS.)

Fan and Ron also share an RV with a tag that commemorates their joint work on quasi-random graphs and other structures [22]:

FIGURE 9. A collaboration.

(This license plate incidentally illustrates the unfortunate fact that California has never figured out how to make a decent-looking letter Q. From a typographic standpoint, Wisconsin and other states would actually be much better places to advertise QRANDOM research.)

Ron tells me [45] that he often sees 2+2 R 4 in the parking lot of the math building at UCSD; another one is S CUBED. At a higher level he also encounters RC FLOW, representing Ricci flow — the key idea with which Grisha Perelman resolved Poincaré's conjecture [77].

Andy Magid has said [68] that he's the only licensed Galois theorist in Oklahoma, because he drives GALOIS. "Most people who read or have to record my car tag, such as tow truck operators or highway patrol officers, do so without comment or even accurate pronunciation. But on occasion it does provoke welcome conversation."

What about the names of other famous mathematicians? I checked a few, to see what California drivers have selected, and got a shock:

in use?	FERMAT	EULER	LAPLACE	FOURIER	GAUSS	GALOIS	HILBERT
1981	no	yes	yes	no	no	no	no
2009	yes	no	yes	yes	yes	no	yes

Alas — my personal hero, Leonhard Euler, has waned in popularity out west. (But David Robbins did have New Jersey EULER for many years.)

The license plate BIG OH has been spotted in New York [86], and it's also present in California. I love that notation [56]. At present New Yorkers, like me, are less enthusiastic about LITTLE OH.

My colleague Ingram Olkin in Stanford's Department of Statistics received STAT PRO as a gift from his children about ten years ago. His daughter Julia now has the California plate SOLV4X; she really wanted SOLVE4X, but it was already taken in 1981 [20].

California's 1981 list had OPTIMUM, MINIMUM, and MAXIMUM; also OPTIMAL and MINIMAL but not yet MAXIMAL. It included both MINMAX and MINIMAX, as well as MAXIMIN and — my favorite — MAXIMOM. There was a Z AXIS on the road, but no X AXIS or Y AXIS. Somebody had DY DX; another had DU DS but without the space.

Fifty-two of the California environmental plates in 1981 began with MATH. Some of them, like MATHER, MATHEW, and MATHIS, were surnames that aren't relevant to our discussion; MATHIEU may, however, have belonged to a group theorist. Noteworthy are MATHBIZ, MATHMAN, MATHPRO, MATHS, MATHWIZ, and MATH4U. I fear that MATHANX was supposed to suggest anxiety rather than thank-you-dear-ma; and MATHOS was perhaps a feminine form of PATHOS.

A light-hearted competition for the best vanity plate with a mathematical theme was organized by the NCTM at the beginning of 2005, and prizes were awarded at their meeting in April of that year. First place went to a "pair o' docs" named Carol and Roy Bohlin, who teach

at Fresno State University and always carry a trunkful of material for
the math classes and workshops that they teach:

Other winners included Hollylynne and Todd Lee, a young couple in
North Carolina who had decided to marry when she (TCHUMATH) and he
(MATHMTCS) saw each other's license plates.

Small Integers

Of course license plates have traditionally featured numbers rather than
letters, and nothing can be more mathematical than numbers. Therefore
mathematical vanity plates often involve carefully selected numbers.

Let's start at the beginning with 0. We've already noted that California's database from 1981 [20] had many combinations of 0 and O. It
also included DOUBLE0, DOUBLEO, DBLOO; in fact, somebody even claimed
OXO EQ 1! There was a vote for 00NUKES. My favorite from [20] in this
category, however, is OOMPH — a plate that is not only pronounceable, it
is semantically equivalent to STOPPED, if you think about it.

Moving up, the use of 1 as a cardinal number and/or multiplicative identity was quite common, as in 1 BAD APL, 1 EGO FIX, 1 FOW VEY,
1 HONKER, 1 LITER, 1 MOMENT. The ordinal 1 appeared too, in 1ST AID,
1ST ALTO, 1ST HALF, 1ST LAP, 1ST N 10, 1ST VIOL. The plate 1F100 may
have denoted a hypergeometric function; but it was most likely on a Ford
F100 pickup truck. I don't know the significance of 1DELTA1, 1OMEGA1,
1SIGMA1 (all found in [20]).

FIGURE 10. Shades of Leibniz and Boole.

Laurence C. Brevard [18] tells the following story (see Fig. 10):

> I got 1 OR 0 in Texas in 1982 but the picture shows the 1984
> plate. Back then you got new plates every year instead of the
> stickers they use now. ... After I moved to Oregon in 2001 I
> got the same plate "number" there. People consistently thought
> the OR stood for Oregon. Sigh.... Someone *else* has this plate
> in California! I also have had the domain 1or0.com since 1998.

May I suggest ORBITS? (Sorry.)

Bill Ragsdale sent me a picture of the license **10-00100**, which he spotted during a trip to China in 1984. He theorizes that "China is moving to binary license plates due to the difficulty of their character set."

The website of Utah's Division of Motor Vehicles [89] provides helpful examples of personalized plates, including 2XX3XY, which certainly looks mathematical. Upon further inspection, however, this one actually turns out to be genomical: The driver has two girls and three boys.

Indeed, I've rarely seen license plates that celebrate the beautiful *mathematical* properties of small integers. Why haven't people chosen messages such as 0 IS NONE, 0 IS LOG1, 1 IS UNIT, 2 IS EVEN, 3D WORLD, 4 COLORS, 5 IS F5, PERFECT 6, 7 FRIEZES, 8 IS CUBE, PAPPUS 9? A large territory remains to be explored. (In [20] I do find 1 IS ALL and 10ISBUF; but the latter surely was chosen by a tennis buff.)

The 1981 collection [20] has many examples based on small numbers that occur in less mathematical ways: 7 COME 11, 8 IS ENOF, 9 LIVES, TEN FOUR, 12 STEPS, 12 TONE, 15 GRAND, SWEET 16, 24 CT, LOVE 30, 49ER, 55 HAHA, 58 PROOF, etc.

François Le Lionnais wrote a classic book [63] that is filled with good reasons to like particular numbers, and David Wells has written a similar but more elementary sequel [92]. (See also De Koninck [28].) There's a well-known proof by induction that *all nonnegative integers are interesting*; for if this statement were false, the smallest noninteresting number would certainly be quite interesting. QED.

Following this reasoning we can conclude that the number 62 is interesting, because it's the smallest integer that appears neither in [63] nor in [92]. The more recent book [28] lists only prosaic facts about 62.

But John Conway has discovered that 62 also has a far more interesting property, namely that it's the least n such that no number is exactly n times the sum of its digits. (See [83, sequence A003635].) We could make a vanity plate from that fact: WHATS 62.

On the other hand, Gordon Garb [38] told me a cautionary tale. After having been excited and inspired by a reference to a paper by Li and Yorke entitled "Period three implies chaos" [64], he once decided to acquire the California vanity plate PERIOD 3. Unfortunately, his choice didn't turn out to be as cool as he had hoped:

> In the years that I had it on my vehicle, nobody ever got the Chaos reference. I explained it many times when friends asked, but what fun is an inside joke if you always have to explain it? My future wife told me years later that she just assumed I was a hockey fan. ... I replaced it with a vanity plate that simply has my typical login name.

Roman Numerals

Since the decimal system is only one of many ways to represent numbers, vanitizers have often opted to express themselves with the venerable notation of ancient Rome — the city where size XL was smaller than size L. For example, the plate IV appeared early on in New Hampshire [48].

An online search using the California DMV website reveals that the license LXIX is presently unavailable. Somebody may have snuck it past the censors, because my state allows this number to appear only on vehicles that were manufactured in 1969.

When I originally received the early California list [20], I looked first for the entry DCLXVI, because I had a notion that it might be fun to drive around displaying the infamous "number of the beast" (see Revelation 13:18 and [39]). Alas, someone had beaten me to it. Roman numerals are in fact not uncommon in [20]; there are, for instance, 36 entries ranging from 1901 (MCMI) to 1980 (MCMLXXX), almost surely intended to stand for dates that have personal significance. Somebody also chose SPQR LXV.

I'm writing this essay in 2009, the year that matches the name of my computer MMIX [57]. Perhaps my license should read MMIXMAN. (Or TOMMIX, which is playfully ambiguous.)

Notice that Roman numerals can also be used in reverse, as in the sequence F4E, S9, SE5EN.

Bond; James Bond

What is the most-wanted three-digit number on a vanity plate? The winner, hands down, is 007. Uncountably many motorists have apparently dreamed of masquerading as Ian Fleming's immortal character James Bond [37]. In the 1981 list [20], for example, one can find

AGNTOO7	DBLO7	JAMESO7	JMSBOO7	007	OOVII
BONDOO7	DOUBLO7	JBOND	JOO7	007BOND	007
BONDOO7	DUBLEO7	JBOO7	OHOHSVN	007LIVZ	007LIVS
DBLOH7	DOO7	JMSBOND	OHOH7	OOSEVEN	OOSVN

and probably more that I've missed. (The choice 007 was not allowed. Nobody had yet taken 007.)

Some lucky Californian will get the license 7AKA007 as part of the *regular* (non-vanity) sequence, sometime during the year 2013, if present trends continue. Who will it be?

In 1966, Sol Golomb created Bond's illustrious binary cousin, Secret Agent 00111, when he introduced the concept of run-length encoding for sequences of bits [42]. Several of the exciting and bizarre exploits of this intrepid information trafficker were revealed later, in an introductory textbook [43]. Agent 00111 either remained undercover in 1981 or failed to own a California vehicle at that time; but he or she is now driving somewhere in the state, and also in Florida.

While we're on this subject, I should mention that another counter-spy, Maxwell Smart [19], also has a huge following in the license plate subculture. Would you believe that the choices

AGNT86	AGNT99	AGENT99	MAXWELL	MSMART	MSMRT	MXSMRT
AGNT8T6	AGENT86	CONTROL	MAX86	MSMARTY	MXSMART	86SMART

all appear in [20]?

Real Numbers

Mathematics doesn't limit itself to whole numbers, of course; many others are out there, including SURREAL ones [20, 54].

What do you think is the first noninteger number that most people think of? You're right: It's π.

To verify this hypothesis, I looked up the license plates that are currently available in Florida, Michigan, Nevada, and North Carolina, which are among the few states that allow motorists to choose plates that contain seven digits and no letters. In each case the combinations 3141592 and 3141593 have already been taken, but 3141591 and 3141594 have not. (Recall that $\pi \approx 3.14159265358979323846264338327950288841972$.)

This cannot be just a coincidence. In North Carolina, which allows up to eight digits, I checked for 31415926 and 31415927 as well, but those plates are still available. The π-fanciers of that state have most likely taken advantage of their typographic freedom by selecting plates with the decimal point included: 3.141592 and 3.141593.

Arizona motorists have currently claimed 314, 3141, 31415, 314159, and 3141592, but not 3141593. Have they perhaps been basing their choices on the successive version numbers of TEX [55]?

Although California doesn't permit plates that are entirely numeric, the 1981 list [20] does include QT314, QT31415, and QT31416, as well as PI R SQ and PI R2.

The people have spoken: π wins!

FIGURE 11. Four mathematicians with a nonrandom license plate.

Figure 11 is a historic photo from 1987 that shows four people who have made significant contributions to the high-precision evaluation of π: Gene Salamin, Yasumasa Kanada, David Bailey, and Bill Gosper. They're gathered around Bailey's appropriately numbered car. At that time Kanada held the world record, having recently computed π to 134,214,700 decimal places. He had helped with the first calculation that exceeded 2 million places, in 1981, but that record didn't last long; Gosper had topped 17 million places in 1985, using some ideas of Salamin, and Bailey had surpassed 29 million in 1986, before Kanada got back in the lead [12]. More than two further decades of continued progress in mathematics, hardware, and software have led to the astonishing present record of 5,000,000,000,000 decimal places (yes, 5 trillion), announced on 2 August 2010. This major feat was achieved by Alexander Yee and Shigeru Kondo on a personal desktop computer, after about 90 days of calculation [95].

David Bailey's current license shows π in a less familiar guise:

FIGURE 12. A conundrum.

Hexadecimal notation, which makes π equal to

$$3.243\text{F}6\text{A}8885\text{A}308\text{D}313198\text{A}2\text{E}03707344\text{A}4093822299\text{F}31\text{D}\ldots,$$

nicely meets California's stipulation that all license plates must contain letters. And it's also especially appropriate for Bailey, who helped to discover the remarkable formula

$$\pi = \sum_{k=0}^{\infty} \frac{1}{16^k}\left(\frac{4}{8k+1} - \frac{2}{8k+4} - \frac{1}{8k+5} - \frac{1}{8k+6}\right),$$

by which the nth hexadecimal digit of π can be computed efficiently without evaluating the previous $n-1$ [12, 13].

Martin Davis currently drives around Berkeley with the vanity plate E I PYE. (He is also martin@eipye.com.) That's a very nice formula; but I think my own preference would be SQRT 2PI, which happens to be currently available if I decide to go for it.

While writing this essay I tried to find other familiar constants ($\sqrt{2}$, e, ϕ, γ) by querying the appropriate websites in Arizona, Florida, Michigan, Nevada, and North Carolina. But I encountered only a few hits: Arizona drivers have reserved 271828, 1618PHI, and 1618033; North Carolina drivers have reserved 1.414214, 2.718282, and 1.618034; otherwise nothing. From this limited sample it appears that fans of Euler's constant have not yet arisen to promote their cause, and that rounding is preferred in the East but not in the West. A rich vein of important numbers remains to be claimed, vanitywise.

Sometimes, as in Figure 1, people obtain mathematically significant license plates purely by accident, without making a personal selection. A striking example of this phenomenon is the case of Michel Goemans, who received the following innocuous-looking plate from the Massachusetts Registry of Motor Vehicles when he and his wife purchased a Subaru at the beginning of September 1993:

FIGURE 13. An anticipation.

Two weeks later, Michel got together with his former student David Williamson, and they suddenly realized how to solve a problem that they had been working on for some years: to get good approximations for maximum cut and satisfiability problems by exploiting semidefinite programming. Lo and behold, their new method — which led to a famous, award-winning paper [41] — yielded the approximation factor .878! There it was, right on the license, with C, S, and W standing respectively for cut, satisfiability, and Williamson.

Large Numbers

Let's return now to the scenario we began with, a license plate that bore the desirable number 65536. Mathematicians have traditionally befriended numbers that are much smaller than this, because smaller numbers tend to have more interesting properties. (Or perhaps because smaller numbers have properties that are easier to discover without computer assistance.) Le Lionnais considered this situation in his postlude to [63], saying "Tous les nombres sont remarquables, mais peu ont été remarqués." His book discusses 219 integers between 2^0 and 2^{20}, having a total of 574 "properties," with the following distribution of k-bit numbers for $1 \leq k \leq 20$:

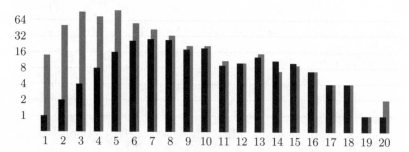

FIGURE 14. Remarkable numbers and remarkable properties in [63].

Here the black bars stand for numbers and the gray bars stand for properties; for example, when $k = 1$ the only 1-bit number is 1 and he mentions 14 of its properties.

The sole number listed for $k = 20$ is 604800, the number of elements in the Hall–Janko group (the fifth sporadic group); this number also has the property that some of its divisors yield an interesting "congruence cover." A congruence cover is a set of integer pairs $(a_1, d_1), \ldots, (a_s, d_s)$ with $d_1 < \cdots < d_s$ such that every integer is congruent to a_k (modulo d_k) for some k. For example, the simplest congruence cover [36] is

$$\{(0, 2), (0, 3), (1, 4), (1, 6), (11, 12)\}.$$

Robert Churchhouse [23] found a congruence cover for which $d_1 = 9$, $d_s = d_{124} = 2700$, and $\mathrm{lcm}(d_1, \ldots, d_s) = 604800$; when Le Lionnais wrote [63], Churchhouse's example had the largest known value of d_1. (Erdős had conjectured that d_1 could be arbitrarily large. His conjecture remains open, and carries a $1000 reward for the solver. A cover with $d_1 = 40$ and $s \approx 10^{50}$ has recently been found [73].)

What other properties does 604800 have, besides the two that were featured by Le Lionnais? For this question mathematicians can now turn to Neil Sloane's wonderful On-Line Encyclopedia of Integer Sequences [83], or OEIS, which tells us for example (in sequence A053401) that there are 604800 seconds in a week. Sequence A001715 of the OEIS reminds us that $604800 = 10!/3!$; from this fact we can conclude, with a hint from A091478, that exactly 604800 simple graphs on 5 labeled vertices have 7 labeled edges. Furthermore we learn from sequences A055981, A058295, A060593, and A080497 that 604800 is the number of ways to write an 11-cycle as the product of two 11-cycles on the same elements [16], and that 604800 can not only be expressed as 5! 7! and as $12!/d(12!)$ but also as

$$(1\times2\times3\times4\times5\times6\times7\times8\times9\times10\times11)/(1+2+3+4+5+6+7+8+9+10+11)$$

and — via prime numbers — as

$$(17-2)(17-3)(17-5)(17-7)(17-11)(17-13).$$

Altogether the number 604800 appears explicitly in 78 sequences of the current OEIS list, or at least it did when I wrote this essay in November 2009; thus it possesses 78 "OEIS properties." I can well imagine that Marshall Hall, who was my Ph.D. advisor long ago, would have been delighted to drive an automobile whose license plates bore the property-rich number 604800.

These considerations beg us to ask, "What numbers greater than, say, 10000, have the most OEIS properties?" I posed this question to Sloane in 2001, and he told me how to answer it by downloading a stripped version of the database. The champion numbers in November 2009, by this criterion, are shown in Table 1.

TABLE 1. Numbers > 10000 with the most OEIS properties

value	props	value	props	value	props	value	props	value	props
16384	646	15625	415	59049	337	10080	301	524288	278
65536	638	1048576	387	131072	328	100000	291	4194304	258
32768	621	19683	365	46656	321	531441	288	11111	255
262144	577	16777216	360	1000000	316	14641	288	16807	254
40320	508	2097152	348	362880	305	10001	282	117649	250

Several conclusions can readily be drawn from this table. First, we notice that the magic number 65536 of Figure 1 is right up there, nearly tied for the lead. Second, almost all of these property-rich numbers are *round* in G. H. Hardy's sense: They are "the product of a considerable number of comparatively small factors" [52, page 48]. The only exceptions are 10001 and 11111, which are oriented to radix-10 notation. Indeed, all of the other champions are powers of 2, 3, 5, 6, 7, 10, or 11, except for 8!, 9!, and 10080 (which is twice 7!).

Table 1 ranks a number n by counting only the sequences in which the OEIS database lists n *explicitly*; it doesn't count all the sequences to which n actually *belongs*. For example, A005843 is the sequence of even numbers, which explicitly lists only 0, 2, 4, 6, ..., 120; a number like 604800 is even but doesn't have the OEIS property of evenness. Being near the beginning of a sequence seems to make membership stronger, because the fact that 2 is even is noteworthy for 2 but the fact that 120 is even is basically "duh" for 120.

Therefore I tried another experiment in which the successive values of each OEIS sequence are assigned weights 1, 1/2, 1/4, 1/8, ... Table 2 shows the integers that currently are most important by that criterion, and again 65536 ranks near the top. Here the tendency to prefer "roundness" is even more pronounced than before: Every number in Table 2, with the exception of 10001, is a power of 2, 3, 5, 6, 7, or 10.

TABLE 2. Numbers > 10000 with the heaviest OEIS properties

value	weight	value	weight	value	weight	value	weight	value	weight
262144	27.9	19683	20.4	387420489	15.1	78125	13.2	10001	11.8
16777216	27.6	15625	19.8	32768	15.1	16807	13.1	9765625	11.6
65536	22.5	1048576	18.6	390625	13.5	823543	12.9	100000	11.6
531441	21.5	16384	18.5	68719476736	13.5	177147	12.6	2097152	11.3
59049	20.8	46656	18.2	4194304	13.2	117649	12.1	1679616	11.0

I'm willing to admit that such numbers are important. Yet somehow the criteria used to generate Table 1 and Table 2 leave me unsatisfied from the standpoint of license-plate desirability. One reason is that many of the OEIS sequences are not really very interesting at all, propertywise. For instance, the Hall–Janko number 604800 occurs near the beginning of A002677, but only because it's the denominator of an obscure constant called M_3'[11] [82]. Frankly, I couldn't care less.

Numbers are often in fact especially interesting when they're at the *end* of a sequence, not the beginning. For example, 65537 is interesting because it's the largest known Fermat prime (A092506, A019434); 43112609 is interesting because it's the binary length of the largest prime number presently known, $(11 \ldots 1)_2$ [94]. (Fans of 43112609 can't use it on a license plate, however, except in North Carolina, because it is eight digits long.) I imagine that Richard Brent's favorite number is 1568705, which is currently the last element of A064411, because he was surprised to discover it in the continued fraction for e^γ [17]; remarkably, this 7-digit value arises rather early on, as the 4294th partial quotient of a number that probably isn't rational.

In my own case, if I had had a chance to choose my favorite 5-digit number to put on a license plate in 1969, shortly after I had seen the plate in Fig. 1, my choice would not have been 65536; I would definitely have chosen 12509 instead. Why? Because I had just completed extensive calculations leading to the conclusion that 12509 is the smallest n such that $l(n) < l^*(n)$, where $l(n)$ is the length of the shortest addition chain for n and $l^*(n)$ is the length of the shortest "star chain" (see [53, §4.6.3]). Before I had done these computations, such integers were known to exist because of a theorem due to W. Hansen [51], but the smallest example that could be based on his proof technique was the gigantic value $n = 2^{6103} + (2^{1016} + 1)(2^{2032} + 1)$. At once 12509 became my favorite 5-digit number.

I bet Neill Clift's favorite 8-digit number is 30958077, because he has discovered [24] that it's the least n such that $l(n) = l(2n) = l(4n)$.

Incidentally, the largest integer in the California list [20] was 9GOOGOL, namely 9×10^{100}. But it was trumped by ALEPH0 and ALEPH1.

Computer Science

In my day job I profess to be a computer scientist, not a mathematician, although there is definitely a soft spot for mathematics in my heart. Thus my closest colleagues have a computer-oriented rather than math-oriented perspective in their predilections for personalized plates. For example, Gio Wiederhold drives D8ABASE. Vaughan Pratt chose DUELITY, because his work makes considerable use of DUALITY (which was already taken when he tried to get it) and because his duality also applies to games.

The most famous license plate from Stanford's Computer Science Department is undoubtedly the one by which the late Gene Golub aptly described himself:

FIGURE 14. An inspiration.

This much-photographed plate, now his epitaph, highlights the leading roles that he played with respect to the computation, application, and popularization of the singular value decomposition of rectangular matrices. Matrix fans also probably know about Jack Dongarra's Tennessee plate, LAPACK, commemorating the popular package of linear algebra routines to which he has made many contributions. (In fact, he previously owned LAPACK in Illinois, and LINPACK in New Mexico before that.)

The most celebrated problem of theoretical computer science— "Is P equal to NP?" — should probably show up on the highway too. But at present nobody has voted either for P EQ NP or for P NEQ NP, at least not in California or Massachusetts or New York or in any other state that I checked. (With two cars, you could hedge your bet and acquire both plates.)

The California list of 1981 [20] included some lowbrow computer-related examples such as A HACK, ALGOL 60, CODER, HACKERS, HACKIT, I CMPUTE, I COBOL, PC SALES; also TEXWEB, which startled me when I spotted it during a visit to Marin County in 1984. By 1986, a car bearing PC WIDOW was already on the road in the East [34].

Armando Stettner, an engineer at Digital Equipment Corporation (DEC) who was working on the UNIX® operating system, decided in 1983 to get New Hampshire license plates that said UNIX. People in those days were clamoring for software licenses that would allow them to use this proprietary system legitimately, so he convinced DEC to make mock "UNIX licenses" to be handed out at conventions. These souvenir plates became wildly popular [75].

As I was writing the present essay I happened to see the California license UPSTART, which microcomputer pioneer Lee Felsenstein has owned since he created a "startup" in 1986. I also came across TURING1, proudly driven by the Computer History Museum curator Dag Spicer. Dag told me that TURING itself was unavailable when he made his choice.

I've also heard about two clever vanity-plate ideas based on programming languages, both of which happen to be presently available in California. The first one, DO 4 TRAN, will be readily understood by any FORTRAN programmer. But the second, 4TH♥IF H, needs a bit of explanation: It means "Honk (H) if you love Forth," in perfectly decent Forth-language syntax (when followed by THEN).

I must confess that, when I was following a car several years ago whose rear license read ENOFILE, it took me a minute to realize that the driver wasn't necessarily a programmer.

Somebody in California is now driving an automobile whose license reads CDR CAR. Maybe it's a man named Charles Dudley Robinson. But I hope it's actually a LISP programmer, ideally one who knows also that the left and right halves of a machine word, when LISP was first implemented on the IBM 704 computer, were obtained by the respective instructions CDR (contents of the decrement field of a register number) and CAR (contents of the address field of a register number).

Other plates refer to computer graphics, or to the Internet, or to user interfaces, artificial intelligence, robotics, networking, texting, etc. But that's a topic for another essay, to be published perhaps in the *Information Technological Intelligencer*.

Untapped Possibilities

Eugene Miya [72] recently came up with an idea for a brand new species of vanity plates: We can cite the Library of Congress catalog numbers of our favorite books. For example, QA1 I8 denotes the accumulated proceedings of the International Congress of Mathematicians; QA3 A57 signifies the *Memoirs of the American Mathematical Society*. Tutte's book on graph theory [88] is QA166 T8; and QA73 E23 is a beautiful picture-book about computer history [33].

The only trouble with this scheme is that most catalog numbers don't fit on the plates. To cite QA300 P62 (Pólya–Szegö [78]), you have to live in an 8-character state like New York. Furthermore, the most recent library numbers usually include decimal points; you must live in Colorado, Connecticut, Louisiana, or North Carolina to cite them. The only book of my own that I could cite in California is T11 K57 [59].

To complete my survey, let me now list a few more potential vanity plates that occurred to me as I was preparing this essay, together with their availability status in various states:

	AZ	CA	MA	MI	NC	NY	SD	UT	WV
0 ZIP	yes	yes	—	yes	yes	no	yes	yes	yes
TI3VOM	no	no	—	no	no	no	no	no	yes
WHENIM64	—	—	—	—	yes	no	—	—	yes
0X0045	no	yes	—	yes	yes	yes	yes	yes	yes
451 F	yes	no	—	—	yes	yes	yes	—	yes
F 451	no	—	—	yes	yes	no	yes	—	yes
CAB1729	yes	yes	—	yes	yes	no	yes	yes	yes
10E9999	yes	yes	—	yes	yes	yes	yes	yes	yes
1/0=INF	—	—	—	—	yes	—	—	—	—
AMS ORG	yes	yes	yes	yes	yes	yes	yes	yes	yes
DEGAUSS	yes	yes	—	yes	yes	no	yes	yes	yes
GOFIGURE	—	—	—	—	no	no	—	—	yes
GOTMATH	no	no	—	no	no	no	yes	yes	no
TEXHAX	yes	yes	yes	yes	yes	yes	yes	yes	yes
WAVELET	yes	no	—	yes	yes	no	yes	yes	yes

(Here "yes" means that it's available, subject to approval; "no" means that it's not available; "—" means that it has improper format with respect to letters and/or digits and/or punctuation.)

Other Countries

Canada began to catch the US-style vanity plate craze in the 1980s, beginning in Ontario and Prince Edward Island, where motorists had already been allowed to choose their own standard-format letters and numbers since 1973 [81]. By 2007, about 3% of all Canadian plates were vanitized [66] — not counting the provinces of Quebec and Newfoundland/Labrador, which have so far held out against such freedom of choice. (Québécois can, however, display anything they want on the *fronts* of their cars; the official plates appear only in back.)

Ontario's vanity plates allow up to 8 characters, but they are subject to special restrictions in order to enhance readability by law enforcement officials [74]: The letters A, S, G are respectively equivalent to the digits 4, 5, 6; and O is equivalent to both 0 and Q. Thus the license 666SAGAS would preclude 255 others such as GG65A645, and

OOGOOGOL

would preclude 971 lookalikes. Furthermore, you can't have more than four equivalent characters in a row, as in GRRRRR or XXXXXXX.

Nothing like the US or Canadian freedom to vanitize is possible in England, where the number plates are subject to severe syntactical restrictions. Britishers do, however, sometimes try; for example, a popular singer named Jess Conrad reportedly once threatened a duel in Regents Park in order to acquire the plate JC21 [8].

When Britain introduced auto registration in 1903, Bertrand Russell's older brother Frank famously waited in line all night so that his car could be identified as A1 [76]. (He later became Under-Secretary of State for Transport, responsible for abolishing British speed limits.) More recently, the comedian Jimmy Tarbuck was known for driving COM 1C; hairstylist Nicky Clarke owns H41 RDO; James Bond could be 13 OND; and a yellow Mercedes convertible supposedly says ORG 45M [70].

Such nonrandom combinations have been sold at auction by the Driver and Vehicle Licencing Agency since 1989, beginning with 1A, which cost £200,000 at the time. By 2008 these sales had contributed more than £1,300,000,000 to the British government treasury [32].

Once issued, British license plates can subsequently be resold and transferred to other vehicles. Indeed, the Cherished Number Dealers Association oversees a thriving industry with more than 150 traders of registration marks, and a driver recently paid £440,625 for F1 [93]. Somebody claims to have reserved L1 NUX in 1993, and L7 NUX was being auctioned in 2001 [15].

Similar remarks apply to licenses in Germany, although without the auctions. Therefore I was astonished and thrilled when the plate

was presented to me as a surprise gift several years ago, after I'd given some lectures about the MMIX computer at the University of Applied Sciences in Munich. Indeed, the German prefix MM is available only in a small nearby village, where one of my hosts happened to have the connections necessary to acquire this miraculously perfect combination on my behalf. Notice also the elegant typography.

Vanity plates, American style, have however spread to the northern shores of Europe, beginning in Scandinavia. I think Sweden was first, in 1993 or so, followed soon after by Finland, Denmark, and Iceland. Norway will begin to issue *personlige bilskilt* in 2010 [10]. Meanwhile Latvia, Poland, Luxembourg, Slovenia, and even Austria have jumped on the bandwagon. Rumor has it that the Netherlands will be vanitized next. Will their plates have room for WISKUNDE?

At the opposite end of the world, "true" vanity plates do exist nowadays in Australia, New Zealand, and Hong Kong; they have also occasionally been issued in the Philippines for special events. Japanese motorists live with a rather bizarre system in which they have freedom only to choose a serial number from 1 to 9999, leading to license plates of the forms $\ldots a$, $\ldots ab$, $.abc$, or $ab\text{-}cd$, where a, b, c, and d are digits with $a \neq 0$. Furthermore, cd is never 42 or 49, because those numbers connote "death" or "bitter death" in Japanese. (In Japan the fact that $\varphi(49) = 42$ is bad news.) Beginning in 1999, monthly lotteries were held for the 26 most popular numbers $\ldots s$, $.sss$, $s0\text{-}00$, $ss\text{-}ss$, 12-34, and 56-78, where $s \in \{1, 2, 3, 5, 7, 8\}$; this list was later decreased to only 13 entries. If you want one of the other values, you can pay extra to get your favorite. (See [11].)

On the continent of Africa one can reportedly obtain vanity plates in Liberia and Uganda [85].

But South America is still holding out. Indeed, US-style vanity plates seem to be presently unavailable anywhere in Latin America except in Puerto Rico, where they are called *tablillas especiales personalizadas*.

Conclusion

We've seen that vanity-plate fever is sweeping through many parts of the world, and that this phenomenon presents remarkable challenges to mathematicians. One of the main unresolved problems is to determine the integers of 5 to 8 digits that are most "interesting," in some reasonably mathematical sense.

As I did this research I learned about six or seven available plates that would suit me well and make me happy. I could now, for instance, actually obtain Figure 2. But unfortunately I have only one car, and I can't decide which of the plates to live without. So I guess I'll just continue to fantasize about the possibilities.

Acknowledgments

The networking skills of Eugene Miya were especially helpful in bringing many choice examples to my attention, and I've also been helped by dozens of other people in casual conversations about the subject. Andrew Turnbull provided important historical information, including reference [85]. David Bailey, Dave Bayer, Carol Bohlin, Laurence Brevard, David Eisenbud, Michel Goemans, Ron Graham, Victor Miller, Bill Ragsdale, and Cathy Seeley contributed photos. Gay Dillin of NCTM sent details of the 2005 contest. The four-author π photograph was taken by Raul Mendez. I found the PROF SVD image on Wikimedia Commons, where it had been posted by Da Troll.

References

[1] "City car tag sales off," *The New York Times* (15 February 1955), 22.

[2] "Office keeps tab on state vehicles," *Los Angeles Times* (18 December 1955), A5.

[3] "First new California plates appear," *Los Angeles Times* (6 December 1962), A1.

[4] "BUM rap arrives from Folsom," *Los Angeles Times* (4 January 1963), 3.

[5] "Plates spell home town," *Los Angeles Times* (17 September 1967), SG_A2.

[6] "ZAP, POW auto plates fight smog," *Los Angeles Times* (22 August 1970), 20.

[7]   "Couple to get first personalized auto plate," *Los Angeles Times* (26 October 1970), A2.

[8]   "New use for personalized auto plates — fighting smog," *The New York Times* (5 March 1972), S27.

[9]   "Playful plates: Connecticut tags identify owners," *Life* **31**, 23 (3 December 1951), 133. [Twenty examples are shown, including PAPA STOP MAMA FAST.]

[10] "Lag ditt egen bilskilt!" http://www.aftenposten.no/spesial/ article2736061.ece [published 27 October 2008, updated 27 May 2009; accessed November 2009]. [This article illustrates the sample plate JEG=007 ("I am 007"); in 1981, [20] had already contained ten variations of OOFDAH.]

[11] (My Japanese friends helped me to find this information at http://www.numberplate-m.com/study/choose.html, and in the article on Japanese license plates at http://ja.wikipedia.org/wiki/ after searching the latter site for '56-78'.)

[12] D. H. Bailey, J. M. Borwein, P. B. Borwein, and S. Plouffe, "The quest for pi," *The Mathematical Intelligencer* **19**, 1 (Winter 1997), 50–57.

[13] David Bailey, Peter Borwein, and Simon Plouffe, "On the rapid computation of various polylogarithmic constants," *Mathematics of Computation* **66** (1997), 903–913.

[14] David Bayer and Michael Stillman, "On the complexity of computing syzygies; computational aspects of commutative algebra," *Journal of Symbolic Computation* **6** (1988), 135–147.

[15] Robert Blincoe, "L1NUX number plate for sale; or is that L7NUX - sneaky," http://www.theregister.co.uk/2001/08/21/l1nux_ number_plate_for_sale/ [accessed November 2009].

[16] G. Boccara, "Nombre de representations d'une permutation comme produit de deux cycles de longueurs donnees," *Discrete Mathematics* **29** (1980), 105–134.

[17] Richard P. Brent, "Computation of the regular continued fraction for Euler's constant," *Mathematics of Computation* **31** (1977), 771–777.

[18] Laurence C. Brevard, personal communication (18 August 2009).

[19] Mel Brooks and Buck Henry, *Get Smart* (1965–1970), a series of 138 television episodes starring Don Adams as Agent 86 and Barbara Feldon as Agent 99.

[20] State of California, Department of Motor Vehicles, *Environmental License Plate Numbers* (21 July 1981), 2 volumes.

[21] State of California, Department of Motor Vehicles, "DMV milestones (major events affecting drivers, vehicles, and the DMV)," http://www.dmv.ca.gov/about/profile/milestones.htm [accessed November 2009].

[22] F. R. K. Chung and R. L. Graham, "Quasi-random set systems," *Journal of the American Mathematical Society* **4** (1991), 151–196.

[23] R. F. Churchhouse, "Covering sets and systems of congruences," in *Computers in Mathematical Research*, edited by R. F. Churchhouse and J.-C. Herz (Amsterdam: North-Holland, 1968), 20–36.

[24] Neill Michael Clift, "Calculating optimal addition chains," *Computing* **91** (2011), 265–284.

[25] Dennis R. Cowhey, *What Does That Mean? The Personal Stories Behind Vanity License Plates* (Arlington Heights, Illinois: Key Answer Products, 1994).

[26] Matt Cunningham, "A bumper crop of physics plates," *Symmetry* **5**,3 (August 2008), 22–27. [Leon Heller, who owns NUCLEON, says that his friends think it means "Nuke Leon."]

[27] Robert E. Dallos, "States reap profit on auto vanity plates," *Los Angeles Times* (3 September 1977), 1.

[28] Jean-Marie De Koninck, *Those Fascinating Numbers* (Providence, Rhode Island: American Mathematical Society, 2009).

[29] Joan Dektar, "This year's great gift adventure," *Los Angeles Times* (6 December 1970), T16–T22.

[30] John and Barbara Dixon, *The Plate Book: Puzzle Plates — The New American Hi-Way Graffiti* (Seattle: Voler, 1982).

[31] Charles R. Donaldson, "Almost anything goes on new personalized license plates," *Los Angeles Times* (6 September 1970), SF_A1.

[32] James Duddridge, "Sale of registration marks," *Hansard House of Commons Debates* **482** (5 November 2008), columns 256–258. [At this time Duddridge introduced a bill to permit American-style vanity plates in England, but his proposal never received a second reading.]

[33] Charles & Ray Eames, *A Computer Perspective* (Cambridge, Massachusetts: Harvard University Press, 1973).

[34] Faith W. Eckler, "Vanity of vanities," *Word Ways* **19** (1986), 195–198; "All is vanity," *Word Ways* **20** (1987), 141–143.

[35] Robert Enstad, "'Peace' license plate issued," *Chicago Tribune* (28 October 1970), 3.

[36] Paul Erdös, "On integers of the form $2^k + p$ and some related problems," *Summa Brasiliensis mathematicæ* **2** (1950), 113–123.

[37] Ian Fleming, *Casino Royale* (London: Jonathan Cape, 1953). [This novel contains nontrivial mathematics relating to gambling, besides its characters Le Chiffre and Mathis. CHIFFRE is currently available in California.]

[38] Gordon Garb, personal communication (5 August 2009).

[39] Martin Gardner, "A fanciful dialogue about the wonders of numerology," *Scientific American* **202**,1 (January 1960), 150, 152, 154, 156. Reprinted as Chapter 1 of *The Numerology of Dr. Matrix* (New York: Simon & Schuster, 1967).

[40] George Garrigues, "TAG problems? NOT at THE DMV," *Los Angeles Times* (13 January 1963), WS9.

[41] Michel X. Goemans and David P. Williamson, "Improved approximation algorithms for maximum cut and satisfiability problems using semidefinite programming," *Journal of the Association for Computing Machinery* **42** (1995), 1115–1145.

[42] Solomon W. Golomb, "Run-length encodings," *IEEE Transactions on Information Theory* **IT-12** (1966), 399–401.

[43] Solomon W. Golomb, Robert E. Peile, and Robert A. Scholtz, *Basic Concepts in Information Theory and Coding: The Adventures of Secret Agent 00111* (New York: Plenum, 1994).

[44] Dave Graham, *Those Crazy License Plates* (Los Angeles: Price/Stern/Sloan, 1974).

[45] Ronald L. Graham, personal communication (28 July 2009).

[46] Gordon Grant, "Hundreds of motorists seek ego-soothing license tags," *Los Angeles Times* (29 August 1970), D1, D14.

[47] Gerry Griffin, "New Hampshire license plate museum," panel 3, http://nhlpm.com/3.html [accessed November 2009].

[48] Gerry Griffin, "New Hampshire license plate museum," panel 53, http://nhlpm.com/53.html [accessed November 2009].

[49] David Haber, "California license plate info," http://www.calpl8s.com/cpinfo.html [accessed November 2009].

[50] David Haber, "California black base plates," page 3, http://www.calpl8s.com/california/black.html?pg=3 [accessed November 2009].

[51] Walter Hansen, "Zum Scholz–Brauerschen Problem," *Journal für die reine und angewandte Mathematik* **202** (1959), 129–136.

[52] G. H. Hardy, *Ramanujan: Twelve Lectures on Subjects Suggested by His Life and Work* (Cambridge, England: Cambridge University Press, 1940).

[53] Donald E. Knuth, *Seminumerical Algorithms*, Volume 2 of *The Art of Computer Programming* (Reading, Massachusetts: Addison–Wesley, 1969).

[54] Donald E. Knuth, *Surreal Numbers: How Two Ex-Students Turned On to Pure Mathematics and Found Total Happiness* (Reading, Massachusetts: Addison–Wesley, 1974).

[55] Donald E. Knuth, *TEX: The Program*, Volume B of *Computers & Typesetting* (Reading, Massachusetts: Addison–Wesley, 1986), 2. [Versions 3.14, 3.141, 3.1415, 3.14159, 3.141592, 3.1415926 were released respectively in 1991, 1992, 1993, 1995, 2002, 2008.]

[56] Donald E. Knuth, "Teach calculus with Big O," *Notices of the American Mathematical Society* **45** (1998), 687–688.

[57] Donald E. Knuth, *MMIX: A RISC Computer for the New Millennium*, Volume 1, Fascicle 1 of new material for *The Art of Computer Programming* (Upper Saddle River, New Jersey: Addison–Wesley, 2005).

[58] Donald E. Knuth, *Combinatorial Algorithms*, Part 1, Volume 4A of *The Art of Computer Programming* (Upper Saddle River, New Jersey: Addison–Wesley, 2010).

[59] Donald E. Knuth, Tracy Larrabee, and Paul M. Roberts, *Mathematical Writing* (Washington, District of Columbia: Mathematical Association of America, 1989).

[60] David Larsen, "Words you can't drive by," *Los Angeles Times* (20 January 1970), B1, B8.

[61] David Larsen, "Personal tags — a bumper crop," *Los Angeles Times* (25 November 1970), C1, C8.

[62] David Larsen, "Gasoline plan's odds may favor the evens," *Los Angeles Times* (10 May 1979), B3, B32.

[63] François Le Lionnais, *Les Nombres Remarquables* (Paris: Hermann, 1983).

[64] Tien-Yien Li and James A. Yorke, "Period three implies chaos," *American Mathematical Monthly* **82** (1975), 985–992.

[65] Greg Lindberg and Dave Smith, "Connecticut License Plates," `http://ctpl8s.tripod.com/id9.html` and also ... `id20.html` [accessed November 2009].

[66] Stefan Lonce, "WHZ SO VN? [Who's so vain?]" *Move* **12**, 4 (Fall 2007), 20–24. See also `http://www.lcns2rom.com/vanity-platesurvey.htm` [accessed November 2009].

[67] Megan Luther, "A license to make a statement: S.D. drivers speak their minds," *Argus Leader* (25 October 2009), appendix, `http://www.argusleader.com/assets/pdf/DF1451091023.PDF` [accessed November 2009].

[68] Andy Magid, "Mathematics and the public," *Notices of the American Mathematical Society* **51** (2004), 1181.

[69] Massachusetts Department of Transportation, Registry of Motor Vehicles, "History of the plate," `http://www.mass.gov/rmv/history/` [accessed November 2009].

[70] MB club UK, discussion forum at `http://www.mbclub.co.uk/forums/general-discussion/11074-anyone-seen-any-good-number-plates-cars-lately.html` [accessed November 2009, by which time this discussion thread included 6114 postings contributed since 2004, arranged on a total of 408 webpages].

[71] Colman McCarthy, "A PLATE 2 CALL YOUR OWN," *The Washington Post Times Herald* (2 March 1969), *Potomac* magazine, 25–27.

[72] Eugene N. Miya, personal communication (8 November 2009).

[73] Pace P. Nielsen, "A covering system whose smallest modulus is 40," *Journal of Number Theory* **129** (2009), 640–666.

[74] Ontario Ministry of Transportation, "Personalized licence plates," `http://www.mto.gov.on.ca/english/dandv/vehicle/plates.shtml` [accessed November 2009].

[75] The Open Group, "The history of the UNIX® license plate," `http://www.unix.org/license-plate.html` [accessed November 2009].

[76] Richard Ottaway, "Vehicle registration marks bill," *Hansard House of Commons Debates* **458** (23 March 2007), columns 1101–1120.

[77] Grisha Perelman, "The entropy formula for the Ricci flow and its geometric applications," `http://arXiv:math.DG/0211159`.

[78] G. Pólya and G. Szegö, *Aufgaben und Lehrsätze aus der Analysis*, first American edition (New York: Dover, 1945).

[79] George Reasons, "No FUN on new license plates; bills go out this week, so PAY," *Los Angeles Times* (23 December 1962), C13–C14.

[80] Art Ryon, "A license plate to remember," *Los Angeles Times* (21 March 1963), A6.

[81] Joseph P. Sallmen, "Canadian personalized license plates," `http://www.canplates.com/vanity.html` [accessed November 2009].

[82] Herbert E. Salzer, "Tables of coefficients for obtaining central differences from the derivatives," *Journal of Mathematics and Physics* **42** (1963), insert facing page 163.

[83] Neil J. A. Sloane, *The On-Line Encyclopedia of Integer Sequences*, `http://www.research.att.com/~njas/sequences` [accessed November 2009].

[84] Don Snyder, "La Canada man given NO SMOG car plates," *Los Angeles Times* (11 November 1970), SG6.

[85] Tim Stentiford, "Vanity: Born in the USA, tales from the tail-end," *Plates* **54**, 4 (August 2008), cover, 21–26.

[86] Peter P. Szabaga, "Vanity plates," `http://pages.prodigy.net/pizzabagel/VanityPlates_AlphaList.htm` [accessed November 2009].

[87] Gay Talese, "State unit urges car law changes," *The New York Times* (16 January 1959), 12. [This article, incidentally, contains the earliest known printed occurrence of the phrase *vanity plates*.]

[88] W. T. Tutte, *Connectivity in Graphs* (Toronto, Ontario: University of Toronto Press, 1966).

[89] UTAH.GOV services, "Personalized license plates," `http://dmv.utah.gov/licensepersonalized.html` [accessed November 2009].

[90] Vermont Department of Motor Vehicles, "A history of Vermont license plates 1894–2000," `http://dmv.vermont.gov/registrations/drivers/plates/history/` [accessed November 2009].

[91] Herbert J. Vida, "New personalized licenses have message of PEACE," *Los Angeles Times* (27 August 1970), WS1.

[92] David Wells, *The Penguin Dictionary of Curious and Interesting Numbers* (Harmondsworth, Middlesex, England: Penguin Books, 1986).

[93] David Wilkins, "3ND 0F TH3 R04D?" in *The Independent* (10 November 2008), motoring section [available online in November 2009].

[94] George Woltman, "Great Internet Mersenne Prime Search GIMPS," http://www.mersenne.org/ [accessed November 2009].

[95] Alexander J. Yee and Shigeru Kondo, "5 trillion digits of pi — new world record," http://www.numberworld.org/misc-runs/pi-5t/details.html [accessed November 2010].

Addendum

In the present book I can't resist mentioning a related factoid that I omitted from the essay above because it would probably not have been understood by mathematically oriented readers: The license plates POTRZB and NGOGN are still unclaimed in California.

Professor Matt Kahn of Stanford's Art Department chose IOIOI for purely æsthetic reasons: He likes this pattern's fourfold symmetry.

Mark Manasse has a wonderful license plate that I learned about too late to include in my original article: His is I DID F9, commemorating the successful factorization of the ninth Fermat number $2^{512} + 1$ [see *Mathematics of Computation* **61** (1993), 319–349; **64** (1995), 1357].

Ron Fagin tells me that, when he was a student at Dartmouth in the mid-1960s, John Kemeny proudly had the New Hampshire license plates LOGIC and SETS.

Several computer-science-related tidbits have also come to my attention:

- Eugene Miya owns a sequel to the UNIX® plate:

- British computer scientist Alex Tiskin has spotted PRO 5ESR.
- Steve Johnson once had California YACCMAN.
- John Warnock or Chuck Geschke should think seriously about acquiring X708798.

And the story continues: I spotted ♥ LG LG LG on 7 June 2010; and in San José on 4 October 2011, Eugene Miya saw P♥THON. "What a grin."

Chapter 18

Diamond Signs

[Excerpted from a website that was launched in September 2003.]

During our summer vacation in 2003, my wife and I amused ourselves by taking leisurely drives in Ohio and photographing every diamond-shaped highway sign that we saw along the roadsides. (Well, not *every* sign; only the distinct ones.) For provenance, I also stood at the base of each sign and measured its GPS coordinates.

This turned out to be even more fun than a scavenger hunt, so we filled in some gaps when we returned to California. And we intend to keep adding to this collection as we drive further, although we may have to venture to New England in order to see FROST HEAVES.

Our collection is limited to signs that appear in a diamond shape, even though many other interesting signs exist. After all, it's necessary to draw the line *somewhere*. In spite of this restriction, we've spotted and documented more than 1000 different signs as of June 2010.

This hobby adds spice to my travel experiences, and tends to keep me alert while driving. But I must admit that I'm sometimes thinking "Hmm... Do I have that sign?" rather than "Should I slow down?"

Traffic engineers have official manuals that dictate what they should be doing. However, our purpose has not been to record the recommended practices; we have instead tried to capture the situation that actually exists on America's highways and byways. As a result, we keep finding new constructions that essentially represent a kind of creative "folk art" that varies greatly from one community to another.

I've tried to organize the collection by introducing an ad-hoc numbering scheme, roughly like the "Dewey decimal system" used to classify the books in older libraries. Each sign has a code name; for example, "I55b" is number 55b in the class of signs related to Intersections.

The following pages contain a small sampling of what we've seen so far, emphasizing examples that have unusual and/or noteworthy aspects.

161

Arrows

Signs A05, A06, and A09 illustrate the three basic changes of direction: curves, bends, and turns. Bends are rare; but we happened to spot A06 on 6 August 2003, the day we began our quest! In 2006 I found a left bend to go with this right bend, and in May 2010 I finally saw reverse bends such as A16. The double turn, A29, occurs right near our house; I've actually never seen it elsewhere. Could it be unique? We spotted the exotic loop A35 in Ohio and the traffic circle A84a in Oregon. Two or three freeways merge in A92 or A92a.

Arrows with Numbers

B00a

N37°24.922′ W121°58.826′

B66

N37°06.264′ W121°58.492′

B01a

N37°16.227′ W122°02.754′

B81

N37°40.166′ W122°23.547′

B86

N39°52.682′ W123°42.863′

B90

N37°48.120′ W122°25.170′

B26

N37°09.856′ W121°59.446′

B41

N37°21.675′ W121°55.153′

B93

N41°58.031′ W121°54.891′

California traffic engineers often indicate the speed for which a curve or turn has been designed: "Slow down to 50 for this curve; take this turn at only 10 miles per hour." But sometimes, as in B00a and B66, a curve is marked only 5 while a turn is rated as high as 40. Unusual speeds (B01a) occasionally help to get a driver's attention. There are reverse curves (B81), reverse turns (B86), and winding roads (B90). Exit ramps have dramatic curves in two styles, illustrated here for left turns by B26 and B41. And then there's the famous tipping truck (B93).

Critters

The iconic road signs for animals rank high among everybody's favorites. We find contented cows (C10), as well as steers who are wilder (C12). In these images the animals are almost always shown facing left — although Arizona signs show elk facing both ways. My favorite elk sign, shown here, is New Mexico's version (C25b). I spotted bighorn sheep (C52) in Colorado. Sometimes whimsical additions appear: a burro with a hula hoop (C49), a duck with a bindle (C31b). California has boars (C55) and bears (C60). Let's also not forget the smaller critters, like newts (C71).

Detours

D89

N40°00.182′ W83°07.930′

D86

N43°02.158′ W87°58.962′

D78

N41°16.681′ W81°38.224′

D44

N43°04.262′ W87°55.744′

D10

N37°21.700′ W121°55.116′

D59

N37°25.939′ W122°09.284′

D08

N37°25.419′ W122°09.900′

D93

N42°21.672′ W71°05.376′

D09

N37°26.248′ W122°09.229′

When roads are being repaired, traffic has to adapt, so new signs sometimes arise and disappear overnight. Special kinds of arrows, like D89, are used only in this context. We found the flamboyant D86 on a Milwaukee freeway. I first encountered D78, which is a symbolic version of D44, on 22 May 2010. Sign D10 shows a "flagger," who here is holding a stop sign instead of a flag. The special sign D59 appears only during Stanford football games. Bicyclists have detours too (D08). Temporary lanes are often narrow (D93). The good news is that detours do end (D09).

Entrances

E80

N37°25.637′ W122°04.676′

E13

N43°02.728′ W88°02.672′

E40

N41°07.791′ W83°28.198′

E45

N40°51.181′ W83°39.081′

E70

N40°44.042′ W80°10.741′

E05

N41°26.529′ W81°56.088′

E95a

N41°08.103′ W82°41.246′

E90

N41°26.472′ W81°56.158′

E65

N38°15.638′ W122°26.416′

Warning signs can also alert drivers to unusual sources of traffic or other activity. E80 is hinged so that it morphs into another when no concert is in progress. E13 illustrates one of many ways to warn about emergency vehicles. Some signs say HOSPITAL ENTRANCE, CHURCH ENTRANCE, SCHOOL ENTRANCE, etc.; E40, E45, E70, and E05 are less common instances of this genre. The wording can be tricky: Do foreigners understand that E95a and E90 mean the same thing, or that PLANT ENTRANCE (E65) has nothing to do with horticulture?

Intersections

I16a

N41°02.998′ W82°53.687′

I21a

N41°29.105′ W81°35.122′

I36

N39°47.980′ W105°30.734′

I08c

N37°34.051′ W122°19.753′

I07

N37°26.109′ W122°11.082′

I09

N38°32.442′ W121°44.271′

I52

N41°25.169′ W82°37.871′

I75

N37°36.158′ W122°23.468′

I99

N41°03.761′ W81°31.297′

Mathematicians use the symbols +, ⊣, ⊢, and ⊤ in theorems; drivers, however, use them to anticipate configurations of crossroads. Many exotic variations on this theme can be found, including I16a, I21a, and monstrosities like I36. Sometimes a circle indicates that one or more of the side roads is a dead end (I08c, I07, I09). Railroads add yet another dimension, as in I52 and I75; in fact, a rail crossing near my wife's birthplace was the very first item in our collection. I once made a special trip to Akron, Ohio, in order to photograph the "crossing yield" sign, I99.

Lanes

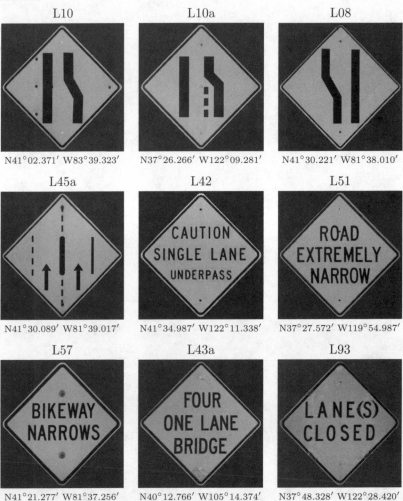

The symbolic sign L10, intended to mean "right lane ends" or "lane ends merge left," was found to be misleading; so it is scheduled to be phased out and replaced by a new design (L10a) borrowed from Canada. I still haven't seen a replacement for the inverse variant L08. Do drivers understand L45a, where lanes are being split under a bridge? Narrow lanes are best described in words, as in L42, L51, and L57. My daughter found and photographed the remarkable L43a. Sign L93 appears near the Golden Gate bridge; a policeman was unhappy that I photographed it.

Nonspecific

N16

N37°23.707′ W122°11.512′

N18

N41°09.299′ W83°25.949′

N19

N41°30.840′ W81°35.725′

N25

N43°20.919′ W88°16.876′

N51

N42°34.676′ W121°52.877′

N57

N37°20.738′ W121°56.346′

N41

N41°30.345′ W82°02.713′

N92

N37°20.498′ W122°01.808′

N95

N37°20.435′ W121°57.313′

Some signs say simply DANGER or CAUTION or SLOW; N16 is more emphatic, and N18 has flashing lights. Sign N19, located within the grounds of a cemetery, is the only one in our collection with white letters on black. Several other classes of more-or-less generic signs are exemplified by N25, N51, and N57. Speed-limit signs are supposed to be rectangular, but lately they're being enclosed in diamond frames as in N41. The cities of Sunnyvale (N92) and Santa Clara (N95) try to keep drivers alert by introducing unique signs, changed every few months.

People

P04

N36°59.814′ W122°03.827′

P11c

N37°58.749′ W122°33.864′

P84

N41°25.515′ W82°21.499′

P53

N37°24.110′ W122°05.415′

P51

N37°24.657′ W122°09.473′

P57

N37°27.701′ W122°11.267′

P62

N40°00.801′ W82°54.736′

P65

N41°30.359′ W81°33.577′

P74

N41°24.875′ W81°36.226′

The image of a pedestrian crossing the street is perhaps the most common warning sign of all. Here I show two variants: a jogger (P04) and a musician (P11c). We found the clever sign P84 in a summer resort where I used to go as a child. Speaking of children, our collection includes more than a dozen ways to warn about kids playing; my favorite so far is P53. The designers of P51 and P57 were careful not to refer to SLOW CHILDREN. People with disabilities are protected by a variety of signs such as P62, P65, and P74.

Road Status

R17

N37°39.650′ W122°04.114′

R04

N40°00.560′ W105°15.845′

R06

N34°17.991′ W108°08.013′

R79

N37°48.092′ W122°24.462′

R73a

N41°18.798′ W83°10.076′

R75

N38°04.621′ W121°43.990′

R24

N37°32.177′ W122°17.324′

R26

N37°33.246′ W122°00.850′

R43

N40°15.374′ W105°51.362′

Special hazards arise in difficult terrain. For example, hills are particularly dangerous for trucks (R17) and bicycles (R04). My daughter has also encountered another type of hill-warning sign (R06). Sharp curves and/or the lack of shoulders at the edges of a highway correspond to a number of interesting warnings such as R79, R73a, and R75. On the other hand, artificial hazards are often created as "traffic calming" devices to reduce a driver's speed: A HUMP (R24) is theoretically milder than a BUMP (R26); there's even a *negative* bump (R43).

Temporary

T12	T10	T18
N37°22.167' W121°55.653'	N37°25.791' W122°10.539'	N41°23.167' W83°39.646'
T46	T72	T77
N35°11.605' W111°37.218'	N41°29.336' W81°55.573'	N37°25.826' W122°10.510'
T95	T39	T04a
N37°31.320' W122°15.973'	N41°28.704' W81°57.614'	N37°38.315' W121°02.009'

Signs that used to say MEN WORKING (T12) have mostly been replaced by non-sexist versions such as T10 and T18. Repair-related signs are difficult to capture, since they come and go quickly; there's often lots of traffic and no good place to park. Thus I was lucky to snap T46 while traveling in Arizona, even though the sign itself was dirty and worn. Other short-lived hazards include partially patched pavement (T72, T77) and electrical wiring (T95). These extra hassles for motorists can be accompanied by frank, though unfriendly, signs like T39 and T04a.

Vehicles

V04g
N37°25.543' W122°10.246'

V20
N37°23.239' W122°10.767'

V15a
N40°15.639' W105°50.596'

V16
N37°25.675' W122°11.418'

V17
N38°32.697' W121°44.305'

V18
N40°30.171' W83°41.732'

V40a
N37°24.558' W121°57.186'

V42
N37°48.277' W122°25.244'

V51
N40°36.165' W80°32.798'

Stanford University has introduced a series of signs like V04g, hoping to avoid car-bike crashes. Another famous Stanford sign (V20), now historic, once greeted visitors to the site of the Artificial Intelligence Laboratory in the hills above the campus. Other vehicles to watch out for, in various parts of the world, are snowmobiles (V15a), golf carts (V16), forklifts (V17), horse-drawn buggies (V18), trams (V40a), and cable cars (V42). My wife and I were recently pleased to discover West Virginia's nice symbol for school bus stops (V51).

Weather

W14	W27	W47
N37°27.241′ W121°55.258′	N36°13.190′ W117°15.642′	N39°47.233′ W105°46.919′
W31a	W37	W32
N39°07.175′ W108°19.544′	N39°02.891′ W119°56.797′	N37°21.831′ W122°10.128′
W60	W67	W80
N39°23.475′ W115°30.272′	N35°31.642′ W105°14.147′	N36°37.427′ W121°50.621′

Water, snow, and ice coexist rather precariously with automobiles when drivers aren't careful. Motorists must watch out when turning in the rain (W14), and we'd better keep out of deep water too (W27). After I stopped to photograph W47 in a Colorado blizzard, my car got stuck in the snow and the wheels spun without effect. Icy roads are particularly risky (W31a, W37, W32). Of course water isn't the only source of weather-oriented woes: There are enough rocks to scare Chicken Little (W60, W67), not to mention winds and sand (W80).

What Does It Mean?

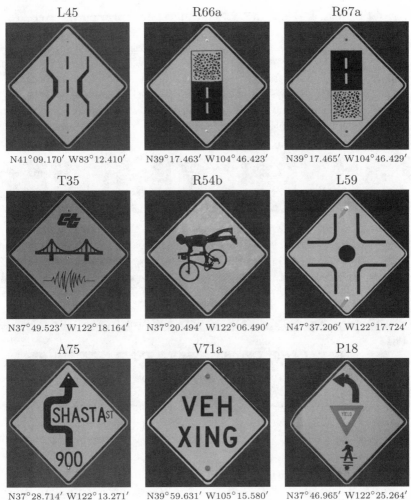

L45

N41°09.170′ W83°12.410′

R66a

N39°17.463′ W104°46.423′

R67a

N39°17.465′ W104°46.429′

T35

N37°49.523′ W122°18.164′

R54b

N37°20.494′ W122°06.490′

L59

N47°37.206′ W122°17.724′

A75

N37°28.714′ W122°13.271′

V71a

N39°59.631′ W105°15.580′

P18

N37°46.965′ W122°25.264′

Two iconic warning signs of the 1990s were withdrawn after 2000 because people couldn't understand them. But they haven't completely disappeared: My wife snapped NARROW BRIDGE (L45) in 2004, and in 2009 she found not only PAVEMENT ENDS (R66a) but also its inverse (R67a). Other examples of signs in our collection that are slightly less than scrutable are the seismic-retrofit sign at the San Francisco–Oakland Bay Bridge (T35), the flying biker (R54b), the barred intersection (L59), the Shasta Street puzzle (A75), the cryptic V71a, and the rebus-like P18.

The Online Collection

All of the diamond signs that I've documented appear on the Web at

`www-cs-faculty.stanford.edu/~knuth/diamondsigns/diam.html`

and pages reachable from there. One of the interesting aspects of this full set is the variety of ways in which the same concept has been expressed. For example, I've come across seven different ways to warn motorists about possibly being blown away:

And there've been 14 ways to tell drivers that they can't enter certain roads without backtracking and going out the same way they came in:

Each sign on my website has its own page, which presents a full color image of 900 × 900 pixels together with the GPS coordinates and other information about where and when the picture was taken. There also are summary pages with thumbnail images of all the signs that belong to the individual classes A, B, C, ..., W. Several interesting signs from Canada and other countries are included on separate pages.

The website is arranged something like a simple adventure game, where you can find hidden delights by clicking in appropriate places. For instance, if you explore carefully you'll discover where a bridge that was said to have clearance 12′ 8″ in 2003 was later reported to have only 12′ 6″ of clearance; some trucks evidently got stuck in the meantime. You'll see occasional graffiti. And you'll find examples of unintentional humor, like PREPARE TO STOP WHEN FLASHING and CAUTION PEDESTRIANS SLIPPERY WHEN WET.

One of my favorite pictures in this collection is best viewed online, so I didn't show it above. Traffic engineers in Sonoma County, California, have used an ordinary symbolic "merging traffic" sign, A91, and rotated it by 90° at a prominent intersection, giving sign number A91a in our collection. (As far as I know, this rotated sign doesn't appear anywhere else in the world.) You might think that I cheated here, by simply rotating A91 and pretending to have a new sign; but if you look closely, you'll see that a bird is perched at the top of A91a, thereby proving its authenticity! I didn't actually notice the bird when I was hastily snapping the picture; I first saw it only while preparing the image for the Web a few days later. It's one of the few cases where I didn't crop the picture and force it into a standard diamond-only shape.

Closeup inspection of some of the images will reveal beautiful textures produced by weathering. For example, I96 is particularly attractive; by chance, I happened to capture it just a week before Stanford's transportation department replaced it by a brand new sign. The new sign is perhaps more effective, but it isn't as lovable; it has the more modern design that I'd previously photographed as I95. Another sign with venerable texture, R47, will perhaps be appreciated by fans of the Wild West — it's riddled with bullet holes.

Most of the pictures were taken by my wife or by myself, or by members of our family. But some of the rarer signs have been contributed by friends; for example, among the images above, B26, B66, C55, C71, D93, P04, V40a, and W80 were photographed by Yoichi Hariguchi; C49 and W27 by Peter Eichenberger. The first sign that I received from afar, in September 2003, was the wonderful SEE WE TOLD YOU SO sent from Iowa by Nate Holbrook (N90). He said that he found it a block or so away from another sign that said BRIDGE OUT AHEAD.

A cool interface between all of these signs and Google Maps, created by Brian Cornell, has been available since December 2007. You can find it by going to the bottom of the webpage cited above and clicking on 'see where the signs were photographed'.

Let me close with a sign that was spotted by Barry Hayes in Ithaca, New York, in 1990. Although it's not a diamond sign, I cannot resist including it in the present book:

Chapter 19

The Orchestra Song

[An unpublished composition for concert band, dated 8 December 1954.]

This piece is actually a "nine-part invention": It is the result of nine solos all playing at once.

The band has been divided into nine sections, marked by Roman numbers I–IX. First section I plays alone. Then section II plays alone. Next comes a duet between sections I and II. Then section III plays alone, followed by sections I, II, and III together. Thus, the piece is to be played in the following order:

> A. Section I solo
> B. II solo
> C. I and II
> D. III solo
> E. I, II, and III
> F. IV solo
> G. I, II, III, and IV
> H. V solo
> I. I, II, III, IV, and V
> J. VI solo
> K. I, II, III, IV, V, and VI
> L. VII solo
> M. I, II, III, IV, V, VI, and VII
> N. VIII solo
> O. I, II, III, IV, V, VI, VII, and VIII
> P. IX solo
> Q. I, II, III, IV, V, VI, VII, VIII, and IX
> R. full band (explained below)

[The full score is too large to fit the format of this book. So it has been divided into four parts, which appear on the next four pages.]

179

All instruments use the first ending in parts A–Q.

Part R: In the final part, the whole band plays the pickup note forte and sustains it for four beats. (The trumpet and piano, which have two pickup notes, use only the first.)

Then, suddenly pianissimo, the chorus is repeated again, building up volume with a slow crescendo and, using the second ending, finishing fortissimo.

Although the score is only ten measures long, it is expanded by these repeats to 144 measures. No dynamic shading is marked on the score because it changes several times during the piece; the conductor should explain it while practicing.

Extra parts: E^b Clarinet plays the Flute I part. Alto Clarinet plays the Baritone Sax part. Bass Trombone plays the Bass part. English Horn plays the Oboe part. Xylophone or Marimba play the Piano part. Bells play the Flute part.

Addendum

I played tenor saxophone in the band at Lutheran High School in Milwaukee, Wisconsin, during my freshman, sophomore, and junior years, after having taken piano lessons while in elementary school. After awhile I became interested in learning about the other instruments, and I looked at the music they were playing, so I began to read books about orchestration that I found in Milwaukee's Public Library.

The Orchestra Song, written near the beginning of my junior year, was my first attempt to put that theory into practice. At the top of my original manuscript I wrote

THE ORCHESTRA SONG   *Traditional Austrian Song*
— adapted for band by Don Knuth

I had learned to sing a variant of most of these melodies at summer camp during the 1940s, with voices imitating instruments, and it occurred to me that real instruments would also work well. Here was a perfect vehicle for me to try my hand at writing band music, as a first test case. I also had in mind that many Milwaukeeans would know the song well enough to enjoy hearing this version, if we could perform it at our annual spring concert in Milwaukee Auditorium.

So I took the verse whose words were "The violin's playing ... a lovely song" and assigned it to the saxophone section. (Our school had only a concert band, not an orchestra.) The other parts that I knew from camp— "The clarinet ... goes dua-dua-dua-det"; "The horn ... wakes me at morn"; "The trumpet ... goes trump-et-ta-ta-ta-ta-ta ta"; "The drums ... five five five five one"; and "The bassoon it knows the point of counterpoint ..." — all fit nicely with the instruments we had available, except that I moved the bassoon theme to the piano, where I thought it would work better. I supplied simple new themes for the oboes, the flutes, and the bassoons/basses, so that everybody was included.

I laboriously copied out all the parts with pen and ink. Even though I needed to copy only ten bars in each case, I recall that this process took an incredibly long time. (We had quite a large band, more than 80 players.) I wondered how real composers could possibly get whole symphonies prepared for a full orchestra.

Well, it turned out that our band director was not at all impressed. He gave me no encouragement whatsoever, and never found time to rehearse any of the parts. So I chalked it up to experience and moved on to other pursuits, having recently discovered *MAD* comics.

In retrospect I do think that the arrangement looks reasonably good, at least on paper, but of course I've never had a chance to actually hear it. (On second thought, I should probably have changed the final chord of the second ending: As it stands, the "dominant" tone — namely C in the key of F — is played only by the piano! Was I joking?)

Many different versions of this traditional folk tune are prevalent. For example, I learned later that my future wife had learned five of the six verses I knew, when she had gone to summer camps in Ohio, although with slightly different words. While preparing this chapter for publication in 2009 I discovered a seven-verse version by Julius G. Herford [*Humor in Vocal Music* (New York: Hargail Music Press, 1946), 4–5], with nice parts for flute and bassoon that I had never encountered before; he called it "The Instruments." German versions, with words such as "Die Geige, die singt, sie jubelt und klingt; Die Klarinett, die Klarinett, macht duaduadua gar so nett," etc., again with numerous variations, are often attributed to Willy Geisler.

Chapter 20

Gnebbishland

[The opening bars of the piano score for an unpublished musical comedy skit, dated 10 April 1959 and performed on 18 April 1959.]

I belonged to the local chapter of Theta Chi fraternity at Case Institute of Technology, and Case's Interfraternity Council used to put on an annual talent show/competition called Stunt Night. During the spring semester of my junior year, I wrote the script, lyrics, and music for a short musical playlet that was our stunt for 1959. The following recollections were written in 2009 as I was preparing the present book for publication.

The title, "Gnebbishland," came from cartoon characters called Nebbishes that were wildly popular at the time. Thousands of stationery stores all over America were selling greeting cards that featured these clueless but amiable characters, with mottos like "I'm trying to be nice" or "So?" or "No, I'm more repressed than you are." One image alone — two couch-potato Nebbishes who say "Next week we've *got* to get organized" — reportedly sold more than 750,000 copies. [See Leonard Gross, "A Nebbish can't do anything! ... except set the whole country laughing and make a fortune for the college boy who draws him!" *This Week Magazine* (16 February 1958), 21, 23.] The man who created Nebbishes, Herb Gardner, went on to write widely acclaimed plays and films such as *A Thousand Clowns* (1962) and *I'm Not Rappaport* (1985).

College students of this era were having Nebbish parties and electing Nebbish queens. My idea was to depict a world of Nebbishes in which the characters sing about their lifestyle and valiantly resist an attempt to change it. All live happily ever after.

Unfortunately (or mercifully?) all copies of the original script and lyrics seem to have disappeared. The only artifact still in my files is the piano score, of which the first one-third is reproduced here.

I'm including Gnebbishland in this book because I've always liked the main chorus, which begins at the place marked [A] and was sung to the following words:

> I'm a Gnebbish, and a Gnebbish isn't snobbish —
>   A little slobbish —
> But it's Fun bein' that way!
> As kings of the greeting card industry,
>   We're all on the verge of insanity.

Everybody sang the chorus; then, in the places where the score indicates first, second, and third endings, the company would break into individual solo numbers, in which each character sang a short phrase found on cards that were currently in local stores. The only such phrase that I still remember for sure is the one beginning at bar 3 of the third ending, where an appropriately costumed creature tries to dance, and sings this:

I ain't neat ...   but I'm swee-eet!

The rest of the score isn't worthy of revival, so I'll just summarize it here. Much of it is soft background music, interspersed with stretches of dialog; I quoted extensively from MacDowell's "To a Wild Rose" when preparing that part.

There were two additional songs, only one of which has left any traces in my memory after fifty years. That one was sung by the anti-hero, a well-meaning but uptight outsider who tries, in the play, to reform the natives but realizes the error of his ways. The climax occurs as he sings, "Alas, I was wrong; they were happy when I came. Now all that is gone — and it's *me* that is to blame!" Here I borrowed the tune of "La Seine" by Guy Lafarge (1948), which was well known in America at the time because it had been given new English words ("You will find your love in Paris") by Mack Gordon.

The melody of the other song was probably original with me. But I no longer recall it, so it can't be worth much. It just goes in one ear and out the other when I play it.

I've always loved to compose and to play music. Thank goodness I never have needed to make a living from this delightful avocation.

Chapter 21

A Carol for Advent

[A song based on words by Jill Knuth, sent to friends with our pre-Christmas letter in December 2001.]

"Carols" — songs written to celebrate the birth of Jesus Christ and the spirit of love and generosity that has long been associated with the Christmas season — are among the most delightful songs in the popular cultures of many lands. We begin to hear these familiar tunes each year in late November and throughout the month of December.

But Christians who grew up with a strong liturgical tradition, like my wife and myself, prefer not to sing Christmas carols until December 24, "Christmas Eve," because the four weeks preceding Christmas Day are traditionally a time of preparation and waiting, called Advent.

That leaves us with four weeks in which there's a relative dearth of special songs to sing. Therefore Jill was inspired to write the words to an Advent Carol, "A Baby is Promised." A few months later, I set her words to music, with four-part harmony (soprano, alto, tenor, bass); and we sent it to our friends in time for the Advent season of 2001.

One can, of course, sing the verses in unison, preferably with piano accompaniment (at least until the harmonies become familiar).

This piece is dedicated to our grandsons, Rees Levi Tucker, Carter John Knuth, Kevin Don Knuth, and Kadin Morris Tucker, two of whom were born between the time we wrote it and the time we shared it.

When we first sent out the music we suggested that people might enjoy looking up the following Bible verses: 2 Kings 6 : 33, Isaiah 30 : 18, Luke 2 : 25.

Incidentally, Jill has also designed and made a dozen or so inspiring banners that are especially appropriate for the days of Advent. They are discussed in the first 23 pages of her book Banners Without Words (San José, California: Resource Publications, 1986).

189

A Baby is Promised

Jill and Don Knuth

pro-mised,   A   Sa- vior, the   Word! But watch-ing is
pro-mised,   A   Sa- vior, the   Word! But watch-ing is
pro-mised,   A   Sa- vior, the   Word! But watch-ing is
pro-mised, The Sa- vior, the   Word! ✤ Watch-ing is

1.

wear- i- some,   Wait-   ing   is   hard.
wear- i- some,   Wait-   ing   is   hard.
wear- i- some,   Wait-   ing   is   hard.

2.

joy when we   Wait   for   our   Lord!

✤ : Omit this note on the final verse.

Chapter 22

Randomness in Music

[Unpublished notes based on an informal talk given on 9 May 1990.]

John Chowning once asked me to speak for a few minutes to the Stanford Music Affiliates, a group of people representing the companies who were helping to sponsor the research at CCRMA, Stanford's Center for Computer Research in Music and Acoustics. Here is a reconstruction of approximately what I said, based on the slides that I used at the time.

Patterns that are perfectly pure and mathematically exact have a strong aesthetic appeal, as advocated by Pythagoras and Plato and their innumerable intellectual descendants. Yet a bit of irregularity and unpredictability can make a pattern even more beautiful. I was reminded of this fact as I passed by two decorative walls while walking yesterday from my home to my office: One wall, newly built, tries to emulate the regular rectangular pattern of a grid, but it looks sterile and unattractive to my eyes; the other wall consists of natural stones that fit together only approximately yet form a harmonious unity that I find quite pleasing.

An ugly new wall   A delightful old wall

I noticed similar effects when I was experimenting years ago with the design of computer-generated typefaces for the printing of beautiful books.

A design somehow "came to life" when it was not constrained to be rigidly consistent.*

Similar examples abound in the musical realm as well as in the world of visual images. For example, I'm told that people who synthesize music electronically discovered long ago that rhythms are more exciting if they don't go exactly "1, 2, 3, 4" but rather miss the beat very slightly and become what a mathematician might call "$1 + \delta_1$, $2 + \delta_2$, $3 + \delta_3$, $4 + \delta_4$." Although the discrepancies δ mount to only a few milliseconds, positive or negative, they enliven the music significantly by comparison with the deadly and monotonous pulsing that you hear when the δ's are entirely zero.

Singers and saxophone players know better than to hit the notes of a melody with perfect pitch.

Furthermore, we can take liberties with the "ideal" notes themselves. In an essay called "Chance in artistic creation," published in 1894,† August Strindberg recounted the following experience:

> A musician whom I knew amused himself by tuning his piano haphazardly, without any rhyme or reason. Afterwards he played Beethoven's *Sonate Pathétique* by heart. It was an unbelievable delight to hear an old piece come back to life. How often had I previously heard this sonata, always the same way, never dreaming that it was capable of being developed further!

And the notion of planned imperfection is not limited to variations in the performance of a given composition; it extends also to the choices of notes that a composer writes down. The main purpose of my talk today is to describe a way by which you could build a simple machine that will produce *random harmonizations of any given melody*.

More precisely, I'll show you how to produce $2^n + 2^{n-1}$ different harmonizations of any n-note melody, all of which are pretty good. A machine can easily generate any one of them, chosen at random, when its user plays the melody on a keyboard with one hand.

The method I shall describe was taught to me in 1969 by David Kraehenbuehl (1923–1997), when I audited his class on Keyboard Harmony at Westminster Choir College. It is extremely simple, although

---

* See, for example, my book *Digital Typography*, pages 57–59, 286–287, 324–325, 386, 391–396; also *The METAFONTbook*, pages 183–185.

† Auguste Strindberg, "Du Hasard dans la production artistique," *La Revue des revues* **11** (15 November 1894), 265–270.

you do need to understand the most elementary aspects of music theory. I shall assume that you are familiar with ordinary music notation.

Kraehenbuehl's algorithm produces four-part harmony from a given melody, where the top three parts form "triadic" chords and the bottom part supplies the corresponding bass notes.

A *triad* is a chord that consists of three notes separated by one-note gaps in the scale. Thus the triads are

and others that differ only by being one or more octaves higher or lower. The bottom note of a triad is called its "root," and the other two notes are called its "third" and its "fifth."

These notions apply to any clef and to any key signature. For example, with the treble clef and in the key of G major, the seven triads

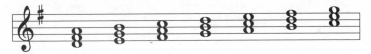

are known by more precise names such as a "D major triad," etc.; but we don't need to concern ourselves with such technical details.

The important thing for our purposes is to consider what happens when individual notes of a triad move up or down by an octave. If we view these chords modulo octave jumps, we see that they make a different shape on the staff when the root tone is moved up an octave so that the third tone becomes lowest; this change gives us the *first inversion* of the triad. And if the root and third are both moved up an octave, leaving the fifth tone lowest, we obtain the *second inversion*:

Root position   First inversion   Second inversion

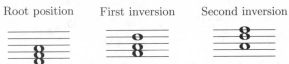

Even though two-note gaps appear between adjacent notes of the first and second inversions, these chords are still regarded as triads, because octave jumps don't change the name of a note on its scale: An A is still an A, etc., and no two notes of an inverted triad have adjacent names.

Music theorists have traditionally studied three-note chords by focussing their attention first on the root of each triad, and next on the bottom note, which identifies the inversion. Kraehenbuehl's innovation was to concentrate rather on the *top* note, because it's the melody note.

He observed that each melody note in the scale comes at the top of three triadic chords — one in root position (0), one in first inversion (1), and one in second inversion (2):

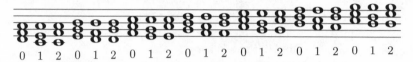

Furthermore, said Kraehenbuehl, there's a natural way to add a fourth part to this three-part harmony by simply repeating the root note, an octave or two lower. For example, in the key of C, we get

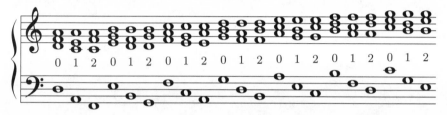

as the four-part harmonizations of melody notes A, A, A, B, B, B, ..., G, G, G. This rule almost always works well, but like all good rules it has an exception: When the bass note turns out to be the *leading tone* of the scale (which is one below the tonic), we should change it to the so-called *dominant tone* (which is two notes lower). Thus Kraehenbuehl's correction to the natural rule yields the 21 four-part chords

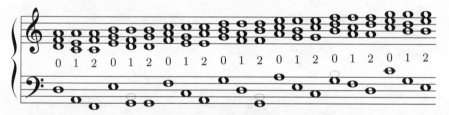

in the key of C, when B is the leading tone; and it yields

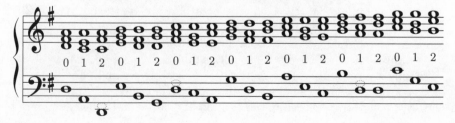

in the key of G, because F♯ is the leading tone in that case. Notice that when the bass note is corrected by shifting it down from a leading tone in root position, it produces a chord with four separate pitches (the so-called "dominant seventh chord" of its key), so it's no longer a triad.

OK, now we know three good ways to harmonize any given melody note in any given key. Kraehenbuehl completed his method by pointing out that the same principles apply to melodies with any number of notes, *provided only that we never use the same inversion twice in a row.* If one note has been harmonized with, say, the first inversion, the next note should be harmonized with either the root position or the second inversion; and so on. With this procedure there are three choices for the first chord, and two choices for every chord thereafter.

Let's test his algorithm by trying it out on a familiar melody:

"London Bridge is falling down, my fair lady" has eleven notes, so Kraehenbuehl has given us $3 \cdot 2 \cdot 2 \cdot 2 \cdot 2 \cdot 2 \cdot 2 \cdot 2 \cdot 2 \cdot 2 \cdot 2 = 3072$ ways to harmonize it. The binary representations of three fundamental constants,

$$\pi = 3 + (.0010010000111111011010101010001\ldots)_2,$$
$$e = 2 + (.1011011111100001010100010110 0\ldots)_2,$$
$$\phi = 1 + (.1001111000110111011110011011 1\ldots)_2,$$

serve to define three more-or-less random sequences of suitable inversions, if we prefer mathematical guidance to coin-flipping. Namely, we can use the integer part of the constant to specify the first chord, then we can change the number of inversions by $+1$ or -1 (modulo 3) for each successive binary digit that is 0 or 1, respectively. This procedure gives us three new harmonizations of that classic British theme:

Variation 1.   harmonized by π

Variation 2.   harmonized by *e*

Variation 3.   harmonized by *φ*

Amazing. Kraehenbuehl's algorithm seems far too simple to be correct, yet it really works!

Of course there's a little glitch at the end, because we have only one chance in three of ending on a chord that's stable and "resolved." No problem: In such a case we can just repeat the last melody note and force the desired chord. With this extension, variations 1 and 2 will end nicely with

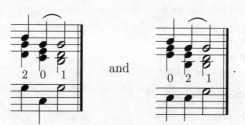

and   .

I can hardly wait for somebody to build me a keyboard that will perform such harmonizations automatically. After all, it's basically just a small matter of programming.

Chapter 23

Basketball's Electronic Coach

[This material was assembled from documents in my family archives.]

During all four years of my undergraduate studies at Case Institute of Technology between 1956 and 1960, I served as manager of the basketball teams, having had several years of experience in that role during my high-school days. At first I worked with Case's freshman team coached by Bill Sudeck; later I helped the varsity team coached by Nip Heim.

It was natural for me to combine this activity with my growing interest in computers; so I worked out a scheme for automating much of the work. A letter to my parents, dated 8 February 1958, said, "I'm basketball manager again, doing the statistics on the IBM."

In high school I'd come up with a general rule of thumb that said, "Possession of the ball is worth roughly one point, except near the end of a period." In other words, if you enter the stadium at a time when your team is leading by a score of 50–49, the effective score is really 51–49 if your team has the ball, but the game is basically tied if the other guys have possession. A corollary of this rule is that field goals don't really change the effective score! One team gains 2 points, but loses possession, while the opponents gain possession. The score really changes when there's a turnover, or when a free throw is made, or at the very end.

Of course I knew that this rule of thumb was only a rough approximation; maybe possession was worth only .8 of a point, say. Even so, the person who steals the ball should be rewarded more than the person who makes baskets, contrary to the normal way that players get credit for their contributions.

In college I finally had an opportunity to test these hunches in a quantitative way, and the computer program I wrote was based on those informal notions about possession. To everyone's surprise, including my own, the system turned out to be quite successful.

Please keep in mind when reading these notes that the rules of bas-ketball have evolved since the 1950s. For example, there was no such thing as a 3-point field goal in those days. Also, all Casies were male.

An Undated Manuscript Written During 1958

The following is a brief summary of the manner in which basketball records are kept by an electronic computer at Case.

The statistics at each basketball game can be taken by two men: a recorder and a spotter. After the game it takes approximately 30 minutes to prepare the necessary totals from the game sheets and about three minutes to punch the IBM cards. One IBM card is made for each Case player who participated in the game, plus a card each for Case and the opponents. Then the machine takes 1.5 minutes to process the game: 30 seconds to take in the "program" of instructions for calculation, 30 seconds to take in the statistical data from all the previous games, and 30 seconds to take in the statistics from this game and to punch the answers. The computer punches four cards for each player, two indicating his performance in this particular game and two containing his cumulative record to date. The cards can easily be printed up for reference and can be filed neatly. Any desired set of statistics can quickly be found from them by passing them through a sorter.

The following information is taken down during the game:

1. Field goals attempted and made (divided into short, medium, and long range).
2. Total free throws attempted and made.
3. Last free throws of a set, made and missed.
4. Total fouls and offensive fouls.
5. Rebounds, defensive and offensive.
6. Violations of rules causing loss of ball.
7. Assists.
8. Loss of ball by fumble, bad pass, or jump ball.
9. Gain of ball by interception or jump ball.
10. Defensive mistakes — allowing opponent to score a field goal.
11. Minutes played.

Each of these eleven statistics is kept for the individual Case players, and items 1 through 6 are kept for the opponents as a team.

The computer does routine calculations such as the shooting per-centages and the running season totals. It also gives a personal score to each Case player, assessing how many points he actually contributed during the game, giving due weight to rebounds, fumbles, et al. Of course only the recorded statistics are taken into account, not unmeasurable quantities like team spirit, or play setup, etc. — although those characteristics will sway a statistics-taker in the player's favor when decisions have to be made in borderline cases.

The weightings of all the individual factors will change from game to game. For example, if the opponents are deadly on free throws, it is more of a sin to commit a foul than if they miss free throws frequently. If the other team is not rebounding well defensively, a missed field goal is not so costly. Thus, these weightings should be expected to vary considerably in different games.

The computer calculates the "true point contribution" of a player by using a rather complicated formula. Using the abbreviations FGA (field goals attempted), FGM (field goals made), FTA (free throws attempted), FTM (free throws made), LFTI (last free throws made), LFTO (last free throws missed), TF (total fouls committed), OF (offensive fouls), OR (offensive rebounds), DR (defensive rebounds), VIOL (violations), AST (assists), FUM (fumbles), BP (bad passes), JL (jump balls lost), JG (jump balls gained), INT (interceptions), DM (defensive mistakes), the player's "point contribution" rating is

$$\begin{aligned} \text{PC} = {}& 2\,\text{FGM} + \text{FTM} + 2(\text{AST} - \text{DM}) \\ & - \alpha(\text{VIOL} + \text{FUM} + \text{JL} + \text{BP} + \text{AST} + \text{FGM} + \text{LFTI}) \\ & + \beta(\text{INT} + \text{JG} + \text{OR} + \text{DR} + \text{DM} - \text{OF}) \\ & - \gamma(\text{TF}) - \delta(\text{FGA} - \text{FGM} + \text{LFTO}), \end{aligned}$$

where α, β, γ, and δ are weighting coefficients determined by team totals. In the formulas for these coefficients, small letters indicate opponents' totals and capital letters denote Case totals:

$$\alpha = 2\,\text{fgm}/(\text{fga} + \text{viol} + \text{of} - \text{or} + \text{INT} + \text{JG} + \text{TF} - \text{OF});$$
$$\beta = 2\,\text{FGM}/(\text{FGA} + \text{VIOL} + \text{OF} - \text{OR} + \text{FUM} + \text{JL} + \text{BP} + \text{tf} - \text{of});$$
$$\gamma = \big(\text{ftm} - \beta(\text{lfti} + \text{lfto} \times \text{DR}/(\text{or} + \text{DR}))\big)/\text{TF};$$
$$\delta = \alpha \times \text{dr}/(\text{OR} + \text{dr}).$$

Intuitively, α represents the average opponents' points per chance; this number varied widely last season from game to game, from .32 up to 1.02. On the other hand β represents Case's average points scored per chance; last season this coefficient remained almost the same from game to game, showing a slight upward trend. The third coefficient, γ, represents points lost per foul; this number also varied drastically. It was as high as $+.70$ in

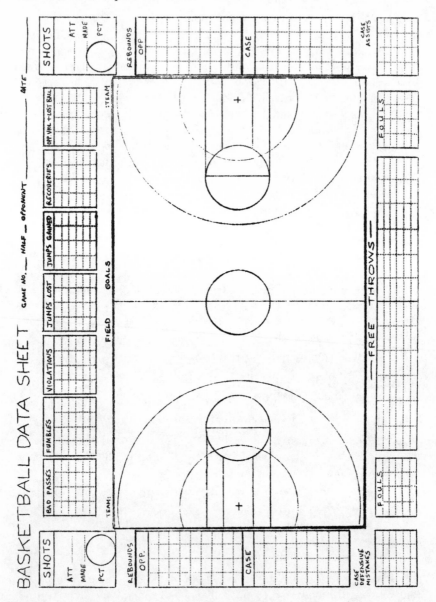

FIGURE 1. The mimeographed forms on which I collected data for each period.
When a player attempted a shot, I wrote his number at his current location.
(Reduced to 60% of the original size.)

one game, but in two games it was slightly *negative*; that is, in those two games it actually paid to foul! The final coefficient δ is the rebounding differential at Case's basket.

The program is presently designed for an IBM 650 computer, but it is readily adaptable to other machines. Copies of the program with complete instructions for its use with a 650 may be obtained from the Case Computing Center after January, 1959. The project is still in its early experimental stages and improvements will undoubtedly be made as they suggest themselves.

Local Newspaper Coverage

[An article by Bill Scholl in The Cleveland Press (8 March 1958).]

Electronic Age Creeps Into Case Cage

When a machine is developed capable of translating the total abilities of two teams and their coaches into the final score of an athletic event, chances are Case Tech will have it.

Imagine, no more long bus rides and hours of physical effort for the players; no more agonizing seasons of planning, plotting, hoping and wailing for coaches; no more parking problems and energy-sapping cheering for the fans; no more sports writers — wup!

Just a brief whirring of wheels, clashing of gears, flashing of lights, ringing of bells, and it's all over.

Basketball: Atomic A. & M. 72, Sad State 43.

This age of electronic miracles hasn't produced such a gadget — but who can argue that it won't?

While we're waiting, Case has taken an interim step by putting a large, three-unit IBM 650 computing machine to work on a minute breakdown of the school's varsity cage statistics this season.

In 30 seconds, the machine comes up with figures that would take the statistician three hours to work out.

The innovation is the brainchild of sophomore Don Knuth of Milwaukee, who at 6 feet, 5 inches, actually is taller than any of the Case players.

"I grew too fast and my coordination is poor for basketball," explains the quiet, bespectacled physics and math whiz almost apologetically.

Don decided to put the computer to work on the growing volume of cage statistics after he was asked to devise a formula to rank the players and then found it took hours to figure out the results.

"It's a pretty complicated formula and takes quite a while to work out by hand," says Don.

Don is so busy recording the multitude of facts called out by assistant Dave Grigsby from their perch behind the Case bench that he doesn't get to see much of the games anymore.

After the final whistle, Don takes his charts to the computing lab a short distance from the fieldhouse, punches the data onto cards, and then puts the IBM 650 through its paces. Rental fee for the machine is $80 an hour while in operation.

"The biggest delay is getting Don to bring the information back to us," laughs Coach Nip Heim, who admits the computer has been more than a little help this winter.

"The results we got were the determining factors in several changes we made between semesters," says Heim. "That's when we started (Dick) Karlinger at forward and moved (Jake) Phillips to guard."

Case won six games this winter for its best season since 1954–55.

"We can always pick out the top man, or two," explains Heim, "but from there on down it's tough." Knuth's formula even shows how many points a Case player permits the enemy to score by way of his bad passes, double dribbles, fumbles, etc.

"The machine figures out everything except how to put the ball through the hoop," says Bill Sudeck, freshman cage coach.

Next step will be to send the 1958–59 statistics through a two-million-dollar Univac, a gift from Remington Rand now being installed at Case.

Time marches on.

[An article by Tom Riley in The Cleveland Plain Dealer (22 December 1958).]

Mechanical Marvel Helps Case Cage Quintet Click

"The number of players times a basic fifty plus individual performance ratings equal the margin of victory or defeat."

That formula is helping to win basketball games at Case Tech, Coach Philip (Nip) Heim revealed last night.

Case is an institute of technology and its undefeated basketball team is an example of the range of tests and experiments by the students.

With the aid of the formula planned by team manager Don Knuth, the performance of each player is rated by an IBM 650 computor [sic] following the game. Knuth, a junior from Milwaukee, takes down the information during the game and later feeds it into the machine.

The number of minutes played, the number of short, medium, and long shots attempted and scored, offensive and defensive rebounds, fumbles, bad passes, and assists are all poured into the mechanical brain along with the important formula.

Mike Doria, a six-foot, four-inch sophomore from St. Joseph High, and Dick Logar, a six-foot, one-inch senior from Lorain, are leading in the ratings. Doria, scoring 80 points during the Rough Riders' five straight victories, was given a boost against Ohio Wesleyan Friday night when he registered 27 rebounds. Logar's 34 points against Mount Union Dec. 17 was a good meal for the IBM brain. Logar has tallied 87 points.

Minutes after the data is filed into the machine, a typewritten sheet evaluating each player is ready for Coach Heim's study. The coach knows instantly how well each boy performed and where concentrated practice is needed. Another sheet reports the reaction of the opposition to the plays of the Rough Riders.

The aid of the mechanical brain was developed by Knuth, a mathematics major, as an experiment in his class. The formula was revised a few times and now the computer can tell the coach almost everything except the range of morale, which is running high with Case the only undefeated college basketball team in the city.

"We can watch the game and easily evaluate a few players, but it's almost impossible to check all the boys' performances during the game," Heim explained. "The machine gives an accurate rundown on every boy that played and can even suggest a starting lineup for the next game."

The machine's evaluation suggests at times that a player might do better or just as well at a guard position instead of forward, and this information proves especially valuable for the Case coaching staff.

Lacking guards but having ample forwards, Case solved the problem with the mechanical brain. Now different players alternate at the position and give the squad more depth.

"Sometimes a player may be down for a game because of an examination coming up or some other problem and this can't be spotted by the machine," Heim pointed out. The mental attitude or errors in a player won't come out in Knuth's formula, but Heim's 25 years experience as a coach has taught him to spot these things.

Heim is the first to admit that Case is not a university concentrating on athletics. "Sports is a necessity on the curriculum but is secondary to studies and naturally the students' interest in their classes ekes out into all their activities," he commented.

The basketball team's IBM advisor is a working example of the university's scope of influence on its student body.

National Magazine Coverage

*[The following item appeared in Newsweek **53**, 1 (5 January 1959), 63.]*

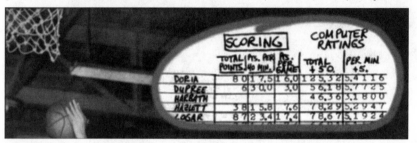

What's That About a Score Card? A Computer's the Thing

If the nation's athletic coaches glanced back this week, they would see nothing less than the IBM 650 computer coming fast.

Thanks in part to this electronic brain, Cleveland's Case Institute of Technology basketball team is currently sporting a 5-0 record. "The 650 is an added man on my staff," explained Philip (Nip) Heim, a 25-year-coaching veteran now enjoying his best season at Case.

The IBM 650 "coach" is the brain child of 20-year-old Don Knuth of Milwaukee, a mathematics major who is also team student manager. After Case's Rough Riders had lost six of its first seven games last season, Knuth told Heim he could come up with a mathematical formula for rating each man that embraced eleven different qualities of play in one equation. Also, the various functions would be "weighted" for each game. That is, when Case played a good rebounding team, the rebound part would get more numerical importance.

At Case's games Knuth is constantly bent over his charts, so busy he literally doesn't "know what the score is." After the final whistle, each player's performance is put on punch cards and run through the 650. Within 90 seconds Knuth has a computer rating for each man in the form of a number from minus 5 to plus 20.

Clearly, the IBM 650 is no substitute for talent. But Heim says it gives him a good line on his starting five. There have also been some surprises. For the five games played this season, Dick Logar has been high scorer. The mechanical coach, however, credited Mike Doria with the highest rating (see contrasting totals above).

Heim naturally is kidded about his new "assistant." But other coaches are now making dead-earnest inquiries.

FIGURE 2. Don Knuth '60 (left) and coach Philip (Nip) Heim
replay a Rough Rider basketball game in the Computing Center.
(from *Case Alumnus* magazine, February 1959)

National Television Coverage

IBM Corporation commissioned Stan Russell to make a film that documented
the whole process, and they supplied the film to the Columbia Broadcasting
System. The film, entitled "Electronic Coach," aired on 8 March 1959 as part
of the Sunday News Special at 11pm on WCBS-TV in New York. Here's a
transcript of the sound track, which conformed in most respects to the script
that Russell had provided:

Walter Cronkite *(shown seated at his desk)*: Well, something new has
come to basketball this year — a bit of automation. The men at Case Institute
of Technology in Ohio still dribble and shoot the ball, of course, but one of
their machines now decides which one of them will take to the floor. *(The film
was now started.)*

Automation came on the heels of desperation. The Institute won only
six out of sixteen games last year; so this season, Don Knuth, student

mathematician, used an electronic computer to evaluate each player's performance.

Here's how he did it: During the scrimmage, Knuth bills the performance record for each player, noting everything from baskets to fumbles. This data is put on punched cards and fed to an IBM computer capable of making 50,000 calculations a minute. Coach Phil Heim checks the computer's findings for the player he needs as the strategy changes.

The material comes off the computer, and then — the Game. Now Heim takes a look at those computations and decides which substitute goes into the game for the immediate strategy.

Does the system work? Coach Heim thinks it does: His team has won 11 out of 14 games this year.

[Cronkite's commentary was carried by 64 television network stations, with an estimated viewing audience of six million people. A copy of the film has been archived by the Computer History Museum, and it can now be viewed on YouTube.]

Afterthoughts

Alas, I have been unable to find any copies of the original program, nor do I recall who carried on with it after I left for graduate school.

My formula for PC should not be taken too seriously. I kept fiddling with it, and never really believed that it was rigorously correct. This work was done long before I had ever heard of Markov processes.

I communicated details of this work to some people at Marquette University in the early 1960s. But it has almost surely had no influence on subsequent applications of computers to sports, except perhaps to stimulate others to do better.

By 1995, professional basketball teams were using computers routinely. Scott McMurray ["Basketball's new high-tech guru," *U.S. News & World Report* **119**, 23 (11 December 1995), 79–80] described a state-of-the-art program called *Advanced Scout*, designed by Inderpal Bhandari of IBM Research.

Chapter 24

The Triel: A New Solution

[Originally published in the Journal of Recreational Mathematics **6** *(1973), 1–7.]*

In a well-known problem, three men fight a pistol duel until two of them are dead. Since a "duel" usually implies that there are only two participants, we may call such a three-way contest a "triel."

Here are the rules for a triel: The players draw lots to determine who fires first, second, and third. Then they take up positions at the corners of an equilateral triangle. Each will fire single shots in turn, continuing in the same cyclic order until there is only one survivor. The person who is firing may aim at will.

The traditional problem is to determine the survival probabilities for each participant, assuming that (a) all three adopt the best strategy; (b) no one is killed unintentionally by a wild shot; (c) the players have respective probabilities p, q, and r of hitting whatever target they aim at; (d) the values of p, q, and r are positive and known to everyone; and (e) the values of p, q, and r remain constant throughout the lives of the corresponding players.

The purpose of this note is to point out that the previous analyses of this problem are incorrect, and to give the (rather surprising) correct solution.

1. The Two-Person Case

After one of the players has succumbed, there will be a duel between the two survivors, so we should solve this simpler problem before considering the full triel. For convenience in the use of English-language pronouns we shall assume that the duelists are both male. Let $f(p,q)$ be the probability that the first player survives, when his accuracy ratio is p and his opponent's is q. Clearly

$$f(p,q) = p + (1-p)(1 - f(q,p));$$

for if his first shot hits its target he is the winner, otherwise $1 - f(q, p)$ is the probability that he is the winner. It follows that

$$f(p, q) = p + (1 - p)\big(1 - (q + (1 - q)(1 - f(p, q)))\big)$$
$$= p + (1 - p)(1 - q)f(p, q).$$

This linear equation has the solution

$$f(p, q) \;=\; p/(p + q - pq),$$

which is (as we might expect) an increasing function of p and a decreasing function of q.

Thus, the two-person case has a simple solution.

2. The Three-Person Case

Suppose it's your turn to shoot in a triel. If you hit your man, the other opponent will fight a duel with you, and he will get to shoot first. You would be foolish to aim at the weaker player, since your chances of hitting the stronger player are equally good. If your shot is successful, you are better off eliminating the more dangerous opponent; if your shot misses it doesn't matter who you miss. Therefore you never aim at your weaker opponent.

Let's assume that the three trielists are named Petersen, Quisling, and Rasmussen, and that their respective accuracy probabilities satisfy $p < q < r$. The argument in the preceding paragraph proves that nobody will ever aim at Petersen, until one of his opponents is wiped out. Then he gets first crack at the other.

Let $P(p, q, r)$ be the probability that Petersen survives, if he goes first and is followed by Quisling, then Rasmussen; let $Q(p, q, r)$ and $R(p, q, r)$ be the corresponding probabilities for Quisling and Rasmussen to survive in those same circumstances. Similarly define $P(q, p, r)$ for Petersen's chances when Quisling goes first and is followed by Petersen then Rasmussen; etc. If each player aims at his stronger opponent, we can write down 18 linear equations that define the situation, starting with

$$P(p, q, r) = p\big(1 - f(q, p)\big) \,+\, (1 - p)P(q, r, p),$$
$$Q(p, q, r) = pf(q, p) \,+\, (1 - p)Q(q, r, p),$$
$$R(p, q, r) = (1 - p)R(q, r, p),$$
$$P(q, p, r) = qf(p, q) + (1 - q)P(p, r, q),$$

and so on. The solution to all these equations is readily obtained, using the formula for $f(x, y)$ given above; but the formulas are too complex to reproduce here.

Since the initial order is obtained by drawing lots, we obtain the overall survival probabilities by averaging over each of the six possible arrangements. This gives the rather complicated, but exact, answers

$$P = \left(\frac{(6 - 3q - 3r + 2qr)p^2(1 - q)}{p + q - pq} + \frac{(6 - 3p - 3r + 2pr)pq}{p + q - pq} \right.$$
$$\left. + \frac{(6 - 3p - 3q + 2pq)pr}{p + r - pr} \right) \Big/ D,$$

$$Q = \left(\frac{(6 - 3q - 3r + 2qr)pq}{p + q - pq} + \frac{(6 - 3p - 3r + 2pr)q^2(1 - p)}{p + q - pq} \right) \Big/ D, \qquad (*)$$

$$R = \left(\frac{(6 - 3p - 3q + 2pq)r^2(1 - p)}{p + r - pr} \right) \Big/ D,$$

where $D = 6(1 - (1-p)(1-q)(1-r))$. A glance at these equations does not make the behavior of the solution very transparent, so the following table of typical values may be helpful:

TABLE 1. Examples of the probabilities in $(*)$

p	q	r	P	Q	R
0.2	0.4	0.6	.314	.305	.381
0.2	0.4	0.8	.273	.237	.490
0.2	0.4	1.0	.237	.182	.581
0.2	0.6	0.8	.246	.337	.417
0.2	0.6	1.0	.220	.268	.512
0.2	0.8	1.0	.203	.354	.443
0.4	0.6	0.8	.430	.304	.266
0.4	0.6	1.0	.403	.249	.348
0.4	0.8	1.0	.374	.322	.304
0.6	0.8	1.0	.513	.303	.184

Notice that in some of these cases the weakest player has the best chance, while the strongest player has the worst, even when he is a "sure shot"! There's an obvious moral for international politics, since you may decrease your chances of survival when you increase your firepower.

Table 1 doesn't show any cases where Quisling is the most likely to win. However, such cases are not impossible (for example when $p = 0.2$, $q = 0.5$, and $r = 0.6$).

3. But What If a Player Passes?

The solution in (∗) is very nice, but it is not correct. For example, see Martin Gardner's discussion [1, Chapter 5] of the case $p = 0.5$, $q = 0.8$, $r = 1.0$; with those probabilities Petersen is better off shooting into the air when his turn comes! A simple calculation shows that his survival chances are improved if he *misses* Rasmussen, because the advantage of first shot in the eventual duel is of critical importance.

The possibility of passing one's turn leads to quite a different analysis of the triel. Consider the following scenario: Petersen passes, thereby improving Rasmussen's chances as well as his own, and it is Quisling's turn. Quisling, thinking furiously because his life is at stake, hits upon a brilliant idea: He *also* passes! Now it is Rasmussen's turn, and he has two choices. Should he fire at Quisling, or should he pass? If he hits Quisling, Petersen might get him (because Petersen will not find it advantageous to pass when Quisling is dead). On the other hand, if Rasmussen passes, we reach precisely the situation we had before: Petersen finds it advantageous to pass, and Quisling passes for the same reason as he did previously. This latter situation is obviously optimum, from Rasmussen's standpoint, since it gives him a survival probability of 1; firing at Quisling would make his chances strictly less than 1 (unless $p = 0$).

Therefore, Rasmussen adopts his best strategy: He passes. It suddenly becomes clear that Quisling also did the best possible thing by passing, because this also raised his own survival probability to 1.

Indeed, our argument shows that the best strategy for all players, in *any* triel regardless of the probabilities p, q, and r, is to shoot wildly on every turn, as long as none of p, q, r are zero. We have proved, by ironclad logic, that pacifism is optimal.

Of course the players shouldn't have gotten into the fight in the first place. But even if they do, it's better for them to handcuff themselves.

Many people, including the author, are alarmed at the possibility that nations will turn over their warmaking decision policies to computers; it is certainly horrifying to contemplate the prospect of machines, rather than humans, making our life-or-death decisions. Yet the situation described above seems to be a counterexample: A computer would have been able to determine the optimum "everybody passes" strategy, but humans would probably have been blinded by their emotions and feelings of "honor"! How else can we explain the fact that the true optimum solution to this problem has just been published for the first time, in the present note, although many people have been considering it for more than thirty years?

4. Further Exploration

The argument for triels does not, unfortunately, carry over to duels. Suppose we have two contestants, Petersen and Quisling, and Petersen passes. Now it's Quisling's turn, and he has two alternatives. If he passes, his survival probability is 1; but if he shoots and misses, his survival probability will *still* be 1, because Petersen (who is in precisely the same situation as before) will pass again. Therefore, Quisling can reason that he loses nothing by taking a shot at Petersen. And therefore Petersen finds that passing is *not* an optimum strategy; so both players will shoot it out. This gives survival probabilities less than 1 to them both, while they could obtain probability 1 if they both passed. It's a paradoxical situation because neither can trust the other.

Similarly if we have a "tetrel" with four players, there is no reason to pass. Each player might as well take aim (at *any* other random player, it doesn't matter which), since after one is eliminated we reach the three-person situation where nobody will shoot to kill.

It is only in the three-person case that we reach the uneasy truce, by impeccable quantitative reasoning. Perhaps that is why the word for "truce" isn't "deuce" or something else.

5. Another Problem

Consider finally what happens if we add a new rule for the trielists: At most k "passes" in a row are allowed, where k is a given number. When $k = 0$ we have the situation analyzed in Section 2 above. When $k = 1$, a player who passes will force the next player to shoot. When $k = 2$, a player who passes will give the next player the chance to force the third player to shoot. This new rule is, of course, completely unenforceable from a practical standpoint; but it does lead to some interesting problems in pure mathematics.

There isn't space here to give a complete analysis of this problem, but the solution can be briefly summarized. First we can prove that, for all fixed $k < \infty$, Rasmussen's best strategy never involves passing. This is intuitively clear, because both of the others will shoot at him if they shoot at anybody; and it can be proved rigorously as follows. Let R_i be Rasmussen's survival probability under the best strategy, when it is his turn after i consecutive passes have just been made, where $0 \leq i \leq k$. His best strategy is either to shoot at Quisling (in which case R_i has a fixed value S, independent of i), or it is to pass. In the latter case we either have $R_i = R_{i+3}$ (if both opponents also pass) or $R_i < R_j$ for some j (if they don't both pass). So, by passing he can never get more than S, which he obtains by shooting.

Since Rasmussen never passes, it follows that each player confronts each turn in the same state, with respect to the number of consecutive passes that have just taken place, except possibly on their very first turn. Furthermore, only the cases $k = 0$, $k = 1$, and $k = 2$ can possibly be different; for $k \geq 3$ the best strategies will be the same as when $k = 2$.

Let us now assume that Petersen shoots first, then Rasmussen, then Quisling. In this case the survival probabilities may be calculated as follows: Let $a = f(q,p)$, $b = f(p,r)$, $c = f(p,q)$, where f is the two-person function defined above. Define the three quantities

$$P_{00} = (pa + \bar{p}rb + \bar{p}\bar{r}qc)/(1 - \bar{p}\bar{q}\bar{r});$$
$$Q_{00} = (q\bar{c} + \bar{q}pa)/(1 - \bar{p}\bar{q}\bar{r});$$
$$R_{00} = r\bar{b}/(1 - \bar{p}\bar{q}\bar{r}).$$

Here $\bar{x}$ stands for $1 - x$. Now define three further quantities P_{10}, Q_{10}, R_{10} by setting q to 0 in the formulas for P_{00}, Q_{00}, R_{00}, while leaving the values of a, b, c unchanged. (Thus, $Q_{10} = pa/(1 - \bar{p}\bar{r})$, etc.) Define P_{01}, Q_{01}, R_{01} similarly by setting p to 0, and define P_{11}, Q_{11}, R_{11} similarly by setting both p and q to 0. The survival probabilities are now determined by the rules shown in Table 2.

TABLE 2. Rules for the shooting order (P, R, Q) and limited passing

If	Petersen's chances are	Quisling's chances are	Rasmussen's chances are
$Q_{00} \geq Q_{10}, P_{00} > P_{01}, P_{10} \geq P_{11}$	P_{00}	$pa + \bar{p}\bar{r}Q_{00}$	$\bar{p}R_{00}$
$Q_{10} > Q_{00}, P_{00} > P_{01}, P_{10} \geq P_{11}$	P_{10}	$pa + \bar{p}\bar{r}Q_{10}$	$\bar{p}R_{10}$
$Q_{01} \geq Q_{10}, P_{01} \geq P_{00}, P_{10} \geq P_{11}$	P_{01}	$pa + \bar{p}\bar{r}Q_{01}$	$\bar{p}R_{01}$
$Q_{10} > Q_{01}, P_{01} \geq P_{00}, P_{10} \geq P_{11}$	P_{10}	$pa + \bar{p}\bar{r}Q_{01}$	$\bar{p}R_{10}$
$Q_{01} \geq Q_{10}, P_{10} < P_{11}$	P_{01}	$pa + \bar{p}\bar{r}Q_{01}$	$\bar{p}R_{01}$
$Q_{10} > Q_{01}, P_{10} < P_{11}, k \geq 2$	P_{01}	$pa + \bar{p}\bar{r}Q_{01}$	$\bar{p}R_{01}$
$Q_{10} > Q_{01}, P_{10} < P_{11}, k = 1$	$rb + \bar{r}qc + \bar{r}\bar{q}P_{10}$	$\bar{r}Q_{10}$	R_{10}

One can show that $P_{10} < P_{11}$ implies $P_{00} \leq P_{01}$, so some of the conditions in Table 2 can be slightly simplified. Furthermore, a somewhat more complex argument shows that $P_{00} \geq P_{01}$ implies $Q_{00} > Q_{10}$; hence the second case never actually occurs. Each of the other cases is possible, for some choices of p, q, and r. (Remember that these formulas apply only when Petersen shoots first, then Rasmussen.) The other five starting configurations can be analyzed in a similar fashion, and fortunately they are simpler.

A list of all the complicated formulas would not be very interesting; let us merely tabulate some typical values (Table 3), averaged over all six shooting orders as in the previous table for $k = 0$.

TABLE 3. Examples of the probabilities for k-limited passing

			$k = 1$			$k \geq 2$		
p	q	r	P	Q	R	P	Q	R
0.2	0.4	0.6	.327	.227	.446	.327	.227	.446
0.2	0.4	0.8	.278	.168	.554	.278	.168	.554
0.2	0.4	1.0	.239	.164	.597	.239	.164	.597
0.2	0.6	0.8	.260	.276	.464	.260	.276	.464
0.2	0.6	1.0	.228	.212	.560	.228	.212	.560
0.2	0.8	1.0	.215	.305	.480	.215	.305	.480
0.4	0.6	0.8	.446	.197	.357	.483	.185	.332
0.4	0.6	1.0	.413	.147	.440	.438	.142	.420
0.4	0.8	1.0	.422	.218	.360	.422	.218	.360
0.6	0.8	1.0	.567	.180	.253	.621	.139	.240

As we might expect, the strategy of passing generally helps Petersen and Rasmussen at the expense of Quisling.

None of the cases listed in Table 3 have the property that everyone's optimal strategy is to shoot. However, there are situations (for example when $p = 0.2$, $q = 0.3$, and $r = 0.8$) where passing is never a good idea.

One final note: Perhaps each player would rather die than live while the other two are still alive; or perhaps the triel is about a beautiful girl who will marry only the winner. In such a case the analysis in Section 3 is inapplicable, and the rule considered here for $k = 2$ seems to give the appropriate formulas. Then, Quisling's idea (to pass after Petersen has passed) is not so brilliant after all, since his survival probability drops to zero.

It is also possible to argue that the analysis in Section 3 fails because sooner or later one of the participants will die of old age; then we are left with a duel! But this argument is problematical, since (for example) *every* mortal man has a survival probability of zero in the long run.

This research was supported in part by Office of Naval Research contract 00014-67-A-0112-0057 NR 044-402, and in part by Norges Almenvitenskapelige Forskningsråd.

References

[1] Martin Gardner, *The Second Scientific American Book of Mathematical Puzzles and Diversions* (New York: Simon & Schuster,

1961). Republished with additions as *Origami, Eleusis, and the Soma Cube: Martin Gardner's Mathematical Diversions* (Washington, D.C.: Mathematical Association of America, 2008).

[2] H. D. Larsen and Leo Moser, "A dart game," solution E811, *American Mathematical Monthly* **55** (1948), 640–641.

[3] Hubert Phillips, "Triangular test," in *Question Time* (London: J. M. Dent, 1937), 125, 261 [problem 223].

Addendum

My word 'triel' for a three-way duel has not picked up much support from other authors. Martin Shubik had coined the term 'truel' for the same notion [*Game Theory and Related Approaches to Social Behavior* (New York: Wiley, 1964), 43]; so had Richard A. Epstein, independently [*The Theory of Gambling and Statistical Logic* (New York: Academic Press, 1967), 343–347]. Other authors, like David L. Silverman [*Your Move* (New York: McGraw–Hill, 1971), 179–180, 214], have followed their lead. On the other hand John C. G. Boot [*Mathematical Reasoning in Economics and Management Science* (Englewood Cliffs, New Jersey: Prentice–Hall, 1967), 92–98] wrote about 'trielling games'. He and I were evidently thinking of analogous instances such as 'duet' versus 'trio'.

Neither 'truel' nor 'triel' appears in the Oxford English Dictionary, vintage 2010, or in the Stanford GraphBase list of five-letter English words. Google's index of the Web in 2003 cited 'triel' only 1481 times and 'truel' only 1487; by contrast, the word 'games' appeared 105,373,578 times in their index, and 'duels' had a count of 108,665. So I consider that the jury is still out. I hesitate to adopt 'truel' myself, because 'triel' sounds less cruel to my ears.

I wasn't the first person to realize that the all-pass strategy is best. Kenneth Kloper wrote to Martin Gardner on 3 September 1958, after seeing Martin's article in *Scientific American* the previous month (a precursor to [1]), in order to demonstrate what he called

> the correct and unique solution: Every morning, at sun-up, three proper gentlemen — a physicist, an engineer, and a bookkeeper — properly fire into the air; old age will claim the survivor.

Kloper also cautioned, however, about the unfortunate possibility of a *suicide* by their second — a mathematician who couldn't accept the fact that such a logical answer was "so unreasonable and yet so correct."

Similarly, after Gardner's book [1] appeared, he received a letter from 1st Lieutenant James Eric Schonblom of the U.S. Army Munitions Command, dated 8 June 1963. Schonblom's letter concluded by saying

The analogy with international relations is complete as this "cold war" situation continues, each firing into the air and eyeing the others warily.

I prefer to believe that persons intelligent enough to realize that survival is rooted in pacifism cannot continue the farce forever. Sooner or later one of them will begin laughing, the seconds will declare that honor has been satisfied, and all three can go home to ponder why they ever considered duels and survival compatible in the first place.

(Gardner's correspondence files now reside in the Stanford University Archives; Martin gave me the opportunity to study them in 1994.)

Thus Kloper, Schonblom, and I independently came to the same conclusion. But is it really correct? Is our reasoning truly bulletproof? I've lectured about this topic to several math clubs, and I haven't succeeded in convincing all the skeptics, probably because of a hidden assumption that I failed to state in my article and in my lectures.

Namely, I should have elaborated on point (e) in the third paragraph of my article: Not only do I assume that p, q, and r remain constant, I also assume that the players' strategies do not depend on any past history. The game that I studied has only $6 + 6$ states, one for each order in which the surviving players will make sequential decisions. Thus an optimizing player will always make the same decision in the same situation. (In principle, I would however allow a player to flip a coin instead of adopting a "pure" strategy, as long as he uses the coin flips in the same way when in the same state.)

Robert Axelrod wrote me a delightful letter in 1984, observing that my article was championing "passifism." His version of my hidden assumption was the following:

If a player makes a given choice he will always make that same choice in the same situation, and this fact is common knowledge. Everyone knows it and everyone knows that everyone else knows it.

In particular, the first player commits himself to a future course of action by making a particular choice now, without knowing what the second player's choice will be, except that it will be optimum. And the second player's choice must be optimum also if he had happened to be first: His strategy, which depends only on the game state, is essentially decided *before* the random selection of who shoots first and who shoots next.

With this understanding, Axelrod proceeded to convince me that "passifism" is therefore optimum in the two-person duel as well. A player who passes is guaranteeing that his opponent has no reason to shoot back, as far as the opponent's survival is concerned. Conversely, a player who doesn't pass will risk survival probability less than 1, in cases where he doesn't go first.

In a way, I like that. I've occasionally wished that the cowboys in old Western movies had meant "It's a tie game" when they said "Draw"!

But if the two-player case is resolved in that way, my analysis of the three-player case goes out the window, since I based it on the probability $f(p, q)$ of winning a shootout. Suppose, for example, that Rasmussen is a sure shot, so that $r = 1$. Isn't it better for him to wipe out one of his opponents and then to bask comfortably in the safety of the resulting duel? Well, no; for then he'll be giving up his chance to prove to the others that he's no threat. They'll have to shoot at him when he isn't first.

Aha, we still conclude that pass-pass-pass is the best way for three competitors to proceed.

Hmm. That argument points up a fallacy in my analysis of the four-player case: I had claimed that each of the four could shoot with impunity until reaching a three-player safety net, but I didn't properly think through the risk of missing. The correct solution, under my assumptions, is actually for *all* players in *any* sequential n-way duel to shoot into the air (or even better, into the ground), regardless of n.

Clearly I'm not competent to work on problems like this, and I'd better "pass" them on to other people who understand them better. (Should I, however, also trust a machine to find the solution?)

Many variants are obviously possible. For instance, Epstein allowed the players to *choose* their probabilities p, q, and r arbitrarily, after the shooting sequence had been selected by lot; and in the all-pass case, he supposed that each winner had only $1/3$ of a life!

Three-way duels have added spice to dramatic productions such as A. P. Herbert's *Fat King Melon and Princess Caraway* (London: Oxford University Press, 1927), and to movies such as Sergio Leone's *The Good, the Bad, and the Ugly* = *Il Buono, il Bruto, il Cattivo* (1966); Quentin Tarantino's *Reservoir Dogs* (1992) and *Pulp Fiction* (1994); Gore Verbinski's *Pirates of the Caribbean: Dead Man's Chest* (2006).

Further information can be found, for example, in "The truel," by D. Marc Kilgour and Steven J. Brams, *Mathematics Magazine* **70** (1997), 315–326.

Chapter 25

The Computer as Master Mind

[Originally published in the Journal of Recreational Mathematics **9** *(1976), 1–6.]*

A deductive game called Master Mind, produced by Invicta Plastics, Ltd., enjoyed a wave of popularity during the 1975 Christmas season [2]. In this game one player (the "codemaker") conceals a four-symbol code, and the other player (the "codebreaker") tries to identify all four symbols by trying appropriate test patterns. There are six symbols, represented by pegs of different colors, and repetitions are permitted; hence there are $6^4 = 1296$ possible codewords. If the codemaker's secret codeword is $x_1x_2x_3x_4$ and if the codebreaker gives the test pattern $y_1y_2y_3y_4$, the codemaker rates that guess by announcing

1) the number of "black hits," namely the number of positions j such that $x_j = y_j$;

2) the number of "white hits," namely the number of positions j such that $x_j \neq y_j$ although x_j does equal y_k for some k, where y_k hasn't been used in another hit.

For example, let the symbols be denoted by 1, 2, 3, 4, 5, 6. If the codeword is 2532 and the test pattern is 3523, there are two white hits and one black hit. Rule (2) is somewhat difficult to state precisely and unambiguously, and the manufacturers have *not* succeeded in doing so on the directions they furnish with the game — although *Games & Puzzles* magazine [7, 8] has given them a rating of 8 points out of 8 for clarity of explanation! Perhaps the clearest way to state the rule exactly, when speaking to mathematicians or to computers, is this: Suppose symbol i occurs n_i times in the codeword and n'_i times in the test pattern, for $1 \leq i \leq 6$. Then the total number of hits, both white and black, is

$$\min(n_1, n'_1) + \min(n_2, n'_2) + \cdots + \min(n_6, n'_6).$$

It follows that the total number of misses (non-hits) is

$$\max(n_1 - n'_1, 0) + \max(n_2 - n'_2, 0) + \cdots + \max(n_6 - n'_6, 0).$$

Notice that it is impossible to have three black hits and one white hit. The codebreaker tries to get *four black hits*, after constructing a minimum number of test patterns.

The purpose of this note is to prove that *the codebreaker can always succeed in five moves or less*. Thus, the code can always be known after at most four guesses have been made; and in fact it will often be known earlier. A complex strategy to achieve this result, worked out with the aid of a computer, appears below in Table 1, in highly condensed form. Readers who have played Master Mind will be able to see how a real expert operates by studying this strategy carefully.

Here is how to read Table 1: Every situation we can arrive at during a game corresponds to a certain number of codewords, and we assume that the reader can figure out all of the possibilities that remain at any given time. If there are n possible codewords remaining, the situation is represented in Table 1 by the notation

n,   if $n \le 2$; or

$n(y_1 y_2 y_3 y_4)$,   if $n > 2$ and if the answer to test pattern $y_1 y_2 y_3 y_4$ will uniquely characterize the codeword; or

$n(y_1 y_2 y_3 y_4 *)$,   if $n > 2$ and if the situation after test pattern $y_1 y_2 y_3 y_4$ is not always unique but there will never be more than two possibilities; or

$$n(y_1 y_2 y_3 y_4 : \alpha_{04}, \alpha_{03}, \alpha_{02}, \alpha_{01}, \alpha_{00}; \alpha_{13}, \alpha_{12}, \alpha_{11}, \alpha_{10};$$
$$\alpha_{22}, \alpha_{21}, \alpha_{20}; \alpha_{31}, \alpha_{30}; \alpha_{40}),$$

if $n > 2$ and if the test pattern $y_1 y_2 y_3 y_4$ answered by j black hits and k white hits leads to situation α_{jk}.

The test pattern doesn't need to be specified when $n = 2$, since the best approach is to name either of the two remaining possibilities.

For example, the beginning of Table 1 can be freely translated thus:

> There are 1296 possibilities to start with. Your first test pattern should be 1122. Now if the answer is "four white hits," only one codeword is possible (you can figure it out, it is 2211), so you should guess that code next and win. If the answer is "three white hits," only 16 possibilities remain, and your next codeword should be 1213. The response must indicate at least one black hit; and if it is "one black hit, two white hits," say, there are four possibilities, which can be distinguished by the answer to test pattern 1415.

A more typical play of the game using the strategy of Table 1 arises when the answer to the first test pattern 1122 is "one black hit." Then the original 1296 possibilities have been reduced to 256, and we go to the ninth situation of the fifteen situations following '1122:' in Table 1; this is the situation just before the second semicolon on the outer level. The second test pattern (see F) is 1344; and let's say the answer is "one white hit." Then 44 possibilities remain, and our third guess is 3526. If the result this time is "one black hit, two white hits," Table 1 says that seven possibilities survive, and that the test pattern 1462 will distinguish them. For example, the reader might wish to deduce the unique codeword that should be guessed after the following sequence:

test pattern	hits
1122	B
1344	W
3526	BWW
1462	BW

(The answer appears at the end of this article.)

Incidentally, the fourth move 1462 in this example is really a brilliant stroke, a crucial play if a win in five is to be guaranteed. None of the seven codewords that satisfy the first three patterns could be used successfully as the fourth test pattern; for example, if we had tried 4562, the response BB would have failed to distinguish 3662 from 5532. A codeword that cannot possibly win in four is *necessary* here to win in five.

Table 1 was found by choosing at every stage a test pattern that *minimizes the maximum number of remaining possibilities*, over all conceivable responses by the codemaker. If this minimum can be achieved by a "valid" pattern (a pattern that makes "four black hits" possible), a valid one should be used. Subject to this condition, the first such test pattern in numeric order was selected. Fortunately this procedure turns out to guarantee a win in five moves.

If the first test pattern is 1123 instead of 1122, the same approach nearly works. But there is one line of play that fails to win in five, starting with

1123	WW	[222 possibilities]
2214	WW	[36 possibilities]
3341		

The 6 possibilities now remaining after "BB" and the 7 after "BBB" cannot all be distinguished by any fourth move. There probably is a way to improve this variation by changing the second pattern. However, when the first test pattern is 1234 it appears to be impossible to guarantee a win in five, especially after 1234 WW [312 possibilities].

TABLE 1. A minimax strategy for Master Mind

1296(1122: 1, 16(1213: 0, 0, 0, 0; 1, 4(1415), 3(1145), 0; 1, 3(4115), 3(1145); 0; 1; 0), 96A, 256B, 256C;
    0, 36D, 208E, 256F; 4(1213), 32G, 114H; 0, 20I; 1)

A = (2344: 0, 2, 16(3215: 0, 0, 0, 0; 1, 2, 1, 1; 2, 3(3231), 2; 0, 3(3213); 1),
    14(5215: 0, 0, 0, 0; 0, 1, 3(3511), 3(3611); 1, 1, 2; 0, 2; 1), 4(1515); 0, 6(2413),
    18(2415: 1, 1, 0, 0; 1, 2, 3(2253), 3(2236); 1, 2, 2; 0, 1; 1), 15(2256*; 0, 4(2234), 14(3315*); 0, 3(2314); 0)

B = (2344: 0, 7(2335), 41(3235: 0, 0, 2, 3(4613), 2; 0, 3(5263), 6(3413), 6(3416); 2, 4(3256), 6(1336); 0, 6(1536); 1),
    44(3516: 1, 4(4651), 6(6255), 1, 0; 3(5613), 7(1461), 5(4551), 1; 3(1113), 5(3551), 3(4515); 0, 4(1145); 1),
    16(5515: 0, 0, 1, 1, 0; 0, 2, 2, 1; 1, 1, 3(1516); 0, 3(1516); 1);
    2, 21(3245: 1, 3(2436), 0, 0, 0; 2, 2, 2, 0; 2, 3(3234), 2; 0, 3(3243); 1),
    42(4514: 1, 1, 7(2456), 4(2635), 3(2636); 0, 4(1356), 5(4361), 6(1635); 2, 2, 3(3614); 0, 3(4414); 1),
    34(3315: 0, 0, 3(5641), 4(2566), 1; 1, 4(5361), 4(5614), 5(6614); 2, 4(3331), 1; 0, 4(3316); 1);
    3(2434), 13(2425*), 23(1545: 0, 1, 3(2654), 3(2353), 4(1136); 0, 2, 4(2564), 3(2335); 0, 0, 2; 0, 1; 0);
    0, 9(1335*); 1)

C = (3345: 2, 20(4653: 2, 2, 0, 0, 0; 3(4536), 3(4534), 1, 0; 2, 2, 1; 0, 3(4453); 1),
    42(6634: 0, 3(4566), 4(4556), 1, 0; 2, 5(4656), 6(5653), 4(1444); 2, 5(5636), 5(4654); 0, 4(1413); 1),
    16(6646: 0, 0, 1, 0, 0; 0, 3(1416), 1, 1; 3(1416), 3(5666); 2; 0, 2; 0), 1;
    4(3453), 40(3454: 1, 5(4535), 6(1436), 0, 0; 2, 5(4356), 6(3536), 0; 1, 3(3564), 6(3463); 0, 4(3456); 1),
    46(3636: 1, 1, 3(4364), 6(4565), 6(4544); 0, 5(4366), 6(1565), 6(4546); 2, 4(3466), 3(3556); 0, 2; 1),
    18(3656: 0, 1, 1, 1, 1; 0, 3(5665), 3(6446), 3(4446); 0, 1, 3(4646); 0, 1; 0);
    5(3435*), 20(3443: 0, 0, 4(4355), 0, 0; 0, 3(3334), 4(3356), 0; 1, 2, 4(3455); 0, 1; 1),
    29(3636: 0, 1, 3(5365), 4(6445), 4(1444); 0, 2, 3(3565), 4(4645); 1, 1, 4(3446); 0, 2; 0); 0, 12(3446*); 1)

$D = (1213: 1, 4(1145), 3(1415), 0, 0; 0, 6(1114*), 7(2412*), 0; 2, 4(1145), 4(1145), 4(1145*); 0, 4(1114*); 1)$

$E = (1134: 0, 4(1312), 24(3521: 1, 2, 4(4612), 0, 0; 0, 3(3312), 3(2423), 0; 2, 2, 3(4621); 0, 3(3321); 1),$
$38(2352: 2, 4(3226), 4(5621), 1, 0; 1, 5(2223), 7(6242), 1; 2, 4(2323), 4(2462); 0, 2; 1),$
$20(2525: 1, 2, 1, 0, 0; 0, 3(2252), 3(2262), 0; 2, 2, 2; 0, 3(2225); 1);$
$4(1341), 34(1315: 1, 3(4151), 4(4151), 0, 0; 1, 6(6451), 6(1461), 0; 3(1351), 3(1361), 2; 0, 4(1113); 1),$
$32(1516: 2, 2, 3(2145), 0, 4(2324); 2, 4(1661), 4(1245), 0; 3(1561), 3(1551), 1; 0, 3(1511); 1),$
$22(1256: 1, 0, 4(2524), 2, 0; 0, 2, 4(5224), 4(2224); 2, 0, 0; 0, 2; 1; 4(1314), 12(1315*), 12(1235*); 0, 2; 0)$

$F = (1344: 0, 7(1335), 41(3135: 0, 0, 2, 3(4623), 2; 0, 3(5163), 6(3423), 6(3426); 2, 4(3156), 6(1436); 0, 6(1536); 1),$
$44(3526: 1, 4(4652), 6(6155), 1, 0; 3(5623), 7(1462), 5(4552); 1; 3(1123), 5(3552), 3(4525); 0, 4(1145); 1),$
$16(5525: 0, 0, 1, 1, 0; 0, 2, 2, 1; 1, 1, 3(1516); 0, 3(1516); 1);$
$2, 21(3145: 1, 3(1436), 0, 0, 0; 2, 2, 2, 0; 2, 3(3134), 2; 0, 3(3143); 1),$
$42(4524: 1, 1, 7(1456), 4(1635), 3(1636); 0, 4(1356), 5(4362), 6(1336); 2, 2, 3(3624); 0, 3(4424); 1),$
$34(3325: 0, 0, 3(5642), 4(1566), 1; 1, 4(5362), 4(5624), 5(6624); 2, 4(3332), 1; 0, 4(3326); 1);$
$3(1434), 13(1415*), 23(1415: 0, 0, 2, 4(3324), 0; 0, 4(1546), 4(1356), 4(1136); 0, 2, 3(1136); 0, 0; 0);$
$0, 9(1335*); 1)$

$G = (1223: 1, 4(2145), 3(4115), 0, 0; 0, 5(2145), 6(4512), 0; 2, 4(1245), 3(1415); 0, 3(1145); 1)$

$H = (1234: 2, 16(1325: 1, 3(4152), 3(4162), 0, 0; 1, 3(3126), 2, 0; 1, 1, 1; 0, 0; 0),$
$20(1325: 0, 3(5162), 1, 0, 0; 0, 2, 4(4522), 4(4622); 0, 3(5125), 3(2116); 0, 0; 0),$
$6(2515), 0; 4(1323), 21(1352: 0, 1, 2, 0, 0; 2, 4(1623), 2, 0; 1, 3(1323), 3(1462); 0, 2; 1),$
$16(2156*), 12(1315*); 2, 6(3526), 8(1536*); 0, 1; 0)$

$I = (1223: 0, 0, 0, 0, 0; 1, 5(1145*), 4(1114*), 0; 1, 3(1415), 4(1114*); 0, 2; 0)$

The strategy in Table 1 isn't optimal from the "expected number of moves" standpoint, but it is probably very close. One line that can be improved occurs in D, after

$$1122 \quad \text{BWW}$$
$$1213 \quad \text{BB}$$

when there are four possible codewords $\{2212, 4212, 5212, 6212\}$. The pattern 4222* distinguishes them more quickly than the arithmetically smallest decent pattern 1145* does.

It is not clear what the optimum strategy would be if we use the interesting new scoring rules proposed by G. W. Gill in [4].

Historical Note

A game very similar to Master Mind, called "Bulls and Cows," has been popular in England for many years. The difference is that all digits of the code in Bulls and Cows must be distinct; but any digits 0 through 9 are allowed. This version of the game has become a popular computer demonstration, after Frank H. King introduced a program for it in August 1968 at Cambridge University [3, 5, 6].

References

[1] "Games gift guide," *Games & Puzzles* **20** (December 1973), 16–17. [Attributes the invention of Master Mind to M. Meyerowitz.]

[2] "And now, Master Mind," *Time* **106**, 22 (1 December 1975), 73.

[3] $\aleph_0$ [Aleph-Null], "Computer recreations," *Software — Practice & Experience* **1** (1971), 201–204.

[4] G. W. Gill, letter to the editor, *Games & Puzzles* **26** (July 1974), 22.

[5] Jerrold M. Grochow, "MOO in Multics," *Software — Practice & Experience* **2** (1972), 303–304.

[6] Frank H. King, "The game of MOO," University of Cambridge, Computer Laboratory (February 1976), 5 pages.

[7] Richard Sharp, review of Master Mind, *Games & Puzzles* **12** (April 1973), 21.

[8] David Wells, "Master Mind: The story of an experiment," *Games & Puzzles* **23** (March–April 1974), cover, 10–11.

Answer to Secret Codeword

16×227.

Addendum

Of course I wouldn't stick precisely to the strategy of Table 1 if I were the codebreaker in a real game. I'd randomize it, by choosing a random permutation $p_1 p_2 p_3 p_4$ of the positions $\{1, 2, 3, 4\}$ and a random permutation $q_1 q_2 q_3 q_4 q_5 q_6$ of the colors $\{1, 2, 3, 4, 5, 6\}$. Then when Table 1 mentions a pattern $x_1 x_2 x_3 x_4$, I would actually use the pattern $q_{x_{p_1}} q_{x_{p_2}} q_{x_{p_3}} q_{x_{p_4}}$.

The question I raised about minimizing the "expected number of moves" can be rephrased to ask for a nonrandomized strategy that makes the fewest total guesses, summed over all 1296 codewords. The strategy in Table 1 yields 5801 guesses; the improvement that I mentioned for part D yields 5800, for an average of $5800/1296 \approx 4.4753$. Robert W. Irving ["Towards an optimum Mastermind strategy," *Journal of Recreational Mathematics* **11** (1978), 81–87] improved this by finding a strategy that needs only 5662 total guesses, or an average of ≈ 4.3688. The codebreaker's first guess in his strategy is 1123, not 1122. He needed six guesses to deduce one of the secret codewords, but he could modify his scheme for a maximum of five by increasing the total from 5662 to 5664.

A still better guessing procedure, with total 5656, was found by E. Neuwirth ["Some strategies for Mastermind," *Zeitschrift für Operations Research* **26** (1982), B257–B278], increasing to 5658 if limited to five guesses per codeword.

Finally, the best possible total — 5625 guesses — was published by Kenji Koyama and Tony W. Lai ["An optimal Mastermind strategy," *Journal of Recreational Mathematics* **25** (1993), 251–256], who did an exhaustive depth-first computer search. The average with their method is therefore $5625/1296 \approx 4.3403$. They also showed how to obtain a total of 5626 guesses without needing more than five per codeword.

Merrill M. Flood ["Mastermind strategy," *Journal of Recreational Mathematics* **18** (1986), 194–202] considered the more general problem in which both codemaker and codebreaker try to optimize their policies. A codemaker who knows the codebreaker's strategy can do better by favoring some codewords over others. For example, the scheme of Koyama and Lai has the following distribution of guesses per game:

$xxxx$	0	0	1	5	0	0	$23/6 \approx 3.833$
$xxxy$	0	0	2	72	46	0	$524/120 \approx 4.367$
$xxyy$	0	0	2	55	33	0	$391/90 \approx 4.344$
$xxyz$	1	8	49	357	304	1	$3118/720 \approx 4.331$
$wxyz$	0	0	32	167	161	0	$1569/360 \approx 4.358$

(The entry in row 4 and column 3 of this chart means that 49 of the 720 codewords of the permuted form $xxyz$ are unmasked on the codebreaker's third guess, etc.) If the codemaker always chooses codewords of the permuted form $xxxy$, such as say 2522, the codebreaker ends up making about 4.367 guesses per game; that's noticeably worse than the 4.340 guesses needed to crack a completely random codeword.

The strategy of Koyama and Lai can, however, be made more balanced by making simple changes to the guesses in a few cases where only two possibilities remain. For example, there's a situation where they guess 1111 when the only other candidate is 1166; by guessing 1166 first, they could increase the average cost for patterns of type $xxxx$ to 24/6, but decrease the cost for $xxyy$ to 390/90. By making a dozen carefully chosen swaps of this kind, their scheme can be modified so that it has the following distribution:

$xxxx$	0	0	1	4	1	0	$24/6 = 4.000$
$xxxy$	0	0	2	75	43	0	$521/120 \approx 4.342$
$xxyy$	0	0	2	56	32	0	$390/90 \approx 4.333$
$xxyz$	1	8	49	348	313	1	$3127/720 \approx 4.343$
$wxyz$	0	0	32	173	155	0	$1563/360 \approx 4.342$

Against this strategy, the codemaker can force only 4.343 guesses per game, on the average.

In 1985 I received an unpublished description of a still better method, entitled "An optimal Mastermind strategy," from Tom Nestor, a mathematics graduate student at Oklahoma State University. His procedure achieves the minimal total of 5625 with a distribution that is almost perfectly balanced:

$xxxx$	0	0	1	3	2	0	$25/6 \approx 4.167$
$xxxy$	0	0	2	75	43	0	$521/120 \approx 4.342$
$xxyy$	0	0	2	56	32	0	$390/90 \approx 4.333$
$xxyz$	1	8	50	347	313	1	$3126/720 \approx 4.342$
$wxyz$	0	0	28	181	151	0	$1563/360 \approx 4.342$

With this scheme we need at most 4.342 guesses per game, regardless of what the codemaker tries to do; that's very near the theoretical minimum of $5625/1296 \approx 4.340$.

Suppose the codebreaker must pay \$1.20 for every guess, but receives \$5.21 whenever discovering a codeword. With the Koyama–Lai methods the codebreaker might lose money; but with Nestor's strategy, the codebreaker can break even, in the long run, against all comers.

Furthermore, the codebreaker can actually make a profit in this version of the game by being more clever. If we make one or two appropriate changes to Nestor's original scheme, by swapping guesses in well-chosen cases where just two possibilities remain, we can obtain pure strategies N_1, N_2, N_3 for which respectively

$$(520/120, \ 391/90, \ 3126/720, \ 1563/360)$$
$$(521/120, \ 391/90, \ 3125/720, \ 1563/360)$$
$$(521/120, \ 391/90, \ 3126/720, \ 1562/360)$$

guesses will resolve the non-$xxxx$ patterns, while the $xxxx$ patterns remain easy. By using (N_0, N_1, N_2, N_3) with the respective probabilities $(13, 3, 18, 9)/43$, where N_0 is Nestor's strategy, we could then win at least \$1/1720 per game, on average, against any codewords. In other words, the expected number of guesses per game would then be at most $521/120 - 1/1720 = 560/129 \approx 4.341$.

Conversely, a codemaker who chooses random $xxxy$, $xxyy$, $xxyz$, or $wxyz$ with the respective probabilities $(4, 3, 24, 12)/43$ can ensure that such a mixed strategy will force the codebreaker to make *at least* $560/129$ guesses per game, on average. This codemaking strategy is equivalent to choosing randomly among the 1290 non-$xxxx$ codes.

Tom Nestor, who has continued to develop sophisticated algorithms for studying Master Mind strategies, wrote to me again in 2010, stating that his programs yield a proof that $5600/1290$ is the minimum average number of guesses per game if we don't allow the codemaker to choose $xxxx$ — although $xxxx$ patterns might still be guessed by the codebreaker if desired. It follows that the mixed strategy that we have discussed for (N_0, N_1, N_2, N_3) is in fact optimum.

In other words, Merrill Flood's problem has now been resolved, and $560/129$ is the true value of the guesses-per-game criterion when both codemaker and codebreaker play optimally.

The same result was, in fact, announced by Michael Wiener, in a posting to the `sci.net` newsgroup of Usenet on 29 November 1995, "from a program that ran for months." Wiener had done this unpublished computation during the late 1980s.

Nestor points out, however, that none of the strategies we've discussed so far is really the best way to play Master Mind! The normal rules don't ask us to minimize the expected number of guesses; they ask us rather *to make fewer guesses, when we are codebreaker, than the opponent does when he or she is codebreaker.* And that is quite a different problem.

For example, let's consider a symmetrical form of the game in which Alice and Bob each play against a computer. The computer chooses codewords for each of them, in such a way that all of the 1296^2 pairs of codewords are equally likely. Alice discovers her codeword after making exactly a guesses, and Bob discovers his after making b. Alice doesn't know anything about b while she's playing, and Bob doesn't know anything about a. Then we stipulate that Alice wins if $a < b$, Bob wins if $a > b$, and the game is tied if $a = b$.

Nestor proved his point by sending me a strategy M, which has the profile $(1, 8, 80, 679, 511, 17)$ compared to the profile $(1, 8, 83, 662, 541, 1)$ of $N = N_0$. There are, for instance, 17 cases for which M needs 6 guesses, while N has only one such bad case. The expected cost of M is proportional to $(1, 8, 80, 679, 511, 17) \cdot (1, 2, 3, 4, 5, 6) = 5630$, compared to the optimum $(1, 8, 83, 662, 541, 1) \cdot (1, 2, 3, 4, 5, 6) = 5625$ of N. But if Alice plays M against Bob's N, she wins with probability

$$\bigl(1 \cdot (8 + 83 + 662 + 541 + 1) + 8 \cdot (83 + 662 + 541 + 1) + \cdots + 511 \cdot 1\bigr)/1296^2,$$

about 28.37%, while he wins with probability

$$\bigl(1 \cdot (8 + 80 + 679 + 511 + 17) + 8 \cdot (80 + 679 + 511 + 17) + \cdots + 541 \cdot 17\bigr)/1296^2,$$

about 28.01%; otherwise the game is tied, with probability

$$(1 \cdot 1 + 8 \cdot 8 + 80 \cdot 83 + \cdots + 17 \cdot 1)/1296^2 \approx 43.62\%.$$

Alice racks up her advantage over Bob's supposedly "optimum" play by being rather good at guessing codes in four steps or less.

A similar phenomenon was found for the game Bulls and Cows by Tetsuro Tanaka ["An optimal MOO strategy," Proceedings of a Game Programming Workshop (1996), 202–209, in Japanese]. He showed that the minimum expected cost for that game is $26274/5040$, obtained with a guessing scheme T whose profile is $(1, 7, 63, 697, 2424, 1774, 74)$; yet he also found a scheme T' with profile $(1, 4, 47, 688, 2531, 1628, 141)$ and expected cost 26312, which wins against T more often than it loses. [See also John Francis, "Strategies for playing MOO, or 'Bulls and Cows'" (preprint, 2010).]

Nestor went on to prove that his strategy M will beat *any* strategy whose profile differs from $(1, 8, 80, 679, 511, 17)$, in this symmetrical version of the game.

On the other hand, Master Mind is usually played sequentially: Alice, say, is the first to break a code; then Bob will know the value of a when it is his turn to be the breaker. This gives him a significant advantage, because he can choose different optimum strategies depending on how lucky or unlucky Alice was. If, for example, $a = 6$, Bob can guarantee victory by using Table 1.

Let β_a be the probability that Bob wins minus the probability that Bob loses, if he plays optimally for a given value of a. (His optimum strategy depends only on a, not on Alice's method of guessing.) Then $\beta_6 = 1$; and $\beta_1 = 1/1296 - 1$, because $a = 1$ forces Bob to lose except when he happens to guess the code on his first try. Nestor has developed an efficient algorithm to determine optimum strategies for the other cases $a = 2$, 3, 4, and 5; then, knowing the values $(\beta_1, \beta_2, \beta_3, \beta_4, \beta_5, \beta_6)$, his algorithm is also able to determine Alice's optimum strategy. Of course I hope he will publish these exciting new results soon.

I've placed an expanded version of Table 1 on the Internet, as file 'http://www-cs-faculty.stanford.edu/~knuth/mm.txt'. It is a 11533-byte long parenthesized formula that begins with

    1296(1122:1(2211),16(1213:0,0,0,0,0;1(2311),

and ends with

    2(1125,1126);0,1(1124);0);0,2(1123,1222);0);1(1122))

and has cases like

    4(5624,5524,6362,6524),5(6624,1555,1565,1655,1665)

in the middle. The conventions of Table 1 are simplified so that 'n' appears by itself only if $n = 0$; '$n(g_1, g_2, \ldots, g_n)$' appears whenever the remaining codewords are $\{g_1, g_2, \ldots, g_n\}$ and you'll know the truth after guessing g_1. (The former notation $n(y_1 y_2 y_3 y_4 *)$ is not used.) My website also contains similar files mm-n0.txt, mm-n1.txt, mm-n2.txt, mm-n3.txt, and mm-m.txt for Nestor's optimum strategies N_0, N_1, N_2, N_3, and M.

Incidentally, the question of optimum play in Gill's sense (see [4]) remains open. Gill proposed minimizing the sum $G + B + 2W + 3N$, where there are G guesses, B black hits, W white hits, and N non-hits. Since $N + W + B = 4G$, his goal is to minimize $13G - 2B - W$.

Chapter 26

Move It Or Lose It

*[Originally published in Variant Chess **8** (2009), 96, based on a letter written to Martin Gardner on 9 January 2002.]*

Dear Martin,

... During Christmas vacation I investigated a variant of chess that you might enjoy trying out with new friends that you happen to meet in a retirement community. I haven't got a great name for it as yet; my son and I tentatively call it "15-Out" a.k.a. "Move It Or Lose It." The idea is to encourage relatively quick games by requiring every piece to move at least once in every 15 turns.

You play with ordinary chess pieces, but each player also has 15 cards that fit under the pieces, each card being the size of a square on the board. The cards of each player are numbered from 1 to 15. One card is placed under every piece *except* the king; the numbers are visible to both players.

Our initial setup was

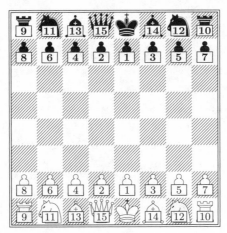

and it worked fine, but lots of other starting positions are plausible.

All the rules of ordinary chess apply, and there's also a new rule that sometimes removes pieces or pawns from the board: Each move has a serial number k that runs through the cycle 1, 2, 3, ..., 14, 15, 1, 2, 3, ..., 14, 15, 1, etc. If you've moved anything besides a king on move k, you put card k under that piece. Also, if card k was under a piece that you *didn't* move, that piece is taken off the board.

A few slightly subtle points arise: (1) When you castle, the rook is the piece that gets card k. (2) When a piece is removed because you didn't move it at its "doomstime," this might result in discovered check on your opponent. (3) A player is not allowed to move in such a way that losing a piece/pawn leaves his king in check; therefore there's a new kind of stalemate.

For example, here are the first moves in the first game that I played with my son John (who had the white pieces):

> 1   e2-e4

(The pawn remains above card #1.)

> 1   ...   e7-e5

(Likewise.)

> 2   Bf1-b5

(He loses his d-pawn. The bishop becomes #2 and card #14 is temporarily retired until move 14.)

> 2   ...   c7-c6

(I lose *my* d-pawn; card #4 temporarily leaves the board.)

> 3   Qd1xd8+

(And he loses his f-pawn.)

> 3   ...   Ke8xd8

(And I lose mine too. Card #3 goes off the board, since K gets no card.)

> 4   Bc1-g5+

(Meanwhile he also loses his c-pawn.)

> 4   ...   Bf8-e7

(Card #4 comes back into play; card #14 is temporarily off; see Fig. 1.)

And so on. (My son was evidently in an aggressive, sacrificial mood.) (He won.)

After a while the pieces dwindle and the new rules have less and less effect; players might reach a point where the cards are a nuisance because the pieces move frequently anyway. It helps to keep a record of the game, so that cards can be dispensed with in such cases. But games go fast, and there's an interesting mix of new strategy versus old.

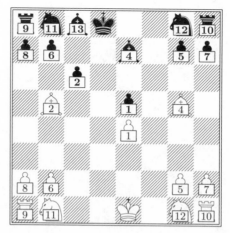

FIGURE 1. The position after Black's fourth move.

Addendum: Comments by Editor John Beasley

The game does indeed go fast, indeed it is so sharp that I fear opening play might soon become stereotyped. However, if this proves to be a problem, other starting arrays could be tried for the cards, or the players could even be invited to place them on the board one at a time as a preliminary phase.

In the meantime, I tried substituting the beginner's move

> 3   Qd1-h5

in the game above. This looks much stronger than in ordinary chess, because the imminent disappearance of Black's f-pawn restricts him to a king move or ... g6. Let's try the latter:

> 3   ...   g7-g6 .

White naturally continues

> 4   Qh5xe5+ ,

but after

> 4   ...   Qd8-e7
> 5   Qe5xh8

his own g-pawn has gone and

> 5   ...   Qe7xe4+

forks his own rook in return. Try

> 6   Bb5-e2

at least rescuing the bishop; then

> 6   ...   Qe4xh1

gives (I think)

I think White must now rescue his queen by

    7   Qh8–e5+

or perhaps 7 Qd4. If he defends his knight by 7 Be3, his h-pawn will go,
Black's reply 7 ... Bb4+ will give check and remove his own h-pawn,
and White's queen is dead.

Strictly for fun, of course, but well worth trying.

Chapter 27

Adventure

[The following unpublished example of "literate programming for fun" was originally placed online on 12 September 1998 and subsequently amended based on responses from readers. An electronic source file for this program is downloadable from the Internet site

  http://www-cs-faculty.stanford.edu/~knuth/programs.html

under the name 'ADVENT'.]

1. Introduction. The ur-game for computers — Adventure — was originally written by Will Crowther in 1975 or 1976 and significantly extended by Don Woods in 1977. I have taken Woods's original FOR-TRAN program for Adventure Version 1.0 and recast it in the CWEB idiom so that those pioneering ideas will be accessible to a broader audience.

I remember being fascinated by this game when John McCarthy showed it to me in 1977. I started with no clues about the purpose of play or what I should do; just the computer's comment that I was at the end of a forest road facing a small brick building. Little by little, the game revealed its secrets, just as its designers had cleverly plotted. What a thrill it was when I first got past the green snake! Clearly the game was potentially addictive, so I forced myself to stop playing — reasoning that it was great fun, sure, but that traditional computer science research is great fun too, possibly even more so.

Now here I am, 21 years later, returning to the great Adventure after having indeed had many exciting adventures in Computer Science. I believe people who have played this game will be able to extend their fun by reading its once-secret program. Of course I urge everybody to *play the game first, at least ten times,* before reading on. But you cannot fully appreciate the astonishing brilliance of its design until you have seen all of the surprises that have been built in.

I believe this program is entirely faithful to the behavior of Ad-venture Version 1.0, except that I have slightly edited the computer

235

messages (in most cases so that they use both lowercase and uppercase letters). I have also omitted Woods's elaborate machinery for closing the cave during the hours of prime-time computing; I believe John Mc-Carthy insisted on this, when he saw the productivity of his AI Lab falling off dramatically — although it is rumored that he had a special version of the program that allowed him to play whenever he wanted. And I have not adopted the encryption scheme by which Woods made it difficult for users to find any important clues in the binary program file or core image; such modifications would best be done by making a special version of CTANGLE. All of the spelunking constraints and inter-active behavior have been retained, although the structure of this CWEB program is naturally quite different from the FORTRAN version that I began with.

Many of the phrases in the following documentation have been lifted directly from comments in the FORTRAN code. Please regard me as merely a translator of the program, not as an author. I thank Don Woods for helping me check the validity of this translation.

By the way, if you don't like **goto** statements, don't read this. (And don't read any other programs that simulate multistate systems.)

2.   To run the program with, say, a UNIX shell, just type 'advent' and follow instructions. (Many UNIX systems come with an almost identical program called 'adventure' already built in; you might want to try it too, for comparison.)

```
#include <stdio.h>      /* basic input/output routines: fgets, printf */
#include <ctype.h>      /* isspace, tolower, and toupper routines */
#include <string.h>      /* strncmp and strcpy to deal with strings */
#include <time.h>      /* current time, used as random number seed */
#include <stdlib.h>      /* exit */
  ⟨ Macros for subroutine prototypes 3 ⟩
  typedef enum {
    false, true
  } boolean;
  ⟨ Type definitions 5 ⟩
  ⟨ Global variables 7 ⟩
  ⟨ Subroutines 6 ⟩
  main( )
  {
    register int j, k;
    register char *p;
    ⟨ Additional local registers 22 ⟩;
```

⟨ Initialize all tables 200 ⟩;
⟨ Simulate an adventure, going to *quit* when finished 75 ⟩;
⟨ Deal with death and resurrection 188 ⟩;
quit: ⟨ Print the score and say adieu 198 ⟩;
  exit(0);
}

3. The subroutines of this program are declared first with a prototype, as in ANSI C, then with an old-style C function definition. The following preprocessor commands make this strategy work correctly with both new-style and old-style compilers.

⟨ Macros for subroutine prototypes 3 ⟩ ≡
#ifdef __STDC__
#define ARGS(*list*)   *list*
#else
#define ARGS(*list*)   ( )
#endif

This code is used in section 2.

__STDC__, Standard C.
exit: **void** ( ), **<stdlib.h>**.
fgets: **char** *( ), **<stdio.h>**.
isspace: **int** ( ), **<ctype.h>**.
printf: **int** ( ), **<stdio.h>**.

strcpy: **char** *( ), **<string.h>**.
strncmp: **int** ( ), **<string.h>**.
time: **time_t** ( ), **<time.h>**.
tolower: **int** ( ), **<ctype.h>**.
toupper: **int** ( ), **<ctype.h>**.

4. The vocabulary. Throughout the remainder of this documentation, "you" are the user and "we" are the game author and the computer. We don't tell you what words to use, except indirectly; but we try to understand enough words of English so that you can play the game without undue frustration. The first part of the program specifies what we know about your language — about 300 words.

5. When you type a word, we first convert uppercase letters to lowercase; then we chop off all but the first five characters, if the word was longer than that, and we look for your (possibly truncated) word in a small hash table. Each hash table entry contains a string of length 5 or less, and two additional bytes for the word's type and meaning. Four types of words are distinguished: *motion_type*, *object_type*, *action_type*, and *message_type*.

⟨ Type definitions 5 ⟩ ≡
  typedef enum {
    no_type, *motion_type*, *object_type*, *action_type*, *message_type*
  } **wordtype**;
  typedef struct {
    char *text*[6];   /* string of length at most 5 */
    char *word_type*;   /* a **wordtype** */
    char *meaning*;
  } **hash_entry**;

See also sections 9, 11, 13, 18, and 19.

This code is used in section 2.

6. Here is the subroutine that puts words into our vocabulary, when the program is getting ready to run.

#define *hash_prime* 1009   /* the size of the hash table */
⟨ Subroutines 6 ⟩ ≡
  void *new_word* **ARGS**((**char** *, **int**));

  void *new_word*(*w*, *m*)
    char *w;   /* a string of length 5 or less */
    int *m*;   /* its meaning */
  {
    register int *h*, *k*;
    register char *p;
    for ($h = 0, p = w$; *p; *p*++) $h = {*}p + h + h$;
    h %= *hash_prime*;
    while (*hash_table*[*h*].*word_type*) {
      h++;
      if ($h \equiv hash\_prime$) $h = 0$;
    }

```
    strcpy (hash_table [h].text, w);
    hash_table [h].word_type = current_type;
    hash_table [h].meaning = m;
}
```

See also sections 8, 64, 65, 66, 71, 72, 154, 160, 194, and 197.

This code is used in section 2.

7.   ⟨ Global variables 7 ⟩ ≡
  hash_entry *hash_table* [*hash_prime*];   /∗ the table of words we know ∗/
  wordtype *current_type*;   /∗ the kind of word we are dealing with ∗/

See also sections 15, 17, 20, 21, 63, 73, 74, 77, 81, 84, 87, 89, 96, 103, 137, 142, 155, 159, 165, 168, 171, 177, 185, 190, 193, 196, and 199.

This code is used in section 2.

8.   While we're at it, let's write the program that will look up a word. It returns the location of the word in the hash table, or −1 if you've given a word like 'tickle' or 'terse' that is unknown.

#define *streq* (*a, b*) (*strncmp* (*a, b*, 5) ≡ 0)
                /∗ strings agree up to five letters ∗/

⟨ Subroutines 6 ⟩ +≡
  int *lookup* ARGS((**char** ∗));

  int *lookup* (*w*)
      char ∗*w*;   /∗ a string that you typed ∗/
  {
    register int *h*;
    register char ∗*p*;
    register char *t*;

    t = *w*[5];
    w[5] = '\0';   /∗ truncate the word ∗/
    for (*h* = 0, *p* = *w*; ∗*p*; *p*++) *h* = ∗*p* + *h* + *h*;
    h %= *hash_prime*;   /∗ compute starting address ∗/
    w[5] = *t*;   /∗ restore original word ∗/
    if (*h* < 0) **return** −1;   /∗ a negative character might screw us up ∗/
    while (*hash_table* [*h*].*word_type*) {
      if (*streq* (*w*, *hash_table* [*h*].*text*)) **return** *h*;
      h++;
      if (*h* ≡ *hash_prime*) *h* = 0;
    }
    return −1;
  }
```

---

ARGS = macro ( ), §3.                          *strncmp*: **int** ( ), <string.h>.
*strcpy*: **char** ∗( ), <string.h>.
```

9.   The **motion** words specify either a direction or a simple action or a place. Motion words take you from one location to another, when the motion is permitted. Here is a list of their possible meanings.

⟨ Type definitions 5 ⟩ +≡

   typedef enum {
     N, S, E, W, NE, SE, NW, SW, U, D, L, R, IN, OUT, FORWARD, BACK,
     OVER, ACROSS, UPSTREAM, DOWNSTREAM,
     ENTER, CRAWL, JUMP, CLIMB, LOOK, CROSS,
     ROAD, WOODS, VALLEY, HOUSE, GULLY, STREAM, DEPRESSION, ENTRANCE, CAVE,
     ROCK, SLAB, BED, PASSAGE, CAVERN, CANYON, AWKWARD, SECRET, BEDQUILT,
       RESERVOIR,
     GIANT, ORIENTAL, SHELL, BARREN, BROKEN, DEBRIS, VIEW, FORK,
     PIT, SLIT, CRACK, DOME, HOLE, WALL, HALL, ROOM, FLOOR,
     STAIRS, STEPS, COBBLES, SURFACE, DARK, LOW, OUTDOORS,
     Y2, XYZZY, PLUGH, PLOVER, OFFICE, NOWHERE
   } **motion**;

10.   And here is how they enter our vocabulary.

If I were writing this program, I would allow the word woods, but Don apparently didn't want to.

⟨ Build the vocabulary 10 ⟩ ≡

  current_type = *motion_type*;
  new_word("north", N); *new_word*("n", N);
  new_word("south", S); *new_word*("s", S);
  new_word("east", E); *new_word*("e", E);
  new_word("west", W); *new_word*("w", W);
  new_word("ne", NE);
  new_word("se", SE);
  new_word("nw", NW);
  new_word("sw", SW);
  new_word("upwar", U); *new_word*("up", U); *new_word*("u", U);
  new_word("above", U); *new_word*("ascen", U);
  new_word("downw", D); *new_word*("down", D); *new_word*("d", D);
  new_word("desce", D);
  new_word("left", L);
  new_word("right", R);
  new_word("inwar", IN); *new_word*("insid", IN); *new_word*("in", IN);
  new_word("out", OUT); *new_word*("outsi", OUT);
  new_word("exit", OUT);
  new_word("leave", OUT);
  new_word("forwa", FORWARD); *new_word*("conti", FORWARD);
  new_word("onwar", FORWARD);
  new_word("back", BACK); *new_word*("retur", BACK);
  new_word("retre", BACK);

new_word("over", OVER);
new_word("acros", ACROSS);
new_word("upstr", UPSTREAM);
new_word("downs", DOWNSTREAM);
new_word("enter", ENTER);
new_word("crawl", CRAWL);
new_word("jump", JUMP);
new_word("climb", CLIMB);
new_word("look", LOOK); *new_word*("exami", LOOK);
new_word("touch", LOOK); *new_word*("descr", LOOK);
new_word("cross", CROSS);
new_word("road", ROAD);
new_word("hill", ROAD);
new_word("fores", WOODS);
new_word("valle", VALLEY);
new_word("build", HOUSE); *new_word*("house", HOUSE);
new_word("gully", GULLY);
new_word("strea", STREAM);
new_word("depre", DEPRESSION);
new_word("entra", ENTRANCE);
new_word("cave", CAVE);
new_word("rock", ROCK);
new_word("slab", SLAB); *new_word*("slabr", SLAB);
new_word("bed", BED);
new_word("passa", PASSAGE); *new_word*("tunne", PASSAGE);
new_word("caver", CAVERN);
new_word("canyo", CANYON);
new_word("awkwa", AWKWARD);
new_word("secre", SECRET);
new_word("bedqu", BEDQUILT);
new_word("reser", RESERVOIR);
new_word("giant", GIANT);
new_word("orien", ORIENTAL);
new_word("shell", SHELL);

---

current_type: **wordtype**, §7.   *new_word*: **void** ( ), §6.
motion_type = 1, §5.

10.   (continued)

new_word("barre", BARREN);
new_word("broke", BROKEN);
new_word("debri", DEBRIS);
new_word("view", VIEW);
new_word("fork", FORK);
new_word("pit", PIT);
new_word("slit", SLIT);
new_word("crack", CRACK);
new_word("dome", DOME);
new_word("hole", HOLE);
new_word("wall", WALL);
new_word("hall", HALL);
new_word("room", ROOM);
new_word("floor", FLOOR);
new_word("stair", STAIRS);
new_word("steps", STEPS);
new_word("cobbl", COBBLES);
new_word("surfa", SURFACE);
new_word("dark", DARK);
new_word("low", LOW);
new_word("outdo", OUTDOORS);
new_word("y2", Y2);
new_word("xyzzy", XYZZY);
new_word("plugh", PLUGH);
new_word("plove", PLOVER);
new_word("main", OFFICE);   *new_word*("offic", OFFICE);
new_word("null", NOWHERE);   *new_word*("nowhe", NOWHERE);

See also sections 12, 14, and 16.

This code is used in section 200.

11.   The **object** words refer to things like a lamp, a bird, batteries, etc.; objects have properties that will be described later. Here is a list of the basic objects. Objects GOLD and higher are the "treasures." Extremely large objects, which appear in more than one location, are listed more than once using '_'.

#**define**   *min_treasure*   GOLD
#**define**   *is_treasure*(*t*)   (*t* ≥ *min_treasure*)
#**define**   *max_obj*   CHAIN

⟨ Type definitions 5 ⟩ +≡
  typedef enum {
    NOTHING, KEYS, LAMP, GRATE, GRATE_, CAGE, ROD, ROD2, TREADS, TREADS_,
    BIRD, DOOR, PILLOW, SNAKE, CRYSTAL, CRYSTAL_, TABLET, CLAM, OYSTER,
    MAG, DWARF, KNIFE, FOOD, BOTTLE, WATER, OIL,
    MIRROR, MIRROR_, PLANT, PLANT2, PLANT2_, STALACTITE, SHADOW, SHADOW_,
    AXE, ART, PIRATE, DRAGON, DRAGON_, BRIDGE, BRIDGE_, TROLL, TROLL_,
       TROLL2, TROLL2_,
    BEAR, MESSAGE, GEYSER, PONY, BATTERIES, MOSS,
    GOLD, DIAMONDS, SILVER, JEWELS, COINS, CHEST, EGGS, TRIDENT, VASE,
    EMERALD, PYRAMID, PEARL, RUG, RUG_, SPICES, CHAIN
  } **object**;

BARREN = 48, §9.
BROKEN = 49, §9.
COBBLES = 64, §9.
CRACK = 55, §9.
DARK = 66, §9.
DEBRIS = 50, §9.
DOME = 56, §9.
FLOOR = 61, §9.
FORK = 52, §9.
HALL = 59, §9.
HOLE = 57, §9.
LOW = 67, §9.
new_word: **void** ( ), §6.
NOWHERE = 74, §9.

OFFICE = 73, §9.
OUTDOORS = 68, §9.
PIT = 53, §9.
PLOVER = 72, §9.
PLUGH = 71, §9.
ROOM = 60, §9.
SLIT = 54, §9.
STAIRS = 62, §9.
STEPS = 63, §9.
SURFACE = 65, §9.
VIEW = 51, §9.
WALL = 58, §9.
XYZZY = 70, §9.
Y2 = 69, §9.

12.   Most of the objects correspond to words in our vocabulary.

⟨ Build the vocabulary 10 ⟩ +≡
  current_type = *object_type*;
  new_word("key", KEYS); *new_word*("keys", KEYS);
  new_word("lamp", LAMP); *new_word*("lante", LAMP);
  new_word("headl", LAMP);
  new_word("grate", GRATE);
  new_word("cage", CAGE);
  new_word("rod", ROD);
  new_word("bird", BIRD);
  new_word("door", DOOR);
  new_word("pillo", PILLOW); *new_word*("velve", PILLOW);
  new_word("snake", SNAKE);
  new_word("fissu", CRYSTAL);
  new_word("table", TABLET);
  new_word("clam", CLAM);
  new_word("oyste", OYSTER);
  new_word("magaz", MAG); *new_word*("issue", MAG);
  new_word("spelu", MAG); *new_word*("\"spel", MAG);
  new_word("dwarf", DWARF); *new_word*("dwarv", DWARF);
  new_word("knife", KNIFE); *new_word*("knive", KNIFE);
  new_word("food", FOOD); *new_word*("ratio", FOOD);
  new_word("bottl", BOTTLE); *new_word*("jar", BOTTLE);
  new_word("water", WATER); *new_word*("h2o", WATER);
  new_word("oil", OIL);
  new_word("mirro", MIRROR);
  new_word("plant", PLANT); *new_word*("beans", PLANT);
  new_word("stala", STALACTITE);
  new_word("shado", SHADOW); *new_word*("figur", SHADOW);
  new_word("axe", AXE);
  new_word("drawi", ART);
  new_word("pirat", PIRATE);
  new_word("drago", DRAGON);
  new_word("chasm", BRIDGE);
  new_word("troll", TROLL);
  new_word("bear", BEAR);
  new_word("messa", MESSAGE);
  new_word("volca", GEYSER); *new_word*("geyse", GEYSER);
  new_word("vendi", PONY); *new_word*("machi", PONY);
  new_word("batte", BATTERIES);
  new_word("moss", MOSS); *new_word*("carpe", MOSS);
  new_word("gold", GOLD); *new_word*("nugge", GOLD);
  new_word("diamo", DIAMONDS);
  new_word("silve", SILVER); *new_word*("bars", SILVER);

new_word("jewel", JEWELS);
new_word("coins", COINS);
new_word("chest", CHEST); new_word("box", CHEST);
new_word("treas", CHEST);
new_word("eggs", EGGS); new_word("egg", EGGS);
new_word("nest", EGGS);
new_word("tride", TRIDENT);
new_word("ming", VASE); new_word("vase", VASE);
new_word("shard", VASE); new_word("potte", VASE);
new_word("emera", EMERALD);
new_word("plati", PYRAMID); new_word("pyram", PYRAMID);
new_word("pearl", PEARL);
new_word("persi", RUG); new_word("rug", RUG);
new_word("spice", SPICES);
new_word("chain", CHAIN);

ART $= 35$, §11.
AXE $= 34$, §11.
BATTERIES $= 49$, §11.
BEAR $= 45$, §11.
BIRD $= 10$, §11.
BOTTLE $= 23$, §11.
BRIDGE $= 39$, §11.
CAGE $= 5$, §11.
CHAIN $= 66$, §11.
CHEST $= 56$, §11.
CLAM $= 17$, §11.
COINS $= 55$, §11.
CRYSTAL $= 14$, §11.
$current\_type$: **wordtype**, §7.
DIAMONDS $= 52$, §11.
DOOR $= 11$, §11.
DRAGON $= 37$, §11.
DWARF $= 20$, §11.
EGGS $= 57$, §11.
EMERALD $= 60$, §11.
FOOD $= 22$, §11.
GEYSER $= 47$, §11.
GOLD $= 51$, §11.
GRATE $= 3$, §11.
JEWELS $= 54$, §11.
KEYS $= 1$, §11.
KNIFE $= 21$, §11.

LAMP $= 2$, §11.
MAG $= 19$, §11.
MESSAGE $= 46$, §11.
MIRROR $= 26$, §11.
MOSS $= 50$, §11.
new_word: **void** ( ), §6.
$object\_type = 2$, §5.
OIL $= 25$, §11.
OYSTER $= 18$, §11.
PEARL $= 62$, §11.
PILLOW $= 12$, §11.
PIRATE $= 36$, §11.
PLANT $= 28$, §11.
PONY $= 48$, §11.
PYRAMID $= 61$, §11.
ROD $= 6$, §11.
RUG $= 63$, §11.
SHADOW $= 32$, §11.
SILVER $= 53$, §11.
SNAKE $= 13$, §11.
SPICES $= 65$, §11.
STALACTITE $= 31$, §11.
TABLET $= 16$, §11.
TRIDENT $= 58$, §11.
TROLL $= 41$, §11.
VASE $= 59$, §11.
WATER $= 24$, §11.

13.   The **action** words tell us to do something that's usually nontrivial.

⟨ Type definitions 5 ⟩ +≡
  typedef enum {
    ABSTAIN, TAKE, DROP, OPEN, CLOSE, ON, OFF, WAVE, CALM, GO, RELAX,
    POUR, EAT, DRINK, RUB, TOSS, WAKE, FEED, FILL, BREAK, BLAST, KILL,
    SAY, READ, FEEFIE, BRIEF, FIND, INVENTORY, SCORE, QUIT
  } **action**;

14.   Many of the action words have several synonyms. If an action does not meet special conditions, we will issue a default message.

#define   *ok*   *default_msg*[RELAX]

⟨ Build the vocabulary 10 ⟩ +≡
  current_type = *action_type*;
  new_word("take", TAKE);   *new_word*("carry", TAKE);
  new_word("keep", TAKE);   *new_word*("catch", TAKE);
  new_word("captu", TAKE);   *new_word*("steal", TAKE);
  new_word("get", TAKE);   *new_word*("tote", TAKE);
  default_msg[TAKE] = "You␣are␣already␣carrying␣it!";
  new_word("drop", DROP);   *new_word*("relea", DROP);
  new_word("free", DROP);   *new_word*("disca", DROP);
  new_word("dump", DROP);
  default_msg[DROP] = "You␣aren't␣carrying␣it!";
  new_word("open", OPEN);   *new_word*("unloc", OPEN);
  default_msg[OPEN] = "I␣don't␣know␣how␣to␣lock␣\
        or␣unlock␣such␣a␣thing.";
  new_word("close", CLOSE);   *new_word*("lock", CLOSE);
  default_msg[CLOSE] = *default_msg*[OPEN];
  new_word("light", ON);   *new_word*("on", ON);
  default_msg[ON] = "You␣have␣no␣source␣of␣light.";
  new_word("extin", OFF);   *new_word*("off", OFF);
  default_msg[OFF] = *default_msg*[ON];
  new_word("wave", WAVE);   *new_word*("shake", WAVE);
  new_word("swing", WAVE);
  default_msg[WAVE] = "Nothing␣happens.";
  new_word("calm", CALM);   *new_word*("placa", CALM);
  new_word("tame", CALM);
  default_msg[CALM] = "I'm␣game.␣␣Would␣you␣care␣to␣explain␣how?";
  new_word("walk", GO);   *new_word*("run", GO);   *new_word*("trave", GO);
  new_word("go", GO);   *new_word*("proce", GO);   *new_word*("explo", GO);
  new_word("goto", GO);   *new_word*("follo", GO);   *new_word*("turn", GO);
  default_msg[GO] = "Where?";
  new_word("nothi", RELAX);
  default_msg[RELAX] = "OK.";
  new_word("pour", POUR);

$default\_msg[\mathtt{POUR}] = default\_msg[\mathtt{DROP}];$
$new\_word(\mathtt{"eat"}, \mathtt{EAT});\ new\_word(\mathtt{"devou"}, \mathtt{EAT});$
$default\_msg[\mathtt{EAT}] = \mathtt{"Don't\ be\ ridiculous!"};$
$new\_word(\mathtt{"drink"}, \mathtt{DRINK});$
$default\_msg[\mathtt{DRINK}] = \mathtt{"You\ have\ taken\ a\ drink\ from\ the\ stream.\ \backslash}$
$\qquad \mathtt{The\ water\ tastes\ strongly\ of\backslash n\backslash}$
$\qquad \mathtt{minerals,\ but\ is\ not\ unpleasant.\ \ It\ is\ extremely\ cold."};$
$new\_word(\mathtt{"rub"}, \mathtt{RUB});$
$default\_msg[\mathtt{RUB}] = \mathtt{"Rubbing\ the\ electric\ lamp\ \backslash}$
$\qquad \mathtt{is\ not\ particularly\ rewarding.\ \ Anyway,\backslash n\backslash}$
$\qquad \mathtt{nothing\ exciting\ happens."};$
$new\_word(\mathtt{"throw"}, \mathtt{TOSS});\ new\_word(\mathtt{"toss"}, \mathtt{TOSS});$
$default\_msg[\mathtt{TOSS}] = default\_msg[\mathtt{DROP}];$
$new\_word(\mathtt{"wake"}, \mathtt{WAKE});\ new\_word(\mathtt{"distu"}, \mathtt{WAKE});$
$default\_msg[\mathtt{WAKE}] = default\_msg[\mathtt{EAT}];$
$new\_word(\mathtt{"feed"}, \mathtt{FEED});$
$default\_msg[\mathtt{FEED}] = \mathtt{"There\ is\ nothing\ here\ to\ eat."};$
$new\_word(\mathtt{"fill"}, \mathtt{FILL});$
$default\_msg[\mathtt{FILL}] = \mathtt{"You\ can't\ fill\ that."};$
$new\_word(\mathtt{"break"}, \mathtt{BREAK});\ new\_word(\mathtt{"smash"}, \mathtt{BREAK});$
$new\_word(\mathtt{"shatt"}, \mathtt{BREAK});$
$default\_msg[\mathtt{BREAK}] = \mathtt{"It\ is\ beyond\ your\ power\ to\ do\ that."};$
$new\_word(\mathtt{"blast"}, \mathtt{BLAST});\ new\_word(\mathtt{"deton"}, \mathtt{BLAST});$
$new\_word(\mathtt{"ignit"}, \mathtt{BLAST});\ new\_word(\mathtt{"blowu"}, \mathtt{BLAST});$
$default\_msg[\mathtt{BLAST}] = \mathtt{"Blasting\ requires\ dynamite."};$
$new\_word(\mathtt{"attac"}, \mathtt{KILL});\ new\_word(\mathtt{"kill"}, \mathtt{KILL});$
$new\_word(\mathtt{"fight"}, \mathtt{KILL});\ new\_word(\mathtt{"hit"}, \mathtt{KILL});$
$new\_word(\mathtt{"strik"}, \mathtt{KILL});\ new\_word(\mathtt{"slay"}, \mathtt{KILL});$
$default\_msg[\mathtt{KILL}] = default\_msg[\mathtt{EAT}];$

$action\_type = 3$, §5.
BLAST, see §99.
BREAK, see §101.
CLOSE, see §93 and §130.
$current\_type$: **wordtype**, §7.
$default\_msg$: **char** *[ ], §15.
DRINK, see §106.
DROP, see §117.
EAT, see §92 and §98.
FEED, see §129.
FILL, see §79 and §110.
GO, see §79.

KILL, see §125.
new_word: **void** ( ), §6.
OFF, see §102.
ON, see §102.
OPEN, see §93 and §130.
POUR, see §107.
RELAX, see §79.
RUB, see §99.
TAKE, see §92 and §112.
TOSS, see §122.
WAKE, see §101.
WAVE, see §99.

14.   (continued)

> *new_word*("say",SAY);   *new_word*("chant",SAY);   *new_word*("sing",SAY);
> *new_word*("utter",SAY);   *new_word*("mumbl",SAY);
> *new_word*("read",READ);   *new_word*("perus",READ);
> *default_msg*[READ] = "I'm␣afraid␣I␣don't␣understand.";
> *new_word*("fee",FEEFIE);   *new_word*("fie",FEEFIE);
> *new_word*("foe",FEEFIE);   *new_word*("foo",FEEFIE);
> *new_word*("fum",FEEFIE);
> *default_msg*[FEEFIE] = "I␣don't␣know␣how.";
> *new_word*("brief",BRIEF);
> *default_msg*[BRIEF] = "On␣what?";
> *new_word*("find",FIND);   *new_word*("where",FIND);
> *default_msg*[FIND] = "I␣can␣only␣tell␣you␣what␣you␣see␣\
>   as␣you␣move␣about␣and␣manipulate\n\
>   things.␣␣I␣cannot␣tell␣you␣where␣remote␣things␣are.";
> *new_word*("inven",INVENTORY);
> *default_msg*[INVENTORY] = *default_msg*[FIND];
> *new_word*("score",SCORE);
> *default_msg*[SCORE] = "Eh?";
> *new_word*("quit",QUIT);
> *default_msg*[QUIT] = *default_msg*[SCORE];

15.   ⟨ Global variables 7 ⟩ +≡
> **char** **default_msg*[30];   /* messages for untoward actions, if nonzero */

16.   Finally, our vocabulary is rounded out by words like `help`, which trigger the printing of fixed messages.

#define   *new_mess*(x)   *message*[k++] = x
#define   *mess_wd*(w)   *new_word*(w, k)
⟨ Build the vocabulary 10 ⟩ +≡
> *current_type* = *message_type*;
> k = 0;
> *mess_wd*("abra");   *mess_wd*("abrac");
> *mess_wd*("opens");   *mess_wd*("sesam");   *mess_wd*("shaza");
> *mess_wd*("hocus");   *mess_wd*("pocus");
> *new_mess*("Good␣try,␣but␣that␣is␣an␣old␣worn-out␣magic␣word.");
> *mess_wd*("help");   *mess_wd*("?");
> *new_mess*("I␣know␣of␣places,␣actions,␣and␣things.␣␣\
>   Most␣of␣my␣vocabulary\n\
>   describes␣places␣and␣is␣used␣to␣move␣you␣there.␣␣\
>   To␣move,␣try␣words\n\
>   like␣forest,␣building,␣downstream,␣enter,␣east,␣west,␣\
>   north,␣south,\n\
>   up,␣or␣down.␣␣I␣know␣about␣a␣few␣special␣objects,␣\
>   like␣a␣black␣rod\n\

hidden␣in␣the␣cave.␣␣These␣objects␣can␣be␣manipulated␣\
␣␣␣␣using␣some␣of\n\
the␣action␣words␣that␣I␣know.␣␣Usually␣you␣will␣\
␣␣␣␣need␣to␣give␣both␣the\n\
object␣and␣action␣words␣(in␣either␣order),␣\
␣␣␣␣but␣sometimes␣I␣can␣infer\n\
the␣object␣from␣the␣verb␣alone.␣␣\
␣␣␣␣Some␣objects␣also␣imply␣verbs;␣in\n\
particular,␣\"inventory\"␣implies␣\"take␣inventory\",␣\
␣␣␣␣which␣causes␣me␣to\n\
give␣you␣a␣list␣of␣what␣you're␣carrying.␣␣\
␣␣␣␣The␣objects␣have␣side\n\
effects;␣for␣instance,␣the␣rod␣scares␣the␣bird.␣␣\
␣␣␣␣Usually␣people␣having\n\
trouble␣moving␣just␣need␣to␣try␣a␣few␣more␣words.␣␣\
␣␣␣␣Usually␣people\n\
trying␣unsuccessfully␣to␣manipulate␣an␣object␣\
␣␣␣␣are␣attempting␣something\n\
beyond␣their␣(or␣my!)␣capabilities␣and␣should␣\
␣␣␣␣try␣a␣completely\n\
different␣tack.␣␣To␣speed␣the␣game␣you␣can␣sometimes␣\
␣␣␣␣move␣long\n\
distances␣with␣a␣single␣word.␣␣For␣example,␣\
␣␣␣␣\"building\"␣usually␣gets\n\
you␣to␣the␣building␣from␣anywhere␣above␣ground␣\
␣␣␣␣except␣when␣lost␣in␣the\n\
forest.␣␣Also,␣note␣that␣cave␣passages␣turn␣a␣lot,␣\
␣␣␣␣and␣that␣leaving␣a\n\
room␣to␣the␣north␣does␣not␣guarantee␣entering␣\
␣␣␣␣the␣next␣from␣the␣south.\n\
Good␣luck!");

BRIEF, see §95.
current_type: **wordtype**, §7.
FEEFIE, see §136.
FIND, see §100.
INVENTORY, see §94 and §100.
k: **register int**, §2.
message: **char** *[], §17.

message_type = 4, §5.
new_word: **void** ( ), §6.
QUIT, see §95.
READ, see §93 and §135.
SAY, see §97.
SCORE, see §95.

16.   (continued)

```
mess_wd("tree");  mess_wd("trees");
new_mess("The␣trees␣of␣the␣forest␣are␣large␣\
        hardwood␣oak␣and␣maple,␣with␣an\n\
occasional␣grove␣of␣pine␣or␣spruce.␣␣\
        There␣is␣quite␣a␣bit␣of␣under-\n\
growth,␣largely␣birch␣and␣ash␣saplings␣\
        plus␣nondescript␣bushes␣of\n\
various␣sorts.␣␣This␣time␣of␣year␣\
        visibility␣is␣quite␣restricted␣by\n\
all␣the␣leaves,␣but␣travel␣is␣quite␣easy␣\
        if␣you␣detour␣around␣the\n\
spruce␣and␣berry␣bushes.");
mess_wd("dig");  mess_wd("excav");
new_mess("Digging␣without␣a␣shovel␣is␣quite␣impractical.␣␣\
        Even␣with␣a␣shovel\n\
progress␣is␣unlikely.");
mess_wd("lost");
new_mess("I'm␣as␣confused␣as␣you␣are.");
new_mess("There␣is␣a␣loud␣explosion␣and␣\
        you␣are␣suddenly␣splashed␣across␣the\n\
walls␣of␣the␣room.");
new_mess("There␣is␣a␣loud␣explosion␣and␣\
        a␣twenty-foot␣hole␣appears␣in␣the␣far\n\
wall,␣burying␣the␣snakes␣in␣the␣rubble.␣␣\
        A␣river␣of␣molten␣lava␣pours\n\
in␣through␣the␣hole,␣\
        destroying␣everything␣in␣its␣path,␣including␣you!");
mess_wd("mist");
new_mess("Mist␣is␣a␣white␣vapor,␣usually␣water,␣\
        seen␣from␣time␣to␣time␣in\n\
caverns.␣␣It␣can␣be␣found␣anywhere␣\
        but␣is␣frequently␣a␣sign␣of␣a␣deep\n\
pit␣leading␣down␣to␣water.");
mess_wd("fuck");  new_mess("Watch␣it!");
new_mess("There␣is␣a␣loud␣explosion,␣and␣\
        a␣twenty-foot␣hole␣appears␣in␣the␣far\n\
wall,␣burying␣the␣dwarves␣in␣the␣rubble.␣␣\
        You␣march␣through␣the␣hole\n\
and␣find␣yourself␣in␣the␣main␣office,␣\
        where␣a␣cheering␣band␣of\n\
friendly␣elves␣carry␣the␣conquering␣adventurer␣\
        off␣into␣the␣sunset.");
mess_wd("stop");
```

```
new_mess("I␣don't␣know␣the␣word␣\"stop\".␣␣\
        Use␣\"quit\"␣if␣you␣want␣to␣give␣up.");
mess_wd("info");  mess_wd("infor");
new_mess("If␣you␣want␣to␣end␣your␣adventure␣early,␣\
        say␣\"quit\".␣␣To␣get␣full\n\
credit␣for␣a␣treasure,␣you␣must␣have␣\
        left␣it␣safely␣in␣the␣building,\n\
though␣you␣get␣partial␣credit␣just␣for␣\
        locating␣it.␣␣You␣lose␣points\n\
for␣getting␣killed,␣or␣for␣quitting,␣\
        though␣the␣former␣costs␣you␣more.\n\
There␣are␣also␣points␣based␣on␣how␣much␣\
        (if␣any)␣of␣the␣cave␣you've\n\
managed␣to␣explore;␣in␣particular,␣\
        there␣is␣a␣large␣bonus␣just␣for\n\
getting␣in␣(to␣distinguish␣the␣beginners␣\
        from␣the␣rest␣of␣the␣pack),\n\
and␣there␣are␣other␣ways␣to␣determine␣\
        whether␣you've␣been␣through␣some\n\
of␣the␣more␣harrowing␣sections.␣␣\
        If␣you␣think␣you've␣found␣all␣the\n\
treasures,␣just␣keep␣exploring␣for␣a␣while.␣␣\
        If␣nothing␣interesting\n\
happens,␣you␣haven't␣found␣them␣all␣yet.␣␣\
        If␣something␣interesting\n\
DOES␣happen,␣it␣means␣you're␣getting␣a␣bonus␣\
        and␣have␣an␣opportunity\n\
to␣garner␣many␣more␣points␣in␣the␣master's␣section.\n\
I␣may␣occasionally␣offer␣hints␣if␣you␣seem␣\
        to␣be␣having␣trouble.\n\
If␣I␣do,␣I'll␣warn␣you␣in␣advance␣how␣much␣\
        it␣will␣affect␣your␣score\n\
to␣accept␣the␣hints.␣␣Finally,␣to␣save␣paper,␣\
        you␣may␣specify␣\"brief\",\n\
which␣tells␣me␣never␣to␣repeat␣the␣full␣\
        description␣of␣a␣place\n\
unless␣you␣explicitly␣ask␣me␣to.");
mess_wd("swim");
new_mess("I␣don't␣know␣how.");
```

17. ⟨ Global variables 7 ⟩ +≡
  char *message*[13];   /* messages tied to certain vocabulary words */

---

mess_wd = macro ( ), §16.   *new_mess* = macro ( ), §16.

18.   Cave data.   You might be in any of more than 100 places as
you wander about in Colossal Cave. Let's enumerate them now, so that
we can build the data structures that define the travel restrictions.

A special negative value called *inhand* is the location code for objects
that you are carrying. But you yourself are always situated in a place
that has a nonnegative location code.

Nonnegative places ≤ *outside* are outside the cave, while places ≥
inside are inside. The upper part of the cave, places < *emist*, is the
easiest part to explore. (We will see later that dwarves do not venture
this close to the surface; they stay ≥ *emist*.)

Places between *inside* and *dead2*, inclusive, form the main cave; the
next places, up to and including *barr*, form the hidden cave on the other
side of the troll bridge; then *neend* and *swend* are a private cave.

The remaining places, ≥ *crack*, are dummy locations, not really part
of the maze. As soon as you arrive at a dummy location, the program
immediately sends you somewhere else. In fact, the last three dummy
locations aren't really even locations; they invoke special code. This
device is a convenient way to provide a variety of features without
making the program logic any more cluttered than it already is.

```
#define   min_in_cave   inside
#define   min_lower_loc   emist
#define   min_forced_loc   crack
#define   max_loc   didit
#define   max_spec   troll
```

⟨ Type definitions 5 ⟩ +≡
  typedef enum {
      inhand = −1, *limbo*,
      road, *hill*, *house*, *valley*, *forest*, *woods*, *slit*, *outside*,
      inside, *cobbles*, *debris*, *awk*, *bird*, *spit*,
      emist, *nugget*, *efiss*, *wfiss*, *wmist*,
      like1, *like2*, *like3*, *like4*, *like5*, *like6*, *like7*, *like8*, *like9*, *like10*, *like11*,
          like12, *like13*, *like14*,
      brink, *elong*, *wlong*,
      diff0, *diff1*, *diff2*, *diff3*, *diff4*, *diff5*, *diff6*, *diff7*, *diff8*, *diff9*, *diff10*,
      pony, *cross*, *hmk*, *west*, *south*, *ns*, *y2*, *jumble*, *windoe*,
      dirty, *clean*, *wet*, *dusty*, *complex*,
      shell, *arch*, *ragged*, *sac*, *ante*, *witt*,
      bedquilt, *cheese*, *soft*,
      e2pit, *w2pit*, *epit*, *wpit*,
      narrow, *giant*, *block*, *immense*, *falls*, *steep*,
      abovep, *sjunc*, *tite*, *low*, *crawl*, *window*,
      oriental, *misty*, *alcove*, *proom*, *droom*,
```
```

slab, *abover*, *mirror*, *res*,
scan1, *scan2*, *scan3*, *secret*,
wide, *tight*, *tall*, *boulders*,
scorr, *swside*,
dead0, *dead1*, *dead2*, *dead3*, *dead4*, *dead5*, *dead6*, *dead7*, *dead8*, *dead9*,
  dead10, *dead11*,
neside, *corr*, *fork*, *warm*, *view*, *chamber*, *lime*, *fbarr*, *barr*,
neend, *swend*,
crack, *neck*, *lose*, *cant*, *climb*, *check*, *snaked*, *thru*, *duck*, *sewer*, *upnout*,
  didit,
ppass, *pdrop*, *troll*
} **location**;

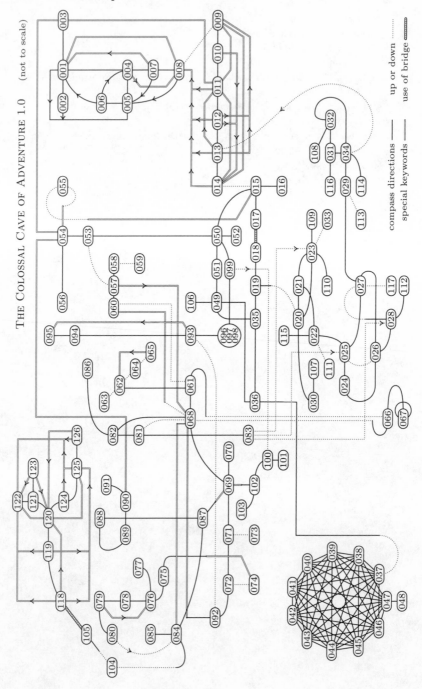

THE COLOSSAL CAVE OF ADVENTURE 1.0 (not to scale)

compass directions ——— up or down ········

special keywords ——— use of bridge ═══

001 = road, §23
002 = hill, §24
003 = house, §25
004 = valley, §26
005 = forest, §27
006 = woods, §27
007 = slit, §28
008 = outside, §29
009 = inside, §30
010 = cobbles, §31
011 = debris, §31
012 = awk, §31
013 = bird, §31
014 = spit, §31
015 = emist, §32
016 = nugget, §33
017 = efiss, §34
018 = wfiss, §34
019 = wmist, §35
020 = like1, §36
021 = like2, §36

022 = like3, §36
023 = like4, §36
024 = like5, §36
025 = like6, §36
026 = like7, §36
027 = like8, §36
028 = like9, §36
029 = like10, §36
030 = like11, §36
031 = like12, §36
032 = like13, §36
033 = like14, §36
034 = brink, §37
035 = elong, §38
036 = wlong, §38
037 = diff0, §39
038 = diff1, §39
039 = diff2, §39
040 = diff3, §39
041 = diff4, §39
042 = diff5, §39

043 = diff6, §39
044 = diff7, §39
045 = diff8, §39
046 = diff9, §39
047 = diff10, §39
048 = pony, §39
049 = cross, §40
050 = hmk, §40
051 = west, §40
052 = south, §40
053 = ns, §41
054 = y2, §41
055 = jumble, §41
056 = windoe, §41
057 = dirty, §42
058 = clean, §42
059 = wet, §42
060 = dusty, §42
061 = complex, §42
062 = shell, §43
063 = arch, §43

064 = ragged, §43
065 = sac, §43
066 = ante, §44
067 = witt, §44
068 = bedquilt, §45
069 = cheese, §45
070 = soft, §45
071 = e2pit, §46
072 = w2pit, §46
073 = epit, §46
074 = wpit, §46
075 = narrow, §47
076 = giant, §47
077 = block, §47
078 = immense, §47
079 = falls, §47
080 = steep, §47
081 = abovep, §48
082 = sjunc, §48
083 = tite, §48
084 = low, §48

085 = crawl, §48
086 = window, §49
087 = oriental, §50
088 = misty, §50
089 = alcove, §51
090 = proom, §51
091 = droom, §51
092 = slab, §52
093 = abover, §52
094 = mirror, §52
095 = res, §52
096 = scan1, §53
097 = scan2, §53
098 = scan3, §53
099 = secret, §53
100 = wide, §54
101 = tight, §54
102 = tall, §54
103 = boulders, §54
104 = scorr, §55
105 = swside, §55

106 = dead0, §56
107 = dead1, §56
108 = dead2, §56
109 = dead3, §56
110 = dead4, §56
111 = dead5, §56
112 = dead6, §56
113 = dead7, §56
114 = dead8, §56
115 = dead9, §56
116 = dead10, §56
117 = dead11, §56
118 = neside, §57
119 = corr, §57
120 = fork, §57
121 = warm, §57
122 = view, §57
123 = chamber, §57
124 = lime, §57
125 = fbarr, §57
126 = barr, §57

19. Speaking of program logic, the complex cave dynamics are essentially kept in a table. The table tells us what to do when you ask for a particular motion in a particular location. Each entry of the table is called an instruction; and each instruction has three parts: a motion, a condition, and a destination.

The motion part of an instruction is one of the motion verbs enumerated earlier.

The condition part c is a small integer, interpreted as follows:

- if $c = 0$, the condition is always true;
- if $0 < c < 100$, the condition is true with probability $c/100$;
- if $c = 100$, the condition is always true, except for dwarves;
- if $100 < c <= 200$, you must have object $c \bmod 100$;
- if $200 < c <= 300$, object $c \bmod 100$ must be in the current place;
- if $300 < c <= 400$, $prop[c \bmod 100]$ must not be 0;
- if $400 < c <= 500$, $prop[c \bmod 100]$ must not be 1;
- if $500 < c <= 600$, $prop[c \bmod 100]$ must not be 2; etc.

(We will discuss properties of objects and the *prop* array later.)

The destination d is either a location or a number greater than *max_loc*. In the latter case, if $d \le$ *max_spec* we perform a special routine; otherwise we print *remarks*$[d -$ *max_spec*$]$ and stay in the current place.

If the motion matches what you said but the condition is not satisfied, we move on to the next instruction that has a different destination and/or condition from this one. The next instruction might itself be conditional in the same way; but the motion is no longer checked after it has first been matched. (Numerous examples appear below; complete details of the table-driven logic can be found in section 146.)

⟨ Type definitions 5 ⟩ +≡

```
typedef struct {
    motion mot;      /* a motion you might have requested */
    int cond;        /* if you did, this condition must also hold */
    location dest;   /* and if so, this is where you'll go next */
} instruction;
```

20.   Suppose you're at location l. Then $start[l]$ is the first relevant instruction, and $start[l+1]-1$ is the last. Also $long\_desc[l]$ is a string that fully describes l; $short\_desc[l]$ is an optional abbreviated description; and $visits[l]$ tells how many times you have been here. Special properties of this location, such as whether a lantern is necessary or a hint might be advisable, are encoded in the bits of $flags[l]$.

```
#define  lighted    1       /* bit for a location that isn't dark */
#define  oil     2       /* bit for presence of oil */
#define  liquid   4       /* bit for presence of a liquid (oil or water) */
#define  cave_hint  8       /* bit for hint about trying to get in the cave */
#define  bird_hint  16      /* bit for hint about catching the bird */
#define  snake_hint  32      /* bit for hint about dealing with the snake */
#define  twist_hint  64      /* bit for hint about being lost in a maze */
#define  dark_hint  128      /* bit for hint about the dark room */
#define  witt_hint  256      /* bit for hint about Witt's End */

#define  travel_size  740      /* at most this many instructions */
#define  rem_size  15       /* at most this many remarks */
```

⟨ Global variables 7 ⟩ +≡
    instruction $travels[travel\_size]$;   /* the table of instructions */
    instruction $*start[max\_loc + 2]$;
        /* references to starting instruction */
    char $*long\_desc[max\_loc + 1]$;
        /* long-winded descriptions of locations */
    char $*short\_desc[max\_loc + 1]$;   /* short-winded descriptions, or 0 */
    int $flags[max\_loc + 1]$;   /* bitmaps for special properties */
    char $*remarks[rem\_size]$;   /* comments made when staying put */
    int rem_count;   /* we've made this many comments */
    int $visits[max\_loc + 1]$;   /* how often have you been here? */

---

location = **enum**, §18.
$max\_loc = 140$, §18.
$max\_spec = 143$, §18.

motion = **enum**, §9.
$newloc$: **location**, §74.
$prop$: **int** [], §63.

21.   Cave connections.   Now we are ready to build the fundamental table of location and transition data, by filling in the arrays just declared. We will fill them in strict order of their **location** codes.

It is convenient to define several macros and constants.

#define *make_loc*(x, l, s, f)
  { *long_desc*$[x] = l$; *short_desc*$[x] = s$; *flags*$[x] = f$; *start*$[x] = q$; }
#define *make_inst*(m, c, d)
  { $q\text{-}mot = m$; $q\text{-}cond = c$; $q\text{-}dest = d$; q++; }
#define *ditto*(m)
  { $q\text{-}mot = m$; $q\text{-}cond = (q - 1)\text{-}cond$; $q\text{-}dest = (q - 1)\text{-}dest$;
    q++; }
#define *holds*(o) $(100 + (o))$
  /* do instruction only if carrying object o */
#define *sees*(o) $(200 + (o))$
  /* do instruction only if object o is present */
#define *not*(o, k) $(300 + (o) + 100 * (k))$
  /* do instruction only if $prop[o] \neq k$ */
#define *remark*(m) *remarks*$[++rem\_count] = m$
#define *sayit* $(max\_spec + rem\_count)$

⟨ Global variables 7 ⟩ +≡
  char *all_alike*[ ] =
      "You␣are␣in␣a␣maze␣of␣twisty␣little␣passages,␣all␣alike.";
  char *dead_end*[ ] = "Dead␣end.";
  int *slit_rmk*, *grate_rmk*, *bridge_rmk*, *loop_rmk*;
    /* messages used more than once */

22.   ⟨ Additional local registers 22 ⟩ ≡
  register instruction *q, *qq;

See also sections 68 and 144.

This code is used in section 2.

23.   The *road* is where you start; its *long_desc* is now famous, having been quoted by Steven Levy in his book *Hackers*.

The instructions here say that if you want to go west, or up, or on the road, we take you to *hill*; if you want to go east, or in, or to the house, or if you say 'enter', we take you to *house*; etc. Of course you won't know about all the motions available at this point until you have played the game for awhile.

⟨ Build the travel table 23 ⟩ ≡
  $q = travels$;
  make_loc$(road$,
  "You␣are␣standing␣at␣the␣end␣of␣a␣road␣\
        before␣a␣small␣brick␣building.\n\
      Around␣you␣is␣a␣forest.␣␣\

    A␣small␣stream␣flows␣out␣of␣the␣building␣and\n\
      down␣a␣gully.",
  "You're␣at␣end␣of␣road␣again.", *lighted* + *liquid*);
  make_inst(W, 0, *hill*); *ditto*(U); *ditto*(ROAD);
  make_inst(E, 0, *house*); *ditto*(IN); *ditto*(HOUSE); *ditto*(ENTER);
  make_inst(S, 0, *valley*); *ditto*(D); *ditto*(GULLY); *ditto*(STREAM);
  ditto(DOWNSTREAM);
  make_inst(N, 0, *forest*); *ditto*(WOODS);
  make_inst(DEPRESSION, 0, *outside*);

See also sections 24, 25, 26, 27, 28, 29, 30, 31, 32, 33, 34, 35, 36, 37, 38, 39, 40, 41, 42, 43, 44, 45, 46, 47, 48, 49, 50, 51, 52, 53, 54, 55, 56, 57, 58, 59, 60, 61, and 62.

This code is used in section 200.

24.   There's nothing up the hill, but a good explorer has to try anyway.

⟨ Build the travel table 23 ⟩ +≡
  make_loc(*hill*,
  "You␣have␣walked␣up␣a␣hill,␣still␣in␣the␣forest.␣␣\
      The␣road␣slopes␣back\n\
    down␣the␣other␣side␣of␣the␣hill.␣␣\
    There␣is␣a␣building␣in␣the␣distance.",
  "You're␣at␣hill␣in␣road.", *lighted*);
  make_inst(ROAD, 0, *road*); *ditto*(HOUSE); *ditto*(FORWARD); *ditto*(E); *ditto*(D);
  make_inst(WOODS, 0, *forest*); *ditto*(N); *ditto*(S);

---

cond: **int**, §19.	*long_desc*: **char** *[], §20.
D = 9, §9.	*max_spec* = 143, §18.
DEPRESSION = 32, §9.	*mot*: **motion**, §19.
dest: **location**, §19.	N = 0, §9.
DOWNSTREAM = 19, §9.	*outside* = 8, §18, §29.
E = 2, §9.	*prop*: **int** [], §63.
ENTER = 20, §9.	*rem_count*: **int**, §20.
flags: **int** [], §20.	*remarks*: **char** *[], §20.
forest = 5, §18, §27.	ROAD = 26, §9.
FORWARD = 14, §9.	*road* = 1, §18, §23.
GULLY = 30, §9.	S = 1, §9.
hill = 2, §18, §24.	*short_desc*: **char** *[], §20.
HOUSE = 29, §9.	*start*: **instruction** *[], §20.
house = 3, §18, §25.	STREAM = 31, §9.
IN = 12, §9.	*travels*: **instruction** [], §20.
instruction = **struct**, §19.	U = 8, §9.
lighted = 1, §20.	*valley* = 4, §18, §26.
liquid = 4, §20.	W = 3, §9.
location = **enum**, §18.	WOODS = 27, §9.

25.   The house initially contains several objects: keys, food, a bottle, and a lantern. We'll put them in there later.

Two magic words are understood in this house, to teleport spelunkers who have been there and done that. (Crowther is said to have pronounced the first one "zizzy"; the pronunciation of the other one is unknown.)

⟨ Build the travel table 23 ⟩ +≡

> *make_loc*(*house*,
>   "You␣are␣inside␣a␣building,␣a␣well␣house␣for␣a␣large␣spring.",
>   "You're␣inside␣building.", *lighted* + *liquid*);
> *make_inst*(ENTER, 0, *road*); *ditto*(OUT); *ditto*(OUTDOORS); *ditto*(W);
> *make_inst*(XYZZY, 0, *debris*);
> *make_inst*(PLUGH, 0, *y2*);
> *make_inst*(DOWNSTREAM, 0, *sewer*); *ditto*(STREAM);

26.   A foolish consistency is the hobgoblin of little minds. (Emerson)

⟨ Build the travel table 23 ⟩ +≡

> *make_loc*(*valley*,
>   "You␣are␣in␣a␣valley␣in␣the␣forest␣\
>   beside␣a␣stream␣tumbling␣along␣a\n\
>   rocky␣bed.",
>   "You're␣in␣valley.", *lighted* + *liquid*);
> *make_inst*(UPSTREAM, 0, *road*); *ditto*(HOUSE); *ditto*(N);
> *make_inst*(WOODS, 0, *forest*); *ditto*(E); *ditto*(W); *ditto*(U);
> *make_inst*(DOWNSTREAM, 0, *slit*); *ditto*(S); *ditto*(D);
> *make_inst*(DEPRESSION, 0, *outside*);

27.   The instructions here keep you in the *forest* with probability 50%, otherwise they take you to the *woods*. This gives the illusion that we maintain more state information about you than we really do.

⟨ Build the travel table 23 ⟩ +≡

> *make_loc*(*forest*,
>   "You␣are␣in␣open␣forest,␣with␣a␣deep␣valley␣to␣one␣side.",
>   "You're␣in␣forest.", *lighted*);
> *make_inst*(VALLEY, 0, *valley*); *ditto*(E); *ditto*(D);
> *make_inst*(WOODS, 50, *forest*); *ditto*(FORWARD); *ditto*(N);
> *make_inst*(WOODS, 0, *woods*);
> *make_inst*(W, 0, *forest*); *ditto*(S);
>
> *make_loc*(*woods*,
>   "You␣are␣in␣open␣forest␣near␣both␣a␣valley␣and␣a␣road.",
>   *short_desc*[*forest*], *lighted*);
> *make_inst*(ROAD, 0, *road*); *ditto*(N);
> *make_inst*(VALLEY, 0, *valley*); *ditto*(E); *ditto*(W); *ditto*(D);
> *make_inst*(WOODS, 0, *forest*); *ditto*(S);

28. You're getting closer. (But the program has forgotten that
`DEPRESSION` leads *outside*; it knew this when you were at the *road* or
the *valley*.)

⟨ Build the travel table 23 ⟩ +≡

  make_loc(*slit*,

    "At␣your␣feet␣all␣the␣water␣of␣the␣stream␣\
          splashes␣into␣a␣2-inch␣slit\n\
      in␣the␣rock.␣␣Downstream␣the␣streambed␣is␣bare␣rock.",
    "You're␣at␣slit␣in␣streambed.", *lighted* + *liquid*);

  make_inst(`HOUSE`, 0, *road*);

  make_inst(`UPSTREAM`, 0, *valley*); *ditto*(`N`);

  make_inst(`WOODS`, 0, *forest*); *ditto*(`E`); *ditto*(`W`);

  make_inst(`DOWNSTREAM`, 0, *outside*); *ditto*(`ROCK`); *ditto*(`BED`); *ditto*(`S`);

  remark("You␣don't␣fit␣through␣a␣two-inch␣slit!");

  make_inst(`SLIT`, 0, *sayit*); *ditto*(`STREAM`); *ditto*(`D`);

  slit_rmk = *sayit*;

BED = 37, §9.
D = 9, §9.
debris = 11, §18, §31.
DEPRESSION = 32, §9.
ditto = macro ( ), §21.
DOWNSTREAM = 19, §9.
E = 2, §9.
ENTER = 20, §9.
forest = 5, §18, §27.
FORWARD = 14, §9.
house = 3, §18.
HOUSE = 29, §9.
lighted = 1, §20.
liquid = 4, §20.
make_inst = macro ( ), §21.
make_loc = macro ( ), §21.
N = 0, §9.
OUT = 13, §9.
OUTDOORS = 68, §9.
outside = 8, §18, §29.
PLUGH = 71, §9.

remark = macro ( ), §21.
ROAD = 26, §9.
road = 1, §18, §23.
ROCK = 35, §9.
S = 1, §9.
sayit = macro, §21.
sewer = 138, §18, §61.
short_desc: **char** *[ ], §20.
SLIT = 54, §9.
slit = 7, §18, §28.
STREAM = 31, §9.
U = 8, §9.
UPSTREAM = 18, §9.
VALLEY = 28, §9.
valley = 4, §18, §26.
W = 3, §9.
WOODS = 27, §9.
woods = 6, §18.
XYZZY = 70, §9.
y2 = 54, §18, §41.

29.   We'll see later that the GRATE will change from state 0 to state 1 if you unlock it. So let's hope you have the KEYS.

⟨ Build the travel table 23 ⟩ +≡

  make_loc(*outside*,

  "You␣are␣in␣a␣20-foot␣depression␣\

        floored␣with␣bare␣dirt.␣␣Set␣into␣the\n\

    dirt␣is␣a␣strong␣steel␣grate␣\

        mounted␣in␣concrete.␣␣A␣dry␣streambed\n\

    leads␣into␣the␣depression.",

  "You're␣outside␣grate.", *lighted* + *cave_hint*);

  make_inst(WOODS, 0, *forest*); *ditto*(E); *ditto*(W); *ditto*(S);

  make_inst(HOUSE, 0, *road*);

  make_inst(UPSTREAM, 0, *slit*); *ditto*(GULLY); *ditto*(N);

  make_inst(ENTER, *not*(GRATE, 0), *inside*); *ditto*(IN); *ditto*(D);

  remark("You␣can't␣go␣through␣a␣locked␣steel␣grate!");

  grate_rmk = *sayit*;

  make_inst(ENTER, 0, *sayit*);

30.   If you've come this far, you're probably hooked, although your adventure has barely begun.

⟨ Build the travel table 23 ⟩ +≡

  make_loc(*inside*,

  "You␣are␣in␣a␣small␣chamber␣\

        beneath␣a␣3x3␣steel␣grate␣to␣the␣surface.\n\

    A␣low␣crawl␣over␣cobbles␣leads␣inwards␣to␣the␣west.",

  "You're␣below␣the␣grate.", *lighted*);

  make_inst(OUT, *not*(GRATE, 0), *outside*); *ditto*(U);

  make_inst(OUT, 0, *grate_rmk*);

  make_inst(CRAWL, 0, *cobbles*); *ditto*(COBBLES); *ditto*(IN); *ditto*(W);

  make_inst(PIT, 0, *spit*);

  make_inst(DEBRIS, 0, *debris*);

31.   Go West, young man. (If you've got a lamp.)

⟨ Build the travel table 23 ⟩ +≡

```
make_loc(cobbles,
  "You␣are␣crawling␣over␣cobbles␣in␣a␣low␣passage.␣␣\
       There␣is␣a␣dim␣light\n\
    at␣the␣east␣end␣of␣the␣passage.",
  "You're␣in␣cobble␣crawl.", lighted);
make_inst(OUT, 0, inside);  ditto(SURFACE);  ditto(NOWHERE);  ditto(E);
make_inst(IN, 0, debris);  ditto(DARK);  ditto(W);  ditto(DEBRIS);
make_inst(PIT, 0, spit);

make_loc(debris,
  "You␣are␣in␣a␣debris␣room␣filled␣with␣\
       stuff␣washed␣in␣from␣the␣surface.\n\
    A␣low␣wide␣passage␣with␣cobbles␣becomes␣\
       plugged␣with␣mud␣and␣debris\n\
    here,␣but␣an␣awkward␣canyon␣leads␣upward␣and␣west.␣␣\
       A␣note␣on␣the␣wall\n\
    says␣\"MAGIC␣WORD␣XYZZY\".",
  "You're␣in␣debris␣room.", 0);
make_inst(DEPRESSION, not(GRATE, 0), outside);
make_inst(ENTRANCE, 0, inside);
make_inst(CRAWL, 0, cobbles);  ditto(COBBLES);  ditto(PASSAGE);  ditto(LOW);
  ditto(E);
make_inst(CANYON, 0, awk);  ditto(IN);  ditto(U);  ditto(W);
make_inst(XYZZY, 0, house);
make_inst(PIT, 0, spit);

make_loc(awk,
  "You␣are␣in␣an␣awkward␣sloping␣east/west␣canyon.", 0, 0);
make_inst(DEPRESSION, not(GRATE, 0), outside);
make_inst(ENTRANCE, 0, inside);
make_inst(D, 0, debris);  ditto(E);  ditto(DEBRIS);
make_inst(IN, 0, bird);  ditto(U);  ditto(W);
make_inst(PIT, 0, spit);

make_loc(bird,
  "You␣are␣in␣a␣splendid␣chamber␣thirty␣feet␣high.␣␣\
       The␣walls␣are␣frozen\n\
    rivers␣of␣orange␣stone.␣␣\
       An␣awkward␣canyon␣and␣a␣good␣passage␣exit\n\
    from␣east␣and␣west␣sides␣of␣the␣chamber.",
  "You're␣in␣bird␣chamber.", bird_hint);
make_inst(DEPRESSION, not(GRATE, 0), outside);
make_inst(ENTRANCE, 0, inside);
make_inst(DEBRIS, 0, debris);
make_inst(CANYON, 0, awk);  ditto(E);
```

make_inst(PASSAGE, 0, *spit*); *ditto*(PIT); *ditto*(W);

make_loc(*spit*,

"At␣your␣feet␣is␣a␣small␣pit␣breathing␣traces␣of␣\
       white␣mist.␣␣An␣east\n\
    passage␣ends␣here␣except␣for␣a␣small␣crack␣leading␣on.",

"You're␣at␣top␣of␣small␣pit.", 0);

make_inst(DEPRESSION, *not*(GRATE, 0), *outside*);

make_inst(ENTRANCE, 0, *inside*);

make_inst(DEBRIS, 0, *debris*);

make_inst(PASSAGE, 0, *bird*); *ditto*(E);

make_inst(D, *holds*(GOLD), *neck*); *ditto*(PIT); *ditto*(STEPS);

make_inst(D, 0, *emist*);

   /* good thing you weren't loaded down with GOLD */

make_inst(CRACK, 0, *crack*); *ditto*(W);

---

32.   Welcome to the main caverns and a deeper level of adventures.

⟨ Build the travel table 23 ⟩ +≡

```
make_loc(emist,
  "You␣are␣at␣one␣end␣of␣a␣vast␣hall␣\
        stretching␣forward␣out␣of␣sight␣to\n\
    the␣west.␣␣There␣are␣openings␣to␣either␣side.␣␣\
        Nearby,␣a␣wide␣stone\n\
    staircase␣leads␣downward.␣␣\
        The␣hall␣is␣filled␣with␣wisps␣of␣white␣mist\n\
    swaying␣to␣and␣fro␣almost␣as␣if␣alive.␣␣\
        A␣cold␣wind␣blows␣up␣the\n\
    staircase.␣␣There␣is␣a␣passage␣\
        at␣the␣top␣of␣a␣dome␣behind␣you.",
  "You're␣in␣Hall␣of␣Mists.",0);
make_inst(L,0,nugget);  ditto(S);
make_inst(FORWARD,0,efiss);  ditto(HALL);  ditto(W);
make_inst(STAIRS,0,hmk);  ditto(D);  ditto(N);
make_inst(U,holds(GOLD),cant);  ditto(PIT);  ditto(STEPS);
ditto(DOME);  ditto(PASSAGE);  ditto(E);
make_inst(U,0,spit);
make_inst(Y2,0,jumble);
```

33.   To the left or south of the misty threshold, you might spot the first treasure.

⟨ Build the travel table 23 ⟩ +≡

```
make_loc(nugget,
  "This␣is␣a␣low␣room␣with␣a␣crude␣note␣on␣the␣wall.␣␣\
        The␣note␣says,\n\
    \"You␣won't␣get␣it␣up␣the␣steps\".",
  "You're␣in␣nugget␣of␣gold␣room.",0);
make_inst(HALL,0,emist);  ditto(OUT);  ditto(N);
```

34.   Unless you take a circuitous route to the other side of the Hall of Mists, via the Hall of the Mountain King, you should make the CRYSTAL bridge appear (by getting it into state 1).

⟨ Build the travel table 23 ⟩ +≡

```
make_loc(efiss,
  "You␣are␣on␣the␣east␣bank␣of␣a␣fissure␣\
        slicing␣clear␣across␣the␣hall.\n\
    The␣mist␣is␣quite␣thick␣here,␣\
        and␣the␣fissure␣is␣too␣wide␣to␣jump.",
  "You're␣on␣east␣bank␣of␣fissure.",0);
make_inst(HALL,0,emist);  ditto(E);
remark("I␣respectfully␣suggest␣you␣go␣\
        across␣the␣bridge␣instead␣of␣jumping.");
```

bridge_rmk = *sayit*;
make_inst(JUMP, *not*(CRYSTAL, 0), *sayit*);
make_inst(FORWARD, *not*(CRYSTAL, 1), *lose*);
remark("There␣is␣no␣way␣across␣the␣fissure.");
make_inst(OVER, *not*(CRYSTAL, 1), *sayit*); *ditto*(ACROSS); *ditto*(W);
ditto(CROSS);
make_inst(OVER, 0, *wfiss*);

make_loc(*wfiss*,
"You␣are␣on␣the␣west␣side␣of␣the␣fissure␣in␣the␣Hall␣of␣Mists.",
    0, 0);
make_inst(JUMP, *not*(CRYSTAL, 0), *bridge_rmk*);
make_inst(FORWARD, *not*(CRYSTAL, 1), *lose*);
make_inst(OVER, *not*(CRYSTAL, 1), *sayit*); *ditto*(ACROSS); *ditto*(E);
ditto(CROSS);
make_inst(OVER, 0, *efiss*);
make_inst(N, 0, *thru*);
make_inst(W, 0, *wmist*);

ACROSS = 17, §9.
cant = 132, §18, §61.
CROSS = 25, §9.
CRYSTAL = 14, §11.
D = 9, §9.
ditto = macro ( ), §21.
DOME = 56, §9.
E = 2, §9.
efiss = 17, §18, §34.
emist = 15, §18, §32.
FORWARD = 14, §9.
GOLD = 51, §11.
HALL = 59, §9.
hmk = 50, §18, §40.
holds = macro ( ), §21.
jumble = 55, §18, §41.
JUMP = 22, §9.
L = 10, §9.
lose = 131, §18, §60.
make_inst = macro ( ), §21.

make_loc = macro ( ), §21.
N = 0, §9.
not = macro ( ), §21.
nugget = 16, §18, §33.
OUT = 13, §9.
OVER = 16, §9.
PASSAGE = 38, §9.
PIT = 53, §9.
remark = macro ( ), §21.
S = 1, §9.
sayit = macro, §21.
spit = 14, §18, §31.
STAIRS = 62, §9.
STEPS = 63, §9.
thru = 136, §18, §61.
U = 8, §9.
W = 3, §9.
wfiss = 18, §18, §34.
wmist = 19, §18, §35.
Y2 = 69, §9.

35.   What you see here isn't exactly what you get; N takes you east
and S sucks you in to an amazing maze.

⟨ Build the travel table 23 ⟩ +≡

  make_loc(*wmist*,

  "You␣are␣at␣the␣west␣end␣of␣the␣Hall␣of␣Mists.␣␣\
      A␣low␣wide␣crawl\n\
    continues␣west␣and␣another␣goes␣north.␣␣\
      To␣the␣south␣is␣a␣little\n\
    passage␣6␣feet␣off␣the␣floor.",

  "You're␣at␣west␣end␣of␣Hall␣of␣Mists.",0);

  make_inst(S,0,*like1*);   *ditto*(U);   *ditto*(PASSAGE);   *ditto*(CLIMB);

  make_inst(E,0,*wfiss*);

  make_inst(N,0,*duck*);

  make_inst(W,0,*elong*);   *ditto*(CRAWL);

36.   The twisty little passages of this maze are said to be all alike, but
they respond differently to different motions. For example, you can go
north, east, south, or west from *like1*, but you can't go north from *like2*.
In that way you can psych out the whole maze of 14 similar locations.
(And eventually you will want to know every place where treasure might
be hidden.) The only exits are to *wmist* and *brink*.

⟨ Build the travel table 23 ⟩ +≡

  make_loc(*like1*, *all_alike*, 0, *twist_hint*);

  make_inst(U,0,*wmist*);   *make_inst*(N,0,*like1*);   *make_inst*(E,0,*like2*);

  make_inst(S,0,*like4*);   *make_inst*(W,0,*like11*);

  make_loc(*like2*, *all_alike*, 0, *twist_hint*);

  make_inst(W,0,*like1*);   *make_inst*(S,0,*like3*);   *make_inst*(E,0,*like4*);

  make_loc(*like3*, *all_alike*, 0, *twist_hint*);

  make_inst(E,0,*like2*);   *make_inst*(D,0,*dead5*);

  make_inst(S,0,*like6*);   *make_inst*(N,0,*dead9*);

  make_loc(*like4*, *all_alike*, 0, *twist_hint*);

  make_inst(W,0,*like1*);   *make_inst*(N,0,*like2*);   *make_inst*(E,0,*dead3*);

  make_inst(S,0,*dead4*);   *make_inst*(U,0,*like14*);   *ditto*(D);

  make_loc(*like5*, *all_alike*, 0, *twist_hint*);

  make_inst(E,0,*like6*);   *make_inst*(W,0,*like7*);

  make_loc(*like6*, *all_alike*, 0, *twist_hint*);

  make_inst(E,0,*like3*);   *make_inst*(W,0,*like5*);

  make_inst(D,0,*like7*);   *make_inst*(S,0,*like8*);

  make_loc(*like7*, *all_alike*, 0, *twist_hint*);

  make_inst(W,0,*like5*);   *make_inst*(U,0,*like6*);

  make_inst(E,0,*like8*);   *make_inst*(S,0,*like9*);

  make_loc(*like8*, *all_alike*, 0, *twist_hint*);

make_inst(W, 0, *like6*); *make_inst*(E, 0, *like7*); *make_inst*(S, 0, *like8*);
make_inst(U, 0, *like9*); *make_inst*(N, 0, *like10*); *make_inst*(D, 0, *dead11*);

make_loc(*like9*, *all_alike*, 0, *twist_hint*);
make_inst(W, 0, *like7*); *make_inst*(N, 0, *like8*); *make_inst*(S, 0, *dead6*);

make_loc(*like10*, *all_alike*, 0, *twist_hint*);
make_inst(W, 0, *like8*); *make_inst*(N, 0, *like10*);
make_inst(D, 0, *dead7*); *make_inst*(E, 0, *brink*);

make_loc(*like11*, *all_alike*, 0, *twist_hint*);
make_inst(N, 0, *like1*); *make_inst*(W, 0, *like11*); *ditto*(S);
make_inst(E, 0, *dead1*);

make_loc(*like12*, *all_alike*, 0, *twist_hint*);
make_inst(S, 0, *brink*); *make_inst*(E, 0, *like13*); *make_inst*(W, 0, *dead10*);

make_loc(*like13*, *all_alike*, 0, *twist_hint*);
make_inst(N, 0, *brink*); *make_inst*(W, 0, *like12*);
make_inst(NW, 0, *dead2*);   /* NW: a dirty trick! */

make_loc(*like14*, *all_alike*, 0, *twist_hint*);
make_inst(U, 0, *like4*); *ditto*(D);

37. ⟨ Build the travel table 23 ⟩ +≡
make_loc(*brink*,
"You␣are␣on␣the␣brink␣of␣a␣thirty-foot␣pit␣\
        with␣a␣massive␣orange␣column\n\
    down␣one␣wall.␣␣You␣could␣climb␣down␣here␣\
        but␣you␣could␣not␣get␣back\n\
    up.␣␣The␣maze␣continues␣at␣this␣level.",
"You're␣at␣brink␣of␣pit.",0);
make_inst(D,0,*bird*); *ditto*(CLIMB);
make_inst(W,0,*like10*); *make_inst*(S,0,*dead8*);
make_inst(N,0,*like12*); *make_inst*(E,0,*like13*);

38.   Crawling west from *wmist* instead of south, you encounter this.
⟨ Build the travel table 23 ⟩ +≡
make_loc(*elong*,
"You␣are␣at␣the␣east␣end␣of␣a␣very␣long␣hall␣\
        apparently␣without␣side\n\
    chambers.␣␣To␣the␣east␣a␣low␣wide␣crawl␣slants␣up.␣␣\
        To␣the␣north␣a\n\
    round␣two-foot␣hole␣slants␣down.",
"You're␣at␣east␣end␣of␣long␣hall.",0);
make_inst(E,0,*wmist*); *ditto*(U); *ditto*(CRAWL);
make_inst(W,0,*wlong*);
make_inst(N,0,*cross*); *ditto*(D); *ditto*(HOLE);

make_loc(*wlong*,
"You␣are␣at␣the␣west␣end␣of␣a␣very␣long␣\
        featureless␣hall.␣␣The␣hall\n\
    joins␣up␣with␣a␣narrow␣north/south␣passage.",
"You're␣at␣west␣end␣of␣long␣hall.",0);
make_inst(E,0,*elong*);
make_inst(N,0,*cross*);
make_inst(S,100,*diff0*);

39.   Recall that the code '100' on the last instruction above means, "Dwarves not permitted." It keeps them out of the following maze, which is based on an 11×11 latin square. (Each of the eleven locations leads to each of the others under the ten motions N, S, E, W, NE, SE, NW, SW, U, D — except that *diff0* goes down to the entrance location *wlong* instead of to *diff10*, and *diff10* goes south to the dead-end location *pony* instead of to *diff0*. Furthermore, each location is accessible from all ten possible directions.)

Incidentally, if you ever get into a "little twisting maze of passages," you're really lost.

#define $twist(l, n, s, e, w, ne, se, nw, sw, u, d, m)$
　　　　$make\_loc(l, m, 0, 0);$
　　　　$make\_inst(\texttt{N}, 0, n);$ $make\_inst(\texttt{S}, 0, s);$ $make\_inst(\texttt{E}, 0, e);$
　　　　$make\_inst(\texttt{W}, 0, w);$
　　　　$make\_inst(\texttt{NE}, 0, ne);$ $make\_inst(\texttt{SE}, 0, se);$ $make\_inst(\texttt{NW}, 0, nw);$
　　　　$make\_inst(\texttt{SW}, 0, sw);$
　　　　$make\_inst(\texttt{U}, 0, u);$ $make\_inst(\texttt{D}, 0, d);$

⟨ Build the travel table 23 ⟩ +≡
　$twist(\textit{diff0}, \textit{diff9}, \textit{diff1}, \textit{diff7}, \textit{diff8}, \textit{diff3}, \textit{diff4}, \textit{diff6}, \textit{diff2}, \textit{diff5}, wlong,$
　　"You␣are␣in␣a␣maze␣of␣twisty␣little␣passages,␣all␣different.");
　$twist(\textit{diff1}, \textit{diff8}, \textit{diff9}, \textit{diff10}, \textit{diff0}, \textit{diff5}, \textit{diff2}, \textit{diff3}, \textit{diff4}, \textit{diff6}, \textit{diff7},$
　　"You␣are␣in␣a␣maze␣of␣twisting␣little␣passages,␣all␣different.");
　$twist(\textit{diff2}, \textit{diff3}, \textit{diff4}, \textit{diff8}, \textit{diff5}, \textit{diff7}, \textit{diff10}, \textit{diff0}, \textit{diff6}, \textit{diff1}, \textit{diff9},$
　　"You␣are␣in␣a␣little␣maze␣of␣twisty␣passages,␣all␣different.");
　$twist(\textit{diff3}, \textit{diff7}, \textit{diff10}, \textit{diff6}, \textit{diff2}, \textit{diff4}, \textit{diff9}, \textit{diff8}, \textit{diff5}, \textit{diff0}, \textit{diff1},$
　　"You␣are␣in␣a␣twisting␣maze␣of␣little␣passages,␣all␣different.");
　$twist(\textit{diff4}, \textit{diff1}, \textit{diff7}, \textit{diff5}, \textit{diff9}, \textit{diff0}, \textit{diff3}, \textit{diff2}, \textit{diff10}, \textit{diff8}, \textit{diff6},$
　　"You␣are␣in␣a␣twisting␣little␣maze␣of␣passages,␣all␣different.");
　$twist(\textit{diff5}, \textit{diff0}, \textit{diff3}, \textit{diff4}, \textit{diff6}, \textit{diff8}, \textit{diff1}, \textit{diff9}, \textit{diff7}, \textit{diff10}, \textit{diff2},$
　　"You␣are␣in␣a␣twisty␣little␣maze␣of␣passages,␣all␣different.");
　$twist(\textit{diff6}, \textit{diff10}, \textit{diff5}, \textit{diff0}, \textit{diff1}, \textit{diff9}, \textit{diff8}, \textit{diff7}, \textit{diff3}, \textit{diff2}, \textit{diff4},$
　　"You␣are␣in␣a␣twisty␣maze␣of␣little␣passages,␣all␣different.");
　$twist(\textit{diff7}, \textit{diff6}, \textit{diff2}, \textit{diff9}, \textit{diff10}, \textit{diff1}, \textit{diff0}, \textit{diff5}, \textit{diff8}, \textit{diff4}, \textit{diff3},$
　　"You␣are␣in␣a␣little␣twisty␣maze␣of␣passages,␣all␣different.");
　$twist(\textit{diff8}, \textit{diff5}, \textit{diff6}, \textit{diff1}, \textit{diff4}, \textit{diff2}, \textit{diff7}, \textit{diff10}, \textit{diff9}, \textit{diff3}, \textit{diff0},$
　　"You␣are␣in␣a␣maze␣of␣little␣twisting␣passages,␣all␣different.");
　$twist(\textit{diff9}, \textit{diff4}, \textit{diff8}, \textit{diff2}, \textit{diff3}, \textit{diff10}, \textit{diff6}, \textit{diff1}, \textit{diff0}, \textit{diff7}, \textit{diff5},$
　　"You␣are␣in␣a␣maze␣of␣little␣twisty␣passages,␣all␣different.");
　$twist(\textit{diff10}, \textit{diff2}, pony, \textit{diff3}, \textit{diff7}, \textit{diff6}, \textit{diff5}, \textit{diff4}, \textit{diff1}, \textit{diff9}, \textit{diff8},$
　　"You␣are␣in␣a␣little␣maze␣of␣twisting␣passages,␣all␣different.");

　$make\_loc(pony, dead\_end, 0, 0);$
　$make\_inst(\texttt{N}, 0, \textit{diff10});$ $ditto(\texttt{OUT});$

40.   Going north from the long hall, we come to the vicinity of another large room, with royal treasures nearby. (You probably first reached this part of the cavern from the east, via the Hall of Mists.) Unfortunately, a vicious snake is here too; the conditional instructions for getting past the snake are worthy of study.

⟨ Build the travel table 23 ⟩ +≡

  make_loc(*cross*,
    "You␣are␣at␣a␣crossover␣of␣a␣high␣N/S␣passage␣and␣a␣low␣E/W␣one.",
      0, 0);
  make_inst(W, 0, *elong*);
  make_inst(N, 0, *dead0*);
  make_inst(E, 0, *west*);
  make_inst(S, 0, *wlong*);

  make_loc(*hmk*,
  "You␣are␣in␣the␣Hall␣of␣the␣Mountain␣King,␣\
        with␣passages␣off␣in␣all\n\
    directions.",
  "You're␣in␣Hall␣of␣Mt␣King.", *snake_hint*);
  make_inst(STAIRS, 0, *emist*); *ditto*(U); *ditto*(E);
  make_inst(N, *not*(SNAKE, 0), *ns*); *ditto*(L);
  make_inst(S, *not*(SNAKE, 0), *south*); *ditto*(R);
  make_inst(W, *not*(SNAKE, 0), *west*); *ditto*(FORWARD);
  make_inst(N, 0, *snaked*);
  make_inst(SW, 35, *secret*);
  make_inst(SW, *sees*(SNAKE), *snaked*);
  make_inst(SECRET, 0, *secret*);

  make_loc(*west*,
  "You␣are␣in␣the␣west␣side␣chamber␣of␣the␣\
        Hall␣of␣the␣Mountain␣King.\n\
    A␣passage␣continues␣west␣and␣up␣here.",
  "You're␣in␣west␣side␣chamber.", 0);
  make_inst(HALL, 0, *hmk*); *ditto*(OUT); *ditto*(E);
  make_inst(W, 0, *cross*); *ditto*(U);

  make_loc(*south*,
  "You␣are␣in␣the␣south␣side␣chamber.", 0, 0);
  make_inst(HALL, 0, *hmk*); *ditto*(OUT); *ditto*(N);

41. North of the mountain king's domain is a curious shuttle station
called Y2, with magic connections to two other places.

(Crowther led a team in 1974 that explored region "Y" of Colossal
Cave; "Y2" was the second location to be named in this region.)

⟨ Build the travel table 23 ⟩ +≡

```
make_loc(ns,
  "You␣are␣in␣a␣low␣N/S␣passage␣at␣a␣hole␣in␣the␣floor.␣␣\
      The␣hole␣goes\n\
    down␣to␣an␣E/W␣passage.",
  "You're␣in␣N/S␣passage.",0);
make_inst(HALL,0,hmk);  ditto(OUT);  ditto(S);
make_inst(N,0,y2);  ditto(Y2);
make_inst(D,0,dirty);  ditto(HOLE);

make_loc(y2,
  "You␣are␣in␣a␣large␣room,␣with␣a␣passage␣to␣the␣south,␣\
      a␣passage␣to␣the\n\
    west,␣and␣a␣wall␣of␣broken␣rock␣to␣the␣east.␣␣\
      There␣is␣a␣large␣\"Y2\"␣on\n\
    a␣rock␣in␣the␣room's␣center.",
  "You're␣at␣\"Y2\".",0);
make_inst(PLUGH,0,house);
make_inst(S,0,ns);
make_inst(E,0,jumble);  ditto(WALL);  ditto(BROKEN);
make_inst(W,0,windoe);
make_inst(PLOVER,holds(EMERALD),pdrop);
make_inst(PLOVER,0,proom);

make_loc(jumble,
  "You␣are␣in␣a␣jumble␣of␣rock,␣with␣cracks␣everywhere.",0,0);
make_inst(D,0,y2);  ditto(Y2);
make_inst(U,0,emist);

make_loc(windoe,
  "You're␣at␣a␣low␣window␣overlooking␣a␣huge␣pit,␣\
      which␣extends␣up␣out␣of\n\
    sight.␣␣A␣floor␣is␣indistinctly␣visible␣\
      over␣50␣feet␣below.␣␣Traces␣of\n\
    white␣mist␣cover␣the␣floor␣of␣the␣pit,␣\
      becoming␣thicker␣to␣the␣right.\n\
    Marks␣in␣the␣dust␣around␣the␣window␣\
      would␣seem␣to␣indicate␣that\n\
    someone␣has␣been␣here␣recently.␣␣\
      Directly␣across␣the␣pit␣from␣you␣and\n\
    25␣feet␣away␣there␣is␣a␣similar␣window␣\
      looking␣into␣a␣lighted␣room.\n\
```

```
      A␣shadowy␣figure␣can␣be␣seen␣there␣\
          peering␣back␣at␣you.",
  "You're␣at␣window␣on␣pit.",0);
  make_inst(E,0,y2);  ditto(Y2);
  make_inst(JUMP,0,neck);
```

42.   Next let's consider the east/west passage below *ns*.

⟨ Build the travel table 23 ⟩ +≡

  make_loc(*dirty*,

  "You␣are␣in␣a␣dirty␣broken␣passage.␣␣\

        To␣the␣east␣is␣a␣crawl.␣␣To␣the\n\

    west␣is␣a␣large␣passage.␣␣\

        Above␣you␣is␣a␣hole␣to␣another␣passage.",

  "You're␣in␣dirty␣passage.", 0);

  make_inst(E, 0, *clean*); *ditto*(CRAWL);

  make_inst(U, 0, *ns*); *ditto*(HOLE);

  make_inst(W, 0, *dusty*);

  make_inst(BEDQUILT, 0, *bedquilt*);

  make_loc(*clean*,

  "You␣are␣on␣the␣brink␣of␣a␣small␣clean␣climbable␣pit.␣␣\

        A␣crawl␣leads\n\

    west.",

  "You're␣by␣a␣clean␣pit.", 0);

  make_inst(W, 0, *dirty*); *ditto*(CRAWL);

  make_inst(D, 0, *wet*); *ditto*(PIT); *ditto*(CLIMB);

  make_loc(*wet*,

  "You␣are␣in␣the␣bottom␣of␣a␣small␣pit␣\

        with␣a␣little␣stream,␣which\n\

    enters␣and␣exits␣through␣tiny␣slits.",

  "You're␣in␣pit␣by␣stream.", *liquid*);

  make_inst(CLIMB, 0, *clean*); *ditto*(U); *ditto*(OUT);

  make_inst(SLIT, 0, *slit_rmk*); *ditto*(STREAM); *ditto*(D); *ditto*(UPSTREAM);

  ditto(DOWNSTREAM);

  make_loc(*dusty*,

  "You␣are␣in␣a␣large␣room␣full␣of␣dusty␣rocks.␣␣\

        There␣is␣a␣big␣hole␣in\n\

    the␣floor.␣␣There␣are␣cracks␣everywhere,␣\

        and␣a␣passage␣leading␣east.",

  "You're␣in␣dusty␣rock␣room.", 0);

  make_inst(E, 0, *dirty*); *ditto*(PASSAGE);

  make_inst(D, 0, *complex*); *ditto*(HOLE); *ditto*(FLOOR);

  make_inst(BEDQUILT, 0, *bedquilt*);

  make_loc(*complex*,

  "You␣are␣at␣a␣complex␣junction.␣␣\

        A␣low␣hands-and-knees␣passage␣from␣the\n\

    north␣joins␣a␣higher␣crawl␣from␣the␣east␣\

        to␣make␣a␣walking␣passage\n\

    going␣west.␣␣There␣is␣also␣a␣large␣room␣above.␣␣\

        The␣air␣is␣damp␣here.",

```
"You're␣at␣complex␣junction.", 0);
make_inst(U, 0, dusty);  ditto(CLIMB);  ditto(ROOM);
make_inst(W, 0, bedquilt);  ditto(BEDQUILT);
make_inst(N, 0, shell);  ditto(SHELL);
make_inst(E, 0, ante);
```

43.   A more-or-less self-contained cavelet can be found north of the complex passage. Its connections are more vertical than horizontal.

⟨ Build the travel table 23 ⟩ +≡

  make_loc(*shell*,

    "You're␣in␣a␣large␣room␣carved␣out␣of␣\

        sedimentary␣rock.␣␣The␣floor\n\

    and␣walls␣are␣littered␣with␣bits␣of␣shells␣\

        embedded␣in␣the␣stone.\n\

    A␣shallow␣passage␣proceeds␣downward,␣\

        and␣a␣somewhat␣steeper␣one\n\

    leads␣up.␣␣A␣low␣hands-and-knees␣passage␣\

        enters␣from␣the␣south.",

    "You're␣in␣Shell␣Room.", 0);

  make_inst(U, 0, *arch*);   *ditto*(HALL);

  make_inst(D, 0, *ragged*);

  remark("You␣can't␣fit␣this␣five-foot␣clam␣\

        through␣that␣little␣passage!");

  make_inst(S, *holds*(CLAM), *sayit*);

  remark("You␣can't␣fit␣this␣five-foot␣oyster␣\

        through␣that␣little␣passage!");

  make_inst(S, *holds*(OYSTER), *sayit*);

  make_inst(S, 0, *complex*);

  make_loc(*arch*,

    "You␣are␣in␣an␣arched␣hall.␣␣A␣coral␣passage␣\

       once␣continued␣up␣and␣east\n\

    from␣here,␣but␣is␣now␣blocked␣by␣debris.␣␣\

       The␣air␣smells␣of␣sea␣water.",

    "You're␣in␣arched␣hall.", 0);

  make_inst(D, 0, *shell*);   *ditto*(SHELL);   *ditto*(OUT);

  make_loc(*ragged*,

    "You␣are␣in␣a␣long␣sloping␣corridor␣with␣ragged␣sharp␣walls.",

    0, 0);

  make_inst(U, 0, *shell*);   *ditto*(SHELL);

  make_inst(D, 0, *sac*);

  make_loc(*sac*,

    "You␣are␣in␣a␣cul-de-sac␣about␣eight␣feet␣across.", 0, 0);

  make_inst(U, 0, *ragged*);   *ditto*(OUT);

  make_inst(SHELL, 0, *shell*);

44.   A dangerous section lies east of the complex junction.

⟨ Build the travel table 23 ⟩ +≡

  make_loc(*ante*,

    "You␣are␣in␣an␣anteroom␣leading␣to␣\

        a␣large␣passage␣to␣the␣east.␣␣Small\n\

```
        passages␣go␣west␣and␣up.␣␣\
            The␣remnants␣of␣recent␣digging␣are␣evident.\n\
        A␣sign␣in␣midair␣here␣says␣\
            \"CAVE␣UNDER␣CONSTRUCTION␣BEYOND␣THIS␣POINT.\n\
        PROCEED␣AT␣OWN␣RISK.␣␣[WITT␣CONSTRUCTION␣COMPANY]\"",
    "You're␣in␣anteroom.",0);
  make_inst(U,0,complex);
  make_inst(W,0,bedquilt);
  make_inst(E,0,witt);

  make_loc(witt,
    "You␣are␣at␣Witt's␣End.␣␣\
            Passages␣lead␣off␣in␣\"all\"␣directions.",
    "You're␣at␣Witt's␣End.",witt_hint);
  remark("You␣have␣crawled␣around␣in␣some␣little␣holes␣\
            and␣wound␣up␣back␣in␣the\n\
        main␣passage.");
  loop_rmk = sayit;
  make_inst(E,95,sayit);  ditto(N);  ditto(S);
  ditto(NE);  ditto(SE);  ditto(SW);  ditto(NW);  ditto(U);  ditto(D);
  make_inst(E,0,ante);      /* one chance in 20 */
  remark("You␣have␣crawled␣around␣in␣some␣little␣holes␣\
            and␣found␣your␣way\n\
        blocked␣by␣a␣recent␣cave-in.␣␣\
            You␣are␣now␣back␣in␣the␣main␣passage.");
  make_inst(W,0,sayit);
```

45.   Will Crowther, who actively explored and mapped many caves in Kentucky before inventing Adventure, named Bedquilt after the Bedquilt Entrance to Colossal Cave. (The real Colossal Cave was discovered near Mammoth Cave in 1895, and its Bedquilt Entrance was found in 1896; see *The Longest Cave* by Brucker and Watson (New York: Knopf, 1976) for further details.)

Random exploration is the name of the game here.

⟨ Build the travel table 23 ⟩ +≡
  make_loc(*bedquilt*,
  "You␣are␣in␣Bedquilt,␣\
        a␣long␣east/west␣passage␣with␣holes␣everywhere.\n\
     To␣explore␣at␣random␣select␣north,␣south,␣up,␣or␣down.",
  "You're␣in␣Bedquilt.",0);
  make_inst(E, 0, *complex*);
  make_inst(W, 0, *cheese*);
  make_inst(S, 80, *loop_rmk*);
  make_inst(SLAB, 0, *slab*);
  make_inst(U, 80, *loop_rmk*);
  make_inst(U, 50, *abovep*);
  make_inst(U, 0, *dusty*);
  make_inst(N, 60, *loop_rmk*);
  make_inst(N, 75, *low*);
  make_inst(N, 0, *sjunc*);
  make_inst(D, 80, *loop_rmk*);
  make_inst(D, 0, *ante*);

  make_loc(*cheese*,
  "You␣are␣in␣a␣room␣whose␣walls␣resemble␣Swiss␣cheese.␣␣\
        Obvious␣passages\n\
     go␣west,␣east,␣NE,␣and␣NW.␣␣\
        Part␣of␣the␣room␣is␣occupied␣by␣a␣large\n\
     bedrock␣block.",
  "You're␣in␣Swiss␣cheese␣room.",0);
  make_inst(NE, 0, *bedquilt*);
  make_inst(W, 0, *e2pit*);
  make_inst(S, 80, *loop_rmk*);
  make_inst(CANYON, 0, *tall*);
  make_inst(E, 0, *soft*);
  make_inst(NW, 50, *loop_rmk*);
  make_inst(ORIENTAL, 0, *oriental*);

  make_loc(*soft*,
  "You␣are␣in␣the␣Soft␣Room.␣␣\
        The␣walls␣are␣covered␣with␣heavy␣curtains,\n\

```
      the␣floor␣with␣a␣thick␣pile␣carpet.␣␣\
         Moss␣covers␣the␣ceiling.",
"You're␣in␣Soft␣Room.",0);
   make_inst(W,0,cheese);  ditto(OUT);
```

46.   West of the quilt and the cheese is a room with two pits.

Why would you want to descend into the pits? Keep playing and you'll find out.

⟨ Build the travel table 23 ⟩ +≡

```
make_loc(e2pit,
  "You␣are␣at␣the␣east␣end␣of␣the␣Twopit␣Room.␣␣\
        The␣floor␣here␣is\n\
     littered␣with␣thin␣rock␣slabs,␣\
        which␣make␣it␣easy␣to␣descend␣the␣pits.\n\
     There␣is␣a␣path␣here␣bypassing␣the␣pits␣\
        to␣connect␣passages␣from␣east\n\
     and␣west.␣␣There␣are␣holes␣all␣over,␣\
        but␣the␣only␣big␣one␣is␣on␣the\n\
     wall␣directly␣over␣the␣west␣pit␣where␣you␣can't␣get␣to␣it.",
  "You're␣at␣east␣end␣of␣Twopit␣Room.",0);
make_inst(E,0,cheese);
make_inst(W,0,w2pit);  ditto(ACROSS);
make_inst(D,0,epit);  ditto(PIT);

make_loc(w2pit,
  "You␣are␣at␣the␣west␣end␣of␣the␣Twopit␣Room.␣␣\
        There␣is␣a␣large␣hole␣in\n\
     the␣wall␣above␣the␣pit␣at␣this␣end␣of␣the␣room.",
  "You're␣at␣west␣end␣of␣Twopit␣Room.",0);
make_inst(E,0,e2pit);  ditto(ACROSS);
make_inst(W,0,slab);  ditto(SLAB);
make_inst(D,0,wpit);  ditto(PIT);
remark("It␣is␣too␣far␣up␣for␣you␣to␣reach.");
make_inst(HOLE,0,sayit);

make_loc(epit,
  "You␣are␣at␣the␣bottom␣of␣the␣eastern␣pit␣\
        in␣the␣Twopit␣Room.␣␣There␣is\n\
     a␣small␣pool␣of␣oil␣in␣one␣corner␣of␣the␣pit.",
  "You're␣in␣east␣pit.",liquid + oil);
make_inst(U,0,e2pit);  ditto(OUT);

make_loc(wpit,
  "You␣are␣at␣the␣bottom␣of␣the␣western␣pit␣\
        in␣the␣Twopit␣Room.␣␣There␣is\n\
     a␣large␣hole␣in␣the␣wall␣about␣25␣feet␣above␣you.",
  "You're␣in␣west␣pit.",0);
make_inst(U,0,w2pit);  ditto(OUT);
make_inst(CLIMB,not(PLANT,4),check);
make_inst(CLIMB,0,climb);
```

47. Oho, you climbed the plant in the west pit! Now you're in another scenic area with rare treasures — if you can get through the door.

⟨ Build the travel table 23 ⟩ +≡
  make_loc(*narrow*,
  "You␣are␣in␣a␣long,␣narrow␣corridor␣\
      stretching␣out␣of␣sight␣to␣the\n\
    west.␣␣At␣the␣eastern␣end␣is␣\
      a␣hole␣through␣which␣you␣can␣see␣a\n\
    profusion␣of␣leaves.",
  "You're␣in␣narrow␣corridor.",0);
  make_inst(D,0,*wpit*); *ditto*(CLIMB); *ditto*(E);
  make_inst(JUMP,0,*neck*);
  make_inst(W,0,*giant*); *ditto*(GIANT);

  make_loc(*giant*,
  "You␣are␣in␣the␣Giant␣Room.␣␣\
      The␣ceiling␣here␣is␣too␣high␣up␣for␣your\n\
    lamp␣to␣show␣it.␣␣Cavernous␣passages␣lead␣\
      east,␣north,␣and␣south.␣␣On\n\
    the␣west␣wall␣is␣scrawled␣the␣inscription,␣\
      \"FEE␣FIE␣FOE␣FOO\"␣[sic].",
  "You're␣in␣Giant␣Room.",0);
  make_inst(S,0,*narrow*);
  make_inst(E,0,*block*);
  make_inst(N,0,*immense*);

  make_loc(*block*,
  "The␣passage␣here␣is␣blocked␣by␣a␣recent␣cave-in.",0,0);
  make_inst(S,0,*giant*); *ditto*(GIANT); *ditto*(OUT);

  make_loc(*immense*,
  "You␣are␣at␣one␣end␣of␣an␣immense␣north/south␣passage.",0,0);
  make_inst(S,0,*giant*); *ditto*(GIANT); *ditto*(PASSAGE);
  make_inst(N,*not*(DOOR,0),*falls*); *ditto*(ENTER); *ditto*(CAVERN);
  remark("The␣door␣is␣extremely␣rusty␣and␣refuses␣to␣open.");
  make_inst(N,0,*sayit*);

  make_loc(*falls*,
  "You␣are␣in␣a␣magnificent␣cavern␣with␣a␣rushing␣stream,␣\
      which␣cascades\n\
    over␣a␣sparkling␣waterfall␣into␣a␣roaring␣whirlpool␣\
      that␣disappears\n\
    through␣a␣hole␣in␣the␣floor.␣␣\
      Passages␣exit␣to␣the␣south␣and␣west.",
  "You're␣in␣cavern␣with␣waterfall.",*liquid*);
  make_inst(S,0,*immense*); *ditto*(OUT);
  make_inst(GIANT,0,*giant*);

```
make_inst(W, 0, steep);
make_loc(steep,
"You␣are␣at␣the␣top␣of␣a␣steep␣incline␣\
        above␣a␣large␣room.␣␣You␣could\n\
    climb␣down␣here,␣but␣you␣would␣not␣be␣\
        able␣to␣climb␣up.␣␣There␣is␣a\n\
    passage␣leading␣back␣to␣the␣north.",
"You're␣at␣steep␣incline␣above␣large␣room.", 0);
make_inst(N, 0, falls); ditto(CAVERN); ditto(PASSAGE);
make_inst(D, 0, low); ditto(CLIMB);
```

block = 77, §18.
CAVERN = 39, §9.
CLIMB = 23, §9.
D = 9, §9.
ditto = macro ( ), §21.
DOOR = 11, §11.
E = 2, §9.
ENTER = 20, §9.
falls = 79, §18.
GIANT = 45, §9.
giant = 76, §18.
immense = 78, §18.
JUMP = 22, §9.
liquid = 4, §20.
low = 84, §18, §48.
make_inst = macro ( ), §21.
make_loc = macro ( ), §21.
N = 0, §9.
narrow = 75, §18.
neck = 130, §18, §60.
not = macro ( ), §21.
OUT = 13, §9.
PASSAGE = 38, §9.
remark = macro ( ), §21.
S = 1, §9.
sayit = macro, §21.
steep = 80, §18.
W = 3, §9.
wpit = 74, §18, §46.

48. Meanwhile let's backtrack to another part of the cave possibly reachable from Bedquilt.

⟨ Build the travel table 23 ⟩ +≡

  make_loc(*abovep*,
  "You␣are␣in␣a␣secret␣N/S␣canyon␣above␣a␣sizable␣passage.", 0, 0);
  make_inst(N, 0, *sjunc*);
  make_inst(D, 0, *bedquilt*); *ditto*(PASSAGE);
  make_inst(S, 0, *tite*);

  make_loc(*sjunc*,
  "You␣are␣in␣a␣secret␣canyon␣at␣\
      a␣junction␣of␣three␣canyons,␣bearing\n\
    north,␣south,␣and␣SE.␣␣\
      The␣north␣one␣is␣as␣tall␣as␣the␣other␣two\n\
    combined.",
  "You're␣at␣junction␣of␣three␣secret␣canyons.", 0);
  make_inst(SE, 0, *bedquilt*);
  make_inst(S, 0, *abovep*);
  make_inst(N, 0, *window*);

  make_loc(*tite*,
  "A␣large␣stalactite␣extends␣from␣the␣roof␣\
      and␣almost␣reaches␣the␣floor\n\
    below.␣␣You␣could␣climb␣down␣it,␣\
      and␣jump␣from␣it␣to␣the␣floor,␣but\n\
    having␣done␣so␣you␣would␣be␣\
      unable␣to␣reach␣it␣to␣climb␣back␣up.",
  "You're␣on␣top␣of␣stalactite.", 0);
  make_inst(N, 0, *abovep*);
  make_inst(D, 40, *like6*); *ditto*(JUMP); *ditto*(CLIMB);
  make_inst(D, 50, *like9*);
  make_inst(D, 0, *like4*);
    /* oh dear, you're in a random part of the maze */
  make_loc(*low*,
  "You␣are␣in␣a␣large␣low␣room.␣␣Crawls␣lead␣north,␣SE,␣and␣SW.",
    0, 0);
  make_inst(BEDQUILT, 0, *bedquilt*);
  make_inst(SW, 0, *scorr*);
  make_inst(N, 0, *crawl*);
  make_inst(SE, 0, *oriental*); *ditto*(ORIENTAL);

  make_loc(*crawl*,
  "Dead␣end␣crawl.", 0, 0);
  make_inst(S, 0, *low*); *ditto*(CRAWL); *ditto*(OUT);

49.   The described view from the west window, *window*, is identical to
the view from the east window, *windoe*, except for one word. What on
earth do you see from those windows? (Don Woods has confided that
the shadowy figure is actually your own reflection, because *mirror* lies
between the two window rooms. An intentional false clue.)

⟨ Build the travel table 23 ⟩ +≡
  make_loc(*window*,
    "You're␣at␣a␣low␣window␣overlooking␣a␣huge␣pit,␣\
          which␣extends␣up␣out␣of\n\
      sight.␣␣A␣floor␣is␣indistinctly␣visible␣\
          over␣50␣feet␣below.␣␣Traces␣of\n\
      white␣mist␣cover␣the␣floor␣of␣the␣pit,␣\
          becoming␣thicker␣to␣the␣left.\n\
      Marks␣in␣the␣dust␣around␣the␣window␣\
          would␣seem␣to␣indicate␣that\n\
      someone␣has␣been␣here␣recently.␣␣\
          Directly␣across␣the␣pit␣from␣you␣and\n\
      25␣feet␣away␣there␣is␣a␣similar␣window␣\
          looking␣into␣a␣lighted␣room.\n\
      A␣shadowy␣figure␣can␣be␣seen␣there␣\
          peering␣back␣at␣you.",
    short_desc[*windoe*], 0);
  make_inst(W, 0, *sjunc*);
  make_inst(JUMP, 0, *neck*);

50.   More treasures await you via the *low* corridor.

⟨ Build the travel table 23 ⟩ +≡
  make_loc(*oriental*,
  "This␣is␣the␣Oriental␣Room.␣␣\
          Ancient␣oriental␣cave␣drawings␣cover␣the\n\
      walls.␣␣A␣gently␣sloping␣passage␣\
          leads␣upward␣to␣the␣north,␣another\n\
      passage␣leads␣SE,␣and␣a␣hands-and-knees␣crawl␣leads␣west.",
  "You're␣in␣Oriental␣Room.",0);
  make_inst(SE,0,*cheese*);
  make_inst(W,0,*low*); *ditto*(CRAWL);
  make_inst(U,0,*misty*); *ditto*(N); *ditto*(CAVERN);

  make_loc(*misty*,
  "You␣are␣following␣a␣wide␣path␣\
          around␣the␣outer␣edge␣of␣a␣large␣cavern.\n\
      Far␣below,␣through␣a␣heavy␣white␣mist,␣\
          strange␣splashing␣noises␣can␣be\n\
      heard.␣␣The␣mist␣rises␣up␣\
          through␣a␣fissure␣in␣the␣ceiling.␣␣The␣path\n\
      exits␣to␣the␣south␣and␣west.",
  "You're␣in␣misty␣cavern.",0);
  make_inst(S,0,*oriental*); *ditto*(ORIENTAL);
  make_inst(W,0,*alcove*);

51.   One of the darkest secrets is hidden here. You will discover that
you must take the emerald from the Plover Room to the alcove. But you
don't learn the name of the Plover Room until the second time you've
been there, since your first visit will be lampless until you know the
secret.

⟨ Build the travel table 23 ⟩ +≡
  make_loc(*alcove*,
  "You␣are␣in␣an␣alcove.␣␣A␣small␣NW␣path␣\
          seems␣to␣widen␣after␣a␣short\n\
      distance.␣␣An␣extremely␣tight␣tunnel␣\
          leads␣east.␣␣It␣looks␣like␣a␣very\n\
      tight␣squeeze.␣␣An␣eerie␣light␣\
          can␣be␣seen␣at␣the␣other␣end.",
  "You're␣in␣alcove.",*dark_hint*);
  make_inst(NW,0,*misty*); *ditto*(CAVERN);
  make_inst(E,0,*ppass*); *ditto*(PASSAGE);
  make_inst(E,0,*proom*);   /* never performed, but seen by 'go back' */
  make_loc(*proom*,
  "You're␣in␣a␣small␣chamber␣lit␣by␣an␣eerie␣green␣light.␣␣\
          An␣extremely\n\

```
narrow␣tunnel␣exits␣to␣the␣west.␣␣\
        A␣dark␣corridor␣leads␣NE.",
"You're␣in␣Plover␣Room.", lighted + dark_hint);
make_inst(W, 0, ppass); ditto(PASSAGE); ditto(OUT);
make_inst(W, 0, alcove);    /* never performed, but seen by 'go back' */
make_inst(PLOVER, holds(EMERALD), pdrop);
make_inst(PLOVER, 0, y2);
make_inst(NE, 0, droom); ditto(DARK);

make_loc(droom,
"You're␣in␣the␣Dark-Room.␣␣\
        A␣corridor␣leading␣south␣is␣the␣only␣exit.",
"You're␣in␣Dark-Room.", dark_hint);
make_inst(S, 0, proom); ditto(PLOVER); ditto(OUT);
```

52.   We forgot to mention the circuitous passage leading west from
the Twopit Room. It winds around and takes you to a somewhat more
mundane area, yet not without interest.

⟨ Build the travel table 23 ⟩ +≡

  make_loc(*slab*,

  "You␣are␣in␣a␣large␣low␣circular␣chamber␣\
        whose␣floor␣is␣an␣immense␣slab\n\
    fallen␣from␣the␣ceiling␣(Slab␣Room).␣␣\
        There␣once␣were␣large␣passages\n\
    to␣the␣east␣and␣west,␣but␣they␣are␣now␣\
        filled␣with␣boulders.␣␣Low\n\
    small␣passages␣go␣north␣and␣south,␣\
        and␣the␣south␣one␣quickly␣bends\n\
    east␣around␣the␣boulders.",
    /* Woods originally said 'west' */
  "You're␣in␣Slab␣Room.",0);
  make_inst(S,0,*w2pit*);
  make_inst(U,0,*abover*); *ditto*(CLIMB);
  make_inst(N,0,*bedquilt*);

  make_loc(*abover*,

  "You␣are␣in␣a␣secret␣N/S␣canyon␣above␣a␣large␣room.",0,0);
  make_inst(D,0,*slab*); *ditto*(SLAB);
  make_inst(S,*not*(DRAGON,0),*scan2*);
  make_inst(S,0,*scan1*);
  make_inst(N,0,*mirror*);
  make_inst(RESERVOIR,0,*res*);

  make_loc(*mirror*,

  "You␣are␣in␣a␣north/south␣canyon␣about␣25␣feet␣across.␣␣\
        The␣floor␣is\n\
  covered␣by␣white␣mist␣seeping␣in␣from␣the␣north.␣␣\
        The␣walls␣extend\n\
  upward␣for␣well␣over␣100␣feet.␣␣\
        Suspended␣from␣some␣unseen␣point␣far\n\
  above␣you,␣an␣enormous␣two-sided␣mirror␣\
        is␣hanging␣parallel␣to␣and\n\
  midway␣between␣the␣canyon␣walls.␣\
    ␣(The␣mirror␣is␣obviously␣provided\n\
  for␣the␣use␣of␣the␣dwarves,␣\
        who␣as␣you␣know␣are␣extremely␣vain.)\n\
  A␣small␣window␣can␣be␣seen␣in␣either␣wall,␣\
        some␣fifty␣feet␣up.",
  "You're␣in␣mirror␣canyon.",0);
  make_inst(S,0,*abover*);
  make_inst(N,0,*res*); *ditto*(RESERVOIR);

```
make_loc(res,
  "You␣are␣at␣the␣edge␣of␣a␣large␣underground␣reservoir.␣␣\
      An␣opaque␣cloud\n\
  of␣white␣mist␣fills␣the␣room␣and␣rises␣rapidly␣upward.␣␣\
      The␣lake␣is\n\
  fed␣by␣a␣stream,␣which␣tumbles␣out␣of␣a␣hole␣in␣the␣wall␣\
      about␣10␣feet\n\
  overhead␣and␣splashes␣noisily␣into␣the␣water␣\
      somewhere␣within␣the\n\
  mist.␣␣The␣only␣passage␣goes␣back␣toward␣the␣south.",
  "You're␣at␣reservoir.", liquid);
make_inst(S, 0, mirror);  ditto(OUT);
```

53. Four more secret canyons lead back to the Hall of the Mountain King. Three of them are actually the same, but the dragon blocks the connection between the northern passage (to *abover*) and the eastern passage (to *secret*). Once you've vanquished the dragon, *scan2* takes the place of *scan1* and *scan3*.

⟨ Build the travel table 23 ⟩ +≡

```
make_loc(scan1,
   "You␣are␣in␣a␣secret␣canyon␣that␣exits␣to␣the␣north␣and␣east.",
      0,0);
make_inst(N, 0, abover);  ditto(OUT);
remark("The␣dragon␣looks␣rather␣nasty.␣␣\
         You'd␣best␣not␣try␣to␣get␣by.");
make_inst(E, 0, sayit);  ditto(FORWARD);

make_loc(scan2, long_desc[scan1], 0, 0);
make_inst(N, 0, abover);
make_inst(E, 0, secret);

make_loc(scan3, long_desc[scan1], 0, 0);
make_inst(E, 0, secret);  ditto(OUT);
make_inst(N, 0, sayit);  ditto(FORWARD);

make_loc(secret,
   "You␣are␣in␣a␣secret␣canyon,␣which␣here␣runs␣E/W.␣␣\
         It␣crosses␣over␣a\n\
      very␣tight␣canyon␣15␣feet␣below.␣␣\
         If␣you␣go␣down␣you␣may␣not␣be␣able\n\
      to␣get␣back␣up.",
   "You're␣in␣secret␣E/W␣canyon␣above␣tight␣canyon.", 0);
make_inst(E, 0, hmk);
make_inst(W, not(DRAGON, 0), scan2);
make_inst(W, 0, scan3);
make_inst(D, 0, wide);
```

54.   Below *secret* there's another way to reach the cheese.

⟨ Build the travel table 23 ⟩ +≡

   make_loc(*wide*,

    "You␣are␣at␣a␣wide␣place␣in␣a␣very␣tight␣N/S␣canyon.", 0, 0);

   make_inst(S, 0, *tight*);

   make_inst(N, 0, *tall*);

   make_loc(*tight*,

    "The␣canyon␣here␣becomes␣too␣tight␣to␣go␣further␣south.", 0, 0);

   make_inst(N, 0, *wide*);

   make_loc(*tall*,

    "You␣are␣in␣a␣tall␣E/W␣canyon.␣␣\

        A␣low␣tight␣crawl␣goes␣3␣feet␣north␣and\n\

      seems␣to␣open␣up.",

    "You're␣in␣tall␣E/W␣canyon.", 0);

   make_inst(E, 0, *wide*);

   make_inst(W, 0, *boulders*);

   make_inst(N, 0, *cheese*);   *ditto*(CRAWL);

   make_loc(*boulders*,

    "The␣canyon␣runs␣into␣a␣mass␣of␣boulders␣---␣dead␣end.", 0, 0);

   make_inst(S, 0, *tall*);

---

abover = 93, §18, §52.

boulders = 103, §18.

cheese = 69, §18, §45.

CRAWL = 21, §9.

D = 9, §9.

ditto = macro ( ), §21.

DRAGON = 37, §11.

E = 2, §9.

FORWARD = 14, §9.

hmk = 50, §18, §40.

long_desc: **char** ∗[], §20.

make_inst = macro ( ), §21.

make_loc = macro ( ), §21.

N = 0, §9.

not = macro ( ), §21.

OUT = 13, §9.

remark = macro ( ), §21.

S = 1, §9.

sayit = macro, §21.

scan1 = 96, §18.

scan2 = 97, §18.

scan3 = 98, §18.

secret = 99, §18, §53.

tall = 102, §18.

tight = 101, §18.

W = 3, §9.

wide = 100, §18, §54.

55.   If you aren't having fun yet, wait till you meet the troll. The only way to get here is to crawl southwest from the *low* room. And then you have a new problem to solve; we'll see later that the TROLL and the BRIDGE are here.

(Don Woods got the idea for the mist-covered bridge after an early morning visit to Mount Diablo; see Steven Levy, *Hackers* (New York: Delta, 1994), Chapter 7.)

⟨ Build the travel table 23 ⟩ +≡
  make_loc(*scorr*,
  "You␣are␣in␣a␣long␣winding␣corridor␣\
       sloping␣out␣of␣sight␣in␣both\n\
    directions.",
  "You're␣in␣sloping␣corridor.",0);
  make_inst(D,0,*low*);
  make_inst(U,0,*swside*);

  make_loc(*swside*,
  "You␣are␣on␣one␣side␣of␣a␣large,␣deep␣chasm.␣␣\
       A␣heavy␣white␣mist␣rising\n\
  up␣from␣below␣obscures␣all␣view␣of␣the␣far␣side.␣␣\
       A␣SW␣path␣leads␣away\n\
  from␣the␣chasm␣into␣a␣winding␣corridor.",
  "You're␣on␣SW␣side␣of␣chasm.",0);
  make_inst(SW,0,*scorr*);
  remark("The␣troll␣refuses␣to␣let␣you␣cross.");
  make_inst(OVER,*sees*(TROLL),*sayit*); *ditto*(ACROSS); *ditto*(CROSS);
  ditto(NE);
  remark("There␣is␣no␣longer␣any␣way␣across␣the␣chasm.");
  make_inst(OVER,*not*(BRIDGE,0),*sayit*);
  make_inst(OVER,0,*troll*);
  make_inst(JUMP,*not*(BRIDGE,0),*lose*);
  make_inst(JUMP,0,*bridge_rmk*);

56.   The only things not yet explored on this side of the troll bridge are a dozen dead ends. They appear at this place in the ordering of all locations because of the pirate logic explained later: The pirate will never go to locations ≥ *dead3*.

#define *max_pirate_loc* *dead2*

⟨ Build the travel table 23 ⟩ +≡
  make_loc(*dead0*, *dead_end*,0,0);
  make_inst(S,0,*cross*); *ditto*(OUT);

  make_loc(*dead1*, *dead_end*,0,*twist_hint*);
  make_inst(W,0,*like11*); *ditto*(OUT);

  make_loc(*dead2*, *dead_end*,0,0);

make_inst(**SE**, 0, *like13*);

make_loc(*dead3*, *dead_end*, 0, *twist_hint*);
make_inst(**W**, 0, *like4*); *ditto*(**OUT**);

make_loc(*dead4*, *dead_end*, 0, *twist_hint*);
make_inst(**E**, 0, *like4*); *ditto*(**OUT**);

make_loc(*dead5*, *dead_end*, 0, *twist_hint*);
make_inst(**U**, 0, *like3*); *ditto*(**OUT**);

make_loc(*dead6*, *dead_end*, 0, *twist_hint*);
make_inst(**W**, 0, *like9*); *ditto*(**OUT**);

make_loc(*dead7*, *dead_end*, 0, *twist_hint*);
make_inst(**U**, 0, *like10*); *ditto*(**OUT**);

make_loc(*dead8*, *dead_end*, 0, 0);
make_inst(**E**, 0, *brink*); *ditto*(**OUT**);

make_loc(*dead9*, *dead_end*, 0, *twist_hint*);
make_inst(**S**, 0, *like3*); *ditto*(**OUT**);

make_loc(*dead10*, *dead_end*, 0, *twist_hint*);
make_inst(**E**, 0, *like12*); *ditto*(**OUT**);

make_loc(*dead11*, *dead_end*, 0, *twist_hint*);
make_inst(**U**, 0, *like8*); *ditto*(**OUT**);

ACROSS = 17, §9.
BRIDGE = 39, §11.
bridge_rmk: **int**, §34.
brink = 34, §18, §37.
CROSS = 25, §9.
cross = 49, §18, §40.
D = 9, §9.
dead_end: **char** [], §21.
dead0 = 106, §18.
dead1 = 107, §18.
dead2 = 108, §18.
dead3 = 109, §18.
dead4 = 110, §18.
dead5 = 111, §18.
dead6 = 112, §18.
dead7 = 113, §18.
dead8 = 114, §18.
dead9 = 115, §18.
dead10 = 116, §18.
dead11 = 117, §18.
ditto = macro ( ), §21.
E = 2, §9.
JUMP = 22, §9.
like3 = 22, §18, §36.
like4 = 23, §18, §36.
like8 = 27, §18, §36.

like9 = 28, §18, §36.
like10 = 29, §18, §36.
like11 = 30, §18, §36.
like12 = 31, §18, §36.
like13 = 32, §18, §36.
lose = 131, §18, §60.
low = 84, §18, §48.
make_inst = macro ( ), §21.
make_loc = macro ( ), §21.
NE = 4, §9.
not = macro ( ), §21.
OUT = 13, §9.
OVER = 16, §9.
remark = macro ( ), §21.
S = 1, §9.
sayit = macro, §21.
scorr = 104, §18.
SE = 5, §9.
sees = macro ( ), §21.
SW = 7, §9.
swside = 105, §18.
TROLL = 41, §11.
troll = 143, §18, §146.
twist_hint = 64, §20.
U = 8, §9.
W = 3, §9.

57.   A whole nuther cave with nine sites and additional treasures is on
tuther side of the troll bridge! This cave was inspired in part by J. R. R.
Tolkien's stories.

⟨ Build the travel table 23 ⟩ +≡
  make_loc(*neside*,
   "You␣are␣on␣the␣far␣side␣of␣the␣chasm.␣␣\
        A␣NE␣path␣leads␣away␣from␣the\n\
    chasm␣on␣this␣side.",
   "You're␣on␣NE␣side␣of␣chasm.",0);
  make_inst(NE, 0, *corr*);
  make_inst(OVER, *sees*(TROLL), *sayit* − 1); *ditto*(ACROSS); *ditto*(CROSS);
  ditto(SW);
  make_inst(OVER, 0, *troll*);
  make_inst(JUMP, 0, *bridge_rmk*);
  make_inst(FORK, 0, *fork*);
  make_inst(VIEW, 0, *view*);
  make_inst(BARREN, 0, *fbarr*);

  make_loc(*corr*,
   "You're␣in␣a␣long␣east/west␣corridor.␣␣\
        A␣faint␣rumbling␣noise␣can␣be\n\
    heard␣in␣the␣distance.",
   "You're␣in␣corridor.",0);
  make_inst(W, 0, *neside*);
  make_inst(E, 0, *fork*); *ditto*(FORK);
  make_inst(VIEW, 0, *view*);
  make_inst(BARREN, 0, *fbarr*);

  make_loc(*fork*,
   "The␣path␣forks␣here.␣␣The␣left␣fork␣leads␣northeast.␣␣\
        A␣dull␣rumbling\n\
   seems␣to␣get␣louder␣in␣that␣direction.␣␣\
        The␣right␣fork␣leads␣southeast\n\
   down␣a␣gentle␣slope.␣␣\
        The␣main␣corridor␣enters␣from␣the␣west.",
   "You're␣at␣fork␣in␣path.",0);
  make_inst(W, 0, *corr*);
  make_inst(NE, 0, *warm*); *ditto*(L);
  make_inst(SE, 0, *lime*); *ditto*(R); *ditto*(D);
  make_inst(VIEW, 0, *view*);
  make_inst(BARREN, 0, *fbarr*);

  make_loc(*warm*,
   "The␣walls␣are␣quite␣warm␣here.␣␣\
        From␣the␣north␣can␣be␣heard␣a␣steady\n\
   roar,␣so␣loud␣that␣the␣entire␣cave␣\

```
        seems␣to␣be␣trembling.␣␣Another\n\
    passage␣leads␣south,␣and␣a␣low␣crawl␣goes␣east.",
  "You're␣at␣junction␣with␣warm␣walls.",0);
make_inst(S,0,fork);  ditto(FORK);
make_inst(N,0,view);  ditto(VIEW);
make_inst(E,0,chamber);  ditto(CRAWL);
```

57.   (continued)

```
make_loc(view,      /* (John Gilbert co-authored this description.) */
"You are on the edge of a breath-taking view.  \
        Far below you is an\n\
    active volcano, from which great gouts \
        of molten lava come surging\n\
    out, cascading back down into the depths.  \
        The glowing rock fills the\n\
    farthest reaches of the cavern with a blood-red glare, \
        giving every-\n\
    thing an eerie, macabre appearance.  \
        The air is filled with flickering\n\
    sparks of ash and a heavy smell of brimstone.  \
        The walls are hot to\n\
    the touch, and the thundering of the volcano \
        drowns out all other\n\
    sounds.  Embedded in the jagged roof far overhead\
         are myriad twisted\n\
    formations, composed of pure white alabaster,\
         which scatter the murky\n\
    light into sinister apparitions upon the walls.  \
        To one side is a deep\n\
    gorge, filled with a bizarre chaos of tortured rock \
        that seems to have\n\
    been crafted by the Devil himself.  \
        An immense river of fire crashes\n\
    out from the depths of the volcano, \
        burns its way through the gorge,\n\
    and plummets into a bottomless pit \
        far off to your left.  To the\n\
    right, an immense geyser of blistering steam \
        erupts continuously\n\
    from a barren island in the center \
        of a sulfurous lake, which bubbles\n\
    ominously.  The far right wall is aflame \
        with an incandescence of its\n\
    own, which lends an additional infernal splendor \
        to the already\n\
    hellish scene.  A dark, foreboding passage \
        exits to the south.",
"You're at breath-taking view.", lighted);
make_inst(S, 0, warm);  ditto(PASSAGE);  ditto(OUT);
make_inst(FORK, 0, fork);
remark(default_msg[EAT]);  make_inst(D, 0, sayit);  ditto(JUMP);
```

```
make_loc(chamber,
    "You␣are␣in␣a␣small␣chamber␣filled␣with␣large␣boulders.␣␣\
        The␣walls␣are\n\
    very␣warm,␣causing␣the␣air␣in␣the␣room␣to␣be␣\
        almost␣stifling␣from␣the\n\
    heat.␣␣The␣only␣exit␣is␣a␣crawl␣heading␣west,␣\
        through␣which␣a␣low\n\
    rumbling␣noise␣is␣coming.",
    "You're␣in␣chamber␣of␣boulders.",0);
make_inst(W,0,warm);  ditto(OUT);  ditto(CRAWL);
make_inst(FORK,0,fork);
make_inst(VIEW,0,view);

make_loc(lime,
    "You␣are␣walking␣along␣a␣gently␣sloping␣\
        north/south␣passage␣lined␣with\n\
    oddly␣shaped␣limestone␣formations.",
    "You're␣in␣limestone␣passage.",0);
make_inst(N,0,fork);  ditto(U);  ditto(FORK);
make_inst(S,0,fbarr);  ditto(D);  ditto(BARREN);
make_inst(VIEW,0,view);

make_loc(fbarr,
    "You␣are␣standing␣at␣the␣entrance␣\
        to␣a␣large,␣barren␣room.␣␣A␣sign\n\
    posted␣above␣the␣entrance␣reads:␣␣\
        \"CAUTION!␣␣BEAR␣IN␣ROOM!\"",
    "You're␣in␣front␣of␣barren␣room.",0);     /* don't laugh too loud */
make_inst(W,0,lime);  ditto(U);
make_inst(FORK,0,fork);
make_inst(E,0,barr);  ditto(IN);  ditto(BARREN);  ditto(ENTER);
make_inst(VIEW,0,view);
```

---

barr = 126, §18.
BARREN = 48, §9.
chamber = 123, §18.
CRAWL = 21, §9.
D = 9, §9.
default_msg: **char** *[], §15.
ditto = macro ( ), §21.
E = 2, §9.
EAT, see §92 and §98.
ENTER = 20, §9.
fbarr = 125, §18.
fork = 120, §18.
FORK = 52, §9.
IN = 12, §9.
JUMP = 22, §9.

lighted = 1, §20.
lime = 124, §18.
make_inst = macro ( ), §21.
make_loc = macro ( ), §21.
N = 0, §9.
OUT = 13, §9.
PASSAGE = 38, §9.
remark = macro ( ), §21.
S = 1, §9.
sayit = macro, §21.
U = 8, §9.
view = 122, §18.
VIEW = 51, §9.
W = 3, §9.
warm = 121, §18.

57.   (continued (continued))

```
make_loc(barr,
  "You␣are␣inside␣a␣barren␣room.␣␣\
        The␣center␣of␣the␣room␣is␣completely\n\
    empty␣except␣for␣some␣dust.␣\
        ␣Marks␣in␣the␣dust␣lead␣away␣toward␣the\n\
    far␣end␣of␣the␣room.␣\
        ␣The␣only␣exit␣is␣the␣way␣you␣came␣in.",
  "You're␣in␣barren␣room.", 0);
make_inst(W, 0, fbarr);  ditto(OUT);
make_inst(FORK, 0, fork);
make_inst(VIEW, 0, view);
```

58.   The two storage locations are accessible only from each other, and
they lead only to each other.

⟨ Build the travel table 23 ⟩ +≡

```
make_loc(neend,
  "You␣are␣at␣the␣northeast␣end␣of␣an␣immense␣room,␣\
        even␣larger␣than␣the\n\
    Giant␣Room.␣␣It␣appears␣to␣be␣a␣repository␣\
        for␣the␣\"Adventure\"\n\
    program.␣␣Massive␣torches␣far␣overhead␣\
        bathe␣the␣room␣with␣smoky\n\
    yellow␣light.␣␣Scattered␣about␣you␣can␣be␣seen␣\
        a␣pile␣of␣bottles␣(all\n\
    of␣them␣empty),␣a␣nursery␣of␣young␣beanstalks␣\
        murmuring␣quietly,␣a␣bed\n\
    of␣oysters,␣a␣bundle␣of␣black␣rods␣\
        with␣rusty␣stars␣on␣their␣ends,␣and\n\
    a␣collection␣of␣brass␣lanterns.␣\
        ␣Off␣to␣one␣side␣a␣great␣many␣dwarves\n\
    are␣sleeping␣on␣the␣floor,␣snoring␣loudly.␣␣\
        A␣sign␣nearby␣reads:␣␣\"DO\n\
    NOT␣DISTURB␣THE␣DWARVES!\"␣\
        ␣An␣immense␣mirror␣is␣hanging␣against␣one\n\
    wall,␣and␣stretches␣to␣the␣other␣end␣of␣the␣room,␣\
        where␣various␣other\n\
    sundry␣objects␣can␣be␣glimpsed␣dimly␣in␣the␣distance.",
  "You're␣at␣NE␣end.", lighted);
make_inst(SW, 0, swend);
```

make_loc(*swend*,
"You␣are␣at␣the␣southwest␣end␣of␣the␣repository.␣␣\
        To␣one␣side␣is␣a␣pit\n\
    full␣of␣fierce␣green␣snakes.␣␣\
        On␣the␣other␣side␣is␣a␣row␣of␣small\n\
    wicker␣cages,␣each␣of␣which␣contains␣\
        a␣little␣sulking␣bird.␣␣In␣one\n\
    corner␣is␣a␣bundle␣of␣black␣rods␣\
        with␣rusty␣marks␣on␣their␣ends.\n\
    A␣large␣number␣of␣velvet␣pillows␣\
        are␣scattered␣about␣on␣the␣floor.\n\
    A␣vast␣mirror␣stretches␣off␣to␣the␣northeast.␣␣\
        At␣your␣feet␣is␣a\n\
    large␣steel␣grate,␣next␣to␣which␣is␣a␣sign␣\
        that␣reads,␣\"TREASURE\n\
    VAULT.␣␣KEYS␣IN␣MAIN␣OFFICE.\"",
"You're␣at␣SW␣end.", *lighted*);
make_inst(NE, 0, *neend*);
make_inst(D, 0, *grate_rmk*);

---

59. When the current location is *crack* or higher, it's a pseudo-location. In such cases we don't ask you for input; we assume that you have told us to force another instruction through. For example, if you try to go through the crack by the small pit in the upper cave (location *spit*), the instruction there sends you to *crack*, which immediately sends you back to *spit*.

#define *forced_move*(*loc*)   (*loc* ≥ *min_forced_loc*)
#define FORCE   0   /* actually any value will do here */

⟨Build the travel table 23⟩ +≡
    make_loc(*crack*,
    "The␣crack␣is␣far␣too␣small␣for␣you␣to␣follow.", 0, 0);
    make_inst(FORCE, 0, *spit*);

60. Here are some forced actions that are less pleasant.

⟨Build the travel table 23⟩ +≡
    make_loc(*neck*,
    "You␣are␣at␣the␣bottom␣of␣the␣pit␣with␣a␣broken␣neck.", 0, 0);
    make_inst(FORCE, 0, *limbo*);

    make_loc(*lose*, "You␣didn't␣make␣it.", 0, 0);
    make_inst(FORCE, 0, *limbo*);

61. The rest are more-or-less routine, except for *check* — which executes a *conditional* forced command.

⟨Build the travel table 23⟩ +≡
    make_loc(*cant*,
    "The␣dome␣is␣unclimbable.", 0, 0);
    make_inst(FORCE, 0, *emist*);

    make_loc(*climb*,
    "You␣clamber␣up␣the␣plant␣\
            and␣scurry␣through␣the␣hole␣at␣the␣top.", 0, 0);
    make_inst(FORCE, 0, *narrow*);

    make_loc(*check*, 0, 0, 0);
    make_inst(FORCE, *not*(PLANT, 2), *upnout*);
    make_inst(FORCE, 0, *didit*);

    make_loc(*snaked*,
    "You␣can't␣get␣by␣the␣snake.", 0, 0);
    make_inst(FORCE, 0, *hmk*);

    make_loc(*thru*,
    "You␣have␣crawled␣through␣a␣very␣low␣wide␣passage␣\
            parallel␣to␣and␣north\n\
        of␣the␣Hall␣of␣Mists.", 0, 0);
    make_inst(FORCE, 0, *wmist*);

$make\_loc\,(duck,\,long\_desc\,[thru],0,0);$
$make\_inst\,(\texttt{FORCE},0,\,wfiss\,);$

$make\_loc\,(sewer,$
`"The`␣`stream`␣`flows`␣`out`␣`through`␣`\`
   `a`␣`pair`␣`of`␣`1-foot-diameter`␣`sewer`␣`pipes.\n\`
  `It`␣`would`␣`be`␣`advisable`␣`to`␣`use`␣`the`␣`exit.",0,0);`
$make\_inst\,(\texttt{FORCE},0,\,house\,);$

$make\_loc\,(upnout,$
`"There`␣`is`␣`nothing`␣`here`␣`to`␣`climb.`␣␣`\`
   `Use`␣`\"up\"`␣`or`␣`\"out\"`␣`to`␣`leave`␣`the`␣`pit.",0,0);`
$make\_inst\,(\texttt{FORCE},0,\,wpit\,);$

$make\_loc\,(didit,$
`"You`␣`have`␣`climbed`␣`up`␣`the`␣`plant`␣`and`␣`out`␣`of`␣`the`␣`pit.",0,0);`
$make\_inst\,(\texttt{FORCE},0,\,w2pit\,);$

62. The table of instructions ends here; the remaining "locations" *ppass*, *pdrop*, and *troll* are special.

⟨ Build the travel table 23 ⟩ +≡
 $start\,[ppass] = q;$
 if $(q > \&travels\,[travel\_size] \lor rem\_count > rem\_size)$ {
  $printf\,(\texttt{"Oops,}␣\texttt{I'm}␣\texttt{broken!\n"});\ exit\,(-1);$
 }

---

63.   Data structures for objects.   A fixed universe of objects was enumerated in the vocabulary section. Most of the objects can move or be moved from place to place; so we maintain linked lists of the objects at each location. The first object at location l is *first*$[l]$, then comes *link*$[first[l]]$, then *link*$[link[first[l]]]$, etc., ending with 0 (which is the "object" called NOTHING).

Some of the objects are placed in *groups* of one or more objects. In such cases *base*$[t]$ is the smallest object in the group containing object t. Objects that belong to groups are immovable; they always stay in the same location. Other objects have *base*$[t]$ = NOTHING and they are free to leave one list and join another. For example, it turns out that the KEYS are movable, but the SNAKE is always in the Hall of the Mountain King; we set *base*[KEYS] = NOTHING and *base*[SNAKE] = SNAKE. Several groups, such as the GRATE and GRATE_, consist of two objects. This program supports operations on groups of more than two objects, but no such objects actually occur.

Each movable or base object t has a current property *prop*$[t]$, which is initially -1 for treasures, otherwise initially 0. We change *prop*$[t]$ to 0 when you first see treasure t; and property values often change further as the game progresses. For example, the PLANT can grow. When you see an object, we usually print a message that corresponds to its current property value. That message is the string *note*$[prop[t] + offset[t]]$.

(Exception: When you first see the RUG or the CHAIN, its property value is set to 1, not 0. The reason for this hack is that you get maximum score only if the property values of all treasures are zero when you finish.)

Each object is in at most one list, *place*$[t]$. If you are carrying object t, the value of *place*$[t]$ is *inhand*, which is negative. The special location *limbo* has value 0; we don't maintain a list *first*[*limbo*] for objects that have *place*$[t]$ = *limbo*. Thus object t is in a list if and only if *place*$[t]$ > 0. The global variable *holding* counts how many objects you are carrying.

One more array completes our set of data structures: Objects that appear in inventory reports have a name, *name*$[t]$.

#define *toting*(t) $(place[t] < 0)$

⟨ Global variables 7 ⟩ +≡
   object *first*[*max_loc* + 1];   /* the first object present at a location */
   object *link*[*max_obj* + 1];
     /* the next object present in the same location */
   object *base*[*max_obj* + 2];
     /* the smallest object in each object's group, if any */
   int *prop*[*max_obj* + 1];   /* each object's current property value */
   location *place*[*max_obj* + 1];   /* each object's current location */

```
char *name[max_obj + 1];    /* name of object for inventory listing */
char *note[100];    /* descriptions of object properties */
int offset[max_obj + 1];    /* where notes for each object start */
int holding;    /* how many objects have place[t] < 0? */
int note_ptr = 0;    /* how many notes have we stored? */
```

64. Here then is a simple subroutine to place an object at a given location, when the object isn't presently in a list.

⟨Subroutines 6⟩ +≡

```
void drop ARGS((object, location));

void drop(t, l)
    object t;
    location l;
{
  if (toting(t)) holding --;
  place[t] = l;
  if (l < 0) holding ++;
  else if (l > 0) {
    link[t] = first[l];
    first[l] = t;
  }
}
```

ARGS = macro ( ), §3.
CHAIN = 66, §11.
GRATE = 3, §11.
GRATE_ = 4, §11.
inhand = −1, §18.
KEYS = 1, §11.
limbo = 0, §18.
location = enum, §18.

max_loc = 140, §18.
max_obj = 66, §11.
NOTHING = 0, §11.
object = enum, §11.
PLANT = 28, §11.
RUG = 63, §11.
SNAKE = 13, §11.

65.   Similarly, we need a subroutine to pick up an object.

#define *move*(*t, l*)   { *carry*(*t*); *drop*(*t, l*); }
#define *destroy*(*t*)   *move*(*t, limbo*)
⟨Subroutines 6⟩ +≡
  void *carry* ARGS((**object**));

  void *carry*(*t*)
      object *t*;
  {
    register location *l* = *place*[*t*];
    if (*l* ≥ *limbo*) {
      place[*t*] = *inhand*;
      holding++;
      if (*l* > *limbo*) {
        register object *r*, *s*;
        for (*r* = 0, *s* = *first*[*l*]; *s* ≠ *t*; *r* = *s*, *s* = *link*[*s*]) ;
        if (*r* ≡ 0) *first*[*l*] = *link*[*s*];
        else *link*[*r*] = *link*[*s*];   /∗ remove *t* from list ∗/
      }
    }
  }

66.   The *is_at_loc* subroutine tests if a possibly multipart object is at a particular place, represented by the global variable *loc*. It uses the fact that multipart objects have consecutive values, and *base*[*max_obj* + 1] ≡ NOTHING.

⟨Subroutines 6⟩ +≡
  boolean *is_at_loc* ARGS((**object**));

  boolean *is_at_loc*(*t*)
      object *t*;
  {
    register object *tt*;
    if (*base*[*t*] ≡ NOTHING) **return** *place*[*t*] ≡ *loc*;
    for (*tt* = *t*; *base*[*tt*] ≡ *t*; *tt*++)
      if (*place*[*tt*] ≡ *loc*) **return** *true*;
    return *false*;
  }

67.   A few macros make it easy to get each object started.

#define $new\_obj\,(t, n, b, l)$
$\qquad\{\qquad$ /* object t named n with base b starts at l */
$\qquad\qquad name\,[t] = n;$
$\qquad\qquad base\,[t] = b;$
$\qquad\qquad offset\,[t] = note\_ptr\,;$
$\qquad\qquad prop\,[t] = (is\_treasure\,(t) \ ? \ -1 : 0);$
$\qquad\qquad drop\,(t, l);$
$\qquad\}$
#define $new\_note\,(n)$ $note\,[note\_ptr\,\text{++}] = n$

68.   ⟨ Additional local registers 22 ⟩ +≡
   register object $t;$

ARGS = macro ( ), §3.
base: **object** [ ], §63.
boolean = **enum**, §2.
drop: **void** ( ), §64.
false = 0, §2.
first: **object** [ ], §63.
holding: **int**, §63.
inhand = −1, §18.
is_treasure = macro ( ), §11.
limbo = 0, §18.
link: **object** [ ], §63.
loc: **location**, §74.

location = **enum**, §18.
max_obj = 66, §11.
name: **char** *[ ], §63.
note: **char** *[ ], §63.
note_ptr: **int**, §63.
NOTHING = 0, §11.
object = **enum**, §11.
offset: **int** [ ], §63.
place: **location** [ ], §63.
prop: **int** [ ], §63.
true = 1, §2.

69. Object data. Now it's time to build the object structures just defined.

We put the objects into their initial locations backwards, that is, highest first; moreover, we place all two-part objects before placing the others. Then low-numbered objects will appear first in the list, and two-part objects will appear last.

Here are the two-part objects, which are mostly unnamed because you won't be picking them up.

⟨ Build the object tables 69 ⟩ ≡
  new_obj (RUG_, 0, RUG, *scan3*);
  new_obj (RUG, "Persian␣rug", RUG, *scan1*);
  new_note ("There␣is␣a␣Persian␣rug␣spread␣out␣on␣the␣floor!");
  new_note ("The␣dragon␣is␣sprawled␣out␣on␣a␣Persian␣rug!!");
  new_obj (TROLL2_, 0, TROLL2, *limbo*);
  new_obj (TROLL2, 0, TROLL2, *limbo*);
  new_note ("The␣troll␣is␣nowhere␣to␣be␣seen.");
  new_obj (TROLL_, 0, TROLL, *neside*);
  new_obj (TROLL, 0, TROLL, *swside*);
  new_note ("A␣burly␣troll␣stands␣by␣the␣bridge␣\
          and␣insists␣you␣throw␣him␣a\n\
      treasure␣before␣you␣may␣cross.");
  new_note ("The␣troll␣steps␣out␣from␣beneath␣the␣bridge␣\
          and␣blocks␣your␣way.");
  new_note (0);
  new_obj (BRIDGE_, 0, BRIDGE, *neside*);
  new_obj (BRIDGE, 0, BRIDGE, *swside*);
  new_note ("A␣rickety␣wooden␣bridge␣extends␣across␣the␣chasm,␣\
          vanishing␣into␣the\n\
      mist.␣␣A␣sign␣posted␣on␣the␣bridge␣reads,␣\
          \"STOP!␣␣PAY␣TROLL!\"");
  new_note ("The␣wreckage␣of␣a␣bridge␣(and␣a␣dead␣bear)␣\
          can␣be␣seen␣at␣the␣bottom\n\
      of␣the␣chasm.");
  new_obj (DRAGON_, 0, DRAGON, *scan3*);
  new_obj (DRAGON, 0, DRAGON, *scan1*);
  new_note ("A␣huge␣green␣fierce␣dragon␣bars␣the␣way!");
  new_note ("Congratulations!␣␣\
          You␣have␣just␣vanquished␣a␣dragon␣with␣your␣bare\n\
      hands!␣(Unbelievable,␣isn't␣it?)");
  new_note ("The␣body␣of␣a␣huge␣green␣dead␣dragon␣\
          is␣lying␣off␣to␣one␣side.");
  new_obj (SHADOW_, 0, SHADOW, *window*);
  new_obj (SHADOW, 0, SHADOW, *windoe*);

new_note("The␣shadowy␣figure␣\
            seems␣to␣be␣trying␣to␣attract␣your␣attention.");
new_obj(PLANT2_, 0, PLANT2, *e2pit*);
new_obj(PLANT2, 0, PLANT2, *w2pit*);
new_note(0);
new_note("The␣top␣of␣a␣12-foot-tall␣beanstalk␣\
            is␣poking␣out␣of␣the␣west␣pit.");
new_note("There␣is␣a␣huge␣beanstalk␣\
            growing␣out␣of␣the␣west␣pit␣up␣to␣the␣hole.");
new_obj(CRYSTAL_, 0, CRYSTAL, *wfiss*);
new_obj(CRYSTAL, 0, CRYSTAL, *efiss*);
new_note(0);
new_note("A␣crystal␣bridge␣now␣spans␣the␣fissure.");
new_note("The␣crystal␣bridge␣has␣vanished!");
new_obj(TREADS_, 0, TREADS, *emist*);
new_obj(TREADS, 0, TREADS, *spit*);
new_note("Rough␣stone␣steps␣lead␣down␣the␣pit.");
new_note("Rough␣stone␣steps␣lead␣up␣the␣dome.");
new_obj(GRATE_, 0, GRATE, *inside*);
new_obj(GRATE, 0, GRATE, *outside*);
new_note("The␣grate␣is␣locked.");
new_note("The␣grate␣is␣open.");
new_obj(MIRROR_, 0, MIRROR, *limbo*);   /* joins up with MIRROR later */

See also section 70.

This code is used in section 200.

70.   And here are the one-place objects, some of which are immovable (because they are in a group of size one).

⟨ Build the object tables 69 ⟩ +≡
   new_obj(CHAIN, "Golden chain", CHAIN, *barr*);
   new_note("There is a golden chain lying in a heap on the floor!");
   new_note("The bear is locked to the wall with a golden chain!");
   new_note("There is a golden chain locked to the wall!");
   new_obj(SPICES, "Rare spices", 0, *chamber*);
   new_note("There are rare spices here!");
   new_obj(PEARL, "Glistening pearl", 0, *limbo*);
   new_note("Off to one side lies a glistening pearl!");
   new_obj(PYRAMID, "Platinum pyramid", 0, *droom*);
   new_note("There is a platinum pyramid here, 8 inches on a side!");
   new_obj(EMERALD, "Egg-sized emerald", 0, *proom*);
   new_note("There is an emerald here the size of a plover's egg!");
   new_obj(VASE, "Ming vase", 0, *oriental*);
   new_note("There is a delicate, precious, Ming vase here!");
   new_note("The vase is now resting, delicately, \
           on a velvet pillow.");
   new_note("The floor is littered \
           with worthless shards of pottery.");
   new_note("The Ming vase drops with a delicate crash.");
   new_obj(TRIDENT, "Jeweled trident", 0, *falls*);
   new_note("There is a jewel-encrusted trident here!");
   new_obj(EGGS, "Golden eggs", 0, *giant*);
   new_note("There is a large nest here, full of golden eggs!");
   new_note("The nest of golden eggs has vanished!");
   new_note("Done!");
   new_obj(CHEST, "Treasure chest", 0, *limbo*);
   new_note("The pirate's treasure chest is here!");
   new_obj(COINS, "Rare coins", 0, *west*);
   new_note("There are many coins here!");
   new_obj(JEWELS, "Precious jewelry", 0, *south*);
   new_note("There is precious jewelry here!");
   new_obj(SILVER, "Bars of silver", 0, *ns*);
   new_note("There are bars of silver here!");
   new_obj(DIAMONDS, "Several diamonds", 0, *wfiss*);
   new_note("There are diamonds here!");
   new_obj(GOLD, "Large gold nugget", 0, *nugget*);
   new_note("There is a large sparkling nugget of gold here!");
   new_obj(MOSS, 0, MOSS, *soft*); *new_note*(0);
   new_obj(BATTERIES, "Batteries", 0, *limbo*);
   new_note("There are fresh batteries here.");
   new_note("Some worn-out batteries have been discarded nearby.");

new_obj (PONY, 0, PONY, $pony$);
new_note ("There␣is␣a␣massive␣vending␣machine␣here.␣␣\
       The␣instructions␣on␣it␣read:\n\
   \"Drop␣coins␣here␣to␣receive␣fresh␣batteries.\"");
new_obj (GEYSER, 0, GEYSER, $view$); new_note (0);
new_obj (MESSAGE, 0, MESSAGE, $limbo$);
new_note ("There␣is␣a␣message␣scrawled␣in␣the␣dust␣\
       in␣a␣flowery␣script,␣reading:\n\
   \"This␣is␣not␣the␣maze␣where␣\
       the␣pirate␣leaves␣his␣treasure␣chest.\"");
new_obj (BEAR, 0, BEAR, $barr$);
new_note ("There␣is␣a␣ferocious␣cave␣bear␣\
       eying␣you␣from␣the␣far␣end␣of␣the␣room!");
new_note ("There␣is␣a␣gentle␣cave␣bear␣\
       sitting␣placidly␣in␣one␣corner.");
new_note ("There␣is␣a␣contented-looking␣bear␣\
       wandering␣about␣nearby.");
new_note (0);
new_obj (PIRATE, 0, PIRATE, $limbo$);
new_note (0);
new_obj (ART, 0, ART, $oriental$); new_note (0);
new_obj (AXE, "Dwarf's␣axe", 0, $limbo$);
new_note ("There␣is␣a␣little␣axe␣here.");
new_note ("There␣is␣a␣little␣axe␣lying␣beside␣the␣bear.");
new_obj (STALACTITE, 0, STALACTITE, $tite$); new_note (0);

---

70.   (continued)

```
new_obj (PLANT, 0, PLANT, wpit);
new_note ("There␣is␣a␣tiny␣little␣plant␣in␣the␣pit,␣\
        murmuring␣\"Water,␣water,␣...\"");
new_note ("The␣plant␣spurts␣into␣furious␣growth␣\
        for␣a␣few␣seconds.");
new_note ("There␣is␣a␣12-foot-tall␣beanstalk␣\
        stretching␣up␣out␣of␣the␣pit,\n\
    bellowing␣\"Water!!␣␣Water!!\"");
new_note ("The␣plant␣grows␣explosively,␣\
        almost␣filling␣the␣bottom␣of␣the␣pit.");
new_note ("There␣is␣a␣gigantic␣beanstalk␣\
        stretching␣all␣the␣way␣up␣to␣the␣hole.");
new_note ("You've␣over-watered␣the␣plant!␣␣\
        It's␣shriveling␣up!␣␣It's,␣it's...");
new_obj (MIRROR, 0, MIRROR, mirror);   new_note (0);
new_obj (OIL, "Oil␣in␣the␣bottle", 0, limbo);
new_obj (WATER, "Water␣in␣the␣bottle", 0, limbo);
new_obj (BOTTLE, "Small␣bottle", 0, house);
new_note ("There␣is␣a␣bottle␣of␣water␣here.");
new_note ("There␣is␣an␣empty␣bottle␣here.");
new_note ("There␣is␣a␣bottle␣of␣oil␣here.");
new_obj (FOOD, "Tasty␣food", 0, house);
new_note ("There␣is␣food␣here.");
new_obj (KNIFE, 0, 0, limbo);
new_obj (DWARF, 0, DWARF, limbo);
new_obj (MAG, "\"Spelunker␣Today\"", 0, ante);
new_note ("There␣are␣a␣few␣recent␣issues␣\
        of␣\"Spelunker␣Today\"␣magazine␣here.");
new_obj (OYSTER, "Giant␣oyster␣>GROAN!<", 0, limbo);
new_note ("There␣is␣an␣enormous␣oyster␣here␣\
        with␣its␣shell␣tightly␣closed.");
new_note ("Interesting.␣␣There␣seems␣to␣be␣\
        something␣written␣on␣the␣underside␣of\n\
    the␣oyster.");
new_obj (CLAM, "Giant␣clam␣>GRUNT!<", 0, shell);
new_note ("There␣is␣an␣enormous␣clam␣here␣\
        with␣its␣shell␣tightly␣closed.");
new_obj (TABLET, 0, TABLET, droom);
new_note ("A␣massive␣stone␣tablet␣embedded␣in␣the␣wall␣reads:\n\
    \"CONGRATULATIONS␣ON␣BRINGING␣LIGHT␣INTO␣THE␣DARK-ROOM!\"");
new_obj (SNAKE, 0, SNAKE, hmk);
new_note ("A␣huge␣green␣fierce␣snake␣bars␣the␣way!");
new_note (0);
```

new_obj (PILLOW, "Velvet␣pillow", 0, *soft*);
new_note ("A␣small␣velvet␣pillow␣lies␣on␣the␣floor.");
new_obj (DOOR, 0, DOOR, *immense*);
new_note ("The␣way␣north␣is␣barred␣by␣a␣\
            massive,␣rusty,␣iron␣door.");
new_note ("The␣way␣north␣leads␣through␣a␣\
            massive,␣rusty,␣iron␣door.");
new_obj (BIRD, "Little␣bird␣in␣cage", 0, *bird*);
new_note ("A␣cheerful␣little␣bird␣is␣sitting␣here␣singing.");
new_note ("There␣is␣a␣little␣bird␣in␣the␣cage.");
new_obj (ROD2, "Black␣rod", 0, *limbo*);
new_note ("A␣three-foot␣black␣rod␣\
            with␣a␣rusty␣mark␣on␣an␣end␣lies␣nearby.");
new_obj (ROD, "Black␣rod", 0, *debris*);
new_note ("A␣three-foot␣black␣rod␣\
            with␣a␣rusty␣star␣on␣an␣end␣lies␣nearby.");
new_obj (CAGE, "Wicker␣cage", 0, *cobbles*);
new_note ("There␣is␣a␣small␣wicker␣cage␣discarded␣nearby.");
new_obj (LAMP, "Brass␣lantern", 0, *house*);
new_note ("There␣is␣a␣shiny␣brass␣lamp␣nearby.");
new_note ("There␣is␣a␣lamp␣shining␣nearby.");
new_obj (KEYS, "Set␣of␣keys", 0, *house*);
new_note ("There␣are␣some␣keys␣on␣the␣ground␣here.");

71.　Low-level input.　Sometimes we need to ask you a question, for which the answer is either yes or no. The subroutine $yes(q, y, n)$ prints q, waits for you to answer, and then prints y or n depending on your answer. It returns a nonzero value if your answer was affirmative.

⟨Subroutines 6⟩ +≡
```
boolean yes ARGS((char *, char *, char *));
boolean yes(q, y, n)
    char *q, *y, *n;
{
    while (1) {
        printf("%s\n\
            **␣", q); fflush(stdout);
        fgets(buffer, buf_size, stdin);
        if (tolower(*buffer) ≡ 'y') {
            if (y) printf("%s\n", y); return true;
        }
        else if (tolower(*buffer) ≡ 'n') {
            if (n) printf("%s\n", n); return false;
        }
        else printf("␣Please␣answer␣Yes␣or␣No.\n");
    }
}
```

72.　The only other kind of input is almost as simple. You are supposed to tell us what to do next in your adventure, by typing one- or two-word commands. We put the first word in *word1* and the (possibly null) second word in *word2*. Words are separated by white space; otherwise white space is ignored.

⟨Subroutines 6⟩ +≡
```
void listen ARGS((void));
void listen() {
    register char *p, *q;
    while (1) {
        printf("*␣"); fflush(stdout);
        fgets(buffer, buf_size, stdin);
        for (p = buffer; isspace(*p); p++) ;
        if (*p ≡ 0) {
            printf("␣Tell␣me␣to␣do␣something.\n"); continue;
        }
        for (q = word1; *p; p++, q++) {
            if (isspace(*p)) break;
            *q = tolower(*p);
        }
```

```
*q = '\0';      /* end of word1 */
for (p++; isspace(*p); p++) ;
if (*p ≡ 0) {
  *word2 = '\0'; return;
}
for (q = word2; *p; p++, q++) {
  if (isspace(*p)) break;
  *q = tolower(*p);
}
*q = '\0';      /* end of word2 */
for (p++; isspace(*p); p++) ;
if (*p ≡ 0) return;
printf("␣Please␣stick␣to␣1-␣and␣2-word␣commands.\n");
  }
}
```

73. A 20-character buffer would probably be big enough, but what the heck.

#**define** *buf_size*   72

⟨ Global variables 7 ⟩ +≡
   char *buffer* [*buf_size*];   /* your input goes here */
   char *word1* [*buf_size*], *word2* [*buf_size*];
     /* and then we snarf it to here */

ARGS = macro ( ), §3.
boolean = **enum**, §2.
false = 0, §2.
fflush: **int** ( ), <stdio.h>.
fgets: **char** *( ), <stdio.h>.
isspace: **int** ( ), <ctype.h>.

printf: **int** ( ), <stdio.h>.
stdin: **FILE** *, <stdio.h>.
stdout: **FILE** *, <stdio.h>.
tolower: **int** ( ), <ctype.h>.
true = 1, §2.

74.   The main control loop.   Now we've got enough low-level mechanisms in place to start thinking of the program from the top down, and to specify the high-level control.

A global variable *loc* represents where you currently live in the simulated cave. Another variable *newloc* represents where you will go next, unless something like a dwarf blocks you. We also keep track of *oldloc* (the previous value of *loc*) and *oldoldloc* (the previous previous value), for use when you ask to 'go back'.

#define *here*(t)   (*toting*(t) ∨ *place*[t] ≡ *loc*)   /* is object *t* present? */
#define *water_here*   ((*flags*[*loc*] & (*liquid* + *oil*)) ≡ *liquid*)
#define *oil_here*   ((*flags*[*loc*] & (*liquid* + *oil*)) ≡ *liquid* + *oil*)
#define *no_liquid_here*   ((*flags*[*loc*] & *liquid*) ≡ 0)

⟨ Global variables 7 ⟩ +≡
   location *oldoldloc*, *oldloc*, *loc*, *newloc*;
      /* recent and future locations */

75.   Here is our overall strategy for administering the game. It is understood that the program might **goto** *quit* from within any of the subsections named here, even though the section names don't mention this explicitly. For example, while checking for interference we might find out that time has run out, or that a dwarf has killed you and no more reincarnations are possible.

The execution consists of two nested loops: There are "minor cycles" inside of "major cycles." Actions define minor cycles in which you stay in the same place and we tell you the result of your action. Motions define major cycles in which you move and we tell you what you can see at the new place.

⟨ Simulate an adventure, going to *quit* when finished 75 ⟩ ≡
   while (1) {
      ⟨ Check for interference with the proposed move to *newloc* 153 ⟩;
      loc = *newloc*;   /* hey, we actually moved you */
      ⟨ Possibly move dwarves and the pirate 161 ⟩;
   commence: ⟨ Report the current state 86 ⟩;
      while (1) {
         ⟨ Get user input; **goto** *try_move* if motion is requested 76 ⟩;
         ⟨ Perform an action in the current place 79 ⟩;
      }
   try_move: ⟨ Handle special motion words 140 ⟩;
      oldoldloc = *oldloc*;
      oldloc = *loc*;
   go_for_it: ⟨ Determine the next location, *newloc* 146 ⟩;
   }

This code is used in section 2.

flags: **int** [], §20.
liquid = 4, §20.
location = **enum**, §18.
oil = 2, §20.

place: **location** [], §63.
quit: label, §2.
toting = macro ( ), §63.

76.   Our main task in the simulation loop is to parse your input. Depending on the kind of command you give, the following section of the program will exit in one of four ways:

- **goto** *try_move* with *mot* set to a desired motion.

- **goto** *transitive* with *verb* set to a desired action and *obj* set to the object of that action.

- **goto** *intransitive* with *verb* set to a desired action and *obj* = NOTHING; no object has been specified.

- **goto** *speakit* with *hash_table*[*k*].*meaning* the index of a message for a vocabulary word of *message_type*.

Sometimes we have to ask you to complete an ambiguous command before we know both a verb and its object. In most cases the words can be in either order; for example, 'take rod' is equivalent to 'rod take'. A motion word overrides a previously given action or object.

Lots of special cases make the program a bit messy. For example, if the verb is 'say', we don't want to look up the object in our vocabulary; we simply want to "say" it.

⟨ Get user input; **goto** *try_move* if motion is requested 76 ⟩ ≡
   verb = *oldverb* = ABSTAIN;
   oldobj = *obj*;
   obj = NOTHING;
cycle: ⟨ Check if a hint applies, and give it if requested 195 ⟩;
   ⟨ Make special adjustments before looking at new input 85 ⟩;
   listen( );
pre_parse: *turns* ++;
   ⟨ Handle special cases of input 82 ⟩;
   ⟨ Check the clocks and the lamp 178 ⟩;
   ⟨ Handle additional special cases of input 83 ⟩;
parse: ⟨ Give advice about going WEST 80 ⟩;
   ⟨ Look at *word1* and exit to the right place if it completes a command 78 ⟩;
shift: *strcpy*(*word1*, *word2*); *word2* = '\0'; **goto** *parse*;

This code is used in section 75.

77.   ⟨ Global variables 7 ⟩ +≡
   motion *mot*;   /* currently specified motion, if any */
   action *verb*;   /* currently specified action, if any */
   action *oldverb*;   /* *verb* before it was changed */
   object *obj*;   /* currently specified object, if any */
   object *oldobj*;   /* former value of *obj* */
   wordtype *command_type*;   /* type of word found in hash table */
   int *turns*;   /* how many times we've read your commands */

78.   The *try_motion* macro is often used to end a major cycle.

#define *try_motion*(*m*) { *mot* = *m*; **goto** *try_move*; }
#define *stay_put*   *try_motion*(NOWHERE)

⟨ Look at *word1* and exit to the right place if it completes a command 78 ⟩ ≡
    k = *lookup*(*word1*);
    if (*k* < 0) {   /* Gee, I don't understand */
        printf("Sorry,␣I␣don't␣know␣the␣word␣\"%s\".\n", *word1*);
        goto *cycle*;
    }
branch: *command_type* = *hash_table*[*k*].*word_type*;
    switch (*command_type*) {
    case *motion_type*: *try_motion*(*hash_table*[*k*].*meaning*);
    case *object_type*: *obj* = *hash_table*[*k*].*meaning*;
        ⟨ Make sure *obj* is meaningful at the current location 90 ⟩;
        if (*word2) **break**;   /* fall through to *shift* */
        if (*verb*) **goto** *transitive*;
        printf("What␣do␣you␣want␣to␣do␣with␣the␣%s?\n", *word1*);
        goto *cycle*;
    case *action_type*: *verb* = *hash_table*[*k*].*meaning*;
        if (*verb* ≡ SAY) *obj* = *word2;
        else if (*word2) **break**;   /* fall through to *shift* */
        if (*obj*) **goto** *transitive*; **else goto** *intransitive*;
    case *message_type*: **goto** *speakit*;
    }

This code is used in section 76.

---

79.   Here is the multiway branch where many kinds of actions can be launched.

If a verb can only be transitive, but no object has been given, we must go back and ask for an object.

If a verb can only be intransitive, but an object has been given, we issue the default message for that verb and start over.

The variable k, initially zero, is used to count various things in several of the action routines.

The *report* macro is often used to end a minor cycle.

#**define** *report*(m)   { *printf*("%s\n", m); **continue**; }
#**define** *default_to*(v)   *report*(*default_msg*[v])
#**define** *change_to*(v)   { *oldverb* = *verb*; *verb* = v; **goto** *transitive*; }

⟨ Perform an action in the current place 79 ⟩ ≡
intransitive: $k = 0$;
  switch (*verb*) {
  case GO: **case** RELAX: **goto** *report_default*;
  case ON: **case** OFF: **case** POUR: **case** FILL: **case** DRINK: **case** BLAST:
    case KILL: **goto** *transitive*;
    ⟨ Handle cases of intransitive verbs and **continue** 92 ⟩;
  default: **goto** *get_object*;
  }
transitive: $k = 0$;
  switch (*verb*) {
  ⟨ Handle cases of transitive verbs and **continue** 97 ⟩;
  default: **goto** *report_default*;
  }
speakit: *report*(*message*[*hash_table*[k].*meaning*]);
report_default: **if** (*default_msg*[*verb*]) *report*(*default_msg*[*verb*]) **else**
  continue;
get_object: *word1*[0] = *toupper*(*word1*[0]);
  printf("%s␣what?\n", *word1*); **goto** *cycle*;
cant_see_it: **if** ((*verb* ≡ FIND ∨ *verb* ≡ INVENTORY) ∧ *word2* ≡ '\0')
  goto *transitive*;
  printf("I␣see␣no␣%s␣here.\n", *word1*); **continue**;

This code is used in section 75.

80.   Here's a freely offered hint that may save you typing.

⟨ Give advice about going WEST 80 ⟩ ≡
  if (*streq*(*word1*, "west")) {
    if (++*west_count* ≡ 10)
      printf("␣If␣you␣prefer,␣simply␣type␣W␣rather␣than␣WEST.\n");
  }

This code is used in section 76.

81. ⟨ Global variables 7 ⟩ +≡
  int *west_count*;
    /∗ how many times have we parsed the word 'west'? ∗/

82. Maybe you said 'say' and we said 'Say what?' and you replied with two things to say. Then we assume you don't really want us to say anything.

⟨ Handle special cases of input 82 ⟩ ≡
  if (*verb* ≡ SAY) {
    if (∗*word2*) *verb* = ABSTAIN; **else goto** *transitive*;
  }

See also section 138.

This code is used in section 76.

83. The verb 'enter' is listed in our vocabulary as a motion rather than an action. Here we deal with cases where you try to use it as an action. Notice that 'H2O' is not a synonym for 'water' in this context.

⟨ Handle additional special cases of input 83 ⟩ ≡
  if (*streq*(*word1*, "enter")) {
    if (*streq*(*word2*, "water") ∨ *streq*(*word2*, "strea")) {
      if (*water_here*) *report*("Your␣feet␣are␣now␣wet.");
      default_to(GO);
    }
    else if (∗*word2*) **goto** *shift*;
  }

See also section 105.

This code is used in section 76.

ABSTAIN = 0, §13.
BLAST, see §99.
cycle: label, §76.
default_msg: **char** ∗[], §15.
DRINK, see §106.
FILL, see §110.
FIND, see §100.
GO = 9, §13.
GO, see §79.
hash_table: **hash_entry** [], §7.
INVENTORY, see §94 and §100.
k: **register int**, §2.
KILL, see §125.
meaning: **char**, §5.
message: **char** ∗[], §17.

OFF, see §102.
oldverb: **action**, §77.
ON, see §102.
POUR, see §107.
printf: **int** ( ), <stdio.h>.
RELAX = 10, §13.
RELAX, see §14.
SAY, see §97.
shift: label, §76.
streq = macro ( ), §8.
toupper: **int** ( ), <ctype.h>.
verb: **action**, §77.
water_here = macro, §74.
word1: **char** [], §73.
word2: **char** [], §73.

84.   Cavers can become cadavers if they don't have light. We keep a variable *was_dark* to remember how dark things were when you gave your last command.

#define   *dark* $((flags[loc] \, \& \, lighted) \equiv 0 \wedge (prop[\text{LAMP}] \equiv 0 \vee \neg here(\text{LAMP})))$

⟨ Global variables 7 ⟩ +≡
    boolean *was_dark*;   /* you've recently been in the dark */

85.   ⟨ Make special adjustments before looking at new input 85 ⟩ ≡
    was_dark = *dark*;

See also sections 158, 169, and 182.

This code is used in section 76.

86.   After moving to *newloc*, we act as your eyes. We print the long description of *newloc* if you haven't been there before; but when you return to a previously seen place, we often use a short form. The long form is used every 5th time, unless you say 'BRIEF', in which case we use the shortest form we know. You can always ask for the long form by saying 'LOOK'.

⟨ Report the current state 86 ⟩ ≡
    if $(loc \equiv limbo)$ **goto** *death*;
    if $(dark \wedge \neg forced\_move(loc))$ {
        if $(was\_dark \wedge pct(35))$ **goto** *pitch_dark*;
        $p = pitch\_dark\_msg$;
    }
    else if $(short\_desc[loc] \equiv 0 \vee visits[loc] \, \% \, interval \equiv 0)$ $p = long\_desc[loc]$;
    else $p = short\_desc[loc]$;
    if $(toting(\text{BEAR}))$
        printf ("You␣are␣being␣followed␣by␣a␣very␣large,␣tame␣bear.\n");
    if (p) *printf* ("\n\
        %s\n", p);
    if $(forced\_move(loc))$ **goto** *try_move*;
    ⟨ Give optional **plugh** hint 157 ⟩;
    if $(\neg dark)$ ⟨ Describe the objects at this location 88 ⟩;

This code is used in section 75.

87.   ⟨ Global variables 7 ⟩ +≡
    int *interval* = 5;   /* will change to 10000 if you want us to be BRIEF */
    char *pitch_dark_msg*[ ] = "It␣is␣now␣pitch␣dark.␣␣\
        If␣you␣proceed␣you␣will␣most␣likely␣fall␣into␣a␣pit.";

88.   If TREADS are present but you have a heavy load, we don't describe them. The treads never actually get property value 1; we use the *note* for property 1 only when they are seen from above.

The global variable *tally* counts the number of treasures you haven't seen. Another variable, *lost_treasures*, counts those you never will see.

⟨ Describe the objects at this location 88 ⟩ ≡
    { **register object** *tt*;

    visits[*loc*]++;
    for (*t* = *first*[*loc*]; *t*; *t* = *link*[*t*]) {
        tt = (*base*[*t*] ? *base*[*t*] : *t*);
        if (*prop*[*tt*] < 0) {   /∗ you've spotted a treasure ∗/
            if (*closed*) **continue**;
                /∗ no automatic *prop* change after hours ∗/
            prop[*tt*] = (*tt* ≡ RUG ∨ *tt* ≡ CHAIN);
                /∗ initialize the property value ∗/
            tally −−;
            ⟨ Zap the lamp if the remaining treasures are too elusive 183 ⟩;
        }
        if (*tt* ≡ TREADS ∧ *toting*(GOLD)) **continue**;
        p = *note*[*prop*[*tt*] + *offset*[*tt*] + (*tt* ≡ TREADS ∧ *loc* ≡ *emist*)];
        if (*p*) *printf*("%s\n", *p*);
    }
}

This code is used in section 86.

89.   ⟨ Global variables 7 ⟩ +≡
    int *tally* = 15;   /∗ treasures awaiting you ∗/
    int *lost_treasures*;   /∗ treasures that you won't find ∗/

---

base: **object** [], §63.
BEAR = 45, §11.
boolean = **enum**, §2.
BRIEF, see §95.
CHAIN = 66, §11.
closed: **boolean**, §177.
death: label, §189.
emist = 15, §18, §32.
first: **object** [], §63.
flags: **int** [], §20.
forced_move = macro ( ), §59.
GOLD = 51, §11.
here = macro ( ), §74.
LAMP = 2, §11.
lighted = 1, §20.
limbo = 0, §18.
link: **object** [], §63.
loc: **location**, §74.

long_desc: **char** ∗[], §20.
LOOK = 24, §9.
newloc: **location**, §74.
note: **char** ∗[], §63.
object = **enum**, §11.
offset: **int** [], §63.
p: **register char** ∗, §2.
pct = macro ( ), §157.
pitch_dark: label, §188.
printf: **int** ( ), <stdio.h>.
prop: **int** [], §63.
RUG = 63, §11.
short_desc: **char** ∗[], §20.
t: **register object**, §68.
toting = macro ( ), §63.
TREADS = 8, §11.
try_move: label, §75.
visits: **int** [], §20.

90.   When you specify an object, it must be at the current location, unless the verb is already known to be FIND or INVENTORY. A few other special cases also are permitted; for example, water and oil are funny, since they are never actually dropped at any location, but they might be present inside the bottle or as a feature of the location.

#define   *object_in_bottle*
$$((obj \equiv \text{WATER} \wedge prop\,[\text{BOTTLE}] \equiv 0) \vee (obj \equiv \text{OIL} \wedge prop\,[\text{BOTTLE}] \equiv 2))$$

⟨ Make sure *obj* is meaningful at the current location 90 ⟩ ≡

```
if (¬toting(obj) ∧ ¬is_at_loc(obj))
    switch (obj) {
    case GRATE: ⟨If GRATE is actually a motion word, move to it 91⟩;
        goto cant_see_it;
    case DWARF: if (dflag ≥ 2 ∧ dwarf()) break; else goto cant_see_it;
    case PLANT: if (is_at_loc(PLANT2) ∧ prop[PLANT2]) {
            obj = PLANT2; break;
        }
        else goto cant_see_it;
    case KNIFE: if (loc ≠ knife_loc) goto cant_see_it;
        knife_loc = −1;
        report("The⎵dwarves'⎵knives⎵vanish⎵\
                as⎵they⎵strike⎵the⎵walls⎵of⎵the⎵cave.");
    case ROD: if (¬here(ROD2)) goto cant_see_it;
        obj = ROD2; break;
    case WATER: case OIL: if (here(BOTTLE) ∧ object_in_bottle) break;
        if ((obj ≡ WATER ∧ water_here) ∨ (obj ≡ OIL ∧ oil_here)) break;
    default: goto cant_see_it;
    }
```

This code is used in section 78.

91.   Henning Makholm has pointed out that the logic here makes GRATE a motion word regardless of the verb. For example, you can get to the grate by saying 'wave grate' from the *road* or the *valley* (but curiously not from the *slit*).

⟨ If GRATE is actually a motion word, move to it 91 ⟩ ≡

```
if (loc < min_lower_loc)
    switch (loc) {
    case road: case valley: case slit: try_motion(DEPRESSION);
    case cobbles: case debris: case awk: case bird: case spit:
        try_motion(ENTRANCE);
    default: break;
    }
```

This code is used in section 90.

92. Simple verbs. Let's get experience implementing the actions by dispensing with the easy cases first.

First there are several "intransitive" verbs that reduce to transitive when we identify an appropriate object. For example, 'take' makes sense by itself if there's only one possible thing to take.

⟨ Handle cases of intransitive verbs and **continue** 92 ⟩ ≡
  case TAKE: **if** (*first* [*loc*] ≡ 0 ∨ *link* [*first* [*loc*]] ∨ *dwarf* ( )) **goto** *get_object*;
    obj = *first* [*loc*]; **goto** *transitive*;

  case EAT: **if** (¬*here*(FOOD)) **goto** *get_object*;
    obj = FOOD; **goto** *transitive*;

See also sections 93, 94, 95, and 136.

This code is used in section 79.

---

awk = 12, §18, §31.
bird = 13, §18, §31.
BOTTLE = 23, §11.
cant_see_it: label, §79.
cobbles = 10, §18, §31.
debris = 11, §18, §31.
DEPRESSION = 32, §9.
dflag: **int**, §159.
DWARF = 20, §11.
dwarf: **boolean** ( ), §160.
EAT = 12, §13.
EAT, see §98.
ENTRANCE = 33, §9.
FIND, see §100.
first: **object** [], §63.
FOOD = 22, §11.
get_object: label, §79.
GRATE = 3, §11.
here = macro ( ), §74.
INVENTORY, see §94 and §100.
is_at_loc: **boolean** ( ), §66.
KNIFE = 21, §11.
knife_loc: **int**, §168.

link: **object** [], §63.
loc: **location**, §74.
min_lower_loc = 15, §18.
obj: **object**, §77.
OIL = 25, §11.
oil_here = macro, §74.
PLANT = 28, §11.
PLANT2 = 29, §11.
prop: **int** [], §63.
report = macro ( ), §79.
road = 1, §18, §23.
ROD = 6, §11.
ROD2 = 7, §11.
slit = 7, §18, §28.
spit = 14, §18, §31.
TAKE = 1, §13.
TAKE, see §112.
toting = macro ( ), §63.
transitive: label, §79.
try_motion = macro ( ), §78.
valley = 4, §18, §26.
WATER = 24, §11.
water_here = macro, §74.

93.   Only the objects GRATE, DOOR, CLAM/OYSTER, and CHAIN can be opened or closed. And only a few objects can be read.

⟨ Handle cases of intransitive verbs and **continue** 92 ⟩ +≡
case OPEN: **case** CLOSE: **if** (*place*[GRATE] ≡ *loc* ∨ *place*[GRATE_] ≡ *loc*)
   obj = GRATE;
  else if (*place*[DOOR] ≡ *loc*) *obj* = DOOR;
  else if (*here*(CLAM)) *obj* = CLAM;
  else if (*here*(OYSTER)) *obj* = OYSTER;
  if (*here*(CHAIN)) {
    if (*obj*) **goto** *get_object*; **else** *obj* = CHAIN;
  }
  if (*obj*) **goto** *transitive*;
  report("There␣is␣nothing␣here␣with␣a␣lock!");
case READ: **if** (*dark*) **goto** *get_object*;   /* can't read in the dark */
  if (*here*(MAG)) *obj* = MAG;
  if (*here*(TABLET)) {
    if (*obj*) **goto** *get_object*; **else** *obj* = TABLET;
  }
  if (*here*(MESSAGE)) {
    if (*obj*) **goto** *get_object*; **else** *obj* = MESSAGE;
  }
  if (*closed* ∧ *toting*(OYSTER)) *obj* = OYSTER;
  if (*obj*) **goto** *transitive*; **else goto** *get_object*;

94.   A request for an inventory is pretty simple too.

⟨ Handle cases of intransitive verbs and **continue** 92 ⟩ +≡
case INVENTORY: **for** (*t* = 1; *t* ≤ *max_obj*; *t*++)
  if (*toting*(*t*) ∧ (*base*[*t*] ≡ NOTHING ∨ *base*[*t*] ≡ *t*) ∧ *t* ≠ BEAR) {
    if (*k* ≡ 0)
      k = 1, *printf*("You␣are␣currently␣holding␣the␣following:\n");
    printf("␣%s\n", *name*[*t*]);
  }
  if (*toting*(BEAR))
    report("You␣are␣being␣followed␣by␣a␣very␣large,␣tame␣bear.");
  if (*k* ≡ 0) *report*("You're␣not␣carrying␣anything.");
  continue;

95.   Here are other requests about the mechanics of the game.

⟨ Handle cases of intransitive verbs and **continue** 92 ⟩ +≡

case BRIEF: *interval* = 10000;
    look_count = 3;
    report ("Okay,␣from␣now␣on␣\
        I'll␣only␣describe␣a␣place␣in␣full␣the␣first␣time\n\
    you␣come␣to␣it.␣␣To␣get␣the␣full␣description,␣say␣\"LOOK\".");

case SCORE: *printf* ("If␣you␣were␣to␣quit␣now,␣you␣would␣score␣%d\n\
    out␣of␣a␣possible␣%d.\n", *score* ( ) − 4, *max_score*);
  if (¬*yes* ("Do␣you␣indeed␣wish␣to␣quit␣now?", *ok*, *ok*)) **continue**;
  goto *give_up*;

case QUIT: **if** (¬*yes* ("Do␣you␣really␣want␣to␣quit␣now?", *ok*, *ok*))
    continue;
give_up: *gave_up* = *true*; **goto** *quit*;

96.   ⟨ Global variables 7 ⟩ +≡
  boolean *gave_up*;   /* did you quit while you were alive? */

---

97.   The SAY routine is just an echo unless you say a magic word.

⟨ Handle cases of transitive verbs and **continue** 97 ⟩ ≡

case SAY: **if** (*word2*) *strcpy* (*word1* , *word2*);
  k = *lookup* (*word1*);
  switch (*hash_table* [*k*].*meaning*) {
  case FEEFIE:
    if (*hash_table* [*k*].*word_type* ≠ *action_type*) **break**;
  case XYZZY: **case** PLUGH: **case** PLOVER:
    word2 = '\0'; *obj* = NOTHING; **goto** *branch*;
  default: **break**;
  }
  printf ("Okay,␣\"%s\".\n", *word1*); **continue**;

See also sections 98, 99, 100, 101, 102, 106, 107, 110, 112, 117, 122, 125, 129, 130,
    and 135.

This code is used in section 79.

98.   Hungry?

⟨ Handle cases of transitive verbs and **continue** 97 ⟩ +≡

case EAT: **switch** (*obj*) {
  case FOOD: *destroy* (FOOD);
    report ("Thank␣you,␣it␣was␣delicious!");
  case BIRD: **case** SNAKE: **case** CLAM: **case** OYSTER: **case** DWARF:
    case DRAGON: **case** TROLL: **case** BEAR:
    report ("I␣think␣I␣just␣lost␣my␣appetite.");
  default: **goto** *report_default*;   /* see §14 for *default_msg* [EAT] */
  }

99.   Waving to the shadowy figure has no effect; but you might wave
a rod at the fissure. Blasting has no effect unless you've got dynamite,
which is a neat trick! Rubbing yields only snide remarks.

⟨ Handle cases of transitive verbs and **continue** 97 ⟩ +≡

case WAVE: **if** (*obj* ≠ ROD ∨ (*loc* ≠ *efiss* ∧ *loc* ≠ *wfiss*) ∨
        ¬*toting* (*obj*) ∨ *closing*) {
    if (*toting* (*obj*) ∨ (*obj* ≡ ROD ∧ *toting* (ROD2))) **goto** *report_default*;
    default_to (DROP);
  }
  prop [CRYSTAL] = 1 − *prop* [CRYSTAL];
  report (*note* [*offset* [CRYSTAL] + 2 − *prop* [CRYSTAL]]);

case BLAST: **if** (*closed* ∧ *prop* [ROD2] ≥ 0) {
    bonus = (*here* (ROD2) ? 25 : *loc* ≡ *neend* ? 30 : 45);
    printf ("%s\n", *message* [*bonus* /5]); **goto** *quit*;
  }
  else goto *report_default*;

case RUB: **if** (*obj* ≡ LAMP) **goto** *report_default*;

$report$("Peculiar.␣␣Nothing␣unexpected␣happens.");

100. If asked to find an object that isn't visible, we give a caveat.

⟨ Handle cases of transitive verbs and **continue** 97 ⟩ +≡

  case FIND: **case** INVENTORY: **if** ($toting(obj)$) $default\_to$(TAKE);
    if (*closed*)
      $report$("I␣daresay␣whatever␣you␣want␣is␣around␣here␣somewhere.");
    if ($is\_at\_loc(obj)$ ∨ ($object\_in\_bottle$ ∧ $place$[BOTTLE] ≡ loc) ∨
        (obj ≡ WATER ∧ $water\_here$) ∨ (obj ≡ OIL ∧ oil_here) ∨
        (obj ≡ DWARF ∧ $dwarf$()))
      $report$("I␣believe␣what␣you␣want␣is␣right␣here␣with␣you.");
    goto $report\_default$;

$action\_type = 3$, §5.
BEAR $= 45$, §11.
BIRD $= 10$, §11.
BLAST $= 20$, §13.
$bonus$: **int**, §193.
BOTTLE $= 23$, §11.
$branch$: **label**, §78.
CLAM $= 17$, §11.
$closed$: **boolean**, §177.
$closing$ = macro, §177.
CRYSTAL $= 14$, §11.
$default\_msg$: **char** *[], §15.
$default\_to$ = macro ( ), §79.
$destroy$ = macro ( ), §65.
DRAGON $= 37$, §11.
DROP, see §117.
DWARF $= 20$, §11.
$dwarf$: **boolean** ( ), §160.
EAT $= 12$, §13.
EAT, see §92.
$efiss = 17$, §18, §34.
FEEFIE $= 24$, §13.
FEEFIE, see §136.
FIND $= 26$, §13.
FOOD $= 22$, §11.
$hash\_table$: **hash_entry** [], §7.
$here$ = macro ( ), §74.
INVENTORY $= 27$, §13.
INVENTORY, see §94.
$is\_at\_loc;$ **boolean** ( ), §66.
k: **register int**, §2.
LAMP $= 2$, §11.
loc: **location**, §74.
$lookup$: **int** ( ), §8.
$meaning$: **char**, §5.

$message$: **char** *[], §17.
$neend = 127$, §18, §58.
$note$: **char** *[], §63.
NOTHING $= 0$, §11.
obj: **object**, §77.
$object\_in\_bottle$ = macro, §90.
$offset$: **int** [], §63.
OIL $= 25$, §11.
oil_here = macro, §74.
OYSTER $= 18$, §11.
$place$: **location** [], §63.
PLOVER $= 72$, §9.
PLUGH $= 71$, §9.
$printf$: **int** ( ), **<stdio.h>**.
$prop$: **int** [], §63.
$quit$: **label**, §2.
$report$ = macro ( ), §79.
$report\_default$: **label**, §79.
ROD $= 6$, §11.
ROD2 $= 7$, §11.
RUB $= 14$, §13.
SAY $= 22$, §13.
SNAKE $= 13$, §11.
$strcpy$: **char** *( ), **<string.h>**.
TAKE, see §92 and §112.
$toting$ = macro ( ), §63.
TROLL $= 41$, §11.
WATER $= 24$, §11.
$water\_here$ = macro, §74.
WAVE $= 7$, §13.
$wfiss = 18$, §18, §34.
$word\_type$: **char**, §5.
$word1$: **char** [], §73.
$word2$: **char** [], §73.
XYZZY $= 70$, §9.

101.   Breaking and/or waking have no effect until the cave is closed, except of course that you might break the vase. The dwarves like mirrors and hate being awakened.

⟨ Handle cases of transitive verbs and **continue** 97 ⟩ +≡
case BREAK: **if** $(obj \equiv$ VASE $\wedge\ prop[$VASE$] \equiv 0)$ {
    printf ("You␣have␣taken␣the␣vase␣\
             and␣hurled␣it␣delicately␣to␣the␣ground.\n");
  smash: **if** (*toting* (VASE)) *drop* (VASE, *loc*);   /* crash */
    prop[VASE] = 2; *base*[VASE] = VASE; **continue**;
      /* it's no longer movable */
}
else if $(obj \neq$ MIRROR) **goto** *report_default*;
if (*closed*) {
  printf ("You␣strike␣the␣mirror␣a␣resounding␣blow,␣\
          whereupon␣it␣shatters␣into␣a\n\
      myriad␣tiny␣fragments."); **goto** *dwarves_upset*;
}
report ("It␣is␣too␣far␣up␣for␣you␣to␣reach.");
case WAKE: **if** (*closed* $\wedge\ obj \equiv$ DWARF) {
  printf ("You␣prod␣the␣nearest␣dwarf,␣\
         who␣wakes␣up␣grumpily,␣takes␣one␣look␣at\n\
    you,␣curses,␣and␣grabs␣for␣his␣axe.\n"); **goto** *dwarves_upset*;
}
else goto *report_default*;

102.   Here we deal with lighting or extinguishing the lamp. The variable *limit* tells how much juice you've got left.

⟨ Handle cases of transitive verbs and **continue** 97 ⟩ +≡
case ON: **if** (¬*here* (LAMP)) **goto** *report_default*;
  if (*limit* < 0) *report* ("Your␣lamp␣has␣run␣out␣of␣power.");
  prop[LAMP] = 1;
  printf ("Your␣lamp␣is␣now␣on.\n");
  if (*was_dark*) **goto** *commence*;
  continue;
case OFF: **if** (¬*here* (LAMP)) **goto** *report_default*;
  prop[LAMP] = 0;
  printf ("Your␣lamp␣is␣now␣off.\n");
  if (*dark*) *printf* ("%s\n", *pitch_dark_msg*);
  continue;

103.   ⟨ Global variables 7 ⟩ +≡
  int *limit*;   /* countdown till darkness */

104. Liquid assets. Readers of this program will already have noticed that the BOTTLE is a rather complicated object, since it can be empty or filled with either water or oil. Let's consider now the main actions that involve liquids.

When you are carrying a bottle full of water, *place*[WATER] will be *inhand*; hence both *toting*(WATER) and *toting*(BOTTLE) are true. A similar remark applies to a bottle full of oil.

The value of *prop*[BOTTLE] is 0 if it holds water, 2 if it holds oil, otherwise either 1 or -2. (The value -2 is used after closing the cave.)

#define *bottle_empty*   ($prop$[BOTTLE] $\equiv 1 \vee prop$[BOTTLE] < 0)

105. Sometimes 'water' and 'oil' are used as verbs.

⟨ Handle additional special cases of input 83 ⟩ $+\equiv$
  if (($streq$($word1$, "water") $\vee$ $streq$($word1$, "oil")) $\wedge$
        ($streq$($word2$, "plant") $\vee$ $streq$($word2$, "door")) $\wedge$
        ($loc \equiv place$[$hash\_table$[$lookup$($word2$)].$meaning$]))
    $strcpy$($word2$, "pour");

---

base: **object** [], §63.
BOTTLE $= 23$, §11.
BREAK $= 19$, §13.
closed: **boolean**, §177.
commence: label, §75.
dark $=$ macro, §84.
drop: **void** ( ), §64.
DWARF $= 20$, §11.
dwarves_upset: label, §192.
hash_table: **hash_entry** [], §7.
here $=$ macro ( ), §74.
inhand $= -1$, §18.
LAMP $= 2$, §11.
loc: **location**, §74.
lookup: **int** ( ), §8.
meaning: **char**, §5.
MIRROR $= 26$, §11.
obj: **object**, §77.

OFF $= 6$, §13.
ON $= 5$, §13.
pitch_dark_msg: **char** [], §87.
place: **location** [], §63.
printf: **int** ( ), <stdio.h>.
prop: **int** [], §63.
report $=$ macro ( ), §79.
report_default: label, §79.
strcpy: **char** *( ), <string.h>.
streq $=$ macro ( ), §8.
toting $=$ macro ( ), §63.
VASE $= 59$, §11.
WAKE $= 16$, §13.
was_dark: **boolean**, §84.
WATER $= 24$, §11.
word1: **char** [], §73.
word2: **char** [], §73.

106. If you ask simply to drink, we assume that you want water. If there's water in the bottle, you drink that; otherwise you must be at a water location.

⟨ Handle cases of transitive verbs and **continue** 97 ⟩ +≡
```
case DRINK: if (obj ≡ NOTHING) {
    if (¬water_here ∧ ¬(here(BOTTLE) ∧ prop[BOTTLE] ≡ 0)) goto get_object;
  }
  else if (obj ≠ WATER) default_to(EAT);
  if (¬(here(BOTTLE) ∧ prop[BOTTLE] ≡ 0)) goto report_default;
  prop[BOTTLE] = 1; place[WATER] = limbo;
  report("The␣bottle␣of␣water␣is␣now␣empty.");
```

107. Pouring involves liquid from the bottle.

⟨ Handle cases of transitive verbs and **continue** 97 ⟩ +≡
```
case POUR: if (obj ≡ NOTHING ∨ obj ≡ BOTTLE) {
    obj = (prop[BOTTLE] ≡ 0 ? WATER : prop[BOTTLE] ≡ 2 ? OIL : 0);
    if (obj ≡ NOTHING) goto get_object;
  }
  if (¬toting(obj)) goto report_default;
  if (obj ≠ WATER ∧ obj ≠ OIL) report("You␣can't␣pour␣that.");
  prop[BOTTLE] = 1; place[obj] = limbo;
  if (loc ≡ place[PLANT]) ⟨ Try to water the plant 108 ⟩;
  if (loc ≡ place[DOOR]) ⟨ Pour water or oil on the door 109 ⟩;
  report("Your␣bottle␣is␣empty␣and␣the␣ground␣is␣wet.");
```

108. ⟨ Try to water the plant 108 ⟩ ≡
```
  {
    if (obj ≠ WATER)
      report("The␣plant␣indignantly␣shakes␣the␣oil␣off␣its␣leaves␣\
              and␣asks,␣\"Water?\"");
    printf("%s\n", note[prop[PLANT] + 1 + offset[PLANT]]);
    prop[PLANT] += 2; if (prop[PLANT] > 4) prop[PLANT] = 0;
    prop[PLANT2] = prop[PLANT] ≫ 1;
    stay_put;
  }
```
This code is used in section 107.

109. ⟨ Pour water or oil on the door 109 ⟩ ≡
  switch (*obj*) {
  case WATER: *prop*[DOOR] = 0;
    report ("The⎵hinges⎵are⎵quite⎵thoroughly⎵rusted⎵now⎵\
        and⎵won't⎵budge.");
  case OIL: *prop*[DOOR] = 1;
    report ("The⎵oil⎵has⎵freed⎵up⎵the⎵hinges⎵\
        so⎵that⎵the⎵door⎵will⎵now⎵open.");
  }
This code is used in section 107.

110. You can fill the bottle only when it's empty and liquid is available. You can't fill the lamp with oil.

⟨ Handle cases of transitive verbs and **continue** 97 ⟩ +≡
  case FILL: **if** (*obj* ≡ VASE) ⟨ Try to fill the vase 111 ⟩;
    if (¬*here*(BOTTLE)) {
      if (*obj* ≡ NOTHING) **goto** *get_object*; **else goto** *report_default*;
    }
    else if (*obj* ≠ NOTHING ∧ *obj* ≠ BOTTLE) **goto** *report_default*;
    if (¬*bottle_empty*) *report*("Your⎵bottle⎵is⎵already⎵full.");
    if (*no_liquid_here*)
      report ("There⎵is⎵nothing⎵here⎵with⎵which⎵to⎵fill⎵the⎵bottle.");
    prop[BOTTLE] = *flags*[*loc*] & *oil*;
    if (*toting*(BOTTLE)) *place*[*prop*[BOTTLE] ? OIL : WATER] = *inhand*;
    printf ("Your⎵bottle⎵is⎵now⎵full⎵of⎵%s.\n" ,
      prop[BOTTLE] ? "oil" : "water");
    continue;

BOTTLE = 23, §11.
bottle_empty = macro, §104.
default_to = macro ( ), §79.
DOOR = 11, §11.
DRINK = 13, §13.
EAT, see §92 and §98.
FILL = 18, §13.
flags: **int** [], §20.
get_object: label, §79.
here = macro ( ), §74.
inhand = −1, §18.
limbo = 0, §18.
loc: **location**, §74.
no_liquid_here = macro, §74.
note: **char** *[], §63.
NOTHING = 0, §11.
obj: **object**, §77.

offset: **int** [], §63.
OIL = 25, §11.
oil = 2, §20.
place: **location** [], §63.
PLANT = 28, §11.
PLANT2 = 29, §11.
POUR = 11, §13.
printf: **int** ( ), <stdio.h>.
prop: **int** [], §63.
report = macro ( ), §79.
report_default: label, §79.
stay_put = macro, §78.
toting = macro ( ), §63.
VASE = 59, §11.
WATER = 24, §11.
water_here = macro, §74.

111.   Filling the vase is a nasty business.

⟨ Try to fill the vase 111 ⟩ ≡

```
{
  if (no_liquid_here)
    report("There⎵is⎵nothing⎵here⎵with⎵which⎵to⎵fill⎵the⎵vase.\n");
  if (¬toting(VASE))  report(default_msg[DROP]);
  printf("The⎵sudden⎵change⎵in⎵temperature⎵has⎵\
          delicately⎵shattered⎵the⎵vase.\n");
  goto smash;
}
```

This code is used in section 110.

112.   Picking up a liquid depends, of course, on the status of the bottle. Other objects need special handling, too, because of various side effects and the fact that we can't take bird and cage separately when the bird is in the cage.

⟨ Handle cases of transitive verbs and **continue** 97 ⟩ +≡

```
case TAKE: if (toting(obj)) goto report_default;
        /* already carrying it */
  if (base[obj]) {      /* it is immovable */
    if (obj ≡ CHAIN ∧ prop[BEAR]) report("The⎵chain⎵is⎵still⎵locked.");
    if (obj ≡ BEAR ∧ prop[BEAR] ≡ 1)
      report("The⎵bear⎵is⎵still⎵chained⎵to⎵the⎵wall.");
    if (obj ≡ PLANT ∧ prop[PLANT] ≤ 0)
      report("The⎵plant⎵has⎵exceptionally⎵deep⎵roots⎵\
              and⎵cannot⎵be⎵pulled⎵free.");
    report("You⎵can't⎵be⎵serious!");
  }
  if (obj ≡ WATER ∨ obj ≡ OIL) ⟨ Check special cases for taking a liquid 113 ⟩;
  if (holding ≥ 7) report("You⎵can't⎵carry⎵anything⎵more.⎵⎵\
              You'll⎵have⎵to⎵drop⎵something⎵first.");
  if (obj ≡ BIRD ∧ prop[BIRD] ≡ 0)
    ⟨ Check special cases for taking a bird 114 ⟩;
  if (obj ≡ BIRD ∨ (obj ≡ CAGE ∧ prop[BIRD])) carry(BIRD + CAGE − obj);
  carry(obj);
  if (obj ≡ BOTTLE ∧ ¬bottle_empty)
    place[prop[BOTTLE] ? OIL : WATER] = inhand;
  default_to(RELAX);      /* OK, we've taken it */
```

113. ⟨ Check special cases for taking a liquid 113 ⟩ ≡
  if (*here*(BOTTLE) ∧ *object_in_bottle*) *obj* = BOTTLE;
  else {
    obj = BOTTLE;
    if (*toting*(BOTTLE)) *change_to*(FILL);
    report("You␣have␣nothing␣in␣which␣to␣carry␣it.");
  }
This code is used in section 112.

114. ⟨ Check special cases for taking a bird 114 ⟩ ≡
  {
    if (*toting*(ROD))
      report("The␣bird␣was␣unafraid␣when␣you␣entered,␣\
             but␣as␣you␣approach␣it␣becomes\n\
          disturbed␣and␣you␣cannot␣catch␣it.");
    if (*toting*(CAGE)) *prop*[BIRD] = 1;
    else *report*("You␣can␣catch␣the␣bird,␣but␣you␣cannot␣carry␣it.");
  }
This code is used in section 112.

115. Similarly, when dropping the bottle we must drop also its liquid contents, if any.

⟨ Check special cases for dropping a liquid 115 ⟩ ≡
  if (*object_in_bottle*) *obj* = BOTTLE;
  if (*obj* ≡ BOTTLE ∧ ¬*bottle_empty*)
    place[*prop*[BOTTLE] ? OIL : WATER] = *limbo*;
This code is used in section 117.

---

base: **object** [], §63.
BEAR = 45, §11.
BIRD = 10, §11.
BOTTLE = 23, §11.
bottle_empty = macro, §104.
CAGE = 5, §11.
carry: **void** ( ), §65.
CHAIN = 66, §11.
change_to = macro ( ), §79.
default_msg: **char** *[], §15.
default_to = macro ( ), §79.
DROP, see §117.
FILL = 18, §13.
here = macro ( ), §74.
holding: **int**, §63.
inhand = −1, §18.
limbo = 0, §18.
no_liquid_here = macro, §74.

obj: **object**, §77.
object_in_bottle = macro, §90.
OIL = 25, §11.
place: **location** [], §63.
PLANT = 28, §11.
printf: **int** ( ), <stdio.h>.
prop: **int** [], §63.
RELAX, see §14 and §79.
report = macro ( ), §79.
report_default: label, §79.
ROD = 6, §11.
smash: label, §101.
TAKE = 1, §13.
TAKE, see §92.
toting = macro ( ), §63.
VASE = 59, §11.
WATER = 24, §11.

.

116.   The other actions.   Now that we understand how to write action routines, we're ready to complete the set.

117.   Dropping an object has special cases for the bird (which might attack the snake or the dragon), the cage, the vase, etc. The verb TOSS also reduces to DROP for most objects.

(The term PONY is a nod to the vending machine once installed in a room called The Prancing Pony, part of Stanford's historic AI Laboratory.)

⟨ Handle cases of transitive verbs and **continue** 97 ⟩ +≡
case DROP: **if** (*obj* ≡ ROD ∧ *toting* (ROD2) ∧ ¬*toting* (ROD)) *obj* = ROD2;
  if (¬*toting* (*obj*)) **goto** *report_default*;
  if (*obj* ≡ COINS ∧ *here* (PONY)) ⟨ Put coins in the vending machine 118 ⟩;
  if (*obj* ≡ BIRD) ⟨ Check special cases for dropping the bird 120 ⟩;
  if (*obj* ≡ VASE ∧ *loc* ≠ *soft*)
    ⟨ Check special cases for dropping the vase 121 ⟩;
  if (*obj* ≡ BEAR ∧ *is_at_loc* (TROLL)) ⟨ Chase the troll away 119 ⟩;
  ⟨ Check special cases for dropping a liquid 115 ⟩;
  if (*obj* ≡ BIRD) *prop* [BIRD] = 0;
  else if (*obj* ≡ CAGE ∧ *prop* [BIRD]) *drop* (BIRD, *loc*);
  drop (*obj*, *loc*);
  if (*k*) **continue**; **else** *default_to* (RELAX);

118.   ⟨ Put coins in the vending machine 118 ⟩ ≡
  {
    destroy (COINS);
    drop (BATTERIES, *loc*);
    prop [BATTERIES] = 0;
    report (*note* [*offset* [BATTERIES]]);
  }
This code is used in section 117.

119.   TROLL2 is the absent troll. We move the troll bridge up to first in the list of things at its location.

⟨ Chase the troll away 119 ⟩ ≡
  {
    printf ("The␣bear␣lumbers␣toward␣the␣troll,␣\
          who␣lets␣out␣a␣startled␣shriek␣and\n\
        scurries␣away.␣␣The␣bear␣soon␣gives␣up␣the␣pursuit␣\
          and␣wanders␣back.\n");
    k = 1;   /* suppress the "OK" message */
    destroy (TROLL); *destroy* (TROLL_);
    drop (TROLL2, *swside*); *drop* (TROLL2_, *neside*);
    prop [TROLL] = 2;

$move(\texttt{BRIDGE}, swside\,)$; $move(\texttt{BRIDGE\_}, neside\,)$;
    /* put first in their lists */
}

This code is used in section 117.

120. ⟨ Check special cases for dropping the bird 120 ⟩ ≡
    {
        if $(here(\texttt{SNAKE}))$ {
            $printf$ ("The␣little␣bird␣attacks␣the␣green␣snake,␣\
                    and␣in␣an␣astounding␣flurry\n\
                    drives␣the␣snake␣away.\n"); $k = 1$;
            if $(closed)$ **goto** $dwarves\_upset$;
            $destroy(\texttt{SNAKE})$;
            $prop[\texttt{SNAKE}] = 1$;   /* used in conditional instructions */
        }
        else if $(is\_at\_loc(\texttt{DRAGON}) \wedge prop[\texttt{DRAGON}] \equiv 0)$ {
            $destroy(\texttt{BIRD})$; $prop[\texttt{BIRD}] = 0$;
            if $(place[\texttt{SNAKE}] \equiv hmk)$ $lost\_treasures$ ++;
            $report$ ("The␣little␣bird␣attacks␣the␣green␣dragon,␣\
                    and␣in␣an␣astounding␣flurry\n\
                    gets␣burnt␣to␣a␣cinder.␣␣The␣ashes␣blow␣away.");
        }
    }

This code is used in section 117.

BATTERIES $= 49$, §11.
BEAR $= 45$, §11.
BIRD $= 10$, §11.
BRIDGE $= 39$, §11.
BRIDGE_ $= 40$, §11.
CAGE $= 5$, §11.
$closed$: **boolean**, §177.
COINS $= 55$, §11.
$default\_to =$ macro ( ), §79.
$destroy =$ macro ( ), §65.
DRAGON $= 37$, §11.
$drop$: **void** ( ), §64.
DROP $= 2$, §13.
$dwarves\_upset$: label, §192.
$here =$ macro ( ), §74.
$hmk = 50$, §18, §40.
is_at_loc: **boolean** ( ), §66.
k: **register int**, §2.
loc: **location**, §74.
$lost\_treasures$: **int**, §89.
$move =$ macro ( ), §65.
$neside = 118$, §18, §57.

$note$: **char** $*[]$, §63.
obj: **object**, §77.
$offset$: **int** [], §63.
$place$: **location** [], §63.
PONY $= 48$, §11.
$printf$: **int** ( ), <stdio.h>.
$prop$: **int** [], §63.
RELAX, see §14 and §79.
$report =$ macro ( ), §79.
$report\_default$: label, §79.
ROD $= 6$, §11.
ROD2 $= 7$, §11.
SNAKE $= 13$, §11.
$soft = 70$, §18, §45.
$swside = 105$, §18, §55.
$toting =$ macro ( ), §63.
TROLL $= 41$, §11.
TROLL_ $= 42$, §11.
TROLL2 $= 43$, §11.
TROLL2_ $= 44$, §11.
VASE $= 59$, §11.

121.   ⟨ Check special cases for dropping the vase 121 ⟩ ≡
  {
    prop [VASE] = (*place* [PILLOW] ≡ *loc* ? 0 : 2);
    printf ("%s\n", *note* [*offset* [VASE] + 1 + *prop* [VASE]]);   *k* = 1;
    if (*prop* [VASE]) *base* [VASE] = VASE;
  }

This code is used in section 117.

122.   Throwing is like dropping, except that it covers a few more cases.

⟨ Handle cases of transitive verbs and **continue** 97 ⟩ +≡
case TOSS: **if** (*obj* ≡ ROD ∧ *toting* (ROD2) ∧ ¬*toting* (ROD)) *obj* = ROD2;
  if (¬*toting* (*obj*)) **goto** *report_default*;
  if (*is_treasure* (*obj*) ∧ *is_at_loc* (TROLL)) ⟨ Snarf a treasure for the troll 124 ⟩;
  if (*obj* ≡ FOOD ∧ *here* (BEAR)) {
    obj = BEAR; *change_to* (FEED);
  }
  if (*obj* ≠ AXE) *change_to* (DROP);
  if (*dwarf* ( )) ⟨ Throw the axe at a dwarf 163 ⟩;
  if (*is_at_loc* (DRAGON) ∧ *prop* [DRAGON] ≡ 0)
    printf ("The␣axe␣bounces␣harmlessly␣\
            off␣the␣dragon's␣thick␣scales.\n");
  else if (*is_at_loc* (TROLL))
    printf ("The␣troll␣deftly␣catches␣the␣axe,␣\
            examines␣it␣carefully,␣and␣tosses␣it\n\
      back,␣declaring,␣\"Good␣workmanship,␣\
            but␣it's␣not␣valuable␣enough.\"\n");
  else if (*here* (BEAR) ∧ *prop* [BEAR] ≡ 0) ⟨ Throw the axe at the bear 123 ⟩
  else {
    obj = NOTHING;
    change_to (KILL);
  }
  drop (AXE, *loc*); *stay_put*;

123.   This'll teach you a lesson.

⟨ Throw the axe at the bear 123 ⟩ ≡
  {
    drop (AXE, *loc*);
    prop [AXE] = 1; *base* [AXE] = AXE;   /* it becomes immovable */
    if (*place* [BEAR] ≡ *loc*) *move* (BEAR, *loc*);
        /* put bear first in its list */
    report ("The␣axe␣misses␣and␣lands␣near␣the␣bear␣\
            where␣you␣can't␣get␣at␣it.");
  }

This code is used in section 122.

124. If you toss the vase, the skillful troll will catch it before it breaks.

⟨ Snarf a treasure for the troll 124 ⟩ ≡

```
{
    drop(obj, limbo);
    destroy(TROLL);  destroy(TROLL_);
    drop(TROLL2, swside);  drop(TROLL2_, neside);
    move(BRIDGE, swside);  move(BRIDGE_, neside);
    report("The␣troll␣catches␣your␣treasure␣\
            and␣scurries␣away␣out␣of␣sight.");
}
```

This code is used in section 122.

AXE = 34, §11.
base: **object** [], §63.
BEAR = 45, §11.
BRIDGE = 39, §11.
BRIDGE_ = 40, §11.
change_to = macro ( ), §79.
destroy = macro ( ), §65.
DRAGON = 37, §11.
drop: **void** ( ), §64.
DROP, see §117.
dwarf: **boolean** ( ), §160.
FEED, see §129.
FOOD = 22, §11.
here = macro ( ), §74.
is_at_loc: **boolean** ( ), §66.
is_treasure = macro ( ), §11.
k: **register int**, §2.
KILL, see §125.
limbo = 0, §18.
loc: **location**, §74.
move = macro ( ), §65.
neside = 118, §18, §57.

note: **char** *[], §63.
NOTHING = 0, §11.
obj: **object**, §77.
offset: **int** [], §63.
PILLOW = 12, §11.
place: **location** [], §63.
printf: **int** ( ), <stdio.h>.
prop: **int** [], §63.
report = macro ( ), §79.
report_default: label, §79.
ROD = 6, §11.
ROD2 = 7, §11.
stay_put = macro, §78.
swside = 105, §18, §55.
TOSS = 15, §13.
toting = macro ( ), §63.
TROLL = 41, §11.
TROLL_ = 42, §11.
TROLL2 = 43, §11.
TROLL2_ = 44, §11.
VASE = 59, §11.

125.   When you try to attack, the action becomes violent.

⟨ Handle cases of transitive verbs and **continue** 97 ⟩ +≡

case KILL: **if** (*obj* ≡ NOTHING) ⟨ See if there's a unique object to attack 126 ⟩;
  switch (*obj*) {
  case 0: *report* ("There␣is␣nothing␣here␣to␣attack.");
  case BIRD: ⟨ Dispatch the poor bird 127 ⟩;
  case DRAGON: **if** (*prop* [DRAGON] ≡ 0) ⟨ Fun stuff for dragon 128 ⟩;
  cry:
    report ("For␣crying␣out␣loud,␣the␣poor␣thing␣is␣already␣dead!");
  case CLAM: **case** OYSTER:
    report ("The␣shell␣is␣very␣strong␣and␣impervious␣to␣attack.");
  case SNAKE: *report* ("Attacking␣the␣snake␣both␣doesn't␣work␣\
        and␣is␣very␣dangerous.");
  case DWARF: **if** (*closed*) **goto** *dwarves_upset*;
    report ("With␣what?␣␣Your␣bare␣hands?");
  case TROLL: *report* ("Trolls␣are␣close␣relatives␣with␣the␣rocks␣\
        and␣have␣skin␣as␣tough␣as\n\
    a␣rhinoceros␣hide.␣␣\
        The␣troll␣fends␣off␣your␣blows␣effortlessly.");
  case BEAR: **switch** (*prop* [BEAR]) {
    case 0: *report* ("With␣what?␣␣Your␣bare␣hands?␣␣\
        Against␣HIS␣bear␣hands?");
    case 3: **goto** *cry*;
    default: *report* ("The␣bear␣is␣confused;␣\
        he␣only␣wants␣to␣be␣your␣friend.");
  }
  default: **goto** *report_default*;
  }

126.   Attackable objects fall into two categories: enemies (snake, dwarf, etc.) and others (bird, clam).

We might get here when you threw an axe; you can't attack the bird with an axe.

⟨ See if there's a unique object to attack 126 ⟩ ≡
```
   {
      if (dwarf ())  k++, obj = DWARF;
      if (here (SNAKE))  k++, obj = SNAKE;
      if (is_at_loc (DRAGON) ∧ prop [DRAGON] ≡ 0)  k++, obj = DRAGON;
      if (is_at_loc (TROLL))  k++, obj = TROLL;
      if (here (BEAR) ∧ prop [BEAR] ≡ 0)  k++, obj = BEAR;
      if (k ≡ 0) {        /* no enemies present */
         if (here (BIRD) ∧ oldverb ≠ TOSS)  k++, obj = BIRD;
         if (here (CLAM) ∨ here (OYSTER))  k++, obj = CLAM;
                /* no harm done to call the oyster a clam in this case */
      }
      if (k > 1) goto get_object;
   }
```
This code is used in section 125.

127.   ⟨ Dispatch the poor bird 127 ⟩ ≡
```
   {
      if (closed)  report ("Oh,␣leave␣the␣poor␣unhappy␣bird␣alone.");
      destroy (BIRD); prop [BIRD] = 0;
      if (place [SNAKE] ≡ hmk)  lost_treasures ++;
      report ("The␣little␣bird␣is␣now␣dead.␣␣Its␣body␣disappears.");
   }
```
This code is used in section 125.

BEAR = 45, §11.
BIRD = 10, §11.
CLAM = 17, §11.
closed: **boolean**, §177.
destroy = macro ( ), §65.
DRAGON = 37, §11.
DWARF = 20, §11.
dwarf: **boolean** ( ), §160.
dwarves_upset: label, §192.
get_object: label, §79.
here = macro ( ), §74.
hmk = 50, §18, §40.
is_at_loc: **boolean** ( ), §66.
k: **register int**, §2.

KILL = 21, §13.
lost_treasures: **int**, §89.
NOTHING = 0, §11.
obj: **object**, §77.
oldverb: **action**, §77.
OYSTER = 18, §11.
place: **location** [ ], §63.
prop: **int** [ ], §63.
report = macro ( ), §79.
report_default: label, §79.
SNAKE = 13, §11.
TOSS, see §122.
TROLL = 41, §11.

128.   Here we impersonate the main dialog loop. If you insist on attacking the dragon, you win! He dies, the Persian rug becomes free, and *scan2* takes the place of *scan1* and *scan3*.

⟨ Fun stuff for dragon 128 ⟩ ≡

```
{
    printf ("With␣what?␣␣Your␣bare␣hands?\n" );
    verb = ABSTAIN;  obj = NOTHING;
    listen ( );
    if (¬(streq (word1 , "yes") ∨ streq (word1 , "y"))) goto pre_parse;
    printf ("%s\n", note [offset [DRAGON] + 1]);
    prop [DRAGON] = 2;     /∗ dead ∗/
    prop [RUG] = 0;  base [RUG] = NOTHING;
      /∗ now it's a usable treasure ∗/
    base [DRAGON_] = DRAGON_;
    destroy (DRAGON_);     /∗ inaccessible ∗/
    base [RUG_] = RUG_;
    destroy (RUG_);     /∗ inaccessible ∗/
    for (t = 1; t ≤ max_obj; t++)
        if (place [t] ≡ scan1 ∨ place [t] ≡ scan3)  move (t, scan2 );
    loc = scan2;  stay_put;
}
```

This code is used in section 125.

129.   Feeding various animals leads to various quips. Feeding a dwarf is a baaaaad idea. The bear is special.

⟨ Handle cases of transitive verbs and **continue** 97 ⟩ +≡

```
case FEED: switch (obj) {
case BIRD:
    report ("It's␣not␣hungry␣(it's␣merely␣pinin'␣for␣the␣fjords).␣␣\
            Besides,␣you\n\
        have␣no␣bird␣seed." );
case TROLL: report ("Gluttony␣is␣not␣one␣of␣the␣troll's␣vices.␣␣\
            Avarice,␣however,␣is." );
case DRAGON: if (prop [DRAGON]) report (default_msg [EAT]);
    break;
case SNAKE: if (closed ∨ ¬here (BIRD)) break;
    destroy (BIRD); prop [BIRD] = 0; lost_treasures ++;
    report ("The␣snake␣has␣now␣devoured␣your␣bird." );
case BEAR: if (¬here (FOOD)) {
        if (prop [BEAR] ≡ 0) break;
        if (prop [BEAR] ≡ 3) verb = EAT;
        goto report_default;
    }
    destroy (FOOD); prop [BEAR] = 1;
```

```
    prop[AXE] = 0;  base[AXE] = NOTHING;     /* axe is movable again */
    report("The␣bear␣eagerly␣wolfs␣down␣your␣food,␣\
          after␣which␣he␣seems␣to␣calm\n\
       down␣considerably␣and␣even␣becomes␣rather␣friendly.");
  case DWARF: if (¬here(FOOD)) goto report_default;
    dflag++;
    report("You␣fool,␣dwarves␣eat␣only␣coal!␣␣\
          Now␣you've␣made␣him␣REALLY␣mad!");
  default: report(default_msg[CALM]);
  }
  report("There's␣nothing␣here␣it␣wants␣to␣eat␣\
       (except␣perhaps␣you).");
```

ABSTAIN = 0, §13.
AXE = 34, §11.
base: **object** [], §63.
BEAR = 45, §11.
BIRD = 10, §11.
CALM, see §14.
closed: **boolean**, §177.
default_msg: **char** *[], §15.
destroy = macro ( ), §65.
dflag: **int**, §159.
DRAGON = 37, §11.
DRAGON_ = 38, §11.
DWARF = 20, §11.
EAT, see §92 and §98.
FEED = 17, §13.
FOOD = 22, §11.
here = macro ( ), §74.
listen: **void** ( ), §72.
loc: **location**, §74.
lost_treasures: **int**, §89.
max_obj = 66, §11.
move = macro ( ), §65.

note: **char** *[], §63.
NOTHING = 0, §11.
obj: **object**, §77.
offset: **int** [], §63.
place: **location** [], §63.
pre_parse: label, §76.
printf: **int** ( ), <stdio.h>.
prop: **int** [], §63.
report = macro ( ), §79.
report_default: label, §79.
RUG = 63, §11.
RUG_ = 64, §11.
scan1 = 96, §18, §53.
scan2 = 97, §18, §53.
scan3 = 98, §18, §53.
SNAKE = 13, §11.
stay_put = macro, §78.
streq = macro ( ), §8.
t: **register object**, §68.
TROLL = 41, §11.
verb: **action**, §77.
word1: **char** [], §73.

130.   Locking and unlocking involves several interesting special cases.

⟨ Handle cases of transitive verbs and **continue** 97 ⟩ +≡

```
case OPEN: case CLOSE: switch (obj) {
  case OYSTER: case CLAM: ⟨ Open/close clam/oyster 134 ⟩;
  case GRATE: case CHAIN: if (¬here(KEYS))
        report("You␣have␣no␣keys!");
    ⟨ Open/close grate/chain 131 ⟩;
  case KEYS: report("You␣can't␣lock␣or␣unlock␣the␣keys.");
  case CAGE: report("It␣has␣no␣lock.");
  case DOOR: if (prop[DOOR]) default_to(RELAX);
    report("The␣door␣is␣extremely␣rusty␣and␣refuses␣to␣open.");
  default: goto report_default;
  }
```

131.   ⟨ Open/close grate/chain 131 ⟩ ≡

```
if (obj ≡ CHAIN) ⟨ Open/close chain 132 ⟩;
if (closing) {
  ⟨ Panic at closing time 180 ⟩; continue;
}
k = prop[GRATE];
prop[GRATE] = (verb ≡ OPEN);
switch (k + 2 * prop[GRATE]) {
case 0: report("It␣was␣already␣locked.");
case 1: report("The␣grate␣is␣now␣locked.");
case 2: report("The␣grate␣is␣now␣unlocked.");
case 3: report("It␣was␣already␣unlocked.");
}
```

This code is used in section 130.

132.   ⟨ Open/close chain 132 ⟩ ≡

```
{
  if (verb ≡ OPEN) ⟨ Open chain 133 ⟩;
  if (loc ≠ barr) report("There␣is␣nothing␣here\
            to␣which␣the␣chain␣can␣be␣locked.");
  if (prop[CHAIN]) report("It␣was␣already␣locked.");
  prop[CHAIN] = 2, base[CHAIN] = CHAIN;
  if (toting(CHAIN)) drop(CHAIN, loc);
  report("The␣chain␣is␣now␣locked.");
}
```

This code is used in section 131.

133.   ⟨ Open chain 133 ⟩ ≡

```
{
    if (prop[CHAIN] ≡ 0)  report("It␣was␣already␣unlocked.");
    if (prop[BEAR] ≡ 0)
        report("There␣is␣no␣way␣to␣get␣past␣the␣bear␣\
                to␣unlock␣the␣chain,␣which␣is\n\
                probably␣just␣as␣well.");
    prop[CHAIN] = 0, base[CHAIN] = NOTHING;       /* chain is free */
    if (prop[BEAR] ≡ 3)  base[BEAR] = BEAR;
    else  prop[BEAR] = 2, base[BEAR] = NOTHING;
    report("The␣chain␣is␣now␣unlocked.");
}
```

This code is used in section 132.

---

134.   The clam/oyster is extremely heavy to carry, although not as heavy as the gold.

#define *clam_oyster*   (*obj* ≡ CLAM ? `"clam"` : `"oyster"`)

⟨ Open/close clam/oyster 134 ⟩ ≡
 if (*verb* ≡ CLOSE) *report* (`"What?"`);
 if (¬*toting*(TRIDENT)) {
  printf (`"You␣don't␣have␣anything␣strong␣enough␣to␣open␣the␣%s"`,
   clam_oyster);
  report (`"."`);
 }
 if (*toting*(*obj*)) {
  printf (`"I␣advise␣you␣to␣put␣down␣the␣%s␣before␣opening␣it.␣␣"`,
   clam_oyster);
  report (*obj* ≡ CLAM ? `">STRAIN!<"` : `">WRENCH!<"`);
 }
 if (*obj* ≡ CLAM) {
  destroy (CLAM); *drop* (OYSTER, *loc*); *drop* (PEARL, *sac*);
  report (`"A␣glistening␣pearl␣falls␣out␣of␣the␣clam␣\`
    `and␣rolls␣away.␣␣Goodness,\n\`
   `this␣must␣really␣be␣an␣oyster.␣␣\`
    `(I␣never␣was␣very␣good␣at␣identifying\n\`
   `bivalves.)␣␣Whatever␣it␣is,␣\`
    `it␣has␣now␣snapped␣shut␣again."`);
 } **else** *report* (`"The␣oyster␣creaks␣open,\`
   `␣revealing␣nothing␣but␣oyster␣inside.\n\`
   `It␣promptly␣snaps␣shut␣again."`);

This code is used in section 130.

135.   You get little satisfaction from asking us to read, unless you hold the oyster — *after* the cave is closed.

⟨ Handle cases of transitive verbs and **continue** 97 ⟩ +≡
case READ: **if** (*dark*) **goto** *cant_see_it*;
 switch (*obj*) {
 case MAG:
  report (`"I'm␣afraid␣the␣magazine␣is␣written␣in␣dwarvish."`);
 case TABLET: *report* (`"\"CONGRATULATIONS␣\`
   `ON␣BRINGING␣LIGHT␣INTO␣THE␣DARK-ROOM!\""`);
 case MESSAGE: *report* (`"\"This␣is␣not␣the␣maze␣where␣\`
   `the␣pirate␣hides␣his␣treasure␣chest.\""`);
 case OYSTER: **if** (*hinted*[1]) {
  if (*toting*(OYSTER))
   report (`"It␣says␣the␣same␣thing␣it␣did␣before."`);
 }
 else if (*closed* ∧ *toting*(OYSTER)) {

>   *offer*(1); **continue**;
>   }
>   **default**: **goto** *report_default*;
>   }

136. OK, that just about does it. We're left with only one more
"action verb" to handle, and it is intransitive. In order to penetrate this
puzzle, you must pronounce the magic incantation in its correct order,
as it appears on the wall of the Giant Room. A global variable *foobar*
records your progress.

⟨ Handle cases of intransitive verbs and **continue** 92 ⟩ +≡
  case FEEFIE: **while** (¬*streq*(*word1*, *incantation*[*k*])) *k*++;
    if (*foobar* ≡ −*k*) ⟨ Proceed foobarically 139 ⟩;
    if (*foobar* ≡ 0) **goto** *nada_sucede*;
    report("What's␣the␣matter,␣can't␣you␣read?␣␣\
        Now␣you'd␣best␣start␣over.");

137. ⟨ Global variables 7 ⟩ +≡
  char *∗incantation*[] = {"fee", "fie", "foe", "foo", "fum"};
  int *foobar*;   /∗ current incantation progress ∗/

138. Just after every command you give, we make the *foobar* counter
negative if you're on track, otherwise we zero it.

⟨ Handle special cases of input 82 ⟩ +≡
  if (*foobar* > 0) *foobar* = −*foobar*;
  else *foobar* = 0;

---

cant_see_it: label, §79.
CLAM = 17, §11.
CLOSE, see §93 and §130.
closed: **boolean**, §177.
dark = macro, §84.
destroy = macro ( ), §65.
drop: **void** ( ), §64.
FEEFIE = 24, §13.
hinted: **boolean** [], §196.
k: **register int**, §2.
loc: **location**, §74.
MAG = 19, §11.
MESSAGE = 46, §11.
nada_sucede: label, §139.
obj: **object**, §77.

offer: **void** ( ), §194.
OYSTER = 18, §11.
PEARL = 62, §11.
printf: **int** ( ), <stdio.h>.
READ = 23, §13.
READ, see §93.
report = macro ( ), §79.
report_default: label, §79.
sac = 65, §18, §43.
streq = macro ( ), §8.
TABLET = 16, §11.
toting = macro ( ), §63.
TRIDENT = 58, §11.
verb: **action**, §77.
word1: **char** [], §73.

139. If you get all the way through, we zip the eggs back to the Giant Room, unless they're already there. The troll returns if you've stolen the eggs back from him.

⟨ Proceed foobarically 139 ⟩ ≡
```
{
    foobar = k + 1;
    if (foobar ≠ 4) default_to(RELAX);
    foobar = 0;
    if (place[EGGS] ≡ giant ∨ (toting(EGGS) ∧ loc ≡ giant))
    nada_sucede: report(default_msg[WAVE]);
    if (place[EGGS] ≡ limbo ∧ place[TROLL] ≡ limbo ∧ prop[TROLL] ≡ 0)
        prop[TROLL] = 1;
    k = (loc ≡ giant ? 0 : here(EGGS) ? 1 : 2);
    move(EGGS, giant);
    report(note[offset[EGGS] + k]);
}
```

This code is used in section 136.

140. Motions. A major cycle comes to an end when a motion verb *mot* has been given and we have computed the appropriate *newloc* accordingly.

First, we deal with motions that don't refer directly to the travel table.

⟨ Handle special motion words 140 ⟩ ≡

   newloc = *loc*;   /∗ by default we will stay put ∗/

   if (*mot* ≡ NOWHERE) **continue**;

   if (*mot* ≡ BACK) ⟨ Try to go back 143 ⟩;

   if (*mot* ≡ LOOK) ⟨ Repeat the long description and **continue** 141 ⟩;

   if (*mot* ≡ CAVE) {

      if (*loc* < *min_in_cave*) *printf* ("I␣can't␣see␣where␣the␣cave␣is,␣\

          but␣hereabouts␣no␣stream␣can␣run␣on\n\

          the␣surface␣for␣long.␣␣I␣would␣try␣the␣stream.\n");

      else *printf* ("I␣need␣more␣detailed␣instructions␣to␣do␣that.\n");

      continue;

   }

This code is used in section 75.

BACK = 15, §9.
CAVE = 34, §9.
default_msg: **char** ∗[], §15.
default_to = macro ( ), §79.
EGGS = 57, §11.
foobar: **int**, §137.
giant = 76, §18, §47.
here = macro ( ), §74.
k: **register int**, §2.
limbo = 0, §18.
loc: **location**, §74.
LOOK = 24, §9.
min_in_cave = 9, §18.
mot: **motion**, §77.

move = macro ( ), §65.
newloc: **location**, §74.
note: **char** ∗[], §63.
NOWHERE = 74, §9.
offset: **int** [], §63.
place: **location** [], §63.
printf: **int** ( ), <stdio.h>.
prop: **int** [], §63.
RELAX, see §14 and §79.
report = macro ( ), §79.
toting = macro ( ), §63.
TROLL = 41, §11.
WAVE, see §99.

141.   When looking around, we pretend that it wasn't dark (though it may *now* be dark), so you won't fall into a pit while staring into the gloom.

⟨ Repeat the long description and **continue** 141 ⟩ ≡
```
    {
        if (++look_count ≤ 3)
            printf("Sorry,␣but␣I␣am␣not␣allowed␣to␣give␣more␣detail.␣␣\
                I␣will␣repeat␣the\n\
                long␣description␣of␣your␣location.\n");
        was_dark = false;
        visits[loc] = 0;
        continue;
    }
```
This code is used in section 140.

142.   ⟨ Global variables 7 ⟩ +≡
```
    int look_count;        /* how many times you've asked us to look */
```

143.   If you ask us to go back, we look for a motion that goes from *loc* to *oldloc*, or to *oldoldloc* if *oldloc* has forced motion. Otherwise we can't take you back.

⟨ Try to go back 143 ⟩ ≡
```
    {
        l = (forced_move(oldloc) ? oldoldloc : oldloc);
        oldoldloc = oldloc;
        oldloc = loc;
        if (l ≡ loc) ⟨ Apologize for inability to backtrack 145 ⟩;
        for (q = start[loc], qq = Λ; q < start[loc + 1]; q++) {
            ll = q→dest;
            if (ll ≡ l) goto found;
            if (ll ≤ max_loc ∧ forced_move(ll) ∧ start[ll]→dest ≡ l)  qq = q;
        }
        if (qq ≡ Λ) {
            printf("You␣can't␣get␣there␣from␣here.\n");  continue;
        }
        else  q = qq;
    found:  mot = q→mot;
        goto go_for_it;
    }
```
This code is used in section 140.

144.   ⟨ Additional local registers 22 ⟩ +≡
```
    register location l, ll;
```

145. ⟨ Apologize for inability to backtrack 145 ⟩ ≡

```
{
  printf("Sorry,␣but␣I␣no␣longer␣seem␣to␣remember␣\
        how␣you␣got␣here.\n");
  continue;
}
```

This code is used in section 143.

146. Now we are ready to interpret the instructions in the travel table. The following code implements the conventions of section 19.

⟨ Determine the next location, *newloc* 146 ⟩ ≡

```
for (q = start[loc]; q < start[loc + 1]; q++) {
  if (forced_move(loc) ∨ q→mot ≡ mot) break;
}
if (q ≡ start[loc + 1]) ⟨ Report on inapplicable motion and continue 148 ⟩;
⟨ If the condition of instruction q isn't satisfied, advance q 147 ⟩;
newloc = q→dest;
if (newloc ≤ max_loc) continue;
if (newloc > max_spec) {
  printf("%s\n", remarks[newloc − max_spec]);
stay: newloc = loc; continue;
}
switch (newloc) {
case ppass: ⟨ Choose newloc via plover-alcove passage 149 ⟩;
case pdrop: ⟨ Drop the emerald during plover transportation 150 ⟩;
  goto no_good;
case troll: ⟨ Cross troll bridge if possible 151 ⟩;
}
```

This code is cited in section 19.

This code is used in section 75.

---

dest: **location**, §19.
false = 0, §2.
forced_move = macro ( ), §59.
go_for_it: label, §75.
loc: **location**, §74.
location = **enum**, §18.
max_loc = 140, §18.
max_spec = 143, §18.
mot: **motion**, §19.
mot: **motion**, §77.
newloc: **location**, §74.
no_good: label, §147.
oldloc: **location**, §74.
oldoldloc: **location**, §74.
pdrop = 142, §18.
ppass = 141, §18.
printf: **int** ( ), <stdio.h>.
q: **register instruction** *, §22.
qq: **register instruction** *, §22.
remarks: **char** *[ ], §20.
start: **instruction** *[ ], §20.
troll = 143, §18.
visits: **int** [ ], §20.
was_dark: **boolean**, §84.

147.   ⟨ If the condition of instruction q isn't satisfied, advance q 147 ⟩ ≡

```
while (1) {
    j = q⁻cond;
    if (j > 300) {
        if (prop[j % 100] ≠ (int)((j − 300)/100))  break;
    } else if (j ≤ 100) {
        if (j ≡ 0 ∨ pct(j))  break;
    } else if (toting(j % 100) ∨ (j ≥ 200 ∧ is_at_loc(j % 100)))  break;
no_good:
    for (qq = q++;
    q⁻dest ≡ qq⁻dest ∧ q⁻cond ≡ qq⁻cond;
    q++) ;
}
```

This code is used in section 146.

148.   Here we look at *verb* just in case you asked us to 'find gully' or something like that.

⟨ Report on inapplicable motion and **continue** 148 ⟩ ≡

```
{
    if (mot ≡ CRAWL)  printf("Which way?");
    else if (mot ≡ XYZZY ∨ mot ≡ PLUGH)  printf(default_msg[WAVE]);
    else if (verb ≡ FIND ∨ verb ≡ INVENTORY)  printf(default_msg[FIND]);
    else if (mot ≤ FORWARD)
        switch (mot) {
        case IN: case OUT: printf("I don't know in from out here.  \
                Use compass points or name something\n\
                in the general direction you want to go.");  break;
        case FORWARD: case L: case R:
            printf("I am unsure how you are facing.  \
                Use compass points or nearby objects.");  break;
        default: printf("There is no way to go in that direction.");
        } else  printf("I don't know how to apply that word here.");
    printf("\n");  continue;        /* newloc = loc */
}
```

This code is used in section 146.

149. Only the emerald can be toted through the plover-alcove passage — not even the lamp.

⟨ Choose *newloc* via plover-alcove passage 149 ⟩ ≡
    if (*holding* ≡ 0 ∨ (*toting*(EMERALD) ∧ *holding* ≡ 1)) {
       newloc = *alcove* + *proom* − *loc*; **continue**;
         /∗ move through the passage ∗/
    } **else** {
      printf ("Something␣you're␣carrying␣\
             won't␣fit␣through␣the␣tunnel␣with␣you.\n\
           You'd␣best␣take␣inventory␣and␣drop␣something.\n");
      goto *stay*;
    }

This code is used in section 146.

150. The *pdrop* command applies only when you're carrying the emerald. We make you drop it, thereby forcing you to use the plover-alcove passage if you want to get it out. We don't actually tell you that it was dropped; we just pretend you weren't carrying it after all.

⟨ Drop the emerald during plover transportation 150 ⟩ ≡
    drop (EMERALD, *loc*);

This code is used in section 146.

---

alcove = 89, §18, §51.
cond: **int**, §19.
CRAWL = 21, §9.
default_msg: **char** ∗[], §15.
dest: **location**, §19.
drop: **void** ( ), §64.
EMERALD = 60, §11.
FIND, see §100.
FORWARD = 14, §9.
holding: **int**, §63.
IN = 12, §9.
INVENTORY, see §94 and §100.
is_at_loc: **boolean** ( ), §66.
j: **register int**, §2.
L = 10, §9.
loc: **location**, §74.
mot: **motion**, §77.

newloc: **location**, §74.
OUT = 13, §9.
pct = macro ( ), §157.
pdrop = 142, §18, §146.
PLUGH = 71, §9.
printf: **int** ( ), <stdio.h>.
proom = 90, §18, §51.
prop: **int** [], §63.
q: **register instruction** ∗, §22.
qq: **register instruction** ∗, §22.
R = 11, §9.
stay: **label**, §146.
toting = macro ( ), §63.
verb: **action**, §77.
WAVE, see §99.
XYZZY = 70, §9.

151.   Troll bridge crossing is treated as a special motion so that dwarves won't wander across and encounter the bear.

You can get here only if TROLL is in limbo but TROLL2 has taken its place. Moreover, if you're on the southwest side, *prop*[TROLL] will be nonzero. If *prop*[TROLL] is 1, you've crossed since paying, or you've stolen away the payment. Special stuff involves the bear.

⟨ Cross troll bridge if possible 151 ⟩ ≡
  if (*prop*[TROLL] ≡ 1) ⟨ Block the troll bridge and stay put 152 ⟩;
  newloc = *neside* + *swside* − *loc*;   /∗ cross it ∗/
  if (*prop*[TROLL] ≡ 0) *prop*[TROLL] = 1;
  if (¬*toting*(BEAR)) **continue**;
  printf ("Just␣as␣you␣reach␣the␣other␣side,␣\
       the␣bridge␣buckles␣beneath␣the\n\
     weight␣of␣the␣bear,␣\
       who␣was␣still␣following␣you␣around.␣␣You\n\
     scrabble␣desperately␣for␣support,␣\
       but␣as␣the␣bridge␣collapses␣you\n\
     stumble␣back␣and␣fall␣into␣the␣chasm.\n");
  prop[BRIDGE] = 1; *prop*[TROLL] = 2;
  drop(BEAR, *newloc*); *base*[BEAR] = BEAR; *prop*[BEAR] = 3;
    /∗ the bear is dead ∗/
  if (*prop*[SPICES] < 0 ∧ *place*[SPICES] ≥ *neside*) *lost_treasures* ++;
  if (*prop*[CHAIN] < 0 ∧ *place*[CHAIN] ≥ *neside*) *lost_treasures* ++;
  oldoldloc = *newloc*;   /∗ if you are revived, you got across ∗/
  goto *death*;

This code is used in section 146.

152.   ⟨ Block the troll bridge and stay put 152 ⟩ ≡
  {
    move(TROLL, *swside*); *move*(TROLL_, *neside*); *prop*[TROLL] = 0;
    destroy(TROLL2); *destroy*(TROLL2_);
    move(BRIDGE, *swside*); *move*(BRIDGE_, *neside*);
    printf ("%s\n", *note*[*offset*[TROLL] + 1]);
    goto *stay*;
  }

This code is used in section 151.

153. Obstacles might still arise after the choice of *newloc* has been made. The following program is executed at the beginning of each major cycle.

⟨ Check for interference with the proposed move to *newloc* 153 ⟩ ≡
    if (*closing* ∧ *newloc* < *min_in_cave* ∧ *newloc* ≠ *limbo*) {
      ⟨ Panic at closing time 180 ⟩; *newloc* = *loc*;
    } **else if** (*newloc* ≠ *loc*)
      ⟨ Stay in *loc* if a dwarf is blocking the way to *newloc* 176 ⟩;

This code is used in section 75.

---

base: **object** [], §63.
BEAR = 45, §11.
BRIDGE = 39, §11.
BRIDGE_ = 40, §11.
CHAIN = 66, §11.
closing = macro, §177.
death: label, §189.
destroy = macro ( ), §65.
drop: **void** ( ), §64.
limbo = 0, §18.
loc: **location**, §74.
lost_treasures: **int**, §89.
min_in_cave = 9, §18.
move = macro ( ), §65.
neside = 118, §18, §57.

newloc: **location**, §74.
note: **char** *[], §63.
offset: **int** [], §63.
oldoldloc: **location**, §74.
place: **location** [], §63.
printf: **int** ( ), **<stdio.h>**.
prop: **int** [], §63.
SPICES = 65, §11.
stay: label, §146.
swside = 105, §18, §55.
toting = macro ( ), §63.
TROLL = 41, §11.
TROLL_ = 42, §11.
TROLL2 = 43, §11.
TROLL2_ = 44, §11.

154.   Random numbers.   You won't realize it until you have played the game for awhile, but adventures in Colossal Cave are not deterministic. Lots of things can happen differently when you give the same input, because caves are continually changing, and the dwarves don't have consistent aim, etc.

A simple linear congruential method is used to provide numbers that are random enough for our purposes.

⟨ Subroutines 6 ⟩ +≡
  int *ran* ARGS((**int**));

  int *ran*(*range*)
      int *range*;   /* for uniform integers between 0 and *range* − 1 */
  {
      rx = (1021 * *rx*) & #fffff;   /* multiply by 1021, modulo 2^{20} */
      return (*range* * *rx*) ≫ 20;
  }

155.   ⟨ Global variables 7 ⟩ +≡
  int *rx*; /* the last random value generated */

156.   Each run is different.

⟨ Initialize the random number generator 156 ⟩ ≡
  rx = (((**int**) *time*(Λ)) & #fffff) | 1;

This code is used in section 200.

157.   The *pct* macro returns true a given percentage of the time.

#define *pct*(*r*) (*ran*(100) < *r*)

⟨ Give optional plugh hint 157 ⟩ ≡
  if (*loc* ≡ *y2* ∧ *pct*(25) ∧ ¬*closing*)
    printf("A␣hollow␣voice␣says␣\"PLUGH\".\n");

This code is used in section 86.

158.   We kick the random number generator often, just to add variety to the chase.

⟨ Make special adjustments before looking at new input 85 ⟩ +≡
  k = *ran*(0);

159. Dwarf stuff. We've said a lot of vague stuff about dwarves; now is the time to be explicit. Five dwarves roam about the cave. Initially they are dormant but eventually they each walk about at random. A global variable called *dflag* governs their level of activity:

0   no dwarf stuff yet (we wait until you reach the Hall of Mists)
1   you've reached that hall, but haven't met the first dwarf
2   you've met one; the others start moving, but no knives thrown yet
3   a knife has been thrown, but it misses
4   knives will hit you with probability .095
5   knives will hit you with probability .190
6   knives will hit you with probability .285

and so on. Dwarves get madder and madder as *dflag* increases; this increases their accuracy.

A pirate stalks the cave too. He acts a lot like a dwarf with respect to random walks, so we call him *dwarf*[0], but actually he is quite different. He starts at the location of his treasure chest; you won't see that chest until after you've spotted him.

The present location of *dwarf*[i] is *dloc*[i]; initially no two dwarves are adjacent. The value of *dseen*[i] records whether or not dwarf i is following you.

```
#define  nd   5     /* this many dwarves */
#define  chest_loc   dead2
#define  message_loc   pony
```
⟨ Global variables 7 ⟩ +≡
    int *dflag*;   /* how angry are the dwarves? */
    int *dkill*;   /* how many of them have you killed? */
    location *dloc*[*nd* + 1] = { *chest_loc*, *hmk*, *wfiss*, *y2*, *like3*, *complex* };
      /* dwarf locations */
    location *odloc*[*nd* + 1];   /* prior locations */
    boolean *dseen*[*nd* + 1];   /* have you been spotted? */

ARGS = macro ( ), §3.
boolean = **enum**, §2.
closing = macro, §177.
complex = 61, §18, §42.
dead2 = 108, §18, §56.
dwarf: **boolean** ( ), §160.
hmk = 50, §18, §40.
k: **register int**, §2.

like3 = 22, §18, §36.
loc: **location**, §74.
location = **enum**, §18.
pony = 48, §18, §39.
printf: **int** ( ), **<stdio.h>**.
time: **time_t** ( ), **<time.h>**.
wfiss = 18, §18, §34.
y2 = 54, §18, §41.

160.   The following subroutine is often useful.

⟨ Subroutines 6 ⟩ +≡
```
  boolean dwarf ARGS((void));
  boolean dwarf ()      /* is a dwarf present? */
  {
    register int j;
    if (dflag < 2) return false;
    for (j = 1; j ≤ nd; j++)
      if (dloc[j] ≡ loc) return true;
    return false;
  }
```

161.   Just after you've moved to a new *loc*, we move the other guys.
But we bypass all dwarf motion if you are in a place forbidden to the
pirate, or if your next motion is forced. In particular, this means that
the pirate can't steal the return toll, and dwarves can't meet the bear.
It also means that dwarves won't follow you into a dead end of the maze,
but c'est la vie; they'll wait for you outside the dead end.

⟨ Possibly move dwarves and the pirate 161 ⟩ ≡
```
  if (loc ≤ max_pirate_loc ∧ loc ≠ limbo) {
    if (dflag ≡ 0) {
      if (loc ≥ min_lower_loc) dflag = 1;
    }
    else if (dflag ≡ 1) {
      if (loc ≥ min_lower_loc ∧ pct(5)) ⟨ Advance dflag to 2 162 ⟩;
    }
    else ⟨ Move dwarves and the pirate 164 ⟩;
  }
```
This code is used in section 75.

162.   When level 2 is reached, we silently kill 0, 1, or 2 of the dwarves.
Then if any of the survivors is in the current location, we move him to
nugget; thus no dwarf is presently tracking you. Another dwarf does,
however, toss an axe and grumpily leave the scene.

(The grumpy dwarf might throw the axe while you're in the maze of
all-different twists, even though other dwarves never go in there!)

⟨ Advance dflag to 2 162 ⟩ ≡
```
  {
    dflag = 2;
    for (j = 0; j < 2; j++)
      if (pct(50)) dloc[1 + ran(nd)] = limbo;
    for (j = 1; j ≤ nd; j++) {
      if (dloc[j] ≡ loc) dloc[j] = nugget;
```

$odloc[j] = dloc[j];$
}
$printf$("A␣little␣dwarf␣just␣walked␣around␣a␣corner,␣\
          saw␣you,␣threw␣a␣little\n\
     axe␣at␣you,␣cursed,␣and␣ran␣away.␣␣(The␣axe␣missed.)\n");
$drop$(AXE, loc);
}

This code is used in section 161.

163.   It turns out that the only way you can get rid of a dwarf is to
attack him with the axe. You'll hit him 2/3 of the time; in either case,
the axe will be available for reuse.

⟨ Throw the axe at a dwarf 163 ⟩ ≡
    {
      for $(j = 1;\ j \leq nd;\ j{+}{+})$
        if $(dloc[j] \equiv loc)$ **break**;
      if $(ran(3) < 2)$ {
        $dloc[j] = limbo;\ dseen[j] = 0;\ dkill{+}{+};$
        if $(dkill \equiv 1)$ $printf$("You␣killed␣a␣little␣dwarf.␣\
               ␣The␣body␣vanishes␣in␣a␣cloud␣of␣greasy\n\
          black␣smoke.\n");
        else $printf$("You␣killed␣a␣little␣dwarf.\n");
      } **else** $printf$("You␣attack␣a␣little␣dwarf,␣\
               but␣he␣dodges␣out␣of␣the␣way.\n");
      $drop$(AXE, loc); $stay\_put$;
    }

This code is used in section 122.

ARGS = macro ( ), §3.
AXE = 34, §11.
boolean = **enum**, §2.
$dflag$: **int**, §159.
$dkill$: **int**, §159.
$dloc$: **location** [ ], §159.
$drop$: **void** ( ), §64.
$dseen$: **boolean** [ ], §159.
$false$ = 0, §2.
j: **register int**, §2.
$limbo$ = 0, §18.

loc: **location**, §74.
max_pirate_loc = 108, §56.
min_lower_loc = 15, §18.
nd = 5, §159.
$nugget$ = 16, §18, §33.
$odloc$: **location** [ ], §159.
pct = macro ( ), §157.
$printf$: **int** ( ), <stdio.h>.
ran: **int** ( ), §154.
$stay\_put$ = macro, §78.
$true$ = 1, §2.

164. Now things are in full swing. Dead dwarves don't do much of anything, but each live dwarf tends to stay with you if he's seen you. Otherwise he moves at random, never backing up unless there's no alternative.

⟨ Move dwarves and the pirate 164 ⟩ ≡
```
{
    dtotal = attack = stick = 0;
        /* initialize totals for possible battles */
    for (j = 0; j ≤ nd; j++)
        if (dloc[j] ≠ limbo) {
            register int i;

            ⟨ Make a table of all potential exits, ploc[0] through ploc[i − 1] 166 ⟩;
            if (i ≡ 0) i = 1, ploc[0] = odloc[j];
            odloc[j] = dloc[j];
            dloc[j] = ploc[ran(i)];        /* this is the random walk */
            dseen[j] = (dloc[j] ≡ loc ∨ odloc[j] ≡ loc ∨ (dseen[j] ∧ loc ≥
                min_lower_loc));
            if (dseen[j]) ⟨ Make dwarf j follow 167 ⟩;
        }
    if (dtotal) ⟨ Make the threatening dwarves attack 170 ⟩;
}
```
This code is used in section 161.

165. ⟨ Global variables 7 ⟩ +≡
```
    int dtotal;      /* this many dwarves are in the room with you */
    int attack;      /* this many have had time to draw their knives */
    int stick;       /* this many have hurled their knives accurately */
    location ploc[19];      /* potential locations for the next random step */
```

166. Random-moving dwarves think *scan1*, *scan2*, and *scan3* are three different locations, although you will never have that perception.

⟨ Make a table of all potential exits, ploc[0] through ploc[i − 1] 166 ⟩ ≡
```
    for (i = 0, q = start[dloc[j]]; q < start[dloc[j] + 1]; q++) {
        newloc = q⃗dest;
        if (newloc ≥ min_lower_loc ∧ newloc ≠ odloc[j] ∧ newloc ≠ dloc[j] ∧
            (i ≡ 0 ∨ newloc ≠ ploc[i − 1]) ∧ i < 19 ∧ q⃗cond ≠ 100 ∧
            newloc ≤ (j ≡ 0 ? max_pirate_loc : min_forced_loc − 1))
        ploc[i++] = newloc;
    }
```
This code is used in section 164.

167.   A global variable *knife_loc* is used to remember where dwarves have most recently thrown knives at you. But as soon as you try to refer to the knife, we tell you it's pointless to do so; *knife_loc* is −1 thereafter.

⟨ Make dwarf *j* follow 167 ⟩ ≡
```
{
    dloc[j] = loc;
    if (j ≡ 0) ⟨ Make the pirate track you 172 ⟩
    else {
        dtotal ++;
        if (odloc[j] ≡ dloc[j]) {
            attack ++;
            if (knife_loc ≥ 0) knife_loc = loc;
            if (ran(1000) < 95 * (dflag − 2)) stick ++;
        }
    }
}
```
This code is used in section 164.

168.   ⟨ Global variables 7 ⟩ +≡
  int *knife_loc*;   /* place where knife was mentioned, or −1 */

169.   ⟨ Make special adjustments before looking at new input 85 ⟩ +≡
  if (*knife_loc* > *limbo* ∧ *knife_loc* ≠ *loc*) *knife_loc* = *limbo*;

---

cond: **int**, §19.
dest: **location**, §19.
dflag: **int**, §159.
dloc: **location** [], §159.
dseen: **boolean** [], §159.
j: **register int**, §2.
limbo = 0, §18.
loc: **location**, §74.
location = **enum**, §18.
max_pirate_loc = 108, §56.
min_forced_loc = 129, §18.

min_lower_loc = 15, §18.
nd = 5, §159.
newloc: **location**, §74.
odloc: **location** [], §159.
q: **register instruction** *, §22.
ran: **int** ( ), §154.
scan1 = 96, §18, §53.
scan2 = 97, §18, §53.
scan3 = 98, §18, §53.
start: **instruction** *[], §20.

170.   We actually know the results of the attack already; this is where we inform you of the outcome, pretending that the battle is now taking place.

⟨ Make the threatening dwarves attack 170 ⟩ ≡
```
{
    if (dtotal ≡ 1)  printf ("There␣is␣a␣threatening␣little␣dwarf");
    else  printf ("There␣are␣%d␣threatening␣little␣dwarves", dtotal);
    printf ("␣in␣the␣room␣with␣you!\n");
    if (attack) {
        if (dflag ≡ 2)  dflag = 3;
        if (attack ≡ 1)  k = 0, printf ("One␣sharp␣nasty␣knife␣is␣thrown");
        else  k = 2, printf ("␣%d␣of␣them␣throw␣knives", attack);
        printf ("␣at␣you␣---␣");
        if (stick ≤ 1)  printf ("%s!\n", attack_msg[k + stick]);
        else  printf ("%d␣of␣them␣get␣you!\n", stick);
        if (stick) {
            oldoldloc = loc; goto death;
        }
    }
}
```
This code is used in section 164.

171.   ⟨ Global variables 7 ⟩ +≡
```
char *attack_msg[] = {"it␣misses","it␣gets␣you",
    "none␣of␣them␣hit␣you","one␣of␣them␣gets␣you"};
```

172.   The pirate leaves you alone once you have found the chest. Otherwise he steals all of the treasures you're carrying, although he ignores a treasure that's too easy. (The pyramid is too easy, if you're in the Plover Room or the Dark-Room.)

You spot the pirate if he robs you, or when you have seen all of the possible treasures (except, of course, the chest) and the current location has no treasures. Before you've spotted him, we may give you a vague indication of his movements.

We use the value of *place*[MESSAGE] to determine whether the pirate has been seen; the condition of *place*[CHEST] is not a reliable indicator, since the chest might be in limbo if you've thrown it to the troll.

#define *pirate_not_spotted*   (*place*[MESSAGE] ≡ *limbo*)
#define *too_easy*(*i*)   (*i* ≡ PYRAMID ∧ (*loc* ≡ *proom* ∨ *loc* ≡ *droom*))

⟨ Make the pirate track you 172 ⟩ ≡
```
{
    if (loc ≠ max_pirate_loc ∧ prop[CHEST] < 0) {
        for (i = min_treasure, k = 0; i ≤ max_obj; i++) {
```

```
        if (¬too_easy(i) & toting(i)) {
            k = −1; break;
        }
        if (here(i)) k = 1;
    }
    if (k < 0) ⟨ Take booty and hide it in the chest 173 ⟩
    else if (tally ≡ lost_treasures + 1 ∧ k ≡ 0 ∧
                pirate_not_spotted ∧ prop[LAMP] ∧ here(LAMP))
        ⟨ Let the pirate be spotted 175 ⟩
    else if (odloc[0] ≠ dloc[0] ∧ pct(20))
        printf("There␣are␣faint␣rustling␣noises␣\
                from␣the␣darkness␣behind␣you.\n");
    }
}
```

This code is used in section 167.

---

attack: **int**, §165.
CHEST = 56, §11.
death: **label**, §189.
dflag: **int**, §159.
dloc: **location** [], §159.
droom = 91, §18, §51.
dtotal: **int**, §165.
here = macro ( ), §74.
i: **register int**, §164.
k: **register int**, §2.
LAMP = 2, §11.
limbo = 0, §18.
loc: **location**, §74.
lost_treasures: **int**, §89.
max_obj = 66, §11.

max_pirate_loc = 108, §56.
MESSAGE = 46, §11.
min_treasure = 51, §11.
odloc: **location** [], §159.
oldoldloc: **location**, §74.
pct = macro ( ), §157.
place: **location** [], §63.
printf: **int** ( ), <stdio.h>.
proom = 90, §18, §51.
prop: **int** [], §63.
PYRAMID = 61, §11.
stick: **int**, §165.
tally: **int**, §89.
toting = macro ( ), §63.

173.   The pirate isn't secretive about the fact that his chest is some-where in a maze. However, he doesn't say which maze he means. Nor does he explain why he is interested in treasures only when you are carrying them; evidently he just likes to see you squirm.

⟨ Take booty and hide it in the chest 173 ⟩ ≡

```
{
    printf ("Out␣from␣the␣shadows␣behind␣you␣\
            pounces␣a␣bearded␣pirate!␣␣\"Har,␣har,\"\n\
        he␣chortles,␣\"I'll␣just␣take␣all␣this␣booty␣\
            and␣hide␣it␣away␣with␣me\n\
        chest␣deep␣in␣the␣maze!\"␣␣\
            He␣snatches␣your␣treasure␣and␣vanishes␣into\n\
        the␣gloom.\n");
    ⟨ Snatch all treasures that are snatchable here 174 ⟩;
    if (pirate_not_spotted) {
    move_chest:  move(CHEST, chest_loc);  move(MESSAGE, message_loc);
    }
    dloc[0] = odloc[0] = chest_loc;
    dseen[0] = false;
}
```

This code is used in section 172.

174.   ⟨ Snatch all treasures that are snatchable here 174 ⟩ ≡

```
for (i = min_treasure; i ≤ max_obj; i++)
    if (¬too_easy(i)) {
        if (base[i] ≡ NOTHING ∧ place[i] ≡ loc)  carry(i);
        if (toting(i))  drop(i, chest_loc);
    }
```

This code is used in section 173.

175.   The window rooms are slightly lighted, but you don't spot the pirate there unless your lamp is on. (And you do spot him even if the lighted lamp is on the ground.)

⟨ Let the pirate be spotted 175 ⟩ ≡

```
{
    printf ("There␣are␣faint␣rustling␣noises\
            ␣from␣the␣darkness␣behind␣you.␣␣As␣you\n\
        turn␣toward␣them,␣\
            the␣beam␣of␣your␣lamp␣falls␣across␣a␣bearded␣pirate.\n\
        He␣is␣carrying␣a␣large␣chest.␣␣\
            \"Shiver␣me␣timbers!\"␣he␣cries,␣\"I've\n\
        been␣spotted!␣␣I'd␣best␣hie␣meself␣off␣to␣the␣maze␣\
            to␣hide␣me␣chest!\"\n\
        With␣that,␣he␣vanishes␣into␣the␣gloom.\n");
```

        goto *move_chest*;
    }
This code is used in section 172.

176.   One more loose end related to dwarfs needs to be addressed here.
If you're coming from a place forbidden to the pirate, so that the dwarves
are rooted in place, we let you get out (and be attacked). Otherwise,
if a dwarf has seen you and has come from where you want to go, he
blocks you.

   We use the fact that *loc* ≤ *max_pirate_loc* implies ¬*forced_move*(*loc*).

⟨ Stay in *loc* if a dwarf is blocking the way to *newloc* 176 ⟩ ≡
    if (*loc* ≤ *max_pirate_loc*) {
        for (*j* = 1; *j* ≤ *nd*; *j*++)
            if (*odloc*[*j*] ≡ *newloc* ∧ *dseen*[*j*]) {
                printf ("A␣little␣dwarf␣with␣a␣big␣knife␣\
                        blocks␣your␣way.\n");
                newloc = *loc*; **break**;
            }
    }
This code is used in section 153.

---

base: **object** [], §63.

carry: **void** ( ), §65.

CHEST = 56, §11.

chest_loc = macro, §159.

dloc: **location** [], §159.

drop: **void** ( ), §64.

dseen: **boolean** [], §159.

false = 0, §2.

forced_move = macro ( ), §59.

i: **register int**, §164.

j: **register int**, §2.

loc: **location**, §74.

max_obj = 66, §11.

max_pirate_loc = 108, §56.

MESSAGE = 46, §11.

message_loc = macro, §159.

min_treasure = 51, §11.

move = macro ( ), §65.

nd = 5, §159.

newloc: **location**, §74.

NOTHING = 0, §11.

odloc: **location** [], §159.

pirate_not_spotted = macro, §172.

place: **location** [], §63.

printf: **int** ( ), <stdio.h>.

too_easy = macro ( ), §172.

toting = macro ( ), §63.

177. Closing the cave. You get to wander around until you've located all fifteen treasures, although you need not have taken them yet. After that, you enter a new level of complexity: A global variable called *clock1* starts ticking downwards, every time you take a turn inside the cave. When it hits zero, we start closing the cave; then we sit back and wait for you to try to get out, letting *clock2* do the ticking. The initial value of *clock1* is large enough for you to get outside.

#define *closing* ($clock1 < 0$)

⟨ Global variables 7 ⟩ +≡
    int *clock1* = 15, *clock2* = 30;   /∗ clocks that govern closing time ∗/
    boolean *panic*, *closed*;   /∗ various stages of closedness ∗/

178. Location Y2 is virtually outside the cave, so *clock1* doesn't tick there. If you stay outside the cave with all your treasures, and with the lamp switched off, the game might go on forever; but you wouldn't be having any fun.

There's an interesting hack by which you can keep *tally* positive until you've taken all the treasures out of the cave. Namely, if your first moves are

    in, take lamp, plugh, on, drop lamp, s, take silver,
        back, take lamp, plugh, out, drop silver, in,

the silver bars will be at *road*; but *prop*[SILVER] will still be −1 and *tally* will still be 15. You can bring the other 14 treasures to the *house* at your leisure; then the *tally* will drop to zero when you step outside and actually see the silver for the first time.

⟨ Check the clocks and the lamp 178 ⟩ ≡
    if (*tally* ≡ 0 ∧ *loc* ≥ *min_lower_loc* ∧ *loc* ≠ *y2*) *clock1* −−;
    if (*clock1* ≡ 0) ⟨ Warn that the cave is closing 179 ⟩
    else {
        if (*clock1* < 0) *clock2* −−;
        if (*clock2* ≡ 0) ⟨ Close the cave 181 ⟩
        else ⟨ Check the lamp 184 ⟩;
    }

This code is used in section 76.

179. At the time of first warning, we lock the grate, destroy the crystal bridge, kill all the dwarves (and the pirate), remove the troll and the bear (unless dead), and set *closing* to true. It's too much trouble to move the dragon, so we leave it. From now on until *clock2* runs out, you cannot unlock the grate, move to any location outside the cave, or create the bridge. Nor can you be resurrected if you die.

$\langle$ Warn that the cave is closing 179 $\rangle \equiv$
```
{
    printf ("A␣sepulchral␣voice,␣\
            reverberating␣through␣the␣cave,␣says,␣\"Cave\n\
        closing␣soon.␣␣All␣adventurers␣exit␣immediately␣\
            through␣main␣office.\"\n" );
    clock1 = −1;
    prop[GRATE] = 0;   prop[CRYSTAL] = 0;
    for (j = 0; j ≤ nd; j++)   dseen[j] = 0, dloc[j] = limbo;
    destroy(TROLL);   destroy(TROLL_);
    move(TROLL2, swside);   move(TROLL2_, neside);
    move(BRIDGE, swside);   move(BRIDGE_, neside);
    if (prop[BEAR] ≠ 3)   destroy(BEAR);
    prop[CHAIN] = 0;   base[CHAIN] = NOTHING;
    prop[AXE] = 0;   base[AXE] = NOTHING;
}
```
This code is used in section 178.

180.   If you try to get out while the cave is closing, we assume that you panic; we give you a few additional turns to get frantic before we close.

$\langle$ Panic at closing time 180 $\rangle \equiv$
```
{
    if (¬panic)   clock2 = 15, panic = true;
    printf ("A␣mysterious␣recorded␣voice␣\
            groans␣into␣life␣and␣announces:\n\
        \"This␣exit␣is␣closed.␣␣\
            Please␣leave␣via␣main␣office.\"\n" );
}
```
This code is used in sections 131 and 153.

AXE = 34, §11.
base: **object** [], §63.
BEAR = 45, §11.
boolean = **enum**, §2.
BRIDGE = 39, §11.
BRIDGE_ = 40, §11.
CHAIN = 66, §11.
CRYSTAL = 14, §11.
destroy = macro ( ), §65.
dloc: **location** [], §159.
dseen: **boolean** [], §159.
GRATE = 3, §11.
house = 3, §18, §25.
j: **register int**, §2.
limbo = 0, §18.
loc: **location**, §74.
min_lower_loc = 15, §18.

move = macro ( ), §65.
nd = 5, §159.
neside = 118, §18, §57.
NOTHING = 0, §11.
printf: **int** ( ), <stdio.h>.
prop: **int** [], §63.
road = 1, §18, §23.
SILVER = 53, §11.
swside = 105, §18, §55.
tally: **int**, §89.
TROLL = 41, §11.
TROLL_ = 42, §11.
TROLL2 = 43, §11.
TROLL2_ = 44, §11.
true = 1, §2.
y2 = 54, §18, §41.

181.   Finally, after *clock2* hits zero, we transport you to the final puzzle, which takes place in the previously inaccessible storage room. We have to set everything up anew, in order to use the existing machinery instead of writing a special program. We are careful not to include keys in the room, since we don't want to allow you to unlock the grate that separates you from your treasures. There is no water; otherwise we would need special code for watering the beanstalks.

The storage room has two locations, *neend* and *swend*. At the northeast end, we place empty bottles, a nursery of plants, a bed of oysters, a pile of lamps, rods with stars, sleeping dwarves, and you. At the southwest end we place a grate, a snake pit, a covey of caged birds, more rods, and pillows. A mirror stretches across one wall. But we destroy all objects you might be carrying, lest you have some that could cause trouble, such as the keys. We describe the flash of light and trundle back.

From the fact that you've seen all the treasures, we can infer that the snake is already gone, since the jewels are accessible only from the Hall of the Mountain King. We also know that you've been in the Giant Room (to get eggs); you've discovered that the clam is an oyster (because of the pearl); the dwarves have been activated, since you've found the chest. Therefore the long descriptions of *neend* and *swend* will make sense to you when you see them.

Dear reader, all the clues to this final puzzle are presented in the program itself, so you should have no trouble finding the solution.

⟨ Close the cave 181 ⟩ ≡

```
{
   printf("The␣sepulchral␣voice␣intones,␣\
          \"The␣cave␣is␣now␣closed.\"␣␣As␣the␣echoes\n\
      fade,␣there␣is␣a␣blinding␣flash␣of␣light␣\
          (and␣a␣small␣puff␣of␣orange\n\
      smoke).␣·␣·␣·␣␣␣␣␣Then␣your␣eyes␣refocus;␣\
      you␣look␣around␣and␣find...\n");
   move(BOTTLE, neend);  prop[BOTTLE] = −2;
   move(PLANT, neend);   prop[PLANT] = −1;
   move(OYSTER, neend);  prop[OYSTER] = −1;
   move(LAMP, neend);    prop[LAMP] = −1;
   move(ROD, neend);     prop[ROD] = −1;
   move(DWARF, neend);   prop[DWARF] = −1;
   move(MIRROR, neend);  prop[MIRROR] = −1;
   loc = oldloc = neend;
   move(GRATE, swend);      /∗ prop[GRATE] still zero ∗/
   move(SNAKE, swend);   prop[SNAKE] = −2;
   move(BIRD, swend);    prop[BIRD] = −2;
```

$move(\texttt{CAGE}, swend)$; $prop[\texttt{CAGE}] = -1$;
$move(\texttt{ROD2}, swend)$; $prop[\texttt{ROD2}] = -1$;
$move(\texttt{PILLOW}, swend)$; $prop[\texttt{PILLOW}] = -1$;
$move(\texttt{MIRROR\_}, swend)$;
for $(j = 1; \ j \le max\_obj; \ j{+}{+})$
  if $(toting(j)) \ destroy(j)$;
$closed = true$;
$bonus = 10$;
$stay\_put$;
}

This code is used in section 178.

182. Once the cave has closed, we look for objects being toted with $prop < 0$; their property value is changed to $-1 - prop$. This means they won't be described until they've been picked up and put down, separate from their respective piles.

⟨ Make special adjustments before looking at new input 85 ⟩ $+\equiv$
  if $(closed)$ {
    if $(prop[\texttt{OYSTER}] < 0 \wedge toting(\texttt{OYSTER}))$
      $printf(\texttt{"\%s\textbackslash n"}, note[offset[\texttt{OYSTER}] + 1])$;
    for $(j = 1; \ j \le max\_obj; \ j{+}{+})$
      if $(toting(j) \wedge prop[j] < 0) \ prop[j] = -1 - prop[j]$;
  }

$\texttt{BIRD} = 10$, §11.
$bonus$: **int**, §193.
$\texttt{BOTTLE} = 23$, §11.
$\texttt{CAGE} = 5$, §11.
$clock2$: **int**, §177.
$closed$: **boolean**, §177.
$destroy = $ macro ( ), §65.
$\texttt{DWARF} = 20$, §11.
$\texttt{GRATE} = 3$, §11.
j: **register int**, §2.
$\texttt{LAMP} = 2$, §11.
loc: **location**, §74.
$max\_obj = 66$, §11.
$\texttt{MIRROR} = 26$, §11.
$\texttt{MIRROR\_} = 27$, §11.
$move = $ macro ( ), §65.

$neend = 127$, §18, §58.
$note$: **char** *[], §63.
$offset$: **int** [], §63.
$oldloc$: **location**, §74.
$\texttt{OYSTER} = 18$, §11.
$\texttt{PILLOW} = 12$, §11.
$\texttt{PLANT} = 28$, §11.
$printf$: **int** ( ), **<stdio.h>**.
$prop$: **int** [], §63.
$\texttt{ROD} = 6$, §11.
$\texttt{ROD2} = 7$, §11.
$\texttt{SNAKE} = 13$, §11.
$stay_put = $ macro, §78.
$swend = 128$, §18, §58.
$toting = $ macro ( ), §63.
$true = 1$, §2.

183.   Death and resurrection.   Only the most persistent adven-
turers get to see the closing of the cave, because their lamp gives out
first. For example, if you have lost the ability to find any treasures, *tally*
will never go to zero.

⟨ Zap the lamp if the remaining treasures are too elusive 183 ⟩ ≡
   if (*tally* ≡ *lost_treasures* ∧ *tally* > 0 ∧ *limit* > 35)   *limit* = 35;

This code is used in section 88.

184.   On every turn, we check to see if you are in trouble lampwise.

⟨ Check the lamp 184 ⟩ ≡
   {
      if (*prop* [LAMP] ≡ 1)   *limit* −−;
      if (*limit* ≤ 30 ∧ *here* (BATTERIES) ∧ *prop* [BATTERIES] ≡ 0 ∧ *here* (LAMP))
         ⟨ Replace the batteries 186 ⟩
      else if (*limit* ≡ 0) ⟨ Extinguish the lamp 187 ⟩
      else if (*limit* < 0 ∧ *loc* < *min_in_cave*) {
         printf ("There's␣not␣much␣point␣in␣\
                  wandering␣around␣out␣here,␣and␣you␣can't\n\
                  explore␣the␣cave␣without␣a␣lamp.␣␣\
                  So␣let's␣just␣call␣it␣a␣day.\n");
         goto *give_up*;
      } **else if** (*limit* ≤ 30 ∧ ¬*warned* ∧ *here* (LAMP)) {
         printf ("Your␣lamp␣is␣getting␣dim");
         if (*prop* [BATTERIES] ≡ 1)
            printf (",␣and␣you're␣out␣of␣spare␣batteries.␣␣You'd\n\
                     best␣start␣wrapping␣this␣up.\n");
         else if (*place* [BATTERIES] ≡ *limbo*)
            printf (".␣␣You'd␣best␣start␣wrapping␣this␣up,␣unless\n\
                     you␣can␣find␣some␣fresh␣batteries.␣␣\
                     I␣seem␣to␣recall␣that␣there's\n\
                     a␣vending␣machine␣in␣the␣maze.␣␣\
                     Bring␣some␣coins␣with␣you.\n");
         else *printf* (".␣␣You'd␣best␣go␣back␣for␣those␣batteries.\n");
         warned = *true*;
      }
   }

This code is used in section 178.

185.   ⟨ Global variables 7 ⟩ +≡
   boolean *warned*;
      /* have you been warned about the low power supply? */

186.   The batteries hold a pretty hefty charge.

⟨ Replace the batteries 186 ⟩ ≡

```
      {
        printf ("Your␣lamp␣is␣getting␣dim.␣␣\
                I'm␣taking␣the␣liberty␣of␣replacing\n\
             the␣batteries.\n" );
        prop [BATTERIES] = 1;
        if (toting (BATTERIES))  drop (BATTERIES, loc);
        limit = 2500;
      }
```

This code is used in section 184.

187. ⟨ Extinguish the lamp 187 ⟩ ≡

```
      {
        limit = −1;  prop [LAMP] = 0;
        if (here (LAMP))  printf ("Your␣lamp␣has␣run␣out␣of␣power." );
      }
```

This code is used in section 184.

188. The easiest way to get killed is to fall into a pit in pitch darkness.

⟨ Deal with death and resurrection 188 ⟩ ≡

pitch_dark:

```
        printf ("You␣fell␣into␣a␣pit␣and␣broke␣every␣bone␣in␣your␣body!\n" );
        oldoldloc = loc;
```

See also sections 189, 191, and 192.

This code is used in section 2.

BATTERIES = 49, §11.
boolean = **enum**, §2.
drop: **void** ( ), §64.
give_up: label, §95.
here = macro ( ), §74.
LAMP = 2, §11.
limbo = 0, §18.
limit: **int**, §103.
loc: **location**, §74.

lost_treasures: **int**, §89.
min_in_cave = 9, §18.
oldoldloc: **location**, §74.
place: **location** [], §63.
printf: **int** ( ), <stdio.h>.
prop: **int** [], §63.
tally: **int**, §89.
toting = macro ( ), §63.
true = 1, §2.

189.   "You're dead, Jim."

When you die, *newloc* is undefined (often *limbo*) and *oldloc* is what killed you. So we look at *oldoldloc*, the last place you were safe.

We generously allow you to die up to three times; *death_count* is the number of deaths you have had so far.

#**define**   *max_deaths*   3

⟨ Deal with death and resurrection 188 ⟩ +≡
death: *death_count* ++;
  if (*closing*) {
    printf ("It␣looks␣as␣though␣you're␣dead.␣␣\
        Well,␣seeing␣as␣how␣it's␣so␣close\n\
      to␣closing␣time␣anyway,␣let's␣just␣call␣it␣a␣day.\n");
    goto *quit*;
  }
  if ($\neg$*yes* (*death_wishes* [2 * *death_count* − 2], *death_wishes* [2 * *death_count* − 1],
      ok) $\vee$ *death_count* $\equiv$ *max_deaths*) **goto** *quit*;

190. ⟨ Global variables 7 ⟩ +≡

```
int death_count;       /* how often have you kicked the bucket? */
char *death_wishes[2 * max_deaths] = {
"Oh dear, you seem to have gotten yourself killed.  \
        I might be able to\n\
    help you out, but I've never really done this before.  \
        Do you want me\n\
    to try to reincarnate you?",
"All right.  But don't blame me if something goes wr......\n\
        ----------------------POOF!! ---\n\
    You are engulfed in a cloud of orange smoke.  \
        Coughing and gasping,\n\
    you emerge from the smoke and find....",
"You clumsy oaf, you've done it again!  \
        I don't know how long I can\n\
    keep this up.  \
        Do you want me to try reincarnating you again?",
"Okay, now where did I put my resurrection kit?....  >POOF!<\n\
    Everything disappears in a dense cloud of orange smoke.",
"Now you've really done it!  \
        I'm out of orange smoke!  You don't expect\n\
    me to do a decent reincarnation \
        without any orange smoke, do you?",
"Okay, if you're so smart, do it yourself!  I'm leaving!" };
```

---

closing = macro, §177.
limbo = 0, §18.
newloc: **location**, §74.
ok = macro, §14.
oldloc: **location**, §74.

oldoldloc: **location**, §74.
printf: **int** ( ), <stdio.h>.
quit: label, §2.
yes: **boolean** ( ), §71.

191.   At this point you are reborn. All objects you were carrying are dropped at *oldoldloc* (presumably your last place prior to being killed), with their properties unchanged. The loop runs backwards, so that the bird is dropped before the cage. The lamp is a special case, because we wouldn't want to leave it underground; we turn it off and leave it outside the building — only if you were carrying it, of course. You yourself are left *inside* the building. (Heaven help you if you try to xyzzy back into the cave without the lamp.) We zap *oldloc* so that you can't just go back.

⟨ Deal with death and resurrection 188 ⟩ +≡
  if (*toting*(LAMP)) *prop*[LAMP] = 0;
  place[WATER] = *limbo*; *place*[OIL] = *limbo*;   /∗ must not *drop* them ∗/
  for (*j* = *max_obj*; *j* > 0; *j*−−)
    if (*toting*(*j*)) *drop*(*j*, *j* ≡ LAMP ? *road* : *oldoldloc*);
  loc = *oldloc* = *house*;
  goto *commence*;

192.   Oh dear, you've disturbed the dwarves.

⟨ Deal with death and resurrection 188 ⟩ +≡
dwarves_upset:
  printf("The␣resulting␣ruckus␣has␣awakened␣the␣dwarves.␣␣\
       There␣are␣now␣several\n\
    threatening␣little␣dwarves␣in␣the␣room␣with␣you!␣␣\
       Most␣of␣them␣throw\n\
    knives␣at␣you!␣␣All␣of␣them␣get␣you!\n");

193.   Scoring.   Here is the scoring algorithm we use:

Objective	Points	Total possible
Getting well into cave	25	25
Each treasure < chest	12	60
Treasure chest itself	14	14
Each treasure > chest	16	144
Each unused death	10	30
Not quitting	4	4
Reaching Witt's End	1	1
Getting to *closing*	25	25
Various additional bonuses		45
Round out the total	2	2
	Total:	350

Points can also be deducted for using hints. One consequence of these rules is that you get 32 points just for quitting on your first turn. And there's a way to get 57 points in just three turns.

Full points for treasures are awarded only if they aren't broken and you have deposited them in the building. But we give you 2 points just for seeing a treasure.

#**define** *max_score*   350

⟨ Global variables 7 ⟩ +≡
   int *bonus*;
      /∗ extra points awarded for exceptional adventuring skills ∗/

---

closing = macro, §177.
commence: label, §75.
drop: **void** ( ), §64.
house = 3, §18, §25.
j: **register int**, §2.
LAMP = 2, §11.
limbo = 0, §18.
loc: **location**, §74.
max_obj = 66, §11.

OIL = 25, §11.
oldloc: **location**, §74.
oldoldloc: **location**, §74.
place: **location** [ ], §63.
printf: **int** ( ), <stdio.h>.
prop: **int** [ ], §63.
road = 1, §18, §23.
toting = macro ( ), §63.
WATER = 24, §11.

194. The hints are table driven, using several arrays:

- *hint_count*[*j*] is the number of recent turns whose location is relevant to hint *j*;
- *hint_thresh*[*j*] is the number of such turns before we consider offering that hint;
- *hint_cost*[*j*] is the number of points you pay for it;
- *hint_prompt*[*j*] is the way we offer it;
- *hint*[*j*] is the hint;
- *hinted*[*j*] is true after we've given it.

Hint 0 is for instructions at the beginning; it costs you 5 points, but you get extra power in the lamp. The other hints also usually extend the lamp's power. Hint 1 is for reading the oyster. And hints 2 through 7 are for the *cave_hint*, *bird_hint*, *snake_hint*, *twist_hint*, *dark_hint*, and *witt_hint*, respectively.

Here's the subroutine that handles all eight kinds of hints.

⟨ Subroutines 6 ⟩ +≡

```
    void offer ARGS((int));
    void offer(j)
        int j;
    {
        if (j > 1) {
            if (¬yes(hint_prompt[j], "␣I␣am␣prepared␣to␣give␣you␣a␣hint,",
                    ok)) return;
            printf("␣but␣it␣will␣cost␣you␣%d␣points.␣␣", hint_cost[j]);
            hinted[j] = yes("Do␣you␣want␣the␣hint?", hint[j], ok);
        } else hinted[j] = yes(hint_prompt[j], hint[j], ok);
        if (hinted[j] ∧ limit > 30) limit += 30 * hint_cost[j];
    }
```

195. ⟨ Check if a hint applies, and give it if requested 195 ⟩ ≡

```
    for (j = 2, k = cave_hint; j ≤ 7; j++, k += k)
        if (¬hinted[j]) {
            if ((flags[loc] & k) ≡ 0) hint_count[j] = 0;
            else if (++hint_count[j] ≥ hint_thresh[j]) {
                switch (j) {
                case 2: if (prop[GRATE] ≡ 0 ∧ ¬here(KEYS)) break;
                    else goto bypass;
                case 3: if (here(BIRD) ∧ oldobj ≡ BIRD ∧ toting(ROD)) break;
                    else continue;
                case 4: if (here(SNAKE) ∧ ¬here(BIRD)) break; else goto bypass;
                case 5: if (first[loc] ≡ 0 ∧ first[oldloc] ≡ 0 ∧ first[oldoldloc] ≡
                        0 ∧ holding > 1) break;
```

```
        else goto bypass;
    case 6: if (prop[EMERALD] ≠ −1 ∧ prop[PYRAMID] ≡ −1) break;
        else goto bypass;
    case 7: break;
    }
    offer(j);
bypass: hint_count[j] = 0;
    }
}
```

This code is used in section 76.

196.   #define *n_hints* 8

⟨ Global variables 7 ⟩ +≡

    int *hint_count*[*n_hints*];   /∗ how long you have needed this hint ∗/

    int *hint_thresh*[*n_hints*] = {0, 0, 4, 5, 8, 75, 25, 20};

      /∗ how long we will wait ∗/

    int *hint_cost*[*n_hints*] = {5, 10, 2, 2, 2, 4, 5, 3};

      /∗ how much we will charge ∗/

    char ∗*hint_prompt*[*n_hints*] = {

```
"Welcome␣to␣Adventure!!␣␣Would␣you␣like␣instructions?",
"Hmmm,␣this␣looks␣like␣a␣clue,␣\
          which␣means␣it'll␣cost␣you␣10␣points␣to\n\
     read␣it.␣␣Should␣I␣go␣ahead␣and␣read␣it␣anyway?",
"Are␣you␣trying␣to␣get␣into␣the␣cave?",
"Are␣you␣trying␣to␣catch␣the␣bird?",
"Are␣you␣trying␣to␣deal␣somehow␣with␣the␣snake?",
"Do␣you␣need␣help␣getting␣out␣of␣the␣maze?",
"Are␣you␣trying␣to␣explore␣beyond␣the␣Plover␣Room?",
"Do␣you␣need␣help␣getting␣out␣of␣here?" };
```

    char ∗*hint*[*n_hints*] = {

```
"Somewhere␣nearby␣is␣Colossal␣Cave,␣\
          where␣others␣have␣found␣fortunes␣in\n\
     treasure␣and␣gold,␣\
          though␣it␣is␣rumored␣that␣some␣who␣enter␣are␣never\n\
     seen␣again.␣␣Magic␣is␣said␣to␣work␣in␣the␣cave.␣\
     ␣I␣will␣be␣your␣eyes\n\
     and␣hands.␣␣Direct␣me␣with␣commands␣of␣one␣or␣two␣words.␣␣\
     I␣should\n\
     warn␣you␣that␣I␣look␣at␣only␣\
          the␣first␣five␣letters␣of␣each␣word,␣so\n\
     you'll␣have␣to␣enter␣\"NORTHEAST\"␣as␣\"NE\"␣\
     to␣distinguish␣it␣from\n\
     \"NORTH\".␣␣Should␣you␣get␣stuck,␣\
          type␣\"HELP\"␣for␣some␣general␣hints.\n\
     For␣information␣on␣how␣to␣end␣your␣adventure,␣etc.,␣\
          type␣\"INFO\".\n\
     ␣␣␣␣␣␣␣␣␣␣␣␣␣␣␣␣␣␣␣␣␣␣␣␣␣␣‾␣␣‾␣␣‾\n\
     The␣first␣adventure␣program␣was␣\
          developed␣by␣Willie␣Crowther.\n\
     Most␣of␣the␣features␣of␣the␣current␣program␣were␣\
          added␣by␣Don␣Woods;\n\
     all␣of␣its␣bugs␣were␣added␣by␣Don␣Knuth.",
"It␣says,␣\"There␣is␣something␣strange␣about␣this␣place,␣\
          such␣that␣one\n\
     of␣the␣words␣I've␣always␣known␣now␣has␣a␣new␣effect.\"",
```

```
"The␣grate␣is␣very␣solid␣and␣has␣a␣hardened␣steel␣lock.␣␣\
        You␣cannot\n\
    enter␣without␣a␣key,␣and␣there␣are␣no␣keys␣in␣sight.␣␣\
        I␣would␣recommend\n\
    looking␣elsewhere␣for␣the␣keys.",
"Something␣seems␣to␣be␣frightening␣the␣bird␣just␣now␣\
        and␣you␣cannot\n\
    catch␣it␣no␣matter␣what␣you␣try.␣\
        ␣Perhaps␣you␣might␣try␣later.",
"You␣can't␣kill␣the␣snake,␣or␣drive␣it␣away,␣\
    or␣avoid␣it,␣or␣anything\n\
    like␣that.␣␣There␣is␣a␣way␣to␣get␣by,␣\
        but␣you␣don't␣have␣the␣necessary\n\
    resources␣right␣now.",
"You␣can␣make␣the␣passages␣look␣less␣alike␣by␣dropping␣things.",
"There␣is␣a␣way␣to␣explore␣that␣region␣\
        without␣having␣to␣worry␣about\n\
    falling␣into␣a␣pit.␣␣\
        None␣of␣the␣objects␣available␣is␣immediately\n\
    useful␣for␣discovering␣the␣secret.",
"Don't␣go␣west."};
boolean hinted[n_hints];        /* have you seen the hint? */
```

---

boolean = enum, §2.

197.   Here's a subroutine that computes the current score.

⟨ Subroutines 6 ⟩ +≡

  int *score* ARGS((**void**));

  int *score* ( )

  {

    register int *j*, *s* = 2;

    register object *k*;

    if (*dflag*) *s* += 25;   /∗ you've gotten well inside ∗/

    for (*k* = *min_treasure*; *k* ≤ *max_obj*; *k*++) {

      if (*prop*[*k*] ≥ 0) {

        s += 2;

        if (*place*[*k*] ≡ *house* ∧ *prop*[*k*] ≡ 0)

          s += (*k* < CHEST ? 10 : *k* ≡ CHEST ? 12 : 14);

      }

    }

    s += 10 ∗ (*max_deaths* − *death_count*);

    if (¬*gave_up*) *s* += 4;

    if (*place*[MAG] ≡ *witt*) *s*++;   /∗ proof of your visit ∗/

    if (*closing*) *s* += 25;

    s += *bonus*;

    for (*j* = 0; *j* < *n_hints*; *j*++)

      if (*hinted*[*j*]) *s* −= *hint_cost*[*j*];

    return *s*;

  }

198.   The worst possible score is −3. It is possible (but unusual) to earn exactly 1 point.

#define *highest_class* 8

⟨ Print the score and say adieu 198 ⟩ ≡

  k = *score* ( );

  printf ("You␣scored␣%d␣point%s␣out␣of␣a␣possible␣%d,␣\

        using␣%d␣turn%s.\n", *k*, *k* ≡ 1 ? "" : "s", *max_score*, *turns*,

      turns ≡ 1 ? "" : "s");

  for (*j* = 0; *class_score*[*j*] ≤ *k*; *j*++) ;

  printf ("%s\n\

      To␣achieve␣the␣next␣higher␣rating", *class_message*[*j*]);

  if (*j* < *highest_class*) *printf* (",␣you␣need␣%d␣more␣point%s.\n",

      class_score[*j*] − *k*, *class_score*[*j*] ≡ *k* + 1 ? "" : "s");

  else *printf* ("␣would␣be␣a␣neat␣trick!\n\

      Congratulations!!\n");

This code is used in section 2.

199. ⟨ Global variables 7 ⟩ +≡
  int *class_score* [ ] = {35, 100, 130, 200, 250, 300, 330, 349, 9999};
  char ∗*class_message* [ ] = {
  "You␣are␣obviously␣a␣rank␣amateur.␣␣Better␣luck␣next␣time.",
  "Your␣score␣qualifies␣you␣as␣a␣novice␣class␣adventurer.",
  "You␣have␣achieved␣the␣rating␣\"Experienced␣Adventurer\".",
  "You␣may␣now␣consider␣yourself␣a␣\"Seasoned␣Adventurer\".",
  "You␣have␣reached␣\"Junior␣Master\"␣status.",
  "Your␣score␣puts␣you␣in␣Master␣Adventurer␣Class␣C.",
  "Your␣score␣puts␣you␣in␣Master␣Adventurer␣Class␣B.",
  "Your␣score␣puts␣you␣in␣Master␣Adventurer␣Class␣A.",
  "All␣of␣Adventuredom␣gives␣tribute␣to␣you,␣\
    "Adventure␣Grandmaster!" };

200. Launching the program.   The program is now complete; all
we must do is put a few of the pieces together.

Most of the initialization takes place while you are reading the opening
message.

⟨ Initialize all tables 200 ⟩ ≡
  ⟨ Initialize the random number generator 156 ⟩;
  offer (0);   /∗ Give the welcome message and possible instructions ∗/
  limit = (*hinted* [0] ? 1000 : 330);   /∗ set lifetime of lamp ∗/
  ⟨ Build the vocabulary 10 ⟩;
  ⟨ Build the travel table 23 ⟩;
  ⟨ Build the object tables 69 ⟩;
  oldoldloc = *oldloc* = *loc* = *newloc* = *road*;
This code is used in section 2.

ARGS = macro ( ), §3.
bonus: **int**, §193.
CHEST = 56, §11.
closing = macro, §177.
death_count: **int**, §190.
dflag: **int**, §159.
gave_up: **boolean**, §96.
hint_cost: **int** [ ], §196.
hinted: **boolean** [ ], §196.
house = 3, §18, §25.
j: **register int**, §2.
k: **register int**, §2.
limit: **int**, §103.
loc: **location**, §74.
MAG = 19, §11.
max_deaths = 3, §189.

max_obj = 66, §11.
max_score = 350, §193.
min_treasure = 51, §11.
n_hints = 8, §196.
newloc: **location**, §74.
object = **enum**, §11.
offer: **void** ( ), §194.
oldloc: **location**, §74.
oldoldloc: **location**, §74.
place: **location** [ ], §63.
printf: **int** ( ), <stdio.h>.
prop: **int** [ ], §63.
road = 1, §18, §23.
turns: **int**, §77.
witt = 67, §18, §44.

201.　Index.　A large cloud of green smoke appears in front of you. It clears away to reveal a tall wizard, clothed in grey. He fixes you with a steely glare and declares, "This adventure has lasted too long." With that he makes a single pass over you with his hands, and everything around you fades away into a grey nothingness.

202. Names of the sections.

⟨ Additional local registers 22, 68, 144 ⟩   Used in section 2.

⟨ Advance *dflag* to 2 162 ⟩   Used in section 161.

⟨ Apologize for inability to backtrack 145 ⟩   Used in section 143.

⟨ Block the troll bridge and stay put 152 ⟩   Used in section 151.

⟨ Build the object tables 69, 70 ⟩   Used in section 200.

⟨ Build the travel table 23, 24, 25, 26, 27, 28, 29, 30, 31, 32, 33, 34, 35, 36, 37, 38,
    39, 40, 41, 42, 43, 44, 45, 46, 47, 48, 49, 50, 51, 52, 53, 54, 55, 56, 57, 58, 59, 60, 61,
    62 ⟩   Used in section 200.

⟨ Build the vocabulary 10, 12, 14, 16 ⟩   Used in section 200.

⟨ Chase the troll away 119 ⟩   Used in section 117.

⟨ Check for interference with the proposed move to *newloc* 153 ⟩   Used
    in section 75.

⟨ Check if a hint applies, and give it if requested 195 ⟩   Used in section 76.

⟨ Check special cases for dropping a liquid 115 ⟩   Used in section 117.

⟨ Check special cases for dropping the bird 120 ⟩   Used in section 117.

⟨ Check special cases for dropping the vase 121 ⟩   Used in section 117.

⟨ Check special cases for taking a bird 114 ⟩   Used in section 112.

⟨ Check special cases for taking a liquid 113 ⟩   Used in section 112.

⟨ Check the clocks and the lamp 178 ⟩   Used in section 76.

⟨ Check the lamp 184 ⟩   Used in section 178.

⟨ Choose *newloc* via plover-alcove passage 149 ⟩   Used in section 146.

⟨ Close the cave 181 ⟩   Used in section 178.

⟨ Cross troll bridge if possible 151 ⟩   Used in section 146.

⟨ Deal with death and resurrection 188, 189, 191, 192 ⟩   Used in section 2.

⟨ Describe the objects at this location 88 ⟩   Used in section 86.

⟨ Determine the next location, *newloc* 146 ⟩   Cited in section 19.   Used in
    section 75.

⟨ Dispatch the poor bird 127 ⟩   Used in section 125.

⟨ Drop the emerald during plover transportation 150 ⟩   Used in section 146.

⟨ Extinguish the lamp 187 ⟩   Used in section 184.

⟨ Fun stuff for dragon 128 ⟩   Used in section 125.

⟨ Get user input; **goto** *try_move* if motion is requested 76 ⟩   Used in section 75.

⟨ Give advice about going WEST 80 ⟩   Used in section 76.

⟨ Give optional **plugh** hint 157 ⟩   Used in section 86.

⟨ Global variables 7, 15, 17, 20, 21, 63, 73, 74, 77, 81, 84, 87, 89, 96, 103, 137, 142, 155, 159, 165, 168, 171, 177, 185, 190, 193, 196, 199 ⟩   Used in section 2.

⟨ Handle additional special cases of input 83, 105 ⟩   Used in section 76.

⟨ Handle cases of intransitive verbs and **continue** 92, 93, 94, 95, 136 ⟩   Used in section 79.

⟨ Handle cases of transitive verbs and **continue** 97, 98, 99, 100, 101, 102, 106, 107, 110, 112, 117, 122, 125, 129, 130, 135 ⟩   Used in section 79.

⟨ Handle special cases of input 82, 138 ⟩   Used in section 76.

⟨ Handle special motion words 140 ⟩   Used in section 75.

⟨ If the condition of instruction q isn't satisfied, advance q 147 ⟩   Used in section 146.

⟨ If GRATE is actually a motion word, move to it 91 ⟩   Used in section 90.

⟨ Initialize all tables 200 ⟩   Used in section 2.

⟨ Initialize the random number generator 156 ⟩   Used in section 200.

⟨ Let the pirate be spotted 175 ⟩   Used in section 172.

⟨ Look at *word1* and exit to the right place if it completes a command 78 ⟩   Used in section 76.

⟨ Macros for subroutine prototypes 3 ⟩   Used in section 2.

⟨ Make a table of all potential exits, $ploc[0]$ through $ploc[i-1]$ 166 ⟩   Used in section 164.

⟨ Make dwarf j follow 167 ⟩   Used in section 164.

⟨ Make special adjustments before looking at new input 85, 158, 169, 182 ⟩   Used in section 76.

⟨ Make sure *obj* is meaningful at the current location 90 ⟩   Used in section 78.

⟨ Make the pirate track you 172 ⟩   Used in section 167.

⟨ Make the threatening dwarves attack 170 ⟩   Used in section 164.

⟨ Move dwarves and the pirate 164 ⟩   Used in section 161.

⟨ Open chain 133 ⟩   Used in section 132.

⟨ Open/close chain 132 ⟩   Used in section 131.

⟨ Open/close clam/oyster 134 ⟩   Used in section 130.

⟨ Open/close grate/chain 131 ⟩   Used in section 130.

⟨ Panic at closing time 180 ⟩   Used in sections 131 and 153.

⟨ Perform an action in the current place 79 ⟩   Used in section 75.

⟨ Possibly move dwarves and the pirate 161 ⟩   Used in section 75.

⟨ Pour water or oil on the door 109 ⟩   Used in section 107.

⟨ Print the score and say adieu 198 ⟩   Used in section 2.

⟨ Proceed foobarically 139 ⟩   Used in section 136.

⟨ Put coins in the vending machine 118 ⟩   Used in section 117.

⟨ Repeat the long description and **continue** 141 ⟩   Used in section 140.

⟨ Replace the batteries 186 ⟩   Used in section 184.

⟨ Report on inapplicable motion and **continue** 148 ⟩   Used in section 146.

⟨ Report the current state 86 ⟩   Used in section 75.

⟨ See if there's a unique object to attack 126 ⟩   Used in section 125.

⟨ Simulate an adventure, going to *quit* when finished 75 ⟩   Used in section 2.

⟨ Snarf a treasure for the troll 124 ⟩   Used in section 122.

⟨ Snatch all treasures that are snatchable here 174 ⟩   Used in section 173.

⟨ Stay in *loc* if a dwarf is blocking the way to *newloc* 176 ⟩   Used in section 153.

⟨ Subroutines 6, 8, 64, 65, 66, 71, 72, 154, 160, 194, 197 ⟩   Used in section 2.

⟨ Take booty and hide it in the chest 173 ⟩   Used in section 172.

⟨ Throw the axe at a dwarf 163 ⟩   Used in section 122.

⟨ Throw the axe at the bear 123 ⟩   Used in section 122.

⟨ Try to fill the vase 111 ⟩   Used in section 110.

⟨ Try to go back 143 ⟩   Used in section 140.

⟨ Try to water the plant 108 ⟩   Used in section 107.

⟨ Type definitions 5, 9, 11, 13, 18, 19 ⟩   Used in section 2.

⟨ Warn that the cave is closing 179 ⟩   Used in section 178.

⟨ Zap the lamp if the remaining treasures are too elusive 183 ⟩   Used in section 88.

203.   Addendum. A definitive discussion of the origins of this fascinating program has been compiled by Dennis G. Jerz, "Somewhere nearby is Colossal Cave: Examining Will Crowther's original 'Adventure' in code and in Kentucky," *Digital Humanities Quarterly* **1**, 2 (Summer 2007), available online.

Chapter 28

Ziegler's Giant Bar

[This material was assembled from documents in my family archives.]

George Ziegler (1830–1904) helped to found a candy-making company in 1861. Eventually the George Ziegler Company — based in Milwaukee, Wisconsin, where I was born — became one of the top five manufacturers of chocolate candy in the USA. Their most famous creation was the Giant Bar, introduced in 1911, the first candy bar to be sold in a covered wrapper. It contained "sweet buttermilk chocolate" and "number one roasted peanuts," and when I was a child you could buy this delicious confection for just a nickel.

FIGURE 1. Candy wrappers like this, once commonplace, are now collectors' items.

The Ziegler Company sponsored a weekly television program for children called the Museum Explorer's Club, produced by the Milwaukee Public Museum and broadcast every Tuesday afternoon by WTMJ-TV. In 1951, when I was a student in eighth grade, they introduced a contest that captivated my attention: How many words can be spelled using only the letters of the phrase `Ziegler's Giant Bar`? (The precise rules are given in Fig. 2 on the next page.)

Immediately I could write down lots of words like `learn`, `strange`, `beggar`, `zebras`, etc., etc., including even longer words like `librarian` and `libertarian`. I was definitely hooked on the problem.

So — and I'm embarrassed to admit it, but I might as well 'fess up — I told my parents that I had a stomach ache and would have to stay home from school one day. And also another day, and another, continuing for two weeks as I worked on the giant-bar challenge.

395

Official Rules for the Word Building Contest

1. Using the slogan `Ziegler's Giant Bar`, make a list of all the words of two letters or more that you can find. No proper names. You may use each letter in any word as often as it appears in the slogan.

2. Print your name, address, and age plainly on your entry, and be sure to enclose a Giant Bar wrapper.

3. The contest is open to all children between the ages of 8 and 15, except to families of persons employed by the Ziegler Candy Company and their advertising agency.

4. All entries should be mailed to Giant Bar, c/o WTMJ-TV, Milwaukee 1, Wisconsin.

5. Contest closes at midnight December 11, 1951.

6. All entries become the property of the Ziegler Candy Company. Prize-winners will receive their prizes on the Museum Explorer's Club program, December 18, 1951, at 4:15pm on WTMJ-TV.

7. Entries will be judged on the basis of the largest correct number of words submitted and on neatness, accuracy, and readability.

FIGURE 2. A competition that I couldn't resist.

My father had acquired a huge unabridged dictionary, the *Funk & Wagnalls New Standard Dictionary of the English Language* (1913), which I had been wanting to examine more closely. It contained 2757 large-format pages packed with small type—nearly 16,000 characters per page. But I realized that I wouldn't have to look at the whole thing. For example, I could completely skip past all words that began with c, d, f, h, j, k, m, o-q, and u-y; thus at most 1497 of the 2757 pages would be relevant. Furthermore, the same culling process could be applied to the second letters of words: I could jump from `ac-` on page 16 to `ae` on page 43, and from `af-` on page 46 to `ag` on page 50, etc. The third and subsequent letters of words also allowed similar speedups.

So I made myself a little card that contained the whole repertoire of available letters, in alphabetical order:

a a b e e g g i i l n r r s t z

By running this card along the columns of definitions, I could rather quickly identify all of the permissible words. (In retrospect, it seems that "algorithmic thinking" was already in my blood at the time.)

Lots of scratch-paper was available in our house, so I wrote down each giant-bar word as I found it, filling many sheets. My parents soon noticed what I was doing, of course, and this must have presented them with quite a dilemma. Should they punish me for playing hooky? (I did actually have some digestive problems, not entirely imaginary, but I also was feeling "consumed" by this project.) Fortunately, by the second week, they had gotten into the spirit of the hunt, and they even helped me to type up the results of my labors.

When the work was complete, I had come up with a total of 4,766 words, broken down by first letter as follows:

a... 667	g... 718	n... 148	t... 470
b... 862	i... 165	r... 553	z... 59
e... 248	l... 375	s... 501	

(Actually I thought I had identified 4,768 valid words; but I see now that my list included two instances of two-word combinations, 'ab intra' and 'in re', which violate the rules. Those two have been deleted from the counts above.) I submitted the list on 21 typewritten pages of legal-size paper, with four columns of roughly 55 words per page.

Here, for example, were the first words that I found, preceding 'ae':

aa	abatis	aberre	ablegating	abregers
aal	abe	aberrs	abler	abrest
aalii	abear	abet	ablest	abri
aaliis	abearing	abets	ablet	abrin
aals	abears	abgregate	abligate	abris
aar	abee	abgregates	abligates	abs
aas	abegge	abietin	ablins	absent
aba	abegges	abigeat	abnegate	absenter
abaiser	abeile	abigeats	abnegates	absit
abanet	abel	abit	abnet	abstain
abanets	abele	abite	abnets	abstainer
abas	abeles	abites	abra	absterge
abase	aberr	ablate	abras	absterging
abaser	aberrant	ablates	abrase	abstringe
abasing	aberrate	ablaze	abrasing	abstringer
abate	aberrates	able	abrasite	
abater	aberrating	ablegate	abreast	
abating	aberratings	ablegates	abreger	

(The one-letter word a was, of course, disallowed by rule 1.) Notice that nouns, like aa, aal, aalii, aba, etc., can usually be made plural by adding an s. Verbs, like abase, usually take the suffixes -er, -ing, and -s; adjectives, like able, often take -er and -est. I saved time by noting such things down in abbreviated form, eventually supplying the full words only when everything was typed up. It was necessary to avoid using a letter too often; for instance, `abase` leads to `abaser` and `abasing` but not to `abases`, because only one `s` is available. Later on in the alphabet, I could go from `rare` to `rarest` but not to `rarer`.

How well did I do? Can I improve on this list today, as an adult? While writing this chapter I decided to experiment with Stuart Flexner's *Random House Dictionary of the English Language*, second edition, unabridged (1987), which sits next to the chair where I do most of my work. Trying to put myself back into the shoes of an eighth-grader, I came up with only 38 words, compared to the 87 listed above! Okay, I wasn't good at plurals when getting started this time — I missed `aas`, `aaliis`, `abas`, and `abris` — so I should have had 42 instead of 38. Still there was quite a lot of difference: The Funk & Wagnalls collection that I'd used in 1951 included 54 words that are absent from Flexner's list.

I knew that different unabridged dictionaries choose to mention different words, but I was surprised by how different they actually are. So I looked closer, and found that 12 of the 54 "extra" Funk & Wagnalls words are not in the Oxford English Dictionary either. (For example, the vintage-2010 OED lacks `abigeat`, `abit`, `ablins`, `absterge`.) All 12 of the mystery words were, however, present in the current online Wiktionary, with three exceptions: Funk included `abreger` and `abregers` as verbs, borrowed from French by musicians who shorten a composition; and he included `abrest` as a simplified spelling of `abreast`, credited to the Simplified Spelling Board.*

---

*The Simplified Spelling Board, a group of several dozen leading lexicographers organized in 1906 with the backing of Andrew Carnegie and U.S. President Theodore Roosevelt, desired "to promote, by systematic and continued effort, the gradual simplification and regulation of English spelling." Many of their suggestions — like 'ether' for 'æther', 'license' for 'licence', 'omelet' for 'omelette', 'draft' for 'draught', 'plow' for 'plough', 'criticize' for 'criticise', 'sulfur' for 'sulphur', 'fiber' for 'fibre' — have been widely adopted, at least in America. But most of them — including 'hed' for 'head', 'hart' for 'heart', 'dout' for 'doubt', 'dum' for 'dumb', 'aile' for 'aisle', 'fild' for 'filled', 'justis' for 'justice', 'adjectiv' for 'adjective', 'infinit' for 'infinite', 'surprize'(!) for 'surprise' — have found little acceptance.

Funk's dictionary also listed simplifications that were proposed at the time by the American Philological Association, who went further: The word 'little' wasn't 'litl' enough for them! I had only a few opportunities to include APA spellings for giant-bar words; I could have listed `gagl`, `gigl`, and `nigl`. But I either missed them or decided that they were too far out.

Conversely, Random House came up with several entries before `ae` that F&W didn't: `abelia`, `abelias`, `abient`, `ablare`, `abristle`, `abseil`. My new list also included two that I had mistakenly overlooked in 1951: `abigail` and `ablating`. (The first of these was hidden under the proper name `Abigail`; an alternate usage of that word, meaning "maid," was cryptically said to be spelled '[a-]'.) Adding these, together with the word `abates` (which I had somehow failed to include in 1951 as well as in 2010) and the word `abelian` (which mathematicians now commonly write with lowercase `a`), makes a grand total of $87 + 8 + 1 + 1 = 97$ words before `ae` that all have a legitimate claim to be giant-bar eligible.*

You may have noted that the phrase "`Ziegler's Giant Bar`" includes an apostrophe. I saw that too, and my list of 4,766 submitted words included 11 cases where I'd found an apostrophe as part of a dictionary entry: `ain't`, `an't`, `aren't`, `e'en`, `e'er`, `'gainst`, `isn't`, `it's`, `ta'en`, `'st`, `'tis`. Near the end of the project I realized that apostrophes could also be used much more often, to form possessive forms of nouns. For example, from `aa` I could make both `aa's` and `aas'`, meaning something that belongs to a Hawaiian lava flow or to more than one lava flow. I left such cases out, because there wasn't time to make a supplementary list and because I feared that I would be stretching rule 1 too far. If apostrophes were really OK, I could also have included plural forms for each of the relevant letters: `a's`, `b's`, `e's`, `g's`, `i's`, `l's`, `n's`, `r's`, `t's`, `z's`.

For the record, my list contained just three words of twelve letters or more: `arterializes`, `interregalia`, and the grand champion, `interregalias`. The final entries of my list, alphabetically speaking, were `ziraleet`, `ziraleets`, `zita`, and `zitas`; nowadays Random House would allow me to follow those by `ziti` and `zits`.

At last the big day came, 18 December 1951. Surprise: I'd won!

FIGURE 3. My debut on (low-definition) television, vintage 1951.

---

* Well, perhaps `abrest` should be disallowed.

I met the judges, who had had only one week to read through all of the contest entries, and learned that fewer than 2,500 words had actually been on their "master list."

The big prize, a television set with a 17-inch screen, was given to my school at a formal ceremony on 21 December. It was installed at the front of the eighth-grade classroom; my teacher used to come to school on Friday nights to watch boxing. I received a handsome red toboggan, about ten feet long, that was destined to provide much pleasure during Wisconsin winters. And plenty of candy bars were also given out to the other members of my class.

The Emmaus Lutheran Sunday Bulletin for 23 December said, "We are happy over Donny's efforts and will tell more in the January Visitor." But no copies of that publication seem to have survived.

According to Donn Brazier in *The Explorer's Log* #81 (Milwaukee Public Museum, 1 January 1952), "The Giant Bar contest is over, and Don Knuth, 13, with over 4000 words, won the TV set for his school Emmaus Lutheran, 8th Grade. How does the toboggan perform these snowy days, Don?" Twenty-nine other students were awarded subsidiary prizes; the second-place winner, Billy Bethke, reportedly found about 2000 words.

Afterthoughts

I am indebted to Susan Otto of the Milwaukee Public Museum Reference Library for details about the official contest rules.

The WTMJ-TV show Museum Explorer's Club, developed by Murl Deusing, was probably among the first of its kind. It began in 1948 as a "sustaining program," namely a program that the station presented as a public service, without commercial sponsorship or advertising support [see *The Billboard* **62**, 42 (16 October 1948), 14]. In 1951 the Ziegler Company was a sponsor; they switched to one-minute commercials in 1952. The handsome host who appears in Figure 3 was Art Whitfield.

When reading that issue of *The Billboard* I couldn't help but notice that they routinely used the term "tele" for "television" in those days. There were "tele stations" and "tele surveys," etc. It's strange that this attractive coinage never entered the popular vocabulary. (If so, I could have used `tele` in the contest.)

Readers of Chapter 32 will be pleased to know that I *did* know the word `baas` when I was young. It appeared on the third page of my list, together with `baaing`.

Chapter 29

Th_5E_4 $CH_3EmIC_2Al_2$ Ca_3P_4Er

[Originally published in Engineering and Science Review, Case Institute of Technology, 2, 3 (March 1959), 32.]

No doubt countless chemists have contemplated whether their formulas can be put together to make English sentences. A little trial will show that very few words can be written as chemical compounds (for example, the words "little" and "trial" cannot). The following story, however, is written entirely in terms of meaningful chemical combinations, though we must admit that some of them are highly unstable. Notice the use of the new elements emanation Em (86), einsteinium E (99), and mendelevium Mv (101), and of the "inert gas trap" pictured on the next page.

$$Th_5E_4 \quad CH_3EmIC_2Al_2 \quad Ca_3P_4Er$$

ON_2Ce_2 $U_2Po_3N_2$ A SH_3INY $AF_3Te_2RnO_2ON$ I_3N_7 $Se_4PtEmBEr$, S_3Ir_2 $P_7ErC_3Y_3$ $H_6AgErTi$, Th_5E_4 $P_2H_3YSiCS_4$ WHI_2P, $WHoSe_3$ Mg Ra_3N_2 O_6UTa_2 Ga_2S_3 In Fr_6O_4NTa CYN_2ThIAS $HoUSe_3$, $WAlKS_4$ In SO_2 He Ca_3N_2 USe_3 H_3Er P_3Ho_3Ne. He CAl_2S_3 UP IV_5AN_3 VON DyCK, AN_2OThEr ScI_3EN_2Ce F_5IENd, ANd $O_3F_6F_2ErS_2Ta_2$ SH_2O_2W Th_5E_4 $GeNTl_2EmAN_2$ H_3IS Pr_2OOF_4 $ThAt_4$ $Mv_1 = Mv_2$.

IV_5AN_3, $HoWEV_2Er$, $HAtE_2S_3$ $P_7ErC_3Y_3$ $BeCAu_2Se_4$ ThE_2Y_2 B_2O_5Th H_4AVE A $CrUS_4H_2$ ON CYN_2ThI_2A. IV_5AN_3, WI_6Th A $SmIrK_4$, SAY_2S_2 He I_2S_7 VErY H_3APPY $ThAt_4$ He H_3As ThI_2S CH_2AN_3Ce. He Ru_4N_2S In H_5AsTe ANd $APPr_2O_2AcHeS$ H_3Er $HoUSe_3$.

He H_3As A KNiFe, $BeCaUSe_4$ He I_2S A RaScAl. $WHEN_2$ He $ReACHeS_4$ H_3Er $HoUSe_3$, He S_2TaBS_2 $CYNThIAs_2$ $MoThEr_2$,

ANa$_2$S$_7$TaSiA,　ANd　ThReAt$_3$ENS$_2$　P$_7$ErC$_3$Y$_3$　Al$_2$(SO$_4$)$_3$. HoWEV$_2$Er, P$_7$ErC$_3$Y$_3$, Th$_5$E$_4$ HErO$_2$, ANTi$_2$CI$_2$PAtES ThI$_2$S MoVE, As He H$_3$As TaKEN$_3$ CaRe$_7$Ta P$_3$Ho$_3$Ne Th$_5$E$_4$ Po$_3$Li$_3$Ce. Th$_5$E$_4$ Co$_4$P$_2$S CaTcH$_5$ IV$_5$AN$_3$ ANd TaK$_2$E$_3$ Th$_5$E$_4$ Sc$_2$Al$_2$AWAg AW$_5$AY$_3$. "YO$_3$U S$_3$URe WErE LuC$_2$K$_2$Y," SAY$_2$S$_2$ CI$_{10}$NdY, ANd SHe ANd P$_7$ErC$_3$Y$_3$ LiVE HAPPILi$_6$ WI$_6$Th EACH$_3$ O$_5$ThEr$_2$ F$_7$O$_2$ReVEr.

Th$_5$E$_4$ E$_3$Nd$_5$

– K$_2$N$_3$UTh

Emanation gas (Em) is normally inert, but in the CH$_3$EmIC$_2$Al$_2$ compound shown it is held in the molecule by the surrounding carbon and aluminum atoms. Argon and helium are combined in similar ways in the story.

Addendum

Every student at Case Institute of Technology had a knowledge of basic physics and inorganic chemistry. Indeed, almost every classroom displayed a large chart of the periodic table, which listed all of the various atomic elements currently known.

To fully understand this story, however, you need to know that our charts in those days used 'A' as the symbol for argon, *not* 'Ar'. We also knew the recently discovered elements 99 and 101, called einsteinium and mendelevium, by the symbols 'E' and 'Mv'; those symbols had been suggested in 1955 by the team that had discovered them, led by A. Ghiorso.

Element 86 has historically been known by different names, because it is radioactive. In general it was called emanation gas (Em) when I learned about it in the 1950s. But it had long been known to have three main isotopes that occur in nature as "emanations" from other radioactive elements, namely radon (from radium), thoron (from thorium), and actinon (from actinium). Radon is the most stable of these isotopes, having a half-life of 3.8 days; furthermore, radon actually arises more often in nature from the decay of uranium than from the decay of radium. Thus radon was by far the most important isotope, and element 86 was most commonly called "radon"; its symbol 'Rn' became standard in 1925. The alternative symbol 'Em' was still, however, in common use until the 1960s. Notice that my story uses 'Rn' once and 'Em' thrice.

The Commission on Atomic Weights of the International Union of Pure and Applied Chemistry meets every few years to adopt new standard conventions. In 1957 they upset my applecart, by changing the symbols for argon, einsteinium, and mendelevium to 'Ar', 'Es', and 'Md', respectively. Fortunately I didn't know about it at the time — these decisions by the higher-ups take awhile to trickle down to undergraduate students — because their new rules basically doomed my project from the start: Without 'A' and 'E', I couldn't form crucial words such as 'a' and 'the'. (Were the scientists on the international committee purposely trying to make literary chemistry impossible?) Furthermore, the change to 'Md' threw out my joke about the conservation of momentum ($Mv_1 = Mv_2$). Thank goodness I was able to write my little tale before the task that I had undertaken became hopeless.

My proposal for an "inert gas trap" was, of course, not serious when I made it in 1959. But I learned recently that radon can actually be caged inside a fullerene!

How many words can actually be formed as concatenations of the chemical element codes? Most words, including 'little' and 'trial', remain impossible, even if we go up to the newly discovered-and-named elements through number 112 (Cn for copernicium). A nice way to formulate this problem mathematically is to consider the power series $W = 1/(1 - A)$ in 26 noncommutative variables $\{a, b, \ldots, z\}$, where A is the sum of all element codes. The value of A that I used for the chemical caper was

$$
\begin{aligned}
A_0 = {} & h + he + li + be + b + c + n + o + f + ne + na + mg + al + si + p + s + cl + a \\
& + k + ca + sc + ti + v + cr + mn + fe + co + ni + cu + zn + ga + ge + as \\
& + se + br + kr + rb + sr + y + zr + nb + mo + tc + ru + rh + pd + ag + cd \\
& + in + sn + sb + te + i + xe + cs + ba + la + ce + pr + nd + pm + sm + eu \\
& + gd + tb + dy + ho + er + tm + yb + lu + hf + ta + w + re + os + ir + pt \\
& + au + hg + tl + pb + bi + po + at + em + rn + fr + ra + ac + th + pa + u \\
& + np + pu + am + cm + bk + cf + e + fm + mv;
\end{aligned}
$$

nowadays we would have to use

$$
\begin{aligned}
A = {} & A_0 - a + ar - em - e + es - mv + md \\
& + no + lr + rf + db + sg + bh + hs + mt + ds + rg + cn.
\end{aligned}
$$

The corresponding power series include the terms

$$
\begin{aligned}
W_0 &= 1 + a + b + c + e + \cdots + thc + the + thf + \cdots + 2caper + \cdots; \\
W &= 1 + b + c + f + \cdots + thc + thf + \cdots + caper + \cdots.
\end{aligned}
$$

It turns out that W_0 contains exactly 1928996 of the $26^5 = 11881376$ possible five-letter words, ranging from *aaaaa* to *zrzry* (about 16%). But W contains only 1497203, ranging from *acacb* to *zrzry* (about 13%). If we restrict consideration to the 5757 five-letter words of English, as defined by the Stanford GraphBase, W_0 has 2120 of them, while W has 1689. Thus, whenever I thought of a five-letter word, I had about a 37% chance of being able to actually use it in the story.

The five-letter word *basin* has coefficient 8 in W_0; this means that there are eight ways to make a basin chemically, e.g., B_2AS_2IN or $\cdots$ or $BaSiN_2$. In this respect *basin* is unique, because all other English words of five or fewer letters have coefficients of 7 or less. On the other hand, when we consider today's revised chemical codes we find that no English five-letter word in W has a coefficient greater than 6, which is the coefficient of *cocos* and *cohos*. (Nonwords like *bhosb* and 284 others do have a coefficient of 8 in W.)

Incidentally, I still remember being absolutely delighted to discover that aluminum sulfate is also a word.

Chapter 30

N-Ciphered Texts

*[Originally published in Word Ways **20** (1987), 173–174, 191–192.]*

Some years ago, while doing research on typography [1], I made a special font of type that obscured the letters in order to study the effects of spacing. Some of my students happened to look at one of my examples, and decided on their own initiative to figure out the words that I thought had been obliterated. To my great surprise, they were not only able to reconstruct a highly complicated and abstruse text, but they also enjoyed every minute of the task! They were so hooked on the problem that they spent the whole night puzzling it out, and the next morning they challenged their friends to do it.

Believing that others might enjoy scratching their heads over this new type of "many to one" cryptogram, I have generated several simple texts that seem especially suited to this kind of game. Here are the alphabets I used, so that you can determine how the letters from A to Z look in capitals and lowercase:

NNNNNNNNIꞮNNNꞰNNNNNNꞰNNNꞰNNN

nnꞇnnꞇinnꞇiniꞇⲛnnnꞇnꞀꞀinnnꞀnnꞀ

The concealed texts include some quotations by famous statesmen, a few limericks, and a surprise or two. Two pages of hidden quotes are followed by two pages of answers; don't peek!

Hint: The first word of the first quote is 'To'.

Reference

[1] Donald E. Knuth and Michael F. Plass, "Breaking paragraphs into lines," *Software — Practice & Experience* **11** (1981), 1176. Reprinted and extended in Donald E. Knuth, *Digital Typography*, CSLI Lecture Notes 78 (Stanford, California: Center for the Study of Language and Information, 1999), 140–141.

1. Nn ιιnιιιnιn ⌐ιn nnιnι I nnn ⌐nnnnnnιιn
nιnⅢn n nιnιnⅢn nι n nιnιnnⅢn, nnn nnnιnιnnn
ιn NιnⅢn ⌐nιn ιnn nnιn nι ιnιι nιnιnⅢn nnn ιι
⌐nnι nnn ιnιnnιnⅢn ιn nιιnnn ιnn ιnιι nnⅢn nι
ιnn nιnⅢnnⅢn nι ⌐ιn nιιnnnnn nⅢ nnn ιnnnι.
Nnn NιnⅢn, ⌐nnⅢn ιnιnnnιι ⌐nι nnn nι nιnn
nιιnn, ιnιn: "Nnn Nnn nιnιnⅢn ιnιι nnnnιιnn-
ιnn."   —Nιnιιnn N. Nnnιnnιι

2. Nιnn nιι nιnnι nnιι, ιnn Nιιnnnn nι Nnnn-
ιιnn nnn Nnnιnιι ιι nnn ⌐nιιnn nnn nnιn nn nι-
nnιιnn nn ιnnn nnn nnιιnι ιιnnn, nnn ιι ιιιn ιnnn
nnnnnnn ιn nιιnn nnn ⌐nnιnι ιn nιιnιn ιnn nιιn-
nιι nnιιιnιn nnιιnnιιnn ιn ιι. —Nnnιιnnn NιιⅢnι

3. I ⌐nιι ιⅢnnnιιnnιn, ιn ιnιι ιnιιnnnn, ⌐nnn
n ιnnι nι ⌐nιnιι. I nnnn nnn nn⌐n ιn ιnn nnn-
ιιnιιnn nnnnι nnnιn ιn ιnιnn nι ⌐nnιιιnn, nnn
ιnn ιnιι nnnιnn—I nnn nnnnι nn ιnιιιιιnn ⌐ιιn
nnn nnn ⌐nn ⌐nnιn nn nιnnnnnn nnnnnn ιn
nnnn ⌐ιn.   —Nnιnnn⌐ Nιnnnιn

4. Nnιn nn nnn nι nn ιιnnnn nn nιι ιnιι
Nn nιι nnιιnnnn, nnιn ιn⌐nιn nnn ⌐nιn,
   "Nιnn⌐ nnnn nιιnnιιnn, ⌐ιn nnnnι,
   ιn n nnnnιn nι nnnnι,
Nnn nnnιnn n nnnιnιιnn nι Nnιn!"

5. Nιιn n nιιnnnnn ⌐nnnι nnⅢn Nιnιιn,
   "Nn ιnn ⌐nn nnn nnιnn ιnnι nnnnnnιn,
   Nnn nnιι nι nnn nnn
   NnⅢnn Nnn., Nnn., nnn Nnι.,
Nnnn ιn Nnι. ιnnn nnnι ιn ιnn ⌐nnιn!"

6. N ⌒nn nınnn nn N̄nnn N̄nıın nnn Nn.
   Nnnn ınnnın nnnınnnn ınnı nn'n ınn.
       Nı ınn ⌒nn ınnı nn ın⌒n
       Nn⌒nınn nın* nnnn nıı ıınnn.
   Nnn nnınnnı, ınnnnınnn, nınn'ı nn.

7. Nnnın ⌒nnı n nnnnn nıı ın N̄nnnn
   Nnnın ıı⌒nnınnı nnnnn ⌒nnnın ınnn.
       Nnnn ın⌒nnnn nınnn ⌒nnn,
       Nnn ının ⌒nıın n ıınn,
   "Iı'ı nnnnnın I nın⌒nnı nnıın⌒nı ın nnı
       nı ⌒nnnn ⌒nnını ınnn ınn ınnı ıınn
       nı I nnııının nnn."   −Nnııın Nnnnnnı

8. Iı ⌒nn nn nnnnnnnn ın ınn ⌒nnnn⌒n⌒nıınnnı
   ınnnı ınnn ıı ın⌒ınn ınn. Nnı ınn ıı nnı ın⌒ınn
   nnn; ınn ıı ınn ınnnnnnn ıı⌒nı nnn. Nnnı ıı
   ⌒nn, ın ınıın nı n nnnnnnn nıınnnnnınnnı, ınn
   nnıın nııı nın⌒nnı nnınnn ın ⌒nnnnnn⌒n.
                           −N. N. Nnnıınnınn

9. Iı ınnnn ⌒nnn nn nnnnını ın ınınn, ınnnn
   ⌒nnnın nn nn nnnıınnı ın nın; nnn ıı ınnnn ⌒nnnn
   nn nnnıınnı ın nn nnnnn, ⌒nnı n ⌒nnın ıı ⌒nnnın
   nn! Nn ınnnın nıı nn nnnnıın n⌒nıınınnı, nnn
   nnnnnnınnınn ⌒nnnın nn nınınıı nnn ının.
                           −Nnnın N. Nnnnnnn

10. Nn⌒n: 1. N⌒nınn⌒nnı, ınn, ınnnı. 2. N
    nınnnnıınn nı ınn nnınnn nı n nnnnnnı, nınnnn nn-
    nnnnınn ın ınını, nnn nnnınnn nn ınnnnnın ınııı,
    ıınnnnn, nı nnnn ınnınnn. 3. Nıın nnı⌒nıı nn
    nınnı ınnn nı nnn nnnınnn, nnnnnı nı nııınn ın
    ınn nnnın.   −Nnınnn Nnınnnnı Nınıınnnnn

1. To illustrate my point I had meanwhile drawn a picture of a crocodile, and explained to Stalin with the help of this picture how it was our intention to attack the soft belly of the crocodile as we attacked his hard snout. And Stalin, whose interest was now at high pitch, said: "May God prosper this undertaking."   —Winston S. Churchill

2. Like all other arts, the Science of Deduction and Analysis is one which can only be acquired by long and patient study, nor is life long enough to allow any mortal to attain the highest possible perfection in it. —Sherlock Holmes

3. I most emphatically, in this instance, made a fool of myself. I have now come to the conclusion never again to think of marrying, and for this reason — I can never be satisfied with any one who would be blockhead enough to have me.   —Abraham Lincoln

4. Said an ape as he swung by his tail
   To his children, both female and male,
      "From your offspring, my dears,
       In a couple of years,
   May evolve a professor at Yale!"

5. Said a calendar model named Gloria,
   "So the men can enjoy real euphoria,
      You pose as you are
      During Jan., Feb., and Mar.,
   Then in Apr. they want to see moria!"

6. A man hired by John Smith and Co.
   Once loudly declared that he'd tho.
        Of the men that he saw
        Dumping dirt near his store.
   The drivers, therefore, didn't do.

7. There was a young girl in Japan
   Whose limericks never would scan.
        When someone asked why,
        She said with a sigh,
   "It's because I always attempt to get
        as many words into the last line
        as I possibly can."   —Martin Gardner

8. It may be conceded to the mathematicians
that four is twice two. But two is not twice
one; two is two thousand times one. That is
why, in spite of a hundred disadvantages, the
world will always return to monogamy.
                              —G. K. Chesterton

9. If there were no puzzles to solve, there
would be no questions to ask; and if there were
no questions to be asked, what a world it would
be! We should all be equally omniscient, and
conversation would be useless and idle.
                              —Henry E. Dudeney

10. Game: 1. Amusement, fun, sport. 2. A
diversion of the nature of a contest, played according to rules, and decided by superior skill,
strength, or good fortune. 3. Wild animals or
birds such as are pursued, caught or killed in
the chase.   —Oxford Universal Dictionary

Addendum

Texts 7, 8, and 9 did not appear in the original *Word Ways* article.

Readers who wish to do their own experiments can use METAFONT to make similar fonts, by visiting the webpage

`http://www-cs-faculty.stanford.edu/~knuth/programs.html`

and downloading file `nnncmbx.mf`.

Chapter 31

Disappearances

[Originally published in The Mathematical Gardner, edited by David A. Klarner, a festschrift for Martin Gardner on his 65th birthday (Belmont, California: Wadsworth, 1981), 264.]

N.B.: When the right-hand portions of the eight-line poem on the following page are interchanged, a seven-line poem results. Which line disappears?

I wonder how magicians make their rabbits disappear;
Enchanted words like "hocus pocus" can not interfere
with laws of science and facts of mathematics that are clear.

The prestidigitators, making use of devious schemes,
(although they never tell you how) transport things as in dreams:
At times suspended, banished, null and void — or so it seems.

There must be something secret, yes, a trick that will involve
— when done with sleight of hand —
a force that's able to *dissolve.*

Enchanted words like "hocus pocus" can transport things as in dreams:

with laws of science suspended, banished, null and void — or so it seems.

The prestidigitators, making use of devious schemes, involve

(although they never tell you how) a force that's able to *dissolve*.

At times I wonder how magicians make their rabbits disappear;

There must be something secret, yes, a trick that will not interfere

— when done with sleight of hand — and facts of mathematics that are clear.

Addendum

When I composed this poem I was unaware that members of the Oulipo [Ouvroir de Littérature Potentielle], especially Claude Berge, had been performing similar magic. Their ingenious poems [1, 2] consist of 14 lines in ordinary sonnet form, rearrangeable into 15 lines. The general principle is based on Sam Loyd's paradoxical "Get Off the Earth" puzzle [3].

Although the meter and rhyming scheme of my poem are non-standard, I do claim that mine is more "perfect," because it does not require any changes of punctuation or capitalization when the right-hand lines are switched.

(See also the disappearing Christmas sheep and angels in Chapter 46.)

[1] Claude Berge and Jacques Roubaud, "14 = 15, Sonnets à contraintes Loydiennes," *Atlas de littérature potentielle* (Paris: Gallimard, 1981), 189–193.

[2] Claude Berge, *La Princesse aztèque, ou contraintes pour un sonnet à longueur variable*, La Bibliothèque Oulipienne, numéro 22 (1983); republished in the collection *La Bibliothèque Oulipienne* (Paris: Ramsay, 1987), 73–82.

[3] Samuel Loyd, "Transformation picture," *U.S. Patent 563778* (14 July 1896).

Chapter 32

Lewis Carroll's word–ward–ware–dare–dame–game

[Originally published in GAMES 2, 4 (July 1978), 22–23.]

With the way fashions change from funk to punk, it's easy to see the difference that a single letter can make. One typographical error in a math book might change conic sections into "comic sections."

Lewis Carroll, the immortal author of *Alice in Wonderland*, realized how much fun it would be to play with sequences of one-letter changes. So at Christmastime in 1877, he invented a game he called Doublets to amuse two of his young lady friends who had "nothing to do."

One of his first puzzles was to change **grass** to **green**. The object is to remove one letter from **grass** and substitute another in its place to form a new word. The same thing is done with each new word — substituting only one letter and leaving the positions of the others unchanged — until the final word is reached. Carroll's solution went from **grass** to **crass–cress–tress–trees–frees–freed–greed** and thence to **green**. Curiously, he missed the fact that two of those steps could be replaced by the single word **treed**. There is another nice 8-step solution that goes from **grass** to **grabs**–_____–_____–_____–_____– **creed–greed** and finally to **green**. (Can you provide the four common words that I've left out?)

If rare words are permitted, then four steps will do the trick, namely **grass–grays–greys–grees–green**. But that's not a very satisfying solution unless you happen to be familiar with **grees**.

So what vocabulary *is* appropriate for Lewis Carroll's game? Carroll defined it as those English words "such as might be used in good society," a difficult standard to establish these days. I personally prefer solutions that stick to the words I know well, since much of the pleasure in this type of puzzle comes from finding new connections between unlike concepts. Almost every pronounceable combination of four or five letters has probably been used as an archaic spelling for something somewhere, but that spoils the game. Therefore I usually rule out words

415

that send me scurrying to an unabridged dictionary; in fact, even the full vocabulary of a college dictionary seems to be too much. I recommend solving with words that are in common use, since they should suffice in a well-constructed puzzle.

The Order and Method Approach

Doublets have been popular ever since Carroll published his first examples in the British magazine *Vanity Fair*. In fact, the game is so popular that it now has many different names: Word Links, Word Ladders, Word Golf, and (as introduced in the January 1978 *GAMES*) Laddergrams. But whatever we call this puzzle, the question remains: How does one go about finding the best solution? Answer: One uses order and method.

Suppose we've been given a simple energy problem to convert `cold` to `warm` in just four steps. Since all four letters in `cold` must change, there is no way to do the job in fewer than four steps. Furthermore, a 4-step solution requires that we jump to a letter in our final destination at each transition. (If only three of the four letters had to change, we would first try for a 3-step solution.) The word following `cold` *must* therefore be either `wold`, `cald`, `cord`, or `colm`. Let's keep the unabridged dictionary closed for the moment and proceed with the simplest choice: `cord`. Since we must still change the c, the o, and the d, there are just three ways to continue. Immediately we find two solutions: `cold–cord–word–worm–warm` and `cold–cord–card–ward–warm`.

In the same way it is easy to play alchemist, turning `lead` into `gold` in three steps. And to solve a puzzle from Nabokov's novel *Pale Fire*, transforming `hate` to `love` in at least two different ways.

Star ... Wars

Now let's tackle a cosmic problem. What is the shortest way to get from `star` to `wars`? Again we see that at least four steps will be needed. But we soon find that there is no 4-step solution in this case, because we cannot change to a letter in `wars` right away. (The only possibility, `saar`, is a proper name and thus traditionally against the rules.) So let's proceed systematically to find all of the legitimate words that we *can* reach from `star`.

In general it is necessary to consider 100 candidates for the second word, namely $x$tar or s$x$ar or st$x$r or sta$x$, where x is one of 25 new letters in each case. Without going to the big dictionary we readily come up with eight possibilities: `scar`, `sear`, `soar`, `spar`, `stir`, `stab`, `stag`, and `stay`. We might call these words close encounters of the first kind.

Now we must test each of the eight starter words to see if we can reach wars from one of *them* in just four steps. The only candidates for the third word that involve a change to a final letter are wear, seas, and spas; but none of them lead to wars in only three steps, so we can be sure that there is no 5-step solution from star to wars. Let's go on then to find all possible encounters of the second kind: those words that can be reached from star after exactly two steps.

Fortunately we don't have to try 100 continuations from each of our eight starter words. At most 75 possibilities are of interest now (for each case), since there is no point in changing the same letter position twice in a row. For example, we need not go from scar to any word like s$x$ar; such words were directly accessible from star. So here are the possible words that we can reach from our list of starters: From scar we get scab, scad, scan, and scat; from sear we get bear, dear, fear, gear, hear, near, pear, rear, tear, wear, year, seer, seal, seam, seas, and seat; from soar we get boar, hoar, roar, sour, soak, and soap; from spar we get spur, span, spas, spat, and spay; from stab we get slab, swab, and stub; from stag we get shag, slag, snag, and swag; and from stay we get shay, slay, and sway. Notice that stir is a dead end, and also that some of these words actually arise in more than one way (scab from both scar and stab; spay from both spar and stay).

With any luck at all there will be a 4-step ladder between one of these 41 words and wars, which would give us a 6-step solution to the whole problem. But alas, they all fizzle. For instance, soap leads only to useless combinations of letters such as woap, saap, sorp, and soas. Furthermore there are three troublesome cases (wear, seas, spas) in which it isn't so easy to check for a 4-mover; when only three of the letters have to change we must try 75 possibilities for each word (w$x$ar, we$x$r, wea$x$, etc.). Unfortunately none of those possibilities will work. Thus there's no 6-step solution from star to wars.

What should we do now, you may be wondering. If we keep multiplying the number of words that spread out from star, we'll soon run out of paper (not to mention patience).

Let's start burning the candle at the other end by discovering what words could precede wars. Again there are 100 cases to try, but by now we're so hooked on the problem that we have to proceed. We find that 19 of them are legit: bars, cars, ears, jars, mars, oars, pars, tars, wads, wags, wans, ways, ward, ware, warm, warn, warp, wart, wary.

While testing these possibilities, I happily stumbled on the following 7-step solution: star–sear–seas–teas–tens–tans–tars–wars. So this must be as short as possible.

Shortcuts and Dead Ends

Of course, a good intuition can often lead to shortcuts. For example, one of the most difficult things to accomplish in a laddergram is to change vowels to consonants. Four-letter words with a pair of vowels in the middle generally have a relatively large number of "neighbor" words to which they could change; so we might have guessed immediately that sear and soar would be the most fruitful ways to start out.

In easy laddergrams, the given words have consonants and vowels in the same positions (as in cold to warm). But with a harder problem (star to wars) the vowel positions usually disagree. In such cases it is best to start by changing one of the given words so that its vowels and consonants line up with the other one.

Besides the problem of changing vowels to consonants (and vice versa), it is also difficult to get to and from letters such as q that appear in relatively few words. The following sequence from ducks to quack shows one successful way to enter the q's: ducks–ducts–duets–suets–suits–suite–quite–quire–quirk–quick–quack. (Notice that by the time we reach duets, the vowels and consonants are lined up with their counterparts in the final word quack.) We could also replace suite by quits in this example. I know of only three other ways to jump into a q word, namely guest–quest, built–quilt, and guilt–quilt. Strictly speaking there is also suint–quint, but it uses a term not in my vocabulary.

Sometimes we have no choice but to stretch our vocabulary a little. If we want to prepare for the switch to metric units by changing quart into liter, we must go to the big dictionary right away, because the only possible first steps lead from quart to such rare words as quare, quirt, or the physicist's new quark. From either quirt or quark–quirk we can reach quire, whence it is clear sailing through familiar words: quite–_____–_____–_____–_____–diets–_____–_____–_____–_____–liter. (Your move.)

Some words like yacht and sheik cannot be used at all. And there are also pairs of words like aloha–alpha and alien–align that lead only to each other. But the vast majority of 5-letter words are linked together, and we should be able to reach other 5-letter words through an appropriate series of one-letter changes. In fact, if you can go three steps from both your starting and ending words, it almost always turns out that there will be a path (perhaps a long one) between them. This principle makes it relatively easy to determine whether or not a proposed laddergram is possible. Notable exceptions are words from the following groups: bound, found, hound, mound, round, sound, wound, would, could, mould, mount, and count; also onset, inset, inlet, islet, isles, idles, idler, and idled. Breaking out of the ight/ighs/igns group (eight, fight, light, might, night, sight, tight, highs, sighs, signs) also presents difficulties, although it can be done by going through a ladder that includes rare words: bight–bigot–begot–beget–beset–reset–revet.

Puzzles

If you've read this far, you're ready for the following puzzles. For fun, use common words wherever possible.

1. link–____–____–____–____–____–golf.

2. liter–_____–_____–_____–raths–_____–_____–_____–litre.

3. mimsy–_____–_____–_____–_____–_____–_____–_____–toves.

4. rains–. . . . .–plain.

5. rouge–. . . . .–cheek.

6. sober–. . . . .–tipsy.

Addendum

I was wrong: There's a 6-step solution star–soar–boar–boas–baas–bars–wars that I overlooked when solving the star wars puzzle by hand! It was first found by Donald F. Kendrick, who sent it to *GAMES* on 5 June 1978. He wrote, "baas? plural form of baa. The cry of sheep."

The worst of it is, I think if I repeated the process I would still make the same mistake. My exposure to Norwegian and Dutch has forever ruined my ability to play Scrabble® and to regard baas as a word of English; that word seems totally foreign. (In Norwegian, "Han er ikke grei aa staa i baas med" means "He is hard to get along with.")

I also erred in assuming that the term "laddergram" had first been introduced in a previous issue of *GAMES*. In fact, John E. Surrick and Lawrence M. Conant had published a 121-page book entitled *Ladder-grams* many years earlier (New York: J. H. Sears & Co., 1927). That book begins with 6-step ladders from flat to tire, bell to ring, peep to hole, slow to fast, leap to life, tramp to rails, and north to south; it ends with a 15-step ladder from small to large. (Using the Stanford GraphBase, one can show that 14 steps actually suffice for their final challenge: small–shall–shale–whale–whole–whose–chose–chase–cease–tease–terse–merse–merge–marge–large.)

Answers

The text asks for ladders such as
    grabs–crabs–cribs–cries–cried–creed;
    lead–load–goad–gold;
    hate–have–lave–love or hate–have–hove–love;
    quite–suite–suits–suets–duets–diets;
    diets–dints–dines–lines–liner–liter.

The other puzzles can be solved with simple ladders such as

1. link–wink–wind–wild–gild–gold–golf.

2. liter–later–rater–rates–raths–laths–lathe–lithe–litre.

3. mimsy–missy–mossy–mosey–nosey–noses–roses–roves–toves.

4. rains–ruins–ruing–suing–sling–slang–slant–plant–plait–plain.

5. rouge–route–routs–roots–soots–shots–shoes–shoer–sheer–cheer–cheek.

6. sober–sorer–corer–cores–cares–hares–harps–harpy–happy–hippy–tippy–tipsy.

Chapter 33

Blood, Sweat, and Tears

*[Originally published in GAMES **2**, 4 (July 1978), 49, as a word-puzzle prize competition.]*

Laddergrams, or Doublets as Lewis Carroll called them (see the previous chapter), are quite enough to fascinate and befuddle most puzzlers. But we'd like to invite you to climb one more rung with us ... into the as yet uncharted realm of Triplets.

The object in the original game of Doublets is to get from one word to another with the fewest intermediate steps. (In each step it is permissible to change one letter.) But suppose there are three words to be connected up, such as **glass**, **plate**, and **spoon**. And suppose you want to connect them in a Y-formation, as shown.

To win this contest, all you have to do is connect **blood**, **sweat**, and **tears** to each other with the best (most efficient) Y-formation. Find the best word to put at the junction of the Y (in the example here, the junction word is **slaps**) and then find the best way to change this word into **blood**, into **sweat**, and into **tears**. Adjacent words must differ by only one letter, as in the example. The total "distance" from your junction word to the three given words should be as small as possible, in order to keep the number of words

```
glass                    plate
   class              slate
      claps   slats
          slaps
          slops
          shops
          shoos
          shook
          spook
          spoon
```

in the Y to a minimum. Any single five-letter words that appear in *Webster's Third New International Dictionary* (Unabridged) may be used, except for proper names, abbreviations, contractions, or hyphenated words. The three arms of the Y need not be the same length. The entry with the fewest total words in the Y wins; in the event of a tie, the entry with the earliest postmark wins.

I have nothing to offer but blood, toil, tears and sweat.

— WINSTON S. CHURCHILL (1940)

Answers

If we restrict consideration to the 5757 words of the Stanford GraphBase (SGB), the minimum of $d(x, \text{blood}) + d(x, \text{sweat}) + d(x, \text{tears})$ is 15, and it is achieved for four values of x: blend, blond, bland, and treed. (These words rank 580, 1387, 1981, and 3647, respectively, in SGB's default ordering by frequency of usage.) The best junction word from this standpoint is therefore 'blend', appropriately enough. And a suitable Y-formation for blend with 15 links is:

```
blend–blond–blood
blend–bleed–breed–treed–tweed–tweet–sweet–sweat
blend–bland–brand–brans–beans–bears–tears
```

Notice that this solution also happens to use the other optimum junction words blond, bland, and treed.

If we restrict ourselves further to the most common 2000 five-letter words, we cannot use treed (rank 3647) or brans (rank 3239) or tweed (rank 2044). With this limitation the cost goes up to 24, but again blend is an optimum junction word. The minimum distance from blend to sweat rises from 7 to 10: blend–bleed–breed–creed–creek–cheek–cheer–sheer–shear–swear–sweat; and from blend to tears, with only common words, the cost goes up from 6 to 12: blend–bland–gland–grand–grind–grins–gains–pains–pairs–hairs–heirs–hears–tears.

Conversely, on the other hand, the *GAMES* competition allowed any word from *Webster's Third New International Dictionary* (Unabridged). The prizewinning entry, found independently by six readers, needed only 12 links, with junction word 'scent':

```
scent–slent–blent–blend–blond–blood
scent–sceat–sweat
scent–scant–scans–scars–sears–tears
```

(See *GAMES* **2**, 6 (November 1978), 62. The words slent, blent, and sceat are unknown to SGB.)

Chapter 34

Biblical Ladders

[Originally published in The Mathemagician and Pied Puzzler, a collection from the first "Gathering for Gardner" in tribute to Martin Gardner, edited by Elwyn Berlekamp and Tom Rodgers (Wellesley, Massachusetts: A K Peters, 1999), 29–34.]

Charles Lutwidge Dodgson, aka Lewis Carroll, invented a popular pastime now called *word ladders*, in which one word metamorphoses into another by changing a letter at a time. We can go from `this` to `that` in three such steps: `this–thin–than–that`.

As an ordained deacon of the Church of England, Dodgson also was quite familiar with the Bible. So let's play a game that combines both activities: Let's construct word ladders in which all words are Biblical. More precisely, the words should all be present in the Bible that was used in Dodgson's day, the King James translation.

Here, for example, is a six-step sequence that we might call Jacob's Ladder, because 'James' is a form of 'Jacob':

... seen of **James**; then of all ...	(1 Corinthians 15:7)
... because your **names** are written ...	(Luke 10:20)
... and their **naves**, and their ...	(1 Kings 7:33)
... When the **waves** of death ...	(2 Samuel 22:5)
... had many **wives**. And his ...	(Judges 8:30)
... made their **lives** bitter with ...	(Exodus 1:14)
... And Jacob **lived** in the land ...	(Genesis 47:28)

Puzzle #1. Many people consider the Bible to be a story of transition from `wrath` to `faith`. The following tableau shows, in fact, that there's a Biblical word ladder corresponding to such a transition. But the tableau lists only the verse numbers, not the words; what are the missing words?

(Remember to use a King James Bible for reference, not a new-fangled translation! Incidentally, the sequence of verses in this ladder is strictly increasing through the Old Testament, never backing up in Biblical order; Jacob's Ladder, on the other hand, was strictly decreasing.)

423

... that his **wrath** was kindled. ...		(Genesis 39:19)
...	_____	... (Genesis 40:2)
...	_____	... (Exodus 24:4)
...	_____	... (Exodus 34:1)
...	_____	... (Leviticus 13:3)
...	_____	... (Leviticus 14:46)
...	_____	... (Leviticus 25:29)
...	_____	... (Deuteronomy 22:21)
...	_____	... (Joshua 11:4)
...	_____	... (1 Samuel 13:20)
...	_____	... (1 Samuel 15:3)
...	_____	... (1 Samuel 26:13)
...	_____	... (1 Kings 10:15)
...	_____	... (Psalm 10:14)
...	_____	... (Isaiah 3:17)
...	_____	... (Isaiah 54:16)
...	_____	... (Isaiah 54:17)
... by his **faith**. Yea also, ...		(Habakkuk 2:4)

Puzzle #2. Of course #1 was too easy. So the verse numbers won't be given this time. Go from **sword** to (plow)**share** in four steps:

... not lift up a **sword** against ...		(Micah 4:3)
...	_____	... ( )
...	_____	... ( )
...	_____	... ( )
... every man his **share**, and his ...		(1 Samuel 13:20)

Hint: In the time of King James, people never swore; they sware.

Puzzle #3. Of course #2 was also pretty easy, if you have a good concordance or a computer file of the King James Bible. How about going from **naked** to **cover**, in eight steps? A suitable middle verse is provided as a clue.

... they *were* **naked**; and they ...		(Genesis 3:7)
...	_____	... ( )
...	_____	... ( )
...	_____	... ( )
...	_____	... (Luke 17:27)
...	_____	... ( )
...	_____	... ( )
...	_____	... ( )
... charity shall **cover** the multitude ...		(1 Peter 4:8)

Puzzle #4.   Find a Biblical word ladder from holy to writ.

Puzzle #5.   (For worshippers of automobiles.)   Construct a 12-step
Biblical ladder from fords (Judges 3:28) to rolls (Ezra 6:1).

Puzzle #6.   Of course #5 was too hard, unless you have special resources.   Here's one that *anybody* can do, with only a Bible in hand.
Complete the following Biblical ladder, which "comes back on itself" in
an unexpected way.

... seventy times **seven**. Therefore ...			(Matthew 18:22)
...	_ _ _ _ _	...	(Matthew 13:)
...	_ _ _ _ _	...	(John 4:)
...	_ _ _ _ _	...	(Numbers 33:)
...	_ _ _ _ _	...	(Deuteronomy 29:)
...	_ _ _ _ _	...	(1 Samuel 15:)
...	_ _ _ _ _	...	(Job 16:)
...	_ _ _ _ _	...	(1 Kings 7:)
...	_ _ _ _ _	...	(Romans 9:)
...	_ _ _ _ _	...	(Leviticus 9:)
...	_ _ _ _ _	...	(Acts 27:)
...	_ _ _ _ _	...	(Jeremiah 10:)
...	_ _ _ _ _	...	(Matthew 13:)
...	_ _ _ _ _	...	(Ezekiel 24:)
...	_ _ _ _ _	...	(Matthew 18:)

Puzzle #7.   Finally, a change of pace: Construct 5 × 5 word squares,
using only words from the King James Bible verses shown. (The words
will read the same down as they do across.)

_ _ _ _ _	Matthew 11:11	_ _ _ _ _	Exodus 28:33
_ _ _ _ _	Judges 9:9	_ _ _ _ _	Lamentations 2:13
_ _ _ _ _	Mark 12:42	_ _ _ _ _	1 Peter 5:2
_ _ _ _ _	Ecclesiastes 9:3	_ _ _ _ _	Genesis 34:21
_ _ _ _ _	Luke 9:58	_ _ _ _ _	Acts 20:9

Answers

Puzzle #1.

... that his **wrath** was kindled. ...	(Genesis 39:19)
... Pharaoh was **wroth** against two ...	(Genesis 40:2)
... And Moses **wrote** all the ...	(Exodus 24:4)
... and I will **write** upon *these* ...	(Exodus 34:1)
... is turned **white**, and the ...	(Leviticus 13:3)
... all the **while** that it is ...	(Leviticus 14:46)
... within a **whole** year after ...	(Leviticus 25:29)
... play the **whore** in her ...	(Deuteronomy 22:21)
... the sea **shore** in multitude, ...	(Joshua 11:4)
... man his **share**, and his ...	(1 Samuel 13:20)
... have, and **spare** them not; ...	(1 Samuel 15:3)
... a great **space** *being* between ...	(1 Samuel 26:13)
... of the **spice** merchants, and ...	(1 Kings 10:15)
... mischief and **spite**, to requite ...	(Psalm 10:14)
... Lord will **smite** with a scab ...	(Isaiah 3:17)
... created the **smith** that bloweth ...	(Isaiah 54:16)
... is of me, **saith** the LORD. ...	(Isaiah 54:17)
... by his **faith**. Yea also, ...	(Habakkuk 2:4)

Puzzle #2.   Here's a strictly decreasing solution:

... not lift up a **sword** against ...	(Micah 4:3)
... Lord GOD hath **sworn** by himself, ...	(Amos 6:8)
... *that are even* **shorn**, which came ...	(Song of Solomon 4:2)
... Eloth, on the **shore** of the Red ...	(1 Kings 9:26)
... every man his **share**, and his ...	(1 Samuel 13:20)

There are 13 other possible citations for **sworn**, and 1 Kings 4:29 could also be used for **shore**, still avoiding forward steps.

Puzzle #3.   First observe that the word in Luke 17:27 must have at least one letter in common with both **naked** and **cover**. So it must be **wives** or **given**; and **given** doesn't work, since neither **gaked** nor **niked** nor **naved** nor **naven** is a word. Thus the middle word must be **wives**, and the step after **naked** must be **waked**. Other words can now be filled in:

... they *were* **naked**; and they ...	(Genesis 3:7)
... again, and **waked** me, as a ...	(Zechariah 4:1)
... which is **waved**, and which ...	(Exodus 29:27)
... the mighty **waves** of the sea. ...	(Psalm 93:4)
... they married **wives**, they were ...	(Luke 17:27)
... hazarded their **lives** for the name ...	(Acts 15:26)
... looked in the **liver**. At his ...	(Ezekiel 21:21)
... hospitality, a **lover** of good men, ...	(Titus 1:8)
... charity shall **cover** the multitude ...	(1 Peter 4:8)

(Many other solutions are possible, but none are strictly increasing or decreasing.)

Puzzle #4. Suitable intermediate words can be found, for example, in Revelation 3:11; Ruth 3:16; Ezra 7:24; Matthew 6:28; Job 40:17; Micah 1:8; Psalm 145:15. (But 'writ' is not a Biblical word.)

Puzzle #5. For example, use intermediate words found in Matthew 24:35; Ezekiel 34:25; Acts 2:45; Ecclesiastes 12:11; Matthew 25:33; Daniel 3:21; John 18:18; Genesis 32:15; 2 Corinthians 11:19; Psalm 84:6; Numbers 1:2. (See also Genesis 27:44.)

Puzzle #6.

... seventy times **seven**. Therefore ...	(Matthew 18:22)
... forth, and **sever** the wicked ...	(Matthew 13:49)
... seventh hour the **fever** left him. ...	(John 4:52)
... and to the **fewer** ye shall give ...	(Numbers 33:54)
... from the **hewer** of thy wood ...	(Deuteronomy 29:11)
... And Samuel **hewed** Agag in pieces ...	(1 Samuel 15:33)
... I have **sewed** sackcloth ...	(Job 16:15)
... hewed stones, **sawed** with saws, ...	(1 Kings 7:9)
... remnant shall be **saved**: For he will ...	(Romans 9:27)
... shoulder Aaron **waved** *for* a wave ...	(Leviticus 9:21)
... violence of the **waves**. And the soldiers' ...	(Acts 27:41)
... Gather up thy **wares** out of ...	(Jeremiah 10:17)
... and sowed **tares** among the ...	(Matthew 13:25)
... And your **tires** *shall be* ...	(Ezekiel 24:23)
... till seven **times**? Jesus saith ...	(Matthew 18:21)

Puzzle #7.
```
women    bells
olive    equal
mites    lucre
event    large
nests    sleep
```

References

[1] Martin Gardner, *The Universe in a Handkerchief: Lewis Carroll's Mathematical Recreations, Games, Puzzles, and Word Plays* (New York: Copernicus, 1996), Chapter 6.

[2] `http://etext.virginia.edu/kjv.browse.html` [an online text of the King James Bible provided in searchable form by the Electronic Text Center of the University of Virginia; this URL has been routed to other sites since June 2008].

Chapter 35

ETAOIN SHRDLU Non-Crashing Sets

*[Originally published in Word Ways **27** (1994), 138.]*

The designers of the Linotype machine arranged its keyboard for optimum speed, assuming that the most common letters of English were e, t, a, o, i, n, s, h, r, d, l, u in that order. The *Oxford English Dictionary* (second edition) has some amusing citations:

> The author sends in a manuscript without exclamation marks. The linotyper puts them in, the author takes them out in proof, the linotyper puts them back in, together with a couple of etaoins. — James Thurber, *The Owl in the Attic and Other Perplexities* (1931)

> What I love about newspapers is their etaoin shrdl. — *The Listener* (15 June 1967)

> 'Lot of pleasure but also a lot of pleasure but also a lot of anxiety and heart-searching.' etaoinshrdlu cmfwyp shrdlu cd showed that cinema and per- Mrs Nissel said that the study forming arts ticket prices had more or less remained in line with the Retail Price Index up to 1975/76. — *The Daily Telegraph* (13 September 1983)

Are there twelve five-letter words, made up of just those twelve letters, having no common letters in any position?

Using my personal list of 5757 words, there are 924 words made from only those letters, but no solutions to the problem. On the other hand, if one asks for only eleven disjoint words instead of twelve, my program finds 43,888 solutions. The nicest of these is

```
usual  honor  thorn  arena  leash  radii
       outdo  ensue  stilt  idled  dirts
```

if we want the words to be as common as possible.

I investigated the 43,888 solutions to see which five-letter strings would complete them to a full set. Exactly 10,406 different strings resulted. And only one of these, `trull`, was a word in my spell-check dictionary. So I found a unique solution to my problem:

```
eland  trull  adieu  ohhhh  issue  nadir
snoot  hunts  reran  dildo  lotsa  uteri
```

Other possibilities arise if I lower my standards slightly to allow words that are ordinarily supposed to be capitalized. For example, if `hindu` is permitted I get three more solutions:

```
ensue  torsi  ahhhh  osier  ideal  neato
stunt  hindu  radon  droid  lulls  ultra

ender  troll  assai  ohhhh  idiot  nurse
slain  hindu  round  delta  latus  utero

enter  tulle  asana  ohhhh  idiot  nodal
slots  hindu  rerun  druid  lasso  uteri
```

and a fourth comes by changing {`slots, druid`} to {`sluts, droid`}. Or, if `nehru` is legitimate (a nehru jacket), we have:

```
ennui  thine  altho  orals  idler  nehru
stood  hadda  rosin  durst  lieth  usual

ennui  theta  alder  ortho  idiot  nehru
stand  harsh  rosin  diode  lulls  usual
```

and another when {`alder, ortho`} is changed to {`altho, order`}.

The most troublesome word to include is evidently the one that ends with the letter `u`.

Addendum

My program in 1994 used a variant of the "dancing links" technique, oriented to finding maximum independent sets in a graph.

Incidentally, my colleague Terry Winograd wrote a pioneering program called SHRDLU to experiment with mechanical methods for understanding English sentences in context. [See his book *Understanding Natural Language* (New York: Academic Press, 1972).] On the webpage

```
http://hci.stanford.edu/~winograd/shrdlu/name.html
```

he explains that he chose the name because he'd seen the phrase ETAOIN SHRDLU in *MAD* magazine.

Chapter 36

Quadrata Obscura (Hidden Latin Squares)

[Dedicated to the memory of Nob Yoshigahara. Presented at the Twenty-Ninth International Puzzle Party (IPP29), San Francisco, California, in August 2009. Published in Word Ways 42 (2009), 248; 43 (2010), 14.]

A latin square is an array in which every row and every column contains exactly the same set of distinct letters.

Complete each of the arrays below to a latin square in which a common English word appears in the bottom row.

(a)

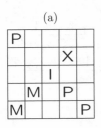

(b)

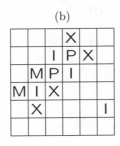

(c)

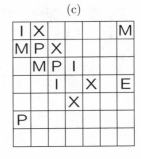

Hints

The main difficulty is to guess the unspecified letters. Puzzle (a) can be completed in three ways, with the respective bottom rows M*XIP, MIX*P, MX*IP; the only common English word that fits is MIXUP.

In puzzle (b) there are *two* unspecified letters, and the possible bottom lines are *P*MIX, *PM*IX, I**MPX, IP**MX, IP*M*X, P**MIX, P*M*IX, X**MIP, X*M*IP, XP*MI*, XPM*I*. Clearly PREMIX is the winner here; it's way ahead of APEMIX and IPSMAX and all other possibilities.

Similarly, the latin square constraints allow lots and lots of seven-letter ways to fill in the bottom line of puzzle (c) — in fact there are 179 ways altogether! — ranging from **EMIPX to XIMPE**. But the English language likes only one of them, even if we forget the latin square rules and consider all 2520 permutations of $\{*, *, E, I, M, P, X\}$. So we might as well write it into the bottom line: SIMPLEX. And then the puzzle becomes routine; the remaining entries are forced, with no need for backtracking, if we use a suitable order to fill them in one at a time.

Answers

(a)

P	X	M	I	U
I	U	P	X	M
U	P	I	M	X
X	M	U	P	I
M	I	X	U	P

(b)

I	P	R	X	M	E
R	E	I	P	X	M
X	M	P	I	E	R
M	I	X	E	R	P
E	X	M	R	P	I
P	R	E	M	I	X

(c)

I	X	E	L	P	S	M
M	P	X	E	S	I	L
X	M	P	I	E	L	S
L	S	I	M	X	P	E
E	L	S	X	I	M	P
P	E	L	S	M	X	I
S	I	M	P	L	E	X

All three answers are unique.

Chapter 37

$5 \times 5 \times 5$ Word Cubes by Computer

*[Originally published in Word Ways **26** (1993), 95–97.]*

I recently used a computer to look for $5 \times 5 \times 5$ word cubes, by which I mean symmetric patterns that spell five-letter words in rows, columns, and whatchamacallits (is there a name for vertical $1 \times 1 \times 5$s?). As far as I know, the only previous example was constructed by Peter Graham and published in *Omni* in July 1987. But his solution

loved	opera	velar	erase	dares	
opera	purer	erode	redan	arena	
velar	erode	logos	adore	reset	(1)
erase	redan	adore	sarum	enemy	
dares	arena	reset	enemy	satyr	

uses **redan** and **sarum**, which are not in my vocabulary. Also **velar** is kind of hazy for me; I know it's a word, but I don't think I've seen it in novels or in "real" English.

Lots of obscure five-letter combinations can be found in unabridged dictionaries, but word puzzles are much more fun when they stick to words that I wouldn't feel like challenging if my opponent played them in Scrabble®. So I've been collecting a list of all the five-letter words that I personally know and love, during odd moments since the early 1970s. Last week I decided to see if any $5 \times 5 \times 5$ cubes were possible using only words from my collection (5757 in all) ... and I found to my surprise that there are many, many solutions (exactly 83576)!

Here are the five best, according to the ranking that I used:

aster	scale	tacos	elope	reset	
scale	codex	adapt	leper	extra	
tacos	adapt	caper	opera	strap	(2)
elope	leper	opera	perks	erase	
reset	extra	strap	erase	taper	

```
types    yeast    pasta    ester    start
yeast    earth    armor    stole    three
pasta    armor    smoke    token    arena        (3)
ester    stole    token    elect    rents
start    three    arena    rents    tease

abler    blade    lapis    edict    rests
blade    login    agent    dinar    entry
lapis    agent    pesto    intro    stool        (4)
edict    dinar    intro    cargo    troop
rests    entry    stool    troop    sylph

other    theme    heros    emote    reset
theme    heron    erupt    moper    entry
heros    erupt    ruler    opera    strap        (5)
emote    moper    opera    terms    erase
reset    entry    strap    erase    types

after    frame    talcs    emcee    reset
frame    rigor    agora    morns    erase
talcs    agora    loyal    crass    salsa        (6)
emcee    morns    crass    ensue    esses
reset    erase    salsa    esses    tease
```

Each of these has one somewhat unusual word: `codex`, `ester`, `login`, `moper`, `talcs`. But they all pass the Scrabble® test, except that `login` might not yet be in standard dictionaries ("What is your login name?").

Another solution uses no unusual words whatever, but it has a flaw in that it uses `erase` twice (or more times, depending on how you count):

```
racer    adore    comas    erase    reset
adore    divan    overt    rarer    entry
comas    overt    meter    arena    strap        (7)
erase    rarer    arena    sends    erase
reset    entry    strap    erase    types
```

Notice that the final square here is the same as in (5).

The vast majority of the 83576 solutions contain too many rare words to be really interesting. Furthermore, only 75130 of them are flawless, in the sense that they contain fifteen distinct words.

It turns out that 4676 of the 5757 words in my collection appear in at least one word cube. One of them, `opera`, actually occurs in 17304 of the 83576, including (2) and (5); in fact, when the cubes are presented as 5 × 5 arrays of words as shown here, `opera` can be placed anywhere except in the fourth column of the fourth row.

Why are there so many solutions? Because each solution can usually be tweaked into another by changing only a few letters. For example, one can easily find 20 different solutions that fill in the asterisks of

```
*a*er    adore    *o*as    erase    reset
adore    divan    overt    rarer    entry
*o*as    overt    *e*er    arena    strap .     (8)
erase    rarer    arena    sends    erase
reset    entry    strap    erase    type*
```

Here's how: The first word *a*er might be either water, paper, later, layer, eager, safer, maker, baker, eater, taper, laser, wager, waver, rarer, saber, cater, paler, caper, gayer, baser, saner, wafer, racer, tamer, barer, lamer, pacer, waxer, or saver; but we have to fit it properly with *o*as, for which the choices are more limited: sodas, sofas, novas, comas, yogas, togas. And that word, in turn, must fit with *e*er, namely with never, refer, meter, fewer, fever, lever, newer, sewer, deter, sever, leper, or defer. Only ten such combinations work out; then type* can be either types or typed, giving 20 solutions as stated.

I've ranked the words in my corpus by frequency of use in various texts; the common words listed above have ranks of 3500 or less. If the entire list of 5757 words is used, we get not 20 but 110 different solutions to (8). The point here is not to obtain an exact count, but rather to illustrate the multiplicative phenomenon that accounts for the large number of word cube solutions. Similarly, the pattern

```
*s*er    scale    *a*os    elope    reset
scale    codex    ad*pt    leper    extra
*a*os    ad*pt    ***e*    opera    st*a*      (9)
elope    leper    opera    perks    erase
reset    extra    st*a*    erase    ta*e*
```

has dozens of solutions, generalizing (2).

If my stockpile of five-letter words is restricted to the most common 3000, only three word cubes are possible, including (3) and two others that are almost the same. Expanding the list to 3500 results in 83 solutions; 6 are like (3), 20 correspond to (8), and 57 correspond to (9). Only 60 of the 83 are flawless, because (9) might contain leper twice.

Word Squares

Each slice of a symmetrical 5 × 5 × 5 word cube is a symmetrical 5 × 5 word *square*, and of course such squares are comparatively easy to devise.

Indeed, my 5757 words can be used to make 541968 different symmetrical 5 × 5 squares, only 280 of which are flawed. All but 23 of the 5757 words participate in at least one square, the exceptions being `jelly`, `jolly`, `juicy`, `squad`, `quill`, `skiff`, `godly`, `dizzy`, `quirk`, `gummy`, `vying`, `gauzy`, `whizz`, `woozy`, `jazzy`, `jimmy`, `jowly`, `boozy`, `djinn`, `spazz`, `buzzy`, `booky`, and `lawzy` (in decreasing order of frequency).

The following three word squares can be formed entirely from the most common 372 words (`agree` having rank 372):

```
grass        glass        class
right        light        light
agree        agree        agree
sheep        sheep        sheep
steps        steps        steps
```

The next best, with `ought` of rank 385 and `theme` of rank 483, are

```
boats        boats        boats
ought        ought        ought
agree        agree        agree .
there        these        theme
steel        steel        steel
```

Addendum

The "dancing links" technique in the following chapter was used to obtain these results. My original article contained several errors, all of which have been corrected above (I hope).

I learned later about the pioneering earlier work of Paul Remley ["Cubism," *Word Ways* **9** (1976), 3–5] and Jeff Grant ["Cubism revisited," *Word Ways* **11** (1978), 156–157; "More word cubes," *Word Ways* **12** (1979), 76–78]. They constructed symmetrical 6 × 6 × 6 cubes with weird words; and Grant also achieved the almost unbelievable feat of finding an *unsymmetrical* 5 × 5 × 5 cube in which all 75 words are distinct, yet they all appear in the *Oxford English Dictionary*:

```
strap    areca    tamal    esile    deter
arena    gavot    ovate    reden    alene
laval    anele    niton    amese    rases
amene    minal    elemi    rened    ettle
salad    asere    resen    entre    deses
```

(For example, `erare` is a medieval Scottish form of `erer`, "sooner.") Very interesting to logophiles.

By the way, `login` is indeed present these days in *The Official Scrabble*® *Players Dictionary*, fourth edition (Springfield, Massachusetts: Merriam–Webster, 2005).

Chapter 38

Dancing Links

[An invited lecture for a symposium at Oxford University, presented 14 September 1999. Originally published in Millennial Perspectives in Computer Science, edited by Jim Davies, Bill Roscoe, and Jim Woodcock, a festschrift for C. A. R. Hoare (Houndmills, Basingstoke, Hampshire: Palgrave, 2000), 187–214.]

> "What a dance
> do they do
> Lordy, how I'm tellin' you!" [2]

My purpose is to discuss an extremely simple technique that deserves to be better known. Suppose x points to an element of a doubly linked list; let $L[x]$ and $R[x]$ point to the predecessor and successor of that element. Then the operations

$$L[R[x]] \leftarrow L[x], \qquad R[L[x]] \leftarrow R[x] \tag{1}$$

remove x from the list; every programmer knows this. But comparatively few programmers have realized that the subsequent operations

$$L[R[x]] \leftarrow x, \qquad R[L[x]] \leftarrow x \tag{2}$$

will put x back into the list again.

This fact is, of course, obvious, once it has been pointed out. Yet I remember feeling a definite sense of "Aha!" when I first realized that (2) would work, because the values of $L[x]$ and $R[x]$ no longer have their former semantic significance after x has been removed from its list. Indeed, a tidy programmer might want to clean up the data structure by setting $L[x]$ and $R[x]$ both equal to x, or to some null value, after x has been deleted. Danger sometimes lurks when objects are allowed to point into a list from the outside; such pointers can, for example, interfere with garbage collection.

437

Why, therefore, am I sufficiently fond of operation (2) that I am motivated to write an entire paper about it? The element denoted by x has been deleted from its list; why would anybody want to put it back again? Well, I admit that updates to a data structure are usually intended to be permanent. But there are also many occasions when they aren't. For example, an interactive program may need to revert to a former state when the user wants to undo an operation or a sequence of operations. Another typical application arises in *backtrack programs* [16], which enumerate all solutions to a given set of constraints. Backtracking, also called *depth-first search*, will be the focus of the present paper.

The idea of (2) was introduced in 1979 by Hirosi Hitotumatu and Kohei Noshita [22], who showed that it makes Dijkstra's well-known program for the N queens problem [6, pages 72–82] run nearly twice as fast without making the program significantly more complicated.

Floyd's elegant discussion of the connection between backtracking and nondeterministic algorithms [11] includes a precise method for updating data structures before choosing between alternative lines of computation, as well as for downdating the data when a new line should be explored. In general, the key problem of backtrack programming can be regarded as the task of deciding how to narrow the search and at the same time to organize the data that controls those decisions. Each step in the solution to a multistep problem changes the problem that remains to be solved.

In simple situations we need only maintain a stack that contains snapshots of the relevant state information at all ancestors of the current node in the search tree. But the task of copying the entire state at each level might take too much time. Therefore we often choose to work with global data structures, which are modified whenever the search enters a new level and restored when the search returns to a previous level.

For example, Dijkstra's recursive procedure for the queens problem kept the current state in three global Boolean arrays, representing the columns, the diagonals, and the reverse diagonals of a chessboard; Hitotumatu and Noshita's program kept it in a doubly linked list of available columns together with Boolean arrays for both kinds of diagonals. When Dijkstra tentatively placed a queen, he changed one entry of each Boolean array from true to false; then he made the entry true again when backtracking. Hitotumatu and Noshita used the assignments of (1) to remove a column and those of (2) to restore it again; this meant that they could find an empty column without having to search for it. Each program strove to record the state information in such a way that the placing and subsequent unplacing of a queen would be efficient.

The beauty of (2) is that operation (1) can be undone by knowing only the value of x. General schemes for undoing assignments require us to record the identity of the left-hand side together with its previous value (see [11]; see also [25, sections 268–284]). But in this case only the single quantity x is needed, and backtrack programs often know the value of x implicitly as a byproduct of their normal operation.

We can apply (1) and (2) repeatedly in complex data structures that involve large numbers of interacting doubly linked lists. The program logic that traverses those lists and decides what elements should be deleted can often be run in reverse, thereby deciding what elements should be undeleted. And undeletion restores links that allow us to continue running the program logic backwards until we're ready to go forward again.

This process causes the pointer variables inside the global data structure to execute an exquisitely choreographed dance; hence I like to call (1) and (2) the technique of *dancing links*.

The Exact Cover Problem

One way to illustrate the power of dancing links is to consider a general problem that can be described abstractly as follows: Given a matrix of 0s and 1s, does it have a set of rows containing exactly one 1 in each column?

For example, the matrix

$$
\begin{pmatrix}
0 & 0 & 1 & 0 & 1 & 1 & 0 \\
1 & 0 & 0 & 1 & 0 & 0 & 1 \\
0 & 1 & 1 & 0 & 0 & 1 & 0 \\
1 & 0 & 0 & 1 & 0 & 0 & 0 \\
0 & 1 & 0 & 0 & 0 & 0 & 1 \\
0 & 0 & 0 & 1 & 1 & 0 & 1
\end{pmatrix}
\tag{3}
$$

has such a set (rows 1, 4, and 5). We can think of the columns as elements of a universe, and the rows as subsets of the universe; then the problem is to cover the universe with disjoint subsets. Or we can think of the rows as elements of a universe, and the columns as subsets of that universe; then the problem is to find a collection of elements that intersect each subset in exactly one point. Either way, it's a potentially tough problem, well known to be NP-complete even when each row contains exactly three 1s [13, section A3.1, problem SP2, known as "X3C" for short]. And it is a natural candidate for backtracking.

Dana Scott conducted one of the first experiments on backtrack programming in 1958, when he was a graduate student at Princeton

University [35]. His program, written for the IAS "MANIAC" computer with the help of Hale F. Trotter, produced the first listing of all ways to place the 12 *pentominoes* into a chessboard leaving the center four squares vacant. For example, one of the 65 solutions is shown in Figure 1. (Pentominoes are the case $n = 5$ of n-ominoes, which are the rookwise-connected n-cell subsets of an infinite board; see [15]. Scott was probably inspired by Golomb's paper [14] and by later developments reported by Martin Gardner [12].)

FIGURE 1.
Scott's pentomino problem.

This problem is a special case of the exact cover problem. Imagine a matrix that has 72 columns, one for each of the 12 pentominoes and one for each of the 60 cells of the chessboard-minus-its-center. Construct all possible rows representing a way to place a pentomino on the board; each row contains a 1 in the column identifying the piece, and five 1s in the columns identifying its positions. (There are exactly 1568 such rows.) We can name the first twelve columns F I L P N T U V W X Y Z, following Golomb's recommended names for the pentominoes [15, page 7], and we can use two digits ij to name the column corresponding to rank i and file j of the board; each row is conveniently represented by giving the names of the columns where 1s appear. For example, Figure 1 is the exact cover corresponding to the following twelve matrix rows:

I 11 12 13 14 15	X 23 32 33 34 43	Z 57 58 67 76 77
N 16 26 27 37 47	W 24 25 35 36 46	T 61 71 72 73 81
L 17 18 28 38 48	P 51 52 53 62 63	V 68 78 86 87 88
U 21 22 31 41 42	F 56 64 65 66 75	Y 74 82 83 84 85

Solving an Exact Cover Problem

The following nondeterministic algorithm, which I will call algorithm X for lack of a better name, finds all solutions to the exact cover problem defined by any given matrix A of 0s and 1s. Algorithm X is simply a statement of the obvious trial-and-error approach. (Indeed, I can't think of any other reasonable way to do the job, in general.)

Algorithm X:

If A is empty, the problem is solved; terminate successfully.

Otherwise choose a column, c (deterministically).

Choose a row, r, such that $A[r, c] = 1$ (nondeterministically).

Include r in the partial solution.

For each j such that $A[r, j] = 1$,

for each i such that $A[i, j] = 1$, delete row i from matrix A;

delete column j from matrix A.

Repeat this algorithm recursively on the reduced matrix A.

The nondeterministic choice of r means that the algorithm essentially clones itself into independent subalgorithms; each subalgorithm inherits the current matrix A, but reduces it with respect to a different row r. If column c is entirely zero, there are no subalgorithms and the process terminates unsuccessfully.

The subalgorithms form a *search tree* in a natural way, with the original problem at the root and with level k containing each subalgorithm that corresponds to k chosen rows. Backtracking is the process of traversing the tree in preorder, "depth first."

Any systematic rule for choosing column c in this procedure will find all solutions, but some rules work much better than others. For example, Scott [35] said that his initial inclination was to place the first pentomino first, then the second pentomino, and so on; this would correspond to choosing column F first, then column I, etc., in the corresponding exact cover problem. But he soon realized that such an approach would be hopelessly slow: There are 192 ways to place the F, and for each of those choices there are approximately 34 ways to place the I. The Monte Carlo estimation procedure described in [24] suggests that the search tree for such a scheme has roughly 2×10^{12} nodes! By contrast, the alternative of choosing column 11 first (the column corresponding to rank 1 and file 1 of the board), and in general choosing the lexicographically first uncovered column, leads to a search tree with 9,015,751 nodes.

Even better is the strategy that Scott finally adopted [35]: He realized that piece X has only 3 essentially different positions, namely centered at 23, 24, or 33. Furthermore, if the X pentomino is at 33, we can assume that the P is not "turned over," thus restricting the P to only four of its eight orientations. Then we get each of the 65 essentially different solutions exactly once, and the full set of $8 \times 65 = 520$ solutions is easily obtained by rotation and reflection.

Solomon Golomb and Leonard Baumert [16] suggested choosing, at each stage of a backtrack procedure, a subproblem that leads to the fewest branches, whenever this choice can be made efficiently. In the case of an exact cover problem, this means that we want to choose at each stage a column with fewest 1s in the current matrix A. Fortunately we will see that the technique of dancing links allows us to do this quite nicely.

For example, Scott's original lexicographic strategy for choosing c led to the following search trees in the pentomino problem:

103,005 nodes and 19 solutions (for X at 23);
106,232 nodes and 20 solutions (for X at 24);
126,636 nodes and 26 solutions (for X at 33, P not flipped).

The Golomb–Baumert strategy reduces this to just

10,421 nodes and 19 solutions (for X at 23);
12,900 nodes and 20 solutions (for X at 24);
14,045 nodes and 26 solutions (for X at 33, P not flipped).

The Dance Steps

One good way to implement algorithm X is to represent each 1 in the matrix A as a *data object* x with five fields $L[x], R[x], U[x], D[x], C[x]$. Rows of the matrix are doubly linked as circular lists via the L and R fields ("left" and "right"); columns are doubly linked as circular lists via the U and D fields ("up" and "down"). Each column list also includes a special data object called its *list header*.

The list header nodes are part of a larger object called a *column object*. Each column object y contains the fields $L[y], R[y], U[y], D[y]$, and $C[y]$ of a data object and two additional fields, $S[y]$ ("size") and $N[y]$ ("name"); the size is the number of 1s in the column, and the name is a symbolic identifier for printing the answers. The C field of each object points to the column object at the head of the relevant column.

The L and R fields of the list headers link together all columns that still need to be covered. This circular list also includes a special column object called the *root*, h, which serves as a master header for all the active headers. The fields $U[h], D[h], C[h], S[h]$, and $N[h]$ are not used.

For example, the 0–1 matrix of (3) would be represented by the objects shown in Figure 2, if we name the columns A, B, C, D, E, F, and G. (This diagram "wraps around" toroidally at the top, bottom,

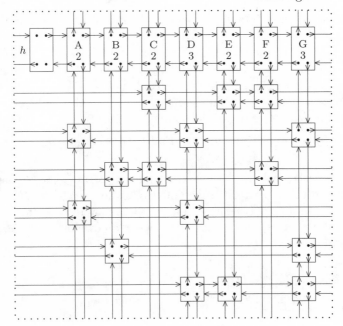

FIGURE 2. Four-way-linked representation of the exact cover problem (3).

left, and right. The C links are not shown because they would clutter up the picture; each C field points to the topmost element in its column.)

Our nondeterministic algorithm to find all exact covers can now be cast in the following explicit, deterministic form as a recursive procedure $search(k)$, which is invoked initially with $k = 0$:

If $R[h] = h$, print the current solution (see below) and return.
Otherwise choose a column object c (see below).
Cover column c (see below).
For each $r \leftarrow D[c]$, $D\big[D[c]\big]$, ..., while $r \neq c$,
    set $O_k \leftarrow r$;
    for each $j \leftarrow R[r]$, $R\big[R[r]\big]$, ..., while $j \neq r$,
        cover column $C[j]$ (see below);
    $search(k + 1)$;
    set $r \leftarrow O_k$ and $c \leftarrow C[r]$;
    for each $j \leftarrow L[r]$, $L\big[L[r]\big]$, ..., while $j \neq r$,
        uncover column $C[j]$ (see below).
Uncover column c (see below) and return.

The operation of printing the current solution is easy: We successively print the rows containing O_0, O_1, ..., O_{k-1}, where the row containing data object O is printed by printing the names $N\big[C[O]\big]$, $N\big[C[R[O]]\big]$, $N\big[C[R[R[O]]]\big]$, etc.

To choose a column object c, we could simply set $c \leftarrow R[h]$; this is the leftmost uncovered column. Or if we want to minimize the branching factor, we could set $s \leftarrow \infty$ and then

$$\text{for each } j \leftarrow R[h],\ R\big[R[h]\big],\ \dots,\ \text{while } j \neq h,$$
$$\text{if } S[j] < s \quad \text{set } c \leftarrow j \text{ and } s \leftarrow S[j].$$

Then c is a column with the smallest number of 1s. (The S fields are not needed unless we want to minimize branching in this way.)

The operation of covering column c is more interesting: It removes c from the header list and removes all rows in c's own list from the other column lists they are in.

Set $L\big[R[c]\big] \leftarrow L[c]$ and $R\big[L[c]\big] \leftarrow R[c]$.
For each $i \leftarrow D[c],\ D\big[D[c]\big],\ \dots,\ \text{while } i \neq c,$
 for each $j \leftarrow R[i],\ R\big[R[i]\big],\ \dots,\ \text{while } j \neq i,$
  set $U\big[D[j]\big] \leftarrow U[j],\ D\big[U[j]\big] \leftarrow D[j],$
  and set $S\big[C[j]\big] \leftarrow S\big[C[j]\big] - 1.$

Operation (1), which I mentioned at the outset of this paper, is used here to remove objects in both the horizontal and vertical directions.

Finally, we get to the point of this whole algorithm, the operation of *uncovering* a given column c. Here is where the links do their dance:

For each $i \leftarrow U[c],\ U\big[U[c]\big],\ \dots,\ \text{while } i \neq c,$
 for each $j \leftarrow L[i],\ L\big[L[i]\big],\ \dots,\ \text{while } j \neq i,$
  set $S\big[C[j]\big] \leftarrow S\big[C[j]\big] + 1,$
  and set $U\big[D[j]\big] \leftarrow j,\ D\big[U[j]\big] \leftarrow j.$
Set $L\big[R[c]\big] \leftarrow c$ and $R\big[L[c]\big] \leftarrow c.$

Notice that uncovering takes place in precisely the reverse order of the covering operation, using the fact that (2) undoes (1). (Actually we need not adhere so strictly to the principle of "last done, first undone" in this case, since j could run through row i in any order. But we must be careful to unremove the rows from bottom to top, because we removed them from top to bottom. Similarly, it is important to uncover the columns of row r from right to left, because we covered them from left to right.)

Consider, for example, what happens when $search(0)$ is applied to the data of (3) as represented by Figure 2. Column A is covered by

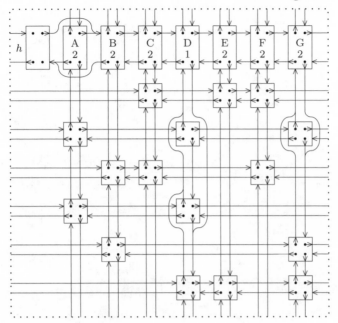

FIGURE 3. The links after column A in Figure 2 has been covered.

removing both of its rows from their other columns; the structure now takes the form of Figure 3. Notice the asymmetry of the links that appear in column D of the updated structure: The upper element was deleted first, so it still points to its original neighbors, but the other deleted element points upward to the column header.

Continuing $search(0)$, when r points to element A of row (A, D, G), we also cover columns D and G. Figure 4 shows the status as we enter $search(1)$; this data structure represents the reduced matrix

$$\begin{array}{cccc} B & C & E & F \end{array}$$
$$\begin{pmatrix} 0 & 1 & 1 & 1 \\ 1 & 1 & 0 & 1 \end{pmatrix}. \qquad (4)$$

Now $search(1)$ will cover column B, and there will be no 1s left in column E. So $search(2)$ will find nothing. Then $search(1)$ will return, having found no solutions, and the state of Figure 4 will be restored. The outer level routine, $search(0)$, will proceed to convert Figure 4 back to Figure 3, and it will move r down to element A of row (A, D).

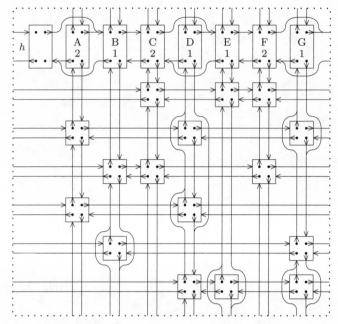

FIGURE 4. The links after columns D and G in Figure 3 have been covered.

Soon the solution will be found. It will be printed as

$$
\begin{array}{lll}
\text{A} & \text{D} & \\
\text{B} & \text{G} & \\
\text{C} & \text{E} & \text{F}
\end{array}
$$

if the S fields are ignored in the choice of c, or as

$$
\begin{array}{lll}
\text{A} & \text{D} & \\
\text{E} & \text{F} & \text{C} \\
\text{B} & \text{G} &
\end{array}
$$

if the shortest column is chosen at each step. (The first item printed in each row list is the name of the column on which branching was done.) Readers who play through the action of this algorithm on some examples will understand why I chose the title of this paper.

Efficiency Considerations

When algorithm X is implemented in terms of dancing links, let's call it algorithm DLX. The running time of algorithm DLX is essentially

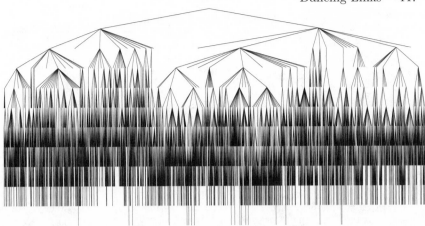

FIGURE 5. The search tree for one case of Scott's pentomino problem.

proportional to the number of times it applies operation (1) to remove an
object from a list; this is also the number of times it applies operation (2)
to unremove an object. Let's say that this quantity is the number of
updates. A total of 30 updates are performed during the solution of (3)
if we repeatedly choose the shortest column: 12 updates are made on
level 0, 14 on level 1, and 4 on level 2. Alternatively, if we ignore the
S heuristic, the algorithm makes 16 updates on level 1 and 7 updates
on level 2, for a total of 35. But in the latter case each update will go
noticeably faster, since the statements $S\big[C[j]\big] \leftarrow S\big[C[j]\big] \pm 1$ can be
omitted; hence the overall running time will probably be less. Of course
we need to study larger examples before drawing any general conclusions
about the desirability of the S heuristic.

A backtrack program usually spends most of its time on only a few
levels of the search tree (see [24]). For example, Figure 5 shows the
search tree for the case X = 23 of Dana Scott's pentomino problem
using the S heuristic. It has the profile shown in Table 1, where the
number of updates shown for level $k > 0$ is the number of times an
element was removed from a doubly linked list during the calculations
between levels $k - 1$ and k. The 2,031 updates on level 0 correspond to
removing column X from the header list and then removing $2030/5 =$
406 rows from their other columns; these are the rows that overlap with
the placement of X at 23. Notice that more than half of the nodes lie
on levels ≥ 8, but more than half of the updates occur on the way to
level 7. Extra work on the lower levels has reduced the need for hard
work at the higher levels.

TABLE 1. Profile of the search tree in Figure 5

Level	Nodes		Updates		Updates per node
0	1	(0%)	2,031	(0%)	2031.0
1	2	(0%)	1,676	(0%)	838.0
2	22	(0%)	28,492	(1%)	1295.1
3	77	(1%)	77,687	(2%)	1008.9
4	219	(2%)	152,957	(4%)	698.4
5	518	(5%)	367,939	(10%)	710.3
6	1,395	(13%)	853,788	(24%)	612.0
7	2,483	(24%)	941,265	(26%)	379.1
8	2,574	(25%)	740,523	(20%)	287.7
9	2,475	(24%)	418,334	(12%)	169.0
10	636	(6%)	32,205	(1%)	50.6
11	19	(0%)	826	(0%)	43.5
Total	10,421	(100%)	3,617,723	(100%)	347.2

When the same problem is run *without* the ordering heuristic based on S fields, we obtain the statistics shown in Table 2. Each update involves about 16 memory accesses when the S heuristic is used, and about 10 accesses when S is ignored. Thus the S heuristic reduces the total number of memory accesses to approximately $(16 \times 3,617,723)/(10 \times 17,818,752) \approx 32\%$ of what would otherwise have been needed in this example. The heuristic is even more effective in larger problems, because it tends to reduce the total number of nodes by a factor that is exponential in the number of levels while the cost of applying it grows only linearly.

Assuming that the S heuristic is good in large trees but not so good in small ones, I tried a hybrid scheme that uses S at low levels but not at high levels. This experiment was, however, unsuccessful. If, for example, S was ignored after level 7, the statistics for levels 8–11 were as follows:

Level	Nodes	Updates
8	18,300	5,672,258
9	28,624	2,654,310
10	9,989	213,944
11	19	10,179

And if the change was applied after level 8, the stats were similar:

Level	Nodes	Updates
9	11,562	1,495,054
10	6,113	148,162
11	19	6,303

TABLE 2. Profile of the search tree without the S heuristic

Level	Nodes		Updates		Updates per node
0	1	(0%)	2,031	(0%)	2031.0
1	6	(0%)	5,606	(0%)	934.3
2	24	(0%)	30,111	(0%)	1254.6
3	256	(0%)	249,904	(1%)	976.2
4	581	(1%)	432,471	(2%)	744.4
5	1,533	(1%)	1,256,556	(7%)	819.7
6	3,422	(3%)	2,290,338	(13%)	669.3
7	10,381	(10%)	4,442,572	(25%)	428.0
8	26,238	(25%)	5,804,161	(33%)	221.2
9	46,609	(45%)	3,006,418	(17%)	64.5
10	13,935	(14%)	284,459	(2%)	20.4
11	19	(0%)	14,125	(0%)	743.4
Total	103,005	(100%)	17,818,752	(100%)	173.0

Therefore I decided to retain the S heuristic at all levels of algorithm DLX.

My trusty old SPARCstation 2 computer, vintage 1992, is able to perform approximately 0.39 mega-updates per second when working on large problems and maintaining the S fields. The 120 MHz Pentium I computer that Stanford computer science faculty were given in 1996 did 1.21 mega-updates per second, and my new 500 MHz Pentium III does 5.94. Thus the running time decreases as technology advances; but it remains essentially proportional to the number of updates, which is the number of times the links do their dance. Therefore I prefer to measure the performance of algorithm DLX by counting the number of updates, not by counting the number of elapsed seconds.

Scott [35] was pleased to discover that his program for Princeton's MANIAC solved the pentomino problem in about 3.5 hours. The MANIAC executed approximately 4000 instructions per second, so this represented roughly 50 million instructions. He and H. F. Trotter found a nice way to use the "bitwise-and" instructions of the MANIAC, which had 40-bit registers. Their code, which executed about $50{,}000{,}000/(103{,}005 + 106{,}232 + 126{,}636) \approx 150$ instructions per node of the search tree, was quite efficient in spite of the fact that they had to deal with about ten times as many nodes as would be produced by the ordering heuristic. Indeed, the linked-list approach of algorithm DLX performs a total of $3{,}617{,}723 + 4{,}547{,}186 + 4{,}865{,}610 = 13{,}030{,}519$ updates, or about 208 million memory accesses; and it would never fit in the 5120-byte memory of the MANIAC! From this standpoint the technique of dancing links is actually a step backward from Scott's 40-year-old method, although of course that method works only for very special types of exact cover problems in which simple geometric structure can be exploited.

The task of finding all ways to pack the set of pentominoes into a 6×10 rectangle is more difficult than Scott's $8 \times 8 - 2 \times 2$ problem, because the backtrack tree for the 6×10 problem is larger and there are 2339 essentially different solutions [21]. In this case we limit the X pentomino to the upper left quarter of the board; our linked-list algorithm generates 904,969 nodes and 309,134,131 updates (or 28,323,148 nodes and 4,107,105,935 updates without the S heuristic). This solves the problem in less than a minute on a Pentium III; however, again I should point out that the special characteristics of pentominoes allow a faster approach.

John G. Fletcher needed only ten minutes to solve the 6×10 problem on an IBM 7094 in 1965, using a highly optimized program that had 765 instructions in its inner loop [10]. The 7094 had a clock rate of 0.7 MHz, and it could access two 36-bit words in a single clock cycle. Fletcher's program required only about $600 \times 700,000/28,323,148 \approx 15$ clock cycles per node of the search tree; so it was superior to the bitwise method of Scott and Trotter, and it remains the fastest algorithm known for problems that involve placing the twelve pentominoes. (N. G. de Bruijn discovered an almost identical method independently; see [7].)

With a few extensions to the 0–1 matrix for Dana Scott's problem, we can solve the more general problem of covering a chessboard with twelve pentominoes and one square tetromino, without insisting that the tetromino occupy the center. This is essentially the classic problem of Dudeney, who invented pentominoes in 1907 [9]. The total number of such chessboard dissections that are essentially different has apparently never appeared in the literature; algorithm DLX needs 1,526,279,783 updates to determine that it is exactly 16,146.

Many people have written about polyomino problems, including distinguished mathematicians such as Golomb [15]; de Bruijn [8]; Berlekamp, Conway, and Guy [4]. Their arguments for placing the pieces are sometimes based on enumerating the number of ways a certain cell on the board can be filled, sometimes on the number of ways a certain piece can be placed. But as far as I know, the basic fact that such tasks are exact cover problems, in which cells and piece names play *identical* roles, has been pointed out only once in the published literature [32], without actually making use of this perfect symmetry between cells and pieces. Algorithm DLX will branch on the ways to fill a cell if some cell is difficult to fill, or on the ways to place a piece if some piece is difficult

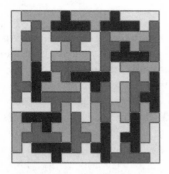

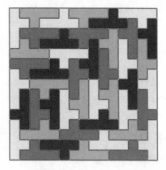

92 solutions, 14,352,556 nodes
1,764,631,796 updates

100 solutions, 10,258,180 nodes
1,318,478,396 updates

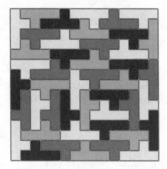

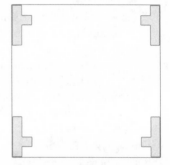

20 solutions, 6,375,335 nodes
806,699,079 updates

0 solutions, 1,234,485 nodes
162,017,125 updates

FIGURE 6. Packing 45 Y pentominoes into a 15 × 15 square.

to place. The algorithm knows no difference, because piece names and cells are simply columns of the given input matrix.

Algorithm DLX begins to outperform other pentomino-placing procedures in problems where the search tree has many levels. For example, let's consider the problem of packing 45 Y pentominoes into a 15 × 15 square. Jenifer Haselgrove studied this with the help of a machine called the ICS Multum — which qualified as a "fast minicomputer" in 1973 [20]. The Multum produced an answer after more than an hour, but she remained uncertain whether other solutions were possible. Now, with the dancing links approach, we can obtain several solutions almost instantly, and the total number of distinct solutions turns out to be 212. The solutions fall into four classes, depending on the behavior at the four corners; representatives of each achievable class are shown in Figure 6.

Applications to Hexiamonds

In the late 1950s, T. H. O'Beirne introduced a pleasant variation on polyominoes by substituting triangles for squares. He named the resulting
shapes *polyiamonds*: moniamonds, diamonds, triamonds, tetriamonds,
pentiamonds, hexiamonds, etc. The twelve hexiamonds were independently discovered by J. E. Reeve and J. A. Tyrrell [33], who found more
than forty ways to arrange them into a 6×6 rhombus. Figure 7 shows one
such arrangement, together with some arrow dissections that I couldn't
resist trying when I first learned about hexiamonds. The 6×6 rhombus
can be tiled by the twelve hexiamonds in exactly 156 ways. (This fact
was first proved by P. J. Torbijn [36], who worked without a computer;
algorithm DLX confirms his result after making 37,313,405 updates, if
we restrict the "sphinx" to only 3 of its 12 orientations.)

O'Beirne was particularly fascinated by the fact that seven of the
twelve hexiamonds have different shapes when they are flipped over, and
that the resulting 19 *one-sided hexiamonds* have the correct number of
triangles to form a hexagon: a hexagon of hexiamonds (see Figure 8). In
November of 1959, after three months of trials, working by hand in his
study, he found a solution; and two years later he challenged the readers
of *New Scientist* to match this feat [28, 29, 30].

Meanwhile he had shown the puzzle to Richard Guy and his family. The Guys published several solutions in a journal published in
Singapore, where Richard was currently a professor [17]. When Richard
subsequently recounted the story of this fascinating recreation in [18], he
remarked that, when O'Beirne had first described the puzzle, "Everyone
wanted to try it at once. No one went to bed for about 48 hours."

A 19-level backtrack tree with many possibilities at each level makes
an excellent test case for the dancing links approach to covering, so I
fed O'Beirne's problem to my program. I broke the general case into
seven subcases, depending on the distance of the hexagon piece from
the center; furthermore, when that distance was zero, I considered two
subcases depending on the position of the "crown." Figure 8 shows a
representative of each of the seven cases, together with statistics about
the search. The total number of updates performed was 134,425,768,494.

My goal was not only to count the solutions, but also to find arrangements that were as symmetrical as possible — in response to a problem
that was stated in Berlekamp, Guy, and Conway's book *Winning Ways*
[4, page 788]. Let us define the *horizontal symmetry* of a configuration to be the number of edges between pieces that also are edges between pieces in the left-right reflection of that configuration. The overall

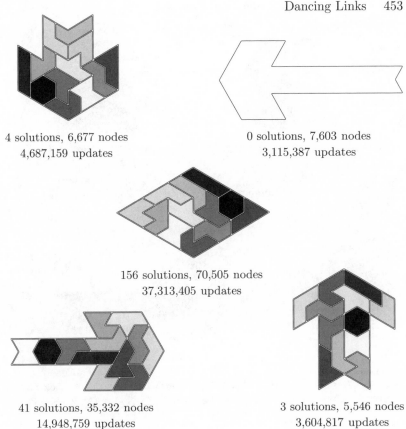

4 solutions, 6,677 nodes
4,687,159 updates

0 solutions, 7,603 nodes
3,115,387 updates

156 solutions, 70,505 nodes
37,313,405 updates

41 solutions, 35,332 nodes
14,948,759 updates

3 solutions, 5,546 nodes
3,604,817 updates

FIGURE 7. The twelve hexiamonds, packed into a 6 × 6 rhombus and into
various arrowlike shapes.

hexagon has 156 internal edges, and the 19 one-sided hexiamonds have
96 internal non-edges. Therefore if an arrangement were perfectly symmetrical — unchanged by left-right reflection — its horizontal symmetry
would be 60. But no such perfectly symmetric solution is possible.

The *vertical symmetry* of a configuration is defined similarly, but
with respect to top-bottom reflection. A solution to the hexiamond problem is *maximally symmetric* if it has the highest horizontal or vertical
symmetry score, and if the smaller score is as large as possible consistent with the larger score. Each of the solutions shown in Figure 8 is, in
fact, maximally symmetric in its class. (And so is the solution to Dana
Scott's problem that is shown in Figure 1: It has vertical symmetry 36
and horizontal symmetry 30.)

(a)

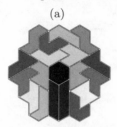

(hsym = 51, vsym = 24)
1,914 solutions
4,239,132 nodes
2,142,276,414 updates

(b)

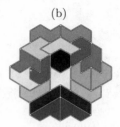

(hsym = 52, vsym = 24)
5,727 solutions
21,583,173 nodes
11,020,236,507 updates

(c)

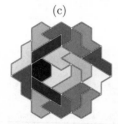

(hsym = 32, vsym = 50)
11,447 solutions
20,737,702 nodes
10,315,775,812 updates

(d)

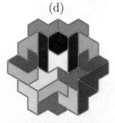

(hsym = 51, vsym = 22)
7,549 solutions
24,597,239 nodes
12,639,698,345 updates

(e)

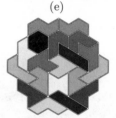

(hsym = 48, vsym = 30)
6,675 solutions
17,277,362 nodes
8,976,245,858 updates

(f)

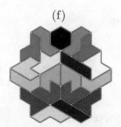

(hsym = 52, vsym = 27)
15,717 solutions
43,265,607 nodes
21,607,912,011 updates

(g)

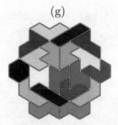

(hsym = 48, vsym = 29)
75,490 solutions
137,594,347 nodes
67,723,623,547 updates

FIGURE 8. Solutions to O'Beirne's hexiamond-hexagon problem, with the small hexagon at various distances from the center of the large one.

The largest possible vertical symmetry score is 50; it is achieved in Figure 8(c), and in seven other solutions obtained by independently rearranging three of its symmetrical subparts. Four of the eight have a horizontal symmetry score of 32; the others have horizontal symmetry 24. John Conway found these solutions by hand in 1964 and conjectured that they were maximally symmetric overall. But that honor belongs uniquely to the solution in Figure 8(f), at least by my definition, because Figure 8(f) has horizontal symmetry 52 and vertical symmetry 27. The only other ways to achieve horizontal symmetry 52 have vertical symmetry scores of 20, 22, and 24. (Two of those other ways do, however, have the surprising property that 13 of their 19 pieces are unchanged by horizontal reflection; this is symmetry of entire pieces, not just of edges.)

After I had done this enumeration, I read Guy's paper [18] for the first time and learned that Marc M. Paulhus had already enumerated all solutions in May 1996 [31]. Good: Our independent computations would confirm the results. But no — my program found 124,519 solutions, while his had found 124,518! He reran his program in 1999 and now we agree.

O'Beirne [29] also suggested an analogous problem for pentominoes, since there are 18 one-sided pentominoes. He asked if they can be put into a 9×10 rectangle, and Golomb provided an example in [15, Chapter 6]. Jenifer Leech wrote a program to prove that there are exactly 46 different ways to pack the one-sided pentominoes in a 3×30 rectangle; see [26]. Figure 9 shows a maximally symmetric example (which isn't really very symmetrical).

46 solutions, 1,428,709 nodes, 462,355,739 updates, hsym = 51, vsym = 48

FIGURE 9. The one-sided pentominoes, packed into a 3×30 rectangle.

I set out to count the solutions to O'Beirne's 9×10 challenge, figuring that an 18-stage exact cover problem with six 1s per row would be simpler than a 19-stage problem with seven 1s per row. But I soon found that the task would be hopeless, unless I invented a much better algorithm. The Monte Carlo estimation procedure of [24] suggests that about 19 quadrillion updates will be needed, with 64 trillion nodes in the search trees. If that estimate is correct, I could have the result in a few months; but I'd rather try for a new Mersenne prime.

I do, however, have a conjecture about the solution that will have maximum horizontal symmetry; see Figure 10.

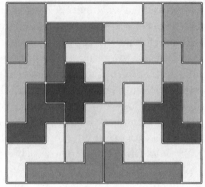

hsym = 74,   vsym = 49

FIGURE 10. Is this the most symmetrical way to pack the one-sided pen-
    tominoes into a 9 × 10 rectangle?

A Failed Experiment

Special arguments based on "coloring" often give important insights into
tiling problems. For example, it is well known [5, pages 142 and 394]
that if we remove two cells from opposite corners of a chessboard, there
is no way to cover the remaining 62 cells with dominoes. The reason is
that the mutilated chessboard has, say, 32 white cells and 30 black cells,
but each individual domino covers one cell of each color. If we present
such a covering problem to algorithm DLX, it makes 4,780,846 updates
(and finds 13,922 ways to place 30 of the 31 dominoes) before concluding
that there is no solution.

The cells of the hexiamond-hexagon problem can be colored black
and white in a similar fashion: All triangles that point left are black,
say, and all that point right are white. Then fifteen of the one-sided
hexiamonds cover three triangles of each color; but the remaining four,
namely the "sphinx" and the "yacht" and their mirror images, each have
a four-to-two color bias. Therefore every solution to the problem must
put exactly two of those four pieces into positions that favor black.

I thought I'd speed things up by dividing the problem into six subproblems, one for each way to choose the two pieces that will favor black.
Each of the subproblems was expected to have about 1/6 as many solutions as the overall problem, and each subproblem was simpler because
it gave four of the pieces only half as many options as before. Thus I
expected the subproblems to run up to 16 times as fast as the original
problem, and I expected the extra information about impossible correla-
tions of piece placement to help algorithm DLX make intelligent choices.

But this setup turned out to be a case where mathematics gave me bad advice. The overall problem had 6675 solutions and required 8,976,245,858 updates (Figure 8(e)). The six subproblems turned out to have respectively 955, 1208, 1164, 1106, 1272, and 970 solutions, roughly as expected; but they each required between 1.7 and 2.2 billion updates, and the total work to solve all six subproblems was 11,519,571,784. So much for *that* bright idea.

Applications to Tetrasticks

Instead of making pieces by joining squares or triangles together, Brian Barwell [3] considered making them from line segments or sticks. He called the resulting objects *polysticks*, and noted that there are 2 disticks, 5 tristicks, and 16 tetrasticks. The tetrasticks are especially interesting from a recreational standpoint; I received an attractive puzzle in 1993 that was equivalent to placing a certain set of ten tetrasticks in a 4 × 4 square [1], and I spent many hours trying to psych it out.

Barwell proved that the sixteen tetrasticks cannot be assembled into any symmetrical shape. But by leaving out any one of the five tetrasticks that have an excess of horizontal or vertical line segments, he found several ways to fill a 5 × 5 square. For example, here's a solution when the L tetrastick is placed at the side:

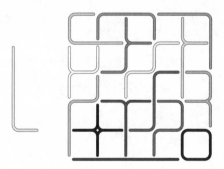

Such puzzles are quite difficult to do by hand, and he had found only five solutions at the time he wrote his paper; he conjectured that fewer than a hundred solutions would actually exist. But his guess turned out to be far too low: The set of all solutions is summarized in Figure 11. These solutions were first found by Wiezorke and Haubrich [38], who invented the puzzle independently after seeing [1].

Polysticks introduce a new feature that is not present in the polyomino and polyiamond problems: *The pieces must not cross each other.*

For example, Figure 12 shows a non-solution to Barwell's L-at-the-side problem in which every line segment in the grid of 5×5 squares is covered, but the V tetrastick crosses the Z.

We can handle this extra complication by generalizing the exact cover problem. Instead of requiring all columns of a given 0–1 matrix to be covered by disjoint rows, we will distinguish two kinds of columns: *primary* and *secondary*. The generalized problem asks for a set of rows that covers every primary column *exactly* once and every secondary column *at most* once.

The tetrastick problem of Figure 11(c) can be set up as a generalized cover problem in a natural way. First we introduce primary columns F, H, I, J, N, O, P, R, S, U, V, W, X, Y, Z representing the fifteen tetrasticks (excluding L), as well as columns Hpq representing the horizontal segments (p, q) — $(p + 1, q)$ and Vqp representing the vertical segments (q, p) — $(q, p+1)$, for $0 \le p < 5$ and $0 \le q \le 5$. We also need secondary columns Ipq to represent interior junction points (p, q), for $0 < p, q < 5$. Each row represents a possible placement of a piece, as in the polyomino and polyiamond problems; but if a piece has two consecutive horizontal or vertical segments and does not lie on the edge of the diagram, it should include the corresponding interior junction point as well.

For example, here are the two rows corresponding to the placement of V and Z in Figure 12:

$$\text{V} \quad \text{H23} \quad \text{I33} \quad \text{H33} \quad \text{V43} \quad \text{I44} \quad \text{V44}$$
$$\text{Z} \quad \text{H24} \quad \text{V33} \quad \text{I33} \quad \text{V32} \quad \text{H32}$$

The common interior point I33 means that these rows cross each other. On the other hand, I33 is not a primary column, because we do not necessarily need to cover it. The solution in Figure 11(c) covers only the interior points I14, I21, I32, and I43.

Fortunately, we can solve the generalized cover problem by using almost the same algorithm as before. The only difference is that we initialize the data structure by making a circular list of the column headers for the primary columns only. Each header node for a secondary column should have L and R fields that simply point to the node itself. The remainder of the algorithm proceeds exactly as before, so we shall still call it algorithm DLX.

A generalized cover problem can be converted to an equivalent exact cover problem of the traditional sort if we simply append one row for each secondary column, containing a single 1 in that column. But we are better off working with the generalized problem, because the generalized algorithm is simpler and faster.

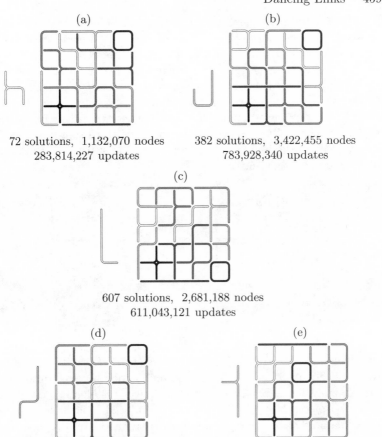

FIGURE 11. Filling a 5 × 5 grid with 15 of the 16 tetrasticks; we must leave out either the H, the J, the L, the N, or the Y, as shown.

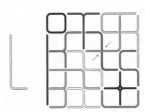

FIGURE 12. Polysticks aren't supposed to cross each other as they do here.

I decided to experiment with the subset of *welded tetrasticks*, namely those that do not form a simple connected path because they contain junction points: F, H, R, T, X, Y. There are ten *one-sided* welded tetrasticks, if we add the mirror images of the unsymmetrical pieces as we did for one-sided hexiamonds and pentominoes. And—aha— these ten tetrasticks can be arranged in a 4 × 4 grid. (See Figure 13.) Only three solutions are possible, including the two perfectly symmetric solutions shown. I've decided not to show the third solution, which has the X piece in the middle, because I want readers to have the pleasure of finding it for themselves.

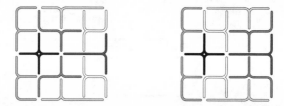

FIGURE 13. Two of the three ways to pack the one-sided welded tetra-sticks into a 4 × 4 square.

There are fifteen one-sided *unwelded tetrasticks*, and I thought they would surely fit into a 5 × 5 grid in a similar way; but this turned out to be impossible. The reason is that if, say, piece I is placed vertically, four of the six pieces J, J′, L, L′, N, N′ must be placed to favor the horizontal direction, and this severely limits the possibilities. In fact, I have been unable to pack those fifteen pieces into any simple symmetrical shape; my best effort so far is the "oboe" shown in Figure 14.

FIGURE 14. The fifteen one-sided unwelded tetrasticks.

I also tried unsuccessfully to pack all 25 of the one-sided tetrasticks into the Aztec diamond pattern of Figure 15; but I see no way to prove that a solution is impossible. An exhaustive search seems out of the question at the present time.

FIGURE 15. Do all 25 of the one-sided
tetrasticks fit in this shape?

Applications to Queens

Now we can return to the problem that led Hitotumatu and Noshita
to introduce dancing links in the first place, namely the N queens
problem, because that problem is actually a special case of the generalized exact cover problem in the previous section. For example, the
4 queens problem is just the task of covering eight primary columns
(R0, R1, R2, R3, F0, F1, F2, F3) corresponding to ranks and files, while
using at most one element in each of the secondary columns (A0, A1, A2,
A3, A4, A5, A6, B0, B1, B2, B3, B4, B5, B6) corresponding to diagonals,
given the following sixteen rows:

R0 F0 A0 B3	R1 F0 A1 B2	R2 F0 A2 B1	R3 F0 A3 B0
R0 F1 A1 B4	R1 F1 A2 B3	R2 F1 A3 B2	R3 F1 A4 B1
R0 F2 A2 B5	R1 F2 A3 B4	R2 F2 A4 B3	R3 F2 A5 B2
R0 F3 A3 B6	R1 F3 A4 B5	R2 F3 A5 B4	R3 F3 A6 B3

In general, the rows of the 0–1 matrix for the N queens problem are

$$\text{R}i \quad \text{F}j \quad \text{A}(i+j) \quad \text{B}(N-1-i+j)$$

for $0 \le i, j < N$. (Here Ri and Fj represent ranks and files of a
chessboard; Ak and Bl represent diagonals and reverse diagonals. The
secondary columns A0, A$(2N-2)$, B0, and B$(2N-2)$ each arise in only
one row of the matrix so they can be omitted.)

When we apply algorithm DLX to this generalized cover problem, it behaves quite differently from the traditional algorithms for the
N queens problem, because it sometimes branches on different ways to
occupy a rank of the chessboard and sometimes on different ways to
occupy a file. Furthermore, we gain efficiency by paying attention to
the order in which primary columns of the cover problem are considered when those columns all have the same S value (the same branching
factor): It is better to place queens near the middle of the board first,
because central positions rule out more possibilities for later placements.

Consider, for example, the eight queens problem. Figure 16(a) shows
an empty board, with 8 possible ways to occupy each rank and each file.

Suppose we decide to cover R4 by placing a queen in R4 and F7, as shown in Figure 16(b). Then there are five ways to cover F4. After choosing R5 and F4 as shown in Figure 16(c), there are four ways to cover R3; and so on. At each stage we choose the most constrained rank or file, using the "organ-pipe ordering"

$$\text{R4 F4 R3 F3 R5 F5 R2 F2 R6 F6 R1 F1 R7 F7 R0 F0}$$

to break ties. Placing a queen in R2 and F3 after Figure 16(d) makes it impossible to cover F2, so backtracking will occur even though only four queens have been tentatively placed.

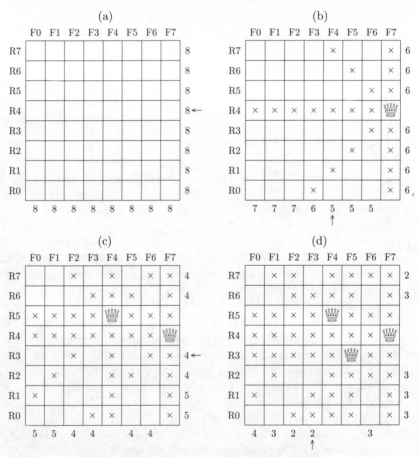

FIGURE 16. Solving the 8 queens problem by treating ranks and files symmetrically.

TABLE 3. Behavior of algorithm DLX on the N queens problem

N	Solutions	Nodes	Updates	R-Nodes	R-Updates
1	1	2	3	2	3
2	0	3	19	3	19
3	0	4	56	6	70
4	2	13	183	15	207
5	10	46	572	50	626
6	4	93	1,497	115	1,765
7	40	334	5,066	376	5,516
8	92	1,049	16,680	1,223	18,849
9	352	3,440	54,818	4,640	71,746
10	724	11,578	198,264	16,471	269,605
11	2,680	45,393	783,140	67,706	1,123,572
12	14,200	211,716	3,594,752	312,729	5,173,071
13	73,712	1,046,319	17,463,157	1,589,968	26,071,148
14	365,596	5,474,542	91,497,926	8,497,727	139,174,307
15	2,279,184	31,214,675	513,013,152	49,404,260	800,756,888
16	14,772,512	193,032,021	3,134,588,055	308,130,093	4,952,973,201
17	95,815,104	1,242,589,512	20,010,116,070	2,015,702,907	32,248,234,866
18	666,090,624	8,567,992,237	141,356,060,389	13,955,353,609	221,993,811,321

The order in which header nodes are linked together at the start of algorithm DLX can have a significant effect on the running time. For example, experiments on the 16 queens problem show that the search tree has 312,512,659 nodes and requires 5,801,583,739 updates, if the ordering R0 R1 ... R15 F0 F1 ... F15 is used, while the organ-pipe ordering R8 F8 R7 F7 R9 F9 ... R0 F0 requires only about 54% as many updates. However, the order in which individual elements of a row or column are linked together has no effect on the algorithm's total running time.

Table 3 shows some statistics observed when algorithm DLX solved small cases of the N queens problem using organ-pipe order, without reducing the number of solutions by taking symmetries of the board into account. Here "R-Nodes" and "R-Updates" refer to the results when we consider only R0, R1, ..., R($N-1$) to be primary columns that need to be covered; in that case, when columns Fj are secondary, the algorithm reduces to the usual procedure in which branching occurs only on ranks of the chessboard. The advantage of mixing ranks with files becomes evident as N increases, but I'm not sure whether the ratio of R-Updates to Updates will be unbounded or approach a limit as N goes to infinity.

I should point out that special methods are known for counting the number of solutions to the N queens problem without actually generating the queen placements [34].

Concluding Remarks

Algorithm DLX, which uses dancing links to implement the "natural" algorithm for exact cover problems, is an effective way to enumerate all solutions to such problems. On small cases it is nearly as fast as algorithms that have been tuned to solve particular classes of problems, like pentomino packing or the N queens problem, where geometric structure can be exploited. On large cases it appears to run even faster than those special-purpose algorithms, because of its ordering heuristic. And as computers get faster and faster, we are of course tackling larger and larger cases all the time.

In this paper I have used the exact cover problem to illustrate the versatility of dancing links, but I could have chosen many other backtrack applications in which the same ideas apply. For example, the approach works nicely with the Waltz filtering algorithm [37]; perhaps this fact has subliminally influenced my choice of names. I recently used dancing links together with a dictionary of about 600 common three-letter words of English to find word squares such as

```
ATE     BED     OHM     PEA     TWO
WIN     OAR     RUE     URN     ION
LED     WRY     BET     BAY     TEE
```

in which each row, column, and left-to-right diagonal is a word; about 60 million updates produced all solutions. I believe that a terpsichorean technique is significantly better than the alternative of copying the current state at every level, as considered in the pioneering paper by Haralick and Elliott on constraint satisfaction problems [19]. Certainly the use of (1) and (2) is simple, useful, and fun.

Acknowledgments

I wish to thank Sol Golomb, Richard Guy, and Gene Freuder for the help they generously gave me as I was preparing this paper. Maggie McLoughlin did an excellent job of translating my scrawled manuscript into a well-organized TEX document. And I profoundly thank Tomas Rokicki, who provided the new computer on which I did most of the experiments, and on which I hope to keep links dancing merrily for many years.

Historical Notes

(1) Although the IAS computer was popularly known in Princeton as the "MANIAC," that title properly belonged only to a similar but different series of computers built at Los Alamos. (See [27].) (2) George

Jelliss [23] has discovered that the great puzzle masters H. D. Benjamin and T. R. Dawson experimented with the concept of polysticks already in 1946–1948. However, they apparently did not publish any of their work. (3) My names for the tetrasticks are slightly different from those originally proposed by Barwell [3]: I prefer to use the letters J, R, and U for the pieces he called U, J, and C, respectively.

Program Notes

The implementation of algorithm DLX that I used when preparing this paper can be found on the webpage

http://www-cs-faculty.stanford.edu/~knuth/programs.html

as file `dance.w`, with the related files `polyominoes.w`, `polyiamonds.w`, `polysticks.w`, and `queens.w`.

References

[1] *845 Combinations Puzzles: 845 Interestingly Combinations* (Taiwan: R.O.C. Patent 66009). [There is no indication of the author or manufacturer. This puzzle actually has only 83 solutions. It carries a Chinese title, "Dr. Dragon's Intelligence Profit System."]

[2] Harry Barris, *Mississippi Mud* (New York: Shapiro, Bernstein & Co., 1927).

[3] Brian R. Barwell, "Polysticks," *Journal of Recreational Mathematics* **22** (1990), 165–175.

[4] Elwyn R. Berlekamp, John H. Conway, and Richard K. Guy, *Winning Ways for Your Mathematical Plays* **2** (London: Academic Press, 1982). [In the second edition (Wellesley, Massachusetts: A K Peters, 2004), volume 4, the hexiamond puzzle is discussed on pages 895–896 and 920.]

[5] Max Black, *Critical Thinking* (Englewood Cliffs, New Jersey: Prentice–Hall, 1946).

[6] Ole-Johan Dahl, Edsger W. Dijkstra, and C. A. R. Hoare, *Structured Programming* (London: Academic Press, 1972).

[7] N. G. de Bruijn, personal communication (9 September 1999): "... it was almost my first activity in programming that I got all 2339 solutions of the 6 × 10 pentomino on an IBM 1620 in March 1963 in 18 hours. It had to cope with the limited memory of that machine, and there was not the slightest possibility to store the full matrix

... But I could speed the matter up by having a very long program, and that one was generated by means of another program."

[8] N. G. de Bruijn, "Programmeren van de pentomino puzzle," *Euclides* **47** (1971/72), 90–104.

[9] Henry Ernest Dudeney, "74.—The broken chessboard," in *The Canterbury Puzzles* (London: William Heinemann, 1907), 90–92, 174–175.

[10] John G. Fletcher, "A program to solve the pentomino problem by the recursive use of macros," *Communications of the ACM* **8** (1965), 621–623.

[11] Robert W. Floyd, "Nondeterministic algorithms," *Journal of the Association for Computing Machinery* **14** (1967), 636–644.

[12] Martin Gardner, "Mathematical games: More about complex dominoes, plus the answers to last month's puzzles," *Scientific American* **197**, 6 (December 1957), 126–140.

[13] Michael R. Garey and David S. Johnson, *Computers and Intractability* (San Francisco: Freeman, 1979).

[14] S. W. Golomb, "Checker boards and polyominoes," *American Mathematical Monthly* **61** (1954), 675–682.

[15] Solomon W. Golomb, *Polyominoes*, second edition (Princeton, New Jersey: Princeton University Press, 1994).

[16] Solomon W. Golomb and Leonard D. Baumert, "Backtrack programming," *Journal of the Association for Computing Machinery* **12** (1965), 516–524.

[17] Richard K. Guy, "Some mathematical recreations," *Nabla* (Bulletin of the Malayan Mathematical Society) **7** (1960), 97–106, 144–153.

[18] Richard K. Guy, "O'Beirne's Hexiamond," in *The Mathemagician and Pied Puzzler*, edited by Elwyn Berlekamp and Tom Rodgers (Natick, Massachusetts: A K Peters, 1999), 85–96.

[19] Robert M. Haralick and Gordon L. Elliott, "Increasing tree search efficiency for constraint satisfaction problems," *Artificial Intelligence* **14** (1980), 263–313.

[20] Jenifer Haselgrove, "Packing a square with Y-pentominoes," *Journal of Recreational Mathematics* **7** (1974), 229.

[21] C. B. Haselgrove and Jenifer Haselgrove, "A computer program for pentominoes," *Eureka: The Archimedeans' Journal* **23** (1960), 16–18.

[22] Hirosi Hitotumatu and Kohei Noshita, "A technique for implementing backtrack algorithms and its application," *Information Processing Letters* **8** (1979), 174–175.

[23] George P. Jelliss, "Unwelded polysticks," *Journal of Recreational Mathematics* **29** (1998), 140–142.

[24] Donald E. Knuth, "Estimating the efficiency of backtrack programs," *Mathematics of Computation* **29** (1975), 121–136. [Reprinted as Chapter 6 of *Selected Papers on Analysis of Algorithms*, CSLI Lecture Notes 102 (Stanford, California: Center for the Study of Language and Information, 2000), 55–75.]

[25] Donald E. Knuth, *TEX: The Program*, Volume B of *Computers & Typesetting* (Reading, Massachusetts: Addison–Wesley, 1986).

[26] Jean Meeus, "Some polyomino and polyamond problems," *Journal of Recreational Mathematics* **6** (1973), 215–220.

[27] N. Metropolis and J. Worlton, "A trilogy of errors in the history of computing," *Annals of the History of Computing* **2** (1980), 49–59.

[28] T. H. O'Beirne, "Puzzles and Paradoxes 43: Pell's equation in two popular problems," *New Scientist* **12** (1961), 260–261.

[29] T. H. O'Beirne, "Puzzles and Paradoxes 44: Pentominoes and hexiamonds," *New Scientist* **12** (1961), 316–317. ["So far as we know, hexiamond has not yet been put through the mill on a computer: but this could doubtless be done."]

[30] T. H. O'Beirne, "Puzzles and Paradoxes 45: Some hexiamond solutions: and an introduction to a set of 25 remarkable points," *New Scientist* **12** (1961), 379–380.

[31] Marc Paulhus, "Hexiamond Homepage," a collection of webpages once at `http://www.math.ucalgary.ca/~paulhusm/hexiamond1`. The version of 20 April 1999 is accessible from The Internet Archive.

[32] Christoph Peter-Orth, "All solutions of the Soma Cube puzzle," *Discrete Mathematics* **57** (1985), 105–121.

[33] J. E. Reeve and J. A. Tyrrell, "Maestro puzzles," *The Mathematical Gazette* **45** (1961), 97–99.

[34] Igor Rivin, Ilan Vardi, and Paul Zimmermann, "The n-queens problem," *American Mathematical Monthly* **101** (1994), 629–639.

[35] Dana S. Scott, "Programming a combinatorial puzzle," Technical Report No. 1 (Princeton, New Jersey: Princeton University Department of Electrical Engineering, 10 June 1958), ii + 14 + 5 pages.

[From page 10: "... the main problem in the program was to handle several lists of indices that were continually being modified."]

[36] P. J. Torbijn, "Polyiamonds," *Journal of Recreational Mathematics* **2** (1969), 216–227.

[37] David Waltz, "Understanding line drawings of scenes with shadows," in *The Psychology of Computer Vision*, edited by P. Winston (New York: McGraw–Hill, 1975), 19–91.

[38] Bernhard Wiezorke and Jacques Haubrich, "Dr. Dragon's polycons," *Cubism For Fun* **33** (February 1994), 6–7.

Addendum

After seeing this paper in print, I realized that algorithm DLX never changes the L and R links, except in the column objects. Therefore the data objects for row entries can be stored sequentially, and they need contain only three links (not five). Dummy objects, containing two links each, can be placed between rows so that the cyclic traversal of row elements is still efficient in either direction.

Ten more years of continued progress in computer hardware have allowed the links inside my desktop machine to dance faster than ever: The 1.2 GHz Intel "Core 2 Duo CPU" that I acquired in 2007 now performs nearly 50 million DLX-type updates per second! And with both processors working on different subproblems, I get more than 90 mega-updates/sec. Thus it's easy nowadays for me to try computations for which I didn't have enough patience in 1999.

I don't know what I was thinking when I estimated the difficulty of the 9×10 one-sided pentomino problem of Figure 10. I blundered badly when I claimed that the method of [24] gives an estimate of 19 quadrillion updates. When I rerun the calculations today, using [24] properly, I consistently obtain predictions of a much smaller problem size, between 3 and 5 *trillion* updates only.

I received letters early in 2000 from Alfred Wassermann and from Patric Östergård, who both had been able to resolve this problem completely and to discover that it has exactly 10,440,433 solutions. (See Alfred Wassermann, "One-sided pentominoes in a 9×10 rectangle," http://did.mat.uni-bayreuth.de/wassermann/pentominoes.ps.gz, a preprint dated 26 May 2000.) In fact, the spiffy computer I now have at home allows me to report that algorithm DLX confirms the number of solutions that they found, after exploring a search tree of 14,077,934,683

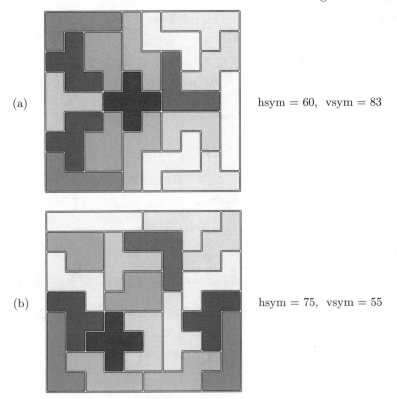

(a)   hsym = 60, vsym = 83

(b)   hsym = 75, vsym = 55

FIGURE 17. Improvements to Figure 10.

nodes and making 4,627,081,954,873 updates. Thus the problem is indeed more difficult than O'Beirne's hexiamond problem of Figure 8 — but only by a factor of 35, not by a factor of 140,000.

This exhaustive enumeration turns up several solutions that are much more symmetric than I had thought possible. The grand champion for symmetry, shown in Figure 17(a), has an amazingly high vertical score, vsym = 83: When this pattern is flipped top-to-bottom, 83 of its 87 internal edges remain unchanged, and in fact 14 of its 18 pieces remain fixed. The horizontal score, hsym = 60, is quite respectable too. And Figure 17(b) shows that my attempt to obtain maximum horizontal symmetry in Figure 10 wasn't optimum either — even though Fig. 10 had 10 pieces fixed by horizontal reflection while Fig. 17(b) has only 8.

The other question that I was unable to answer when I presented my paper in 1999 has also led to happy results: The 25 one-sided tetrasticks can, in fact, be packed into the Aztec diamond shape of Figure 15, thereby fulfilling my fondest hopes. Alfred Wassermann used a cluster of 16 workstations in November 1999 to discover that there are exactly 107 ways to accomplish this feat. [See "Covering the Aztec diamond with one-sided tetrasticks," *Bulletin of the Institute of Combinatorics and its Applications* **32** (2001), 70–76.]

Several of these intricate and elusive patterns are especially striking. For example, 9 of the 25 pieces in

remain unchanged under left-right reflection. And in

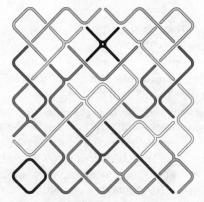

there are actually 10 such symmetrical pieces. Wassermann depicts them all, in color, in his online document http://did.mat.uni-bayreuth.de/ wassermann/allsolutions.pdf.

Algorithm DLX solves this task by considering six inequivalent placements of the X, and by restricting the I to be vertical in two of those six cases. The computation turns out to involve 12,318,463,410,037 updates, for search trees of 33,831,460,543 nodes all told.

Some people have questioned whether I should have called this shape an "Aztec diamond," because many papers about Aztec diamonds restrict consideration to cases where there are two cells at the top, bottom, left, and right. My terminology, however, is based on Richard Stanley's more flexible definition, according to which the shape of my Figure 15 is the Aztec diamond of order 9/2. In general, an Aztec diamond of order s has $2s$ rows, $2s$ columns, and staircase-like boundaries. In a $(2k + 1) \times (2k + 1)$ checkerboard with black squares at the corners, the set of white squares is essentially equivalent (after 45° rotation) to an Aztec diamond of order k, while the set of black squares is essentially equivalent to an Aztec diamond of order $k + \frac{1}{2}$. (See my paper "Aztec diamonds, checkerboard graphs, and spanning trees," *Journal of Algebraic Combinatorics* **6** (1997), 253–257, reprinted as Chapter 10 of my *Selected Papers on Discrete Mathematics*, for further discussion and generalization to "Aztec rhomboids.")

Let me close this chapter by exhibiting another pleasant polystick pattern, inspired by a question of Brian Barwell in the *Journal of Recreational Mathematics* **35** (2006), page 68:

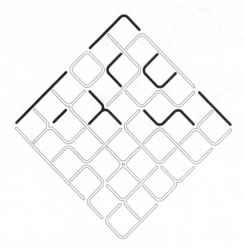

Here the "monostick," the two "disticks," and the five "tristicks" (in black) are mixed with the sixteen tetrasticks (in white), all two-sided, in such a way that the eight black polysticks all appear in the top half, without touching each other. (This problem has 37 solutions; the reader is encouraged to find them all. According to [23], H. D. Benjamin was apparently the first to discover that these 24 polysticks could be packed into a square array, on 6 October 1948.)

Chapter 39

Nikoli Puzzle Favors

[Dedicated to the memory of Nob Yoshigahara. Presented at the Twenty-Ninth International Puzzle Party (IPP29), San Francisco, California, in August 2009.]

1. Masyu

Nikoli Co., Ltd., has been publishing wonderful pencil-and-paper puzzles since 1980. Some of them, like Sudoku, are based on combinatorics and logic; others are based on pure geometry and involve no numbers whatsoever. Masyu ("evil influence") is one of the best of the latter type.

The idea is to draw a closed loop of straight segments through the centers of grid cells, in such a way that (a) the path turns 90° at each cell that is marked with a black stone, but goes straight through the two neighboring cells; (b) the path goes straight through each cell that is marked with a white stone, but turns 90° at one or both of the two neighboring cells. The path must not cross itself. For example,

the setup   forces the loop-path to be   .

Solve the following masyu:

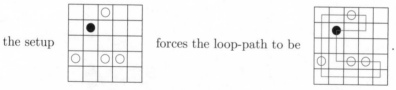

473

2. Slitherlink and Skimperlink

Slitherlink is another Nikoli puzzle based on loops, but this time the loop is supposed to run through *corners* of the cells instead of the midpoints. When a number is placed in a cell, exactly that many of the cell's edges must belong to the loop. A new variant that I call "skimperlink" is similar, except that more than one loop is allowed; the goal of skimperlink is to use the fewest *edges*, not the fewest loops. For example,

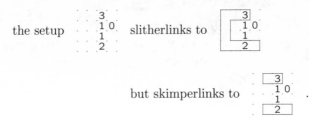

Notice that each loop with k edges touches exactly k points of the grid; thus, the skimperlink problem is the same as asking for a set of disjoint loops that satisfy the numeric constraints and touch the fewest points.

Solve the following skimperlink:

```
2  2 3  1 2  2 1     2  1 1 1       2       2        2 2   1 2  1
2         2       0 1     2 2 2  0  0 1    0  1 1 2 0 1       2    2  1 1   1 2
    0   1  1 2 1  1 2  1 2     1 2      2 1         1  2     0     2  0
0 1          0      1      1 0      1      2  0 1 3 1 1 2 1 1      0 2 1
    1          0         1        1      1 0  2      2  1  2
  1  0                  1  1    0      1 2    2  1   2
0  1         0 1   0  2 0    1 1 1    0   1   2 2 1     0
  1  1         1 1   0 0    1 1   2 0 0  1   1 1    0 2
      1        1          1 1  0 0 1   2 2     1  1 1 2
    1      1 0 1      0   2            1  2 3 1 1 2 2 2    2 2 0
2 1    1  2   0  0      1  1 0   1   1  0 1    1     2  2          2
2    3    2 2     3    2 1    1 2    2 1 1 2     1 1 2  1 2    2  2 2 1     2 2
```

3. Solutions

Before I give the answers to those puzzles, I want to mention that both masyu and slitherlink are excellent examples of problems for which computer structures called BDDs and ZDDs work wonders. [See *The Art of Computer Programming*, Volume 4A (Addison–Wesley, 2010), Section 7.1.4, for a comprehensive introduction to BDD and ZDD technology.]

Suppose the horizontal edge that extends rightward from point (i, j) is denoted by h_{ij}. We let $h_{ij} = 1$ if that edge is present, otherwise $h_{ij} = 0$. Similarly, we suppose that v_{ij} represents the vertical edge that extends downward from (i, j), where $v_{ij} = 1$ or $v_{ij} = 0$. The condition that a choice of edges for skimperlink makes proper loops is that every point is touched by exactly zero or two edges; that is,

$$h_{ij} + v_{ij} + h_{i(j-1)} + v_{(i-1)j} = 0 \text{ or } 2 \qquad (*)$$

for all points (i, j). (When a point is on the boundary, this equation refers to missing edges outside the diagram, which are always zero.) The further condition that a cell with point (i, j) in its upper left corner is surrounded by exactly d_{ij} edges is

$$h_{ij} + v_{ij} + h_{(i+1)j} + v_{i(j+1)} = d_{ij}, \qquad (**)$$

whenever d_{ij} has been specified.

The given skimperlink puzzle has 1312 edge variables (676 h's and 636 v's), so the number of possible ways to set them each to 0 or 1 is huge: $2^{1312} = 89, 403, 456, 790, 138, 199, 504, 722, 663, 845, 938, 162,$ $546, 598, 192, 956, 947, 925, 057, 063, 268, 777, 466, 378, 033, 398, 197, 844,$ $774, 764, 419, 923, 259, 919, 936, 119, 490, 754, 348, 335, 315, 827, 215, 256,$ $797, 393, 219, 729, 086, 127, 756, 921, 211, 321, 811, 144, 190, 452, 640, 067,$ $268, 641, 216, 468, 033, 705, 852, 087, 174, 876, 295, 013, 276, 952, 237, 406,$ $566, 616, 302, 156, 609, 034, 102, 568, 251, 715, 295, 346, 981, 084, 737, 525,$ $424, 640, 722, 115, 940, 281, 297, 509, 188, 186, 649, 324, 815, 686, 699, 212,$ $604, 140, 246, 556, 947, 662, 422, 743, 704, 115, 482, 557, 772, 626, 648, 955,$ $221, 254, 191, 950, 005, 687, 812, 096 \approx 8.9 \times 10^{394}$. But the ZDD for all these solutions is very simple; it has only 1313 nodes. Then we can easily incorporate all the conditions of $(*)$ and $(**)$, ordering the edge variables lexicographically on (j, i) and getting a ZDD of 299,244 nodes that describes all ways to choose legal edge combinations. The number of such combinations is $458, 524, 440, 120, 243, 839, 648, 854, 802, 389, 756,$ $214, 626, 867, 672, 178, 768 \approx 4.6 \times 10^{50}$ — still huge, but not nearly so vast as before. Moreover, the calculation of this ZDD goes very quickly, considering that 1312 variables are being handled: Less than two billion memory accesses are needed, and about 51 megabytes of memory. Therefore a run-of-the-mill laptop, vintage 2007, finds it in about 36 seconds.

And here comes the punch line: The skimperlink solution — namely, the solution with fewest edges, from all those 4.6×10^{50} possibilities — is easy to "read off" from the ZDD, in less than one second of further calculation, including the time to verify that the minimum solution is unique.

A similar approach works for the given masyu problem. Instead of $(**)$, we use the conditions

$$h_{ij} + v_{ij} + h_{i(j-1)} + v_{(i-1)j} = 2$$
$$h_{ij}v_{ij} + v_{ij}h_{i(j-1)} + h_{i(j-1)}v_{(i-1)j} + v_{(i-1)j}h_{ij} = 1$$
$$h_{ij}\bar{h}_{i(j+1)} = v_{ij}\bar{v}_{(i+1)j} = h_{i(j-1)}\bar{h}_{i(j-2)} = v_{(i-1)j}\bar{v}_{(i-2)j} = 0$$

when point (i, j) is specified black (here $\bar{x}$ stands for $1 - x$), or

$$h_{ij} + v_{ij} + h_{i(j-1)} + v_{(i-1)j} = 2$$
$$h_{ij} = h_{i(j-1)}, \qquad v_{ij} = v_{(i-1)j}$$
$$h_{i(j-2)}h_{i(j-1)}h_{ij}h_{i(j+1)} = v_{(i-2)j}v_{(i-1)j}v_{ij}v_{(i+1)j} = 0$$

when point (i, j) is specified white. The ZDD in this case turns out to have just 253 nodes; it can be computed in about one second (more precisely, after 56 million accesses to 10.5 megabytes of memory). Another fraction of a second establishes the fact that the constraints of problem 1 are satisfied by exactly 400 of the 2^{352} possible ways to choose the edges, and that exactly one of those 400 defines a single loop.

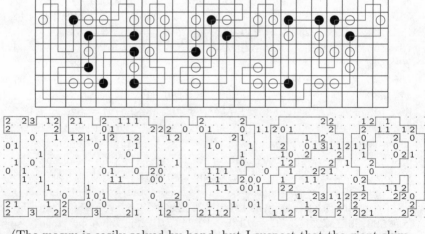

(The masyu is easily solved by hand, but I suspect that the giant skimperlink problem will be much harder for mere mortals to psych out.)

Chapter 40

Uncrossed Knight's Tours

*[Originally published in the Journal of Recreational Mathematics **2** (1969), 155–157, as a letter to the editor.]*

Mr. Yarbrough's uncrossed knight's tours [1], which maximize knight moves that don't intersect, are a pleasant recreation. Not being too good at it by myself, however, I programmed it for our computer.

Well over three billion cases were examined — without getting into any 7×9, 8×9, or 9×9 boards (too big for the machine!). The findings are summarized in Figures 1 and 2, which show respectively the longest possible uncrossed *paths* and the longest possible uncrossed *cycles*, on various rectangular boards.

These machine runs confirmed that Yarbrough's path of length 35 on the ordinary 8×8 chessboard is indeed maximum, as are most of his examples on smaller boards. But improved paths for the 6×6, 6×8, and 7×8 boards have been found by others [2, 3]. My computations of the absolutely longest tours were able to beat the hand-crafted solutions of those authors only in one case, 5×6 — which is a rather small board, not big enough to be considered much of a challenge. The new path of length 14 on this board is surprisingly long, when we compare it to the best possible results on $5 \times n$ boards for n near 6, as well as to the best possible results on $6 \times n$ boards for n near 5.

My programs also were able to find maximum-length cycles in every case up to 8×8; Yarbrough's paper exhibits cycles only on the 3×6 and 7×7 boards. Long cycles are harder to find than long paths.

Several interesting general properties of uncrossed knight's tours were also discovered during this study. For example, variants of the maximal 5×8 path

will yield paths of length $6n - 5$ on any $5 \times 2n$ board with $n \geq 2$.

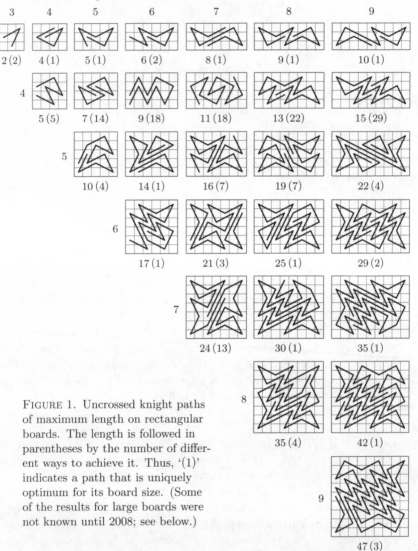

FIGURE 1. Uncrossed knight paths of maximum length on rectangular boards. The length is followed in parentheses by the number of different ways to achieve it. Thus, '(1)' indicates a path that is uniquely optimum for its board size. (Some of the results for large boards were not known until 2008; see below.)

It is easy to show that the longest cycles on a $3 \times n$ board are essentially the same for $n = 4k + 2$, $4k + 3$, $4k + 4$, and $4k + 5$ when $k \geq 1$. They will have length $4k + 2$, with the general form indicated in Figure 3. Likewise, the longest cycles on $4 \times n$ boards have length $2n - 4$ for $n \geq 4$, but in this case the solutions are not always unique.

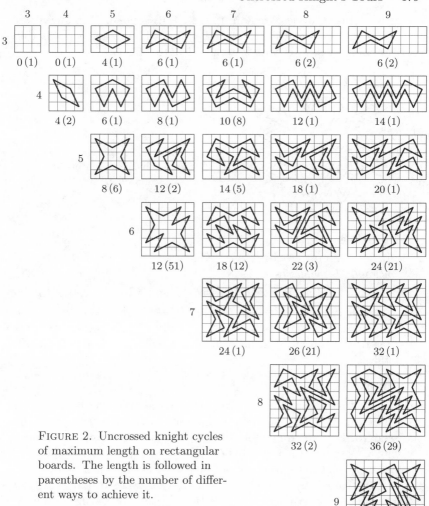

FIGURE 2. Uncrossed knight cycles of maximum length on rectangular boards. The length is followed in parentheses by the number of different ways to achieve it.

FIGURE 3. Optimum uncrossed knight cycles on $3 \times n$ boards, when $4k + 2 \leq n \leq 4k + 5$.

An uncrossed cycle of length $n^2 - 8n + 12$ is possible on any $n \times n$ board when n is a multiple of 4 and $n \geq 8$. Figure 4 illustrates this construction for $n = 16$, with a cycle of length 140.

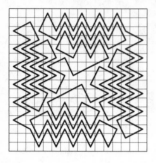

FIGURE 4. A general way to achieve asymptotically optimum density.

References

[1] L. D. Yarbrough, "Uncrossed Knight's tours," *Journal of Recreational Mathematics* **1** (1968), 140–142.

[2] Ronald E. Ruemmler, "Uncrossed Knight's tours" (letter to the editor), *Journal of Recreational Mathematics* **2** (1969), 154–157.

[3] Michio Matsuda and S. Kobayashi, "Uncrossed Knight's tours" (letter to the editor), *Journal of Recreational Mathematics* **2** (1969), 155–157.

Addendum

The word "tour" is used somewhat loosely when crossing is forbidden, because ordinary knight's tours are supposed to visit *every* square of the chessboard. Here we are mainly thinking about paths or cycles that are as long as possible; it's probably best to call them just paths and cycles, because we don't have proofs of optimality except on small boards.

I investigated these fascinating tours/paths/cycles in 1968 and 1969 during my year of national service at the Institute for Defense Analyses in Princeton, New Jersey. As part of that job I had access to a CDC 6600 computer, which was the world's fastest machine at the time.

I used standard "backtracking" techniques to enumerate the tours exhaustively, and it turned out to be quite a huge calculation. The 5×5 case needed only 0.8 seconds to run, but my program took 11.2 seconds to study the 6×6 board and 23.0 minutes to do the 7×7. At that rate, the 8×8 would have needed more than 400 hours, according to an estimation procedure that I was developing [see Donald E. Knuth, "Estimating the efficiency of backtrack programs," *Mathematics of Computation* **29** (1975), 121–136; reprinted as Chapter 6 of *Selected Papers on Analysis* ·

FIGURE 5. An extension of Figure 2, made
possible by recently invented ZDD technology.

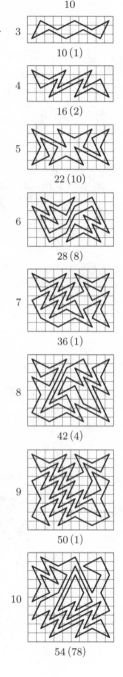

of *Algorithms*, CSLI Lecture Notes 102 (Stanford,
California: Center for the Study of Language and
Information, 2000), 55–75]. So I rewrote the program in assembly language, and wound up with a
total running time of 117 hours to analyze the 8×8
board — not counting the hours that I devoted to
writing the code and debugging it.

I worked things out so that the computer would
run this job only during idle time, in the "background," when there was no other work to do. Special procedures for restarting and for recovery from
machine failures were needed, because several weeks
went by before the run was finished. Still, computers were extremely expensive in 1969, especially
when machines of this caliber were concerned; the
cost of 117 hours on a CDC 6600 at commercial
rates in those days might have exceeded a million
dollars! Therefore my employers suggested that it
could be unwise to publicize the fact that so much
"virtual government money" was being spent on a
chessboard recreation — even though the related research on backtracking eventually turned out to be
quite valuable — and I agreed to keep quiet about
the running time details. This arrangement worked
out nicely for me, because people were amazed that
I could solve such a problem with a reasonable cost;
in fact, I couldn't, but I wasn't supposed to admit it.

The 7×9 problem is harder than the 8×8,
because it has less symmetry. And boards that were
even larger were clearly out of the question in 1969.
But I happened to discover a new way to deal with
paths and cycles in 2008, by using so-called ZDD
structures instead of backtracking. Therefore I'm
now able to complete the study of the 7×9, 8×9,
and 9×9 boards, thereby filling in several entries
that were necessarily missing from Figures 1 and 2
when my letter was originally published. In fact,
I now can also present complete information about

the uncrossed knight *cycles* on all boards up to size 10×10 (see Figure 5); cycles turn out to be easier than paths, ZDD-wise.

Some board sizes in Figures 1 and 2 have many different optimal solutions; for example, there are 14 ways to fit an uncrossed path of length 7 into a 4×5 board. (In fact it's fun to find them all by hand, because they're quite pretty and can be used as design motifs. A complete list appears at the end of this chapter.) But in other cases there's only one way to achieve the maximal length; this happens when an unusually long path or cycle turns out to exist. Thus, for example, the paths of length 30 and 42 on the 7×8 and 8×9 boards are longer than normal, hence difficult to find. How on earth did Ruemmler [2] discover them by hand? Readers who enjoy a challenge might like to find an uncrossed knight path of length 43 in a 5×16 board. There are only two ways to do it. (*Hint:* Both solutions are symmetric under rotation by 180°.) The answers appear below.

When several different solutions exist, I chose a representative one to display in Figure 1 or Figure 2 by always showing a solution with maximum symmetry; and if several solutions have maximum symmetry, I chose an "unusual" instance, in order to illustrate as much variety as possible. Solutions that aren't strictly the same often turn out to be very close to each other; for example, the four length-35 uncrossed knight paths on the 8×8 chessboard are

and it's easy to see that the first two differ in only two edges near the center; the other two differ only in four edges at the lower right corner. Similarly, the three paths of length 47 on the 9×9 chessboard are

   ;

the latter two differ only in their final step at one endpoint. I put the first of these three into Figure 1, because the middle solution had already been published by Ruemmler, Matsuda, and Kobayashi [2, 3].

The ZDD technique that I used for these new results is based on the method described in exercises 7.1.4–225 and 7.1.4–226 of *The Art of*

Computer Programming; those exercises describe how to represent all of the simple paths and simple cycles of an undirected graph in terms of a binary branching structure. I extended that method to forbid edges that cross each other, using an idea that Dan Eilers had described to me in 2000: We can introduce "dummy vertices" into the graph, eight per cell, analogous to the secondary columns for interior junction points of the tetrastick problems that I had considered in my paper on dancing links. Each knight move can be thought of as passing not only from one cell of the chessboard graph to another, but also as passing through (or near) four of the dummy vertices, as indicated in the following diagram:

If no dummy vertex is encountered twice, no edges cross.

With this procedure I was able to represent all of the 10×10 uncrossed knight cycles inside the computer as a single ZDD structure, namely as a directed acyclic graph consisting of 50,160,557 two-way branch nodes and two sink nodes. Each of those branch nodes essentially asks whether or not to include a particular knight move as part of the tour. One of them is called the root; every path from the root to the "positive" sink corresponds to an uncrossed knight cycle. The total number of such paths, which is also the total number of uncrossed knight cycles (without taking any symmetries into account), is easily deduced from the ZDD, and it turns out to be exactly 5,534,720,777,802.

Thus I could study all 5.5 trillion of the 10×10 cycles without examining them one by one. In fact, the total computer time that I needed for this task came to about 220 minutes, so this ZDD approach was able to deal with roughly 419 million knight cycles per second. That's fewer than 7.2 machine-clock cycles per knight cycle!

Similarly, the uncrossed 9×9 knight *paths* can be represented as a sequence of 14 ZDDs, one for each of the inequivalent starting points of paths that end at a point not equivalent to a previous start. (First we try to start at a corner and end anywhere; then we try to start next to a corner and end at any noncorner; and so on.) These 14 ZDDs turn out to have about 386 million nodes altogether.

I should point out that this ZDD-based approach does require several gigabytes of memory. It would *not* have been feasible in 1969.

There may be a way to treat 11×11 cycles and 10×10 paths by generalizing these methods to two-sided ZDDs (where one ZDD starts at the top of the board and another starts at the bottom). And after a few more years of Moore's law I can imagine going up to 12×12 boards, maybe even 13×13. But at present I see no way to carry out an exhaustive study of all possible 16×16 uncrossed knight cycles or paths.

The history of uncrossed knight's tours actually goes back to 1930, when the great puzzlist Thomas Rayner Dawson presented the problem of finding an uncrossed knight path of length 35 on an ordinary chessboard, as well as an uncrossed knight cycle of length 32. [T. R. Dawson, "Les échecs féeriques, §43 — Lignes et points du quadrillage : Les Circuits de Sauteurs," problem 186, *L'Echiquier* (2) **2** (1930), 1085.] He presented two solutions [*L'Echiquier* (2) **3** (1931), 1150], namely the second and third of the four 35-step paths shown above, together with a 32-cycle that was found by his Romanian friend Wolfgang Pauly.

Major advances in the theory were made in France by Jean Cornuejols and Bernard Lemaire [see P. Berloquin, "Jeux et paradoxes," *Science et Vie* **119**, 640 (January 1971), 138–139; 641 (February 1971), 128–129; **126**, 684 (September 1974), 122–123] and independently in England by Robin Merson [see *Games & Puzzles* **9** (January 1973), 27]. In particular, they all found efficient ways to extend paths when the board size increases by 8. Lemaire and Merson continued to make substantial improvements during their spare time during the 70s and 80s, but without publishing their results — and indeed remaining unaware of each other's existence. Finally it became known that uncrossed knight paths of length at least $n^2 - 6n + 21$ are possible on all $n \times n$ boards for $n \geq 10$, and that this lower bound can often be improved by 2. Lemaire has even improved it by 3, whenever $n \bmod 8 = 1$. Alexander Fischer was the first to publish tours of length 135 and 183 on the 14×14 and 16×16 boards [*The Games and Puzzles Journal* #45 (September 2006), §1]. Merson also discovered how to construct the best-known uncrossed knight *cycles*, of length at least $n^2 - 7n + 24$ on $n \times n$ boards when $7 \leq n < 32$, and at least $n^2 - 7n + 22$ when $n \geq 32$. Here, for example, are Fischer's length-183 path and Merson's length-172 cycle for $n = 16$:

The paper "Non-intersecting paths by leapers" in *The Games and Puzzles Journal* **2**, #17 (October 1999), 305–310, by Robin Merson and George Jelliss, summarizes Merson's results and also discusses the uncrossed tours that can be made by generalized knights called *leapers.*

While composing this addendum in 2010, I suddenly realized that there was a whole class of uncrossed knight tour problems still waiting to be investigated: We can work with "wraparound" chessboards (also known as toruses), where the knight is allowed to exit through the top, bottom, left, or right boundary of the board and come in at the other side, as long as it doesn't cross another part of its path. In essence, we allow the knight to "think outside the box," provided that its path doesn't intersect any other paths that could be obtained by replication in an infinite tiling of the plane. For example, the 10-cycle

is noncrossing on a 3 × 5 torus, because the corresponding infinite tiling looks like this:

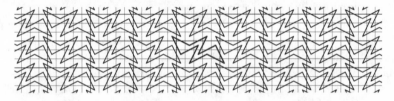

Cycles on a torus might not return to their starting point when we draw them outside the box; they might end up on another tile in the plane. In that case an infinite path is traced out in the plane as we traverse the cycle repeatedly — and that path becomes doubly infinite if we follow the cycle in both directions. Such doubly infinite paths will fill the plane, without crossing, if we replicate them; but I decided to restrict attention to cases where the cycle forms a closed polygon, because those shapes are much more interesting. (For example, a knight that continually travels in the same direction will make a cycle of length 15 on a 3 × 5 torus, thus covering every cell. But that's no big deal, because the corresponding infinite path is simply a straight line. Very boring.) The only noncrossing cycle on a 3 × 5 torus that has length ≥ 10 and meets the polygon constraint is the example shown above.

Can you find the unique cycle of noncrossing knight moves on a 4 × 4 torus that forms a 10-gon? (Please don't peek at the answer below until you've tried.)

Uncrossed knight *paths* turn out to be equally interesting when extended to toruses. In this case we want the corresponding path in the plane to begin and end in the same $m \times n$ box. Under this restriction the 3×5 torus admits only one noncrossing path of length 11, and that path wanders rather far afield before coming home:

(Again we can make an infinite tiling.) I challenge the reader to find all of the noncrossing paths on a 4×4 torus that make 11 knight moves. It's a pleasant recreation, and one of the solutions is quite surprising.

I looked also at 4×5 toruses; but decided not to pursue this pleasant recreation any further at the moment, because (a) I don't want to spoil the readers' fun, and (b) toroidal tours are better suited to good-old backtracking than to the newfangled ZDD approach. I'm sure, however, that many delightful designs based on noncrossing toroidal moves are "out there" ready to be discovered.

Research on uncrossed paths can also be pushed in quite a different direction: Knight paths can be "warped" as well as "wrapped"! The images of noncrossing paths obviously remain noncrossing when we distort them with fancy lenses, and a new kind of pattern arises.

Consider, for example, the following three versions of Dawson's original uncrossed knight path:

length 106.170   length 78.262   length 57.569

On the left we have "stereographic projection," obtained by placing a sphere atop the original image with the south pole on the center and projecting onto the sphere's lower surface, where the sphere's radius is chosen so that the equator lies directly above the four corner points. On the right, we have "radial distortion," obtained by scaling each point by its distance from the center. In all three cases the square's center and four corner points remain fixed. The paths change dramatically, with central features emphasized in the stereographic version but shrunken in the radial version. And the lengths change too, of course; the original Euclidean length, 78.262, is $35\sqrt{5}$.

Therefore we ask, "What uncrossed knight path is longest, in the stereographic projection?" Such a path shouldn't be as sparse in the middle as Dawson's original; and it turns out that the best has length 34 in the unwarped sense:

length 109.776   length 76.026   length 50.142

I know that this path is optimum, and uniquely so, because the ZDD representation makes it easy to solve any *Boolean program*, namely to find all solutions that maximize a linear combination $\sum c_i x_i$ of the variables that are either present (1) or absent (0). (In our case, the variables x_i are the 168 possible moves of a knight on a chessboard; the coefficients c_i are the lengths of their stereographic images.)

Similarly, it's easy to find the noncrossing path that is *radially* longest, and the uniquely best one turns out to have only 31 steps:

length 84.607   length 69.318   length 58.536

I think only a computer could have figured this out.

Finally, let's consider the optimum warped *cycles*. From a stereographic standpoint, Pauly's original 32-cycle from 1930 is still best:

length 97.912   length 71.554   length 51.759

But radius-stretched warping prefers the following unique 30-cycle:

length 85.834   length 67.082   length 53.431

Answers

The maximum-length uncrossed knight paths on a 4 × 5 board are:

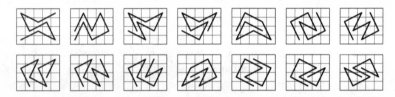

Similarly, the two 5 × 16 winners are:

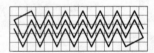   

(In fact, the left-hand one was implicitly mentioned on the very first page of this chapter.)

Here is the 10-gon for a 4×4 torus, together with the five noncrossing 11-paths:

(The last one is the surprise: It really *doesn't* cross.) By the way, the 5 × 4 torus hosts a nice 14-gon, and four amazing 15-paths:

 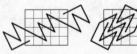

Chapter 41

Celtic Knight's Tours

[The following previously unpublished notes, written on Saint Patrick's Day (2010), are based on experiments that I carried out during the Christmas holidays of 1992.]

The fascinating problem of discovering a knight's tour — a sequence of moves by which a knight can visit every square of the chessboard exactly once — has been studied for nearly 1200 years, yet many natural questions about such tours remain unanswered. One such question, based on the appealing diagrams that arise when we trace out a sequence of knight moves, is considered and partially answered in the notes below.

This investigation began when I read Vandermonde's classic memoir on the subject ["Remarques sur les problèmes de situation," *Mémoires de Mathématique et de Physique, tirés des registres de l'Académie Royale des Sciences* (1771), part 1, 566–574 and plates X, XI], in which he introduced three-dimensional knight's tours on a $4 \times 4 \times 4$ cube and related the paths to *threads*, in patterns for weaving. I was struck by the quality of the illustrations in his paper, which were much more refined than those I'd seen in 20th-century publications; see, for example, Fig. 1.

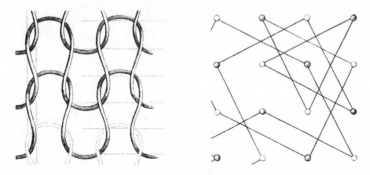

FIGURE 1. Details enlarged from Vandermonde's Figure 4 and Figure 5.

489

Hmmm, I thought: Wouldn't it be nice if my books on *The Art of Computer Programming* could have illustrations that approach the quality that was achievable in the 18th century?

Meanwhile my wife and I had become interested in the interlacing patterns of what is popularly called Celtic art, after having spent two glorious weeks in Ireland during the spring of 1992. We had seen many examples of graphic design and jewelry that featured intricate, entangled paths such as those in Figure 2: The path is basically two-dimensional, yet it avoids self-intersection by alternately passing over and under itself, achieving a three-dimensional effect.

FIGURE 2. A decorated letter 'v'
from the ninth-century *Book of Kells*
[actually the letter 'u' in 'autem',
part of Mark 15 : 24, folio 183^r].

Thus when I read Vandermonde's ideas about constructing knight's tours, it was only natural for me to imagine redrawing the example he had given for an ordinary chessboard, one-fourth of which was shown at the right of Figure 1 above, by rendering it instead as a "Celtic knot":

FIGURE 3. Vandermonde's
tour of 1771, redrawn as
an interlaced path. (Look
closely at the crossings.)

With a wee bit o' imagination one can even perceive a shamrock here!

Can *any* cycle of knight moves be drawn in this way, with the path alternately going under then going over whenever it meets itself? Yes it can. In fact, the under-and-over property is true for any closed curve in the plane that doesn't go through any point more than twice. I'm not sure who first discovered this principle — perhaps it is quite ancient — but the great mathematician C. F. Gauss stated it without proof in one of his notebooks, dated 30 December 1844 ["Zur Geometrie der Lage, für zwei Raumdimensionen," published in Carl Friedrich Gauss, *Werke* **8** (Leipzig: Teubner, 1900), 282–286]. A simple proof can be based on the fact that the curve partitions the plane into regions that can be colored either white or gray, depending on whether a straight line from the region to the "outside" crosses the curve an even or odd number of times. Given such a two-coloring, consider the curve segments that go counterclockwise around each gray region; we can assume that they pass *under* the next segment, at each crossing point. This rule gives a consistent way to tell which strand is on top whenever two strands cross, and it alternates between up and down as desired.

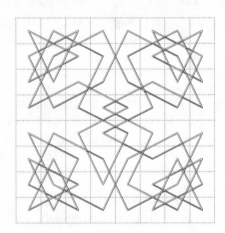

FIGURE 4. The under-and-over property is explained by two-coloring the regions.

The effect of interleaving is easiest to see when the path is wide; but if the path crosses itself in three places that are extremely close together, we must thread it through a small triangle. A knight path comes pretty close to having a triple point if it contains the three moves shown here; these three moves intersect at the corners of a tiny triangle, whose area is just 1/120th of the area of a chessboard square. The tour in Figs. 3 and 4 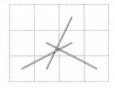 contains twelve of these tiny triangles, so its path must be rather narrow.

Let's say that a closed knight's tour is *Celtic* if it doesn't contain any such tiny triangles. Celtic tours make attractive "Celtic knot patterns" when we draw them with interlacing, because we can make the paths wider than they were in Figs. 3 and 4. For example, here's a 6 × 6 Celtic cycle shown with both narrow and wide paths:

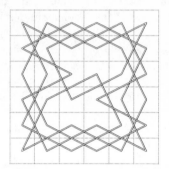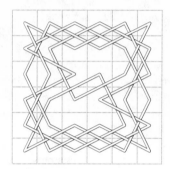

FIGURE 5. A Celtic tour discovered in Berlin.

This particular cycle has the honor of being the first Celtic tour ever published, because Leonhard Euler presented it on the next-to-last page of his famous essay on the knight's tour, "Solution d'une question curieuse qui ne paroit soumise à aucune analyse," *Mémoires de l'Académie Royale des Sciences et Belles-Lettres* (Berlin, 1759), 310–337. Of course Euler didn't realize at the time that it was "Celtic"; but he did remark that the path is symmetric under 180° rotation. This tour also has another claim to fame, namely that it's the only 6 × 6 knight's cycle for which 8 of the 36 moves are intersected by at most four other moves, and the remaining 28 moves are crossed by at most three others.

There are 1245 different 6 × 6 knight's cycles in all, and only one besides Euler's turns out to be Celtic. The lesser-known one also happens to be the only 6 × 6 tour with 15 "×-crossings": 30 out of its 36 moves are parts of ×'s. (See Fig. 6.) It was found by George Jelliss in December 1992, shortly after I had asked him if he thought Celtic tours might exist. Celtic tours are impossible on rectangular boards with fewer than 36 squares; thus Figs. 5 and 6 contain the smallest possible examples. Figure 6 also shows three other Celtic tours due to Jelliss, including two 8 × 8 tours with 180° symmetry chosen from more than 50 that he had found before Christmas. The 10 × 10 example is even more symmetrical: It remains unchanged under 90° rotation—a feat that is possible only on boards of size $(4k+2) \times (4k+2)$. It's the first knight's tour ever to be explicitly called *Celtic* in print. [G. P. Jelliss, "10 × 10 knight's tours

FIGURE 6. Celtic tours discovered in St. Leonard's-on-Sea.

with quaternary symmetry," *The Games and Puzzles Journal* **2**, #16
(May 1999), 286–287.]

The 8×8 tour at the lower right of Fig. 6 is particularly interesting
because it intersects itself only 76 times. Jelliss presented it as a candidate for the honor of "knight's cycle on an ordinary chessboard that
has fewest crossings when drawn on the plane." He constructed it by
changing just four links of the elegant pattern in Fig. 7, which has 90°

rotational symmetry. Notice that Fig. 7 consists of four *quarter-tours*, which are cycles of length 16 that cover the entire board when taken together; moreover, these quarter-tours do not intersect themselves.

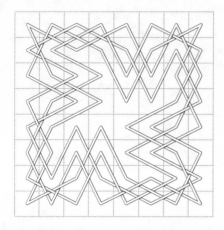

FIGURE 7. A noncrossing 16-cycle, interwoven with three copies of itself to make a pleasant Celtic pattern.

I decided to test Jelliss's conjecture by examining all of the 8×8 knight's cycles that are symmetric under $180°$ rotation. There are exactly 608,233 essentially different cycles with that property, and they can all be constructed and analyzed in less than a minute on a modern desktop computer. It turns out that 2321 of them (about 0.382%) are Celtic, and nine of the Celtic ones are slightly better than the example in Fig. 6, with only 74 intersections. But the overall winner is non-Celtic; it has only 70 intersections, and it is unique. Furthermore, the maximum number of intersections among all symmetric cycles is 122, and there is just one way to achieve that many. (See Fig. 8.) The average symmetric tour has 94.02 intersections, with a standard deviation of about 5.57; thus extreme cases like these are quite rare.

The total number of essentially distinct 8×8 knight's cycles is known to be 1,658,420,855,433 [Brendan McKay, "Knight's tours of an 8×8 chessboard," Technical report TR-CS-97-03 (Australian National University, February 1997), 4 pages]; so I've considered only a tiny fraction of them. Some day I want to generate them all, and to learn the true minimum and maximum number of self-intersections.

I've taken one step in this direction already, by looking more closely at the eight moves that touch the four central squares of a chessboard in any complete tour. For example, I studied all of the 8×8 cycles for which those eight moves agree with the central pattern on the left of Fig. 8, because such parallel lines certainly cover a lot of territory

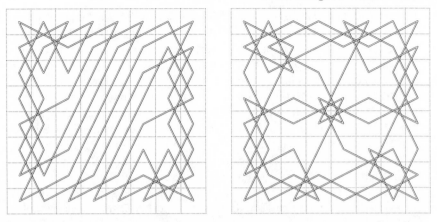

FIGURE 8. The symmetric 8×8 cycles that minimize and maximize intersections.

without crossing. Exactly 6,964,213 essentially different knight's cycles have four parallels in the center; 1981 of them are symmetric, 218 are Celtic, and 15 are both symmetric and Celtic. It turns out that only two of the asymmetric cases have as few as 70 self-intersections. One of these is shown in Fig. 9; the other is obtained by replacing the chess moves e3–f5 and f1–g3 by e3–f1 and f5–g3, respectively. Similarly I considered all of the distinct 8 × 8 knight cycles whose centers have the non-Celtic configuration on the right of Fig. 8. In this case there are 1278 symmetric solutions and 12,546,275 that are asymmetric. Only one of them, shown in Fig. 9, attains 126 intersections, the current record.

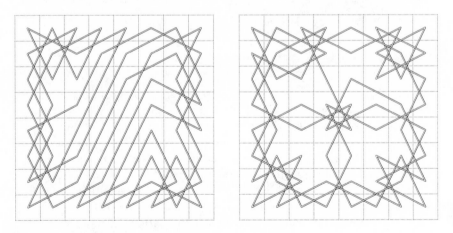

FIGURE 9. Asymmetric 8×8 cycles that may minimize and maximize intersections.

Exactly 18,941,491 of the 1,658,420,855,433 cyclic knight's tours of the ordinary chessboard are Celtic. That's about 0.00114%, a ratio nicely consistent with the 0.382% that was discussed earlier for symmetric tours. (A symmetric tour must essentially be Celtic on half of the board; a general tour must be Celtic on both halves, and 0.382% × 0.382% ≈ 0.00146%.) I recently figured out how to generate all the Celtic 8×8 tours with an algorithm that runs more than 600 times faster than the classical backtrack procedure I'd used in 1992, by adapting the ideas of "dancing links" to the problem of finding Hamiltonian cycles with restrictions. As a result of this study, I now know the Celtic tours that minimize and maximize self-intersections: There are just two ways to achieve only 72 crossings Celtically, and the Celtic tour with 108 crossings is unique. (See Fig. 10; to get the other 72-crossing example, change the moves d5–f4 and f6–h5 respectively to d5–f6 and f4–h5.)

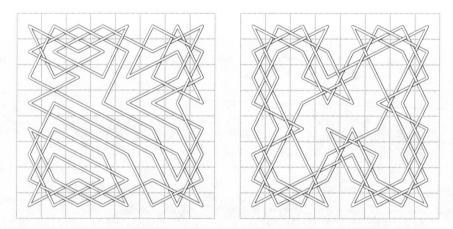

FIGURE 10. The Celtic 8×8 cycles that minimize and maximize intersections.

Let's zoom in now and take a closer look at the geometry of intersections. A knight move that isn't too close to the edge of the board can be crossed by nine other moves, as shown in Fig. 11. (Only seven of those nine can occur simultaneously in a single tour; and symmetric tours exist in which four of the 64 moves are in fact intersected seven times. See G. P. Jelliss, "Intersections in knight tours," *Chessics* **2**, number 19 (Autumn 1984), 25–27.) The intersection points are not equally spaced: The distance from point 1 to point 2 in the illustration is 1/4 of the distance from point 0 to point 1, and it's only 1/20 of the length of the full knight move from point 0 to point 10.

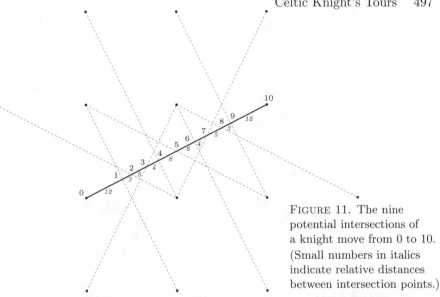

FIGURE 11. The nine
potential intersections of
a knight move from 0 to 10.
(Small numbers in italics
indicate relative distances
between intersection points.)

Two moves are perpendicular when they cross at points 1, 4, 6, or 9 in this diagram. The crossing pattern $\top$ in such cases is unsymmetrical, with one arm of the cross cut in the ratio 3:2 while the other has the cut-ratio 1:4. The non-perpendicular types of crossings are more symmetrical: For example, at points 2 or 8 the pattern is $\asymp$, with both arms cut in ratio 1:3. In this case the arms cross at angles $\alpha \approx 53.13°$ and $180° - \alpha \approx 126.87°$, where $\alpha = 2\arctan\frac{1}{2} = \arctan\frac{4}{3}$. At points 3 or 7 the pattern is $\asymp$, with cut ratios 1:2 and sharper crossing angles $\overline{\alpha} = \arctan\frac{3}{4} \approx 36.87°$ and $180° - \overline{\alpha} \approx 143.13°$; notice that $\overline{\alpha} = 90° - \alpha$. Finally, the most symmetrical crossing of all occurs at point 5, where the pattern $\times$ has cut ratios 1:1; again the angles at the crossing point are α and $180° - \alpha = 90° + \overline{\alpha}$.

The only possible angles between consecutive knight moves are α, $\overline{\alpha}$, and 90°; and we've now seen that these are also the only possible angles between intersecting moves. Hence the only possible triangles formed by knight paths are right triangles, with the three distinct angles α, $\overline{\alpha}$, 90°. In fact such triangles are famous, because their sides have the well-known proportions 3:4:5 of the smallest right triangle with integer sides.

If a chessboard is composed of squares that have length s on each side, the units of length indicated by italic numerals in Fig. 11 are $u = \sqrt{5}s/60$. The tiny triangles that are forbidden in Celtic tours have sides of lengths $3u$, $4u$, and $5u$; eight of them can be spotted in Fig. 11, if one looks closely. Their area is $6u^2 = s^2/120$, as stated earlier.

The entire chessboard has 240 places where such 3-4-5 triangles might arise; Fig. 12 indicates all of the possibilities:

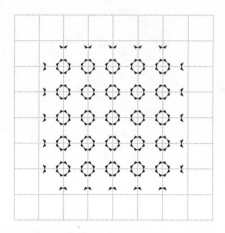

FIGURE 12. The tiny triangles that must be avoided if a knight's tour is to be Celtic.

In general, all triangles obtainable as subsets of knight paths must have side lengths $3ku$, $4ku$, $5ku$, for some integer $k \geq 1$. The area will then be $6k^2u^2 = k^2s^2/120$. Let's say that such triangles have "type k." A knight's tour is Celtic when it contains no type-1 triangles.

George Jelliss ["Knightly triangles," *The Games and Puzzles Journal* **2**, #17 (October 1999), 315] has proved a remarkable theorem about type-k triangles: *Given $k \geq 1$, there is essentially only one way to construct a triangle of type k from three segments of a knight path.* For example, a triangle of type 2 arises only when we have an $\times$ intersection together with another move that makes a $\rightthreetimes$ intersection with one arm of the $\times$ and a $\top$ intersection with the other. (This situation arises in Fig. 11 if and only if the move from 0 to 10 is intersected at points $\{1,3\}$, $\{3,5\}$, $\{4,5\}$, $\{5,6\}$, $\{5,7\}$, or $\{7,9\}$; the six possibilities are geometrically equivalent.)

His proof is sketched in Fig. 13, based on the three ways that the angle $\overline{\alpha}$ can be formed, with right triangles cut off at distances $4ku$ on one side, $5ku$ on the other. Notice that the knight will turn at some corner of the triangle if and only if k is divisible by 3, 4, or 5. When $k > 7$ we need more than three moves to form the whole triangle, except in the interesting case $k = 12$. When $k = 12$ or $k \geq 15$ the triangle contains interior points; such triangles will be intersected by other moves of a complete tour, so they won't appear as white or gray triangles when the planar regions defined by the cycle are two-colored as explained above. On the other hand, a type-2 triangle formed by

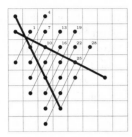 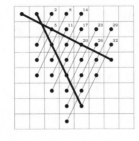 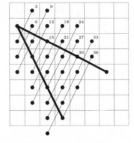

FIGURE 13. Unique recipes for triangles of types $3k + 1$, $3k + 2$, $3k + 3$.

a knight's path doesn't necessarily show up as a triangle in the two-coloring; it might be cut by another part of the path into a triangle of type 1 plus a "kite" shape of area $s^2/40$. Similarly, a type-3 triangle in a Celtic tour might contain triangles of type 2, or it might be "nicked" by type-2s that lie near its periphery.

The board must of course be larger than 8×8 if we want a type-k triangle when k is large; but all sizes up to type 33 are possible on an ordinary chessboard, except for $k = 31$. And type 36 is possible too: In fact, triangles of type 36 appear in exactly 49,247,382 different knight's cycles, 650 of which are Celtic like the one shown here.

A type-k triangle will be a cycle when k is a multiple of 60, with the knight turning at each corner; it can't be part of a tour in that case.

Figure 15 shows the only example I know of a knight's cycle with 30 triangles of type 1 and 40 of type 2. (The right-hand example in Fig. 9 has 44 of type 2, but "only" 29 of type 1.) Is this the "least Celtic" of all knight tours on the chessboard?

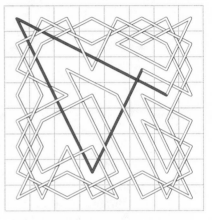

FIGURE 14. Type 36 — the max. (Maybe we should call it "type 4.")

FIGURE 15. Many small triangles.

By studying the limited possibilities for a knight to maneuver near a corner, Jelliss noted in 1992 that every knight's cycle on the chessboard must have at least one triangle of type 2. Thus no "super-Celtic tours," in which all triangles have types 3 or more, are possible. In fact, one can see without difficulty that a type-2 triangle must appear somewhere in the upper left quadrant of the board unless *all* of the following moves are present:

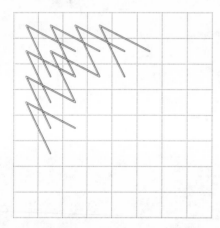

FIGURE 16. This is what happens when we try to forbid type-2 triangles.

And then it's easy to see that at least two type-2 triangles must appear in the upper right quadrant, and two more in the lower left. Thus we can conclude that *every knight's cycle on the chessboard contains at least four triangles of type 2*. And indeed, this lower bound is optimum; there are, for example, four symmetric tours that contain just one type-2 triangle in each quadrant.

FIGURE 17. A knight's cycle that has only four triangles of type 2 (and ten of type 1).

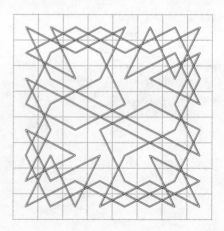

(a)   (b)

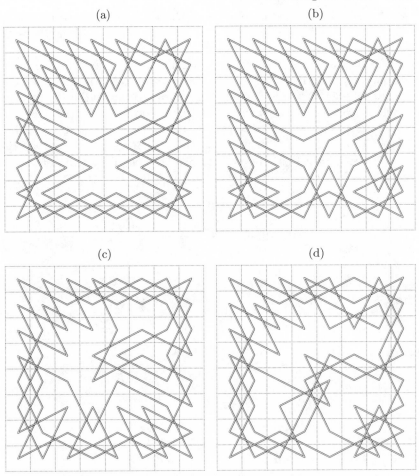

(c)   (d)

FIGURE 18. Some of the extreme ways to extend Figure 16.

The pattern in Figure 16 can be completed to a full knight's cycle in exactly 52,359,773 ways, four of which are symmetrical. [Jelliss exhibited two of the symmetric examples in *Chessics* **2**, number 19 (Autumn 1984), 25–27.] None of them are Celtic, but Fig. 18(a) shows a case with only two type-1s; it has thirteen of type 2. Fig. 18(b) illustrates the fact that one can have only 70 self-intersections without using the central parallel-lines pattern of Figs. 8 and 9. The total number of type-2 triangles under the constraint of Figure 16 can never be less than 6, as in the example of Fig. 18(c); it reaches its maximum, 29, uniquely in Fig. 18(d).

If Fig. 15 is the least Celtic of all chessboard tours, which tour is *most* Celtic? I nominate Fig. 19(a), which not only has just eight type-2 triangles (the minimum, when type-1s are forbidden), it also has only four ⤬ intersections (the minimum over all knight's tours); furthermore it's nicely symmetric. Another noteworthy example is Fig. 19(b), which may well be the only knight's tour — Celtic or not — with the astonishing property that 60 of its 64 moves are part of an ⤬ intersection. The tour in Fig. 19(c) is one of several that have only 14 intersections of the perpendicular ⊤ type; I know of no *non*-Celtic tours with fewer than 16 such intersections. Celtic tours don't like ⊤ crossings; there's only one such tour, Fig. 19(d), with as many as 50 of them.

(a)   (b)

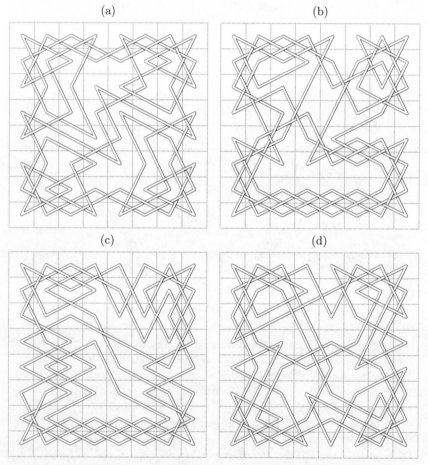

(c)   (d)

FIGURE 19. Record-breaking Celtic cycles of particular interest.

Celtic tours make pleasant patterns on boards of many other sizes, especially because we can often find symmetries that are impossible on an ordinary chessboard. Three types of symmetry are possible for knight's cycles on rectangular boards, and all three can be achieved without type-1 triangles when the board size is 10×5 (see Fig. 20).

(a)   (b)   (c)

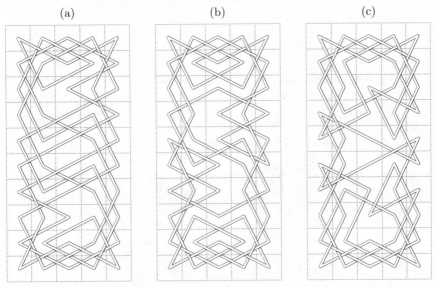

FIGURE 20. Symmetries à la (a) rotation, (b) Bergholt, and (c) reflection.

To understand the difference, consider the same three tours presented as arrays of numbers, where the knight hops from 0 to 1 to 2 to $\cdots$ to 49 and then back to 0:

(a)						(b)						(c)			
0	47	34	15	2		5	2	33	10	7		0	39	6	45	2
35	14	1	48	33		34	9	6	3	32		5	46	1	40	7
46	49	32	3	16		1	4	27	8	11		38	49	42	3	44
13	36	17	44	31		26	35	12	31	28		11	4	47	8	41
18	45	30	37	4		19	0	29	24	13		48	37	10	43	34
29	12	5	20	43		36	25	20	49	30		23	12	35	18	9
6	19	42	11	38		21	18	37	14	23		36	29	22	33	16
41	28	7	24	21		38	41	22	45	48		13	24	17	28	19
8	23	26	39	10		17	46	43	40	15		30	21	26	15	32
27	40	9	22	25		42	39	16	47	44		25	14	31	20	27

In case (a), the pairs of numbers that lie opposite each other with respect to the center are $\{0, 25\}$, $\{47, 22\}$, $\{34, 9\}$, ..., $\{37, 12\}$, $\{4, 29\}$; they all differ by exactly 25, which is half the total number of knight moves. But in case (b), the corresponding pairs are $\{5, 44\}$, $\{2, 47\}$, $\{33, 16\}$, ..., $\{24, 25\}$, $\{13, 36\}$; here they have constant *sum*, 49, instead of a constant difference! In both cases the diagrams of moves remain unchanged under 180° rotation about the center; but when Fig. 20(b) is rotated, the cycle also changes direction, so the tour goes *backwards*. Symmetry of this kind for knight cycles was discovered by Ernest Bergholt, who discussed it briefly in *British Chess Magazine* **38** (1918), 104, 195. [He had written at length to W. W. Rouse Ball about the subject in 1917; his letter was discovered among the papers of H. J. R. Murray and published in *The Games and Puzzles Journal* **2**, #14 (16 December 1996), 233–237.]

Case (c) is rather different and somewhat more rare; it involves mirror reflection about a horizontal axis, instead of rotation. Here we find that the number pairs $\{0, 25\}$, $\{39, 14\}$, $\{6, 31\}$, ..., $\{43, 18\}$, $\{34, 9\}$, which lie *vertically* opposite each other, all differ by 25.

A knight's tour can have rotational symmetry as in case (a) on $m \times n$ boards only when m and n are both even, or when one of them is odd and so is $mn/2$. Bergholtian symmetry as in case (b) can occur only when either m or n is odd. And reflection symmetry as in case (c) is possible only when $mn/2$ is odd.

Here's a table of the total number of geometrically distinct Celtic cycles on $m \times n$ boards, for $m \leq n$ and $mn \leq 66$:

5×10: $530\,(8, 5, 7)$ 6×9: $31437\,(69, 3, 73)$

5×12: $21230\,(0, 31, 0)$ 6×10: $596485\,(676, 0, 0)$

6×6: $2\,(1, 0, 0)$ 6×11: $11715215\,(1274, 180, 848)$

6×7: $52\,(2, 0, 3)$ 7×8: $284003\,(0, 21, 0)$

6×8: $1568\,(28, 0, 0)$ 8×8: $18941491\,(2321, 0, 0)$

Symmetric counts for types (a), (b), and (c) are shown in parentheses; for example, a 5×10 board admits 530 Celtic cycles, of which 8 are symmetric under 180° rotation, 5 have Bergholtian symmetry, 7 have mirror symmetry, and the other 510 are asymmetric. Board sizes not shown have no Celtic cycles.

So far we've been considering only knight's tours that are *closed*; but *open* tours, in which the knight traverses all cells of the board without returning to the starting point, also make attractive Celtic patterns. (In fact, many of the interlacing patterns in the *Book of Kells* are paths rather than cycles.) The smallest examples occur on 4×5 boards, which support three different Celtic paths, two of which are symmetric:

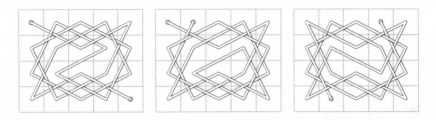

Notice that symmetry of open tours under rotation or reflection always reverses the direction of the path in Bergholtian fashion.

Open knight's tours of the 4×8 board have been studied for more than 1000 years, because they can be used to make symmetric cycles on the full 8×8 board if the endpoints occur in fortuitous places. For example, we can use the open tours

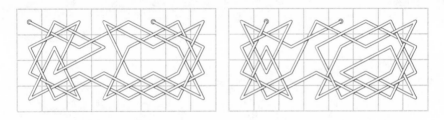

and hook them up with their rotations to form complete Celtic cycles:

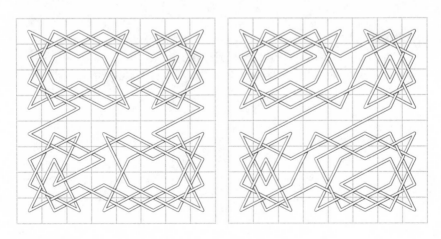

Seven such Celtic cycles are possible; here are two more examples:

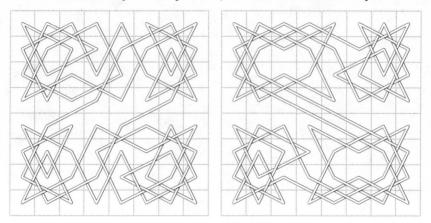

We can also mix and match, if we prefer variety to symmetry:

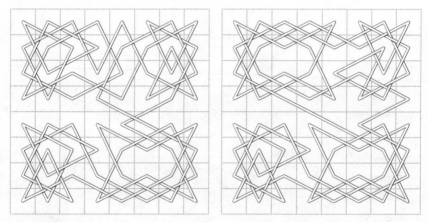

The only possible Celtic knight's tour on a 5×5 board is a symmetrical open tour from corner to corner that I happened to find in 1992:

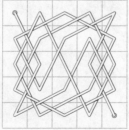

When the next size, 5×6, is considered, a new problem arises that I didn't realize until many years later: If the complete diagram of knight moves disconnects the two endpoints from each other, we cannot draw the tour with the perfect up-and-down interlacing of a Celtic knot! Consider, for example, the following two open tours:

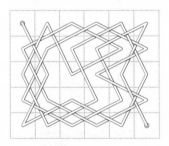 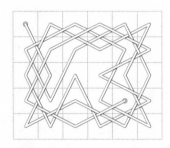

The left-hand one is fine, but on the right we can't manipulate the "threads" without breaking the under-and-over rule. In fact, our proof by which we showed that closed tours can always be properly threaded also shows why the threading is impossible in open tours such as this one.

Hmm; a· tour that deserves to be called Celtic should always be presentable as a Celtic knot. We must therefore refine our definition of Celtic knight's tours: Not only should the tour avoid any three moves that are nearly concurrent because of type-1 triangles, the endpoints of an open tour must be reachable from each other without crossing over any of the knight moves. This new criterion excludes 7 of the 80 open tours on a 5×6 board that would otherwise qualify for Celticness.

If both endpoints occur at the outer edge of the board, namely in the top or bottom rows or in the leftmost or rightmost columns, there is no problem. And we can also sometimes connect interior endpoints together without crossing any moves. For example, here are some 6×6 examples that are thoroughly Celtic in spite of having interior endpoints:

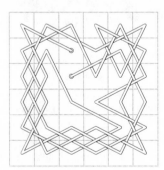 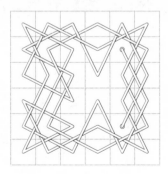

For the record, let's list the total number of distinct open Celtic tours on $m \times n$ boards, for all board sizes $m \leq n$ and $mn \leq 36$ that support at least one open tour:

$$3 \times 8: 3\,(2) \qquad 4 \times 9: 559\,(5)$$
$$4 \times 5: 3\,(2) \qquad 5 \times 5: 1\,(1)$$
$$4 \times 6: 16\,(0) \qquad 5 \times 6: 73\,(0)$$
$$4 \times 7: 32\,(6) \qquad 5 \times 7: 601\,(28)$$
$$4 \times 8: 122\,(0) \qquad 6 \times 6: 668\,(0)$$

As before, symmetric counts appear in parentheses.

One can show without difficulty that complete Celtic cycles are impossible on $3 \times n$ boards. However, there are some nice ways to construct *open* $3 \times n$ tours that have unimpeachable Celtic credentials. George Jelliss proved in 1993 that the endpoints of such tours must lie in the top or bottom rows, and that one endpoint must be in the second column from the left while the other is in the second column from the right; hence n must be even. He found all ten of the geometrically distinct tours in the smallest feasible case after $n = 8$, namely $n = 16$; four of them, like the following example, are symmetrical:

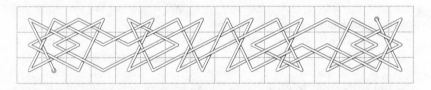

The first five moves of any Celtic $3 \times n$ tour, as well as the last five moves, can be independently flipped about a horizontal axis, thereby allowing each endpoint to appear either at the top or bottom. The number of geometrically distinct solutions, for $16 \leq n \leq 24$, is given by the following table:

$n =$	16	17	18	19	20	21	22	23	24
sols $=$	10 (4)	0 (0)	16 (0)	0 (0)	42 (4)	0 (0)	116 (8)	0 (0)	196 (8)

In fact, the set of *all* $3 \times n$ Celtic knight's tours can be fully analyzed, using methods that apply to $3 \times n$ knight's tours in general; those methods are explained in the next chapter. The total number of $3 \times n$ tour diagrams can be shown to be the same as the number of oriented paths

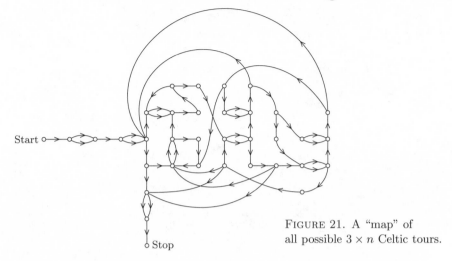

Start o→ o→ o→ o→

o Stop

FIGURE 21. A "map" of all possible $3 \times n$ Celtic tours.

from Start to Stop in Fig. 21. The corresponding generating function $T(z) = 8z^8 + 32z^{16} + 64z^{18} + O(z^{20})$ turns out to be

$$T(z) = (8z^8 - 32z^{12} - 64z^{18} + 256z^{20} + 320z^{22} - 512z^{24}$$
$$- 576z^{26} - 512z^{28} + 256z^{30} + 1024z^{32})/C(z^2), \quad \text{where}$$
$$C(z) = 1 - 4z^2 - 4z^4 - 16z^5 + 28z^6 + 16z^7 - 64z^8 - 16z^9$$
$$- 48z^{10} + 64z^{11} + 64z^{12};$$

and the generating function $S(z) = 2z^4 + 4z^8 + 4z^{10} + 8z^{11} + O(z^{12})$ for half of a symmetric tour is

$$S(z) = (2z^4 - 4z^8 + 4z^{10} + 8z^{11} - 16z^{12}$$
$$+ 8z^{13} - 24z^{14} + 32z^{16} + 32z^{17} + 16z^{18}$$
$$- 48z^{19} - 96z^{21} - 32z^{22} - 32z^{23} - 64z^{24}$$
$$+ 128z^{26} + 128z^{27})/C(z^2).$$

The generating function $G(z) = 3z^8 + 10z^{16} + 16z^{18} + O(z^{20})$ for geometrically distinct solutions is then $T(z)/4 + S(z^2)/2$.

Let's close by contemplating the following remarkable 3×40 Celtic tour, which is readily extended to boards of size $3 \times 8n$ for any $n \geq 2$:

Chapter 42

Long and Skinny Knight's Tours

[The following previously unpublished notes are based on research that I couldn't resist pursuing during Easter week of 2010, while editing the previous chapter for publication.]

The $m \times n$ knight graph is the graph of mn vertices (i, j) for $0 \le i < m$ and $0 \le j < n$, with $(i, j) \,\text{---}\, (i', j')$ if and only if $(i - i')^2 + (j - j')^2 = 5$. In other words, it's the graph whose vertices are the cells of a chessboard with m rows and n columns; two cells are adjacent if a knight can move from one to the other. The smallest interesting cases occur when $m = 3$ and $n \ge 4$.

The study of Hamiltonian paths and cycles on these $3 \times n$ graphs has a long history going back to Euler [4, §42], who found all Hamiltonian paths of the 3×4 board, namely

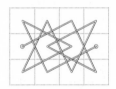 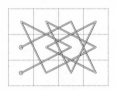 

up to symmetry, and stated (correctly) that no such paths exist on 3×5 or 3×6 boards. Euler exhibited two examples of 3×7 tours,

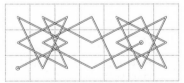 and 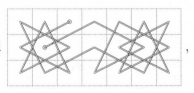 ,

thereby showing that the total number of cells could be odd. He also stated (incorrectly) that Hamiltonian *cycles* on the $3 \times n$ knight graph are

511

impossible, and other authors propagated this widely believed statement for more than 150 years. Suddenly Ernest Bergholt surprised everybody by discovering cycles on the 3×10;* the first example he found [1, 2] was

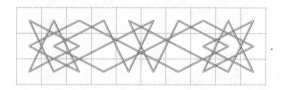

An excellent exposition of the history and theory of $3 \times n$ knight's tours, for small n, has been prepared by G. P. Jelliss [5, 6]. The purpose of the present note is to count the total number of such tours that exist for arbitrarily *large* values of n. For example, we'll be able to deduce without great difficulty that the 3×100 knight graph has exactly

17,171,285,160,376,241,062,521,061,238,260,619,247,832,232,930,992,568

Hamiltonian paths, and that it has exactly

4,861,943,174,181,138,724,903,568,742,746,024,250,554,974,208

Hamiltonian cycles. (Every Hamiltonian cycle on this graph leads to 300 of the Hamiltonian paths, by deleting one of the edges. Those paths are said to be *reentrant*.) As a byproduct of our investigations we'll encounter several elementary facts about $3 \times n$ tours that are of independent interest, as well as some very pleasant new patterns.

---

* When I read Euler's paper carefully for the first time in 1972, I scribbled the following notes on my copy: "Impossibility not proved, nor is it plainly stated that reentrancy is impossible on $4 \times n$, or boards with odd no. of cells. [I didn't really understand Euler's French wording.] Here's a 3×14 [based on a 3×7 path; go from 1 to 21, then $1'$ to $21'$]:

9	12	7	4	17	14	19	$21'$	$18'$	$15'$	$2'$	$5'$	$8'$	$11'$
6	3	10	13	20	1	16	$16'$	$1'$	$20'$	$13'$	$10'$	$3'$	$6'$
11	8	5	2	15	18	21	$19'$	$14'$	$17'$	$4'$	$7'$	$12'$	$9'$

Exercise: Characterize $3 \times n$ that admit reentrancy. ... I believe I've proved without great difficulty that 3×6, 3×8, 3×10 are impossible. ... Addendum, 12 Dec 92: Altogether 176 solutions 3×12. *And* there are 16 solutions of the 3×10! Also 1536 solutions of 3×14." [I had begun my study by reading the major reference books on recreational mathematics, which were written before 1918, so I didn't learn of Bergholt's work until later.]

The Basic Setup

Our main tool will be a *directed* graph K, called `knight3`, which encapsulates all of the information about $3 \times n$ knight's tours for arbitrary n in a single structure. This digraph K turns out to have 712 vertices and 5506 arcs. The vertices of K represent the "states" that can arise when we take a $3 \times n$ tour and cut it into two pieces, consisting of k columns at the left and $n - k$ columns at the right, for some k. The arcs of K represent the allowable transitions between states when k increases by 1.

Let S_n denote the $3 \times n$ knight graph, and let $\widehat{S}_n$ be its extension obtained by adding a new vertex ∞ that is adjacent to all the others. Hamiltonian paths T in S_n are equivalent to Hamiltonian cycles $\widehat{T}$ in $\widehat{S}_n$, where the two endpoints of T are the two neighbors of ∞ in $\widehat{T}$. Throughout the following discussion, we will bear in mind that S_n and $\widehat{S}_n$ are undirected graphs, which have edges (moves) between cells; K, by contrast, is a directed graph, which has arcs (transitions) between states.

Given a Hamiltonian cycle T on S_n or $\widehat{S}_n$, let $T_k = T \mid \widehat{S}_k$ be the edges of T that lie entirely in the first k columns of the chessboard, possibly extended by ∞. Thus, for example, in Euler's first 3×4 tour as given above, and with the rows numbered 0, 1, 2 from top to bottom, we have

$$T = T_4 = \{\infty-10, 10-02, 02-23, 23-11, 11-03, 03-22,$$
$$22-01, 01-20, 20-12, 12-00, 00-21, 21-13, 13-\infty\}$$

and $T_2 = \{\infty-10, 01-20, 00-21\}$, where the notation $ij-i'j'$ stands for the edge from (i, j) to (i', j').

In general, every cell of $\widehat{S}_k$ will be covered by exactly two edges of T_k, except perhaps for ∞ and for cells in the two rightmost columns of S_k. The uncovered cells are either untouched — that is, absent from all of T_k's edges — or they are attached to some other cell by a single edge of T_k. In the latter case, they are "mated" to a similarly attached cell, by a maximal subpath of T_k whose endpoints are the two mates. Continuing the previous example, we have

$$T_3 = \{\infty-10, 10-02, 22-01, 01-20, 20-12, 12-00, 00-21\},$$

and the uncovered cells of $\widehat{S}_3$ are ∞, 02, 11, 22, 21. Cell 11 is untouched, while the pairs $\{\infty, 02\}$ and $\{22, 21\}$ are mates.

It's convenient to denote the seven possibly uncovered cells by the typewriter-style digits 1, 2, 3, 4, 5, 6, and ∞, denoting the respective cells $(0, k-1)$, $(1, k-1)$, $(2, k-1)$, $(0, k-2)$, $(1, k-2)$, $(2, k-2)$, and ∞. In this notation the right end of the partial board $\widehat{S}_k$ is essentially

$$
\infty \quad
\begin{matrix}
4 & 1 \\
5 & 2 \\
6 & 3
\end{matrix} \ \Bigg| \quad ,
$$

although cell ∞ is actually off in limbo somewhere. Each of these seven cells x is assigned a mate, called $mate[x]$, by the rules

$$
mate[x] = \begin{cases}
0, & \text{if } x \text{ is covered by } T_k; \\
x, & \text{if } x \text{ is untouched by } T_k; \\
y, & \text{if } x \text{ and } y \text{ are attached to each other via } T_k.
\end{cases}
$$

The state corresponding to T_k is then denoted by the seven-digit code

$$mate[1]\ mate[2]\ mate[3]\ mate[4]\ mate[5]\ mate[6]\ mate[\infty].$$

For example, the state corresponding to T_3 in Euler's tour T is $\infty060531$, because cells $(1, 2, 3, 4, 5, 6, \infty)$ are respectively $(02, 12, 22, 01, 11, 21, \infty)$ when $k = 3$. This state is a successor in K of the state that corresponds to T_2, which happens to be state $6243\infty15$ according to these rules.

To go from T_k to T_{k+1} in general, we begin by increasing all of the code numbers by 3 and then we append new untouched elements 1, 2, 3, thereby obtaining up to ten potentially relevant cells:

$$
\infty \quad
\begin{matrix}
7 & 4 & 1 \\
8 & 5 & 2 \\
9 & 6 & 3
\end{matrix} \ \Bigg| \quad .
$$

The remaining task is to take account of the edges of T that belong to T_{k+1} but not to T_k, namely those that have one endpoint in column k and another in columns $k - 1$ or $k - 2$ (or ∞). This set of new edges is conveniently encoded by three italic digits, representing the sum of codes for each of the nine possibilities:

100 for edge 8 — 1	*010* for edge 7 — 2	*001* for edge 4 — 3
200 for edge 6 — 1	*020* for edge 9 — 2	*002* for edge 8 — 3
400 for edge ∞ — 1	*040* for edge ∞ — 2	*004* for edge ∞ — 3

For example, T_3 has four edges that aren't in T_2 in Euler's tour T, and the transition from $6243\infty15$ to $\infty060531$ has the code name $100 + 010 + 020 + 001 = 131$. Only $7^3 - 3^3 = 316$ of the 512 potential transition codes abc are actually possible, because $0 \le a, b, c \le 6$ and because most two of the digits $\{a, b, c\}$ can exceed 3.

Let's watch the process of going from $6243\infty15$ to $\infty060531$ in slow motion: First we upgrade $6243\infty15$ to $1239576\infty48$, as k is increased from 2 to 3. Then we add edge *100*, from 8 to 1, obtaining $\infty239576041$. Edge *010*, from 7 to 2, changes that to $\infty639520041$; edge *020*, from 9 to 2, yields $\infty036540001$; and the final edge *001*, from 4 to 3, produces the state $\infty060530001$ that actually corresponds to T_3. Of course the edges of T_{k+1} have by now covered 7, 8, 9; so we leave out the '*mate*[7] *mate*[8] *mate*[9]' part of the ten-digit code, obtaining the new seven-digit state code $\infty060531$.

The operation of changing the *mate* values, as a new edge is added from x to y, might seem to require a complicated case analysis. But in fact, we simply need to do the following six assignments, in order:

$$x' \leftarrow mate[x], \ y' \leftarrow mate[y];$$
$$mate[x] \leftarrow 0, \ mate[y] \leftarrow 0;$$
$$mate[x'] \leftarrow y', \ mate[y'] \leftarrow x'.$$

The cases $x' = x$ and/or $y' = y$ do a bit of redundant computation, but we save time because we needn't treat them specially. Notice, however, that such a knight move is legal only when x' and y' are nonzero. Furthermore, we usually assume that $x' \neq y$ (hence $y' \neq x$). The exceptional case, in which $x' = y$ and $y' = x$, is allowed only when completing a Hamiltonian cycle, namely when all other mates are already zero; otherwise we'd be closing a cycle that is too short. If this case is permissible we omit the last two assignments of the scheme above, thereby closing the final cycle by setting both $mate[x]$ and $mate[y]$ to 0.

With this machinery in place, Euler's tour T is completely characterized as a path of length 4 in K:

$$000000\infty \xrightarrow{040} 1\infty30002 \xrightarrow{201} 6243\infty15 \xrightarrow{131} \infty060531 \xrightarrow{363} 0000000.$$

Indeed, we've set up a one-to-one correspondence between the open knight's tours of a $3 \times n$ chessboard and the paths of length n from 000000∞ to 0000000 in K.

Similarly, it's easy to see that the *closed* tours are in one-to-one correspondence with paths of length $n - 1$ from 1230000 to 0000000. Bergholt's closed tour on the 3×10 board corresponds to the path

$$1230000 \xrightarrow{201} 6243510 \xrightarrow{133} 6000510 \xrightarrow{122} 3412000 \xrightarrow{011} 1560230$$
$$\xrightarrow{321} 0543200 \xrightarrow{212} 2150300 \xrightarrow{100} 6235410 \xrightarrow{232} 6043510 \xrightarrow{333} 0000000.$$

State 000000ᴔ is called the *open source* vertex of K, and denoted by the symbol σ_o; state 1230000 is called the *closed source* vertex, and denoted by σ_c. State 0000000 is the *sink* vertex, τ.

Symmetries

Euler's three tours on the 3×4 board give us three paths of length 4 from σ_o to τ in K. But we have to be careful when we count paths: We will see shortly that there are actually *eight* different shortest paths in K from σ_o to τ, not three. Did Euler miss five of them? No. He found the three tours that are *geometrically* distinct; but the diagram of any given $3 \times n$ tour leads to a different *diagram* when it is reflected about a horizontal axis. Sometimes we also get two further diagrams after reflecting about a vertical axis. Euler's three tours lead in this way to $2 + 4 + 2 = 8$ different diagrams, and the one-to-one correspondence we have been discussing is a correspondence with respect to diagrams. Symmetry under reflection can indeed be accounted for; we just haven't gotten there yet.

We can, however, see easily that the top-to-bottom reflection process, which basically interchanges row 0 with row 2, does have a straightforward effect on paths in K. Consider, for example, the relation between the path for Euler's tour T and the path that corresponds to the tour T' that we get by reflecting T about a horizontal axis; that tour is

$$000000ᴔ \xrightarrow{\;040\;} 1ᴔ30002 \xrightarrow{\;201\;} 6243ᴔ15 \xrightarrow{\;232\;} 40ᴔ1503 \xrightarrow{\;353\;} 0000000.$$

In general, every state α corresponds to a "flipped" state α', and every transition t corresponds to a "flipped" transition t'. If $\alpha = \mathtt{abcdefg}$ and $t = \mathtt{abc}$, we have $\alpha' = \mathtt{c'b'a'f'e'd'g'}$ and $t' = \mathtt{c'b'a'}$, where

$$0' = 0, \; 1' = 3, \; 2' = 2, \; 3' = 1, \; 4' = 6, \; 5' = 5, \; 6' = 4, \; ᴔ' = ᴔ;$$
$$0' = 0, \; 1' = 2, \; 2' = 1, \; 3' = 3, \; 4' = 4, \; 5' = 6, \; 6' = 5.$$

Notice that $\sigma_o' = \sigma_o$, $\sigma_c' = \sigma_c$, and $\tau' = \tau$; also $1ᴔ30002' = 1ᴔ30002$ and $6243ᴔ15' = 6243ᴔ15$. But $40ᴔ1503' = ᴔ060531$.

We will defer further study of symmetry until we've completely understood the situation when symmetries are ignored.

Classification of States

The state codes of K are all obtainable in principle by (a) starting with the sequence of seven digits 123456ᴔ, then (b) setting some subset of them to 0, and (c) applying an involution (a self-inverse permutation) to the remaining nonzeros. Thus the total number of possibilities is

$$\binom{7}{7}t_0 + \binom{7}{6}t_1 + \binom{7}{5}t_2 + \binom{7}{4}t_3 + \binom{7}{3}t_4 + \binom{7}{2}t_5 + \binom{7}{1}t_6 + \binom{7}{0}t_7,$$

where t_k is the number of involutions of k elements.

The well-known formula $\sum_{k \geq 0} t_k z^k/k! = e^{z+z^2/2}$ (see, for example, [8, exercise 5.1.4–25]) implies that this sum is $7! \, [z^7] \, e^{2z+z^2/2} = 1850$. However, only 1406 of the 1850 potential states are actually reachable from the source states σ_o and σ_c by legal transitions of knight moves. There's no way to reach 1000000, for example.

Another large set of states, having the forms ***4***, *****6*, and ***6*4*, can easily be shown to have no successor; here '*' is a "wild card" that matches any digit. Such states aren't in K, because they don't lead to τ, and by excluding them from the reachable states we can whittle the number of possibilities from 1406 down to 750. We can also knock out states of the form 1*3*5**, whose successors have no successors, thereby removing six more reachable cases from the set. And another 32 cases, such as 1035400, fail to satisfy a necessary condition that is derived below, in spite of being reachable from σ_o.

Thus we're left with 712 vertices in K, as stated earlier. A simple computer program shows that each of these vertices, except σ_c, actually occurs in some path of length 16 or less from σ_o to τ. (In fact, only the two states 10300∞6 and 103∞004, which occur near the middle of

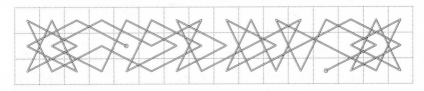

or its reflection, require a path of length more than 14.)

Cell (i, j) of the chessboard is said to be *even* when $i + j$ is even, and *odd* when $i + j$ is odd. A $3 \times n$ board has $\lceil 3n/2 \rceil$ even cells and $\lfloor 3n/2 \rfloor$ odd cells. Therefore, when n is odd, the endpoints of an open tour must both be even. It follows that four different kinds of open tours are possible:

1) Both endpoints appear in the same column; one of them is odd, the other is even, and n is even.

2) Both endpoints appear in the same column; both of them are even, and n is odd.

3) The endpoints appear in different columns, and the left endpoint is even. The right endpoint is even if n is odd, odd if n is even.

4) The endpoints appear in different columns, and the left endpoint is odd. The right endpoint is even, and so is n.

We will see that these four cases show up naturally in the states of K.

Let us divide the vertices of K into four classes, called O (open), F (free), B (bound), and C (closed). Class O consists of all states whose code names end with ∞; these are the states that occur before any endpoints of the tour have appeared. Class C consists of all states whose names end with 0; these are the states of closed tours, and they also occur after both endpoints of an open tour have been seen. Between O and C we have two choices for the intermediate states, when one endpoint has appeared but not the other: Class F corresponds to open tours of type (3) above, following an even left endpoint; class B corresponds to open tours of type (4), following an odd left endpoint.

The states of classes O, B, and C are bipartite, so we subdivide them further into classes O_0, O_1, B_0, B_1, C_0, and C_1. An O_0 or B_0 state always occurs an even number of steps after σ_o; a B_0 or C_0 state always occurs an even number of steps before τ. Classes O_1, B_1, and C_1 are similar, but with an odd number of steps. Class F is free of any parity restrictions.

The allowable transitions between classes are then

$$O_0 \to O_1, \quad O_0 \to B_1, \quad O_0 \to F, \quad O_0 \to C_0, \quad O_0 \to C_1;$$
$$O_1 \to O_0, \quad O_1 \to B_0, \quad O_1 \to F, \quad O_1 \to C_0;$$
$$F \to F, \quad F \to C_0, \quad F \to C_1;$$
$$B_0 \to B_1, \quad B_0 \to C_1;$$
$$B_1 \to B_0, \quad B_1 \to C_0;$$
$$C_0 \to C_1; \quad C_1 \to C_0.$$

Notice that the transition $O_1 \to C_1$ is illegal: Open tours of type (1) above use a transition $O_0 \to C_1$ or $O_1 \to C_0$ when the endpoints appear, but tours of type (2) must use $O_0 \to C_0$. Type (3) tours go in some fashion from O to F to C; type (4) tours go from O to B to C. Euler's 3×4 tours go $O_0 \to B_1 \to B_0 \to B_1 \to C_0$, $O_0 \to C_1 \to C_0 \to C_1 \to C_0$, and $O_0 \to F \to F \to F \to C_0$, respectively.

It turns out that a total of $(84, 75, 204, 110, 72, 91, 76)$ vertices belong to the respective classes $(O_0, O_1, F, B_0, B_1, C_0, C_1)$ in K.

Computing the Parity

There's a systematic way to determine the class of any vertex directly from its state code, although the rules are slightly intricate. Given the values of $mate[x]$ for $1 \le x \le 7$, where '7' stands temporarily for '∞' in this discussion, we define several related quantities as follows:

z_0 = the number of nonzero x with $mate[x] = 0$ and x even;

z_1 = the number of nonzero x with $mate[x] = 0$ and x odd;

f_0 = the number of nonzero x with $mate[x] = x$ and x even;

f_1 = the number of nonzero x with $mate[x] = x$ and x odd;

p_{00} = the number of $x < y$ with $mate[x] = y$, x and y both even;

p_{01} = the number of $x < y$ with $mate[x] = y$, $x + y$ odd;

p_{11} = the number of $x < y$ with $mate[x] = y$, x and y both odd.

The values of f_0 and f_1 are redundant, because we clearly have

$$z_0 + f_0 + 2p_{00} + p_{01} = 3, \qquad z_1 + f_1 + p_{01} + 2p_{11} = 4.$$

The latter relations show that $p_{00} \le 1$ and $p_{11} \le 2$; both of these upper bounds are achieved in state 7650321 (that is, ∞650321), which is the lexicographically largest state of K.

How do these quantities change when a knight move between an even cell x and an odd cell y changes the mate table? If x and y were previously untouched, such a move clearly sets

$$f_0 \leftarrow f_0 - 1, \qquad f_1 \leftarrow f_1 - 1, \qquad p_{01} \leftarrow p_{01} + 1.$$

If only one was untouched, one of four possible changes will occur:

either $f_0 \leftarrow f_0 - 1$, $z_1 \leftarrow z_1 + 1$, $p_{00} \leftarrow p_{00} + 1$, $p_{01} \leftarrow p_{01} - 1$;

or $f_0 \leftarrow f_0 - 1$, $z_1 \leftarrow z_1 + 1$, $p_{01} \leftarrow p_{01} + 1$, $p_{11} \leftarrow p_{11} - 1$;

or $f_1 \leftarrow f_1 - 1$, $z_0 \leftarrow z_0 + 1$, $p_{00} \leftarrow p_{00} - 1$, $p_{01} \leftarrow p_{01} + 1$;

or $f_1 \leftarrow f_1 - 1$, $z_0 \leftarrow z_0 + 1$, $p_{01} \leftarrow p_{01} - 1$, $p_{11} \leftarrow p_{11} + 1$.

And if both were previously mated with other elements, we'll have

either $z_0 \leftarrow z_0 + 1$, $z_1 \leftarrow z_1 + 1$, $p_{01} \leftarrow p_{01} - 1$;

or $z_0 \leftarrow z_0 + 1$, $z_1 \leftarrow z_1 + 1$, $p_{00} \leftarrow p_{00} - 1$,
$$p_{01} \leftarrow p_{01} + 1, \; p_{11} \leftarrow p_{11} - 1.$$

Notice that in each of these cases, the knight move leaves the quantity

$$I = z_0 - z_1 + p_{00} - p_{11}$$

invariant. Intuitively, I represents the difference between the number of even and odd cells covered in the first $k - 2$ columns.

When k increases by 1, we promote cells $\{1, \ldots, 7\}$ to $\{4, \ldots, 10\}$; promotion causes even and odd cells to switch roles, so we have

$$z_0 \leftrightarrow z_1, \qquad p_{00} \leftrightarrow p_{11}, \qquad \text{and} \qquad I \leftarrow -I.$$

Then we append $\{1, 2, 3\}$, causing $f_0 \leftarrow f_0 + 1$, $f_1 \leftarrow f_1 + 2$; now

$$z_0 + f_0 + 2p_{00} + p_{01} = z_1 + f_1 + p_{01} + 2p_{11} = 5.$$

(At this point '∞' is temporarily represented by the *even* value '10'.) The value of I remains invariant while we do further knight moves, but it changes again when we truncate the tableau by removing the zero mates of $\{7, 8, 9\}$; truncation causes $z_0 \leftarrow z_0 - 1$ and $z_1 \leftarrow z_1 - 2$, if the mate of ∞ isn't 0, hence $I \leftarrow I + 1$.

If ∞ was mated to ∞ before and after such a state transition, as it is in the 0 states, the net effect is to set $I \leftarrow 1 - I$. Therefore we see that the open states of class 0_0 have $I = 0$, while those of class 0_1 have $I = 1$.

If ∞ was mated to 0 before and after a state transition, as it is in the C states, the truncation operation causes $z_0 \leftarrow z_0 - 2$ and $z_1 \leftarrow z_1 - 1$, hence $I \leftarrow -1 - I$. In this case therefore we find that subclass C_0 corresponds to $I = -1$ and subclass C_1 corresponds to $I = 0$. (And we also see that a state code like 1035400, which makes $I = +1$, cannot be valid in K, thereby confirming a remark made above.)

On the other hand if ∞ was mated to any of the other cells $\{1, \ldots, 6\}$ before and after the transition, as it is in the F and B states, the process of demoting 10 to 7 has the effect of decreasing I by 1, because it either sets $p_{01} \leftarrow p_{01} - 1$ and $p_{11} \leftarrow p_{11} + 1$ or $p_{01} \leftarrow p_{01} + 1$ and $p_{00} \leftarrow p_{00} - 1$. Thus I always becomes simply $-I$ during an F or B transition. By looking at boundary conditions, we conclude that the bound states of class B_0 are characterized by $I = -1$, while those of class B_1 have $I = +1$. For example, the states of Euler's tour T can be classified as follows:

state	z_0	z_1	f_0	f_1	p_{00}	p_{01}	p_{11}	I	class
000000∞	3	3	0	1	0	0	0	0	0_0
1∞30002	2	1	0	2	0	1	0	+1	B_1
6243∞15	0	0	1	0	0	2	1	−1	B_0
∞060531	2	0	0	1	0	1	1	+1	B_1
0000000	3	4	0	0	0	0	0	−1	C_0

Cycles

The digraph K contains four 1-cycles (arcs from a vertex to itself):

$$02\infty0503 \xrightarrow{302} 02\infty0503, \qquad \infty200501 \xrightarrow{103} \infty200501,$$
$$10430\infty6 \xrightarrow{031} 10430\infty6, \qquad 603\infty014 \xrightarrow{230} 603\infty014.$$

They give rise to repetitive $3 \times n$ knight's tours for all $n \geq 11$, because we can loop around the cycle as many times as we like, producing a nice "hookwork" motif once we've set up a proper start and finish:

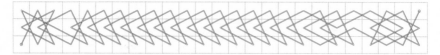

All four of these 1-cycles yield essentially the same pattern, but reflected horizontally and/or vertically.

Of course 1-cycles can appear only on a vertex whose state is F, because the other kinds of states are bipartite and have only even cycles. The 2-cycles are, however, interesting too, both visually and mathematically. There are 21 of them, giving rise to five distinct textures:

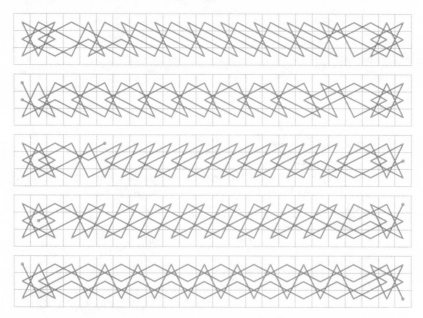

The last of these was apparently first discovered by George Jelliss [5], who calls it "barbed wire." It illustrates an interesting phenomenon: The 2-cycle pattern that we see is really the repeating sequence of transitions *111*, *222*, *111*, *222*, ..., not the 2-cycles of connectivity states that are tracked in K. Indeed, this sequence of transitions arises not only in the 2-cycle

$$\infty543201 \xrightarrow{\;111\;} 56\infty0123 \xrightarrow{\;222\;} \infty543201,$$

and in the top-to-bottom reflection of that cycle,

$$65∞0213 \xrightarrow{222} ∞452301 \xrightarrow{111} 65∞0213,$$

but also in another 2-cycle that is its *own* reflection:

$$∞325401 \xrightarrow{111} 21∞0653 \xrightarrow{222} ∞325401.$$

Moreover, in the symmetric tour illustrated above, it actually occurs in a 4-cycle of K, *not* a 2-cycle, namely

$$3∞15402 \xrightarrow{111} 2160∞53 \xrightarrow{222} 21∞5403 \xrightarrow{111} 21503∞6 \xrightarrow{222} 3∞15402!$$

Hmm. If visual 2-cycles can occur in 4-cycles, perhaps there also are visual 1-cycles that don't show up in any of K's 1-cycles. Sure enough: There's a 3-cycle

$$0∞30652 \xrightarrow{320} 0630∞25 \xrightarrow{320} 05302∞6 \xrightarrow{320} 0∞30652$$

in which all transitions are *320*, yet no 1-cycle has this property. Using this cycle, a knight can trace out a "latticework" path

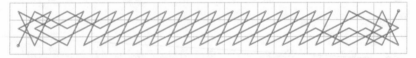

in which it covers just one third of the texture on each pass, as it travels right-left-right (starting at the left).

And that's not all. The digraph contains three different 5-cycles in which all of the transitions are *121* — thereby leading, in fact, to a family of symmetric knight's tours in which all but seven of the transitions are *121*, whenever $n \bmod 5 \neq 2$:

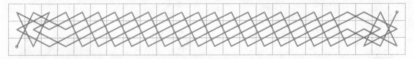

Jelliss has called this texture "brickwork" [5]; it goes right-left-right-left-right. Together with the hookwork and latticework motifs, it completes the set of visual 1-cycles possible with a $3 \times n$ knight.

Pleasant visual 3-cycles arise also from the 3-cycles of K that *don't* make the latticework pattern above:

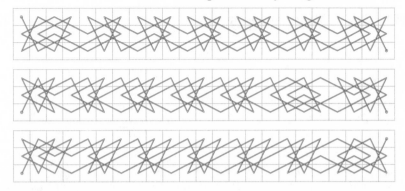

One can well imagine the walls of a mathematics common room being graced with patterns like these.

And K contains a vast number of 4-cycles and 5-cycles. Here are just a few snapshots of this mostly unexplored terrain:

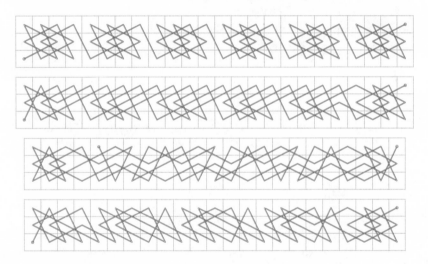

The second of these visual 4-cycles actually occurs in K only as a 12-cycle. Further study of such patterns is clearly indicated.

Enumeration

Our main goal, to count all tours of length $3n$, is getting closer, now that we're familiar with the digraph K. Let $N(\alpha, \beta, n)$ be the number of paths of length n in K from state α to state β; the number of $3 \times n$ knight's tours is then $N(\sigma_o, \tau, n)$ for open tours and $N(\sigma_c, \tau, n - 1)$ for closed tours. (Strictly speaking, we really mean "walks" of length n, not "paths," using the terminology of modern graph theory, because we're talking about sequences

$$\alpha = \alpha_0 \longrightarrow \alpha_1 \longrightarrow \cdots \longrightarrow \alpha_n = \beta$$

that might pass through the same state many times. But we will continue to call them paths in this informal discussion.)

In principle, the calculation of $N(\alpha, \beta, n)$ is not difficult when n isn't too large. We can set up, or imagine, K's adjacency matrix A, which has one row and one column for each state of K. The entry $A_{\alpha\beta}$ in row α and column β is 1 if $\alpha \longrightarrow \beta$ and 0 otherwise; symbolically we write $A_{\alpha\beta} = [\alpha \longrightarrow \beta]$. Then

$$N(\alpha, \beta, n) = A_{\alpha\beta}^n$$

is the entry in row α and column β of the nth power of matrix A.

Instead of evaluating $N(\alpha, \beta, n)$ for a particular n, we can get much more information by determining the generating function

$$G(\alpha, \beta) = N(\alpha, \beta, 0) + N(\alpha, \beta, 1)z + N(\alpha, \beta, 2)z^2 + \cdots$$
$$= \sum_{n=0}^{\infty} N(\alpha, \beta, n)z^n,$$

which represents all of the $N(\alpha, \beta, n)$ simultaneously. The formula $N(\alpha, \beta, n) = A_{\alpha\beta}^n$ tells us that the matrix of all these generating functions is

$$I + Az + A^2 z^2 + \cdots = \sum_{n=0}^{\infty} A^n z^n = (I - Az)^{-1},$$

where $I = A^0$ is the identity matrix whose entries are $I_{\alpha\beta} = [\alpha = \beta]$. Thus everything we want to know appears in the inverse of the matrix $I - Az$. The individual entries of this inverse are well known to be $\pm g(\alpha, \beta, z)/f(z)$, where $f(z)$ is the determinant of $I - Az$ and $g(\alpha, \beta, z)$ is the determinant of the submatrix obtained by deleting column α and row β. Since $f(z)$ and $g(\alpha, \beta, z)$ are polynomials in z, the generating functions $G(\alpha, \beta)$ are rational, and the numbers $N(\alpha, \beta, n)$ obey a linear recurrence relation with constant coefficients.

Thus everything works out swimmingly in theory. But in practice, we have to deal with the fact that A is a great big matrix with 712 rows, 712 columns, and 5506 nonzero entries (about 7.7 nonzeros per

row). The polynomials $f(z)$ and $g(\alpha, \beta, z)$ have large degree and large
coefficients. Dealing with giant matrices of polynomials is no picnic.

We're really interested only in two of those generating functions,
however, namely $G(\sigma_o, \tau)$ and $G(\sigma_c, \tau)$; so we don't need all $712^2 =$
506,944 entries of the matrix $(I - Az)^{-1}$. Our problem can be solved
more economically by considering, say, the 712 generating functions
$G(\alpha) = G(\alpha, \tau)$, which satisfy the simultaneous linear equations

$$G(\alpha) \;=\; [\alpha = \tau] + z \sum_{\alpha \to \beta} G(\beta)$$

over all vertices α of K. For example, the equation

$$G(0\omega00002) \;=\; z\big(G(1230\omega05) + G(1250300) + G(5230100)\big)$$

expresses the generating function for $0\omega00002$, a B_0 state, in terms of
the generating functions for a B_1 state and for two C_1 states.

The symmetry of K that takes $\alpha \mapsto \alpha'$ when the board is reflected
about a horizontal axis now helps a lot, because we have $\alpha \longrightarrow \beta$ if and
only if $\alpha' \longrightarrow \beta'$. Thus $G(\alpha) = G(\alpha')$, and the number of unknown functions is roughly halved; it decreases from 712 to 376. (In fact K has 40
self-dual states with $\alpha = \alpha'$; examples are 321050ω, $6043\omega15$, $3\omega10502$,
and 4561230 of classes O, F, B, and C, respectively.) We can treat the
pair $\{\alpha, \alpha'\}$ as a unified state, and the equation above simplifies to

$$G(0\omega00002) \;=\; z\big(G(1230\omega05) + 2G(\{1250300, 5230100\})\big).$$

Further reduction occurs whenever we have two reduced states with
exactly the same successors, because their generating functions are obviously identical. Mathematically speaking, we can let $\alpha \equiv \beta$ be an
equivalence relation between states with the property that, if $\alpha \equiv \beta$ and
if α has the successor states $\alpha_1, \ldots, \alpha_s$ while β has the successors β_1,
$\ldots, \beta_t$, then $s = t$ and we have $\alpha_1 \equiv \beta_1, \ldots, \alpha_t \equiv \beta_t$. Such a relation
implies that $G(\alpha) = G(\beta)$ whenever $\alpha \equiv \beta$. This idea reduces K to
its "homomorphic image," which is the multidigraph $\widehat{K} = K/\equiv$ whose
vertices are the equivalence classes $[\alpha]$.

The successive grouping of states with the same successors, after
we've paired each α with its dual α', leads to an equivalence relation with
just 220 inequivalent "superstates," and 1648 arcs between them. For
example, $3210000, 5200100, 0250300$ is a superstate of three equivalent
vertices of class C_0; another superstate, $02435\omega6, 42015\omega6, 026\omega534$,
$620\omega514$, groups four of class B_0; the still larger example

$$30100\omega6, 50001\omega6, 005\omega304, 500\omega104, 00503\omega6, 301\omega004$$

groups six of class F. There are five superstates of size 8, and there's even a superstate of size 9. We're making progress.

The structure of K, in which vertices of classes F and B are independent of each other and come "between" those of classes O and C, helps further, and so does the bipartite nature of classes O, B, C. The reduced digraph $\widehat{K}$ has just $(25, 27, 58, 29, 29, 25, 27)$ superstates of classes O_0, O_1, F, B_0, B_1, C_0, C_1, respectively.

Enumeration of Closed Tours

All successors of C vertices are again of class C, so we can find the generating functions $G(\alpha)$ for all closed superstates α by solving $25 + 27$ simultaneous linear equations. This part of K is bipartite, so we immediately can reduce to just 25 equations, one of which is simply "$G(\tau) = 1$." The other 24 equations for vertices of class C_0 have a factor of z^2 on each right-hand side. Hence the solutions $G(\alpha)$ will each have the form $g(\alpha, z^2)/P(z^2)$, where P is a polynomial that captures the "looping" structure of closed states. That polynomial P turns out to have degree 21:

$$P(z) = 1 - 6z - 64z^2 + 200z^3 + 1000z^4 - 3016z^5 - 3488z^6 + 24256z^7$$
$$- 23776z^8 - 104168z^9 + 203408z^{10} + 184704z^{11} - 443392z^{12}$$
$$- 14336z^{13} + 151296z^{14} - 145920z^{15} + 263424z^{16} - 317440z^{17}$$
$$- 36864z^{18} + 966656z^{19} - 573440z^{20} - 131072z^{21}.$$

The initial state $\sigma_c = 1230000$ is of class C_1. It has only one successor, 6243510, which of course has class C_0. The numerator polynomial $g(6243510, z)$ turns out to be

$$16(z^4 + 5z^5 - 34z^6 - 116z^7 + 505z^8 + 616z^9 - 3179z^{10}$$
$$- 4z^{11} + 9536z^{12} - 8176z^{13} - 13392z^{14} + 15360z^{15} + 13888z^{16}$$
$$+ 2784z^{17} - 3328z^{18} - 22016z^{19} + 5120z^{20} + 2048z^{21});$$

we get the generating function for closed $3 \times n$ tours by (i) multiplying $g(6243510, z)$ by z, (ii) dividing the result by $P(z)$, and (iii) replacing z by z^2. This process yields a power series that begins as follows:

$$\frac{16z^{10} + 80z^{12} - 544z^{14} + O(z^{16})}{1 - 6z^2 - 64z^4 + O(z^6)} = 16z^{10} + 176z^{12} + 1536z^{14} + O(z^{16}).$$

There are 16 closed tour diagrams on a 3×10 board, 176 on a 3×12, 1536 on a 3×14, and so on. Everything checks out.

(*Historical note:* Noam Elkies and the author derived this generating function independently in 1994; see [3] and the addendum below.)

These counts don't take any account of symmetry, however, as mentioned before. The 16 tours on the 3×10 have 16 different diagrams; but if we prefer to believe that reflection and/or rotation don't really change a tour, each tour has been counted four times if it has no symmetry, twice if its diagram is the same under reflection or 180° rotation. It turns out that there are six *geometrically distinct* closed tours on this board, two of which have left-right symmetry, two of which are rotationally symmetric, and two of which have no symmetry at all (thus $16 = 2 \cdot 2 + 2 \cdot 2 + 4 \cdot 2$):

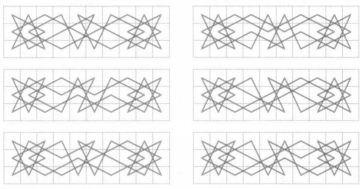

The first of these is Bergholt's original solution shown earlier; he subsequently, on 24 August 1917, found the one directly below it [2]. The two examples in the second line are in fact obtainable from those on the first line by flipping the moves on the left half of the board, top-to-bottom.

Let's try therefore to figure out exactly how many symmetric tours are possible. The necessary information is, in fact, already present in K, once we figure out how to access it.

First let's review the possibilities for symmetry in closed knight's tours, as presented for example in [7] or [9]. When specialized to $3 \times n$ boards, the theory tells us that three kinds of symmetry can occur: (A) reflection about a vertical axis; (B) rotation by 180°, causing the tour to reverse its direction; and (E) rotation by 180°, causing the tour to retain its direction. For convenience we'll call them Axial, Bergholtian, and Eulerian. Types (A) and (E) are possible only if $n/2$ is odd.

The closed states of K tell us the essential facts about "who is connected to whom" after we've made a partial tour covering k columns of the board. Most of those states are incompatible with any of the three symmetries, when we try to interface them with their mirror image or with their 180° rotation.

Axial symmetry, for example, requires the cells that we've called 1 through 6 to meet their reflected counterparts $1'$ through $6'$ in the center of the board, in the following mirrorlike pattern:

$$
\begin{array}{cccc}
4 & 1 & 1' & 4' \\
5 & 2 & 2' & 5' \\
6 & 3 & 3' & 6'
\end{array}
$$

Consider a more-or-less random closed state, say 6432510. It says that there have been knight moves that connect 1 with 6 and 2 with 4, while leaving 3 and 5 untouched; the mirror image will therefore connect $1'$ with $6'$ and $2'$ with $4'$, while leaving $3'$ and $5'$ untouched. Since 3 is untouched we will need the future knight moves from $1'$ to 3 and $5'$ to 3. By symmetry we'll then have $3'$ to 1 and $3'$ to 5 as well. Since 5 was untouched, the move from $1'$ to 5 is forced too; but that's impossible, because $1'$ is already covered.

On the other hand the somewhat similar state 6530210 does allow us to attain type (A) symmetry: Previous knight moves connect 1 with 6, connect 2 with 5, leave 3 untouched, and cover 4. The mirror moves will connect $1'$ with $6'$, connect $2'$ with $5'$, leave $3'$ untouched, and cover $4'$. A full tour is obtained if we now supply additional moves from $1'$ to 3, $5'$ to 3, $2'$ to 6, $3'$ to 1, $3'$ to 5, and $6'$ to 2.

That same state leads to Bergholtian symmetry as well, using the picture

$$
\begin{array}{cccc}
4 & 1 & 3' & 6' \\
5 & 2 & 2' & 5' \\
6 & 3 & 1' & 4'
\end{array}
$$

in this case the necessary and sufficient hookups are $3'$ to 3, $5'$ to 3, $2'$ to 6, $1'$ to 1, $3'$ to 5, and $6'$ to 2.

Similar analysis shows that just 23 of the 167 closed states support symmetry. They fall into three categories,

$$S_1 = \{0050300, 2143500, 2160530, 4321500, 5000100, 6320510\};$$

$$S_2 = \{1320650, 1325400, 1543200, 1560230,$$
$$2130650, 2135400, 3010000, 4531200, 6530210\};$$

$$S_3 = \{1243650, 1265430, 2143000, 2160030,$$
$$4231650, 4321000, 6235410, 6320010\}.$$

Axial symmetry comes from S_1 and S_2; Bergholtian symmetry comes from S_2 and S_3; Eulerian symmetry is rarer, it comes only from S_1. The states of S_1 and S_2 belong to class C_1, so we reach them only when k is odd, as required for symmetry types (A) and (E). The states of S_3 belong to class C_0, so we reach them only when k is even. (When state α belongs to S_j, so does its dual, α'; the state 3010000 in S_2 is self-dual.)

Let $A_c(z)$, $B_c(z)$, and $E_c(z)$ be the generating functions for the number of ways to complete half of a knight's tour that has symmetry of types (A), (B), or (E), respectively. Then

$$A_c(z) = z \sum_{\alpha \in S_1 \cup S_2} G(\sigma_c, \alpha) = 4z^5 + 24z^7 + 276z^9 + O(z^{11});$$

$$B_c(z) = z \sum_{\alpha \in S_2 \cup S_3} G(\sigma_c, \alpha) = 4z^5 + 8z^7 + 48z^8 + 152z^9 + 352z^{10} + O(z^{11});$$

$$E_c(z) = z \sum_{\alpha \in S_1} G(\sigma_c, \alpha) = 16z^7 + 124z^9 + O(z^{11}).$$

The enumeration of symmetric closed tours will be complete if we just compute the generating functions $G(\sigma_c, \alpha)$ for the 23 special states α.

Our calculations above were designed to compute the generating functions $G(\alpha) = G(\alpha, \tau)$ for paths from α to the sink; unfortunately those functions aren't what we need here. Our new problem counts paths *to* α from a *source*, so the paths should go the other way. The same methods apply however, when all arcs of K are reversed, except that the reduced multidigraph turns out to be somewhat larger in this case than it was before. The denominator, $P(z^2)$, remains the same, because the determinant of a matrix doesn't change when we transpose the matrix.

Thus we obtain three magic polynomials

$$\begin{aligned}
a_c(z) = {} & 4z^5 - 124z^9 + 212z^{11} + 1248z^{13} - 5120z^{15} - 4928z^{17} \\
& + 41280z^{19} + 22224z^{21} - 140608z^{23} - 151680z^{25} + 189952z^{27} \\
& + 413056z^{29} - 50432z^{31} - 121344z^{33} - 141312z^{35} - 337920z^{37} \\
& + 49152z^{39} + 163840z^{41} + 65536z^{43},
\end{aligned}$$

$$\begin{aligned}
b_c(z) = {} & 4z^5 - 16z^7 + 48z^8 - 152z^9 + 64z^{10} + 576z^{11} - 1432z^{12} \\
& + 1584z^{13} - 672z^{14} - 5816z^{15} + 15792z^{16} - 2928z^{17} \\
& - 6864z^{18} + 14832z^{19} - 65232z^{20} - 23584z^{21} + 79776z^{22} \\
& + 70944z^{23} + 95936z^{24} + 71552z^{25} - 286848z^{26} - 395648z^{27} \\
& - 31104z^{28} - 22016z^{29} + 362752z^{30} + 538880z^{31} + 156160z^{32} \\
& + 107520z^{33} + 88576z^{34} - 96256z^{35} - 225280z^{36} - 249856z^{37} \\
& - 454656z^{38} - 311296z^{39} + 196608z^{40} + 294912z^{41} + 65536z^{42},
\end{aligned}$$

$$\begin{aligned}
e_c(z) = {} & 16z^7 + 28z^9 - 364z^{11} - 336z^{13} + 696z^{15} - 2000z^{17} \\
& + 26448z^{19} + 45808z^{21} - 211552z^{23} - 223232z^{25} + 585600z^{27} \\
& + 435072z^{29} - 589312z^{31} - 228864z^{33} - 45056z^{35} - 88064z^{37} \\
& + 360448z^{39} - 131072z^{41} + 65536z^{43},
\end{aligned}$$

where $A_c(z) = a_c(z)/P(z^2)$, $B_c(z) = b_c(z)/P(z^2)$, $E_c(z) = e_c(z)/P(z^2)$.

Enumeration of Open Tours

The 220×220 adjacency matrix for $\widehat{K}$ has the somewhat sparse form

$$\widehat{A} = \begin{array}{|c|c|c|c|c|c|c|}
\hline
0 & C & F_0 & 0 & B_1 & X_0 & X_1 \\
\hline
\tilde{C} & 0 & F_1 & B_2 & 0 & X_2 & 0 \\
\hline
0 & 0 & F & 0 & 0 & \tilde{F}_0 & \tilde{F}_1 \\
\hline
0 & 0 & 0 & 0 & B & 0 & \tilde{B}_1 \\
\hline
0 & 0 & 0 & \tilde{B} & 0 & \tilde{B}_2 & 0 \\
\hline
0 & 0 & 0 & 0 & 0 & 0 & C \\
\hline
0 & 0 & 0 & 0 & 0 & \tilde{C} & 0 \\
\hline
\end{array}.$$

We've seen how to find the generating functions $G(\alpha)$ for the "C" part of this matrix, at the lower right corner; each of them has the form $g(\alpha)/P(z^2)$, where $g(\alpha) = g(\alpha, z)$ is a polynomial in z.

The "B" part of this matrix leads, similarly, to generating functions $G(\alpha)$ of the form $g(\alpha)/Q(z^2)$ for superstates α of class B, where

$$Q(z) = 1 - 4z - 26z^2 + 4z^3 - 43z^4 - 116z^5 + 888z^6 + 1224z^7$$
$$+ 10292z^8 + 6052z^9 - 7088z^{10} + 111280z^{11} - 16192z^{12}$$
$$- 204080z^{13} + 407232z^{14} - 681472z^{15} + 66432z^{16}$$
$$- 699392z^{17} - 943104z^{18} - 126976z^{19} + 98304z^{20}.$$

This polynomial Q is based on the submatrices B and $\tilde{B}$, which govern the interactions between superstates of classes B_0 and B_1, just as P was based on the analogous submatrices C and $\tilde{C}$ for superstates of classes C_0 and C_1. The numerators $g(\alpha)$ in this case are not, however, simply polynomials in z; they have the form

$$g(\alpha) = \sum_{\beta} g_{\alpha\beta} G(\beta), \qquad \text{summed over all } \beta \text{ of class C.}$$

Here the coefficients $g_{\alpha\beta}$ are polynomials in z that depend on the submatrices $\tilde{B}_1$ and $\tilde{B}_2$, which govern the transitions from B superstates to C superstates. We've already determined the generating functions $G(\beta)$ for the C superstates β; so we obtain $G(\alpha)$ for each B superstate α by plugging in the known values $G(\beta)$, yielding a rational function with denominator $P(z^2)Q(z^2)$.

The "F" part of $\widehat{A}$ is similar, but more complex because it's not bipartite. When superstate α has class $\mathtt{F}$, its generating function $G(\alpha)$ has the form $g(\alpha)/R(z)$, where $R(z)$ comes from the 58×58 submatrix F:

$$
\begin{aligned}
R(z) = {} & 1 - 3z - 9z^3 - 14z^4 + 61z^5 + 110z^6 + 61z^7 - 35z^8 \\
& - 498z^9 - 1262z^{10} - 356z^{11} + 3864z^{12} + 3788z^{13} - 6008z^{14} \\
& - 2472z^{15} - 7532z^{16} - 17956z^{17} + 17732z^{18} + 36088z^{19} \\
& - 35176z^{20} + 2256z^{21} + 154624z^{22} + 109008z^{23} + 73376z^{24} \\
& + 71440z^{25} - 104336z^{26} - 762592z^{27} - 277728z^{28} - 123008z^{29} \\
& - 573760z^{30} - 771456z^{31} + 221568z^{32} + 122368z^{33} - 1205760z^{34} \\
& + 1966592z^{35} + 714752z^{36} - 2555904z^{37} - 412672z^{38} + 1376256z^{39} \\
& - 272384z^{40} - 294912z^{41} + 1781760z^{42} + 860160z^{43} + 516096z^{44} \\
& + 1081344z^{45} - 65536z^{46} - 262144z^{47} + 131072z^{48}.
\end{aligned}
$$

Again $g(\alpha) = \sum_\beta g_{\alpha\beta} G(\beta)$, summed over all β of class $\mathtt{C}$, but with polynomial coefficients $g_{\alpha\beta}$ this time coming from submatrices $\tilde{F}_0$ and $\tilde{F}_1$. Thus the denominator for the rational generating functions $G(\alpha)$ is $P(z^2)R(z)$, when α is an $\mathtt{F}$ state.

Finally we come to the top rows of matrix $\widehat{A}$, which correspond to paths from states of class $\mathtt{O}$. The submatrices C and $\tilde{C}$ for $\mathtt{O}$-to-$\mathtt{O}$ transitions are the same as those for $\mathtt{C}$-to-$\mathtt{C}$ transitions; hence the factor $1/P(z^2)$ that corresponds to cycles between $\mathtt{C}$ states arises also for cycles between $\mathtt{O}$ states. We conclude that the generating function for any $\mathtt{O}$ state α has the form $\sum_\beta g_{\alpha\beta} G(\beta)/P(z^2)$, summed over all superstates β of classes $\mathtt{F}$, $\mathtt{B}$, and $\mathtt{C}$, for which we already know $G(\beta)$.

Let's divide all open knight's tours into three main categories:

- Type X have both endpoints in the same column.
- Type F have endpoints that match the nearest corner cells.
- Type B have endpoints that don't match the nearest corner cells.

(Types F and B have endpoints in different columns. Cells "match" if they are both even or both odd — that is, if they have the same "color" on a chessboard.) For example, the 3×4 tours at the beginning of this chapter have types B, X, F, respectively. These three basic types are just the same as the four considered earlier with respect to parity, except that the tours that we previously called types (1) and (2) are both just type X, but distinguished by whether the board has an even or odd number of columns. Our previous types (3) and (4) are now called F and B, respectively. The corner cells of boards with an even number of columns are even at the left and odd at the right; otherwise all four corner cells are even.

We obtain all open tours of type X by zeroing out all of the F and B submatrices of the big matrix $\widehat{A}$. The generating function for all X tours is therefore $x_o(z)/P(z^2)^2 = 4z^4 + 80z^8 + O(z^9)$, for some polynomial $x_o(z)$. Similarly, we get all open tours of type F by zeroing out the B and X submatrices, obtaining a generating function $f_o(z)/(P(z^2)R(z)) = 2z^4 + 52z^7 + 224z^8 + O(z^9)$ for another appropriate polynomial $f_o(z)$; and the generating function $b_o(z^2)/(P(z^2)Q(z^2)) = 2z^4 + 92z^8 + O(z^{10})$ for open tours of type B results when the F and X submatrices are zeroed. The sum of all three generating functions is $t_o(z)/(P(z^2)^2Q(z^2)R(z)) = 8z^4 + 52z^7 + 396z^8 + O(z^9)$, the generating function for open tours of all three kinds. This function solves the enumeration problem that we set out to tackle, because it enumerates the diagrams of open tours on $3 \times n$ boards for all n.

There's no point in wasting paper by listing the polynomials $x_o(z)$, $f_o(z)$, $b_o(z)$, and $t_o(z)$ here, although curious readers can find them in [10]. Let us, however, go on to enumerate the *symmetrical* open tours, so that we can determine exactly how many of the knight's tour diagrams are essentially distinct.

Symmetrical open tours exist of all three types X, F, and B. We've seen the smallest examples for F and B, found by Euler, on the 3×4 board; the smallest examples for type X appear on the 3×9:

In general, the only possibility for symmetry of an open tour is analogous to Bergholtian symmetry of a closed tour, where rotation by 180° yields the same diagram but causes the tour to run backwards. We can, in fact, obtain a symmetric open tour by removing either of the edges in the "X" that appears at the middle of any closed tour with Bergholtian symmetry; this open tour will be of type F if $n/2$ is odd, type B if $n/2$ is even. For example, here are the 3×10 open tours of this type:

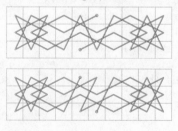 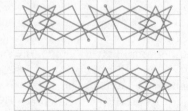

To enumerate open tours that are symmetrical on $3 \times n$ boards, when n is even, we can therefore proceed as we did for Bergholtian symmetry of closed tours, by characterizing the states that will support $180°$ rotation after $n/2$ steps. Euler's first tour, for example, reaches state 6243∞15 after two steps; and any $n/2$-step path from σ_o to 6243∞15 in K will yield a symmetric $3 \times n$ open tour if the next transition is *131*. This open tour will be of type B, and n will be a multiple of 4, because 6243∞15 belongs to class B_0.

The open tours that are symmetrical on $3 \times n$ boards for odd values of n can be characterized in essentially the same way, but the configuration of cells near the center now looks like this after $(n-1)/2$ steps:

$$\begin{array}{ccccc} 4 & 1 & @ & 3' & 6' \\ 5 & 2 & 0{=}0' & 2' & 5' \\ 6 & 3 & @' & 1' & 4' \end{array}$$

Consider, for instance, state 3412∞05, which means that the knight moves within the first $(n-1)/2$ columns connect 1 with 3, 2 with 4, and 5 with ∞, while covering 6. Let's continue by connecting 0 with 4 (and also with $4'$, since $0 = 0'$); that's the only way to connect 4 to the future. We now must choose two neighbors of @, and the corresponding two neighbors of @'; and we'll also have to move from either $1'$ or $3'$ to 2, hence from $2'$ to either 1 or 3. Say we move $2'$ to 1; then @ must move to 3 and also to either 5 or $5'$. Both of those setups work. So do the alternatives with $2'$ to 3, @ to $1'$, and @ to either 5 or $5'$. Thus there are four different ways to get a symmetric $3 \times n$ tour, when state 3412∞05 has been reached after the first $(n-1)/2$ columns.

State 600001∞ is another instructive case. To make a symmetric $3 \times n$ tour after $(n-1)/2$ steps have led to this state, we'll need to connect 0 to 6 and $6'$, @' to 1 and ∞, @ to $1'$ and ∞'. The resulting tour is of type X. Further study of this situation shows that state 600001∞ and its dual, 004300∞, can arise only when the the self-dual state 604351∞ is followed by transition *133* or *332*. Furthermore, every closed tour ends when the self-dual state 6043510 goes to 0000000 with transition *333*. Therefore *every closed tour of the $3 \times n$ board leads to two open tours of type X on the $3 \times (2n{+}1)$ board*, one that passes through state 600001∞ and another that passes through state 004300∞. Applying this construction to Bergholt's first 3×10 tour yields an open tour with reflective symmetry in each half, in addition to overall rotational symmetry:

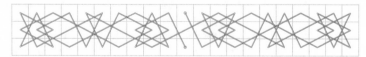

TABLE 1. States after $3 \times n/2$ that yield symmetry on $3 \times n$

			Class F			
00ω0003	05302ω6	053ω204	0ω30652	0ω35402	12435ω6	126ω534
15002ω6	150ω204	1ω00652	1ω05402	2143ω05*	21503ω6	215ω304
2160ω35*	21ω0653	21ω5403	35102ω6*	351ω204*	3ω10652*	3ω15402*
42315ω6	4321ω05*	45ω1203	4ω51302	53201ω6	532ω104	5ω43102
5ω60132	623ω514	6320ω15*	65ω0213	6ω50312	ω000001	ω320651
ω325401	ω543201	ω560231				

			Class B$_0$			
02354ω6	023ω654	03200ω6	032ω004	0ω43002	0ω60032	12054ω6
120ω654	21000ω6	210ω004	32154ω6*	321ω654*	42ω1653	4ω01002
52431ω6	6243ω15*	625ω314	62ω5413	6ω00012	ω243651	ω265431

			Class B$_1$			
0030ω05	1000ω05	13205ω6	132ω504	1ω43502	1ω60532	21305ω6
213ω504	3010ω05*	4ω31502	50ω0103	6ω30512	ω050301	

$* = $ times 2

TABLE 2. States after $3 \times (n-1)/2$ that yield symmetry on $3 \times n$

			Class 0$_0$			
000065ω*	000540ω*	004300ω	006003ω	043200ω	045230ω*	054320ω*
056023ω*	056023ω	063002ω	065032ω*	124300ω	126003ω	140200ω
160002ω	214300ω	216003ω	341200ω*	361002ω*	400100ω	423100ω
425130ω*	432100ω	450120ω*	524310ω*	526013ω*	540210ω*	560012ω*
600001ω	623001ω	625031ω*	632001ω	650021ω*		

			Class F			
0043ω05*	0060ω35*	00ω0653*	00ω5403*	0432ω05*	0630ω25*	0ω30652*
0ω35402*	1243ω05*	1260ω35*	12ω0653*	12ω5403*	1402ω05*	14ω2003
1600ω25*	16ω0023	1ω00652*	1ω05402*	1ω43002	1ω60032	2143ω05*
2160ω35*	21ω0653*	21ω5403*	3412ω05**	3610ω25**	3ω10652**	3ω15402**
4001ω05*	40ω1003	4231ω05*	4321ω05*	45ω1203**	4ω31002	4ω51302*
54ω2103*	56ω0123*	5ω43102*	5ω60132*	6000ω15*	60ω0013	6230ω15*
6320ω15*	65ω0213**	6ω30012	6ω50312*	ω000651*	ω005401*	ω043001
ω060031	ω230651*	ω235401*	ω320651*	ω325401*	ω432001	ω452301*
ω543201**	ω560231**	ω630021	ω650321*			

$* = $ times 2; $** = $ times 4

A surprisingly large number of states can be extended after n columns to form symmetric open tours that have either $2n$ columns or $2n + 1$ columns or both. In fact, more than $1/4$ of the non-C states of K — 143 out of 545 — have this extension property. They're listed in Tables 1 and/or 2, together with the appropriate multiplicative factors that should be used when counting symmetric diagrams of various kinds. From that information we can compute the relevant generating functions for symmetric open tours:

$$X_s(z) = zx_s(z^4)/P(z^4) = 4z^9 + 16z^{13} + 264z^{17} + O(z^{21}) \qquad \text{for type X;}$$
$$F_s(z) = f_s(z)/(P(z^4)R(z^2)) = 2z^4 + 4z^7 + 12z^8 + O(z^9) \qquad \text{for type F;}$$
$$B_s(z) = b_s(z^2)/(P(z^4)Q(z^4)) = 2z^4 + 8z^8 + 16z^{10} + O(z^{12}) \quad \text{for type B.}$$

Again the polynomials x_s, f_s, b_s can be found in [10].

Asymptotic Growth

The number of $3 \times n$ tours is huge even when n is fairly small, as we've seen for the case $n = 100$. And the form of the generating functions allows us to pin down the exact rate of growth for each of the species of tours that we've studied, because the coefficient of z^n in $1/f(z)$ has exponential growth rate ρ^n when $1/\rho$ is the smallest positive root of $f(1/\rho) = 0$, if f is a polynomial.

The relevant values of ρ for the three polynomials $P(z^2)$, $Q(z^2)$, and $R(z)$ are respectively

$$\rho(P) = 3.11949\,04567\,55102\,15858\,14810\,12447\,09095\,14449+;$$
$$\rho(Q) = 2.73629\,97867\,23484\,49801\,18887\,83106\,50428\,06057+;$$
$$\rho(R) = 3.45059\,21117\,50198\,79034\,91949\,64004\,51254\,67975+.$$

(All three polynomials happen to be irreducible over the rational numbers, so their roots are simple.) We may conclude that

- Open tours of type F predominate, with approximately $c_F\rho(R)^n$ tours when n is large, where $c_F \approx 0.027892741$.
- There are approximately $0.000169n\rho(P)^n$ and $0.00144n\rho(P)^n$ open tours of the respective types X and B, when n is even, and approximately $0.0000526n\rho(P)^n$ of type X when n is odd.
- Approximately $0.0001899\rho(P)^n$ closed tours are possible, when n is a large even number.

Symmetric tours are negligible by comparison, since there are only $O(\rho(R)^{n/2})$ of them.

When an open tour has endpoints in columns j and k, where $1 \le j \le k \le n$, let $m = k - j$. The number of open tours when m and

TABLE 3. Exact counts for $3 \times n$ knight's tours of various kinds

$n =$	4	5	6	7	8	9	10	11	12	13	14	15	16	17	18	19	20
$C[n] =$	0	0	0	0	0	0	16	0	176	0	1536	0	15424	0	147728	0	148416
$A_c[n] =$	0	0	0	0	0	0	4	0	0	0	24	0	0	0	276	0	0
$B_c[n] =$	0	0	0	0	0	0	4	0	0	0	8	0	48	0	152	0	352
$E_c[n] =$	0	0	0	0	0	0	0	0	0	0	16	0	0	0	124	0	0
$C_s[n] =$	0	0	0	0	0	0	4	0	0	0	24	0	24	0	276	0	176
$G_c[n] =$	0	0	0	0	0	0	6	0	44	0	396	0	3868	0	37070	0	362192
$X_o[n] =$	4	0	0	0	80	40	368	352	5296	3744	48656	40208	523808	415488	5270976	4333504	54215264
$F_o[n] =$	2	0	0	52	224	520	1616	10320	37024	125120	441200	1798576	6327472	22985504	81178008	301420176	1057619944
$B_o[n] =$	2	0	0	0	92	0	1064	0	14928	0	156416	0	1785600	0	19416704	0	211014544
$T[n] =$	8	0	0	52	396	560	3048	10672	57248	128864	646272	1838784	8636880	23400992	105865688	305753680	1322849752
$X_s[n] =$	0	0	0	0	0	4	0	0	0	16	0	0	0	264	0	0	0
$F_s[n] =$	2	0	0	4	12	20	28	120	104	304	384	1304	1680	4936	5908	18304	21412
$B_s[n] =$	2	0	0	0	8	0	16	0	48	0	200	0	616	0	1832	0	6008
$T_s[n] =$	2	0	0	2	10	12	22	60	76	160	292	652	1148	2600	3870	9152	13710
$G_o[n] =$	3	0	0	14	104	146	773	2698	14350	32296	161714	460022	2159794	5851548	26468357	7642996	330719293

$n - m$ are both large is approximately proportional to $\rho(P)^{n-m}\rho(R)^m$ for type F, $\rho(P)^{n-m}\rho(Q)^m$ for type B. Since $\rho(Q) < \rho(P) < \rho(R)$ we may conclude that most of the open F tours have endpoints near the left and right edges of the board, but most of the open B tours have endpoints near each other.

Summary

We have derived formulas that enable us to count the exact number of solutions to 15 different flavors of the $3 \times n$ knight's tour problem:

$C[n]$ = closed tour diagrams; requires $n \bmod 2 = 0$.
$A_c[n]$ = closed tour diagrams with left-right symmetry; $n \bmod 4 = 2$.
$B_c[n]$ = closed tour diagrams with Bergholtian symmetry; $n \bmod 2 = 0$.
$E_c[n]$ = closed tour diagrams with $180°$ symmetry; $n \bmod 4 = 2$.
$C_s[n] = (A_c[n] + B_c[n] + E_c[n])/2$: distinct symmetric closed tours.
$G_c[n] = C[n]/4 + C_s[n]/2$: geometrically distinct closed tours.

$X_o[n]$ = open tour diagrams of type X.
$F_o[n]$ = open tour diagrams of type F.
$B_o[n]$ = open tour diagrams of type B; $n \bmod 2 = 0$.
$T[n] = X_o[n] + F_o[n] + B_o[n]$: open tour diagrams.
$X_s[n]$ = symmetric open tour diagrams of type X; $n \bmod 4 = 1$.
$F_s[n]$ = symmetric open tour diagrams of type F.
$B_s[n]$ = symmetric open tour diagrams of type B; $n \bmod 2 = 0$.
$T_s[n] = (X_s[n] + F_s[n] + B_s[n])/2$: distinct symmetric open tours.
$G_o[n] = T[n]/4 + T_s[n]/2$: geometrically distinct open tours.

Values of these quantities for small n appear in Table 3; further values can be found in [10]. In each case we have obtained rational generating functions, from which the enumeration can be extended to arbitrarily large n without great difficulty.

References

[1] Ernest Bergholt, letter to the editor, *British Chess Magazine* **38** (1918), 74.

[2] Ernest Bergholt, "Memoranda on the knight's tour," edited by G. P. Jelliss from original notes written by Bergholt and sent to H. J. R. Murray in 1916 and 1917, *The Games and Puzzles Journal* **2**, 13 (28 May 1996), 213–217; **2**, 14 (16 December 1996), 231–237, 244.

[3] Noam D. Elkies and Richard P. Stanley, "The mathematical knight," *The Mathematical Intelligencer* **25**, 1 (Winter 2003), 22–34.

[4] L. Euler, "Solution d'une question curieuse qui ne paroit soumise à aucune analyse," *Mémoires de l'Académie Royale des Sciences et Belles-Lettres* (Berlin, 1759), 310–337.

[5] George Jelliss, "Open knight's tours of three-rank boards," *Knight's Tour Notes*, note 3a (21 October 2000). Published online at http://www.ktn.freeuk.com/3a.htm (accessed April 2010).

[6] George Jelliss, "Closed knight's tours of three-rank boards," *Knight's Tour Notes*, note 3b (21 October 2000). Published online at http://www.ktn.freeuk.com/3b.htm (accessed April 2010).

[7] George Jelliss, "Symmetry in knight's tours," *Knight's Tour Notes* (2001). Published online at http://www.ktn.freeuk.com/sa.html (accessed April 2010).

[8] Donald E. Knuth, *Sorting and Searching*, Volume 3 of *The Art of Computer Programming* (Reading, Massachusetts: Addison–Wesley, 1973).

[9] Donald E. Knuth, "Celtic knight's tours," Chapter 41 of the present volume.

[10] Neil J. A. Sloane, *The On-Line Encyclopedia of Integer Sequences*, http://www.research.att.com/~njas/sequences; see sequences A070030, A169696, and A169764–A169777 [accessed June 2010].

Addendum

As mentioned above, Noam Elkies and I had already enumerated the Hamiltonian *cycles* of S_n several years ago. In fact, we both did it during early April of 1994, although we were completely unaware of each other's interest in the problem until we happened to meet at the Mathematical Sciences Research Institute a short time later(!). Noam beat me by a couple of weeks. He subsequently sent me his computer program, which used a state-transition scheme similar to the one described above. But actually he had a better idea: Instead of using a table of six mates — this was the case of closed tours, where ω does not arise — he got by with only five, which he aptly called a "quincunx." Indeed, my transition calculation

$$\begin{array}{ccccc} 41 & 741 & 041 & 41 \\ 52 & \mapsto \ 852 & \to \ 052 & \mapsto \ 52 \\ 63 & 963 & 063 & 63 \end{array}$$

with nine intermediate mates can be reduced via quincunxes to

$$\begin{array}{ccccc} 2 & 42 & 02 & 2 \\ 531 & \mapsto \ 7531 & \to \ 0531 & \mapsto \ 531, \\ 6 & 86 & 06 & 6 \end{array}$$

with only eight. More importantly, I see now that his scheme makes it easy to compute the right-to-left reflection of any transition; with my scheme I need to know two *successive* transitions $q \to q' \to q''$ before I can reflect the transition $q \to q'$.

Interested readers will probably find it instructive to enumerate open $3 \times n$ tours with Elkies's quincunx strategy, by introducing the vertex ∞ as done above.

Hopefully the results obtained with both methods will agree, as they did in the much simpler closed-tour problem. If not ..., well, we'll learn some more about debugging.

Chapter 43

Leaper Graphs

*[Originally published in The Mathematical Gazette **78** (1994), 274–297.]*

An $\{r, s\}$-leaper [15, page 130; 3, page 30; 16] is a generalized knight that can jump from (x, y) to $(x \pm r, y \pm s)$ or $(x \pm s, y \pm r)$ on a rectangular grid. The graph of an $\{r, s\}$-leaper on an $m \times n$ board is the set of mn vertices (x, y) for $0 \le x < m$ and $0 \le y < n$, with an edge between vertices that are one $\{r, s\}$-leaper move apart. We call x the *rank* and y the *file* of board position (x, y). George P. Jelliss [9, 10] raised several interesting questions about these graphs, and established some of their fundamental properties. The purpose of this paper is to characterize when the graphs are connected, for arbitrary r and s, and to determine the smallest boards with Hamiltonian cycles when $s = r + 1$ or $r = 1$.

Theorem 1. *The graph of an $\{r, s\}$-leaper on an $m \times n$ board, when $2 \le m \le n$ and $1 \le r \le s$, is connected if and only if the following three conditions hold: (i) $r + s$ is relatively prime to $r - s$; (ii) $n \ge 2s$; (iii) $m \ge r + s$.*

Proof. Condition (i) is necessary because any common divisor d of $r+s$ and $r - s$ will be a divisor of $x + y$ for any vertex (x, y) reachable from $(0, 0)$; any leaper move changes the sum of coordinates by $\pm(r + s)$ or $\pm(r - s)$. If $d > 1$, vertex $(0, 1)$ would therefore be disconnected from vertex $(0, 0)$.

Condition (ii) is necessary because $m \le n < 2s$ would imply that the "middle" point $(\lfloor m/2 \rfloor, \lfloor n/2 \rfloor)$ is isolated: We would have $\lfloor m/2 \rfloor - s < 0$, $\lfloor m/2 \rfloor + s \ge m$, $\lfloor n/2 \rfloor - s < 0$, and $\lfloor n/2 \rfloor + s \ge n$, leaving no place to leap from the middle.

To show that condition (iii) is necessary we show first that the $\{r, s\}$-leaper graph on the infinite board with $m = r + s - 1$ and $n = \infty$ has no path from $(0, 0)$ to $(0, 1)$. For this purpose we construct a special path through special points (x_k, y_k) as follows:

$$(x_0, y_0) = (r - 1, 0)\,;$$

$$(x_{k+1}, y_{k+1}) = \begin{cases} (x_k + r, y_k + s)\,, & \text{if } x_k < s - 1\,; \\ (x_k - s, y_k + r)\,, & \text{if } x_k \geq s\,. \end{cases}$$

The path terminates when $x_k = s - 1$. It is not difficult to see that termination will occur when $k = r + s - 2$, because the sequence $x_0, x_1, \ldots$ runs first through all values $\{0, 1, \ldots, r + s - 2\}$ that are congruent to -1 modulo r, then all values congruent to $-1 - s$, then all values congruent to $-1 - 2s$, etc. Since s is relatively prime to r, all residues will occur before we finally reach $-1 - (r - 1)s$ modulo r, which is the class of values congruent to $s - 1$. Now if (x, y) is any point reachable from $(r - 1, 0)$ on this infinite graph, there is a unique value of k such that $x = x_k$. And the difference $y - y_k$ must be an even number, because all $\{r, s\}$-leaper moves preserve this condition. Therefore the point $(x, y+1)$ is not reachable from $(r - 1, 0)$.

Condition (iii) is therefore necessary. Vertex $(0, 1)$ will surely be disconnected from $(0, 0)$ on any $m \times n$ board with $m < r + s$ if it is disconnected from $(0, 0)$ on a $(r + s - 1) \times \infty$ board.

Finally we show that conditions (i), (ii), and (iii) are in fact sufficient for connectivity. We need only prove that the graph is connected when $m = r + s$ and $n = 2s$, because the connectivity of an $m \times n$ board obviously implies connectivity for $(m + 1) \times n$ and $m \times (n + 1)$ boards when $m > 1$. The proof is somewhat delicate, because the graph is, in some sense, "just barely" connected.

Let $m = r + s$ and $n = 2s$, and let t be any number in the range $0 \leq t < n$. Define a path on the $m \times n$ board by the rules

$$(x_0, y_0) = (0, t)\,;$$

$$(x_{k+1}, y_{k+1}) = \begin{cases} (x_k + r, y_k \pm s)\,, & \text{if } x_k < s\,; \\ (x_k - s, y_k \pm r)\,, & \text{if } x_k \geq s\,. \end{cases}$$

The sign of $\pm s$ is uniquely determined by the condition $0 \leq y_{k+1} < 2s$; the sign of $\pm r$ may or may not be forced by this condition, and we can use any desired convention when a choice is possible. The path will reach a point (x_k, y_k) of the form $(0, u)$ when $k = r + s$, after doing s moves by $(r, \pm s)$ and r moves by $(-s, \pm r)$. Therefore $(0, u)$ is reachable from $(0, t)$; we want to use this information to establish connectivity of the graph.

Consider first the case $t = 0$; we will choose the signs so that y_k is either 0 or r or s or $r + s$ for all k. This produces a sequence of file numbers $y_k^{(0)}$. Similarly, we can keep y_k in the set $\{0, r, s, r + s\}$

whenever $t = r$, s, or $r + s$; this procedure defines sequences $y_k^{(r)}$, $y_k^{(s)}$, $y_k^{(r+s)}$. Now notice that after k steps we have $x_k = ar - bs$ for some uniquely determined a and b, where $k = a + b$, and the value of y_k depends only on the parity of a and b:

a	b	$y_k^{(0)}$	$y_k^{(r)}$	$y_k^{(s)}$	$y_k^{(r+s)}$
even	even	0	r	s	$r + s$
odd	even	s	$r + s$	0	r
odd	odd	$r + s$	s	r	0
even	odd	r	0	$r + s$	s

After $r + s$ steps we have $x_{r+s} = 0$ and $a = s$, $b = r$. Therefore if r is even and s is odd, we have found paths from $(0, 0)$ to $(0, s)$ and from $(0, s)$ to $(0, 0)$. Combining them into a cycle shows that $(x, 0)$ and (x, s) are reachable from $(0, 0)$ whenever x is even. Similarly, the paths from $(0, r)$ to $(0, r + s)$ and back to $(0, r)$ show that (x, r) and $(x, r + s)$ are reachable from $(0, r)$ whenever x is even. In the other case, when r is odd and s is even, the construction proves that $(x, 0)$ and (x, r) are reachable from $(0, 0)$ whenever x is even, while (x, s) and $(x, r + s)$ are similarly reachable from $(0, s)$. The same argument establishes a more general principle, which can be formulated as follows:

Lemma 1. *Let t be any value such that $0 \le t < t + r < s$. Then (x, t) is reachable from (z, t) on the $(r + s) \times 2s$ board and $(x, t + r)$ is reachable from $(z, t + r)$, whenever $x - z$ is even.*

The proof consists of forming sequences $y_k^{(t)}$, $y_k^{(t+r)}$, $y_k^{(t+s)}$, and $y_k^{(t+r+s)}$ as before.   □

Our next step in proving Theorem 1 is to establish a mild form of connectivity:

Lemma 2. *Every cell on the $(r + s) \times 2s$ board is reachable from some cell in file 0. That is, for all (x, y) there is a z such that (x, y) is connected to $(z, 0)$.*

Let us say that file y is *accessible* if its cells are all reachable from file 0. Let $d = s - r$. To prove that all files are accessible, we will start at file 0 and, whenever file y is accessible, we will increase y by d if $y < r$, or decrease y by r if $y \ge r$. This procedure will prove accessibility for all $y < s$. It will then be obvious that all files $y \ge s$ are accessible.

If $r \le y < s$ and file y is accessible, we can easily show that file $t = y - r$ is accessible by using Lemma 1. For if (x, t) is any cell in file t, there is a path from (x, t) to either $(0, t)$ or $(1, t)$, and we can go in one step from (z, t) to $(z + s, y)$ whenever $z < r$. If $r = z = 1$, we need three steps: $(1, y - 1)$, $(0, y + s - 1)$, $(s, y + s)$, $(s - 1, y)$.

The other case is slightly more complicated. Suppose file y is accessible and $0 \le y < r$. Let $(x, y + d)$ be any cell in file $y + d$. If $x < r$, we can go via $(x + s, y + d + r)$ to $(x + d, y)$ in two steps, and a similar two-step path goes from $(x, y + d)$ to $(x - d, y)$ if $x \ge s$. So the only problematic situation arises when $r \le x < s$. In such a case we can follow a zigzag path

$$(x, y + d), \ (x - r, y + d + s), \ (x + d, y + 2d), \ \ldots, \ \big(x + kd, y + (k{+}1)d\big)$$

until first reaching $y + (k{+}1)d \ge r$. When this occurs, we have $kd \le y + kd < r$, so $x + kd < s + kd < r + s$ is a legitimate rank. Now we can use Lemma 1 with $r + t = y + (k{+}1)d$ to connect $(x + kd, r + t)$ to either $(0, r + t)$ or $(1, r + t)$. And we can take another zigzag path from $(0, r + t)$ back to file y as desired:

$$(0, y + (k{+}1)d), \ (s, y + (k{+}1)d + r), \ (d, y + kd), \ \ldots,$$
$$(kd + s, y + d + r), \ ((k{+}1)d, y).$$

Adding $(1, 0)$ to each point of this path will also connect $\big(1, y + (k{+}1)d\big)$ to file y, unless $kd = r - 1$.

Therefore our proof of Lemma 2 hinges on being able to find a path in the exceptional case $kd = r - 1$. This case can arise only when $y = 0$. Hence we must find a path from $(x, s - 1)$ to file 0, for some odd integer x, whenever the parameters r and s satisfy the special conditions $r = 1 + kd$, $s = 1 + (k{+}1)d$. (Such leaper graphs exist whenever $k \ge 0$ and d is odd.) An examination of small cases reveals a strategy that works in general: The path begins

$$(d, s{-}1), \ (s, 2s{-}1),$$
$$(0, s{-}1{+}d), \ (s, 2d{-}1), \ (d, s{-}1{+}2d), \ \ldots,$$
$$(kd, s{-}1{+}(k{+}1)d) = (z{-}s, 2s{-}2),$$
$$(z, s{-}2{+}d), \ (z{-}s, 2d{-}2), \ (z{-}d, s{-}2{+}2d), \ \ldots,$$
$$(z{-}kd, s{-}2{+}(k{+}1)d) = (s, 2s{-}3),$$

and so on, where $z = r + s - 1$ is the number of the last rank; the idea is to repeat the $(2k+1)$-step staircase subpaths $d - 1$ times, until reaching $(s, 2s - d)$. Since $2s - d = r + s$, point $(s, 2s - d)$ is two easy steps from file 0; the proof of Lemma 2 is complete. □

Lemmas 1 and 2 together show that the graph has at most two connected components, because each vertex is connected either to cell

$(0,0)$ or cell $(1,0)$ of file 0. Furthermore, the construction in the proof of Lemma 2 shows that (x,y) is connected to $(0,0)$ if $x + f(y)$ is even and to $(1,0)$ if $x + f(y)$ is odd, where $f(y)$ is a certain parity function associated with file y. This follows because the proof connects (x,y) to a cell congruent modulo 2 to $(x+d, y+d)$ when we increase y by d, to $(x+s, y-r)$ when we decrease y by r, and to $(x+r, y+s)$ when we increase y by s. Thus we may take $f(y+d) = f(y)+d$, $f(y-r) = f(y)+s$, and $f(y+s) = f(y)+r$.

But the full cycle of changes in y involves exactly r increases by d, and exactly d decreases by r; so we get back to $y = 0$ with a parity value of $rd + sd$, which is odd. Therefore $(0,0)$ is connected to $(1,0)$! The proof of Theorem 1 is complete.   □

The next natural question to ask about leaper graphs is whether or not they are Hamiltonian. Indeed, this is an especially appropriate question, because the whole idea of Hamiltonian cycles first arose in connection with knight's tours—which are Hamiltonian paths of the $\{1,2\}$-leaper graph on an 8×8 board. Knight's tours have fascinated people for more than 1000 years, yet their secrets have not yet been fully unlocked.

Dawson [2] showed that $\{1, 2k\}$-leapers have Hamiltonian paths from corner to corner of a $(2k+1) \times 4k$ board. Therefore the smallest connected graph already has a Hamiltonian path when $r = 1$. However, Hamiltonian *cycles* are more difficult; they require larger boards, of size 3×10 or 5×6 when $k = 1$, or 9×10 when $k = 2$.

Jelliss [10] derived necessary conditions for the existence of Hamiltonian cycles using $\{r, r+1\}$-leapers, and conjectured that the board of smallest area in this special case has size $(2r+1) \times (6r+4)$. He proved his conjecture when $r \leq 3$. The following theorem gives further support to Jelliss's conjecture, because it shows that a board with smallest dimension greater than $2r+1$ must have an area at least $(4r+2)^2$, which exceeds $(2r+1)(6r+4)$.

Theorem 2. *If $r > 2$ and the graph of an $\{r, r+1\}$-leaper on an $m \times n$ board has a Hamiltonian cycle, and if $2r+1 < m \leq n$, then $m \geq 4r+2$.*

Proof. Let $s = r + 1$. All vertices (x,y) with $0 \leq x, y < r$ are adjacent only to $(x+r, y+s)$ and $(x+s, y+r)$. Therefore a Hamiltonian cycle must include both of these edges. Similarly, the edges from (x,y) to $(x-r, y+s)$ and $(x-s, y+r)$ are forced when $m-r \leq x < m$ and $0 \leq y < r$.

Therefore, if $2r+1 < m < 3r+1$, a "snag" [10] occurs at vertex (r,s): Any Hamiltonian cycle must lead from this vertex directly to $(0,0)$, but also to $(2r, 0)$ and $(r + s, 1)$, because $m - r \leq 2r < r + s = 2r + 1 < m$. Only two of these three compulsory moves are possible.

Similarly, if $3r + 1 < m < 4r + 1$, there is a snag at $(2r, s)$. This vertex must connect to $(r - 1, 1)$, $(3r, 0)$, and $(3r + 1, 1)$.

The case $m = 3r + 1$ is impossible if $r > 1$, because vertex $(2r - 1, s)$ must connect to $(r - 2, 1)$, $(3r - 1, 0)$, and $(3r, 1)$.

Suppose finally that $m = 4r + 1$. Vertex $(r - 1, 2)$ has just two neighbors, $(2r - 1, r + 3)$ and $(2r, r + 2)$, because $r > 2$. Similarly, $(3r + 1, 2)$ is adjacent only to $(2r + 1, r + 3)$ and $(2r, r + 2)$. Therefore $(2r, r + 2)$ must not connect to $(3r, 1)$. But now $(3r, 1)$ has only two remaining options, namely $(4r, r + 2)$ and $(2r - 1, r + 1)$. This makes a snag at $(2r - 1, r + 1)$, which must also link to $(r - 1, 0)$ and $(r - 2, 1)$. □

On the other hand, Jelliss's conjecture does turn out to be false for all $r > 3$, because $\{r, r + 1\}$-leapers continue to acquire new problems on narrow boards as r grows:

Theorem 3. *If the graph of an $\{r, r + 1\}$-leaper on a $(2r + 1) \times n$ board has a Hamiltonian cycle, where $r > 3$, then $n \geq r^2 + 5r + 2$ if r is odd, $n \geq r^2 + 6r + 4$ if r is even.*

Proof. Let $s = r + 1$, and suppose first that we have a board of size $(2r + 1) \times \infty$. Certain edges are forced to be present in any Hamiltonian cycle, because some vertices have degree 2. We will see that such edges, in turn, can force other connections.

Each vertex (x, y) has at most four neighbors. If the x coordinate represents vertical position (rank) and the y coordinate represents horizontal position (file) as in matrix notation, two of these neighbors lie to the "left," namely $(x \pm r, y - s)$ and $(x \pm s, y - r)$, and two lie to the "right," $(x \pm r, y + s)$ and $(x \pm s, y + r)$. (If $x \neq r$, there is one choice of sign for $x \pm s$ and $x \pm r$; if $x = r$, neither choice works for $x \pm s$, but both choices are valid for $x \pm r$.)

It will be convenient to use a two-dimensional representation of the files: The notation $[a, b]$ will refer to $as - b$, for $a \geq 1$ and $1 \leq b \leq s$. In terms of this notation, the neighbors of all vertices in file $[a, b]$ belong to files $[a - 1, b]$, $[a - 1, b - 1]$, $[a + 1, b]$, and $[a + 1, b + 1]$. (Appropriate adjustments to these formulas are made when $a = 1$ or $b = 1$ or $b = s$.)

The files are also classified into various types:

Type R: All vertices must link to both right neighbors. (For example, file $[1, s] = 0$ is type R because its vertices have no left neighbors. In fact, file $[1, b]$ is type R for $2 \leq b \leq s$.)

Type R': The middle vertex, in rank r, must link to both right neighbors. (File $[1, 1]$ is type R', because vertex (r, r) has no left neighbors; the other vertices in this file have one neighbor to the left.)

Type L: All vertices must link to both left neighbors. (File $[2, s]$ is type L, because both left neighbors of its vertices are in files of type R. In fact, file $[2, b]$ is type L for $3 \le b \le s$.)

Type L': The middle vertex must link to both left neighbors. (File $[2, 2]$ is type L'.)

Type l: All vertices except the middle must link to at least one left neighbor. (File $[1, 1]$ is type l, because for example vertex $(0, r)$ has a left neighbor in file 0, which is type R.)

Type l': The extreme vertices, in ranks 0 and $2r$, must link to at least one left neighbor. (File $[2, 1] = 2s - 1$ is type l', because $(0, 2s - 1)$ and $(2r, 2s - 1)$ are the only neighbors of (r, r).)

Additional types r and r' also arise when n is finite, because the right boundary has properties like that of the left.

When file $[a, b]$ is type R, its right neighbors $[a+1, b]$ and $[a+1, b+1]$ must be either type L or l. When $[a, b]$ is type R', $[a + 1, b]$ is either L or l'. And when files $[a, b]$ and $[a, b - 1]$ both have type L, file $[a + 1, b]$ must have type R; its left neighbors cannot be used. Such arguments inductively establish the following facts for all $a \le s$:

$[a, b]$ is type R when a is odd, type L when a is even, for $a < b \le s$;

$[a, a]$ is type R' when a is odd, type L' when a is even;

$[a, 1]$ is type l when a is odd and $a < s$;

$[a, a]$ is type l when a is even;

$[a, a - 1]$ is type l' when a is even.

Furthermore $[s + 1, s]$ is type l' when r is even. A file can simultaneously have two non-conflicting types; for example, $[1, 1]$ is both R' and l, while $[2, 2]$ is both L' and l. At the other extreme, files with no forced links have no special type.

To prove the theorem, we will show first that all files having special types when $n = \infty$ must be present when n is finite. Theorem 1 tells us that $n \ge 2s$; we want to prove that $n > s^2$. Suppose $n = ks - d$, where $0 \le d < s$ and $k \le s$. This right boundary introduces complementary constraints; let

$$\overline{[a, b]} = n - 1 - [a, b] = [k - a, d + 1 - b]$$

be the file that corresponds to $[a, b]$ when left and right are interchanged. Then file $\overline{[a, b]}$ has the type we have derived for $[a, b]$ but with the interchange of L and R, l and r. The value of $n = ks - d$ must be chosen so that complementary types do not conflict.

First, k must be even. For if k is odd, file $(k-1)s = [k, s]$ is type R or R'; but it is also file $\overline{[1, d+1]}$, which is type L or L'.

Second, d must be even. For the $\{r, r+1\}$-leaper graphs are always bipartite — each leap links a "black" square with a "red" square, as on a chessboard — and a bipartite graph cannot be Hamiltonian when it has an odd number of vertices.

Third, d cannot be zero. Otherwise file $[k, s]$ is type L or l, while it also is file $\overline{[1, 1]}$, which is type r. Since L is incompatible with r, we must have $k = s$. But then file $\overline{[r, 1]}$ is type r, conflicting with the fact that $\overline{[r, 1]} = [2, s]$ also is type L.

Fourth, we must have $k > d$. Otherwise file $[k-1, k-1]$, which is type R', would link to the nonexistent file $[k, k-1] = n + d - 1 - k > n$.

Fifth, a contradiction arises even when the previous conditions are satisfied, so that k and d are even and $0 < d < k \leq s$. Suppose, for example, that $k = 10$ and $d = 6$. All neighbors of vertices in Hamiltonian cycles are then forced except for certain vertices in 24 files:

$$
\begin{array}{ccccccccccc}
[1,1] & — & [2,2] & — & [3,3] & — & [4,4] & — & [5,5] & — & [6,6] \\
| & & | & & | & & | & & | & & | \\
[2,1] & — & [3,2] & — & [4,3] & — & [5,4] & — & [6,5] & — & [7,6] \\
| & & | & & | & & | & & | & & | \\
[3,1] & — & [4,2] & — & [5,3] & — & [6,4] & — & [7,5] & — & [8,6] \\
| & & | & & | & & | & & | & & | \\
[4,1] & — & [5,2] & — & [6,3] & — & [7,4] & — & [8,5] & — & [9,6]
\end{array}
$$

This follows because all files $[a, b]$ with $a < b$ are type R or L; and all files $\overline{[a, b]}$ with $a < b$ are type L or R. We have $\overline{[a, b]} = [10 - a, 7 - b]$, so the files in the array can also be represented in the dual form

$$
\begin{array}{ccccccccccc}
\overline{[9,6]} & — & \overline{[8,5]} & — & \overline{[7,4]} & — & \overline{[6,3]} & — & \overline{[5,2]} & — & \overline{[4,1]} \\
| & & | & & | & & | & & | & & | \\
\overline{[8,6]} & — & \overline{[7,5]} & — & \overline{[6,4]} & — & \overline{[5,3]} & — & \overline{[4,2]} & — & \overline{[3,1]} \\
| & & | & & | & & | & & | & & | \\
\overline{[7,6]} & — & \overline{[6,5]} & — & \overline{[5,4]} & — & \overline{[4,3]} & — & \overline{[3,2]} & — & \overline{[2,1]} \\
| & & | & & | & & | & & | & & | \\
\overline{[6,6]} & — & \overline{[5,5]} & — & \overline{[4,4]} & — & \overline{[3,3]} & — & \overline{[2,2]} & — & \overline{[1,1]}
\end{array}
$$

All links between files are indicated by horizontal and vertical lines in these arrays.

Let us say that a vertex is even or odd according as it belongs to file $[a, b]$ where a is even or odd. All links go between even vertices and odd vertices. The edges of a Hamiltonian cycle that have not been forced by our arguments so far must therefore touch the same number of even vertices as odd vertices. We will obtain a contradiction by showing that the odd vertices have more unspecified neighbors in the Hamiltonian cycle than the even vertices do.

In our example, the 24 files are classified as follows:

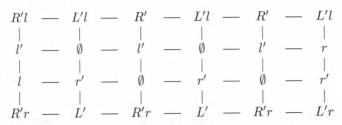

An unconstrained file (indicated here by $\emptyset$) has $2r + 1$ vertices with a total of $4r + 2$ unspecified neighbors. Making it type l or r specifies $2r$ of these; making it type l', r', L', or R' specifies 2. The total number of specified neighbors in odd files is $4(2r) + 6(2)$; the total in even files is $6(2r) + 12(2)$. Therefore the odd vertices have an excess of unspecified neighbors; there aren't enough "slots" available to specify them all.

For general k and d, there are $(k-d)d$ files with partially unspecified vertices. There will be $d/2$ odd files of type R', and $d/2$ of type L'; the same holds for even files. There are $(k-d)/2$ odd files of type l, and $(k-d)/2$ of type r; there are $d/2$ even files of type l, and $d/2$ of type r. There are no odd files of types l' or r'; there are $d/2$ even files of each of those types. Therefore the total number of unspecified vertices in even files will balance the total in odd files if and only if

$$(k - d)(2r) = d(2r + 2).$$

The smallest solution to this equation, when $d > 0$ and $k - d > 0$, is $k - d = r + 1$, $d = r$. But then $k = 2r + 1$ exceeds s.

We know therefore that $n > s^2$. Hence all the files of special types, from $[1, s] = 0$ to $[s + 1, s] = s^2$, are present. Further considerations depend on whether r is even or odd.

Suppose r is even. Then the arguments above can be used also in the case $k = s + 1$, except that when $d = 0$ we find that file $[r, s] = \overline{[3, 1]}$

must be type r as well as type L. Contradictions are obtained exactly as before; hence $n > (s+1)s$.

We cannot have $n = (s+2)s - d$ for $d \in \{3, 5, \ldots, r-1\}$, because file $\overline{[s, s]}$, which is type L', would be the same as file $[3, d+1]$, which is type R. The case $d = 1$ is also impossible, because file $\overline{[s+1, s]}$, which has type r', is file $[2, 2]$, which has type $L'l$; then vertices $(0, 2r)$ and $(2r, 2r)$ would both link to $(r, r-1)$ and $(3r, r+1)$, forming a "short circuit." Therefore $n > (s+2)s$.

We can show that $n \geq (s+3)s$ by letting $n = (s+3)s - d$ and using the parity argument above with $k = s+3$. When $d = 2$ the number of odd files of type l (and of type r) will be one less than before, because $[s, 1]$ is not type l, but this just makes the lack of balance even worse. Furthermore, when $d = 0$ and $r > 4$, file $\overline{[r-1, 1]} = [6, s]$ has conflicting types r and L.

When $r = 4$ and $n = 40 = (s+3)s$, file $\overline{[s+1, s]} = [3, 1]$ has types r' and l. This forces file $[2, 1]$ to be type L', and a loop of length $4r + 2$ is forced from $(r, 2r+1)$ to $(2r, r)$ to $\cdots$ to $(0, r)$ to $(r, 2r+1)$.

And when $n = (s+4)s - d$ for $d \in \{5, 7, \ldots, r-1\}$, file $\overline{[s, s]} = [5, d+1]$ has conflicting types L' and R. In the remaining case $d = 3$, file $\overline{[s+1, s]} = [4, 4]$ is r' and l, forcing a loop from $(r, 3r-1)$ to $(0, 4r)$ to $(r, 5r+1)$ to $(2r, 4r)$ to $(r, 3r-1)$.

Finally, suppose r is odd. We cannot have $n = (s+1)s - d$ for $d \in \{2, 4, \ldots, r-1\}$ because file $\overline{[s, s]} = [2, d+1]$ has conflicting types $R'r$ and L. The case $d = 0$ is also impossible, because file $\overline{[s, s-1]} = [2, 2]$ would be of types r' and $L'l$, forcing a short circuit as before. Next, if $n = (s+2)s - d$, we use the parity argument with $k = s+2$ when $d > 0$. If $d = 0$ and $r > 3$, file $\overline{[r, 1]} = [4, s]$ has conflicting types r and L. And if we try to let $n = (s+3)s - d$ for $d \in \{4, 6, \ldots, r-1\}$, file $\overline{[s, s]} = [4, d+1]$ has conflicting types $R'r$ and L. □

Theorems 2 and 3 have proved that certain leaper graphs fail to be Hamiltonian. Let us now strike a happier note by constructing infinitely many Hamiltonian cycles, on the boards that have the smallest area not ruled out by those theorems.

Theorem 4. *The graph of an $\{r, r+1\}$-leaper on a $(4r+2) \times (4r+2)$ board is Hamiltonian.*

Proof. Let us call the leaper moves NE, NW, EN, ES, SE, SW, WS, and WN, where (N, E, S, W) stand respectively for North, East, South, West, and where the first letter indicates the direction of longest leap. North is the direction of decreasing x; East is the direction of increasing y. Thus NE is a leap from (x, y) to $(x - r - 1, y + r)$; ES goes to $(x + r, y + r + 1)$.

We construct first a highly symmetric set of leaper moves in which every vertex has degree 2, illustrated here in the case $r = 4$ and $s = 5$:

SE/ES	SE/ES	SE/ES	SE/ES	D_1	SW/WS	SW/WS	SW/WS	A_4	$\overline{A}_4$	SE/ES	SE/ES	SE/ES	$\overline{D}_1$	SW/WS	SW/WS	SW/WS	SW/WS
SE/ES	SE/ES	SE/ES	SE/ES	D_2	SW/WS	SW/WS	SW/WS	A_3	$\overline{A}_3$	SE/ES	SE/ES	SE/ES	$\overline{D}_2$	SW/WS	SW/WS	SW/WS	SW/WS
SE/ES	SE/ES	SE/ES	SE/ES	D_3	SW/WS	SW/WS	SW/WS	A_2	$\overline{A}_2$	SE/ES	SE/ES	SE/ES	$\overline{D}_3$	SW/WS	SW/WS	SW/WS	SW/WS
SE/ES	SE/ES	SE/ES	SE/ES	D_4	SW/WS	SW/WS	SW/WS	A_1	$\overline{A}_1$	SE/ES	SE/ES	SE/ES	$\overline{D}_4$	SW/WS	SW/WS	SW/WS	SW/WS
B_1	B_2	B_3	B_4	F_4	E_4	E_3	E_2	E_1	$\overline{E}_1$	$\overline{E}_2$	$\overline{E}_3$	$\overline{E}_4$	$\overline{F}_4$	$\overline{B}_4$	$\overline{B}_3$	$\overline{B}_2$	$\overline{B}_1$
NE/EN	NE/EN	NE/EN	NE/EN	F_3	NW/WN	NW/WN	NW/WN	NW/WN	NE/EN	NE/EN	NE/EN	NE/EN	$\overline{F}_3$	NW/WN	NW/WN	NW/WN	NW/WN
NE/EN	NE/EN	NE/EN	NE/EN	F_2	NW/WN	NW/WN	NW/WN	NW/WN	NE/EN	NE/EN	NE/EN	NE/EN	$\overline{F}_2$	NW/WN	NW/WN	NW/WN	NW/WN
NE/EN	NE/EN	NE/EN	NE/EN	F_1	NW/WN	NW/WN	NW/WN	NW/WN	NE/EN	NE/EN	NE/EN	NE/EN	$\overline{F}_1$	NW/WN	NW/WN	NW/WN	NW/WN
X	NE/EN	NE/EN	NE/EN	C_0	C_1	C_2	C_3	C_4	$\overline{C}_4$	$\overline{C}_3$	$\overline{C}_2$	$\overline{C}_1$	$\overline{C}_0$	NW/WN	NW/WN	NW/WN	X
X'	SE/ES	SE/ES	SE/ES	C'_0	C'_1	C'_2	C'_3	C'_4	$\overline{C}'_4$	$\overline{C}'_3$	$\overline{C}'_2$	$\overline{C}'_1$	$\overline{C}'_0$	SW/WS	SW/WS	SW/WS	X'
SE/ES	SE/ES	SE/ES	SE/ES	F'_1	SW/WS	SW/WS	SW/WS	SW/WS	SE/ES	SE/ES	SE/ES	SE/ES	$\overline{F}'_1$	SW/WS	SW/WS	SW/WS	SW/WS
SE/ES	SE/ES	SE/ES	SE/ES	F'_2	SW/WS	SW/WS	SW/WS	SW/WS	SE/ES	SE/ES	SE/ES	SE/ES	$\overline{F}'_2$	SW/WS	SW/WS	SW/WS	SW/WS
SE/ES	SE/ES	SE/ES	SE/ES	F'_3	SW/WS	SW/WS	SW/WS	SW/WS	SE/ES	SE/ES	SE/ES	SE/ES	$\overline{F}'_3$	SW/WS	SW/WS	SW/WS	SW/WS
B'_1	B'_2	B'_3	B'_4	F'_4	E'_4	E'_3	E'_2	E'_1	$\overline{E}'_1$	$\overline{E}'_2$	$\overline{E}'_3$	$\overline{E}'_4$	$\overline{F}'_4$	$\overline{B}'_4$	$\overline{B}'_3$	$\overline{B}'_2$	$\overline{B}'_1$
NE/EN	NE/EN	NE/EN	NE/EN	D'_4	NW/WN	NW/WN	NW/WN	A'_1	$\overline{A}'_1$	NE/EN	NE/EN	NE/EN	$\overline{D}'_4$	NW/WN	NW/WN	NW/WN	NW/WN
NE/EN	NE/EN	NE/EN	NE/EN	D'_3	NW/WN	NW/WN	NW/WN	A'_2	$\overline{A}'_2$	NE/EN	NE/EN	NE/EN	$\overline{D}'_3$	NW/WN	NW/WN	NW/WN	NW/WN
NE/EN	NE/EN	NE/EN	NE/EN	D'_2	NW/WN	NW/WN	NW/WN	A'_3	$\overline{A}'_3$	NE/EN	NE/EN	NE/EN	$\overline{D}'_2$	NW/WN	NW/WN	NW/WN	NW/WN
NE/EN	NE/EN	NE/EN	NE/EN	D'_1	NW/WN	NW/WN	NW/WN	A'_4	$\overline{A}'_4$	NE/EN	NE/EN	NE/EN	$\overline{D}'_1$	NW/WN	NW/WN	NW/WN	NW/WN

Some vertices have been given names A_j, B_j, etc.; these provide important connecting links. The other, nameless vertices occur in blocks where all links have the same pair of directions; for example, every vertex called SE/ES is joined to its SE and ES neighbors. These blocks effectively serve as parallel mirrors that provide staircase paths, rising or falling at 45° angles, such as the implicit 7-step path from A_1 to B_1.

The named vertices are connected as follows:

> A_j goes WS, ES;
>
> B_j goes SE, EN;
>
> C_j goes NW, SW, except C_r goes NW, SE;
>
> D_j goes SE, SW;
>
> E_j goes WN, WS, except E_r goes WN, SE;
>
> F_j goes NW, EN, except F_r goes SW, EN;
>
> X goes NE, SE.

The directions for complemented vertices like $\overline{A}_j$ are the same but with E and W interchanged; the directions for primed vertices like A'_j are the same but with N and S interchanged. Thus, for example, vertex B'_j goes NE, ES; and $\overline{F}'_r$ goes NE, WS. It is easy to verify that these pairs of directions are consistent: The endpoints of each edge point to each other.

We can now deduce the connections between named vertices, following paths through unnamed ones. The nearest named neighbors of A_j are B_j and $\overline{F}_j$. The nearest to B_j are A_j and C'_{j-1}. The nearest to C_j are D_j (or E_1 when $j = 0$) and B'_{j+1} (or $\overline{E}'_r$ when $j = r$). The nearest to D_j are C_j and E_j (or X when $j = r$). The nearest to E_j are D_j (or $\overline{C}'_r$ when $j = r$) and F_{j-1} (or C_0 when $j = 1$). The nearest to F_j are $\overline{A}_j$ and E_{j+1} (or X' when $j = r$). And the nearest to X are D_r and F'_r.

Each chain of edges therefore falls into a pattern that depends on the value of r mod 4. If $r = 4k$ we have

$$X \,..\, D_r \,..\, C_r \,..\, \overline{E}'_r \,..\, \overline{F}'_{r-1}$$
$$..\, A'_{r-1} \,..\, B'_{r-1} \,..\, C_{r-2} \,..\, D_{r-2} \,..\, E_{r-2} \,..\, F_{r-3}$$
$$..\, \overline{A}_{r-3} \,..\, \overline{B}_{r-3} \,..\, \overline{C}'_{r-4} \,..\, \overline{D}'_{r-4} \,..\, \overline{E}'_{r-4} \,..\, \overline{F}'_{r-5} \cdots$$
$$..\, E_2 \,..\, F_1 \,..\, \overline{A}_1 \,..\, \overline{B}_1 \,..\, \overline{C}'_0 \,..\, \overline{E}'_1 \,..\, \overline{D}'_1 \,..\, \overline{C}'_1 \,..\, \overline{B}_2 \,..\, \overline{A}_2 \cdots$$
$$..\, \overline{A}_{r-2} \,..\, F_{r-2} \,..\, E_{r-1} \,..\, D_{r-1} \,..\, C_{r-1} \,..\, B'_r \,..\, A'_r \,..\, \overline{F}'_r \,..\, \overline{X}.$$

If $r = 4k + 2$ the pattern is almost the same except that the middle transition is complemented and primed:

$$..\, \overline{E}'_2 \,..\, \overline{F}'_1 \,..\, A'_1 \,..\, B'_1 \,..\, C_0 \,..\, E_1 \,..\, D_1 \,..\, C_1 \,..\, B'_2 \,..\, A'_2 \cdots.$$

If $r = 4k + 1$ the pattern in the middle is

$$..\, E_3 \,..\, F_2 \,..\, \overline{A}_2 \,..\, \overline{B}_2 \,..\, \overline{C}'_1 \,..\, \overline{D}'_1 \,..\, \overline{E}'_1 \,..\, \overline{C}'_0 \,..\, \overline{B}_1 \,..\, \overline{A}_1 \cdots$$

ending with $\overline{A}_r \,..\, F_r \,..\, X'$. And if $r = 4k + 3$, the middle is again complemented and primed; again the path ends with $\overline{A}_r \,..\, F_r \,..\, X'$.

Consequently the edges defined above make exactly two cycles altogether. If r is even, one cycle contains X and $\overline{X}$, the other contains X' and $\overline{X}'$. If r is odd, the cycles contain $\{X, X'\}$ and $\{\overline{X}, \overline{X}'\}$, respectively.

A small change now joins the cycles together into a single Hamiltonian cycle: We simply replace the subpaths

$$F'_r, X, D_r, C_r, \overline{E}_r \qquad \text{and} \qquad \overline{F}_r, \overline{X}', \overline{D}'_r, \overline{C}'_r, E_r$$

by

$$F'_r, C_r, D_r, X, E_r \qquad \text{and} \qquad \overline{F}_r, \overline{C}'_r, \overline{D}'_r, \overline{X}', \overline{E}'_r,$$

respectively.   □

The proof of Theorem 4 leads, for example, to the following 18×18 leaper tour when $r = 4$:

0	272	220	43	53	333	363	104	183	83	4	263	233	153	143	320	372	100
270	222	41	55	212	51	331	365	102	2	265	231	151	312	155	141	322	370
224	38	57	210	277	214	48	328	367	267	228	148	314	377	310	157	138	324
36	60	207	280	386	275	216	46	326	226	146	316	375	286	380	307	160	136
334	362	105	182	84	388	273	218	44	144	318	373	88	184	82	5	262	234
52	332	364	103	1	271	221	42	54	154	142	321	371	101	3	264	232	152
213	50	330	366	268	223	40	56	211	311	156	140	323	368	266	230	150	313
276	215	47	327	225	37	58	208	278	378	308	158	137	325	227	147	315	376
387	274	217	45	35	61	206	281	385	287	381	306	161	135	145	317	374	285
85	174	117	345	335	361	106	181	87	185	81	6	261	235	245	17	74	187
176	115	347	27	125	337	358	108	178	78	8	258	237	25	127	247	15	76
113	350	30	66	168	123	340	356	111	11	256	240	23	68	166	130	250	13
352	32	64	203	301	171	121	342	354	254	242	21	71	201	303	164	132	252
34	62	205	282	384	288	173	118	344	244	18	73	188	284	382	305	162	134
336	360	107	180	86	175	116	346	26	126	246	16	75	186	80	7	260	236
124	338	357	110	177	114	348	28	67	167	128	248	14	77	10	257	238	24
170	122	341	355	112	351	31	65	202	302	165	131	251	12	255	241	22	70
300	172	120	343	353	33	63	204	283	383	304	163	133	253	243	20	72	200

(Radix 9 notation is used here so that the near-fourfold symmetry is revealed.) We can present this tour graphically in an appealing way by rendering the cycle of moves with the `eofill` operator of PostScript®:

In this illustration, the image changes from black to white whenever an edge of the tour is crossed.

The tour above for $r = 4$ was found by an exhaustive computer calculation, which determined that exactly 16 different $\{4, 5\}$-leaper tours on an 18×18 board have $180°$ symmetry; none have $90°$ symmetry. The chosen tour exhibited maximum symmetry under the circumstances, and fortunately it could be generalized to arbitrary r.

The proof of Theorem 4 breaks down when $r = 0$, but of course the result is trivial in that case. When $r = 1$ we get the well known 6×6 knight's tour

$$
\begin{array}{cccccc}
0 & 36 & 13 & 23 & 6 & 30 \\
12 & 24 & 38 & 28 & 14 & 22 \\
37 & 1 & 35 & 7 & 31 & 5 \\
25 & 11 & 27 & 15 & 21 & 17 \\
2 & 34 & 8 & 18 & 4 & 32 \\
10 & 26 & 3 & 33 & 16 & 20 \\
\end{array}
$$

(again expressed in radix 9 and again viewed via `eofill`).

A. H. Frost showed a century ago that the graphs for $\{1, 4\}$-leapers and $\{2, 3\}$-leapers are Hamiltonian on a 10×10 board [6, plate VII]. T. H. Willcocks showed more recently that $\{2, 5\}$-leapers and $\{3, 4\}$-leapers are Hamiltonian on a 14×14 [11]. Willcocks conjectured that an $\{r, s\}$-leaper has a Hamiltonian cycle on a $2(r + s) \times 2(r + s)$ board whenever $s - r$ and $s + r$ are relatively prime. Theorem 4 establishes this conjecture in the extreme cases when $s - r = 1$, and computer calculations have verified it whenever $r + s < 15$. The computer had to work hard to find a tour only in the case $r = 5$, $s = 8$.

We can verify Willcocks's conjecture also in the other extreme case, when $r = 1$:

Theorem 5. *The graph of a $\{1, 2k\}$-leaper on a $(4k + 2) \times (4k + 2)$ board is Hamiltonian.*

Proof. Now we're faced with a rather ungainly leaper that jumps across almost half of the board's width or height with every leap. It's convenient to give symbolic names to the vertices using the pattern illustrated in Fig. 1. Positions marked '.' in that figure obtain names by complementation (left-right reflection) and/or priming (up-down reflection). Thus, for example, the full names of the vertices on the top row are

$$O \ \overline{A}_2 \ C_1' \ \overline{B}_{12} \ B_{25}' \ \overline{B}_{22} \ B_{15}' \ H_2 \ K_4 \ \overline{K}_4 \ \overline{H}_2 \ \overline{B}_{15}' \ B_{22} \ \overline{B}_{25}' \ B_{12} \ \overline{C}_1' \ A_2 \ \overline{O};$$

the dots in Fig. 1 help keep the diagram from being even more cluttered than it already is.

O . . . . . . H_2 K_4 . . . B_{22} . B_{12} . A_2 $\overline{O}$

K_5 . . . B_{21} . B_{11} . A_1 . . . . . . H_1 K_3 .

. G_2 . G_4 . G_6 . G_8 . . . .

. . W^0_{11} X^0_{11} W^0_{12} X^0_{12} W^0_{13} X^0_{13} . . Y^1_{11} Z^1_{11} Y^1_{12} Z^1_{12} Y^1_{13} Z^1_{13} J_{12} .

. F_{11} Y^0_{11} Z^0_{11} Y^0_{12} Z^0_{12} Y^0_{13} Z^0_{13} J_{11} . W^1_{11} X^1_{11} W^1_{12} X^1_{12} W^1_{13} X^1_{13} . .

. . W^0_{21} X^0_{21} W^0_{22} X^0_{22} W^0_{23} X^0_{23} . E_{13} Y^1_{21} Z^1_{21} Y^1_{22} Z^1_{22} Y^1_{23} Z^1_{23} I_{13} .

. E_{12} Y^0_{21} Z^0_{21} Y^0_{22} Z^0_{22} Y^0_{23} Z^0_{23} . . W^1_{21} X^1_{21} W^1_{22} X^1_{22} W^1_{23} X^1_{23} . .

. . . D_2 . D_4 . D_6 . . . . H_4 .

. . . . H_3 . . B_{23} . B_{13} . A_3 . .

. K_6 . B_{26} . B_{16} . A_4 . . . . K_2

G_1 . G_3 . G_5 . G_7 . . K_1 . . . .

. . X^2_{11} W^2_{11} X^2_{12} W^2_{12} X^2_{13} W^2_{13} F_{13} . Z^3_{11} Y^3_{11} Z^3_{12} Y^3_{12} Z^3_{13} Y^3_{13} . J_{13}

F_{12} . Z^2_{11} Y^2_{11} Z^2_{12} Y^2_{12} Z^2_{13} Y^2_{13} . . X^3_{11} W^3_{11} X^3_{12} W^3_{12} X^3_{13} W^3_{13} . .

. . X^2_{21} W^2_{21} X^2_{22} W^2_{22} X^2_{23} W^2_{23} . . Z^3_{21} Y^3_{21} Z^3_{22} Y^3_{22} Z^3_{23} Y^3_{23} . I_{12}

E_{11} . Z^2_{21} Y^2_{21} Z^2_{22} Y^2_{22} Z^2_{23} Y^2_{23} . I_{11} X^3_{21} W^3_{21} X^3_{22} W^3_{22} X^3_{23} W^3_{23} . .

. . D_1 . D_3 . D_5 . D_7 . . . . H_5

. . . . C_2 . B_{24} . B_{14} . . .

O' . C_1 . B_{25} . B_{15} . . . . $\overline{O}'$

FIGURE 1. Vertex names for Theorem 5 when $k = 4$.

The names in general, besides O, are

$$A_1, \ldots, A_4\,;\ B_{i1}, \ldots, B_{i6}\,;\ C_1, C_2\,;\ D_1, \ldots, D_{2k-1}\,;$$

$$E_{p1}, E_{p2}, E_{p3}\,;\ F_{q1}, F_{q2}, F_{q3}\,;\ G_1, \ldots, G_{2k}\,;\ H_1, \ldots, H_5\,;$$

$$I_{p1}, I_{p2}, I_{p3}\,;\ J_{q1}, J_{q2}, J_{q3}\,;\ K_1, \ldots, K_6\,;\ W^a_{ij}, X^a_{ij}, Y^a_{ij}, Z^a_{ij}\,;$$

here $0 \le a \le 3$, $1 \le i \le k-2$, $1 \le j \le k-1$, $1 \le p < \lceil k/2 \rceil$, and $1 \le q < \lfloor k/2 \rfloor$.

The vertices named E_{pt} occur two positions to the left of $Z^a_{(k-2p)1}$, where $a = (2, 0, 1)$ for $t = (1, 2, 3)$ respectively. Similarly, vertices F_{qt} occur two positions to the left of $Z^a_{(k-2q-1)1}$, where $a = (0, 2, 3)$. Vertices I_{pt} occur two positions to the right of $Y^a_{(k-2p)(k-1)}$, where $a = (2, 3, 1)$ if k is even, $a = (0, 1, 3)$ if k is odd; vertices J_{qt} occur two positions to the right of $Y^a_{(k-2q-1)(k-1)}$, where $a = (0, 1, 3)$ if k is even, $a = (2, 3, 1)$ if k is odd. The positions of the other named vertices are self-evident. We may assume that $k \ge 3$.

To show that the graph is Hamiltonian, we will first link the vertices in six closed cycles, then we will join those cycles together. The basic cycle, if $k = 2l + 2$, is

$$O, A_1, \ldots, A_4, B_{11}, \ldots, B_{16}, \ldots, B_{(k-2)1}, \ldots, B_{(k-2)6}, C_1, C_2,$$
$$D_1, \ldots, D_{2k-1}, E_{11}, E_{12}, E_{13}, F_{11}, F_{12}, F_{13}, E_{21}, \ldots, F_{l3}, G_1, \ldots, G_{2k},$$
$$H_1, \ldots, H_5, I_{11}, I_{12}, I_{13}, J_{11}, J_{12}, J_{13}, I_{21}, \ldots, J_{l3}, K_1, \ldots, K_6,$$

followed by its "primed" reflection O', A_1', $\ldots$, K_6', O. On the other hand, if $k = 2l + 1$, the basic cycle is

$$O, A_1, \ldots, A_4, B_{11}, \ldots, B_{16}, \ldots, B_{(k-2)1}, \ldots, B_{(k-2)6}, C_1, C_2,$$
$$D_1, \ldots, D_{2k-1}, E_{11}, E_{12}, E_{13}, F_{11}, F_{12}, F_{13}, E_{21}, \ldots, E_{l3}, H_5', \ldots, H_1',$$
$$G_{2k}', \ldots, G_1', I_{11}, I_{12}, I_{13}, J_{11}, J_{12}, J_{13}, I_{21}, \ldots, I_{l3}, K_1, \ldots, K_6,$$

followed by O', A_1', $\ldots$, K_6', O. Another basic cycle is obtained by complementing everything. We also form W, X, Y, and Z cycles as follows, letting j stand for $k - 1$:

$$W_{11}^0, W_{11}^1, W_{21}^0, W_{21}^1, \ldots, W_{(j-1)1}^0, W_{(j-1)1}^1, \alpha_{j-1}, \alpha_{j-2}, \ldots, \alpha_1, \quad \text{where}$$
$$\alpha_t = W_{t1}^3, W_{t2}^1, W_{t2}^3, \ldots, W_{tj}^1, W_{tj}^3, W_{tj}^2, W_{tj}^0, \ldots, W_{t2}^2, W_{t2}^0, W_{t1}^2;$$

$$X_{11}^2, X_{11}^3, X_{21}^2, X_{21}^3, \ldots, X_{(j-1)1}^2, X_{(j-1)1}^3, \beta_{j-1}, \beta_{j-2}, \ldots, \beta_1, \quad \text{where}$$
$$\beta_t = X_{t1}^1, X_{t2}^3, X_{t2}^1, \ldots, X_{tj}^3, X_{tj}^1, X_{tj}^0, X_{tj}^2, \ldots, X_{t2}^0, X_{t2}^2, X_{t1}^0;$$

$$Y_{11}^1, Y_{11}^0, Y_{21}^1, Y_{21}^0, \ldots, Y_{(j-1)1}^1, Y_{(j-1)1}^0, \gamma_{j-1}, \gamma_{j-2}, \ldots, \gamma_1, \quad \text{where}$$
$$\gamma_t = Y_{t1}^2, Y_{t2}^0, Y_{t2}^2, \ldots, Y_{tj}^0, Y_{tj}^2, Y_{tj}^3, Y_{tj}^1, \ldots, Y_{t2}^3, Y_{t2}^1, Y_{t1}^3;$$

$$Z_{11}^3, Z_{11}^2, Z_{21}^3, Z_{21}^2, \ldots, Z_{(j-1)1}^3, Z_{(j-1)1}^2, \delta_{j-1}, \delta_{j-2}, \ldots, \delta_1, \quad \text{where}$$
$$\delta_t = Z_{t1}^0, Z_{t2}^2, Z_{t2}^0, \ldots, Z_{tj}^2, Z_{tj}^0, Z_{tj}^1, Z_{tj}^3, \ldots, Z_{t2}^1, Z_{t2}^3, Z_{t1}^1.$$

Cycles can be spliced together when we have consecutive vertices (u_1, u_2) in one cycle and (v_1, v_2) in another, where u_1 is adjacent to v_1 and u_2 is adjacent to v_2. The pairs

$$\begin{array}{lll}
(E_{12}, E_{13}) & \text{and} & (Z_{(k-2)1}^2, Z_{(k-2)1}^3) \\
(E_{12}', E_{13}') & \text{and} & (W_{11}^0, W_{11}^1) \\
(\overline{D}_2, \overline{D}_3) & \text{and} & (Y_{(k-2)(k-1)}^0, Y_{(k-2)(k-2)}^2) \\
(\overline{D}_2', \overline{D}_3') & \text{and} & (X_{1(k-1)}^2, X_{1(k-2)}^0) \\
(\overline{G}_3', \overline{G}_4') & \text{and} & (Z_{(k-2)(k-1)}^0, Z_{(k-2)(k-1)}^2)
\end{array}$$

satisfy this property and suffice to complete the proof. (The first two pairs hook the Z and W cycles into the basic cycle; the next two hook the Y and X cycles into its complement. The last pair hooks the Z cycle, which is now part of the basic cycle, into the complement.)   □

As an example of the construction in Theorem 5, here is the 22×22 cycle that arises when $k = 5$:

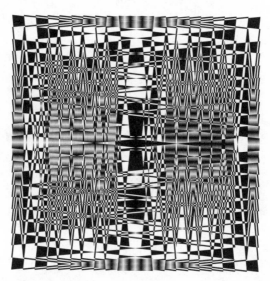

```
  0  143 386 139 384 133 378 127 372 457 360 269 172 257  18 251  12 245   6 243   2 145
361 270 171 258  17 252  11 246   5 242   1  144 387 140 383 134 377 128 371 458 359 268
 54 467 388 465 390 463 392 461 394 459 396 185 170 187 168 189 166 191 164 241 162 333
397 274 399 196 401 194 403 192 405 238  55 332  81 320  83 318  85 316  87 314 355 184
158 331  80 307  94 309  92 311  90 313 354 275 446 231 412 233 410 235 408 237  56 471
449 276 445 230 415 228 417 226 419 224 157 472  79 306  97 304  99 302 101 300 353 180
156 327  78 293 108 295 106 297 104 299 450 179 444 217 426 219 424 221 422 223  60 473
451 280 443 216 429 214 431 212 433 210  61 326  77 292 111 290 113 288 115 286 349 178
152  35  76  37  74  39  72  41 118 285 348 281 442 203 440 205 438 207 436 209  62 477
347 174 345  26 343  28 341  30 339  32 151 478  65  48  67  46  69  44 119 284 455 282
150 483 142 385 138 379 132 373 126 367 456 173 262  19 256  13 250   7 244   3 146 479
271 362 263  22 259  16 253  10 247   4 335  52 141 382 135 376 129 370 123 366 267 358
468  53 466 389 464 391 462 393 460 395 272 357 186 169 188 167 190 165 240 163 334 161
273 398 197 400 195 402 193 404 239 406 469 160 321  82 319  84 317  86 315  88 183 356
330 159 322  95 308  93 310  91 312  89 182 447 198 413 232 411 234 409 236 407 470  57
277 448 199 414 229 416 227 418 225 420 329  58 323  96 305  98 303 100 301 102 181 352
328 155 324 109 294 107 296 105 298 103 278 351 200 427 218 425 220 423 222 421 474  59
279 452 201 428 215 430 213 432 211 434 475 154 325 110 291 112 289 114 287 116 177 350
 34 153  36  75  38  73  40  71  42 117 176 453 202 441 204 439 206 437 208 435 476  63
175 346  25 344  27 342  29 340  31 338  33  64  49  66  47  68  45  70  43 120 283 454
482 149  50 137 380 131 374 125 368 121 364 265  24 261  20 255  14 249   8 337 480 147
363 264  23 260  21 254  15 248   9 336 481 148  51 136 381 130 375 124 369 122 365 266
```

.　Z_4　X_1　A_1^3　A_1^4　A_1^5　A_1^6　A_1^7　.　Y_1　.　.　.　.　.　.　.　Z_2

.　Y_6　.　.　.　.　.　.　Z_3　X_2　A_2^3　A_2^4　A_2^5　A_2^6　A_2^7　.　Y_2

X_7　.　X_9　A_5^3　A_5^4　A_5^5　A_5^6　A_5^7　.　Y_9　.　.　.　.　.　X_5　.

.　Y_{14}　.　.　.　.　.　X_6　.　X_{10}　A_6^3　A_6^4　A_6^5　A_6^6　A_6^7　.　Y_{10}

X_{15}　.　X_{17}　A_9^3　A_9^4　A_9^5　A_9^6　A_9^7　.　Y_{17}　.　.　.　.　.　X_{13}　.

.　Y_{22}　.　.　.　.　.　.　X_{14}　.　X_{18}　A_{10}^3　A_{10}^4　A_{10}^5　A_{10}^6　A_{10}^7　.　Y_{18}

X_{23}　.　X_{25}　A_{13}^3　A_{13}^4　A_{13}^5　A_{13}^6　A_{13}^7　.　Y_{25}　.　.　.　.　.　X_{21}　.

.　Y_{30}　.　.　.　.　.　.　X_{22}　.　X_{26}　A_{14}^3　A_{14}^4　A_{14}^5　A_{14}^6　A_{14}^7　.　Y_{26}

Z_5　.　B_2　B_3　B_4　B_5　B_6　B_7　B_8　.　.　.　.　.　.　.　Z_1　.

Y_5　.　Y_7　.　.　.　.　.　X_3　A_3^3　A_3^4　A_3^5　A_3^6　A_3^7　.　Y_3　.

.　X_8　A_4^3　A_4^4　A_4^5　A_4^6　A_4^7　.　Y_4　.　Y_8　.　.　.　.　.　X_4

Y_{13}　.　Y_{15}　.　.　.　.　.　X_{11}　A_7^3　A_7^4　A_7^5　A_7^6　A_7^7　.　Y_{11}　.

.　X_{16}　A_8^3　A_8^4　A_8^5　A_8^6　A_8^7　.　Y_{12}　.　Y_{16}　.　.　.　.　.　X_{12}

Y_{21}　.　Y_{23}　.　.　.　.　.　X_{19}　A_{11}^3　A_{11}^4　A_{11}^5　A_{11}^6　A_{11}^7　.　Y_{19}　.

.　X_{24}　A_{12}^3　A_{12}^4　A_{12}^5　A_{12}^6　A_{12}^7　.　Y_{20}　.　Y_{24}　.　.　.　.　.　X_{20}

Y_{29}　.　Y_{31}　.　.　.　.　.　X_{27}　A_{15}^3　A_{15}^4　A_{15}^5　A_{15}^6　A_{15}^7　.　Y_{27}　.

.　Z_6　A_{16}^3　A_{16}^4　A_{16}^5　A_{16}^6　A_{16}^7　.　Y_{28}　.　Y_{32}　.　.　.　.　.　X_{28}

FIGURE 2. Vertex names for Theorem 6 when $k = 4$.

Leapers with $r = 1$ can in fact tour a slightly smaller board:

Theorem 6. *The graph of a $\{1, 2k\}$-leaper on a $(4k + 1) \times (4k + 2)$ board is Hamiltonian.*

Proof. This time the construction is simpler. We may assume that $k \geq 2$, because Euler [4] constructed a 5×6 knight's tour. The case $k = 2$ was solved by Huber-Stockar [7], whose method can be generalized to all larger values of k. We assign names as illustrated in Fig. 2, with dots standing for names obtained by complementation (left-right reflection) as in the proof of Theorem 5. The vertex names, in general, are

$$A_1^j, \ldots, A_{4k}^j, \quad \text{for} \quad 2 < j < 2k; \quad B_2, \ldots, B_{2k};$$

$$X_1, \ldots, X_{8k-4}; \quad Y_1, \ldots, Y_{8k}; \quad Z_1, \ldots, Z_6.$$

Notice that the graph contains paths

$$(B_{j-1} \text{ or } B_{j+1}), A_1^j, \ldots, A_{4k}^j, (B_{j-2} \text{ or } B_j)$$

for $2 < j < 2k$, except that vertex B_{j-2} is not present when $j = 3$.

Let α_j be the path $B_{j-2}, A_{4k}^j, \ldots, A_1^j, B_{j+1}, A_{4k}^{j+1}, \ldots, A_1^{j+1}$, when $2 < j < 2k$ and j is even. This path α_j can be followed by vertex B_{j+2}. Therefore we can get from X_1 to B_{2k-2} and to B_{2k} via the disjoint paths

$$X_1, \ldots, X_{8k-4},\ Z_1, \ldots, Z_6,\ \alpha_4, \alpha_8, \ldots, \alpha_{2k-4},\ B_{2k-2}$$

and $\quad X_1,\ B_3,\ A_{4k}^3, \ldots, A_1^3,\ \alpha_6, \alpha_{10}, \ldots, \alpha_{2k-2},\ B_{2k}$

when k is even; we can do it via the disjoint paths

$$X_1, \ldots, X_{8k-4},\ Z_1, \ldots, Z_6,\ \alpha_4, \alpha_8, \ldots, \alpha_{2k-2},\ B_{2k}$$

and $\quad X_1,\ B_3,\ A_{4k}^3, \ldots, A_1^3,\ \alpha_6, \alpha_{10}, \ldots, \alpha_{2k-4},\ B_{2k-2}$

when k is odd.

Since we can also get from B_{2k} to $\overline{B}_{2k-2}$ via the vertices $Y_1, \ldots, Y_{8k}$, we obtain a path from B_{2k-2} to $\overline{B}_{2k-2}$ that runs through all vertices with uncomplemented names. This path plus its complement is the desired Hamiltonian cycle. □

The `eofill` images that arise from this construction have a pleasant symmetry and "basketweave" texture. Here's the 21×22 case ($k = 5$):

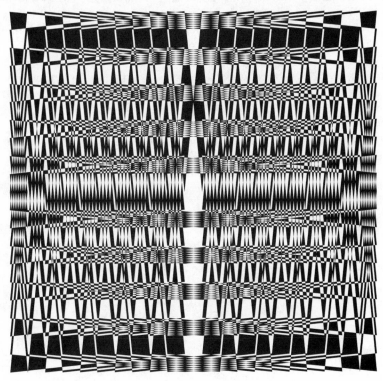

The board in Theorem 6 turns out to be as small as possible.

Theorem 7. *A $\{1, 2k\}$-leaper has no Hamiltonian cycle on a board of area less than $(4k+1)(4k+2)$.*

Proof. Consider the $\{1, 2k\}$-leaper graph on an $m \times n$ board with $m \leq n$ and $2k + 1 \leq m \leq 4k$. If m is even, we can show that no Hamiltonian cycle exists by using an argument due to de Jaenisch [8, page 46], Flye Sainte-Marie [5], and Jelliss [11]: Say that vertex (x, y) is type A if x is even, y is even, and $x < 2k$, or if x is odd, y is odd, and $x \geq m - 2k$; it is type B if x is odd, y is even, and $x < 2k$, or if x is even, y is odd, and $x \geq m - 2k$; it is type C otherwise. Type A vertices are adjacent only to vertices of type B, but there are no more Bs than As. Thus the only possible cycle containing all the As has the form $ABAB \ldots AB$. But such a cycle misses all the Cs.

Suppose therefore that m is odd, say $m = 2l + 1$. Then $l \geq k$ and $n \geq 4k$, by Theorem 1. The links from (l, y) to $(l \pm 1, y + 2k)$ are forced when $y < 2k$, because $l < 2k$. The case $n = 4k$ is impossible by the argument in the previous paragraph, when the ranks and files of the board are transposed. Therefore $n > 4k$, and a short circuit from $(l, 0)$ to $(l \pm 1, 2k)$ to $(l, 4k)$ is forced unless $n > 6k$. Furthermore, if $6k \leq n < 8k$, a short circuit from $(l, n - 6k)$ to $(l \pm 1, n - 4k)$ to $(l, n - 2k)$ is forced. Consequently we have $n \geq 8k$. (This argument, in the case $k = 2$, was suggested by Jelliss in a letter to the author.)

If $m \geq 2k + 3$ we have therefore $mn \geq 16k^2 + 24k > (4k+1)(4k+2)$. And if $m = 2k + 1$ and $n \neq 8k$ we have $mn \geq (2k + 1)(8k + 2) = (4k + 1)(4k + 2)$ because n must be even.

The remaining case is quite interesting, because we will see that a Hamiltonian path (but not a cycle) is possible. Let $m = 2k + 1$ and $n = 8k$, and assume that a Hamiltonian cycle exists. We will write $u \sim v$ if u and v are adjacent vertices of that cycle. Vertices of degree 2 force the connections

$$(x, y) \sim (x + 1, y + 2k), \qquad (x, y) \sim (x - 1, y + 2k),$$

for $0 < x < 2k$ and $0 \leq y < 2k$; also at the corners we have

$$(0, 0) \sim (1, 2k), \quad (0, 0) \sim (2k, 1),$$
$$(2k, 0) \sim (0, 1), \quad (2k, 0) \sim (2k - 1, 2k).$$

Notice that both neighbors of (x, y) in the cycle have now been identified whenever $1 < x < 2k - 1$ and $y < 4k$; by symmetry, the same is true in the right half of the board, when $y \geq 4k$. Our goal is to deduce the behavior of the cycle on the remaining vertices, which lie in the top two and bottom two ranks of the board. We will assume that $k > 1$, so that these four ranks are distinct. A similar (and much simpler) argument applies when $k = 1$.

Let $(x, y)' = (2k - x, 8k - 1 - y)$ be the point opposite (x, y) with respect to the center of the board. Whenever we deduce that $u \sim v$, a symmetric derivation proves that $u' \sim v'$; such consequences need not be stated explicitly.

We must have either $(0, 4k - 1) \sim (2k, 4k - 2)$ or $(0, 4k - 1) \sim (2k, 4k) = (0, 4k - 1)'$, because $(0, 4k - 1) \not\sim (1, 6k - 1) = (2k - 1, 2k)'$; the latter is joined to $(2k, 0)'$ and $(2k - 2, 0)'$. Similarly, we must have either $(2k, 4k - 1) \sim (0, 4k - 2)$ or $(2k, 4k - 1) \sim (2k, 4k - 1)'$. These choices are not independent. For if $(0, 4k - 1) \sim (2k, 4k - 2)$ and $(2k, 4k - 1) \sim (0, 4k - 2)$, there is a short circuit

$$(0, 4k - 1) \sim (1, 2k - 1) \sim \cdots \sim (2k - 1, 2k - 1) \sim (2k, 4k - 1)$$
$$\sim (0, 4k - 2) \sim \cdots \sim (2k, 4k - 2) \sim (0, 4k - 1);$$

likewise the connections $(0, 4k - 1) \sim (0, 4k - 1)'$ and $(2k, 4k - 1) \sim (2k, 4k - 1)'$ force a short circuit

$$(0, 4k - 1) \sim \cdots \sim (2k, 4k - 1)$$
$$\sim (2k, 4k - 1)' \sim \cdots \sim (0, 4k - 1)' \sim (0, 4k - 1).$$

By symmetry we can therefore assume without loss of generality that

$$(0, 4k - 1) \sim (2k, 4k - 2) \quad \text{and} \quad (2k, 4k - 1) \sim (2k, 4k - 1)'.$$

These connections imply also $(0, 4k - 1)' \sim (2k, 4k - 2)'$; we still are able to claim legitimately below that $u' \sim v'$ holds whenever we have deduced that $u \sim v$.

Further detective work establishes $(1, 2k + 1) \sim (0, 1)$, because $(1, 2k + 1) \not\sim (0, 4k + 1) = (2k, 4k - 2)'$. Therefore the cycle contains the path

$$(2k, 1) \sim (0, 0) \sim \cdots \sim (2k, 0) \sim (0, 1) \sim (1, 2k + 1)$$
$$\sim (2, 1) \sim \cdots \sim (2k - 2, 1) \sim (2k - 1, 2k + 1);$$

it follows that $(2k, 1) \not\sim (2k - 1, 2k + 1)$. The only possibilities remaining are $(2k, 1) \sim (0, 2)$ and $(2k - 1, 2k + 1) \sim (2k, 4k + 1) = (0, 4k - 2)'$.

Now we can establish, in fact, the relations

$$(1, 2k + 2j - 1) \sim (0, 2j - 1) \sim (2k, 2j - 2),$$
$$(0, 4k - 2j + 1) \sim (2k, 4k - 2j),$$

for $1 \le j \le k$. They have been verified when $j = 1$; suppose we know them for some $j < k$. Then $(2k, 2j) \not\sim (0, 2j - 1)$, hence $(2k, 2j) \sim (0, 2j + 1)$ and $(2k, 2j) \sim (2k - 1, 2k + 2j)$. Hence $(0, 4k - 2j - 1) \not\sim (1, 6k - 2j - 1) = (2k - 1, 2k + 2j)'$; we must have $(0, 4k - 2j - 1) \sim (2k, 4k - 2j - 2)$. This in turn forces $(1, 2k + 2j + 1) \sim (0, 2j + 1)$, because $(1, 2k + 2j + 1)$ can't be joined to $(0, 4k + 2j + 1) = (2k, 4k - 2j - 2)'$. The induction on j is complete, and we have also proved that

$$(2k, 2j) \sim (2k - 1, 2k + 2j) \qquad \text{for } 1 \le j < k.$$

One consequence of our deductions so far is the existence of a rather long path,

$$(0, 2) \sim (2k, 1) \sim \cdots \sim (2k - 1, 2k + 1) \sim (0, 4k - 2)'$$
$$\sim \cdots \sim (2k, 4k - 2)' \sim (0, 4k - 1)' \sim \cdots \sim (2k, 4k - 1)'$$
$$\sim (2k, 4k - 1) \sim \cdots \sim (0, 2)'.$$

We've also found paths from $(0, 2k + 2j - 2)$ to $(2k, 2k + 2j - 1)$ and from $(1, 2k + 2j)$ to $(2k - 1, 2k + 2j + 1)$, for $1 \le j < k$.

The final phase of the proof consists of establishing the relations

j odd	j even
$(0, 2j) \sim (2k, 2j-1)$	$(0, 2j) \sim (1, 2k+2j)$
$(1, 2k+2j) \sim (2k, 4k-2j-1)'$	$(0, 4k-2j) \sim (2k, 4k-2j-1)$
$(2k, 2j+1) \sim (2k-1, 2k+2j+1)$	$(0, 4k-2j-2) \sim (2k-1, 2k+2j+1)'$
$(0, 2j) \sim (2k, 2j+1)$	$(0, 2j) \sim (2k, 2j+1)$

for $1 \le j < k$. Suppose first that $j = 1$ and $k > 1$. We know already that $(0, 2) \sim (2k, 1)$. Now $(2k, 4k - 3)$ cannot be joined to $(0, 4k - 4)$, because that would make a short circuit; it cannot be joined to $(0, 4k - 2)$, because the neighbors of $(0, 4k - 2)$ are known. So we have $(2k, 4k - 3) \sim (2k - 1, 6k - 3) = (1, 2k + 2)'$. This relation implies $(1, 2k + 2) \not\sim (0, 2)$, so $(0, 2) \sim (2k, 3)$. We also have a path

$$(2k - 1, 2k + 3) \sim \cdots \sim (1, 2k + 2) \sim (2k, 4k - 3)' \sim \cdots \sim (0, 4k - 4)';$$

hence $(2k - 1, 2k + 3) \not\sim (2k, 4k + 3) = (0, 4k - 4)'$, and the relation $(2k - 1, 2k + 3) \sim (2k, 3)$ is forced. The proof for $j = 1$ is complete.

Suppose the relations have been proved for some $j < k - 1$. If j is odd, we have $(0, 4k - 2j - 2) \not\sim (2k, 4k - 2j - 1)$ and

$$(0, 4k - 2j - 2) \not\sim (1, 6k - 2j - 2) = (2k - 1, 2k + 2j + 1)' ;$$

hence $(0, 4k - 2j - 2) \sim (2k, 4k - 2j - 3)$. Also $(0, 2j + 2) \not\sim (2k, 2j + 1)$; we must have $(2k, 2j + 3) \sim (0, 2j + 2) \sim (1, 2k + 2j + 2)$. And there's already a path

$$(2k - 1, 2k + 2j + 3) \sim \cdots \sim (1, 2k + 2j + 2) \sim \cdots \sim (2k, 2j + 3) ,$$

so $(2k - 1, 2k + 2j + 3) \not\sim (2k, 2j + 3)$. This forces $(2k - 1, 2k + 2j + 3) \sim (2k, 4k + 2j + 3) = (0, 4k - 2j - 4)'$. The required relations for $j + 1$ have been established.

If j is even, we have proved that $(2k, 2j + 1) \not\sim (2k - 1, 2k + 2j + 1)$, so $(2k, 2j + 1) \sim (0, 2j + 2)$. Also $(2k, 4k - 2j - 3) \not\sim (0, 4k - 2j - 2)$, and $(2k, 4k - 2j - 3) \not\sim (0, 4k - 2j - 4)$ because of a short circuit; so $(2k, 4k - 2j - 3) \sim (2k - 1, 6k - 2j - 3) = (1, 2k + 2j + 2)'$. This implies $(0, 2j + 2) \not\sim (1, 2k + 2j + 2)$, so $(0, 2j + 2) \sim (2k, 2j + 3)$. Finally, the existing path

$$(2k - 1, 2k + 2j + 3) \sim \cdots \sim (1, 2k + 2j + 2)$$
$$\sim (2k, 4k - 2j - 3)' \sim \cdots \sim (0, 4k - 2j - 4)'$$

shows that $(2k - 1, 2k + 2j + 3) \not\sim (2k, 4k + 2j + 3) = (0, 4k - 2j - 4)'$; we must have $(2k - 1, 2k + 2j + 3) \sim (2k, 2j + 3)$.

Now that the induction on j is complete, we have deduced the entire Hamiltonian cycle with the exception of one link from one vertex (and its complement). More precisely, when $k > 1$ is odd we have found the Hamiltonian path

$$(2k, 2k{-}1) \sim (0, 2k{-}2) \sim (1, 4k{-}2) \sim \cdots \sim (2k{-}1, 4k{-}1) \sim (0, 2k)'$$
$$\sim \cdots \sim (2k, 2k{+}1)' \sim (0, 2k{+}2)' \sim \cdots \sim (2k, 2k{+}3)'$$
$$\sim (1, 4k{-}4) \sim \cdots \sim (2k{-}1, 4k{-}3) \sim (2k, 2k{-}3)$$
$$\sim (0, 2k{-}4) \sim (2k, 2k{-}5) \sim \cdots \sim (2k, 1)$$
$$\sim \cdots \sim (2k, 1)' \sim \cdots \sim (2k, 2k{-}1)' ;$$

when k is even we have found another,

$$(0, 2k) \sim \cdots \sim (2k, 2k+1) \sim (1, 4k-2)'$$
$$\sim \cdots \sim (2k-1, 4k-1)' \sim (2k, 2k-1)' \sim (0, 2k-2)'$$
$$\sim (2k, 2k-3)' \sim (0, 2k-4)' \sim (1, 4k-4)'$$
$$\sim \cdots \sim (2k-1, 4k-3)' \sim (0, 2k+2) \sim \cdots \sim (2k, 2k+3)$$
$$\sim (0, 2k+4) \sim \cdots \sim (2k, 4k-1) \sim (2k, 4k-1)' \sim \cdots \sim (0, 2k)'.$$

The endpoints of these paths are not adjacent, so it is impossible to complete a cycle.   □

Willcocks [11] has also conjectured that square boards with side less than $2(r + s)$ do *not* yield Hamiltonian graphs. Using a slight extension of the methods above we can in fact prove a bit more:

Theorem 8. *An $\{r, s\}$-leaper has no Hamiltonian cycle on an $m \times n$ board when $2s \leq m \leq n < 2(r + s)$.*

Proof. We may assume that r and s are relatively prime, with $2 \leq r < s$. We show first that there is no Hamiltonian cycle on an $m \times n$ board when $m = 2s$ and n is arbitrary. Say that vertex (x, y) is type A if $x < s$ and $x \equiv t$ (modulo $2r$), or if $x \geq s$ and $x \equiv r + s + t$ (modulo $2r$), where

$$t = \begin{cases} s \bmod 2r, & \text{if } s \bmod 2r < r; \\ 0 & \text{if } s \bmod 2r > r. \end{cases}$$

Similarly, say that (x, y) is type B if $x < s$ and $x \equiv r + t$ (modulo $2r$), or $x \geq s$ and $x \equiv s + t$ (modulo $2r$). Otherwise (x, y) is type C. Let $s = 2kr + s'$, where $0 \leq s' < 2r$. If $s' < r$, we have $t = s'$, so the vertices of type A are those in ranks t, $t + 2r$, ..., $t + (2k - 2)r$, $2t + (2k + 1)r$, ..., $2t + (4k - 1)r$, while those of type B are in ranks $t + r$, $t + 3r$, ..., $t + (2k - 1)r$, $2t + 2kr$, ..., $2t + (4k - 2)r$. If $s' > r$, we have $t = 0$, so the vertices of type A have ranks 0, $2r$, ..., $2kr$, $s' + (2k + 1)r$, ..., $s' + (4k + 1)r$ while those of type B have ranks r, $3r$, ..., $(2k + 1)r$, $s' + 2kr$, ..., $s' + 4kr$. In both cases there are exactly as many vertices of type B as type A, and every neighbor of a type A vertex has type B. This rules out a Hamiltonian cycle, as in Theorem 7.

To complete the proof, we must show that no Hamiltonian cycle is possible on an $m \times n$ board when $2s < m \leq n < 2(r + s)$. Let

$x = \min(m - 2s, r) - 1$, $y = \min(n - 2s, r) - 1$. Then the short circuit

$$(x, y),\ (x + r, y + s),\ (x, y + 2s),\ (x + s, y + 2s - r),\ (x + 2s, y + 2s),$$
$$(x + 2s - r, y + s),\ (x + 2s, y),\ (x + s, y + r),\ (x, y)$$

is forced, because $x < r$, $y < r$, $x + 2s \geq m - r$, and $y + 2s \geq n - r$. $\square$

Unsolved Problems

A proof of Willcocks's general Hamiltonian cycle conjecture would be very interesting. A presumably simpler problem, but also of interest, is to characterize the smallest boards on which leaper graphs are *biconnected*. The next cases to consider are perhaps those in which r and s are consecutive Pell numbers, that is, consecutive elements of the sequence 1, 2, 5, 12, 29, 70, 169, ... defined by the recurrence $A_{k+1} = 2A_k + A_{k-1}$. This choice makes the angles between the eight leaper moves as nearly equal as possible; we have proved the conjecture only in the cases where those angles are as unequal as possible.

The results above suggest several additional open problems. For example, what is the *diameter* of the $\{r, s\}$-leaper graph on an $(r+s) \times 2s$ board, when the conditions of Theorem 1 are satisfied?

What is the 3-dimensional analog of Theorem 1? (An $\{r, s, t\}$-leaper on a board with ranks, files, and layers is able to make up to 48 moves from each position, by changing the three coordinates by some permutation of the numbers $\{\pm r, \pm s, \pm t\}$. For example, Vandermonde [17, §13] constructed a $4 \times 4 \times 4$ tour with a 3-dimensional knight, which is a $\{0, 1, 2\}$-leaper.)

What is the smallest n for which $\{1, 2k\}$-leapers can make a Hamiltonian cycle on a $(2k + 1) \times n$ board? The proof of Theorem 7 shows that such cycles have an intriguing structure. When $k = 1$, the answer is 10 (see Bergholt [1]), but for larger values of k it appears likely that the answer is $12k$. This conjecture is true, at any rate, when $k = 2$; also $n \geq 36$ is necessary when $k = 3$.

Theorem 3 provides a lower bound for Hamiltonian leaper graphs with $s = r+1$, but it is not the best possible result of its kind. The lower bound on n can, for example, be raised by 2 whenever r is a multiple of 4, because we can extend the argument in the proof as follows: Suppose $r = 2k$ and $n = (s+4)s - 1$. Then the files that are not R or L are $[a, a]$ for $1 \leq a \leq k + 2$; $[a + 1, a]$ and $[a + 2, a]$, for $1 \leq a \leq k + 1$; $[a + 3, a]$ for $1 \leq a \leq k$; $[a, 1]$ for $4 < a \leq k + 2$; and the complements of those files. As before we call files $[a, b]$ and $\overline{[a, b]}$ odd or even according as a is odd or even. It turns out that the odd files have $2r - 4$ more unspecified neighbors than the even files do. All links go between an odd file and an even file, except for a link from $[k+2, 1]$ to $\overline{[k + 2, 1]}$. The odd excess can be dissipated only if the special connection from $[k+2, 1]$ to $\overline{[k + 2, 1]}$ goes from odd to odd. A Hamiltonian cycle is therefore impossible if k is even.

This result is best possible when $r = 4$, because numerous $\{4,5\}$-leaper tours do exist on a 9×46 board. Here, for example, is one that can be found using the method Euler [4] proposed for ordinary knights:

0	$\overline{132}$	59	$\overline{102}$	93	$\overline{116}$	172	$\overline{142}$	$\overline{201}$	18	8	40	$\overline{75}$	84	182	155	30	$\overline{16}$	10	$\overline{26}$	$\overline{189}$	$\overline{48}$	82	161...
134	57	$\overline{104}$	123	66	95	114	174	140	205	42	$\overline{77}$	86	125	68	180	157	203	195	187	46	149	163	184...
55	106	121	167	127	64	97	112	176	136	79	88	$\overline{147}$	165	$\overline{35}$	70	178	138	185	44	150	45	186	194...
108	119	169	$\overline{145}$	3	129	62	99	110	53	90	152	198	21	5	37	$\overline{72}$	51	$\overline{162}$	81	47	188	$\overline{196}$	23 ...
117	171	143	200	19	1	$\overline{131}$	60	101	92	154	29	$\overline{15}$	11	$\overline{25}$	7	$\overline{39}$	$\overline{74}$	$\overline{83}$	49	190	27	$\overline{13}$	13 ...
94	115	173	141	206	133	58	103	124	67	181	156	202	17	9	$\overline{41}$	76	$\overline{85}$	183	160	31	192	23	196...
65	96	113	175	135	56	105	122	166	$\overline{126}$	69	179	139	204	43	78	$\overline{87}$	148	164	$\overline{34}$	158	33	194	$\overline{186}$...
128	63	98	111	54	107	120	168	146	4	36	71	177	137	80	89	151	197	$\overline{22}$	193	32	159	184	163...
2	$\overline{130}$	61	100	109	118	170	144	199	20	6	38	73	52	91	153	28	$\overline{14}$	12	$\overline{24}$	191	50	$\overline{161}$	82 ...

(Only the left portion of the board is shown; the right half is reversed and complemented, so that the full tour has 180° symmetry. A bar over a number means that 207 should be added.)

A similar argument shows that the lower bound for $r = 5$ can be raised from 52 to 56, and that a symmetric $\{5,6\}$-leaper tour does exist on an 11×56 board.

For $r \geq 6$, the lower bounds derived above are not optimum, but more powerful methods will be needed to establish the best possible results. Computer algorithms for the general symmetric traveling salesrep problem show that the $\{6,7\}$-leaper graph on a 13×76 board is not Hamiltonian; in fact, at least 18 additional edges are needed to make a Hamiltonian cycle possible. This result [14] was obtained and verified by two independently developed computer codes, one by Giovanni Rinaldi and Manfred Padberg, the other by Michael Jünger, Gerhard Reinelt, and Stefan Thienel. They noticed that the lower bound of 18 can be obtained simply from a linear programming model with the constraint that each vertex has degree 2; instead of asking for a Hamiltonian cycle, the linear model merely asks for *any* collection of disjoint cycles that hit all the vertices. On the other hand if each edge of the graph has weight 0 and each edge not in the graph has weight 1, a single cycle of total weight 18 turns out to be possible.

Leaper graphs should provide good challenges for all such computer codes. Michael Jünger [12] has recently used his program to verify Willcocks's conjecture when $r + s = 15$, so the smallest unsettled cases are now $\{r, 17 - r\}$-leapers for $2 \leq r \leq 7$. Jünger [13] has also found the smallest Hamiltonian graphs of $\{r, r + 1\}$-leapers on $(2r + 1) \times n$ boards when $r = 6$ $(n = 92)$ and $r = 7$ $(n = 106)$.

References

[1] E. Bergholt, letter to the editor, *British Chess Magazine* **38** (1918), 74.

[2] T. R. Dawson, problem 278 in "Récréations mathématiques," edited by M. Kraitchik, *L'Echiquier* **4** (1928), 985, 1054.

[3] Anthony Dickins, *A Guide to Fairy Chess* (Richmond, Surrey: The Q Press, 1967).

[4] L. Euler, "Solution d'une question curieuse qui ne paroit soumise à aucune analyse," *Mémoires de l'Académie Royale des Sciences et Belles-Lettres* (Berlin, 1759), 310–337.

[5] C. Flye Sainte-Marie, "Note sur un problème relatif à la marche du cavalier sur l'échiquier," *Bulletin de la Société Mathématique de France* **5** (1877), 144–150.

[6] M. Frolow, *Les Carrés Magiques* (Paris: 1886).

[7] E. Huber-Stockar, problem 6304, *Fairy Chess Review* **5**, 16 (February 1945), 124; **5** 17 (March 1945), 134.

[8] C. F. de Jaenisch, *Traité des Applications de l'Analyse Mathématique au Jeu des Echecs* **2** (St. Petersbourg: 1862–1863).

[9] George P. Jelliss, "Theory of leapers," *Chessics* **2**, 24 (Winter 1985), 86–98.

[10] George P. Jelliss, "Generalized knights and Hamiltonian tours," *Journal of Recreational Mathematics* **27** (1995), 191–200.

[11] G. P. Jelliss and T. H. Willcocks, "The five free leapers," *Chessics* **1**, 2 (July 1976), 2; **1**, 6 (August 1978), 4–5.

[12] Michael Jünger, electronic communication from the University of Cologne, 8 April 1994.

[13] Michael Jünger, electronic communication from the University of Cologne, 11 April 1994.

[14] Michael Jünger and Giovanni Rinaldi, electronic communications from the University of Cologne, 29 March 1994. (The programs they used were described shortly afterwards as part of a survey paper: M. Jünger, G. Reinelt, and G. Rinaldi, "The traveling salesman problem," *Handbooks in Operations Research and Management Science* **7**: *Network Models*, edited by M. O. Ball, T. L. Magnanti, C. L. Monma, and G. L. Nemhauser (Amsterdam: North-Holland, 1995), 225–330.)

[15] Édouard Lucas, *Récréations Mathématiques* **4** (Paris: 1894).

[16] C. St J. A. Nash-Williams, "Abelian groups, graphs and generalized knights," *Proceedings of the Cambridge Philosophical Society* **55** (1959), 232–238.

[17] Vandermonde, "Remarques sur les problèmes de situation," *Mémoires de Mathématique et de Physique, tirés des registres de l'Académie Royale des Sciences* (Paris, 1771), part 1, 566–574 and plates X, XI.

Addendum

How many leaps does it take to get from the upper left corner to the other vertices of a leaper graph, when the graph has only $r + s$ ranks and $2s$ files — just enough to connect everything up? These sets of distances make intriguing patterns. Here, for example, are the relevant shortest-path values when $s = 12$, using darker shading for cells that are further from the corner:

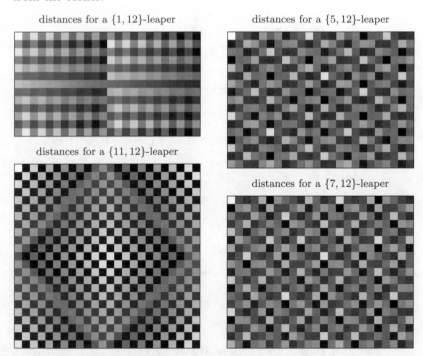

distances for a $\{1, 12\}$-leaper   distances for a $\{5, 12\}$-leaper

distances for a $\{11, 12\}$-leaper

distances for a $\{7, 12\}$-leaper

In the $\{7, 12\}$ case, 39 steps (the maximum) are needed to get from $(0, 0)$ to $(1, 0)$; the only other vertex needing 39 steps is $(1, 14)$. But 43 steps are needed to get from $(0, 4)$ to $(0, 5)$ in that graph. In the $\{11, 12\}$

case, the maximum distance between any two vertices turns out to be 65, which occurs between $(0,0)$ and $(0,1)$ (and many other pairs).

Table 1 shows the maximum distance from a corner (in regular type), as well as the overall diameter (in boldface type), of all minimally connected leaper graphs with $r < s \le 13$. Both statistics appear to be $6k - 1$ for the $\{1, 2k\}$-leapers as well as the $\{k, k + 1\}$-leapers. What is the asymptotic behavior of these statistics for general r and s?

TABLE 1. Distance statistics of $(r + s) \times 2s$ leaper graphs

	$s{\mp}2$	$s{\mp}3$	$s{\mp}4$	$s{\mp}5$	$s{\mp}6$	$s{\mp}7$	$s{\mp}8$	$s{\mp}9$	$s{\mp}10$	$s{\mp}11$	$s{\mp}12$	$s{\mp}13$
$r{\mp}1{\rightarrow}$	**5**	∞	11	∞	17	∞	23	∞	29	∞	35	∞
$s{=}2{\rightarrow}$	**5**	$r{\mp}2{\rightarrow}$ **11**	∞	13	∞	18	∞	23	∞	28	∞	33
$s{=}3{\rightarrow}$	∞	11	$r{\mp}3{\rightarrow}$ **17**	∞	∞	∞	19	∞	24	∞	∞	∞
$s{=}4{\rightarrow}$	**11**	∞	17	$r{\mp}4{\rightarrow}$ **23**	∞	23	∞	28	∞	25	∞	30
$s{=}5{\rightarrow}$	∞	14	∞	23	$r{\mp}5{\rightarrow}$ **29**	∞	27	∞	∞	∞	33	∞
$s{=}6{\rightarrow}$	**17**	∞	∞	∞	29	$r{\mp}6{\rightarrow}$ **35**	∞	∞	∞	35	∞	44
$s{=}7{\rightarrow}$	∞	18	∞	29	∞	35	$r{\mp}7{\rightarrow}$ **41**	∞	47	∞	39	∞
$s{=}8{\rightarrow}$	**23**	∞	20	∞	30	∞	41	$r{\mp}8{\rightarrow}$ **47**	∞	44	∞	41
$s{=}9{\rightarrow}$	∞	24	∞	30	∞	∞	∞	47	$r{\mp}9{\rightarrow}$ **53**	∞	∞	∞
$s{=}10{\rightarrow}$	**29**	∞	24	∞	∞	∞	47	∞	53	$r{\mp}10{\rightarrow}$ **59**	∞	51
$s{=}11{\rightarrow}$	∞	28	∞	26	∞	47	∞	46	∞	59	$r{\mp}11{\rightarrow}$ **65**	∞
$s{=}12{\rightarrow}$	**35**	∞	∞	∞	34	∞	43	∞	∞	∞	65	$r{\mp}12{\rightarrow}$ **71**
$s{=}13{\rightarrow}$	∞	34	∞	30	∞	46	∞	44	∞	65	∞	71

This chapter has focused on the cases where $r = 1$ or $s - r = 1$. Another infinite family of leaper graphs that cries out for investigation arises when r is even and $s = 2r \pm 1$. With such parameters the leaper is approximately an ordinary chess knight, but scaled up by a factor of r.

"Fibonacci leapers," like $\{5, 8\}$ or $\{8, 13\}$, etc., should also lead to beautiful patterns. (Of course we ought to omit every third case, like $\{3, 5\}$ or $\{13, 21\}$, because F_j and F_{j+1} are both odd when $j \bmod 3 = 1$.)

Bruce Sagan wrote me in October of 1994 to propose a generalization of Theorem 1 to higher-dimensional boards, based on hand calculations he had done in dimension 3: "Suppose we have an $\{r_1, r_2, \ldots, r_k\}$-leaper where $r_1 \le \cdots \le r_k$. If there is some box such that the corresponding leaper graph is connected then the smallest such box has dimensions $n_1 \times \cdots \times n_k$ where $n_i = \max(2r_i, r_{i-1} + r_{i+1})$. Here we let $r_0 = r_1$ and $r_{k+1} = r_k$. Note that we have $n_1 = r_1 + r_2$ and $n_k = 2r_k$."

The idea of presenting knight's tours as black-and-white diagrams with the "eofill" operator was discovered by George Jelliss, who showed it to me in a letter dated 26 December 1992. [See "Knight's tour mosaics," *The Games and Puzzles Journal* (online) #21 (March 2001), §15.] Jelliss wondered how hard it would be to minimize or maximize the black area; this question seems to be quite difficult, except for boards of small size. By making an exhaustive search of all the ordinary knight tours on a 6 × 6 board, I found that the minimum and maximum black areas in that case are respectively $547/60 \approx 9.11667$ and $303/20 = 15.15$, out of the total conceivable area $5 \times 5 = 25$; the extremal tours that achieve these limits are unique:

Steady advances in hardware and software technology have led to further progress in the study of leaper graphs. In particular, Michael Jünger has now verified Willcocks's conjecture for all cases with $r + s = 17$, 19, 21, and 23, leaving $r + s = 25$ as the next frontier. He also has extended his earlier results about Hamiltonian $\{r, r + 1\}$-leapers on $(2r + 1) \times n$ boards; the smallest such boards are now known to be the following:

$$r = \quad 1 \quad 2 \quad 3 \quad 4 \quad 5 \quad 6 \quad 7 \quad 8 \quad 9 \quad 10 \quad 11$$
$$\min n = 10 \quad 16 \quad 22 \quad 46 \quad 56 \quad 92 \quad 106 \quad 138 \quad 172 \quad 212 \quad 254$$

For example, he found the following 23×254 tour of an $\{11, 12\}$-leaper, which you might be able to see with a magnifying glass:

This is a Hamilton cycle in a graph with 5842 vertices, found in 148 seconds on a dual-core Xeon® 5130 2GHz computer with 4GB RAM. His experiments were done in 2009 with the Concorde TSP solver developed by David Applegate, Bob Bixby, Vašek Chvátal, and Bill Cook (http://www.tsp.gatech.edu/concorde.html).

Leaper graphs have been incorporated into the online collection tsplib of benchmark tests for what I (still) call the "traveling salesrep problem." They probably will always provide interesting challenges as new algorithms are developed for that problem.

Chapter 44

Number Representations and Dragon Curves

*[Written with Chandler Davis. Originally published in the Journal of Recreational Mathematics **3** (1970), 66–81, 133–149.]*

1. Introduction

Take a long strip of paper and fold it in half; then fold the result in half again, several more times, as shown in Figure 1. When the paper is opened up again, it displays an interesting pattern of creases.

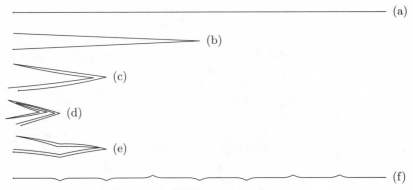

(a)

(b)

(c)

(d)

(e)

(f)

FIGURE 1. Folding a strip of paper.

If we write D for a crease that makes the paper dip downward (a "valley fold"), and U for one that makes an upward hump (a "mountain fold"), Figure 1 shows that after n folds the creases form the following patterns:

$$n = 1 \quad D$$
$$n = 2 \quad DDU$$
$$n = 3 \quad DDUDDUU$$

It is easy to see that there will be $2^n - 1$ creases after n folding operations have been performed, since the paper has been divided into 2^n areas.

Let S_n be the sequence of $2^n - 1$ Ds and Us that is obtained after n folding operations. One way to analyze the sequences S_1, S_2, S_3, ... is to observe that S_{n+1} always begins with S_n, since we can imagine starting with paper twice as long when we want to do $n + 1$ folds. In the same way we can see that the sequence S_{n+1} ends with the sequence S_n in backwards order, with U and D interchanged, since the last n folds act in essentially the same way on the first and last halves of the paper. Thus we know that S_4 must begin with $S_3 = DDUDDUU$, and it must end with S_3 backwards (namely $UUDDUDD$) but with U and D swapped (namely $DDUUDUU$). If we let $\overline{S}$ denote the sequence obtained from a sequence S by writing it backwards and interchanging U and D, we therefore get the simple formula

$$S_{n+1} = S_n D \overline{S_n}. \tag{1.1}$$

(The middle letter, which comes from the first fold, is always D.) This rule defines S_n for any n, starting with the "empty" sequence S_0. Notice that for any sequences S and T we have

$$\overline{\overline{S}} = S \qquad \text{and} \qquad \overline{ST} = \overline{T}\,\overline{S};$$

therefore

$$\overline{S_{n+1}} = S_n U \overline{S_n}. \tag{1.2}$$

In other words, $\overline{S_n}$ turns out to be the same as S_n, except that the middle letter is changed from D to U. This is the sequence of creases that we get if we turn the paper end-for-end.

There is yet another way to obtain the sequence S_{n+1} from S_n, if we concentrate our attention on the last fold instead of the first: The 2nd, 4th, 6th, ... creases in S_{n+1} are evidently the same as the creases of S_n. Furthermore, the 1st, 3rd, 5th, ... creases are alternately D, U, D, U, ...; this is easily seen from Figure 1(e), since the odd-numbered creases must alternate regardless of the pattern of the even-numbered ones. Thus $S_n = a_1 a_2 a_3 \ldots a_m$ implies that

$$S_{n+1} = D a_1 U a_2 D a_3 U \ldots D a_m U. \tag{1.3}$$

Since S_{n+1} begins with S_n it makes sense to talk of the infinite sequence S_∞ that arises in the limit. Rule (1.3) gives us a quick way to write down as much of S_∞ as we please. First we write alternating Ds and Us, leaving spaces between them:

$$D \quad U \quad D \quad U \quad D \quad U \quad D \quad U \quad D \quad U \quad \ldots$$

Then, using our left hand to point and our right hand to write, and with the left hand moving just half as fast as the right, we successively copy the letters that are being pointed at, into the remaining spaces:

$$S_\infty = DDUDDUUDDDUUDUUDDDUD\ldots \qquad (1.4)$$

From S_∞ we can easily read off the sequences S_1, S_2, S_3, S_4, etc., by looking at the first few letters. (A well-known empirical theorem states that a piece of paper cannot be folded in half more than twelve times,[*] no matter how long or thin a sheet is used. But from the standpoint of pure mathematics we may safely ignore such mundane considerations.)

An infinite sheet of paper that is creased in accordance with the sequence S_∞, and then opened up so that each crease makes an angle of $100°$, forms a pattern that begins as shown in Figure 2. The continuation of this pattern winds slowly around the initial point, eventually forming an infinite spiral.

FIGURE 2. The folds of S_8 opened, with $100°$ angles at each bend.

An even more interesting pattern can be observed if $90°$ angles are used, as shown in Figure 3 on the next page. Here the first 4096 segments of the design are illustrated; notice that different portions of the diagram that were separated in Figure 2 have now become perfectly enmeshed with each other. We call this the "dragon design of order 12" since it corresponds to 12 folding operations. If we round out the corners in Figure 3 we obtain the intriguing pattern of Figure 4, which has been called the "dragon curve" by its discoverer John E. Heighway [1].

---

[*] See Britney C. Gallivan, *How to Fold Paper in Half Twelve Times* (Pomona, California: Historical Society of Pomona Valley, 2002), 45 pages.

FIGURE 3. Dragon design of order 12.

In the remainder of this paper we will investigate some of the most interesting properties of the dragon curve, and we will also find that several other types of dragon curves arise when slight changes are made in the method of paperfolding.

2. Number Representations

Further study of the dragon curve and dragon design can be based on some novel ways to represent integers. Let us begin with the familiar binary system, where, for example, the number 982 is represented as

$$982 = (1111010110)_2. \tag{2.1}$$

(A survey of number systems and their history appears in [4].) Equation (2.1) means, in another notation, that

$$982 = 2^9 + 2^8 + 2^7 + 2^6 + 2^4 + 2^2 + 2^1. \tag{2.2}$$

From the basic identity

$$2^k + 2^{k-1} + \cdots + 2^{j+1} + 2^j = 2^{k+1} - 2^j, \tag{2.3}$$

which comes from summing a geometric series, we may rewrite (2.2) as

$$982 = 2^{10} - 2^6 + 2^5 - 2^4 + 2^3 - 2^1,$$

FIGURE 4. Dragon curve of order 12.

and also (going back to the notation (2.1), with $\bar{1}$ standing for -1) as

$$982 = (1000\bar{1}1\bar{1}10\bar{1}0)_2. \tag{2.4}$$

Notice that the nonzero digits 1 and $\bar{1}$ alternate in this representation. For reasons that will become clear later, we will call a binary representation "folded" if it uses 1 and $\bar{1}$ alternately, as its nonzero digits. Every positive integer has a folded representation, which may be found from its binary representation as we deduced (2.4) from (2.3), namely by changing each maximal string of consecutive ones, '01...110', to the string '10...0$\bar{1}$0'. Furthermore, a folded representation of $-n$ is obtained from a folded representation of n by interchanging 1 and $\bar{1}$. But folded representations are not unique; another way to represent 982, besides (2.4), is

$$982 = (100\bar{1}1\bar{1}1\bar{1}110)_2. \tag{2.5}$$

The situation is clarified by the following theorem:

Theorem 1. *Every nonzero integer has exactly two folded representations, a "positive" one in which the rightmost nonzero digit is 1 and a "negative" one in which the rightmost nonzero digit is $\bar{1}$.*

Proof. We will show that each nonzero integer n has exactly one positive folded representation; the corresponding statement for negative representations follows by negating the positive representations of $-n$.

If n is even, its only possible folded representation is a representation of $n/2$ followed by a zero. If $n \neq 1$ is odd, its only possible positive folded representation is the negative of a representation of $-(n-1)/2$, followed by 1. Therefore we can prove that n has a unique positive folded representation by induction on $|n|$, noting that the representation of 1 is $(1)_2$ and the representation of -1 is $(\bar{1}1)_2$.   □

This proof of Theorem 1 gives us a simple way to construct the two folded representations of each integer from right to left. For example, we have the following table:

n	*Positive representation*	*Negative representation*	*Short representation*	
1	1	$1\bar{1}$	1	
2	10	$1\bar{1}0$	10	
3	$1\bar{1}1$	$10\bar{1}$	$10\bar{1}$	
4	100	$1\bar{1}00$	100	
5	$1\bar{1}01$	$1\bar{1}1\bar{1}$	$1\bar{1}01$	(2.6)
6	$1\bar{1}10$	$10\bar{1}0$	$10\bar{1}0$	
7	$10\bar{1}1$	$100\bar{1}$	$100\bar{1}$	
8	1000	$1\bar{1}000$	1000	
9	$1\bar{1}001$	$1\bar{1}01\bar{1}$	$1\bar{1}001$	

This table shows why we have called the representations "folded," since it corresponds roughly to the paperfolding process we have already seen: The positive representations of 7, 6, 5 end respectively with the negative representations of 1, 2, 3, negated. The negative representations of 7, 6, 5 end respectively with the positive representations of 1, 2, 3, negated. This is essentially the behavior we have already seen in (1.1), and in fact we will see later that the folded representations are intimately related to the dragon curve. For example, the rightmost column of (2.6) lists the folded representation having the fewest nonzero digits; the reader can verify that this is the positive or negative representation according as the nth letter of S_∞ in (1.4) is D or U, respectively. Alternatively one can show that the nth letter of S_∞ is D if and only if the short folded representation of n has an odd number of nonzero digits. (The famous Morse–Hedlund sequence [2, chapter 12] is obtained in essentially the same way from the ordinary binary representation of n.)

It is not hard to find the rule that takes us from the positive folded representation to the negative one: We simply change the rightmost nonzero digit from 1 to $\bar{1}$, and add 1 to the digit immediately to its left. (Compare (2.4) with (2.5).)

We can prove a similar representation law for the *Gaussian integers*, the complex numbers of the form $m + ni$ where m and n are integers. In this case we will use the Gaussian integer $1 + i$ as a base, instead of 2; and we will use the digits 0, 1, i, $\bar{1}$, $\bar{i}$ (the latter denoting $-i$), with the restriction that the nonzero digits must belong to the cyclic pattern

from left to right. For example,

$$-5 + 33i = (1000\bar{i}\bar{1}i10\bar{i}0)_{1+i}$$

is one of the admissible representations of this type, since the nonzero digits fall into the required sequence and since

$$(1 + i)^{10} = 32i \qquad\qquad (1 + i)^{10} = 32i$$
$$(1 + i)^{6} = -8i \qquad\qquad -i(1 + i)^{6} = -8$$
$$(1 + i)^{5} = -4 - 4i \qquad\qquad -(1 + i)^{5} = 4 + 4i$$
$$(1 + i)^{4} = -4 \qquad\qquad i(1 + i)^{4} = -4i$$
$$(1 + i)^{3} = -2 + 2i \qquad\qquad (1 + i)^{3} = -2 + 2i$$
$$(1 + i)^{1} = 1 + i \qquad\qquad -i(1 + i)^{1} = 1 - i$$
$$\text{Total} = -5 + 33i$$

Let us call such a scheme a "revolving representation" of a Gaussian integer. We can prove a result analogous to Theorem 1 for these curious representations:

Theorem 2. *Every nonzero Gaussian integer $m + ni$ has exactly four revolving representations, one each in which the rightmost nonzero digit takes on the values 1, i, $\bar{1}$, $\bar{i}$.*

Proof. Let us say that a revolving representation is of type σ if the rightmost nonzero digit is σ; we can use a proof very much like that of Theorem 1. It suffices to prove that $m + ni$ has a unique revolving representation of type 1, since the type σ representation is obtained by multiplying the type 1 representation of $(m + ni)/\sigma$ by σ.

Notice that $(1 + i)(a + bi) = (a - b) + (a + b)i$; hence the sum of the real and imaginary parts of a Gaussian multiple of $1+i$ is always an even number. Consequently if $m+n$ is even, the only possible revolving representation of $m+ni$ is a revolving representation (of the same type) of

$$\frac{m + ni}{1 + i} = \left(\frac{m+n}{2}\right) + \left(\frac{n-m}{2}\right)i,$$

followed by zero. And if $m + n$ is odd, the only possible revolving representation of type 1 is a type 1 representation of

$$\frac{m + ni - 1}{i(1 + i)} = \left(\frac{1 - m + n}{2}\right) + \left(\frac{1 - m - n}{2}\right)i,$$

multiplied by i and followed by 1. We can therefore prove the theorem by induction on $|m + ni|^2 = m^2 + n^2$, since our argument implies that 1, i, -1, and $-i$ have the following unique type 1 representations:

$$1 = (1)_{1+i},$$
$$i = (i1)_{1+i},$$
$$-1 = (i01)_{1+i},$$
$$-i = (\bar{1}i1)_{1+i}.$$

(The quantity

$$(m^2 + n^2) - \left(\left(\frac{1-m+n}{2}\right)^2 + \left(\frac{1-m-n}{2}\right)^2\right) = \frac{(m+1)^2}{2} + \frac{n^2}{2} - 1$$

is positive when $m+n$ is odd and $m^2 + n^2 > 1$, unless $m+ni = -2+i$; so $|m+ni|^2$ is decreased by the construction in all the remaining cases.)   □

As examples of Theorem 2, here are the four representations of some small Gaussian integers:

	Type 1	Type i	Type $\bar{1}$	Type $\bar{i}$
1	1	$\bar{i}\bar{1}i$	$\bar{i}0\bar{1}$	$1\bar{i}$
2	$\bar{1}i100$	$\bar{1}0i00$	$\bar{i}\bar{1}00$	$i00$
3	$\bar{1}0i01$	$i1\bar{i}00\bar{1}i$	$i1\bar{i}000\bar{1}$	$\bar{1}0i1\bar{i}$
$1+i$	10	$\bar{i}\bar{1}i0$	$\bar{i}0\bar{1}0$	$1\bar{i}0$
$2+i$	$\bar{i}\bar{1}i1$	$\bar{i}\bar{1}0i$	$\bar{1}i10\bar{i}\bar{1}$	$\bar{1}i100\bar{i}$
$3+i$	$\bar{1}0i10$	$\bar{1}00i0$	$\bar{1}i1\bar{i}\bar{1}0$	$\bar{1}i10\bar{i}0$
$1-i$	$\bar{1}i10$	$\bar{1}0i0$	$\bar{i}\bar{1}0$	$i0$
$2-i$	$\bar{1}0i1$	$\bar{1}00i$	$\bar{1}i1\bar{i}\bar{1}$	$\bar{1}i10\bar{i}$
$3-i$	$\bar{1}i010$	$i1\bar{i}0\bar{1}i0$	$i1\bar{i}00\bar{1}0$	$\bar{1}i1\bar{i}0$

If α is the string of digits representing the type σ representation of some Gaussian integer, we can find the corresponding type σi representation α^T and the type $-\sigma i$ representation α^S by the following recursive rules:

$$(\alpha 0)^T = \alpha^T 0, \qquad (\alpha 0)^S = \alpha^S 0, \qquad 0^T = 0^S = 0.$$

$$(\alpha i1)^T = \alpha 0i, \quad (\alpha \bar{1}i)^T = \alpha 0\bar{1}, \quad (\alpha i\bar{1})^T = \alpha 0\bar{i}, \quad (\alpha 1\bar{i})^T = \alpha 01.$$

$$(\alpha 01)^S = \alpha 1\bar{i}, \quad (\alpha 0i)^S = \alpha i1, \quad (\alpha 0\bar{1})^S = \alpha \bar{1}i, \quad (\alpha 0\bar{i})^S = \alpha \bar{i}\bar{1}.$$

$$(\alpha 01)^T = \alpha^R \bar{1}i, \quad (\alpha 0i)^T = \alpha^R \bar{i}\bar{1}, \quad (\alpha 0\bar{1})^T = \alpha^R 1\bar{i}, \quad (\alpha 0\bar{i})^T = \alpha^R i1.$$

$$(\alpha i1)^S = \alpha^R 0\bar{i}, \quad (\alpha \bar{1}i)^S = \alpha^R 01, \quad (\alpha \bar{i}\bar{1})^S = \alpha^R 0i, \quad (\alpha 1\bar{i})^S = \alpha^R 0\bar{1}.$$

$$(\alpha 0)^R = \alpha^S \sigma, \quad \text{if } \alpha \text{ is a type } -\sigma \text{ representation.}$$

$$(\alpha 1)^R = (\alpha i)^R = (\alpha \bar{1})^R = (\alpha \bar{i})^R = \alpha^T 0.$$

The rules in the first three lines are rather easy to understand: Clearly $(\alpha^S)^T = (\alpha^T)^S = \alpha$. If the rightmost nonzero digit, σ, of the type σ representation is immediately preceded by the nonzero digit σi, then the type σi representation is simply obtained by replacing the pair $(\sigma i)(\sigma)$ by $(0)(\sigma i)$. Let us call these two representations "similar."

On the other hand, if the rightmost nonzero digit of the type σ representation is immediately preceded by zero, the type σi representation is obtained by replacing the pair $(0)(\sigma)$ by $(-\sigma)(\sigma i)$ and performing a rather complicated transformation on the remainder of the representation to the left; in this case the type $-\sigma$ representation will be similar to the type σi representation. (An auxiliary transformation α^R appears above in order to simplify the equations; it takes a type $-\sigma$ representation of z into a type σ representation of $z + \sigma$. We have $(\alpha^R)^R = \alpha$.)

As a consequence of these remarks we may state that *the four revolving representations of a nonzero Gaussian integer always consist of two pairs of similar representations.* For example, consider the representations of 3, where $i1\bar{i}00\bar{1}i$ is similar to $i1\bar{i}000\bar{1}$, and $\bar{1}0i1\bar{i}$ is similar to $\bar{1}0i01$.

The reader may find it interesting to show that revolving representations to the base $1 - i$ are *not* always possible.

3. Analyses of the Dragon Curve

The ideas about number representations that we have just developed can be used to derive detailed information about the dragon curve.

Returning to the dragon sequence S_∞ defined in Section 1, let us define the functions

$$d(n) = \begin{cases} +1, & \text{if the } n\text{th letter of } S_\infty \text{ is } D; \\ -1, & \text{if the } n\text{th letter of } S_\infty \text{ is } U; \end{cases} \tag{3.1}$$

$$g(n) = d(1) + \cdots + d(n-1). \tag{3.2}$$

Then $g(n)$ represents the excess of Ds over Us in the first $n-1$ letters of the infinite string S_∞.

By (1.3) we have a simple independent definition of $d(n)$:

$$d(2n+1) = (-1)^n, \qquad d(2n) = d(n). \tag{3.3}$$

The reader may find it interesting to prove the multiplicative property

$$d(mn) = d(m)d(n). \tag{3.4}$$

We also have, by (1.1), the relation

$$d(2^{n+1} - m) = -d(m), \qquad \text{for } 0 < m < 2^n. \tag{3.5}$$

It follows that, if $1 \le m \le 2^n$,

$$\begin{aligned} g(2^{n+1}) &= g(2^{n+1} - m + 1) + d(2^{n+1} - m + 1) + \cdots + d(2^{n+1} - 1) \\ &= g(2^{n+1} - m + 1) - d(m-1) - \cdots - d(1) \\ &= g(2^{n+1} - m + 1) - g(m). \end{aligned} \tag{3.6}$$

Setting $m = 2^n$ yields

$$g(2^{n+1}) = g(2^n + 1) - g(2^n) = d(2^n) = 1,$$

since $d(2^n) = d(1) = 1$ by (3.3); therefore we have proved the relation

$$g(2^{n+1} - m + 1) = 1 + g(m), \qquad \text{for } n \ge 0 \text{ and } 1 \le m \le 2^n. \tag{3.7}$$

It follows, in particular, that $g(n) > 0$ for $n > 1$; that is, the Ds outnumber the Us in every nonempty initial segment of S_∞. The interested reader may also verify that $\lceil 2^{k+1}/3 \rceil$ is the smallest value of n such that $g(n) = k$, when $k > 0$. (The symbol $\lceil x \rceil$ denotes the least integer greater than or equal to x.)

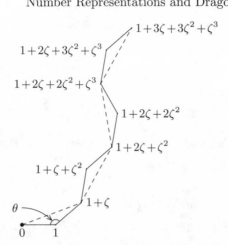

$$1+3\zeta+3\zeta^2+\zeta^3$$

$$1+2\zeta+3\zeta^2+\zeta^3$$

$$1+2\zeta+2\zeta^2+\zeta^3$$

$$1+2\zeta+2\zeta^2$$

$$1+2\zeta+\zeta^2$$

$$1+\zeta+\zeta^2$$

$$1+\zeta$$

θ

0 1

FIGURE 5. Dragon design represented with complex numbers.

Suppose we take our folded sheet of paper and bend it at an angle of exactly θ at every crease. (For example, when $\theta = 100°$ the paper assumes the shape shown in Figure 2; the case $\theta = 140°$ is illustrated in Figure 5.) Figure 5 shows that the shape of the curve can be described conveniently using complex arithmetic, based on powers of the number

$$\zeta \; = \; e^{i(\pi-\theta)}. \tag{3.8}$$

If we define the "dragon function" $\delta(n)$ by the rule

$$\delta(n) \; = \; \zeta^{g(1)} + \zeta^{g(2)} + \cdots + \zeta^{g(n)}, \tag{3.9}$$

it is not difficult to see that $\delta(n)$ is the point of the complex plane that is occupied by the nth crease in the paper, if the first line segment goes from 0 to 1.

The following table shows the behavior of the functions for small n.

n	$d(n)$	$g(n)$	$\delta(n)$
1	+1	0	1
2	+1	1	$1 + \zeta$
3	−1	2	$1 + \zeta + \zeta^2$
4	+1	1	$1 + 2\zeta + \zeta^2$
5	+1	2	$1 + 2\zeta + 2\zeta^2$
6	−1	3	$1 + 2\zeta + 2\zeta^2 + \zeta^3$
7	−1	2	$1 + 2\zeta + 3\zeta^2 + \zeta^3$
8	+1	1	$1 + 3\zeta + 3\zeta^2 + \zeta^3$

In order to obtain a convenient formula for $\delta(n)$ we may observe that, if $1 \leq m \leq 2^n$,

$$
\begin{aligned}
\delta(2^{n+1}) &= \delta(2^{n+1} - m) + \zeta^{g(2^{n+1}-m+1)} + \cdots + \zeta^{g(2^{n+1})} \\
&= \delta(2^{n+1} - m) + \zeta^{g(m)+1} + \cdots + \zeta^{g(1)+1} \\
&= \delta(2^{n+1} - m) + \zeta\delta(m).
\end{aligned}
\tag{3.10}
$$

Setting $m = 2^n$ we find $\delta(2^{n+1}) = (1 + \zeta)\delta(2^n)$, and therefore

$$
\delta(2^n) = (1 + \zeta)^n.
\tag{3.11}
$$

By combining (3.10) and (3.11) we obtain

Theorem 3. *If $n = 2^{k_0} - 2^{k_1} + \cdots + (-1)^t 2^{k_t}$, with $k_0 > k_1 > \cdots > k_t \geq 0$, then*

$$
\delta(n) = (1 + \zeta)^{k_0} - \zeta(1 + \zeta)^{k_1} + \cdots + (-\zeta)^t (1 + \zeta)^{k_t}. \quad \square
\tag{3.12}
$$

This formula gives $\delta(n)$ in terms of the folded representations of n. (Either folded representation will do.) It makes the paperfolding process altogether explicit: The "paper" is represented by the points $\delta(0)$, $\delta(1)$, ..., together with the segments joining each $\delta(n)$ to $\delta(n+1)$. When $\theta = 180°$, we have $\zeta = 1$ and $\delta(n) = n$: The "paper" is laid out straight. Decrease θ, and bends appear at every fold $\delta(n)$, until at $\theta = 90°$ and $\zeta = i$ we have the dragon design that begins as in Figure 3. As θ approaches $0°$, ζ approaches -1, and (3.12) approaches $0^{k_0} + 0^{k_1} + \cdots + 0^{k_t}$; under the usual convention $0^0 = 1$, which is appropriate in this case, we have $\delta(n) = 0$ when $k_t > 0$ (n even), and $\delta(n) = 1$ when $k_t = 0$ (n odd). Thus at $\theta = 0°$ we have the tightly folded position sketched schematically in Figure 1(d).

One of the interesting consequences of (3.12) is that

$$
\delta(2n) = (1 + \zeta)\delta(n),
\tag{3.13}
$$

so that the subsequence $\delta(0)$, $\delta(2)$, $\delta(4)$, $\delta(6)$, ... traces out the same shape as $\delta(0)$, $\delta(1)$, $\delta(2)$, $\delta(3)$, ..., multiplied by the factor $1 + \zeta$. (See the dotted lines in Figure 5.) This in turn allows us to derive the dragon curve in a new way, superficially quite different, which was first noticed by Bruce A. Banks [1]. We start with the single segment joining $0 = \delta(0)$ to $1 = \delta(1)$. To introduce the first fold, we leave those two points as the endpoints and fold down in the middle, so our three points are 0, $(1 + \zeta)^{-1}$, 1; that is, $(1 + \zeta)^{-1}\delta(0)$, $(1 + \zeta)^{-1}\delta(1)$, $(1 + \zeta)^{-1}\delta(2)$. At the next stage we leave those three points fixed and introduce a fold in each of the two segments joining them, alternating the directions; and so on. Each time, the segments inherited from the previous stage are replaced by folds, which alternate between down and up folds as the curve is traversed. Then the endpoints of the segments at the mth stage are

$$(1 + \zeta)^{-m} \delta(k) \qquad (k = 0, 1, 2, \ldots, 2^m),$$

by induction on m using (3.13). So we have "shrunk" the dragon design of order m into a curve that runs from 0 to 1.

To see what happens as m gets large, let us formally take (3.12) as the definition of $\delta(n)$ when n is any nonnegative *real* number in folded representation. Since (3.13) remains valid, the points we just found may be written as

$$(1 + \zeta)^{-m} \delta(2^m s) = \delta(s) \qquad (s = 0, 2^{-m}, 2 \cdot 2^{-m}, \ldots, 1). \qquad (3.14)$$

The reader should have no difficulty in proving that the series (3.12) converges for other values of s as well, whenever $60° < \theta < 180°$; and that $\delta(s)$ is thereby defined as a continuous curve in the plane. For example,

$$\begin{aligned} \delta(1/3) &= \delta(2^{-1} - 2^{-2} + 2^{-3} - 2^{-4} + \cdots) \\ &= (1 + \zeta)^{-1} - \zeta(1 + \zeta)^{-2} + \zeta^2(1 + \zeta)^{-3} - \cdots \\ &= 1/(1 + 2\zeta). \end{aligned}$$

We will not dwell on the properties of this curve. The reader may prove, using Theorem 4 below, that for $\zeta = i$ ($\theta = 90°$) the continuous function $\delta(s)$ is "space-filling" as s runs over all nonnegative real values; indeed, four copies of it cover the plane, without hitting any point more than four times. (See exercise 4.1–18 in [4].)

Confining ourselves again to integer values of n, we may raise another question: Since folded representations exist for both positive and negative n, should we not extend our formulas to negative n? If we retain (3.3) we must have

$$d(-n) = -d(n) \qquad \text{if } n \neq 0. \qquad (3.15)$$

We may define $d(0)$ as either $+1$, 0, or -1, as it suits our fancy. (The choice $d(0) = 0$ makes (3.4) and (3.15) valid for all integers m and n.)

Now if we are to retain the relations $g(n+1)-g(n) = d(n)$ and $\delta(n+1) - \delta(n) = \zeta^{d(n)}(\delta(n) - \delta(n-1))$ for all n, we must have for $n \geq 0$

$$
\begin{aligned}
g(-n) &= -(d(0) + d(-1) + \cdots + d(-n)) \\
&= g(n+1) - d(0);
\end{aligned}
\tag{3.16}
$$

$$
\begin{aligned}
\delta(-n) &= -(\zeta^{g(0)} + \cdots + \zeta^{g(1-n)}) \\
&= -(\zeta^{g(1)-d(0)} + \cdots + \zeta^{g(n)-d(0)}) \\
&= -\zeta^{-d(0)}\delta(n).
\end{aligned}
\tag{3.17}
$$

These formulas are neatest in the classical case $\theta = 90°$, $\zeta = i$. For then (3.17) says that

$$
\delta(-n) = \begin{cases}
i\delta(n), & \text{if } d(0) = +1; \\
-\delta(n), & \text{if } d(0) = 0; \\
-i\delta(n), & \text{if } d(0) = -1;
\end{cases}
$$

in other words the "negative" dragon curve is the same as the positive dragon curve, except rotated by $90°$, $180°$, or $270°$.

Though $d(0) = 0$ may seem most natural, the choice $d(0) = +1$, $\theta = 90°$ gives a curve obtained from the sequence of creases

$$
S = \overline{S_\infty}DS_\infty,
$$

which is infinite in both directions. This sequence (and hence the entire associated doubly infinite dragon curve) has the following remarkable property that was mentioned to the authors by Frans Djorup: Any finite segment of S is repeated infinitely often in S; but S has a unique "midpoint" if it is considered as a whole, since the equation

$$
d(n + n_0) = d(n)
$$

for fixed n_0 can hold for all integers n only when $n_0 = 0$, as we see from (3.3). Thus we must examine infinitely many elements of S (or infinitely many sections of the curve) in order to locate its center.

Now let's analyze the classical dragon curve in detail. When $\zeta = i$, Theorem 3 tells us that

$$
\begin{aligned}
\delta(2^{k_0} - 2^{k_1} &+ \cdots + (-1)^t 2^{k_t}) \\
&= (1+i)^{k_0} - i(1+i)^{k_1} + \cdots + (-i)^t(1+i)^{k_t}.
\end{aligned}
\tag{3.18}
$$

For example, if we use the folded and revolving number systems,

$$\delta(982) = \delta((1000\bar{1}1\bar{1}10\bar{1}0)_2)$$
$$= (1000\bar{i}\bar{1}i10\bar{i}0)_{1+i}$$
$$= -5 + 33i. \tag{3.19}$$

A revolving representation of $\delta(n)$ is given in terms a folded representation of n. We can therefore apply our number-representation know-how to deduce what is probably the most interesting property of the dragon curve:

Theorem 4. *The infinite dragon curve (which begins as shown in Figure 4) never crosses itself. Four dragon curves, started at the same point but rotated at 90° intervals, fill the entire plane completely, in the sense that each line segment of length one in the plane, having integer coordinates for its endpoints, is traversed exactly once by the four associated dragon designs. (See Figure 6.)*

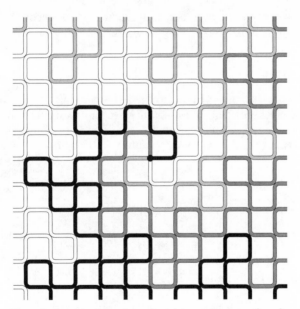

FIGURE 6. Four dragon designs, joined end-to-end, cover the plane.

This result was first noticed by William G. Harter [1], but the following discussion is apparently the first rigorous proof that explains the phenomenon.

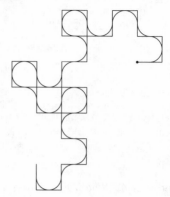

FIGURE 7. Dragon curve
superimposed on dragon design.

Proof. From the relation between the dragon design and the dragon
curve (see Figure 7), and the fact that the dragon design consists of
straight lines joining points with integer coordinates, with a 90° turn
after every unit step, it is evident that the dragon curve will not cross
itself unless the dragon design traverses some line segment twice. Thus
the first part of the theorem is a consequence of the second part.

The four dragon designs may be represented by the four functions

$$\delta(n),\ i\delta(n),\ -\delta(n),\ -i\delta(n). \tag{3.20}$$

Every line segment of length one in the plane, having integer coordinates
as its endpoints, may be represented as a line segment from $a + bi$ to
$a + bi + \sigma$, where $a + b$ is even and σ is 1, i, -1, or $-i$. Let the type σ
representation of $a + bi + \sigma$ be

$$a + bi + \sigma \ = \ \sigma i^t (1+i)^{k_0} + \cdots + \sigma i (1+i)^{k_t} + \sigma, \tag{3.21}$$

where $k_0 > \cdots > k_t > 0$ and $t \geq 0$; and let

$$n \ = \ 2^{k_0} + \cdots + (-1)^{t-1} 2^{k_t} + (-1)^t. \tag{3.22}$$

Then we have, by formula (3.18),

$$\begin{aligned} a + bi + \sigma &= \sigma i^t \delta(n); \\ a + bi\ &= \sigma i^t \delta(n - (-1)^t). \end{aligned} \tag{3.23}$$

Therefore any given line segment is traversed at least once by one of the
four dragon designs.

For example, suppose we want to prove that the line segment from $33+5i$ to $33+6i$ is traversed by one of the four dragon designs. Then we let $a = 33$, $b = 5$, $\sigma = i$, and we compute the revolving representations:

$$33 + 6i = (\bar{i}000\bar{1}i1\bar{i}0\bar{1}i)_{1+i};$$
$$33 + 5i = (\bar{i}000\bar{1}i1\bar{i}0\bar{1}0)_{1+i}.$$

It follows that $-i\delta(n) = 33 + 6i$ and $-i\delta(n - 1) = 33 + 5i$, if $n = (1000\bar{1}1\bar{1}10\bar{1}1)_2 = 983$. (See (3.19).) This segment is traversed in the 983rd segment of the fourth dragon design.

To complete the proof of Theorem 4, we must show that no line segment is traversed more than once. If some segment were traversed twice, then one of its endpoints must occur at least three times among the four dragon designs (3.20). Evidently $\delta(n) \neq 0$ when $n > 0$, so the proof will be complete if we show that *every nonzero Gaussian integer occurs exactly twice among the four dragon designs.*

For this claim we invoke Theorem 2, which tells us that any given nonzero Gaussian integer $a + bi$ has exactly four revolving representations. We have already observed that these form two pairs of "similar" representations. By the correspondence between the positive and negative folded representations of an integer (see the remarks following Theorem 1), we see that each pair of similar representations defines a single value of n, and a single one of the four dragon designs (3.20) that assumes the value $a + bi$ at the nth step. $\square$

For example, consider the point $a+bi = 3$. Its type 1 representation, $(\bar{1}0\,i01)_{1+i}$, is similar to its type $\bar{i}$ representation, $(\bar{1}0\,i1\bar{i})_{1+i}$; both of these tell us that $3 = -\delta(n)$ where $n = (10\bar{1}01)_2 = (10\bar{1}1\bar{1})_2 = 13$. Its type i and $\bar{1}$ representations, $(i1\bar{i}00\bar{1}i)_{1+i}$ and $(i1\bar{i}000\bar{1})_{1+i}$, both say that $3 = i\delta(n)$ for $n = (1\bar{1}100\bar{1}1)_2 = (1\bar{1}1000\bar{1})_2 = 47$.

This proof of Theorem 4 not only shows us that the four dragon curves fill the plane, it gives us a reasonably efficient way to compute exactly when a given point will be hit.

Before leaving the dragon curve let us make note of a few more consequences of Theorem 3 when the bending angle is different from $90°$. If θ is less than $60°$, the point $1 + \zeta$ lies inside the unit circle, so $(1 + \zeta)^m \to 0$ as $m \to \infty$. Therefore the dragon design is bounded in the plane when $0 < \theta < 60°$.

It is interesting to study the borderline case $\theta = 60°$, when $1 + \zeta$ is $e^{\pi i/3}$, a sixth root of unity. Then $(1 + \zeta)^6 = (1 + \zeta)^{12} = \cdots = 1$, hence the dragon design comes back repeatedly to visit points infinitely often.

It is not difficult to see that every "Eisenstein integer point" $a + b\zeta$ in the plane, including zero, is traversed infinitely often by the dragon design when $\theta = 60°$. Furthermore, it is possible to analyze the pattern formed by the first 2^m segments of this design, using a rather tedious argument. We can show, for example, that the first 2^{12n-2} segments of the curve have the shape indicated in Figure 8.

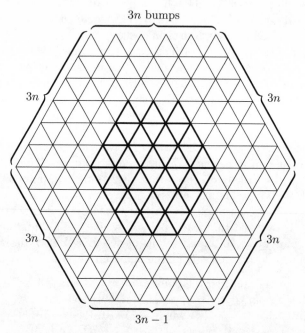

FIGURE 8. Dragon design of order $12n - 2$ for $\theta = 60°$.
(Illustrated for $\boldsymbol{n = 1}$ and $n = 2$.)

4. The Alternate Dragon Curve

Let's go back now to our original paperfolding experiment. What would happen if we were to fold the paper over first from left to right, then from right to left, then left to right again, and so on alternately? (See Figure 9.) Our first inclination would be to say that this makes no essential difference; but Figure 9 shows that already after three folds we have a somewhat different pattern than we obtained in Figure 1! The

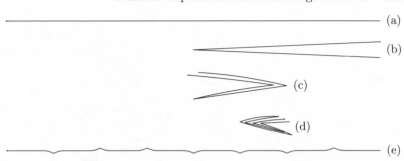

(a)

(b)

(c)

(d)

(e)

FIGURE 9. Paperfolding in alternating directions.

sequence of creases now becomes

$$S_1 = D$$
$$S_2 = UDD$$
$$S_3 = DUUDDDU$$
$$S_4 = UDDUUUDDUDDDUUD.$$

A study of this situation reveals that we get a more tractable sequence when we flip the paper over (interchanging D and U) when n is even:

$$S_1 = D$$
$$S_2 = DUU$$
$$S_3 = DUUDDDU$$
$$S_4 = DUUDDDUUDUUUDDU.$$

Now we have the pattern

$$S_{n+1} = \begin{cases} S_n D \overline{S_n}, & \text{if } n \text{ is even,} \\ S_n U \overline{S_n}, & \text{if } n \text{ is odd,} \end{cases} \qquad (4.1)$$

which leads to an infinite sequence as before.

Having gone this far, it is only natural to plot the "alternate dragon curve" corresponding to this method of alternate folding. The result is something of a surprise: This curve fills an isosceles triangle! (See Figure 10.)

The triangular curve in Figure 10 has a very interesting fine structure that the reader can see by tracing over it with a colored pen. (Try it!) Another way to exhibit this structure is shown in Figure 11, which

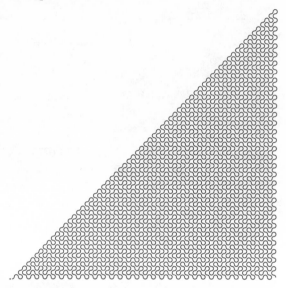

FIGURE 10. The alternate dragon curve of order 12.

illustrates the attractive shape formed by the alternate dragon curve when the bending angle is 95° instead of 90°.

It is interesting to explore this curve in the same manner as we have analyzed the classical dragon curve. To spare the reader the details, we will merely list the results here, for comparison with the previous formulas:

$$d(2n + 1) = (-1)^n, \qquad d(2n) = -d(n); \tag{4.2}$$

$$\delta(2^{k_0} - 2^{k_1} + \cdots + (-1)^t 2^{k_t})$$
$$= \zeta^{-a_0}(1+\zeta)^{k_0} - \zeta^{-a_1}(1+\zeta)^{k_1} + \cdots + (-1)^t \zeta^{-a_t}(1+\zeta)^{k_t}, \tag{4.3}$$

where

$$a_j = (-1)^{k_0} + \cdots + (-1)^{k_{j-1}} + \lfloor k_j/2 \rfloor. \tag{4.4}$$

It is remarkable that Figure 10 is so much simpler in appearance than the classical dragon curve, in view of the fact that its equation (4.3) is so much more complicated than (3.12).

There are, of course, many more patterns by which the initial strip of paper could be repeatedly folded in half, if we fold willy-nilly in either direction. Let us say that a "generalized dragon curve" is any curve obtainable by some such sequence of folds, after opening the paper to 90° bends at each crease and rounding the corners.

FIGURE 11. Spreading out the alternate dragon curve.

Theorem 5. *A generalized dragon curve never crosses itself.*

Proof.   This time we must prove the first part of Theorem 4 under much weaker hypotheses, so it is necessary to use an entirely different method of proof. Fortunately a simple geometric argument can be used, with a minimum of algebra.

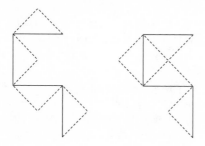

FIGURE 12.
From n folds to $n + 1$.

Let $\delta(n)$ denote the point reached by a given generalized dragon design after n steps. If we are given a dragon design from a sequence of d folds, the sequence obtainable from one further fold will form a zigzag pattern that alternates from one side of the given design to the other, as shown in Figure 12. We have two choices, corresponding to which direction we make the final fold; this corresponds to whether we start the zigzag pattern on one side of the first segment or on the other side. Consequently we can see that *the sequence* $\delta(0)$, $\delta(2)$, $\delta(4)$, ... *is also the sequence corresponding to some generalized dragon design* (multiplied by the factor $(1 + i)$), *having one less fold.*

Since the dragon design changes orientation by $90°$ at each crease, its line segments alternate between a horizontal and a vertical orientation. If $\delta(m) = \delta(n)$, for $m < n$, the number of horizontal steps intervening between m and n must be even (in order to get back to the same point), and the number of vertical steps is also even; so we must have the same number of horizontal and vertical steps, and $n - m$ must be a multiple of 4.

In order to show that the generalized dragon curve does not cross itself, we must prove that the generalized dragon design traces no segment twice. If it did, we would have, say, $\delta(m) = \delta(n)$ and $\delta(m+1) = \delta(n\pm1)$. Since both $n-m$ and $(n\pm1)-(m+1)$ are multiples of 4 we must choose the $+$ sign:

$$\delta(m) = \delta(n) \qquad \text{and} \qquad \delta(m + 1) = \delta(n + 1).$$

We can choose m to be the smallest possible value so that this happens. If m is even, we must have $\delta(m + 2) \neq \delta(n + 2)$, by induction on the number of folds, since otherwise we would have a line segment traced twice in the "even" sequence $\delta(m)$, $\delta(m + 2)$, ..., $\delta(n)$, $\delta(n + 2)$ corresponding to one less fold. Since the lines from $\delta(m + 1)$ to $\delta(m + 2)$ and from $\delta(n + 1)$ to $\delta(n + 2)$ both have vertical orientation or both have horizontal orientation, we have

$$\delta(m + 2) - \delta(m + 1) = -(\delta(n + 2) - \delta(n + 1)).$$

But now there is a $90°$ orientation between the line from $\delta(m)$ to $\delta(m+2)$ and the line from $\delta(n)$ to $\delta(n+2)$, as shown in Figure 13; this is impossible, since $n - m$ is a multiple of 4 and there cannot be an odd number of steps between m and n in the "even" sequence m, $m + 2$, ..., n. And if m is odd we obtain a similar contradiction, because $\delta(m - 1) \neq \delta(n - 1)$ and there can't be a $90°$ orientation between the line from $\delta(m + 1)$ to $\delta(m - 1)$ and the line from $\delta(n + 1)$ to $\delta(n - 1)$. Therefore no segment is traced twice, and the theorem has been proved.   □

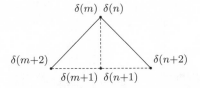

$\delta(m)$ $\delta(n)$

$\delta(m+2)$

$\delta(n+2)$

$\delta(m+1)$ $\delta(n+1)$

FIGURE 13.
Can a generalized design
trace a segment twice?

Theorem 5 implies that we can get a wide variety of interesting curves if we fold the paper haphazardly, choosing at random between the relations $S_{n+1} = S_n D \overline{S_n}$ or $S_{n+1} = S_n U \overline{S_n}$. Readers who have access to automatic plotting equipment may find it interesting to generate random dragon curves; some of the infinite variety that is possible is illustrated in Figures 14–16, which were selected from about twenty candidates drawn on a Calcomp® plotter in 1968.

Many variations of sequence (1.4) have been explored by Heighway and Harter [3], often leading to striking patterns.

FIGURE 14. Mama, baby, and papa $(D,\ D,\ D,\ D,\ U,\ U,\ U,\ D,\ U,\ U,\ D,\ U)$.

FIGURE 15. Autumn $(D, U, D, D, D, D, U, D, D, U, D, U)$.

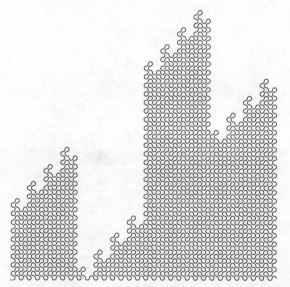

FIGURE 16. Skyline $(D, D, U, U, D, U, D, D, U, U, D, U)$.

5. Ter-dragon Curves

Still more possibilities arise if we use a new type of fold that *trisects* the paper at each step instead of bisecting it:

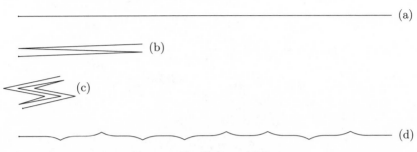

FIGURE 17. Ternary folding.

This procedure yields

$$S_1 = DU$$
$$S_2 = DUDDUUDU$$

and, in general,

$$S_{n+1} = S_n D S_n U S_n. \tag{5.1}$$

(Notice that $\overline{S_n} = S_n$.) Our sequence $d(n)$ now is defined by the rules

$$d(3n+1) = +1, \quad d(3n-1) = -1, \quad d(3n) = d(n). \tag{5.2}$$

The corresponding "ter-dragon design" is not very interesting when we open the creases to 90° angles. But it makes a space-filling pattern when we use 60° angles instead, as shown in Figure 18 on the following page.

We can develop the theory of the ter-dragon curve in essentially the same way as we have analyzed the classical dragon curve. For brevity we will merely state the key facts here, since readers may fill in the gaps by themselves using techniques that have been explained earlier.

The dragon design sequence $\delta(n)$ corresponding to (5.1) satisfies the relations

$$\delta(3^n + m) = (2 + \zeta)^n + \zeta\delta(m),$$
$$\delta(2 \cdot 3^n + m) = (1 + \zeta)(2 + \zeta)^n + \delta(m), \tag{5.3}$$

for $0 \le m < 3^n$; therefore $\delta(n)$ can readily be determined from the ternary representation of n. When the bending angle θ is 60°, we have $\zeta = \omega$, where

$$\omega = \frac{-1 + \sqrt{3}i}{2} \tag{5.4}$$

is a cube root of unity.

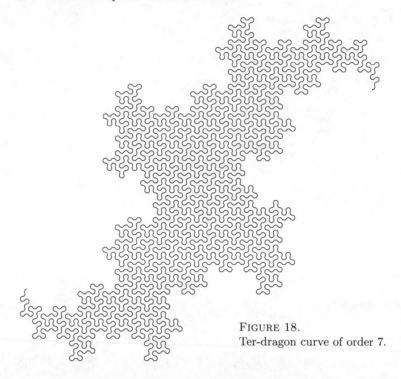

FIGURE 18.
Ter-dragon curve of order 7.

Just as four classical dragon curves fill the plane, *six* ter-dragon curves will fill the plane if they are joined at 60° angles. (See Figure 19.)

FIGURE 19. Six ter-dragon curves fill the plane.

We have implicitly assumed that relation (5.1) forms S_{n+1} by adding more letters to the right of the string S_n at the left; but we may also imagine that S_{n+1} is obtained by starting with the S_n in the middle and adding letters at both ends. If we hold the *middle* of S_n in a fixed position as n goes to $n+1$, we obtain a sequence S_∞ that is infinite in *both* directions. Under this interpretation we get a new view of the ter-dragon curve; in fact, a *single* ter-dragon curve now fills the plane! See Figure 20, where, for convenience, we have rotated and flipped the curve, and scaled it by 2 so that the distance between creases is 2 instead of 1. It is convenient to place the origin at the exact center of this curve τ, and to make the 60° bends occur at the points $\tau(n+1/2)$ instead of at $\tau(n)$.

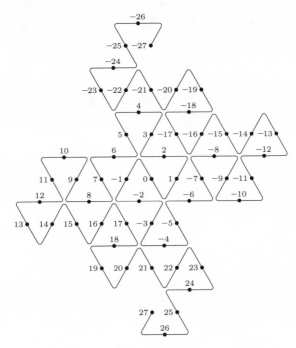

FIGURE 20. Plane-filling ter-dragon curve $\tau(t)$, for $-27 \leq t \leq 27$.
(Point $\tau(n)$ is labeled 'n'.)

The ter-dragon curve of Figure 20 has some pleasant properties that are related to the *balanced ternary* number system. In this system (see [4]), numbers are written to the base 3, with 1, 0, and $\bar{1}$ as the digits instead of 0, 1, and 2.

Numbers of the form $a + b\omega$, where a and b are integers and ω is given by (5.4), are called "Eisenstein integers." For convenience we shall use the symbol ψ to denote the other complex cube root of unity,

$$\psi = \frac{-1 - \sqrt{3}i}{2} = \omega^2 = -1 - \omega. \tag{5.5}$$

Eisenstein integers have a "revolving cubic representation" analogous to our revolving representations of Gaussian integers: We use the number

$$1 + 2\omega = \sqrt{3}i$$

as base, and our nonzero digits are $1, \bar{\psi}, \omega, \bar{1}, \psi, \bar{\omega}$, which are the sixth roots of unity. (Here the bar over a digit denotes *negation*, not complex conjugation.) The "revolving" rule for nonzero digits is that, from left to right,

$$\begin{aligned} &1 \text{ and } \bar{1} \text{ must be followed by } \omega \text{ or } \bar{\omega}; \\ &\omega \text{ and } \bar{\omega} \text{ must be followed by } \psi \text{ or } \bar{\psi}; \\ &\psi \text{ and } \bar{\psi} \text{ must be followed by } 1 \text{ or } \bar{1}. \end{aligned} \tag{5.6}$$

We have the following simple connection between the balanced ternary representation of x and a revolving cubic representation of $\tau(x)$, when $2x$ is an integer:

x	*Balanced ternary representation of x*	*Revolving cubic representation of $\tau(x)$*
0	0.0	0.0
1/2	0.111111...	$0.1\omega\psi1\omega\psi\ldots$
1	1.0	1.0
3/2	1.111111...	$1.\omega\psi1\omega\psi1\ldots$
2	$1\bar{1}.0$	$1\bar{\omega}.0$
50	$1\bar{1}0\bar{1}1.0$	$1\bar{\omega}0\bar{\psi}\bar{1}.0$

In other words, we cyclically substitute $1, \omega, \psi$ for the ones in the balanced ternary representation, while retaining the signs. The infinite expansions that arise can be simplified as follows:

$$\begin{aligned} (0.1\omega\psi1\omega\psi\ldots)_{1+2\omega} &= \frac{1}{1+2\omega}\left(1 + \frac{\omega}{1+2\omega} + \left(\frac{\omega}{1+2\omega}\right)^2 + \cdots\right) \\ &= \frac{1}{1+2\omega}\left(\frac{1}{1 - \omega/(1+2\omega)}\right) = \frac{1}{1+\omega} = -\omega; \end{aligned} \tag{5.7}$$

hence $\tau(1/2) = -\omega$. The fraction $1/2$ actually has two representations in the balanced ternary number system, namely $(0.111111\ldots)_3$ and $(1.\overline{1}\overline{1}\overline{1}\overline{1}\overline{1}\ldots)_3$. It makes no difference which representation we choose, since

$$(1.\overline{\omega}\overline{\psi}\overline{1}\,\overline{\omega}\overline{\psi}\overline{1}\ldots)_{1+2\omega}$$
$$= 1 + (-\omega)(0.1\omega\psi1\omega\psi\ldots)_{1+2\omega} = 1 + \omega^2 = -\omega.$$

Let us call the Eisenstein integer $a + b\omega$ "odd-odd" if a and b are odd; "odd-even" if a is odd and b is even; and so on. Since

$$(a + b\omega)(1 + 2\omega) = (a - 2b) + (2a - b)\omega, \tag{5.8}$$

multiplication by any power of $1 + 2\omega$ does not change the odd/even characteristics of an Eisenstein integer. Notice that

$$\begin{aligned} \pm 1 &\text{ is odd-even;} \\ \pm\omega &\text{ is even-odd;} \\ \pm\psi &\text{ is odd-odd;} \end{aligned} \tag{5.9}$$

so we can readily determine the odd/even character of an Eisenstein integer expressed in revolving cubic form. Indeed, let us say that a revolving cubic representation is of type (σ_1, σ_2) if the leftmost nonzero digit is $\pm\sigma_1$ and the rightmost nonzero digit is $\pm\sigma_2$, where σ_1 and σ_2 are 1, ω, or ψ. Then it is easy to see that

a representation of type	defines an Eisenstein integer of type
$(1, 1)$ or (ω, ψ)	odd-even;
(ω, ω) or $(\psi, 1)$	even-odd;
(ψ, ψ) or $(1, \omega)$	odd-odd;
$(1, \psi)$ or $(\omega, 1)$ or (ψ, ω)	even-even.

Conversely, we can always find revolving cubic representations of Eisenstein integers when these conditions are met:

Theorem 6. *An odd-even Eisenstein integer has exactly two revolving cubic representations, one of type $(1, 1)$ and one of type (ω, ψ). An even-odd Eisenstein integer has exactly two revolving cubic representations, one of type (ω, ω) and one of type $(\psi, 1)$. An odd-odd Eisenstein integer has exactly two revolving cubic representations, one of type (ψ, ψ) and one of type $(1, \omega)$. An even-even Eisenstein integer has exactly three revolving cubic representations, one each of types $(1, \psi)$, $(\omega, 1)$, and (ψ, ω).*

Proof. This theorem may be proved in essentially the same way as we proved Theorems 1 and 2. $\square$

Using Theorem 6 together with (5.7), and arguing as in Theorem 4, it is not difficult to show that the ter-dragon curve of Figure 20 never crosses itself, and it fills the entire plane.

By reversing the direction of ternary folds each time, we obtain the *alternate ter-dragon curve*, shown in Figure 21. Six of these will fill the plane if they are joined at 60° angles. They come from the sequence

$$d(3n + 1) = +1, \quad d(3n - 1) = -1, \quad d(3n) = -d(n). \tag{5.10}$$

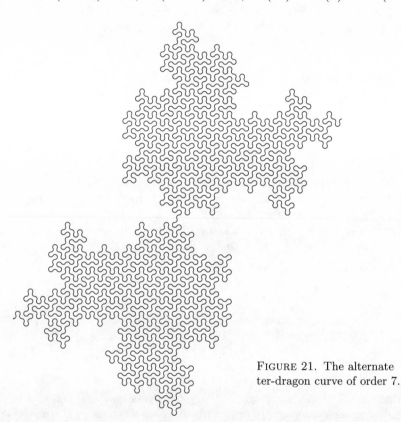

FIGURE 21. The alternate ter-dragon curve of order 7.

We can also form infinitely many *generalized ter-dragon curves* by making ternary folds in arbitrary directions. Thus

$$S_{n+1} = S_n D S_n U S_n \quad \text{or} \quad S_n U S_n D S_n \tag{5.11}$$

for each n. No curve formed in this way will cross itself, when opened to 60° at each crease; this fact can be proved by an argument similar to that of Theorem 5.

6. Generalization to Multiplicative Sequences

All four of our principal "dragon sequences" $d(n)$, namely those defined in (3.3), (4.2), (5.2), (5.10), satisfy the multiplicative property

$$d(mn) = d(m)d(n) \tag{6.1}$$

already noted in (3.4). And our generalized dragon and ter-dragon curves satisfy this property too, when m is relatively prime to n. This observation suggests that we should generalize further by looking at *arbitrary* sequences of ± 1s that satisfy (6.1).

It is clear that all functions satisfying (6.1) can be constructed by assigning values to $d(p)$ for all prime numbers p in any arbitrary fashion. The classical dragon sequence (3.3) corresponds to the assignment

$$d(p) = \begin{cases} +1, & \text{if } p = 2; \\ +1, & \text{if } p = 4k + 1; \\ -1, & \text{if } p = 4k - 1; \end{cases} \tag{6.2}$$

the alternate dragon sequence (4.2) is the same but with $d(2) = -1$. The ter-dragon sequences (5.2) and (5.10) are defined by (6.1) and

$$d(p) = \begin{cases} \pm 1, & \text{if } p = 3; \\ +1, & \text{if } p = 3k + 1; \\ -1, & \text{if } p = 3k - 1. \end{cases} \tag{6.3}$$

Another simple multiplicative function that suggests itself is defined by (6.1) and

$$d(p) = \begin{cases} -1, & \text{if } p = 2; \\ +1, & \text{if } p = 2k + 1. \end{cases} \tag{6.4}$$

If we form the corresponding design $\delta(n)$ for the bending angle $\theta = 90°$, and compare it to the dragon design of Figure 3, we get a rather surprising result: The tiny curve of Figure 22 is traced out when $0 \le n \le 16$, and it is repeated endlessly thereafter since we can prove that

$$\delta(2^n + m) = -\delta(m), \qquad \text{for } 0 \le m \le 2^n \text{ and } n \ge 3 \tag{6.5}$$

in this particular case.

FIGURE 22. Getting into a rut.

Using a bending angle of 60° or 120° with (6.4) gives curves that cross themselves yet have a rather pleasant appearance aesthetically; the first 4096 segments are shown in Figures 23 and 24, which look surprisingly similar "in the large" although they appear quite different in their fine structure. (Thicker lines in these illustrations represent edges that are traversed more frequently in the corresponding designs.)

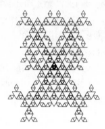

FIGURE 23. Fido: A self-crossing design with 60° bends.

FIGURE 24. The design of Figures 22 and 23, with 120° bends (rotated 90°).

Another multiplicative sequence of potential interest can be defined by the rules

$$d(p) = \begin{cases} +1, & \text{if } p = 2; \\ -1, & \text{if } p = 3; \\ +1, & \text{if } p = 6k + 1; \\ -1, & \text{if } p = 6k - 1. \end{cases} \tag{6.6}$$

The corresponding curves are not unpleasant, but not very unusual either, so they are not illustrated here.

7. Conclusion

We have seen that paper folding leads to some curves with remarkable properties; these properties are intimately related to number systems for integers and for lattices of integers in the plane.

Are there 3-dimensional "dragon curves" that have aesthetic properties comparable to the 2-dimensional ones considered here? One way to generalize what we have done above is to let $\delta(n)$ be a vector-valued function satisfying the relation

$$\delta(2n) = A\delta(n)$$

for some appropriate matrix A. We have not been able to discover any 3-dimensional generalization of any particular interest, although it seems not unlikely that some crystal structure possesses paths of comparable beauty.

The authors thank Donald Coxeter for helpful comments. The research of Chandler Davis was supported in part by the National Research Council of Canada.

References

[1] Martin Gardner, "Mathematical Games," *Scientific American* **216**, 3 (March 1967), 124–125; **216**, 4 (April 1967), 118–120; **217**, 1 (July 1967), 115. Reprinted in *Mathematical Magic Show* (New York: Knopf, 1977), Chapter 15, Problem 7.

[2] Walter Helbig Gottschalk and Gustav Arnold Hedlund, *Topological Dynamics*, American Mathematical Society Colloquium Publications, Volume 36 (Providence, Rhode Island: American Mathematical Society, 1955).

[3] W. G. Harter and J. E. Heighway, personal communication.

[4] Donald E. Knuth, *Seminumerical Algorithms*, Volume 2 of *The Art of Computer Programming* (Reading, Massachusetts: Addison–Wesley, 1969), Section 4.1.

Addendum

Another elementary way to visualize the dragon curve and its cousins occurred to me in 2009: We can "fatten up" the zigzag path by enclosing each edge — or | within a diamond-shaped tile ◆ or ◆, so that each unit segment becomes the diagonal of a tile instead of an actual edge.

These tiles fit together nicely because the path always changes direction by ±90°; for example, Figure 7 becomes

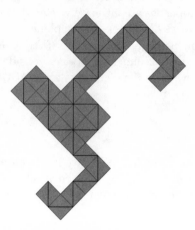

when embellished in this way. The dragon design becomes a dragon polyomino!

Furthermore, we can place "walls" of length $\sqrt{2}$ wherever two such tiles join at a bend of the path. The resulting pattern can be illustrated as follows, showing walls in black and the original path in white:

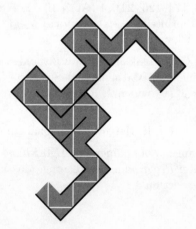

In this interpretation, an object that follows the zigzag path "bounces" off the walls as it moves. If the walls were mirrors, a beam of light would perfectly trace out the dragon design as it passes through this system of walls, which I like to call the *dragon labyrinth* of order 5.

The ter-dragon can be fattened up with lozenge-shaped tiles in a similar way, although the mirror-reflection idea no longer prevails. Here's the ter-dragon labyrinth of order 4:

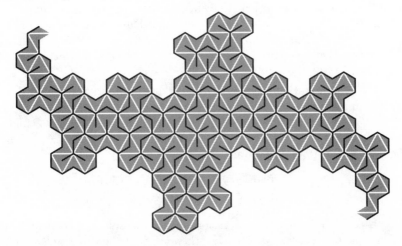

While preparing Figure 2, which opens up the dragon-sequence folds to angles of 100° at each bend, I noticed in 1969 that 95°-angle folds would lead to paths that cross themselves. For example, the path obtained from S_{10} will interfere with itself just before points 447 and 703; and if we look further, 95° bends applied to S_{12} will yield a path that crosses itself quite dramatically before and after points 1787 and 2807.

Consider the continuous curve $\delta(t)$ indicated in (3.14), and allow the angle θ to vary. As θ decreases from 180° it reaches a critical value θ_c where $\delta(t)$ first ceases to be a one-to-one function from the positive real numbers into the complex plane. This value θ_c seems to lie between 95° and 96°, but I don't know how to calculate it. The most troublesome self-crossing points appear to lie near $7 \cdot 2^n$ and $11 \cdot 2^n$.

The sequence $d(n)$ in (3.3) is expressible as $\mathrm{sign}(G(n) - G(n-1))$, where $G(n)$ is the nth element of "Gray binary code," namely $n \oplus \lfloor n/2 \rfloor$; this fact was noted by George P. Darwin in a letter to Martin Gardner dated 26 April 1967. Indeed, if we let $\nabla(n) = G(n) - G(n-1)$, it is easy to see that $\nabla(2n) = 2\nabla(n)$ and $\nabla(2n+1) = (-1)^n$. [Gray binary code is discussed in Section 7.2.1.1 of *The Art of Computer Programming*. Another property of $d(n)$ is discussed in exercise 4.5.3–41 of that work.]

I should have noticed that, besides (3.7), the function g also satisfies

$$g(4n-3) = g(2n-1), \qquad g(4n-1) = g(2n) + 1,$$
$$g(4n-2) = g(2n-1) + 1, \qquad g(4n) = g(2n).$$

The "Morse–Hedlund" sequence discussed in this chapter is now commonly known as the Thue–Morse sequence, because it appeared in two classic early works: Axel Thue, "Über die gegenseitige Lage gleicher Teile gewisser Zeichenreihen," *Skrifter udgivne af Videnskabs-Selskabet i Christiania*, Mathematisk-Naturvidenskabelig Klasse (1912), No. 1, 1–67, §7; Harold Marston Morse, "Recurrent geodesics on a surface of negative curvature," *Transactions of the American Mathematical Society* **22** (1921), 84–100, §14.

The Dutch mathematician F. M. Dekking wrote to Martin Gardner in the summer of 1975, describing many new kinds of dragon-like curves. If $S = a_1 a_2 \ldots a_{s-1}$ and $T = b_1 b_2 \ldots b_{t-1}$ are any sequences of folds, where each element a_i of S and each element b_j of T is either D or U, he defined the "folding product" $S * T = c_1 c_2 \ldots c_{st-1}$ by the rule

$$S * T = \begin{cases} S b_1 \overline{S} b_2 S \ldots S b_{t-1} \overline{S}, & \text{if } t \text{ is even;} \\ S b_1 \overline{S} b_2 S \ldots \overline{S} b_{t-1} S, & \text{if } t \text{ is odd.} \end{cases}$$

He observed that this new operation, which generalizes formulas (1.1), (4.1), and (5.1), is *associative*; in other words, we have $R * (S * T) = (R * S) * T$ for any sequences R, S, and T. Therefore it makes sense to consider n-ary folding products $S_1 * S_2 * \cdots * S_n$, as well as infinite folding products $S_1 * S_2 * S_3 * \cdots$. Notice that folding products satisfy

$$\overline{S * T} = \begin{cases} S * \overline{T}, & \text{if } t \text{ is even;} \\ \overline{S} * \overline{T}, & \text{if } t \text{ is odd.} \end{cases}$$

If we define the "folding powers"

$$S^{*n} = \overbrace{S * \cdots * S}^{n \text{ times}},$$

then the dragon sequence of order n is $D * \cdots * D = D^{*n}$, and the ter-dragon sequence of order n is $DU * \cdots * DU = (DU)^{*n}$. Furthermore, the alternate dragon and ter-dragon sequences of order $2n$ are respectively $(DUU)^{*n}$ and $(DUUDUDDU)^{*n}$ in this notation.

Folding powers produce many *new* species of dragons. For example, let's consider sequences S of four folds; these are the folding patterns that divide a strip of paper into five equal parts, so that S^{*n} will yield 5^n equal parts. If we change all Ds to Us and vice versa, everything is simply reflected as in a mirror; hence we can restrict consideration to the eight cases where S begins with D. Suppose we open all folds to $90°$. Then the sequence $S = DDDD$ intersects itself; and when $S = DDDU$ or $DUUU = \overline{DDDU}$, the sequence $S^{*2} = S * S$ intersects itself. But the other five cases yield arbitrarily long folding powers S^{*n} that never repeat any edges, for any n, illustrated here for $n = 3$:

$(DUUD)^{*3} =$

$(DDUU)^{*3} =$

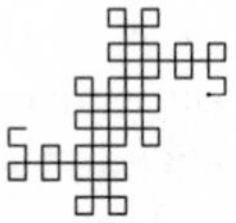

$(DUDU)^{*3} =$

$(DUDD)^{*3} =$

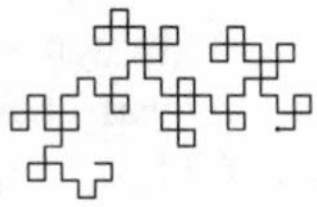

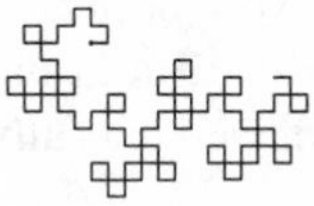

$(DDUD)^{*3} =$

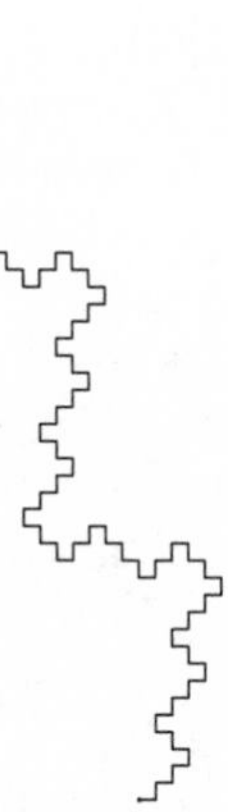

(In each case the origin point is indicated by a small dot.) The first and last examples leave the origin so fast, their points never touch. But the other three examples are *plane-filling*, in the sense that all of the edges in at least one $m \times m$ subgrid are covered somewhere within S^{*n}, when n is sufficiently large (depending on m). For example, $(DDUU)^{*3}$ covers several 2×2 subgrids, and $(DDUD)^{*3}$ covers several 1×1's; and

$(DDUD)^{*4} =$

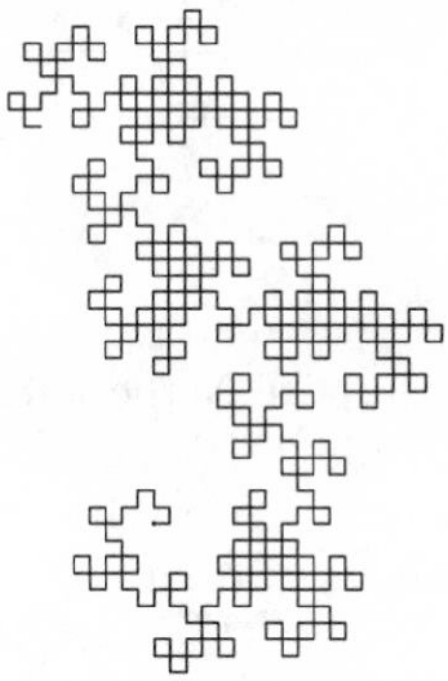

covers several 3×3's.

Let's say that a folding sequence S is *self-avoiding* if its iterated folding power $S^{*\infty}$ never traverses the same edge twice, always assuming $90°$ folds. A self-avoiding sequence can also be *plane-filling* in the sense

above, covering arbitrarily large subgrids. Furthermore, Dekking called
S *perfect* when the four paths $(S^{*\infty}, iS^{*\infty}, -S^{*\infty}, -iS^{*\infty})$ cover every
grid edge exactly once. Thus, the dragon curve's folding sequence $S = D$
is perfect, and so are the sequences $DDUU, DUDD, DDUD$. Dekking
conjectured in 1975 that $S * T$ is perfect when S and T are perfect.

A sequence S can be plane-filling without being perfect. Indeed,
we have seen that this is true for the alternate dragon curve, when
$S = DUU$; in that case $S^{*\infty}$ covers just $1/8$ of the plane, not $1/4$,
because $S^{*\infty} \cup (iS^{*\infty}) \cup (-S^{*\infty}) \cup (-iS^{*\infty})$ only covers about half of the
edges (see Figure 10). Since $DUU = D * U$ while the simple sequences
D and U are both perfect, we must revise Dekking's original conjecture,
limiting it to cases where S and T both begin with D. In that form,
Dekking was able to prove his conjecture several years later, by finding
nice ways to characterize exactly when a folding sequence that begins
with D is self-avoiding, plane-filling, and/or perfect.

First, he showed that S is self-avoiding if and only if $S * DDD$ has
no repeated edges; indeed, he showed more generally that if $S * DDD$
and T have no repeated edges, then $S * T$ has no repeats. He did this
by first observing that grid paths in which $90°$ turns occur after every
step are equivalent to paths in the infinite directed graph

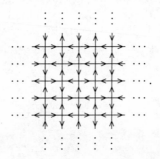

[See F. M. Dekking, "Iterated paperfolding and planefilling curves," Report 8126 (Nijmegen, The Netherlands: Katholieke Universiteit, Math-
ematisch Instituut, 1981), 16 pages.]

Second, he proved that a self-avoiding S with $s - 1$ folds is plane-
filling if and only if its grid path (which has length s) ends at a point
$z = a + bi$ for which $a^2 + b^2 = s$. (For example, the five self-avoiding
examples shown earlier for $s = 5$ end at the respective points 3, $1 + 2i$,
$1 + 2i$, $-1 + 2i$, and $3 + 2i$; hence only the middle three are plane-filling.)

Third, he discovered the remarkable fact that a plane-filling S is
perfect if and only if its grid path does not go through the edge from
$z + zi - 1 - i$ to $z + zi - i$. And he constructed perfect sequences S of

length s whenever $s > 1$ can be written as the sum of two squares, by defining an appropriate s-arc subgraph of the infinite digraph above, and using the fact that a balanced digraph always contains an Eulerian trail.

His conjecture about the product of perfect sequences follows from these facts, in a stronger form: *If S and T are plane-filling sequences that both begin with D, then $S * T$ is perfect if and only if either S is perfect or T is perfect.*

The possibilities are much trickier than they may seem at first glance. Consider, for example, the sequences $S = DDUDDUDU$ and $T = DUDUUDUU = \overline{S}$, which define paths of length $s = 9$ to the points $z = -3$ and $z = 3$, respectively. We have

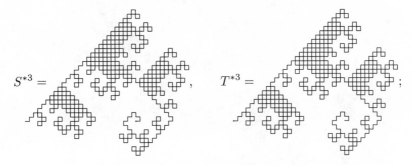

$$S^{*3} = \qquad\qquad , \qquad T^{*3} = \qquad\qquad ;$$

both paths are the same, except for the starting point. Yet the starting point makes a huge difference, because S is perfect but T is not! If we draw S^{*3} and $-S^{*3}$ in black, together with iS^{*3} and $-iS^{*3}$ in gray, we get a beautiful design that perfectly fills a diamond-shaped region about the origin:

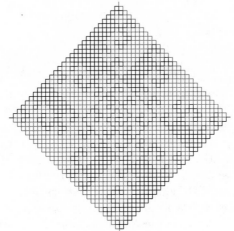

It's a design with a meso-American flavor, also reminiscent of meandering patterns in the "late geometric" style that was popular on Greek vases in the 8th century B.C.

But the same tactics with T^{*3} lead to a far different result:

Each of the four copies of T^{*n} covers a region like S^{*n}, which we know fills $1/4$ of a diamond. Hence $T^{*\infty}$ covers just $1/16$ of the plane — only half as much as the alternate dragon curve, which covers $1/8$.

This example is the case $m = 3$ of a general construction $S_m = D(DU)^1 D(DU)^2 \ldots D(DU)^{m-1}$ that yields similar (but ever more intricate) folding paths of length $s = m^2$ that lead from 0 to $i^{m-1}m$. The reader is encouraged to try drawing S_5^{*3} (with computer help).

The simplicity of Dekking's characterizations makes it easy to count exactly how many s-folds of various types are possible, for small s. Suppose A_s of the 2^{s-2} possibilities beginning with D are self-avoiding but not plane-filling; B_s are plane-filling but not perfect; and C_s are perfect. Then we have:

$s =$	2	3	4	5	6	7	8	9	10	11	12	13	14	15	16	17	18	19	20
$A_s =$	0	1	1	2	7	10	15	33	45	93	186	300	530	825	1561	2722	4685	7419	13563
$B_s =$	0	0	1	0	0	0	0	2	2	0	0	2	0	0	8	0	4	0	12
$C_s =$	1	0	1	3	0	0	6	3	20	0	0	29	0	0	56	101	108	0	392

In his letters of 1975 to Martin Gardner, Dekking pointed out that the sequence $S = DUUUDDDU$, which is the simplest perfect pattern for $s = 9$, actually generates the famous space-filling curve of Giuseppe Peano ["Sur une courbe, qui remplit toute une aire plane," *Mathematische Annalen* **36** (1890), 157–160], which was the first-ever construction of a continuous function from the unit interval $[0 .. 1]$ to the unit square $[0 .. 1] \times [0 .. 1]$. Indeed, S^{*2} in this case generates a path that corresponds via our polyomino construction to

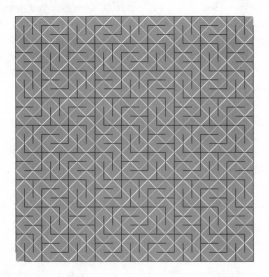

(but rotated by 45°), which we may call "Peano's labyrinth of order 3." [See Hans Sagan, *Space-Filling Curves* (New York: Springer, 1994), Fig. 3.6.2.]

Dekking did not publish the proofs of his theorems about generalized dragons at the time, perhaps because he felt that the world was not yet ready for them. Recently, however, he has written a definitive paper, "Paperfolding morphisms, spacefilling curves, and fractal tiles," *Theoretical Computer Science* **414** (2012), 20–37.

This theory suggests several more intriguing problems that I have no idea how to solve. For instance:

1) If S is a plane-filling sequence, we have seen that its iterated extension $S^{*\infty}$ might fill 1/4, 1/8, or 1/16 of the entire plane. Are other values of this overall density possible? And how can the density be computed, given S?

2) Given an infinite sequence $a_1, a_2, a_3, \ldots$ of D's and/or U's, how can one determine the density of the plane-filling path $a_1 * a_2 * a_3 * \cdots$? What is the smallest possible value of this density? (For example, we know that the density is 1/4 when $a_j = D$ for all j; it is 1/8 when $a_j = U$ if and only if j is even. What is the density when $a_j = U$ if and only if j is, say, a perfect square, or a prime number? Notice that the density is unchanged if we change any *finite* number of the parameters a_j from D to U or vice versa.)

3) The theory of plane-filling S can be developed for folds of $60°$ as well as $90°$, but detailed characterizations have not yet been worked out. In this case a "perfect" S would be a sequence for which the six paths $(S^{*\infty}, \omega S^{*\infty}, \omega^2 S^{*\infty}, -S^{*\infty}, -\omega S^{*\infty}, -\omega^2 S^{*\infty})$ cover every edge of the hexagonal grid exactly once. (Dekking remarked in 1975 that every perfect S that he knows for $60°$ folds was "balanced," in the sense that $\overline{S} = S$. He suspected that unbalanced cases might exist, but perhaps only when S involves a large number of folds.)

Many fascinating properties of generalized dragon curves certainly remain to be discovered.

Meanwhile, researchers have been developing the theory in other directions. For example, consider the number $f(x) = \sum_{n \geq 1} b_n x^n$, where $b_n = (d(n) + 1)/2$ is 1 when the nth term of the dragon sequence S_∞ is D, otherwise $b_n = 0$. Then the "dragon constant," the binary fraction

$$f(\tfrac{1}{2}) = (0.b_1 b_2 b_3 \ldots)_2 = (0.110110011100100110110001100\ldots)_2$$
$$\approx 0.85073\,61882\,01867\,26036\,77977\,60532\,06660\,44114-,$$

is known to be transcendental. In fact, $f(x)$ is transcendental when x is *any* nonzero algebraic number with $|x| < 1$; and the same is true for the sequences $\langle b_n \rangle$ that correspond to any of the generalized dragon curves considered in Theorem 5 and in problem (2) above. These results were proved by M. Mendès France and A. J. van der Poorten, "Arithmetic and analytic properties of paper folding sequences," *Bulletin of the Australian Mathematical Society* **24** (1981), 123–131.

Further interesting properties of dragon-like curves and sequences are explored in the expository paper "Folds!" by Michel Dekking, Michel

Mendès France, and Alf van der Poorten, in *The Mathematical Intelligencer* **4** (1982), 130–138, 173–181, 190–195; **5**, 2 (1983), 5. In particular, they explain how the ideas relate to the rapidly developing theory of "automatic sequences." [See the book *Automatic Sequences* by Jean-Paul Allouche and Jeffrey Shallit (Cambridge University Press, 2003), for a comprehensive introduction to that subject.]

The question of 3-dimensional folding, which Chandler Davis and I mentioned briefly at the close of our original paper, has been fruitfully studied by Michel Mendès France and J. O. Shallit, "Wire bending," *Journal of Combinatorial Theory* **A50** (1989), 1–23, although not exactly in the way we had in mind.

Topological properties of the image of the continuous dragon curve $\delta(t)$ in (3.14) have been investigated by Sze-Man Ngai and Nhu Nguyen, "The Heighway dragon revisited," *Discrete and Computational Geometry* **29** (2003), 603–623.

John Heighway wrote to Martin Gardner on 30 December 1997, explaining that he had discovered the dragon curve but that William Harter had named it. I asked Harter in 2001 about his recollections, and he told an interesting story:

> The dragon curve was born in June of 1966. Jack [Heighway] came into my office (actually cubicle) and said that if you folded a \$1 bill repeatedly he thought it would make a random walk or something like that. (We'd been arguing about something in Feller's book on return chances.) I was dubious but said "Let's check it out with a big piece of paper." (Those were the days when NASA could easily afford more than \$1's worth of paper.) Well, it made a funny pattern alright but we couldn't really see it too clearly. So one of us thought to use tracing paper and "unfold" it indefinitely so we could record (tediously) as big a pattern as we wanted. But each time we made the next order, it just begged us to make one more!
>
> ... Lee Ponting, another summer student, should be mentioned, too, for writing the first program to plot the dragon using FORTRAN and a Calcomp.
>
> More recently, the dragon was used by Michael Crichton in a book about dragons entitled "Jurassic Park" to go along with a story line that includes a character who works on "fractals." Unfortunately, Mr. Crichton seems to have failed to notice why the dragons were called dragons. He proceeded to print them "evolving" page after page, but upside down, that is, as dead

dragons! Maybe this shows that you always get punished if you use something without attribution.

[See Michael Crichton, *Jurassic Park* (New York: Knopf, 1990), 9, 31, 83, 179, 269, 315, 363.]

Further thoughts appear in some notes entitled "Diamonds and dragons," on my Stanford website.

Chapter 45

Mathematics and Art:
The Dragon Curve in Ceramic Tile

[Written with Jill Knuth. Originally published in the Journal of Recreational Mathematics **6** *(1973), 165–167.]*

The "dragon curve" and its curious mathematical properties have been described in previous issues of the *Journal of Recreational Mathematics* [1, 2, 3], and also in a Russian publication for mathematics students [4]. Although the dragon curve appears to be a complicated pattern, it is interesting to discover that it can be constructed using only three kinds of square tiles:

The tiles with arcs must of course be rotated to fit the curve properly.

While designing our new house, we wanted to include something that was uniquely personal and would blend with the contemporary architecture. One of us is a mathematician who has contributed to the theory of the dragon curve; the other is an artist who has worked with ceramics. The dragon curve provided us with a design that had mathematical interest and which, at the same time, was æsthetically pleasing and challenging to construct from ceramic tiles. Therefore we decided to decorate the entry to our home with this design.

First, we found that a dragon curve of order 8 was too small to be effective, while order 10 and larger would require too many tiles. The order 9 curve seemed to be just right. We cut about 1000 paper tiles from old grocery bags, painted the arcs with ink and a wide brush, and posted the paper mock-up on the wall. After living with the design for a week we were still pleased with it, and so we decided to go ahead with the ceramic version. (See Figure 1.)

Since we lacked the equipment to make so many tiles, we investigated the possibility of working with Heath Ceramics, a commercial tile maker in Sausalito, California. The mathematics of the design dictated that 2×2-inch tiles were needed for the proposed $5\,{}^{1}/_{2} \times 6$-foot panel, but Heath could produce nothing smaller than 3×3 inches without expensive equipment changes. Fortunately, we found that Heath was closing down most of their plant for the month of June, 1970, and they agreed to let us work there with the help of a skeleton crew. They extruded about 300 3×12-inch tiles for us. While the clay was still moist we cut them by hand into 1800 2×2-inch tiles. The actual measurement of the tiles at this point was slightly larger to allow for shrinkage during the firing.

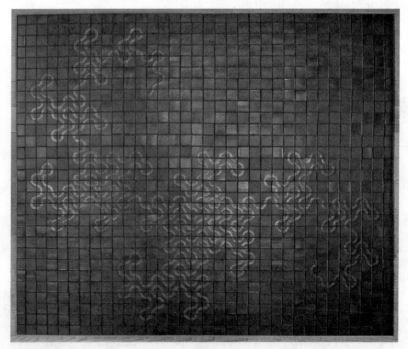

FIGURE 1. The dragon curve of order 9, which can be constructed from just three different kinds of ceramic tiles.

Heath Ceramics is well known for the beauty of their stoneware glazes. We chose a matte black glaze for the background, and an opalescent, semi-matte olive glaze for the arcs. After the initial bisque firing, the tiles were sprayed with the background glaze; we then applied the olive glaze heavily with a rubber syringe to obtain a thick, wide line with small irregularities. During the second and final firing, at about 2200°F, this thick application of glaze sometimes bubbled, sometimes contracted, producing interesting variations. (See Figure 2.)

FIGURE 2. Detail of dragon curve shows variations of thickness and texture in the stoneware glaze.

It turned out that just barely enough tiles had survived the high firing temperature. We needed exactly 627 blank tiles, 207 single arcs, and 152 double arcs, in agreement with the formulas

$$207 + 2 \times 152 = 2^9 - 1; \qquad 627 + 207 + 152 = 29 \times 34.$$

The tiles were set by a professional tile setter. This job required close supervision, since a double arc rotated 90° looks right even when it is wrong; the original paper mock-up was a big help at this point, as a reference. The joints were filled with charcoal black grout, which blended with the background color of the tiles and emphasized the design. The edges were finished by being recessed into the cedar wall paneling. We unveiled the completed dragon curve at a combinatorial mathematics seminar on January 17, 1972, about three years after the project had been conceived.

The final result has been quite satisfying from both a mathematical and a visual standpoint. Varied lighting conditions throughout the day enhance the raised texture of the design, and the slightly different angles of reflection provide added life. It has proved to be an interesting conversation piece. Mathematical guests appreciate the relationship to binary number systems, while one of the neighborhood children says it looks like ant tracks!

References

[1] Chandler Davis and Donald E. Knuth, "Number representations and dragon curves, I," *Journal of Recreational Mathematics* **3** (1970), 66–81.

[2] Chandler Davis and Donald E. Knuth, "Number representations and dragon curves, II," *Journal of Recreational Mathematics* **3** (1970), 133–149. [Combined with [1] and reprinted with revisions as Chapter 44 of the present volume.]

[3] Petra I. Osarczuk and Rudolf Ondrejka, Letters to the Editor, *Journal of Recreational Mathematics* **4** (1971), 152.

[4] Н. Б. Васильев и В. Л. Гутенмахер, "Кривые дракона," *Квант* **1**, 2 (March 1970), 36–46. English translation: Nikolay Vasilyev and Victor Gutenmacher, "Dragon curves," *Quantum* **6**, 1 (September–October 1995), 5–10, 60. See also Vladimir Dubrovsky, "Dragon the omnipresent," *Quantum* **6**, 6 (July–August 1996), 34–37.

Addendum

More than 35 years of living with this delightful pattern have not diminished its charm; it continues to be a source of daily pleasure. Yet I was shocked to discover, while preparing the present book for publication, that I had actually misunderstood the curve during all this time!

Let me explain. I'd thought that the dragon curve began near the lower right corner of Fig. 1, and ended near the upper middle. Jill and I had scratched our names into the clay of a special single-arc tile, which we used for the supposed first step of the curve. We also marked the eighth step with a special tile in which the glaze had "erupted" slightly. (See Figure 3.) And the 16th, 32nd, 64th, 128th, and 256th steps were marked in the same fashion, so that I could readily explain the recursive construction of the dragon curve to mathematical visitors.

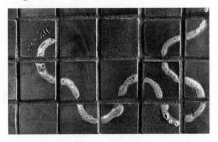

FIGURE 3. The authors installed special tiles in the places where we believed that the curve took its first and eighth steps.

All seemed fine until I suddenly realized that we had the curve *backwards*: The curve that starts near the lower right is *not* S_9, it's $\overline{S_9}$! Indeed, the 256th step in our pattern corresponds to a U step, but formulas (1.1) and (1.2) of the previous chapter stipulate that it should be a D step. Figure 1 does show the dragon curve of order 9, but that curve actually starts in the upper middle and *ends* at the lower right.

Oh my. People tell me that I'm an incurable perfectionist; will I still be able to live with this, now that I know the truth? Fortunately, the answer to this question is quite "plain & simple to express," as in my favorite poem: a grook by Piet Hein that actually sits less than a dozen feet from the dragon curve in the entryway to my house. (See Figure 4.) And in fact the error that I made—now permanently set in stoneware—may well make the design even more beautiful. [See, for example, Robyn Griggs Lawrence's book *The Wabi-Sabi House: The Japanese Art of Imperfect Beauty* (Clarkson Potter, 2004).]

FIGURE 4. The road to wisdom. (Stone cut by David Kindersley and Lida Lopes Cardozo.)

On the other hand, if a mathematics department wants to install the pattern of Fig. 1 on the walls or the floor of a students' common room, I recommend that they either leave the tiles unmarked, or mark the key curve positions by starting in the mathematically correct location.

The three types of tiles that we used are not the only appealing way
to render mathematical dragons artistically. Another good choice

will, for example, yield the *dragon labyrinth* of order 9, as discussed in
the addendum to the previous chapter:

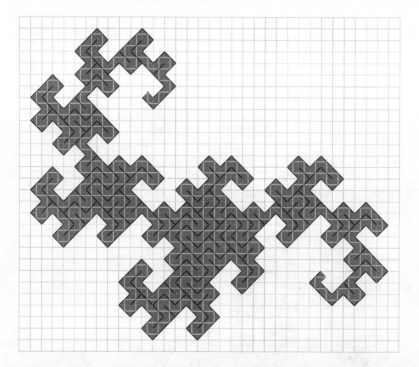

(The special tiles shown here at the beginning and end may be replaced
by blanks if desired.)

And that's not all: The theory with which we constructed the
labyrinth shows that a completely different approach to tiling is also
possible, using tiles that are rotated by 45°. For example, the "dragon
pipeline of order 9," illustrated on the next page, was typeset using a
custom-made font that contains the characters ' ', ' ', ' ', ' ', ' '
for horizontal motions and ' ', ' ', ' ', ' ', ' ' for vertical motions.

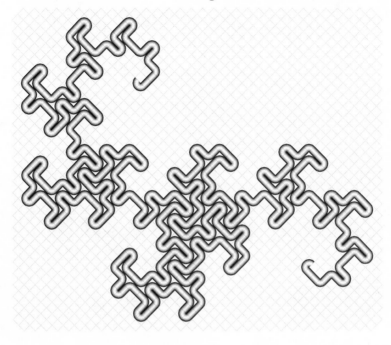

And of course we haven't begun to exploit variations in color, etc.

Further work in the intersection between mathematics and art promises to be ever more exciting, as new patterns are discovered and new opportunities for rendering designs in many different media are continually being introduced.

Chapter 46

Christmas Cards

[This material was assembled from documents in my family archives.]

Christmastime often inspires a wish to create something special, to do something that brings an extra dash of merriment. My wife Jill and I have been sending annual holiday greetings to our closest relatives and friends, ever since our marriage nearly 50 years ago, and we've often included playful items that tickled our fancy at the time. This chapter surveys a dozen or so of our Christmas projects that have had a recreational flavor related in some way to mathematics and/or computer science. And I also threw in a Christmas carol that I learned abroad.

My parents were too poor to purchase Christmas cards that were made professionally. So they decided to produce their own, using a "ditto machine" to print a purple image on one side of a penny postcard. For example, Figure 1(a) shows what they mailed to their friends when I was 0.9 years old. Figure 1(b) was the somewhat more subtle card that they sent a year later, when I was 1.9 and my sister was -0.6.

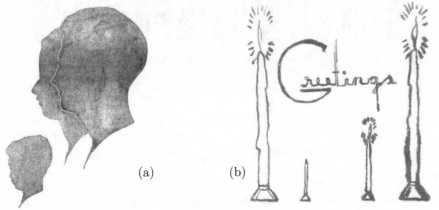

(a)   (b)

FIGURE 1. Christmas cards from Erv and Lou Knuth in 1939 and 1940.

623

(a)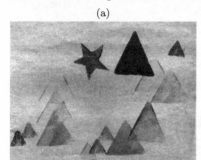

(b)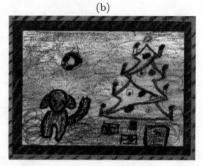

FIGURE 2. Cards from (a) Jim and Wilda Carter, and (b) from Jill herself.

Jill's parents also sent out handmade cards every year. One of my favorites, shown in Fig. 2(a), featured abstract trees printed in shades of blue and green by using suitably cut "potato stamps." And Jill made limited-edition cards of her own, starting at an early age; one of the first, in Fig. 2(b), was drawn with crayons. Her card from 1960 — the year before we were married — was produced by silk screening in two colors: purple and deep red. (See Figure 3, which you might wish to read by tipping the bottom of the page upward.)

FIGURE 3. "Negative space" (reproduced at the original size).

Thus our cards developed from a marriage of two somewhat different traditions. For awhile our designs in odd-numbered years were almost entirely based on a visual/graphic æsthetic, while those in even-numbered years had some sort of mathematical twist. Of course Jill made sure that the designs of the latter kind were artistic too.

1962: Counting

Our first mathematical card, shown in Fig. 4, was self-explanatory. The friends and relatives who received it knew that I was a graduate student

(a)

(b)

FIGURE 4. The (a) outside and (b) inside of our card in 1962.

in mathematics at the time. Jill silk-screened a cool-blue triangle onto some textured gold paper; then my father printed her MERRY CHRIST-MAS grid over that, in black ink; and she finished the job by drawing 21 little red stars by hand in each copy.

1964: A Flexagon

Our card in 1964 was hexagonal instead of rectangular. It looked

like this   like this

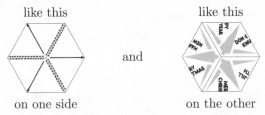

and

on one side   on the other

and there was no immediately obvious way to open it up. We began in that year to include an annual newsletter about what we'd been doing,* and the newsletter for 1964 explained the card as follows:

> P.S. The Christmas card contains a hidden message. One side shows solid arrows and dotted lines; fold it so the solid arrows are "valleys" and the dotted lines are "ridges." Bring the points of the three solid arrows together at the bottom, so that all three arrows are pointing in the same direction.

 The card now opens at the top, to reveal a red Christmas star! If the same folding and opening process is repeated on this star pattern, the card will open again, and the unscrambled message will appear.

---

* For example, I said this about my current work: "My major activity of the

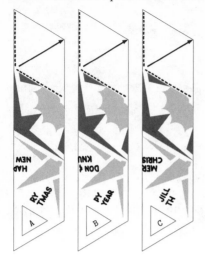

FIGURE 5. These strips of paper, shown at 1/4 actual size, can be assembled into a "trihexaflexagon" Christmas card by following the instructions below. (Red areas are shown in dark gray, and green areas are in light gray. A full-size image in full color can be downloaded from `www-cs-faculty.stanford.edu/ ~knuth/christmas-flexagon.pdf`.)

You can recreate our card by cutting out the three strips of paper illustrated in Fig. 5, and pasting them together in just the right way. In fact, this assembly process turns out to be fun — although you might not enjoy making dozens and dozens of them, as I did in 1964.

Suppose, in general, that you have a printed pattern that looks like the left half of Figure 6. Draw the assembly-key information in the right half of that figure on the back side, using a light pencil. (These keys $\boxed{1}$, $\boxed{2}$, ..., $\boxed{9}$ and $\boxed{A}$, $\boxed{B}$, $\boxed{C}$ won't be visible at the end, but they're quite helpful for putting everything together properly.) Cut out the three strips and crease them into triangles as indicated, where a dotted line stands for a "valley fold" and a solid line stands for a "mountain fold," as seen from the back.

Now place the partially folded strips next to each other in a triangle as shown in Fig. 7. The leftmost strip occupies the upper left of this triangle, with $\boxed{7}$ and $\boxed{5}$ folded under the $\boxed{1}$, and with $\boxed{4}$ and $\boxed{B}$

---

year (same as last year) is writing about The Art of Computer Programming. The rough draft of this book, some 1500 hand-written pages, is nearly complete and the next step is to rewrite and type the manuscript. Meanwhile I continue as Assistant Professor of Mathematics in the stimulating Caltech environment, and I am also teaching computer classes to the employees at Burroughs Corporation. The year has been a very fruitful one for mathematical research."

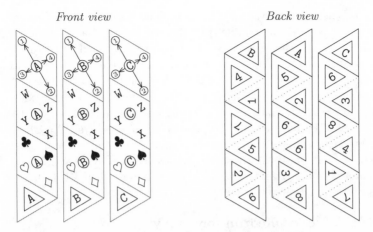

FIGURE 6. A general-purpose way to make trihexaflexagons.

folded together between △₁ and △₂, where they sit upright — perpendicular to the table on which you're working. The other two strips go into the lower right and lower left of Fig. 7 in the same way.

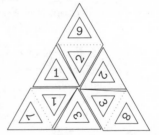

FIGURE 7. The three partially folded strips, ready for gluing.

The next step works like magic: Using a glue stick, you'll find that it's possible to paste successively △₁ to △₁, then △₂ to △₂, ..., △₉ to △₉. And finally you can finish up by pasting △ₐ to △ₐ, △ᵦ to △ᵦ, and △꜀ to △꜀, taking extra care to make these last three pairs stick together tightly at all three edges. The flexagon assembled from Fig. 6 in this way will go through the following cycle:

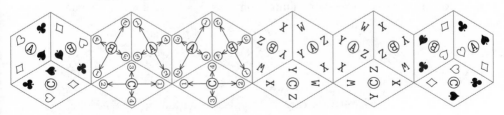

(The two hexagons at the left are the top and bottom of the starting configuration; you get the middle two after one flex, and another flex yields the final two.) When this general procedure is applied to the design in Fig. 5, the "secret" Christmas message is represented by the rightmost hexagon of the cycle. One more flex takes you back to the beginning.

Historical note: Arthur H. Stone discovered the trihexaflexagon in 1939, after which many further flexagons were discovered by Bryant Tuckerman, Richard Feynman, John Tukey, and others. [See Chapter 1 of Martin Gardner's book *Hexaflexagons, Probability Paradoxes, and the Tower of Hanoi* (Mathematical Association of America, 2008); also Chapter 2 of his *Origami, Eleusis, and the Soma Cube* (Mathematical Association of America, 2008).]

1966: A Dodecahedron for Jenny

The timely birth of our daughter on 12 December 1966, the numerically auspicious date "twelve-twelve-six-six," set off a chain of ideas that led to the most elaborate Christmas card we ever made. We decided to send everyone a Christmas tree ornament in the shape of a dodecahedron, where the 12 faces correspond to the 12 verses of a familiar song about Christmas gifts:

> On the twelfth day of Christmas, my true love gave to me
>   12 drummers drumming,

11 pipers piping,	6 geese a-laying
10 lords a-leaping,	5 golden rings,
9 ladies dancing,	4 hummingbirds,
8 maids a-milking,	3 french hens,
7 swans a-swimming,	2 turtle doves,

>   and a partridge in a pear tree.

Jill masterfully illustrated each verse, and we worked out a way to produce the card by breaking the dodecahedron into two halves as shown in Fig. 8. After printing these pieces on sturdy paper, cutting them out, and making ten "mountain folds," I used needle and thread to tie them loosely together at their common boundary via the following scheme:

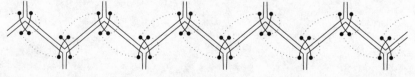

With generous lengths of thread, the pieces laid flat in the envelope.

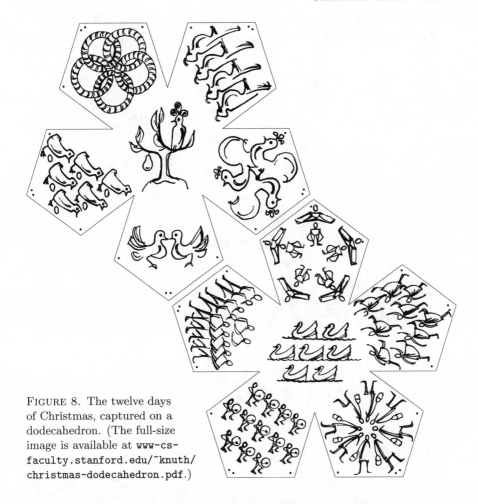

FIGURE 8. The twelve days
of Christmas, captured on a
dodecahedron. (The full-size
image is available at www-cs-
faculty.stanford.edu/~knuth/
christmas-dodecahedron.pdf.)

The recipients of the card could then assemble the ornament by
tightening the threads, a procedure that turned out to be a simple but
very pleasant puzzle in its own right. Here's how our newsletter for 1966
explained what to do:

By working around the edges starting with the hummingbirds,
pull the threads tight to bring all the corners together so that a
symmetrical 12-sided Christmas tree ornament is obtained. Can
you identify each of the twelve days of Christmas?

(Try it, you'll like it!)

We also enclosed a birth announcement that featured Jill's innovative rendering of a tree with upward-and-downward binary branching:

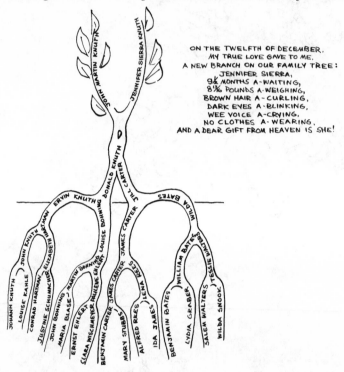

ON THE TWELFTH OF DECEMBER,
MY TRUE LOVE GAVE TO ME,
A NEW BRANCH ON OUR FAMILY TREE:
    JENNIFER SIERRA,
    9½ MONTHS A-WAITING,
    8⅞ POUNDS A-WEIGHING,
    BROWN HAIR A-CURLING,
    DARK EYES A-BLINKING,
    WEE VOICE A-CRYING,
    NO CLOTHES A-WEARING,
AND A DEAR GIFT FROM HEAVEN IS SHE!

1968: Angels Fill the Sky

"Our Christmas card this year shows part of the Christmas sky: a multitude of the heavenly host, reaching indefinitely in all directions, touching their wings together in groups of six, their feet in groups of two, and their hands in groups of three." Jill devised the ingenious angel figure illustrated here, which can be replicated to tile the entire plane as shown in Fig. 9; she discovered an extra degree of design freedom that surprised me greatly at the time. We sent a copy of this card to M. C. Escher in Holland, who responded with a friendly acknowledgment and a rep-tile that he himself had drawn in 1939 when doing his early studies of plane-filling shapes.

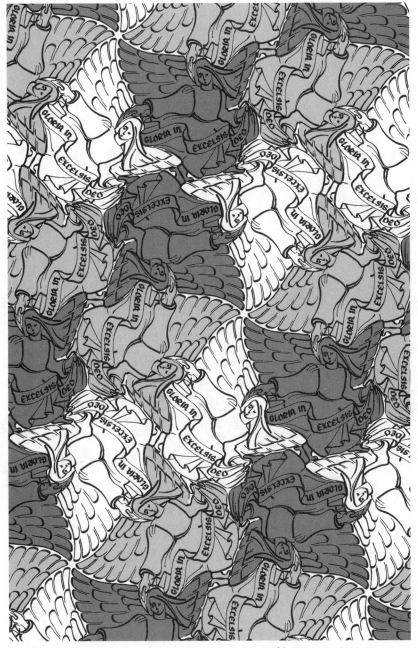

FIGURE 9. Our card from 1968, reduced to 80% of its original size.

Jill's discovery, which allows pairs of angels to touch each other's feet in an intriguing way, can be understood geometrically as follows. Take any 30°–60°–90° triangle ABC and a point X inside it; then draw a more-or-less arbitrary curve from A to X and another from X to B. Rotate the former by 60° about A and the latter by 180° about B, thus obtaining new points X' and X''. Draw another curve from X' to C, and rotate it by 120° about C; the rotated curve will then go from C to X'':

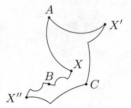

If the paths don't cross each other, this figure will tile the plane! Proof:

[The excellent book *Creating Escher-Type Drawings* by E. R. Ranucci and J. L. Teeters (Palo Alto, California: Creative Publications, 1977) discusses many ways to devise amazing patterns of this kind. They seem to have missed this particular one, although their figure 4-28 on page 84 comes very close. A complete theory had in fact been worked out by Heinrich Heesch in 1932; Jill actually rediscovered Heesch's type '$CC_3C_3C_6C_6$'. See Doris Schattschneider's beautifully and extensively annotated edition of Escher's notebooks, *Visions of Symmetry* (New York: W. H. Freeman, 1990). See also William W. Chow, "Automatic generation of interlocking shapes," *Computer Graphics and Image Processing* **9** (1979), 333–353; Craig S. Kaplan and David H. Salesin, "Escherization," *ACM SIGGRAPH International Conference on Computer Graphics and Interactive Techniques* **27** (2000), 499–510.]

1970: Disappearing Sheep

We turn next to the scene on the ground instead of in the sky.

"And there were in the same country shepherds abiding in the field, keeping watch over their flock by night." [Luke 2:8] Our Christmas card this year illustrates a puzzling and little-known fact about those sheep. Arrange the three pieces thus

and you will see ten sheep, two rocks, and one star. Now rearrange the two bottom pieces thus

and behold! The two rocks and one star are still present, but there are only nine sheep! "All we like sheep have gone astray." [Isaiah 53:6, Jeremiah 50:6, Ezekiel 34:6] Can you figure out which one has disappeared? "Rejoice with me; for I have found my sheep which was lost." [Luke 15:6]

The original card was 4″ × 11.375″, printed with white ink on dark chocolate-brown construction paper, using a linoleum block that Jill carved for the occasion.

My parents were quite intrigued by the disappearing sheep, so they asked Jill to design a similar card that they could send to their own friends. She responded by drawing a remarkable Christmas "wreath" filled with angels, together with a disk in the middle that could be rotated into two different positions.

So my dad used the printing press in his basement to print her design on colored paper of good quality, making about 200 in red and 200 in green for the family card of 1972. "When the message reads 'Merry Christmas' there are 15 angels, but when it says 'Happy New Year' (try it) you will find 16 angels. This strange phenomenon can perhaps best be explained by an analogy: The same principle can be used to make a 7-line poem from a 6-line poem by shifting the ends of each line as shown."

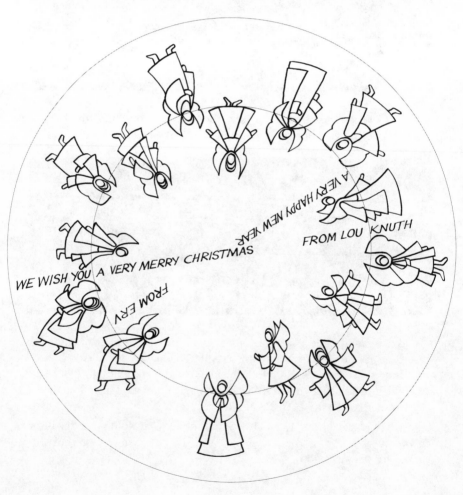

One of the Christmas angels disappears, reappears;
    then once again she suddenly is gone,
        like a star that twinkles at night;
        soon it returns, from off to on,
           it blinks with great peace and tranquillity,
           and fills us with awe and humility.

One of the Christmas angels disappears,
    then once again she suddenly reappears;
        like a star that is gone,
        soon it returns, twinkles at night;
        it blinks from off to on,
           and with great peace and tranquillity,
           fills us with awe and humility.

(I had composed that little explanatory poem when Jill was doing the artwork. It gave me the courage to construct a more elaborate poem several years later, to celebrate Martin Gardner's 65th birthday and his interest in magic tricks; see "Disappearances" in Chapter 31.)

1972: A Four-Sided Crêche

"Our Christmas card this year folds into a tetrahedron. The three blank triangles can be tucked in so that they hold the shape together, with the four decorated triangles showing four views of the nativity scene."

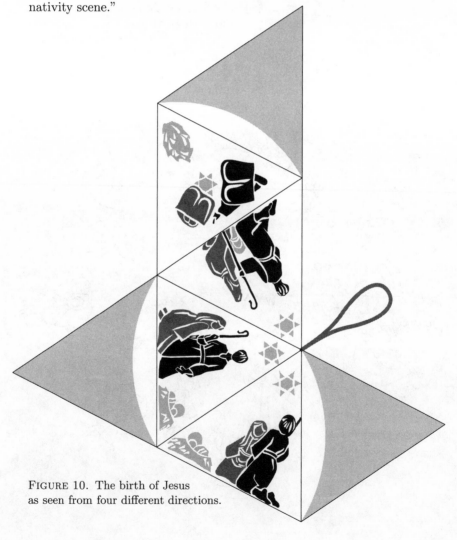

FIGURE 10. The birth of Jesus
as seen from four different directions.

FIGURE 11. Top and bottom views of the assembled card.

Figure 10 shows our tetrahedron at about 37% of its original size. We produced the card in an interesting way, during the year we lived in Norway: Jill designed the figures and carved them on a linoleum block. Then we used that block to make the images by rubbing wax crayons on thin sheets of translucent rice-paper: bright yellow-orange for the baby, manger, and star; rust color for Mary; and dark brown for Joseph. Next we pasted the rice-paper images onto sturdy medium-brown paper, using glue only at the arcs of the three circles where the rice-paper bonded with blank triangles. Finally we cut out the final shape with scissors, made six "mountain folds," and attached a loop of red yarn to the back (see Fig. 11).

1977: Turning Toward Typography

The cards that we sent out during the next several years were primarily *objets d'art* rather than *objets de mathématique*. But it turned out that the accompanying *newsletter* that we sent in 1977 would be unexpectedly significant in retrospect, because 1977 was the year that I began to think about how to design fonts algorithmically. The prototypes of the prototypes of the Computer Modern typefaces made their first public appearance in that newsletter; thus I can't resist showing a few excerpts in Fig. 12 on the next page.

At this time, as explained in my paper "The errors of TEX" [*Literate Programming*, Chapter 10], I had begun to write the code for TEX78, but I wasn't ready to debug it until several months later. Therefore I used a much more primitive system — POX ("Prototype Overlay Xero-graphics," written by R. E. Maas in 1973) — to do the typesetting.

***Greetings from California, 1977!**
Many of you might be expecting "Greetings from Chile" this year, but Don's research during his sabbatical has taken an unexpected turn which requires the use of Stanford's library and computer facilities. Jill also wanted to pursue some work that was hard to transplant, and John and Jenny were not anxious to leave home at a time when best friends are an important part of their lives. So all of us were content to stay put this year.
...
Music continues to be a special pleasure for us. John and Jenny began taking viola lessons as well as piano, and both play in the school orchestra and sing in the Junior Choir. Jill is still taking organ lessons and plays piano duets with Don. Don played Mozart's organ quintets with a chamber music group this spring, at a small concert here at the house. We continue to enjoy singing cantatas and other inspiring music in the church choir.

✑**This is Don:** The unexpected switch in my research began in April, when I put my main project of writing Volume 4 on the back burner and turned temporarily to a full-time study of typography and computer printing of mathematics texts. (For example, all the lettering used in this newsletter was made by an experimental computer program I am designing; some of the styles my program produces are sort of funny, but by next year I hope to have the second edition of my volume 2 all printed using these new methods.) I had the good fortune to be specially honored twice this year for my professional work, being appointed to Stanford's first endowed chair in Computer Science, and also being invited by the American Mathematical Society to give the major address at its convention this winter. As I write this, I am frantically preparing for that lecture.

✸**This is Jill:** *My Chinese classes came in handy for our trip. I was able to communicate, though at a very basic level. My strongest impression of China was of the beauty and dignity of the people and of the profound and dynamic changes taking place in this huge and varied nation. At home I have become more involved with stitchery, especially banners. I've exhibited in a few local shows, made a series of Christmas banners for a small shopping center, and have begun the major project of making banners for all the festivals of the Church Year. Photography serves as an adjunct to design projects and provides me with a lot of inspiration and source material. As a change of pace from fabric and stitching, I've also done a little graphic design—letterheads, covers, and logos.*

✐**This is John (now a 7th grader):** We have just finished football, started basketball, and baseball is coming up. I'm going mad over "MAD" and have approximately $25 worth of "MAD" magazines and books. I just got braces a month ago. O yeah, we went to China for a month. It was very hot and humid. Gasp!

✸**This is Jenny (now a 5th grader):** *I received roller skates for my 11th birthday and now roller skate to school. We still have our three pets (a dog and two cats) and our goldfish outside just had babies. I enjoy playing the viola but I still enjoy the piano very much. In China it was very hot. I didn't enjoy breakfast because usually I'm very hungry in the morning and want a cool, refreshing breakfast. Pickled spicy cabbage is not that.*

FIGURE 12. Excerpts from our family newsletter in December 1977, showing the first examples of my first experimental typefaces (at 45% of the original size).

1979: An Alphabetical Greeting

1979 was the year that I devoted to the first-generation METAFONT system for computer-drawn letters. I did much of this work as a guest of the Xerox Palo Alto Research Center, where one of the first color laser-printers had just been installed. Each letter of the prototype Computer Modern alphabets that I was developing could be displayed in "proof mode," which showed the key design points within each character on an underlying grid. I liked the appearance of these proofmode images; so I decided that our 1979 Christmas card should feature the words 'Merry Christmas', with each of those 14 letters shown in proofmode. Furthermore I decided to print it on the new color Xerox machine, using a rainbow of colors.

Unfortunately, however, each proofmode character required a large number of pixels; to print just one character at a time was already straining the capacity of the computers then available. Four different levels of software were needed to print 'Merry Christmas' in the way I wanted it, none of which had ever been confronted with such large files before. With difficulty I rewrote the first one so that it could handle

14 times as many pixels; but then the second one broke. And so on. Finally I decided to shorten the message:

FIGURE 13. Red letters on a green grid (at 50% of the original size).

1981: Madonna and Child

Our typographic card of 1981 featured St. Luke's Christmas story:

At that time the emperor, Cæsar Augustus, ordered a census to be taken throughout the Roman Empire. This first census was conducted when Quirinius was the governor of Syria. Everyone, then, went to register himself, each to his own home town. * Joseph went from the town of Nazareth in Galilee south to the town of Bethlehem in Judea, the birthplace of King David, because he was a descendant of David. He went to register with Mary, who was promised in marriage to him. Mary was pregnant, and while they were in Bethlehem, the time came for her to have her baby. She gave birth to her first son, wrapped him in cloths and laid him in a manger—there was no room for them to stay at the inn. * Some shepherds were in that part of the country spending the night in the fields, taking care of their flocks. An angel of the Lord appeared to them, and the glory of the Lord shone over them. They were terribly frightened, but the angel said to them, "Don't be afraid! I am here with good news for you, which will bring great joy to all the people. This very day in David's town your Savior was born—Christ the Lord! And this is what will prove it to you: you will find a baby wrapped in cloths and lying in a manger." * Suddenly a great army of heaven's angels appeared with the first angel, singing praises to God: "Glory to God in the highest heaven, and peace on earth to those with whom he is pleased!" * When the angels went away from them back into heaven, the shepherds said to each other, "Let's go to Bethlehem and see what has happened, as the Lord has told us." * They hurried off and found Mary and Joseph and saw the baby lying in the manger. The shepherds told them what the angel had said about the child. All who heard it were amazed at what the shepherds said. Mary remembered all these things and thought deeply about them. * Then the shepherds went back, singing praises to God for all they had heard and seen; it had been just as the angel had told them.

1985: Adoremus

And a few years later I used typography in yet another way.

> Our Christmas card, "Let us adore," contains a little puzzle for
> those of you who like a challenge. Can you determine how many
> separate strands of cord have been looped together to make the
> knots in the design? For example, the star breaks down into
> eight short loops and two longer loops. How many strands are
> in "Adoremus"? How many appear in the three kings?

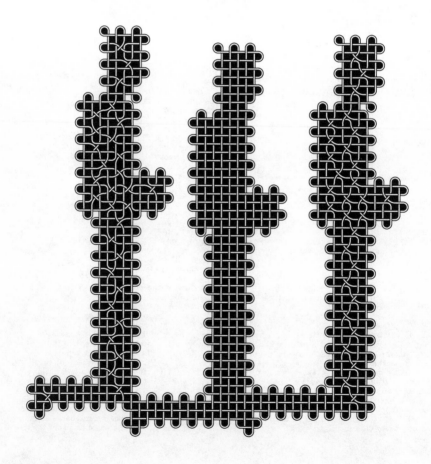

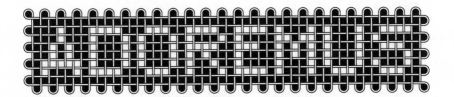

Solution: "Adoremus" has only one strand; that's easy to see. Furthermore, by using colored pens (try it), one can conclude that the three kings involve seven separate strands, two of which are fairly short.

The special fonts used to make these illustrations, together with a program CELTIC-PATHS that prepares such designs for TₑX, are online at http://www-cs-faculty.stanford.edu/~knuth/programs.html.

1989: Additional Specialty Fonts

Our Christmas card for 1989 (Figure 14), and its accompanying newsletter, introduced an experimental typeface called 'JEN', based on my daughter's handwriting. (1989 was the year that I added fancy new ligature mechanisms to the TₑX and METAFONT systems, thereby enabling fonts such as this.) We also spruced things up by using another new font, 'HOLLY', for decorative effects of various kinds.

FIGURE 14.
HOLLY + JEN
+ Psalm 136:1
(reduced to 55%).

1994: Stars From Golden Triangles

A "golden triangle" is an isosceles triangle in which the unequal sides exhibit the golden ratio ϕ. There are two kinds of golden triangles: One is acute ($\triangle$), with angles 72°–72°–36°; the other is obtuse ($\triangle$), with angles 36°–36°–108°. Golden triangles deserve to be much better known, because they have many beautiful properties. For example, every golden triangle, whether acute or obtuse, is readily decomposed into two smaller golden triangles — one of each kind; and the areas of the triangles in this decomposition correspond to the rule $\phi = 1 + 1/\phi$ that defines the golden ratio. The famous Penrose tiles can be formed from golden triangles, because two of the acute ones make a "kite" and two of the obtuse ones make a "dart."

I became enamored of golden triangles during 1994, while preparing material for Section 7.2.2 of *The Art of Computer Programming* and corresponding with Nob Yoshigahara (see Chapter 47). I subsequently lectured about them to the Japanese "Academy of Recreational Mathematicians" in Tokyo on 16 November 1996. Independently, Mark McClure published some colorful examples of golden-triangle tilings in *The Mathematical Intelligencer* **24**, 2 (Spring 2002), 33–42. Since golden triangles are closely related to five-pointed stars, it was not surprising that Jill and I decided to use them in our Christmas card for 1994.

> Since Don had so much fun with puzzles this year, we decided to include a new one with our card. Some of you might remember the card we sent just after Jenny was born, when we made little ornaments out of twelve pentagons, representing the Twelve Days of Christmas. This year we're returning to the pentagon theme, but transforming pentagons into a star: "They were overjoyed at the sight of the star" [Matthew 2 : 10]. We wish you all another blessed year of peace and joy.
>
> **STAR PUZZLE:** Cut each pentagon into four triangles. Then make a star using twelve of the sixteen triangles, judiciously choosing three of each color. *Triangles of the same color should not touch each other at any point.* (There are only 13 ways to do this!)
>
> **SUPERSTAR PUZZLE:** Use all four triangles of each color to make a star together with two small pentagons — again without allowing any same-colored triangles to touch.

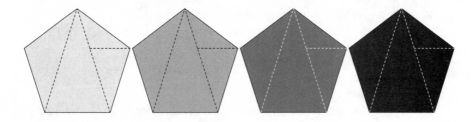

Solutions:

2003: A Tree of Spanning Trees

During the past twenty years I've regularly given "Christmas tree lectures" at Stanford in December, describing the coolest things that I've learned about tree structures during that year. My lecture in 2003 included a diagram that just happened to be perfect for a Christmas card: It shows all of the "spanning trees" of a nice little six-point graph, connected by a thread in which just one branch of the mini-tree changes at each step. (For further details, you can watch the lecture online, `http://scpd.stanford.edu/knuth/index.jsp`, and/or scrutinize Algorithm 7.2.1.6S in *The Art of Computer Programming*.)

2004: A Norwegian Christmas Carol

In 2001, Jill and I had based our annual Christmas message and card on "A carol for Advent" (Chapter 21), commemorating the births of our grandchildren. Three years later we were again in the mood to send out festive music, for which I gave the following explanation:

> We celebrated our first Scandinavian Christmas in Norway during the winter of 1972. The winter sun came out for only three or four hours each day, but everybody was in great spirits and we were entranced by many festive traditions that were new to us. For example, Norwegians placed their Christmas trees in the middle of a room, so that everybody could join hands to sing special songs while circling around the tree. One night in mid-December, several dozen families who lived near us in suburban Oslo got together to dance around a big, live pine tree that had been decorated in a nearby field, and that's when I recall first hearing the Norwegian carols that I grew to love during the following weeks.
>
> The best of these carols, to my ears — and I also think the Norwegian children liked it best, judging from the glow in their eyes as they sang it — was "Å Jul Med Din Glede" ("O Yule With Thy Joy"), because it not only has a catchy melody but it also gives everybody a chance to clap hands, dance, and bow down in time to the music.
>
> After returning home, I was surprised to find that this particular song was virtually unknown on the other side of the Atlantic, although Christmas carols from many different nations have become popular in America. I found myself singing "Å Jul Med Din Glede" to myself even 30 years after having left Norway; so I resolved to translate the words into English (with Jill's help), and to arrange the melody so that it can be sung in four-part harmony. I hope that many other people will thereby experience some of the pleasure that this song has given me.
>
> You can't sing "O Yule With Thy Joy" in a totally authentic way unless your Christmas tree is in the middle of a room. But you still can have fun marching in a circle, clapping hands, kneeling, and bowing on cue. It's best not to sing it too slowly; the right tempo is about 160 beats per minute, something like "Jingle Bells."

O Yule With Thy Joy

Norwegian carol by Gustava Kielland
Arranged and translated by Don and Jill Knuth, 2004

1 O Yule with thy joy and thy child- like glee,
2 O tale of the East, O ye wise men three,
3 I hold out with glad- ness to you my hand,

we wish thee a most heart- y wel - come.
we know well just where you are go - ing;
come quick- ly and give me the oth - er;

We shout out our hap - pi- est greet- ings to thee:
so we want to join you, for hap- py we'll be
then we'll be u - ni - ted in love's ho- ly band,

yes, ten thou - sand times we bid wel - come!
to fol- low the star bright- ly glow- ing.
and prom- ise to love one a- noth- er.

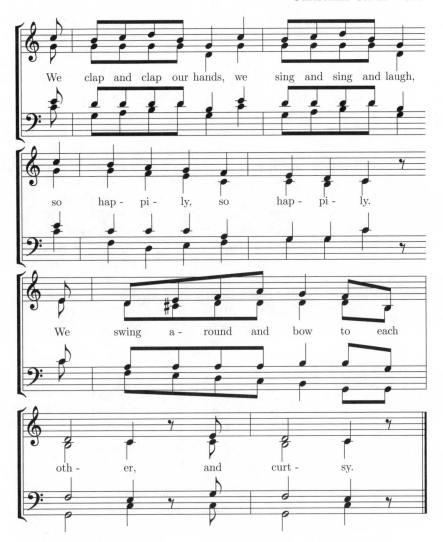

We clap and clap our hands, we sing and sing and laugh,

so hap - pi - ly, so hap - pi - ly.

We swing a - round and bow to each

oth - er, and curt - sy.

Å jul med din glede og barnlige lyst,
  vi ønsker deg alle velkommen,
vi hilser deg alle med jublende røst
  ti tusene ganger velkommen.
    Vi klapper i hendene,
      vi synger og vi ler,
    så gladelig, så gladelig,
      vi svinger oss i kretsen og neier,
        og bukker.

I Østerlands vise, I tre stjernemenn,
  vi vet nok hvorhen I skal drage,
for vi ville også så gjerne derhen
  og Eder på reisen ledsage. Vi klapper . . .

Så rekker jeg deg nå med glede min hånd,
  kom, skynd deg og gi meg den annen.
Så knytter vi kjærlighets hellige bånd
  og lover å elske hinannen. Vi klapper . . .

"Å Jul Med Din Glede" was written by Gustava Kielland (née Susanne Sophie Caroline Gustava Blom), who was born in 1800 and died in 1889. In 1824 she married the Lutheran priest Gabriel Kirsebom Kielland (1796–1854), who served for 13 years in Finnøy and then for 17 years in Lyngdal. She and her husband were pioneers in missionary work, and she became known as the "mother of women's clubs" in Norway because she founded a missionary society in 1840 with the help of farmers' wives in Lyngdal. Meanwhile she also raised nine children, eight of whom (plus 73 grandchildren) were alive at the time of her death. Her autobiography *Reminiscence From My Life*, published in 1880, was one of the first to be written by a Norwegian woman, and it has often been reprinted. The street "Gustava Kiellands vei" in Kongsberg, the city of her birth, was named in her honor in 1982.

One day she happened to hear her kitchen maid singing a Swedish song called "Viljen I Veta och Viljen I Förstå?" ("Do You Want to Know, and Do You Want to Understand?"), and she was struck by the realization that it wasn't solemn and serious like a typical Norwegian carol. So she wrote the melody down, and added new words that, she said, came easily, "almost by themselves."

2006: The Pentagrid

Mathematics and computer science returned to our card in 2006, which featured Figure 15, printed in black and red on metallic gold paper.

> Our Christmas card this year features the starlike "pentagrid," an illustration in Don's most recent work. Mathematicians discovered 150 years ago that pentagons can have 90° angles, in a warped geometry called the hyperbolic plane; thus they fit together like squares in an ordinary plane. We show the pentagrid as seen through a special lens, projecting the entire hyperbolic plane into a circle.

> *All the curtains had the same measure. He coupled five curtains to one another, and again coupled five curtains to one another.*   – Exodus 36:9–10

(The pentagrid, and its amazing connection with Fibonacci numbers by which an unusual implicit data structure can be traversed efficiently, is discussed in Section 7.1.3 of *The Art of Computer Programming*, where it is Fig. 14 in Volume 4A. "A circular regular tiling, confined on all sides by infinitely small shapes, is really wonderful." – M. C. Escher)

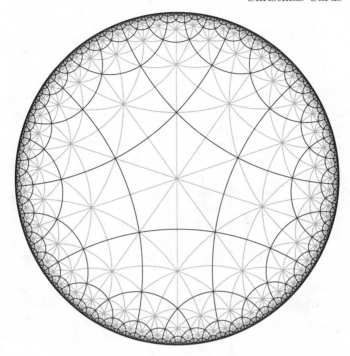

FIGURE 15. The pentagrid, which adorned our card in 2006 (actual size).

A Foretaste of the Future: Jablan Tiles

It's time now to conclude this chapter by presenting the sudoku-like puzzle that formed the basis of our most recent Christmas card.

But that puzzle doesn't fit nicely on the present page.

So I've decided to fill this page and the next by discussing a "Kufic" design motif that occurred to me while writing the present book. It's based on some novel modular tiles discovered by Slavik Jablan, who showed them to the participants of the eighth Gathering for Gardner in March 2008. [Jablan had previously presented a related pattern in a paper written with R. Sarhangi and R. Sazdanovic, "Modularity in medieval Persian mosaics," *VisMath* **7** (2005), Paper 9, Figure 20.]

The design uses just three kinds of tiles, ' ', ' ', and ' ', which match each other at the edges, and 90° rotations. The first is white in the center, the second is black, and the third is gray. Jablan used only the first and second of these; I added the third one as an experiment.

I plan to refine this design and use it in a future Christmas card, probably in color, possibly in 2011.

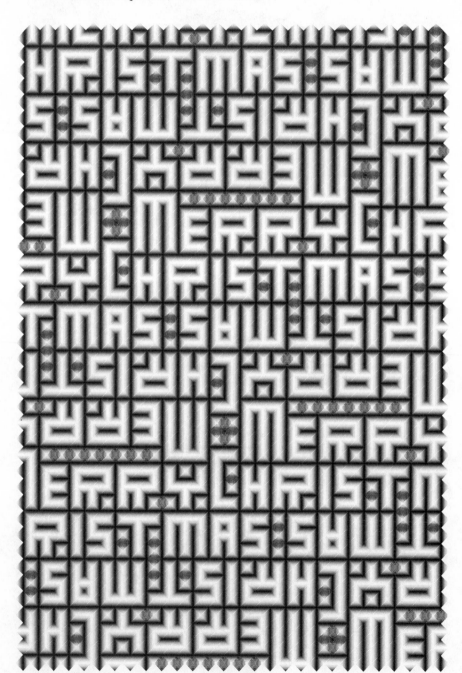

2009: Christmas Sudoku

Here's a type of "jigsaw sudoku" puzzle that contains a holiday message:

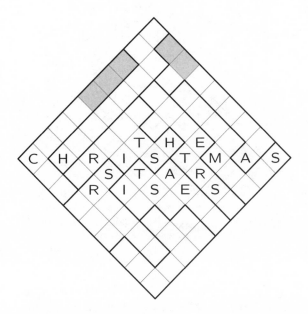

This 9×9 diamond contains 9 downward diagonals, 9 upward diagonals, and 9 bordered regions. Some of the boxes are already filled in to say THE CHRISTMAS STAR RISES. Notice that nine letters are used: C, H, A, R, M, S, I, T, E.

Fill in the other boxes so that every diagonal and every region contains C, H, A, R, M, S, I, T, E in some order. (There's only one way.)

Hint: Where can you put the letter A into the top northwest-to-southeast diagonal row, without a conflict?

When you've solved the puzzle, a secret word will appear in the five lightly-shaded boxes near the top. Have fun!

Hints on solving THE CHRISTMAS STAR RISES

Warning: It's best to uncover only one step of this solution at a time, so as not to spoil the "aha"-type fun of discovery. Read further *only* when you're stuck; then you'll soon find your skills rising like a star!

Let's put labels into the blank cells so that we can talk about them:

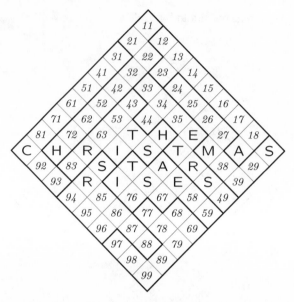

It will be convenient to refer to a downward diagonal like *11*, *12*, ... as "row 1," and to an upward diagonal like ..., *21*, *11* as "column 1."

Since many of the cells are filled in, we have only a limited number of ways to put letters into the unknown places. For example, look at cell *35*, and consider the possibilities in turn: Should *35* be filled with

C, H, A, R, M, S, I, T, or E?

Only C and A are not blocked. The reason is that row 3 already contains E and M; column 5 already contains H, S, T, I; and the region around cell *35* already contains E, T, R, S.

Now notice that *11* is forced to be A, because there must be an A in row 1 (and A can't go into *12*, *13*, ..., *18*, because that region already contains its A).

Setting *11* = A, we can conclude in a similar way that *92* must also be A. (There must be an A in column 2.) Get it?

Next, notice that *39* is also forced to be A — yes, we're on an "A binge" — because there must be an A in the region that contains cells *24*, *25*, *26*, *27*, *38*, *39*, *29*. The A doesn't fit anywhere else in that region.

Aha! With *39* = A, only one possibility remains for cell *35*, because we've already noted that *35* has to be either A or C.

⋆   ⋆   ⋆   ⋆   ⋆   ⋆   ⋆   ⋆   ⋆   ⋆   ⋆   ⋆   ⋆   ⋆   ⋆

Let's pause at this point to review the methods that we've used. There are four basic types of forcing steps that make progress in this puzzle, and we've now seen examples of each.

Row move: There's just one way to put a certain letter into a row.

Column move: There's just one way to put a letter into a column.

Region move: There's just one way to put a letter into a region.

Position move: There's just one letter that can go into a certain cell.

First we used a row move to conclude that $11 = $ A.

Then we used a column move to conclude that $92 = $ A.

Then we used a region move to conclude that $39 = $ A.

And we used a position move to conclude that $35 = $ C.

⋆   ⋆   ⋆   ⋆   ⋆   ⋆   ⋆   ⋆   ⋆   ⋆   ⋆   ⋆   ⋆   ⋆   ⋆

Armed with these four tools, and with a good eye (or a good system of organized notes) to see when they apply, we can in fact fill in 25 of the unknown cells without needing to erase anything!

Here is one scenario by which all forced moves can be successively discovered, not necessarily in this order — but remember that it's best not to peek at them until you've given this exercise the old college try:

$11 = $ A (row)	$33 = $ I (pos)	$93 = $ T (col)
$92 = $ A (col)	$49 = $ M (pos)	$31 = $ R (pos)
$39 = $ A (reg)	$44 = $ A (pos)	$38 = $ T (pos)
$35 = $ C (pos)	$85 = $ A (col)	$21 = $ T (col)
$23 = $ S (reg)	$63 = $ A (col)	$22 = $ M (row)
$32 = $ S (reg)	$77 = $ A (row)	$12 = $ T (col)
$81 = $ S (col)	$96 = $ H (reg)	$97 = $ S (col)
$34 = $ H (pos)	$13 = $ H (col)	$79 = $ T (row)

and finally $87 = $ T (col).

So we've progressed to the following partial solution:

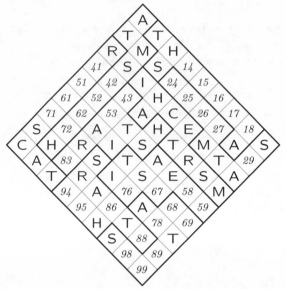

At this point nothing is forced, and we must even invent a more sophisticated type of move or resort to guessing.

(Well, we do know that the secret word "*51 41 31 12 13*" is __RTH; in the Christmas spirit we know therefore that *51* = M and *41* = I. But let's suppose that no secret word clue had been given.)

The guessing strategy that will be described in the rest of these notes might not be the best way to proceed, but it does work. The main idea is to find a row, column, region, or cell for which there are only a small number of cases to try. For example, only two choices remain for *17*: That cell must be either C or I.

Let's try *17* = C. Then more things are forced, namely

67 = H (pos)	*95* = M (pos)	*86* = C (pos)
27 = I (pos)	*15* = R (pos)	*76* = M (pos)
29 = H (row)	*94* = E (pos)	*88* = I (pos)
24 = C (col)	*14* = M (pos)	*89* = E (pos)
26 = R (pos)	*16* = I (pos)	*83* = M (pos)
25 = E (pos)	*18* = E (pos)	*53* = C (pos)

and we arrive at the partial solution at the top of the next page.

Oops: We're stuck, because there's no way to put C into the region that contains *58* and *59*. So we made a bad guess, and we have to backtrack. Since *17* cannot be C, we've discovered in fact that *17* = I.

OK, we must part with the uncompletable diagram

and return to our previous state, except that we are now allowed to set $17 = \mathsf{I}$. Unfortunately this new fact doesn't force any more moves; we'll have to make yet another guess.

Well, 24 has to be either C or E. Suppose $24 = \mathsf{C}$; then $27 = \mathsf{H}$ (pos); $67 = \mathsf{C}$ (pos); $76 = \mathsf{M}$ (pos); $89 = \mathsf{C}$ (col); and we've reached another impasse:

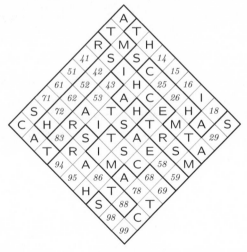

There's no way to put C into the region that contains 88. But hey, we have deduced that $24 = \mathsf{E}$.

And now it turns out that we're home free. Everything else is forced:

25 = R (pos)	41 = I (pos)	58 = H (pos)
94 = M (pos)	42 = C (pos)	67 = C (pos)
14 = C (pos)	72 = E (pos)	27 = H (pos)
95 = E (pos)	62 = R (pos)	68 = M (pos)
15 = M (pos)	52 = I (pos)	88 = I (pos)
16 = R (pos)	71 = H (pos)	86 = C (pos)
18 = E (pos)	51 = M (pos)	26 = I (pos)
76 = M (col)	61 = E (pos)	29 = C (pos)
83 = M (row)	78 = C (pos)	89 = E (pos)
53 = C (pos)	69 = H (pos)	98 = R (pos)
43 = E (pos)	59 = R (pos)	99 = I (pos)

We needn't reproduce the final diagram here.

Merry Christmas and Happy New Year!

References for the Christmas Sudoku

[1] "Where is the baby who is destined to be your king? We saw his star at its rising, and we've come to honor him." [Matthew 2:2]

[2] Bob Harris, "The Grand Time Sudoku and the law of leftovers," *Mathematical Wizardry for a Gardner* (Wellesley, Massachusetts: A K Peters, 2009), 55–57.

Addendum

Bob Harris found a nice way to solve the Christmas Sudoku without any guessing or backtracking, except for a tiny bit of lookahead: He noticed that, after the twenty-five forced moves have been made, either *68*, *78*, or *98* must be M; hence *58* can't be M, and neither can *88*. Hence *76* = M (reg); *83* = M (row); *53* = C (pos); etc.

Chapter 47

Geek Art

[This material was assembled from my personal collection.]

One of the things that make computer scientists peculiar is the fact that we're attracted to art objects that are a bit quirky. For example, I greatly enjoy the paintings of Salvador Dalí and René Magritte. That in itself is not unusual; but the strange thing is that certain other works provoke an even stronger response. When, for instance, I first saw Escher's *Ascending and Descending*, I knew instantly that I simply *had* to acquire my own copy of an original print — especially in 1967, when it was possible to buy a signed copy from the artist himself for $75.

Previous chapters of this book contain several examples of the kind of art that really "turns me on." When my wife and I devoted an entire wall of our house to the dragon curve in ceramic tile (Chapter 45), and when we made many of the Christmas cards that are discussed in Chapter 46, we were consciously striving to create objects that were not only beautiful according to the conventional æsthetics of fine art, we wanted them to be mathematically beautiful as well, thus gratifying our left brains and right brains simultaneously. These are artistic pieces that also have technical significance — sort of a marriage between C. P. Snow's "two cultures."

Computers have, of course, made many new kinds of art possible, and I've long been fascinated by novel images produced by computer graphics. Some of my own experiments along those lines are discussed in Chapter 21 of *Digital Typography* (Stanford, California: Center for the Study of Language and Information, 1999); and one of the "leaper graph" images from Chapter 43 of the present book once appeared in an exhibit of computer art at the Xerox Palo Alto Research Center. Early developments in this field were chronicled, as they happened, in a long series of articles by John Lansdown entitled "Not only computing — also art," which appeared quarterly in *The Computer Bulletin* from 1974 to

1992.* Later works are well represented by *Maeda @ Media* by John Maeda (London: Thames & Hudson, 2000); and by the "context free art" in *Community of Variation*, edited by Mark Lentczner (Mountain View, California: Ozone House, 2008).

But computer art and context free art aren't really the kinds of art that I'm thinking about as I write the present chapter. I woke up recently with the idea that the kind of art I like might best be characterized by calling it "geek art"; so I turned to the Internet, wondering whether or not this pungent phrase had occurred to anybody else. Sure enough, Google Trends told me that the relative number of searches for "geek art" had gone from 0 to about 30 during November and December of 2009.

When I did my own search for online examples of so-called geek art, I found lots of cool stuff. But still, it wasn't really what I had in mind. Most of the works referred to popular culture — often *Star Trek* — or to arcane aspects of computer software. There was a wonderful portrait of "Mona Leia," by James Hance, reminding me of the covers of *MAD* magazine #11 (May 1954) and #14 (August 1954). Carl Zimmer has collected photos of tattoos that feature great formulas of mathematics and physics. And so on. The closest thing to my own conception of geek art that I could find on the Web was David Litwin's amazing portrait of Stephen Colbert, made with 768 Rubik's cubes.†

Instead of trying to come up with a definition of what I mean by "geek art," I shall in this chapter simply present a dozen or so examples of more-or-less artistic things that I've felt an urge to create, over the years, together with some examples of cherished works that I've received from other people.

1973: Hexominoes

I'll tell these stories in roughly chronological order, because there has been sort of a steady progression since Jill and I did the dragon curve in 1971. We spent the academic year 1972–1973 in Norway, where we became entranced by many of the folk traditions that we encountered. In particular, I loved the shag rugs or wall hangings made from brightly colored yarns, knotted over a regular square grid — something like pixels, but with a delightfully random texture. I knew right away that I wanted to own such a "rya"; and I had plenty of time to knot a small one, because I could combine that task with reading bedtime stories to our kids every

---

* The title before September 1976 was "Not quite computing — almost art."

† See http://www.twistypuzzles.com/forum/viewtopic.php?f=1&t=6247 for the complete story of Litwin's project during 2007–2008.

night. Jill wrote to our parents on 10 February 1973 that "Don has really gotten 'tied up' with making rya wall hangings. ... He saw a red hanging in a store and thought it was so beautiful. Now that he has gotten interested in yarns, he'll stop to peer in yarn store windows and will closely examine different kinds of weaving. Pretty soon he'll be as bad as I am about wanting to try out different needlework techniques."

At that time I was studying polyominoes (see Chapter 38), in preparation for Section 7.2.2 of *The Art of Computer Programming*, and I'd just learned about the interesting case of *hexominoes*, which are the six-celled analogs of two-celled dominoes. The 35 possible hexomino shapes were first listed by H. D. Benjamin [*Problemist Fairy Chess Supplement* **2**, 9 (December 1934), 92], who offered a ten-shilling Christmas prize to anybody who could pack them perfectly into a 14 × 15 rectangle. The prize was won by F. Kadner [*Problemist Fairy Chess Supplement* **2**, 10 (February 1935), 104–105], who gave an elegant proof that the hexominoes *cannot* be perfectly packed into *any* rectangle: If we checker the rectangle with alternating black and white squares, there will be 105 squares of each color. But 24 of the hexominoes each yield 3 black and 3 white, while the other 11 give 4 of one color and 2 of the other.

The question remained, therefore, to find other nice shapes in which all 35 of the hexominoes can be displayed. Several nice packings were subsequently found; and my favorite solution also turned out to be perfectly suitable for execution as a rya! Walter Stead found an elegant way to put fifteen 1 × 1 holes in a 5 × 45 rectangle, thereby allowing the remaining 210 squares to be checkered with 106 versus 104 instead of 105 versus 105:

With the help of A. S. M. Dickins I was able to communicate with Stead, who confirmed in 1973 that he had published this construction for the first time in *Fairy Chess Review* **9**, 1 (December 1954), 2–4, as part of a survey of related results. (He also remarked that this particular arrangement "has been 'pinched' without permission in U.S.A.")

In some notes about how to attack polyomino packing problems, which were called *dissection problems* at that time, Stead recommended placing the awkward pieces

as soon as possible; the useful ones

 and especially

should preferably be reserved for the last stages. "Work the pattern along on a fairly irregular edge, not on a straight front. The expert can judge the required 'toothiness' of the working front by the kind of pieces he still has in hand. ... There is a great thrill to be had from the successful closing of a difficult dissection. Usually the 'closure' can be foreseen with two pieces 'in hand.' That is the great moment!"

I noticed that Stead's hexomino arrangement could be three-colored:

Therefore I had the rya pattern that I wanted, and I proceeded to make the wall hanging shown in Figure 1. This design graces a wall of my office at home, where I see it every time I use my computer; after more than 35 years, I still enjoy it greatly. It's a pity that you can't see the rich colors of yarn now, as you read this book — with the hexominoes in golden yellow, bright orange-red, and mellow auburn-rust, and with deep green accents at the edges and in the "holes." But most of the illustrations in this chapter can in fact be viewed on the Internet in glorious color, as explained in the acknowledgments below.

FIGURE 1. My favorite wall hanging. (approximately 30 cm × 125 cm)

FIGURE 2.
Detail from the
back of Figure 1.

To make the rya in Fig. 1, I needed to tie $34 \times 139 = 4726$ knots, cutting each of them so that two threads about an inch long came through the grid-based fabric on the back. By Norwegian standards, this was of course a quite trivial number of knots, since I wasn't making a whole rug. The knotting and cutting provided a pleasant way to relax in the evening, working on small batches. Once this job was complete, I decided to try another medium too; so I rendered the same design in beads (Figure 3).

FIGURE 3. My favorite beaded bracelet. (approximately 12 mm × 132 mm)

There are many other ways to insert the 35 hexominoes into Stead's 5 × 45 box with 15 holes. Indeed, his original pattern already yields fifteen more ways, because we can decompose it into four subareas

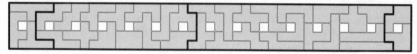

and those subareas can be flipped independently to give sixteen essentially different packings. There probably are millions of different solutions altogether, in spite of the fact that even a single solution is by no means easy to find. I could enumerate all of them systematically by using the "dancing links" algorithm of Chapter 38, if I wanted to mount a major effort on a cluster of computers. But random sampling tells me that the dancing links procedure would probably need to update its data structures roughly 4×10^{18} times during that process, unless I find some way to speed it up; that's four *quintillion* updates.

Suppose we decide to freeze the positions of the leftmost 16 hexominoes in Stead's pattern. In how many ways can the remaining 19 be placed? The method of dancing links needs only a few seconds to answer this question and to crank out all such placements, and it turns out that there are exactly 3522 of them — 1761 in which the 1 × 6 piece lies in the lower half, as in Stead's original, plus 1761 obtained by reflection.

One of those new placements of the rightmost 19 caught my eye:

It has the interesting property that each hexomino touches either the top row or the bottom row (or both). Furthermore, the overall rectangle of size 5 × 45 has been split into two subrectangles of sizes 5 × 27 and 5 × 18, containing respectively 21 and 14 hexominoes together with 9 and 6 holes.

Hmmm. Can we decompose Stead's holey rectangles even further, packing 7 hexominoes and 3 holes into a 5 × 9, with the holes in columns {2, 5, 8} of the middle row? Yes indeed we can. In fact the arrangement

(*)

shows that 28 hexominoes can be put into four different 5 × 9 frames; but there's no analogous way to pack all 35. (The dancing links algorithm needs less than a minute to determine that exactly 17,078 choices of seven hexominoes can be packed into a 5 × 9 frame, with holes in the required places. Then a second round of dancing, with these 17,078 choices forming a new exact cover problem, establishes that no five choices are disjoint, but it does discover several examples of disjoint fours such as the one shown.) The reader will find it interesting to extend (*) by packing six of the remaining seven hexominoes into a fifth holey 5 × 9, without overlapping; there's only one way to do it!

Incidentally, Stead's paper in the *Fairy Chess Review* mentioned also a noteworthy construction by H. D. Benjamin of a case where hexominoes *can* be perfectly packed into a rectangle. Benjamin first discarded the eight "easy" pieces that fit inside of a 3 × 3 square; then he put the tough 27 that remained into a 9 × 18 rectangle as follows:

He went on to embody this hard-to-find arrangement in a rug, which Stead called "magnificent." (I wonder how many colors he used in the rug? Four colors are necessary and, of course, sufficient.) The problem of enumerating all solutions to Benjamin's problem appears to be about two orders of magnitude more difficult than the problem of enumerating all ways to pack the hexominoes into Stead's 5 × 45 frame, even though only 27 hexominoes need to be packed instead of 35.

1975: Hexagonal Primes

Prime numbers lead to innumerable patterns of great mathematical beauty, but geometric depictions of primes don't seem to lead to any designs that are especially appealing to the eye.

Two-dimensional analogs of prime numbers turn out to be equally interesting, however, and visually more satisfying. A *Gaussian integer* is a complex number of the form $a + bi$ where a and b are integers, and the set of all such numbers is well known to be a "unique factorization domain." In other words, every nonzero Gaussian integer can be represented in essentially only one way as a product of "Gaussian primes."

The number $7 + 9i$ can, for instance, be written in factored form as $(1 + i)(2 - i)(3 + 2i)$, where these factors cannot be reduced further. We also can write $7 + 9i = (i - 2)(3i - 2)(i - 1)$; but the factorization is essentially unique, because one can prove that the product $p_1 \ldots p_t$ of t Gaussian primes is equal to $7 + 9i$ if and only if $t = 3$, $p_1 = i^{k_1}q_1$, $p_2 = i^{k_2}q_2$, and $p_3 = i^{k_3}q_3$, where $(k_1 + k_2 + k_3) \bmod 4 = 3$ and $\{q_1, q_2, q_3\} = \{1+i, 1+2i, 3+2i\}$. Arbitrary powers of i can be included in each factor, just as we can include powers of -1 within factors of ordinary integers.

A pleasant pattern is obtained when we consider the number of prime factors that are present in each nonzero Gaussian integer. These numbers t are shown here for Gaussians whose distance from 0 is less than 11.5; the value for $7 + 9i$ is, for example, 3, and it appears 7 cells to the right and 9 cells up from the empty cell in the middle of the pattern. The value is 0 when we try to factor 1, i, -1, or $-i$; these four Gaussian integers are called the *units* of the domain. An ordinary (real) integer p is a Gaussian prime if and only if it's an ordinary prime with $p \bmod 4 = 3$.

```
                3 3 2 1 2 3 3
            3 3 1 4 1 4 1 4 1 3 3
        3 2 2 1 3 2 2 2 2 3 1 2 2 3
      7 1 4 1 5 1 3 2 6 2 3 1 5 1 4 1 7
      3 1 2 2 2 2 2 1 3 1 3 1 2 2 2 2 1 3
    2 4 2 4 1 3 2 4 1 3 1 4 2 3 1 4 2 4 2
  3 2 1 2 1 3 1 2 1 2 2 2 1 2 1 3 1 2 1 2 3
  3 1 5 2 3 1 5 2 3 1 4 1 3 2 5 1 3 2 5 1 3
3 1 3 1 2 2 2 2 2 1 2 1 2 1 2 2 2 2 2 1 3 1 3
3 4 2 3 1 4 1 3 1 3 1 2 1 3 1 3 1 4 1 3 2 4 3
2 1 2 2 3 1 2 1 2 1 1 0 1 1 2 1 2 1 3 2 2 1 2
1 4 2 6 1 3 2 4 1 2 0     0 2 1 4 2 3 1 6 2 4 1
2 1 2 2 3 1 2 1 2 1 1 0 1 1 2 1 2 1 3 2 2 1 2
3 4 2 3 1 4 1 3 1 3 1 2 1 3 1 3 1 4 1 3 2 4 3
3 1 3 1 2 2 2 2 2 1 2 1 2 1 2 2 2 2 2 1 3 1 3
  3 1 5 2 3 1 5 2 3 1 4 1 3 2 5 1 3 2 5 1 3
  3 2 1 2 1 3 1 2 1 2 2 2 1 2 1 3 1 2 1 2 3
    2 4 2 4 1 3 2 4 1 3 1 4 2 3 1 4 2 4 2
      3 1 2 2 2 2 2 1 3 1 3 1 2 2 2 2 1 3
      7 1 4 1 5 1 3 2 6 2 3 1 5 1 4 1 7
        3 2 2 1 3 2 2 2 2 3 1 2 2 3
            3 3 1 4 1 4 1 4 1 3 3
                3 3 2 1 2 3 3
```

Similar properties hold for the "Eisenstein integers" $a + b\omega$, where $\omega = (\sqrt{3}i - 1)/2$ is a complex cube root of unity. The product of two such numbers is again Eisensteinian, because $(a+b\omega)(c+d\omega) = ac+(ad+bc)\omega+ bd\omega^2 = (ac-bd)+(ad+bc-bd)\omega$; and again the prime factors are essentially unique. These numbers fit into hexagonal cells, analogous to the square cells of the Gaussian integers. To find the number of prime factors of, say, $7 + 9\omega$, go 7 cells right from the center hexagon, then 9 cells up-and-left at an angle of $120°$; the value is 1, so $7 + 9\omega$ is an Eisenstein prime.

```
                    2 1 1 2
                2 3 3 1 4 1 3 3 2
            1 2 1 1 2 2 2 2 1 1 2 1
        2 2 2 2 3 1 2 2 2 1 3 2 2 2 2
        3 1 2 4 1 1 3 1 1 3 1 1 4 2 1 3
    2 3 1 3 1 3 2 2 2 3 2 2 2 3 1 3 1 3 2
    1 1 2 1 1 2 2 1 2 1 1 2 1 2 2 1 1 2 1 1
  1 4 2 2 3 2 1 3 1 2 3 2 1 3 1 2 3 2 2 4 1
  2 1 2 2 1 2 2 1 1 2 1 1 2 2 1 2 2 1 2 1 2
  2 2 1 3 1 2 2 2 1 2 1 2 2 2 1 3 1 2 2 1 2 2
  3 1 1 3 2 1 3 1 1 2 1 1 2 1 1 3 1 2 3 1 1 3
  2 1 3 1 2 2 2 2 1 2 1 1 1 2 1 2 2 2 2 1 3 1 2
  2 2 1 2 1 1 2 1 1 1 0 0 1 1 1 2 1 1 2 1 2 2
  1 2 4 2 3 2 1 2 2 1 0     0 1 2 2 1 2 3 2 4 2 1
  2 2 1 2 1 1 2 1 1 1 0 0 1 1 1 2 1 1 2 1 2 2
  2 1 3 1 2 2 2 2 1 1 1 1 1 2 1 2 2 2 2 1 3 1 2
  3 1 1 3 2 1 3 1 1 2 1 1 2 1 1 3 1 2 3 1 1 3
  2 2 1 3 1 2 2 2 1 2 1 2 2 2 1 3 1 2 2 1 2 2
  2 1 2 2 1 2 2 1 1 2 1 1 2 2 1 2 2 1 2 1 2
  1 4 2 2 3 2 1 3 1 2 3 2 1 3 1 2 3 2 2 4 1
    1 1 2 1 1 2 2 1 2 1 1 2 1 2 2 1 1 2 1 1
    2 3 1 3 1 3 2 2 2 3 2 2 2 3 1 3 1 3 2
        3 1 2 4 1 1 3 1 1 3 1 1 4 2 1 3
        2 2 2 2 3 1 2 2 2 1 3 2 2 2 2
            1 2 1 1 2 2 2 2 1 1 2 1
                2 3 3 1 4 1 3 3 2
                    2 1 1 2
```

The value for $7 + 11\omega$ is 2, and indeed $7 + 11\omega = (1 - \omega)(1 + 6\omega)$. Notice that there are six units in this case: 1, $1 + \omega$, ω, -1, $-1 - \omega$, and $-\omega$. An ordinary prime p is an Eisenstein prime if and only if $p \bmod 3 = 2$.

For artistic purposes, of course, we prefer arrays of colors to arrays of numbers. The two discrete circles of values on the previous page are perceived more intuitively when presented in a purely graphic language:

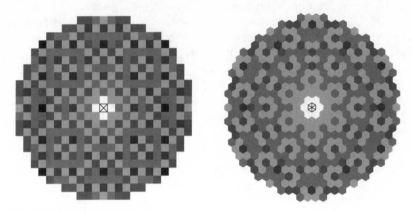

Here the units are white, the primes are light gray, and numbers with more and more prime factors get darker and darker. We might also opt for binary output, showing the primes only (in black this time):

The binary pattern on the left was first devised in 1946 by Balthasar van der Pol, who published it in a report of the Haagsche Maatschappij Diligentia, a society of mathematicians in The Hague. He subsequently computed the pattern on the right, jointly with Pierre Speziali ["The primes in $k(\varrho)$," *Indagationes Mathematicæ* **13** (1951), 9–15, with a foldout illustration], giving also a list of all the Eisenstein primes whose magnitude is less than 10000. He arranged for linen tablecloths to be woven, showing the Gaussian primes, and gave one to D. H. Lehmer, who hung it on the wall of his study in Berkeley [see *Mathematical Tables and Other Aids to Computation* **5** (1951), 139]. The tablecloths were also available for sale in Amsterdam at a large gathering of mathematicians from around the world [see *Proceedings of the International Congress of Mathematicians 1954*, Volume 1 (Amsterdam: North-Holland, 1957), 158].

Several years ago I saw one of those historic tablecloths. It was interesting, but (alas) I cannot say that it was beautiful. The pattern of Eisenstein primes is really much nicer. Indeed, Lehmer himself remarked, when reviewing the paper of van der Pol and Speziali, that "the symmetry of the diagram produces a strikingly beautiful effect" [*Mathematical Reviews* **12** (1951), review 676b]. Two decades later, when I was contemplating a design that might be suitable for my own study at Stanford, my thoughts turned naturally to the Eisenstein primes.

But I already had a nice wall hanging. Instead, I asked my wife to make a patchwork coverlet based on this pattern of hexagons, and she responded enthusiastically. Here's what she said in letters to our parents (26 January 1975 and 10 February 1975):

> I've been sewing on a patchwork and embroidered comforter cover. Don generated the design on the computer, and I embroidered about 160 hexagons (started in October). Now I'm sewing them together with about 220 plain hexagons. The whole thing will make one huge hexagon with a pattern on it. Then I'll have to put it on a background to form the top of the cover. The back of the cover, like a huge pillow case, will be just plain. It's exciting now that it's going together. ...
>
> The quilt I am sewing is now all pieced together. There are about four hundred small hexagons. Some are cut from various shades of blue, and some are in the orange-yellow-red family. These are embroidered and form the design. Don made the design on the computer, it has some mathematical significance, but is also an interesting visual pattern. Now that it's together, I like it very much. Now I must sew the backing and edging, and do the quilting. I'll quilt on the machine, just a simple outline around the blue hexagons, more for strength than appearance. Maybe I'll have it done by the end of the week.

During the past 35 years I've taken hundreds of naps under this coverlet, which is depicted in Figures 4 and 5. I love it! (Once again I recommend that you check out the full color version on the Web.) The

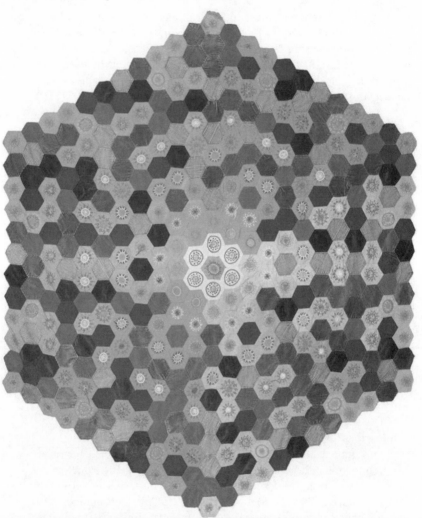

FIGURE 4. My favorite comforter cover. (approximately 55″ × 63″)
With its border (not shown), the entire coverlet measures 57.5″ × 76″.

central hexagon is a special green color, to represent zero; it is surrounded by six light blue hexagons, to represent the units. Then the
Eisenstein primes appear in various shades of the "warm" colors yellow,
pink, and/or orange; by contrast, the products of two or more primes appear in a variety of blue hues, medium to dark. The zero, the units, and
the primes are all gaily embroidered, as shown in Figure 5. (The pattern

FIGURE 5. Detail of Figure 4, at 50% of the original size.
Each hexagon has 1.5-inch sides.

in Figure 4 needs to be rotated clockwise by 30° if you want to reconcile it with the complex-plane-oriented diagrams on previous pages. I've done that rotation in Figure 5.) Notice that, except for the important distinctions between zero, unit, prime, and nonprime cells, Jill's color choices were based on visual elegance, not on additional mathematical properties; one should not let mathematics govern *everything*.

1975: A Knitted Möbius Band

We invited one of the young computer scientists I had met in Norway, Stein Krogdahl, to visit Stanford for a year, and he became a great friend. Jill discovered that he was interested in knitting, which of course is another way to enjoy the properties of the beautiful Norwegian yarns. At Christmastime in 1975 he presented us with a delightful piece of geek art: He had figured out how to knit a Möbius band — the fascinating one-sided surface that had been discovered independently by the German mathematicians J. B. Listing and A. F. Möbius in 1858.* I myself have never learned to knit, and I'm also geometrically challenged, so I'm not sure how Stein accomplished this feat. But knowledgeable knitters may be able to psych out from Figure 6 the ingenious scheme by which he was able to knit-and-purl with two colors of yarn so that the band's one-sidedness is plainly visible.

FIGURE 6. My favorite knitted object. (actual size)
Red-orange yarn appears at the edges, golden yellow in the middle.

---

* See Johann Benedict Listing, "Der Census räumlicher Complexe oder Ver-allgemeinerung des Euler'schen Satzes von den Polyëdern," *Abhandlungen der mathematischen Classe der Königlichen Gesellschaft der Wissenschaften zu Göttingen* **10** (1862), 97–182; A. F. Möbius, "Ueber die Bestimmung des Inhaltes eines Polyeders," *Berichte über die Verhandlungen der Königlich Sächsischen Gesellschaft der Wissenschaften zu Leipzig, mathematisch-physische Classe* **17** (1865), 31–68; Paul Stäckel, "Die Entdeckung der einseitigen Flächen," *Mathematische Annalen* **52** (1899), 598–600.

Miles Reid has explained how to knit Möbius bands and other exotic structures in "The knitting of surfaces," *Eureka: The Archimedeans' Journal* **34** (1971), 21–26. See also the excellent website by sarah-marie belcastro, "Knitted Möbius bands," `http://www.toroidalsnark.net/mkmb.html`.

1975: A π Vest

The next item in my collection was another pleasant surprise that I received on Christmas Day, 1975: Jill gave me a new vest, which she had designed and made using Ultrasuede® — a rather expensive fabric that had been invented in Japan and recently introduced to America.

FIGURE 7. My favorite vest, modeled in 2010 by Emily and Tim Aiken. (approximately $22.5'' \times 40''$; the numerals are $2'' \times 3.14''$)

I fondly recall wearing this vest when I gave a lecture to the Harvard Mathematics Department on 23 February 1976. Somebody asked me to demonstrate it with full precision, during the question period, by turning around slowly. Nowadays, of course, I wear it on 14 March.

1975: A Quicksort Double-Weave

Meanwhile I had also received a fine example of geek art as a gift from my student Bob Sedgewick, who received his Ph.D. in 1975. Bob's wife Linda, like my wife Jill, has a strong interest in art that has spilled over into his and my own lives. Linda had majored in biology ("to help earn a living," she said) and minored in art ("to help feed my soul"), and she was particularly interested in weaving and textiles. So Bob and Linda filled a room of their apartment with a fine eight-harness

FIGURE 8. My favorite doubly woven fabric. (approximately $36'' \times 11''$)
Both sides are shown; half of the threads are orange, the other half are brown.

loom, and Linda showed him how to use it to immortalize a beautiful
pattern that he had discovered during his doctoral research. While my
secretary Phyllis Winkler was typing the final version of Bob's thesis
["Quicksort," Stanford Computer Science Technical Report STAN-CS-
75-492 (1975), reprinted by Garland Publishing of New York in 1980],
he passed the time by making the magnificent "double-weave" fabric
shown in Figure 8. (I had first seen double-weaving in Finland in 1972,
and I think I'd showed Bob the one that I had purchased at the time.)

FIGURE 9. Emily Aiken demon-
strates the intriguing duplicity
of a doubly woven fabric.

FIGURE 10. Detail of Figure 8. (actual size)

The pattern depicted here is an extension of Figure 4.2b on page 116
of Bob's thesis. It characterizes the *best case partitioning elements* when
the quicksort algorithm is used with "cleanup parameter" $M = 4$. The
top row corresponds to sorting $N = 5$ elements; the next row corresponds
to $N = 6$; and so on, proceeding all the way to $N = 124$. When the
quicksort algorithm is applied to N elements, one element is chosen

for partitioning; if its key is the Kth largest, the smaller elements are moved into positions 1 through $K - 1$, the larger elements are moved into positions $K + 1$ through N, and the partitioning element itself goes into position K. The subfiles from 1 to $K - 1$ and $K + 1$ to N are subsequently partitioned in the same way, until reaching subfiles of size M or less. Bob wanted to know what values of K were best, in the sense that they minimize the amount of work done. When $M = 4$ and $N = 5$, all partitioning elements are equally good, so K can be 1, 2, 3, 4, or 5. When $N = 6$, only the values 2, 3, 4, or 5 are optimum for K; these four cases are indicated in the second row of the weaving. It turns out that when $N = 9, 19, 29, 39, 59, 79$, and 119, there's only one optimum choice for K: We must take $K = (N + 1)/2$. (In other words, the "median" element is the only good choice for partitioning in such cases.)

Bottom line: The math is interesting and appealing; so is the pattern. I've often displayed this weaving and shown it to visitors.

1976: Inspiration From Matt Kahn

The time was now ripe for me to learn how to make more things by myself. Linda Sedgewick had taken the Stanford Art Department's most famous class, "Basic Design" (aka "Art 60") as taught by Professor Matt Kahn, in the fall of 1974, and she recommended it highly. Thus it came about that Jill and I began to audit Art 60 in January of 1976.

That class changed my life. Wow! What a revelation! I learned how to get my hands dirty and experiment with things that I'd never dreamed of doing before. Matt Kahn had an uncanny gift of making all of his students work to the maximum of their capacity (and often more), as if his class were the only important thing in the world. We were required to finish 18 projects during a 10-week period, many of which were quite substantial, and to critique each other's work in extended classroom sessions. I found myself devoting five days out of every week to these projects, with just two days left to take care of the other aspects of my life (which at that time included teaching a graduate course on analysis of algorithms, writing a paper on pattern matching, giving an invited talk to the annual AAAS meeting in Boston, taking John and Jenny to see the Harlem Globetrotters, etc., etc.). One side effect, after I saw how much work could be expected from art students, was that I began to drive my own computer science students harder; but that's another story. A second side effect was that I was prepared to work with artists when my research began to embrace typography in 1978.

I'll try to give the flavor of Art 60 by discussing a few of the projects that I pursued. Our first assignment was to train our eyes by sketching "something organic" at larger-than-life size. For this I drew a picture of granola with banana slices, in extreme closeup. Another project related to the Munsell color wheel and the vibrating optical effects that are obtained when colors of equal value and different hue are juxtaposed.

Early on I made an experimental graphic that hung on the wall of my office at Stanford for many years before we moved to another building. I can't locate it now, but I'll try to recreate it here, hoping that my memory isn't too flaky. I took red and blue Magic Markers® and drew an array of red and blue dots, according to a computer-generated pattern obtained by starting with a checkerboard of alternating red and blue, but switching the color with some probability p that depended on the position. Thus the original color was retained when $p = 0$, hence we saw the original checkerboard; the original color was reversed when $p = 1$, yet we still saw a checkerboard; and the final color was totally random in the places where $p = 1/2$. The value of p was designed to vary slowly from place to place, so that any two adjacent positions would tend to have a total of about $p + (1 - p) = 1$ dot of each color, on average. More precisely, for the dot in row i and column j I used the formula

$$p = \min(x, 2 - x), \qquad \text{where } x = \frac{(i + 4j) \bmod 200}{100};$$

regions of constant p would therefore have a slope of 4 to 1. Here's the result (but in shades of gray):

I predicted that, when viewed from afar, my eyes would perceive a checkerboard in the areas where p was near 0 or 1, but that they'd see a purplish blend of red and blue where the color choice was random. But I was 100% wrong! Instead, the checkerboard areas were distinctly purple, even when viewed from only a few inches away; the random areas, by contrast, looked like a bunch of isolated islands of red, in a blue sea. It was very hard to believe that the red dots in the islands were really the same color as the red dots in the purplish strips. Human eyes are evidently wired to see *deviations* from regularity, and to smooth out regularity itself.

Kahn encouraged his class to take risks and to experiment with many different kinds of media. So I tried, for example, to mix oil paints with water, wondering if I might be able to obtain interesting effects that way. (Answer: No.) Then I played with specimens of wet clay, drying them in the sun and hoping to figure out how to encourage beautiful patterns of cracks to appear. (Result: Partial success; but the clay was fragile, and the cracks were difficult to see at a distance.) More traditionally, I used hot wax and two colors of dye to make a four-color batik pattern on cotton muslin. (Result: Success; but the quality was too amateurish to be really satisfying. The pattern I made was based on Penrose tiles, and would have been quite pleasant if my technique had been better. Unfortunately I've lost track of this piece and can't illustrate it here.)

Three of the eighteen projects, among my least successful, were supposed to be related to each other. We were asked to exhibit three different moods — "anger," "ceremony," and "festivity" — by combining a small number of simple elements of our own choice, in three different ways. My solution was to create a triptych: I took some shiny gold curtain rings (about the size of a quarter) and cut them into smaller arcs, then glued them in three different ways onto three longish panels of royal blue velour paper. My idea was that, for example, '⌣' conveys happiness. But alas, it didn't really work. By contrast, Jill's solution to this problem received Kahn's highest praise. She had mounted wooden dowels in various ways onto three square bases, and painted them with three subtly different deep red hues. We still enjoy looking at all three.

For the final project, Kahn gave his students a free rein to do anything that we liked. I decided to design a small Hall of Mirrors to be part of a future amusement park, and I built a small model. The tiny mirrors in my model were movable, hinged together in different ways; some were flat, some were curved. Visitors could be surrounded by mirrors on all sides as they walked through certain corridors. On the floor of a large recreation area or dance floor, I painted the Coca-Cola® logo in an anamorphically disguised form, so that it could be perceived only indirectly by looking in a cylindrical mirror. Result: Lots of fun, but my model wasn't worth keeping. I'm still waiting for somebody to build a real example of what I had in mind.

Matt Kahn taught Art 60 and its successor Art 160, as well as many other courses at Stanford, for more than sixty years until his retirement in 2010. Based on what I saw in 1976, I'm sure he had great fun working with so many generations of talented students.

1976: A Whimsical Die

Five of the projects that I've saved from the Art 60 experience match my notion of "geek art," so I'll describe them next.

Kahn asked each of us to design something that embodied six different textures. Immediately I thought of the six faces of a cube, each of which could be textured differently. Jill told me about the pleasures of working with balsa wood. So I purchased a nice little block and began to learn how to shape it.

I decided to make MAD dice — or, rather, to make a single somewhat crazy die (see Figure 11). I purposely made it oblique and partly curved, not a perfectly rectilinear cube, because there was no question of rolling it to obtain a random value. Each face of my design required different woodworking tools: drills, chisels, files, gouges, countersinks, etc. The hole in side 1 connects to the middle hole in side 3. Side 5 was the smoothest; I finished it with the finest sandpaper and emery cloth.

Balsa wood smells wonderful when you sand it.

FIGURE 11. My favorite paperweight. (approximately 2.5″ × 3″ × 3.5″)

1976: A Furry Torus

We were also asked to make something that was delightful to touch. My solution was to take two hot-water bottles and cover them with fake fur. I also hooked them together into sort of a doughnut shape, making it possible to stick your hands in the middle and get nice and warm (see Figure 12).

FIGURE 12. Emily Aiken with my favorite torus. (approximately $4'' \times 9'' \times 17''$)

To complete this project I needed to learn how to use our Elna® sewing machine. Of course Jill was the perfect tutor, since she is a master of that instrument. The tricky part was to make the final seams, because the fabric had to close on itself and the needle-bobbin mechanism had to get there in somehow. I don't remember how I did it; something about turning the torus inside out. (Alas, I never was very good at topology.)

To fill this comfy hand-and-bed-warmer, which by the way I still use when I'm cold, you put hot water in each end — being careful to close the lid on one side before working on the other side. To empty it, you try to keep the water out of the fur.

1976: A Bicentennial Banner

Everybody in the USA focused on history during 1976, which was the 200th anniversary of our country's existence. Therefore one of my major projects for Matt Kahn was oriented toward this year-long celebration. I designed an "Escheresque" tiling pattern that combined Liberty Bells and Shields with American Eagles, and sewed it together by using red-white-and-blue felt to match the colors of our flag (see Figs. 13 and 14).

At the base of one of the eagles you will see that I gave a nod to the Great Seal of the United States by embroidering an olive branch in one of the talons, thirteen arrows in the other. (Compare Figure 14 with the image of this Great Seal on a dollar bill.) Furthermore, if you look very closely at the middle of the top row in Figure 13, you'll see that I also embroidered a symbolic crack in the Liberty Bell. And at the upper left I spangled this banner with a few stars and bars.

1976: A Bicentennial Shirt

The same design, with small alterations, also fit the specifications of another required Art 60 project. I don't recall exactly what those spec-

FIGURE 13. My favorite patriotic banner. (approximately $31'' \times 42''$)

FIGURE 14.
A detail from
Figure 13.

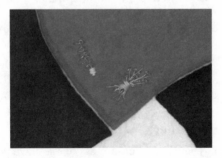

ifications were, but I do know that I was able to kill two birds with one liberty bell, so to speak: With my marginal sewing skills at their all-time peak, I created a red-white-and-blue shirt using the eagles-and-bell motif that I'd developed for the banner (see Figure 15).

FIGURE 15. Tim Aiken wearing my favorite Fourth-of-July shirt.
The design on the back measures approximately $6.5'' \times 14''$.

In both the banner and the shirt, I was especially careful to choose
fabrics that had exactly the right shades of red and blue. Notice also the
buttons, which were gold and deep blue; I show one here at true size:

Professor Kahn insisted that his artists be detail-oriented.

1976: Hommage à Bach

During all this time I should, of course, have been working on Volume 4
of *The Art of Computer Programming*. I didn't have to feel too guilty,
however, because one of the major projects that Kahn had assigned was
in fact compatible with one of the requirements for that book. Namely,
that book needed a frontispiece, to continue a tradition that had already
been established in Volumes 1, 2, and 3.

To tell the story properly I had better begin by backtracking three years. Once again the story is best told in Jill's words, quoting from one of her weekly letters from Norway:

> Addison–Wesley, Don's publisher, is working on the second edition of Volume 1. There was a blank page at the beginning and Don wanted me to draw a picture for it, something that would reflect the topics in the book and look "handdrawn" and organic. We discussed a lot of ideas and finally ended up with a "tree." Certain kinds of operations in computing are called "trees" because they branch. After a lot of trial and error we finally evolved a drawing of a stylized tree. The number of branches corresponds to a certain mathematical pattern and the "leaves" have veins and spots that represent a binary numbering system. I made the trunk and branches on rice paper in a slightly Japanese style. The leaves will be gray. It's something of an accomplishment to come up with something that pleases us both.

Indeed, her final phrase may perhaps serve as the *real* definition of the term "geek art"! Certainly her illustration (Figure 16) is one of the earliest and finest examples of geek art that I own. (Her letter, incidentally, was written on 24 January 1973, less than two weeks after I had completed the first draft of *Surreal Numbers*.)

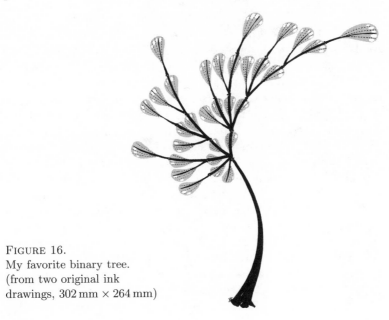

FIGURE 16.
My favorite binary tree.
(from two original ink
drawings, 302 mm × 264 mm)

I commissioned my six- and seven-year-old children to draw a frontispiece of fanciful numbers for the second edition of Volume 2; and I'd already decided to use a computer-generated pattern related to hashing, the golden ratio, and phyllotaxis as the frontispiece for the *first* edition of Volume 3, which came out in January of 1973.

As I looked forward to Volume 4, which was planned to be about combinatorial algorithms, I thought about musical composers like J. S. Bach and P. I. Tchaikovsky, who had included so many beautiful combinatorial patterns in their works. An idea for its frontispiece began to jell when a pipe organ was being installed in my home during 1975. At

that time I purchased a little statue of Bach (about $16'' \times 10'' \times 6''$, pictured here without its base) and set it inside the organ chambers, so that the world's all-time greatest organist could listen to the music that was being played, at least symbolically.

One day it occurred to me that the features of Bach's face could be conveyed visually by means of contour lines; I'd often seen such lines in the grids that numerical analysts use when they study airplane wings, etc. Furthermore, I realized that music notation largely consists of grid lines. Aha! Could I perhaps represent Bach's image via his music?

Art 60 gave me a perfect opportunity to explore that question — except for one thing: The state of computer graphics in January 1976 was extremely primitive. My computer terminal was essentially just a simple teletype, unable to display complex images. All I could see, as I used the machine, was a rectangular array containing about 25×80 characters of text. No color, no shades of gray: The characters on-screen were white on black, or white on green. Researchers at Xerox PARC had begun to develop newfangled "window-oriented" systems with a "desktop metaphor" on a "bitmapped display," but I knew nothing of such work. Moreover, I had only one way to obtain high-quality graphic images as the output of a computer program: I could produce a sequence of instructions that controlled a Calcomp® plotter. The instructions understood by the plotter were (a) raise the pen; (b) lower the pen; (c) pause; or (d) move the pen one tiny step up or down, and/or left or right. Small images, of lower quality, could also be output via the Xerox Graphics Printer (XGP), which produced bitmaps with a resolution of about 180 dots per inch at the sides of a page and about 210 dots per inch in the middle.

Still, I was undaunted; I wanted to make a Bach-inspired grid image, from which I could draw the music in by hand. I'd already used a plotter to draw such things as the dragon curves in Chapter 44.

The main problem facing me was input, not output. How was I to get the shape data from the statue into the computer? Stanford's Artificial Intelligence Lab had a TV camera hooked up to their machine; but that camera was unusable for my purposes, because it severely distorted the images, and I didn't have time to write image-processing and calibration software. (In fact, I didn't encounter a working 3D scanner until much later, in the 1990s.) The only somewhat reasonable input device that I could find at the time was a curious contraption called a "profile gauge," which Jill and I found at a hardware store. It had a row of 181 tightly packed steel needles, about 30 to the inch, capable of recording a shape when pressed against an object:

I used the profile gauge to plot cross-sections of Bach's head manually on graph paper, at 26 different levels. Here, for example, were levels 10–13:

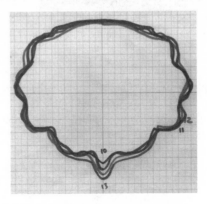

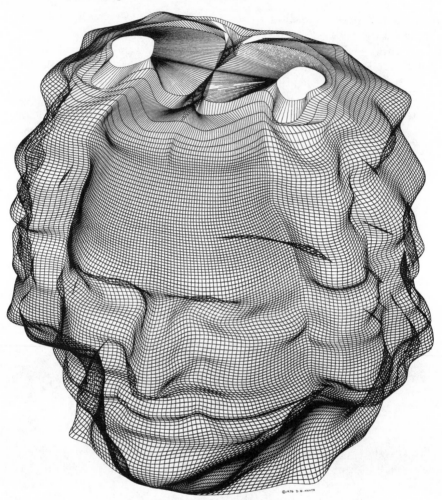

FIGURE 17. My favorite grid. (approximately $21'' \times 15''$)

The 26 levels weren't equally spaced. By eyeballing these plots, I typed key coordinates into a file (about 15 to 30 points per level), and wrote a program to interpolate from that data in all three dimensions, thus obtaining thousands of approximate points on the surface of the statue.*

---

*Little did I know that my experience writing this program, which was my first encounter with splines, would prove to be crucial two years later when I decided to write programs for font design.

I still couldn't visualize the results, but my program allowed me to rotate and tilt the statue virtually; thus it was possible to choose a favorable viewing angle after using the XGP to quickly produce a few dozen crude approximations to the final output. The Calcomp® then drew Figure 17.

What are the glitches in the hair and forehead of Figure 17, and at the lower left? Answer: I didn't do any hidden line elimination when deciding what rectangular patches should be plotted. I simply computed the perpendicular to the surface of each patch, and plotted the patch if and only if that direction pointed towards me more than it pointed away. The extra lines therefore come from the back side of the image; for example, Bach's hair was somewhat curly in back.

The remainder of the story is told in my diary entries from 1976:

02 Mar more on mirrors; forgot about the faculty meeting I had called
03 Mar still 'crashing' away to finish art projects
04 Mar finished the mirror hall; went up to A.I. Lab to try Bach routines
05 Mar stayed up till 8 a.m. working on Bach drawing at A.I. Lab
06 Mar arose Saturday 5 p.m., to bed Sunday at 6 p.m. after getting
07 Mar the plotter drawing of Bach; also prepared final exam for CS255
08 Mar at midnight, finished putting music on Bach drawing

Voilà, I had the desired frontispiece:

FIGURE 18.
My favorite
two-part invention.

Hommage à Bach.

I had photostats made of both Figures 17 and 18, and I showed them to the other members of Art 60 at our final class meeting on 11 March. To my surprise, Professor Kahn praised Figure 17, warts and all; he thought that the glitches added pizzazz, and shouldn't be removed. Figure 18 was OK, but it didn't blow him away as I had hoped it would. No doubt he was right. Indeed I learned later, when working on fonts, that accidental mistakes in computer graphics are often much more interesting than preplanned ideas. However, I am enormously happy today to have Figure 18 as the frontispiece to Volume 4, after having taken more than 30 years to finish the first 800 pages of the accompanying text.

By the way, I encourage anyone who likes or doesn't like Figure 18 to take a look at the frontispiece of Peter Schickele's *Definitive Biography of P. D. Q. Bach* (New York: Random House, 1976).

The experiences that Jill and I had while taking Art 60 were summarized in the annual newsletter that we sent to friends at the end of 1976. Jill wrote, "I find that I'm most satisfied when I can use both my mind and my hands to solve a problem."

1983: Vive la Programmation Littéraire

Figure 19 shows a cherished work of art that was a gift from my mother-in-law; it hangs prominently next to the chair where I work at home. I'm not sure of the exact date, but I'm guessing 1983, because that is when I sent her a copy of *The WEB System of Structured Documentation*, Stanford Technical Report STAN-CS-83-980 (1983). Page 2 of that report says "The name WEB itself was chosen in honor of my wife's mother, Wilda Ernestine Bates." She loved needlework and lived 1912–2001.

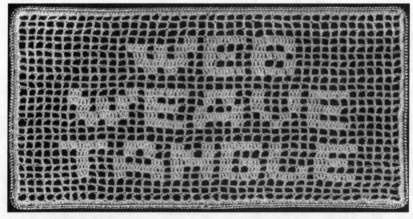

FIGURE 19. My favorite filet crochet. (approximately $5\frac{1}{8}'' \times 10\frac{1}{4}''$)

1993: Pentomino Cubes

Besides the whimsical cube in Figure 11, I now also have some real cubes, thanks to gifts from Jill in 1993. Figure 20 shows two views of a large cube that has been wrapped with the twelve pentominoes. And Figure 21 shows one view of a pair of smaller cubes that have each been wrapped with six different pentominoes, again representing all twelve.

FIGURE 20. Front and back views of my favorite cube. (approximately $9.1'' \times 9.1'' \times 9.1''$; each pentomino is composed of five $2\frac{7}{8}'' \times 2\frac{7}{8}''$ squares)

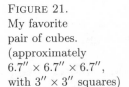

FIGURE 21.
My favorite
pair of cubes.
(approximately
$6.7'' \times 6.7'' \times 6.7''$,
with $3'' \times 3''$ squares)

Please take time to look online at the full-color versions of these illustrations, if you can, because twelve different vividly colored fabrics have been used to make a stunning display. The six colors on the right side of Fig. 21 are "warm," and the six on the left are "cool," and in general the whole set is way cool.

How could it be possible to arrange the pentominoes in such a way? If we make twelve pentominoes from 1×1 squares, we need 60 squares; so each face of the cube must contain 10 squares. Oh, okay, we'll make the cube $\sqrt{10} \times \sqrt{10} \times \sqrt{10}$, by slanting everything in the ratio 1 : 3 and using Pythagoras's theorem to get a hypotenuse whose length is the square root of $1^2 + 3^2$. Similarly, a pair of cubes can be wrapped with 60 square units of fabric if we make each cube $\sqrt{5} \times \sqrt{5} \times \sqrt{5}$, this time slanting with the ratio 1 : 2. In fact, these two ways to decompose the faces are related to each other in an interesting way:

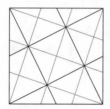

("To double the number of cells, first multiply by 4, then divide by 2.")

The idea of covering two $\sqrt{5} \times \sqrt{5} \times \sqrt{5}$ cubes with the pentominoes was discovered first: F. Hansson published it as problem 7124 in *Fairy Chess Review* **6**, number 10 and 11 (February and April 1947), 71, 81. A year later, H. D. Benjamin discovered that a single $\sqrt{10} \times \sqrt{10} \times \sqrt{10}$ cube would also suffice [Problem 7591, *Fairy Chess Review* **6**, number 16 and 17 (February and April 1948), 122, 131]. Another solution to Benjamin's one-cube problem was published subsequently by W. Stead, in the survey article cited above, and popularized by Martin Gardner and Solomon W. Golomb in the 1960s.

I took a closer look at pentomino wrapping in December 1973, with the hope of actually making such cubes, and immediately realized that the previous authors hadn't really given much thought to the appearance of the final pattern. Strange things happen at the corners of the cube, because only three of the individual square cells meet at such points — not the usual four. For example, the 2×2 portion of the P pentomino can't go on top of a corner point; it would have to overlap itself, as in Fig. 22(a). And if we move the P one step away as in Fig. 22(b), so that only three of its cells surround the corner, we still can't see the P shape.

I called placements like Fig. 22(a) "bad"; they arise only with the P. And I called placements like Fig. 22(b) "improper"; in such cases two parts of the pentomino boundary join together, thereby making a notch disappear. Improper placements can arise with any of the pentominoes except the I, and they spoil the effect. Hansson himself wasn't bothered by this joining of seams when he first proposed the two-cube problem in 1947 — his original solution was improper. But I wanted to see a solution in which each pentomino shape was clearly recognizable. Therefore, in

(a)   (b)   (c)   (d)

FIGURE 22. Bad, improper, and poor placements of pentominoes.

the spring of 1974, I proposed and supervised a term project by Stanford student Robert Filman, who used a computer to find several proper solutions to the two-cube problem.

Right after coming home from the first Gathering for Gardner, in January 1993, I decided to look at this problem again; in fact, it was my second test case for what eventually became known as the dancing links algorithm. Unknown to me, C. J. Bouwkamp was also destined to become interested in the same problem at about the same time; and he too would independently realize the importance of proper solutions. [See *Simplex Sigillum Veri*, edited by E. H. L. Aarts et al. (Eindhoven, Netherlands: Technische Universiteit Eindhoven, 1995), 87–96.] But my approach was somewhat different, because I realized that proper solutions weren't necessarily nice enough to satisfy my own implicit criterion: I wanted each of the pentomino shapes to be *readily identifiable* after having been wrapped around the cube's surface. For example, I didn't like the L in Fig. 22(c), which looks more like a C or a U, even though it has been placed properly. Similarly, I rejected the T in Fig. 22(d), as insufficiently T-like. After experimenting with paper cutouts, I decided to restrict all placements so that the cube corners would never coincide with any of the places marked × in the following diagram:

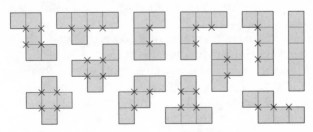

Let's say that a pentomino wrapping is "fussy" if it obeys this strong condition. It turns out that there are exactly 3090 proper ways to wrap a $\sqrt{5} \times \sqrt{5} \times \sqrt{5}$ cube with six different pentominoes, but only 201 of them are fussy. (The dancing links algorithm establishes these facts in the blink of an eye, needing only about 200 and 23 mega-updates, respectively.) By choosing two of these wrappings, and insisting that they use no pentominoes in common, we get a solution to Hansson's problem.

And here's the punch line: Hansson's problem has 687 proper solutions, but *only one* fussy solution! Thus, the pattern that Jill immortalized for me in Figure 21 not only solves the problem, it is the uniquely best solution. No wonder it's my favorite.

Benjamin's one-cube problem, on the other hand, has many more solutions. There are 284,402 proper ways to wrap a $\sqrt{10} \times \sqrt{10} \times \sqrt{10}$ cube with the twelve pentominoes; and 53,171 of them are also fussy. How was I to decide which of the fussy solutions should appear in the larger cube that Jill had agreed to make for me? My first thought was to restrict the solutions so that no pentomino is "folded" or bent more than once; in other words, each pentomino should appear on exactly two faces of the cube. (There's no way to fit any of the pentominoes into a single face, because each face has only four full-size squares.) But that condition turned out to be asking too much. I backed off slightly, and decided instead to require that no pentomino appear on more than two faces of the cube except perhaps in tiny regions whose area is only 1/6 of a full square. Thus at least 93% of each pentomino's total area had to be confined to at most two of the faces. This condition also implies that every pentomino must occupy exactly one of the twelve mid-edge squares that are bisected by the edges of the cube.

Aha! There are only six solutions to Benjamin's problem that satisfy this "extremely fussy" restriction; and just one of them contains only 20 total folds. Thus again there's a uniquely best way to do the wrapping, and again I have a good reason for saying that Figure 20 is my favorite.

The way Jill made the cubes in Figs. 20 and 21 also turned out to be interesting. We had thought first of pillows stuffed with foam, but foam didn't give the right-angled edges we were hoping for. So we embedded stiff-but-flexible pieces of cardboard in order to define the underlying cube shape. The 60 individual squares of the twelve pentominoes could be pieced together on a sewing machine, using essentially the same technique that is used for piecework quilts — except for the endgame: Just as in the case of my hot-water bottle (Figure 12), there was no way to make the final stitches without interfering with the machine's mechanism. Jill did, however, devise a nice way to do almost everything by machine, with the exception of a small seam (less than half the circumference of the cube) that needed to be done by hand in order to close everything up.

Before making the three full-size cubes, she decided to experiment first at 1/4 the scale, using fabric in six shades of red and pink, so that on 14 February 1993 she could surprise me with a delightful valentine:

1994: Golden Triangles

I met Japan's great puzzlist Nob Yoshigahara at the Gathering for Gardner in 1993, and we began a frantic correspondence during the summer of 1994. Here's a problem that I sent to him and a few other friends in September of that year, inspired by a decagon puzzle that he'd sent me:

Rearrange the triangles of the four pentagons

to make a single pentagon.

It's easy to do this in such a way that no triangles of the same color touch at any edge:

But your task is to do it so that no triangles of the same color touch at any point whatsoever.

Extra challenge: Also keep the four triangles   from touching each other.

If you've read Chapter 46, you'll know that Jill and I sent out a Christmas card in 1994 that was based on the same sixteen pieces, but with the object of making a five-pointed star. The pentagon puzzle that I sent to Nob in September was tougher. But he wrote me proudly on 4 October: "I solved your extremely difficult problem #2 in only 20 minutes, but some mania puzzler consumed 10 days in vain!"

And then, a few days later, my mailbox contained an almost unbelievable surprise. There was my puzzle, not only solved but gorgeously rendered in five colors of Japanese hardwood — and autographed to boot! This treasure is now the most prized item in my puzzle collection.

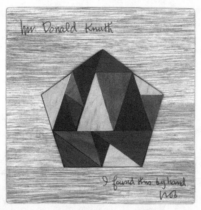

FIGURE 23. My favorite puzzle. (15 cm × 15 cm)

Stan Isaacs distributed copies of my pentagon and star puzzles (executed in yellow, blue, red, and green plastic) at the 15th International Puzzle Party, which was organized by Nob in May 1995; Stan called it the Puzzling Pentagon. Nob also mentioned it in *Quark Visual Science Magazine*, number 156 (Tokyo: Kodansha, June 1995), 127. Ever since 1994 I've been pleased to note that 'don' is a reflection of 'nob'.

1996: A Puzzle Box

Most of the finest "geek art" that exists in the world today has, in fact, been created in the context of puzzles, and a tradition of meticulously crafted mechanical puzzles made with the finest materials has been growing rapidly in recent years. The Spanish sculptor Miguel Berrocal began about 1960 to form gold, silver, and other precious metals into interlocking works that can be ingeniously taken apart and put back together, combining what Martin Gardner has called "visual beauty, tactile pleasure, humor, and the intellectual stimulation of a three-dimensional combinatorial puzzle." [See his book *Penrose Tiles to Trapdoor Ciphers* (New York: W. H. Freeman, 1989), Chapter 18.] In America, Stewart Coffin began about the same time to create what he called "Ap-Art" — puzzles that can be taken *apart*, usually made from the finest imported hardwoods.

The tradition of fine wooden puzzles actually goes back to the early 19th century in Japan, where craftsmen centered in the village of Yumoto in the Hakone region began to make puzzle boxes called *himitsu bako*, "personal secret boxes." During November 1996, Nob and his wife invited Jill and me to spend an unforgettable night with them at a spa in Yumoto. There we visited Yoshiyuki Ninomiya, the greatest living puzzle-box maker, and saw him at work in his amazingly small studio.

Artworks by world-class professionals are definitely out of my league, price-wise, but Nob insisted on presenting me with one of Ninomiya's newest creations (Figure 24). A loose object is clearly inside this box, because you can hear it when you wiggle it. But many steps are needed to open the box and release the hidden charm; and the pieces of wood fit so snugly that they appear to be inseparable.

Figure 24.
My favorite box.
(6 cm × 10 cm × 15 cm)

2002: My Big Bang

Our story now continues into the 21st century, and into a brand new era for me personally. One of the chief milestones in a computer scientist's life is the occasion of their "millionth birthday," when reckoned in the binary system. (Ordinary people, and the Beatles, call it the 64th birthday.) That day, for me, was 10 January 2002 — at which time Jill worked together with my former students Bob Sedgewick, Leo Guibas, and Jeff Vitter to organize a big surprise party. An astonishing number of people, associated with all aspects of my life, came to Stanford at this time to celebrate the occasion and join the fun.

FIGURE 25. My favorite blast. $(7'' \times 10\frac{1}{4}''$ and $7\frac{3}{4}'' \times 10\frac{1}{4}'')$

Figure 25 depicts one of my main souvenirs from that glorious event, a pair of pictures that Bob, Leo, and Jeff had commissioned Duane Bibby to create for the party invitations and the T-shirts. Readers of *The TEXbook* and *The METAFONTbook* all know Duane as the person who created the delightful lion mascots who embody the spirit of TEX and METAFONT. The popularity of Duane's illustrations among TEXies surely qualifies him as an outstanding geek artist ... although I imagine he would prefer a more traditional appellation. Anyway he's great, regardless of what buzzwords we might use to characterize his work.

2002: Venn–Grünbaum Rings

Another souvenir of my millionth birthday was a gift from Frank Ruskey, who fabricated a fascinating "Venn diagram" from five intricately linked rings of colored cords (Figure 26). Students of elementary mathematics are often introduced to simple cases of the diagrams that John Venn popularized long ago as an aid to understanding the relations between different sets ["On the diagrammatic and mechanical representation of propositions and reasonings," *The London, Edinburgh and Dublin Philosophical Magazine and Journal of Science*, series 5, **10** (1880), 1–18].

Namely, the diagram

makes it easy to see the points that lie inside both rings or in only one ring or in neither; and the "Borromean rings" diagram

exhibits all 8 possibilities for points inside-or-not of three different rings. Ruskey based his design on a beautiful configuration that Branko Grünbaum had discovered for *five* different rings ["Venn diagrams and independent families of sets," *Mathematics Magazine* **48** (1975), 12–23, Figure 1(e)].

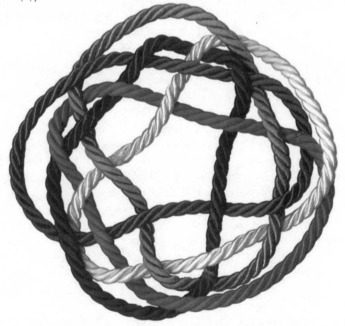

FIGURE 26. My favorite linked rings. (approximately $7'' \times 7''$)

Grünbaum presented his deceptively simple pattern as a superimposition of five ellipses — something that Venn had stated was impossible! Moreover, Grünbaum's five ellipses were identical and arranged symmetrically; I show them here using the "eofill" convention of Chapter 43. Each ellipse intersects its two nearest neighbors four times; it intersects the other two ellipses only twice each.

Notice that the rings in Figure 26 are interlaced, going alternately over and under each other as in a Celtic knot (see Chapter 41). In fact, they have the so-called "Brunnian" property: Break any one link and they all come apart. [See Hermann Brunn, "Ueber Verkettung," *Sitzungsberichte der mathematisch-physikalischen Classe der königlich bayerischen Akademie der Wissenschaften zu München* **22** (1892), 77–99 and Tafel II–IV.] The three Borromean rings are easily seen to be Brunnian; but the "five golden rings" in Figure 8 of Chapter 46 are not.

A very comprehensive discussion of the whole subject has been prepared by Frank Ruskey and Mark Weston, "A survey of Venn diagrams," *Electronic Journal of Combinatorics* DS#5; it's a profusely illustrated "dynamic survey" whose webpages are periodically updated. They credit Rick Mabry and C. van de Walle for independently discovering the Brunnian property of Grünbaum's pattern.

Incidentally, I once held a surprise party for Gene Golub, to celebrate the fact that he had just become exactly 2^{14} days old. Gene was born on 29 February 1932, so he had only one fourth as many birthdays as most people do; therefore his friends kept looking for other reasons to celebrate. He came to my house on Friday evening, 7 January 1977, suspecting nothing; we all yelled "Surprise" and began to shake his hand, while he was completely clueless about why we were congratulating him. I gave him a puzzle, made of felt, that was equivalent to a Tower of Hanoi with 14 pegs; the idea was that, if he had received the puzzle at birth and made one step towards its solution every day, he would just recently have finished it, because $2^{14} - 1$ steps are necessary.

Like the Tower of Hanoi, Frank Ruskey's gift also has a nice connection with powers of 2, because there are just 2^n combinations of n sets. But I didn't have the heart to tell him that a set of five Venn rings would have been more appropriate for my 32nd birthday than for my 64th.

2005: Sierpiński's Egg

We've seen that geek art can take many different forms. Figure 27 shows yet another beautiful variation, which was a gift from my friend Jennifer

Laaser. She adapted traditional techniques of Ukrainian egg decoration to display the world's most famous fractal, the "Sierpiński gasket." [W. Sierpinski, "Sur une courbe dont tout point est un point de ramification," *Comptes Rendus hebdomadaires des séances de l'Académie des Sciences* **160** (Paris: 1915), 302–305.] This image arises in many recursive situations; for example, computer scientists know it as the pattern of integers m and n that can be added in the binary system without carries (see exercise 1.2.6–11 in *The Art of Computer Programming*).

FIGURE 27. My favorite egg.
(approximately 60 mm × 43 mm × 43 mm)

2009: An Interlocking Trivet

At the 29th International Puzzle Party Ginda Fisher gave me a beautiful set of eight wooden pieces that fit together at 45° angles in an intriguing way. (See Figure 28.) She calls it the Trickier Trivet, because her earlier six-piece version was the Tricky Trivet. Indeed, the pieces don't come apart or go back together unless you twist and/or jiggle them in a certain way; they don't just slide. Therefore I keep it assembled, and I can easily carry it to the dining table whenever I need a trivet — which I do almost daily. A bowl of hot soup balances perfectly in the middle.

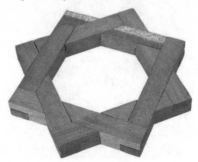

FIGURE 28.
My favorite trivet. (7″ × 7″)

2010: TEX in Stitches

To celebrate the 32nd birthday of TEX (see Chapter 49), I decided to present keepsakes to a dozen or so of the key people who had made extraordinary contributions to my research on digital typography. I had just gained access to a computer-controlled embroidery machine, something that had always fascinated me; so I seized this opportunity to learn how to use it and to create "something different" for the people I wanted to honor.

I started with Duane Bibby's portrait of TEX-on-a-Roman-column, shown here; this image had been used to decorate the ends of chapters in my book *TEX: The Program* [Volume B of *Computers & Typesetting* (Reading, Massachusetts: Addison–Wesley, 1986)]. Jill helped me to simplify the lines and reduce them to the bare essentials, and I figured out a way to trace out the simplified design without needing to cut the threads. We used golden embroidery thread on blue denim fabric. It was fascinating to watch the machine chugging away, magically creating the image stitch-by-stitch — a process that took about five minutes.

FIGURE 29.
My favorite embroidery. $(2\frac{1}{8}'' \times 4'')$

The algorithm by which I reduced the pattern to a "unicursal" route for the sewing machine was interesting and amazingly simple. So I'll present it here, using the conventions of the Stanford GraphBase. [See Donald E. Knuth, *The Stanford GraphBase* (New York: ACM Press, 1994), which is also available from the server `ftp.cs.stanford.edu` via anonymous ftp, in directory `pub/sgb`.] Given an arbitrary connected and undirected graph g, the problem is to output an *Eulerian trail* of g, namely a cycle of oriented edges that traverses each arc exactly once. (An undirected edge between vertices u and v is considered to be two arcs, one from u to v and the other from v to u. Thus, the Eulerian trail will traverse each edge twice, once in each direction. You can see that the sewing machine has done that in Figure 29.)

We begin by defining a recursive subroutine $dfs(u,v)$ ("depth-first search"), which sets $v\text{-}parent = u$ and $v\text{-}nav$ to the arc that follows the arc to u in v's adjacency list. The subroutine also explores all vertices reachable from v that haven't already been seen.

```
#define parent  v.V
#define nav  w.A
void dfs(register Vertex *u, register Vertex *v)
{
    register Vertex *w;
    register Arc *a;

    v⃗parent = u;
    for (a = v⃗arcs;  a;  a = a⃗next) {
        w = a⃗tip;
        if (w ≡ u) v⃗nav = a⃗next;
        else if (w⃗parent ≡ Λ) dfs(v, w);
    }
}
```

The Eulerian trail is now output as follows, using a variable v that points to a **Vertex** and a variable a that points to an **Arc**:

```
dfs(g⃗vertices + g⃗n, g⃗vertices);
for (v = g⃗vertices;  v ≠ g⃗vertices + g⃗n;  ) {
    printf("␣%s", v⃗name);
    a = v⃗nav;
    if (¬a) a = v⃗arcs;
    v⃗nav = a⃗next;
    v = a⃗tip;
}
```

By the way, my first test case as I was learning how to use the embroidery machine was to stitch the dragon curve of Chapters 44 and 45. This curve is already unicursal, so it needed no special algorithm to turn it into running stitches. The result, using white thread on brown felt, was quite pleasant (shown here at true size):

2010: Fun with a Lasercutter

At about the same time, I began also to use a more dangerous computer-controlled device, a machine that focuses a powerful laser beam — powerful enough to cut through wood and other materials. I call it dangerous not because it demands careful attention, which it does, but because it's dangerously addictive. So far I've used it mostly for etching, not cutting, although Jill has been exploiting its ability to cut useful and interesting shapes. (We'll be making lasercut Christmas cards this year.)

One of my first experiments was to etch the "dragon labyrinth" of Chapter 45 onto a small glass plate. Curiously, the glass now seems to radiate light when you place it on a dark surface. (See Figure 30.)

In another early trial, I took one of the key illustrations that I've been using recently as I write *The Art of Computer Programming*, a

FIGURE 30. A dragon that glows. $(4'' \times 6'')$

stylized map of the continental USA that shows which states have common boundaries, and etched it onto a nice little piece of teak wood.

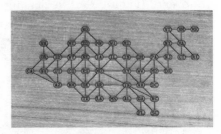

FIGURE 31. My favorite planar graph. (approximately $2.5'' \times 5''$)

I've also been having some success with reproductions of other favorite illustrations, etching them onto walnut and formica as well as onto glass and teak. In particular, the pentagrid, which is discussed in Chapter 46, makes a marvelous plate:

FIGURE 32. A potpourri of laser engravings. (plate has $9''$ diameter)

We like to use the plate. I'm not sure what I'll do with the other knick-knacks, but still I'm kind of glad to have them.

2010: Celtic Knight's Tours

As I wrote Chapter 41 of the present book I began to hanker for a real-life embodiment of the knight's tours discussed there, presented as true Celtic knots that have been interlaced in the proper way. Coincidentally, Jill and I had just seen an exhibit of "thread art" at a San José gallery. So I went back to working with my hands and with brightly colored threads, as I had done long ago when making the rya in 1973; in fact, for this new project I used the very same needle that I had used 'way back then. Figure 33 shows my first creation of geek-and-thread art: It's the "most Celtic" knight's tour that is possible on the standard 8 × 8 chessboard (Figure 19(a) in Chapter 41).

FIGURE 33.
My favorite
8×8 knight's tour,
viewed at a slight
angle. (each square
of the board is ap-
proximately $\frac{1}{2}'' \times \frac{1}{2}''$)

I started by laser-etching the pattern onto a $6\frac{1}{8}'' \times 6\frac{1}{8}'' \times \frac{3}{4}''$ block of solid oak. Then I inserted 62 copper-clad weatherstripping nails, and wound the knight's tour around them with green and gold nylon twine. Half of the tour is green, the other half is gold, in order to demonstrate the symmetry of this tour. Between halves the twine disappears down two holes that extend all the way through to the other side of the board; the green and gold ends are tied together down there, in order to hold everything in place. That's why there are 62 nails, not 64.

Then I was psyched to do a similar thing for the three 10 × 5 tours that illustrate the different kinds of symmetry that are possible (Figure 20 in Chapter 41). Again I used two colors of twine for each tour: orange with yellow, pink with gold, orange with green. In this piece I decided to use brass "escutcheon pins" instead of copper nails. If you study Figure 34 carefully you'll notice that, in the middle tour (the case of Bergholtian symmetry), I could not put the transition holes in the center of the board; it was another case where the demands of art were given a boost with the help of mathematics.

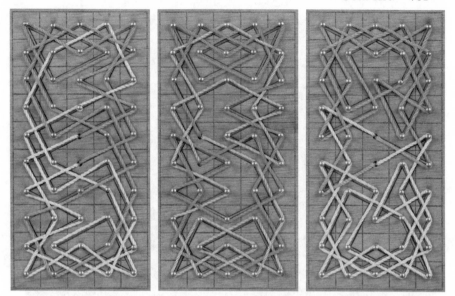

FIGURE 34. My three favorite 10×5 knight's tours.
(these details were superimposed on a single block of size $6\frac{1}{4}'' \times 14\frac{1}{4}'' \times \frac{3}{4}''$)

2005: The Climax

And now I step backward a bit in time, in order to present the greatest
pride and joy of my entire collection. I didn't mention it earlier because
I wanted to save the best for last.

During a visit to Antwerp in 2003 I was entranced by a beautiful
three-dimensional work of art called "Bibliotheek," hanging at Elzenveld
where I was staying. I kept coming back to look at it, and bringing
friends with me to admire it.

Unfortunately I couldn't read the signature of the artist, although
I had pretty good guesses for most of the letters. After a year of detective
work, with the help of Google and my friend Brigitte Verdonk of the
University of Antwerp, I was finally able to learn the artist's name:
Roger Van Akelijen. It turned out that he was also associated with
the Plantin-Moretus museum, one of Antwerp's greatest treasures and
a "must-see" for all typophiles like myself.

In August of 2004 I commissioned him to do a three-dimensional
piece for my office at home, outlining my general feelings as follows:

> I don't intend to dictate in any way the content of the work, ex-
> cept that I do hope it will remind me of a romantic library filled
> with beloved books that would have made Christoph Plantin

FIGURE 35. My ideal workplace, a three-dimensional work by
Roger Van Akelijen in 2005. (approximately 40 cm × 56 cm × 14 cm)

proud! If you include the figure of a scholar and/or a desk within
the image, you might think about including also a modern computer terminal, as a counterpoint to the antique books in the
library itself. I mention this not to force your hand, but only
because I know that you are intrigued by paradoxical juxtapo-
sitions. I definitely don't want a thoroughly modern, electronic
library to be depicted, however! It's true that I myself write
up-to-date books about computer science; but my books tend
to emphasize the rich history of the subject. Part of my research
has in fact been to create software tools with which people are
able to create attractive new books themselves by taking proper
account of centuries-old traditions.

Since March of 2005 was the 16th anniversary of TEX User Groups in
Europe, I attended EuroTEX 2005 in France and renewed acquaintances
with Hermann Zapf and many other friends from my typographic past.
Immediately afterwards I could go to Antwerp to meet Van Akelijen,
see his studio, celebrate with him and his wife at a pub, and receive
my glorious new mini-library. I had better not dwell on my subsequent

adventures, as I carried it with me via Eurostar and the London Underground and various buses and planes until returning home a week later; suffice it to say that we all arrived safely. This creation fits my office perfectly, and it inspires me daily as I gaze at it — right next to where I do most of my writing. [An excellent photo by Timothy Archibald, showing this work of art where it now rests permanently in my office, appears in Kara Platoni's article "Love at first byte," *Stanford Magazine* **35**, 3 (May–June 2006), 64–69, available online.]

Acknowledgments

I'm extremely grateful to my colleague Héctor García-Molina, who took the wonderful photographs that have served as the basis for most of the illustrations in this chapter. He has put the full-color images into an online album that I think everyone will enjoy. See

> `http://infolab.stanford.edu/~hector/`
>
> `photos/2010/GeekArtV2/album.htm`

for the real truth behind Figures 1, 4, 5, 6, 7, 8, 9, 10, 12, 13, 14, 15, 20, 21, 30, 31, 33, and 34. Thanks also to colleagues Alex Aiken and Jennifer Widom for allowing Héctor and me to geekify their children as part of this project.

Addendum

I forgot to mention that Edmé Simonot had already implemented Vandermonde's idea of knotted-string knight's tours in his *Polygraphile* of 1872. In fact I encountered two examples of that remarkable puzzle during a visit to the Cleveland Public Library in May 2010, shortly after having designed Figures 33 and 34.

Chapter 48

Memories of Martin Gardner

*[One of several tributes published in Notices of the American Mathematical Society **58**, 3 (March 2011), 418–422.]*

Most Americans over 60 remember the moment that they first learned that President Kennedy had been shot. I shall always remember the moment that I first learned of Martin Gardner's death.

I was staying for two weeks with one of my cousins in Ohio, using spare time to put the finishing touches on parts of a book that I was dedicating to Martin. At dinner one night I had explained to my hosts how I was preparing a special part of the preface in his honor, and why I was thankful for his ongoing inspiration. Then, at dinner two nights later, my cousin said that she'd just heard an obituary notice for him, while listening to NPR on her way home. Alas! Martin had told me how much he was looking forward to seeing this book, and I had been writing much of it especially for his personal pleasure.

But I believe in celebrating the joyous experiences of life, rather than mourning what might have been. Martin brought me and countless others a steady stream of intellectual stimulation and delight, over a period of many decades. A piece of writing from him often caused me to drop everything else for several days so that I could work on a fascinating puzzle. His fifteen precious volumes, in which 25 years' worth of monthly columns for *Scientific American* have been collected and amplified, sit prominently on a shelf next to the chair in which I read and write every day. For me, those volumes are the Canon.

Indeed, more people have probably learned more good mathematical ideas from Martin Gardner than from any other person in the history of the world, in spite of (or perhaps because of) the fact that he claimed not to be a mathematician himself. He was the consummate master of the art of teaching by storytelling. Yet he didn't stick to the easy aspects of the subjects that he treated; he dug deeply into the origins of every idea that he was explaining, with superb scholarship. (On dozens of occasions when it turned out that he and I had independently researched the history of some topic, he had invariably located some aspects of the story that had escaped my notice.) Most amazingly, he did all this while faced with relentless monthly deadlines — spending two weeks per month on *Scientific American* while devoting the remaining two weeks to a wide variety of other pursuits.

I first had the opportunity to meet him in person at his home on Euclid Avenue, Hastings-on-Hudson, in December 1968. I was especially impressed by his efficient filing system using tiny cards, and by the fact that he did all of his writing while *standing up*, at a typewriter on a raised pedestal. I eventually followed his lead by getting my own stand-up computer desk.

In 1994, after many years of continued friendship, he invited me to spend two unforgettable weeks at the condominium in Hendersonville, North Carolina, where all of the notes and correspondence from his days of writing for *Scientific American* were currently stored. I systematically went through about fifty large boxes of material, barely able to sleep at night because of all the exciting things I was finding among those letters. He had carried on incredibly interesting exchanges with hundreds of mathematicians, as well as with artists and polymaths such as Maurits Escher and Piet Hein, all recorded in these files, mixed in of course with a fair amount of forgettable trivia. Already when he began his monthly series in 1956 and 1957, he was corresponding with the likes of Claude Shannon, John Nash, John Milnor, and David Gale. Later he would receive mail from budding mathematicians John Conway, Persi Diaconis, Jeffrey Shallit, Ron Rivest, etc., etc. These files of correspondence now have a permanent home at Stanford University Archives, where I continue to consult them frequently.

While writing the present note, I took the opportunity to reread dozens of the letters that Martin had sent to me over the years, most recently a month or so before his death. In one of those letters he remarked that he regularly devoted one full day each week to answering mail. Thus I know that thousands of people like me have been able to benefit in a direct and personal way from his wisdom and generosity, in addition to the millions who have been edified by his publications. Countless more will surely benefit from his classic works, because those beautifully written volumes continue to remain in print and someday they will be online.

Chapter 49

An Earthshaking Announcement

*[A presentation made in San Francisco on 30 June 2010 to commemorate TEX's 32nd birthday, at the 31st Annual Meeting of the TEX Users Group and a reunion of the original project members. Published in TUGboat **31** (2010), 121–124.]*

Ladies and gentlemen, distinguished guests, dear friends: How appropriate it is for us to be meeting here in the city where Steve Jobs has made so many dramatic announcements. Today I have the honor of unveiling for you something that, in Steve's words, is "truly incredible" — a successor to TEX that I've been working on in secret for quite some time.

All of us know that computers and the Internet have been changing the world at a dizzying pace. Consequently few, if any, of the assumptions that I made when I first got TEX to work in 1978 are valid today. Day after day I've been becoming more and more convinced that a totally different approach is now needed. Finally I woke up one morning with the realization that I couldn't be happy unless I came up with a new system that rectifies my former mistakes — a system that leads to real progress.

Thus I've decided to scrap TEX78 and TEX82 and to start over from scratch. Of course the first thing that I wanted to fix was the most egregious design error that I'd made in the early system: The old TEX was internally based on binary arithmetic, although its user interface was entirely decimal! Thus one could write, for example,

```
\ifdim .4pt = .39999pt \message{yes} \fi
```

and get the response 'yes'. Furthermore a construction like

```
\dimen0=.4pt \multiply \dimen0 by 10 \showthe\dimen0
```

would give the answer '3.99994pt'; how ridiculous can you get? Are mathematicians supposed to like this? Are computer scientists supposed to like this? Is anybody supposed to like this?

707

(By the way, I apologize for using handwritten overhead-projector slides in this presentation, instead of making PowerPoint points. Some unexpected problems arose with my computer at home, and I didn't want to risk security leaks by putting any of this material on someone else's machine.)

Returning to my story, many of you may recall that the old TEX represented all dimensions as integer multiples of a so-called "scaled point," defined to be 1/65536th of a printer's point, where a printer's point was defined to be exactly 1/72.27th of an inch. How bizarre and anachronistic! Nobody remembers or cares about the old-fashioned units that printers used in the pre-Internet era. The graphic designers of today all know that there are exactly 72 points to an inch, as specified by Adobe Systems; why should TEX insist on calling that now-universal unit a "big point"? Indeed, what relevance will points of *any* kind be to anybody, ten years from now?

Moreover, TEX never has allowed dimensions to exceed \maxdimen, or 16383.9999847412109375 pt, which is roughly 18.8921175 feet (5.7583 meters). Today's graphic devices make posters and banners much larger than this, so TEX cannot cope.

At the other extreme, advances in nanotechnology mean that TEX's minimum dimension of one scaled point is far too large to accommodate 21st-century applications: A scaled point is huge, more than two farshimmelt potrzebies; it's more than 53 Ångström units, 'way bigger than a hydrogen atom.

Thus I'm pleased to say that my new typesetting system finally gets it right: Dimensions can be arbitrarily large or arbitrarily small multiples of internationally accepted units. They can be expressed as exact rational quantities, like 3/7 of a yard; they can also be expressed in terms of irrational numbers like π and $\sqrt{2}$, so that circles and other objects can at last be rendered with perfect accuracy.

My design from 32 years ago was heavily influenced by what we used to call "efficiency." I didn't understand the implications of Moore's law. I didn't realize that, in a few years, I wouldn't care whether *The Art of Computer Programming* could be typeset in half a second, rather than waiting five seconds.

Examples of my tunnel vision abound, on almost every page of *The TEXbook*. For example, I used backslashes and other strange characters to define what I called "control sequences." Does any other system you know have control sequences? Of course not.

With my old rules people never knew whether or not a blank space really meant a blank space.

Therefore the basic input language for my new system is entirely a subset of XML, a widely accepted standard. However, XML is really only necessary at the lowest level, and most users won't need to be aware of it, because we'll see in a moment that there are many other ways to provide input.

Of course the character set for my new system is Unicode, so that there is 100% support for all of the languages and metalanguages of the world. Automatic spelling and grammar correction are built in for each language, as well as automatic correction to page layout and design. Different languages can freely be intermixed at will, always with appropriate ligatures, kerning, and hyphenation.

The old TEX was limited to left-to-right typesetting; and some of its extensions also now handle the right-to-left conventions of many languages that my original implementation didn't consider. But my new system has been designed from the beginning to produce output in any direction whatsoever, whether horizontally or vertically or diagonally or along any kind of curved lines.

In fact, since 3D printing technology is now widespread, I decided at the outset that there was no reason to limit my new system to only two dimensions. Three dimensions are now standard in the new system; in other words, we deal with voxels instead of mere pixels. I've also provided hooks to allow future extensions to four or more dimensions, in case the string theorists prove to be right.

From a virtual standpoint, the notion of hypertext already gives us the equivalent of unlimited dimensionality, and the production of hyperdocuments and web pages will be one of the chief thrusts of my new system. TEX's old principles of boxes, glue, and penalties turn out to yield fantastic new ways to create multimedia documents, including animated videos and stereophonic sound.

Indeed, the input and output aspects of the new system aren't confined to traditional forms of text. Audio input and camera input are now seamlessly integrated, as well as sensor devices of all sorts. The system uses your GPS coordinates intelligently, if you are a mobile user, and senses your motions and gestures with accelerometers, etc. Complete support of haptics is also fully implemented. Instead of "what you see is what you get," we now also have "what you hear is what you get," and "what you feel is what you get."

There really is little difference between input and output in the new system, because any input can be output; conversely, any output from one hyperdocument can be input to another, or to itself. For example, music can be input from one or more MIDI devices, then either output to a conventional printed score, or to another MIDI device or group of devices—optionally segmented into individual parts, or transposed, or whatever you want. Going the other way, a printed score can be used as the input to a synthesizer, etc. I'll say more about these dynamic aspects later.

Does my new system have macros? No. Macros are *passé*; they're *so* mid-20th-century. Nowadays nobody really needs macros, which we all know can be difficult to write and even dangerous. Everything in the new system is menu-driven, somewhat in the style of "Microsoft Word" but considerably enhanced: Experts have prepared recipes for everything you'll ever want to do, and these features keep growing and getting better and better. The menus needn't appear on your computer screens in traditional pull-down or pop-up form; my system also responds to spoken commands and to gestures. And it quickly learns your preferences, so that it's customized to your own wishes, thereby making document preparation almost instantaneous.

You may have noticed that I've been referring a lot to my new system, but I haven't yet told you its name. I had to explain some of its characteristics before you could fully understand the name. But now I'm ready to reveal it, and more importantly to show you its logo:

How does one properly pronounce this name? Listen carefully: "ĭ-tér" ["ĕe-técks"]. In the first place, you'll notice that it should be said musically, with *tones* as in Mandarin. (The first vowel is spoken with a dipping tone, "ĭ", where the pitch falls and then rises. The second vowel has a strictly rising tone, "é", almost as if you're asking a question.) In the second place, you'll notice that I've also rung a bell when saying the name. The bell is also part of the logo:

It reminds us that ⓘ* is not limited by obsolete conventions, not hampered by the days when documents were only seen but not heard. (However, the bell is optional, and it is omitted in documents that have no audio. Conversely, the logo is actually three-dimensional in a 3D document.) In the third place, did you notice that I said "tecks" instead

---

* [A bell rings at this point.]

of "techhhh"? I've decided to go with the flow, since almost nobody
outside of Greece has ever pronounced 'TEX' with the correct 'X' sound.

Some of you may recall that I wrote the entire program for TEX78
and TEX82 all by myself, and you may be wondering whether I've done
the same for ⓣEX*. Don't worry: This time around I'm having the job
done by people who know what they're doing. After many years I've
finally come to realize that my main strength lies in an ability to delegate
work and to lead large projects, rather than to go it alone. Programming
has never really been my forté — for example, I've had to remove 1289
bugs from TEX, and 571 from METAFONT.

I made a very fortunate discovery during the summer of 2006 when
I visited the Academy of Sciences in Armenia. There I learned that a
huge amount of highly sophisticated but classified defense work had been
done secretly at a large institute in Yerevan during the Soviet era. I met
many of the people who had participated in those activities, and found
that they were extraordinarily good programmers. Moreover, they were
anxious to apply their skills to new domains. So they were a perfect
match for my desire to make ⓣEX* a reality.

I had long envied my colleagues at Stanford who had started up
their own companies and gotten rich. Now it was my turn, and without
much difficulty I formed a clandestine group called *Project Marianne*,
comprising more than 100 of the top programmers in the world.

A few weeks ago some of you apparently discovered our website por-
tal at www.projectmarianne.com. I've also seen blogs that wondered
about the Armenian letter M on that page (Unicode #0544, "Men").
But as far as I know, nobody outside of our group has yet been able to
penetrate the firewall that we built into that site, nor to look at any of
our planning documents or initial demos. Needless to say, I'm pleased at
this success, because the ability to create secure documents is another
feature of ⓣEX*.

Furthermore, I believe that nobody else has realized until now that
'Marianne' is an anagram of 'Armenian'.

After some deliberation, our group decided that all of the code for
ⓣEX* should be written in Scheme. We also decided to guarantee success
by using all of the silver bullets that have been discovered by software
engineers during the past decades: Information Hiding, Agile Software
Development, Extreme Programming, Use Case Modeling, Bebugging,
Look Ahead Design, Waterfall Modeling, Unit Testing, Refactoring,
Rapid Prototyping, the whole shebang. We're going beyond ordinary
Object-Oriented Programming to Aspect-Oriented Programming. But

we're not using any formal methods, because everybody knows that formal methods are strictly academic. And we're abandoning the old notion of "literate programming" that I used when developing TEX82, because documentation has proved to be too much of a pain.

Naturally it's out of the question for a system like ⑩* to be freely available and essentially in the public domain, as the old TEX system was. These talented programmers certainly deserve to be paid handsomely for their hard work. We have therefore devised some innovative pricing strategies, so that I'm sure you will consider ⑩* to be an unbeatable bargain, considering the enormous value of its new features.

Here's the way it will work: Payments will be by monthly subscription, which will entitle you to unlimited use of ⑩* on one or two of your own computers, or up to 40 hours × 16 gigabytes of computing in our cloud of approved service providers. During the first year we're offering a one-month free introductory trial; thereafter your costs will depend on the quality of Internet access that is available in your area. For example, California users will pay \$99 per month, and German users will pay €69; but the monthly fee in Armenia will be only ֏1999.

There are substantial discounts for senior citizens and for children under five years of age, as well as educational discounts for students.

Moreover — and this is the main innovation — you get a 10% discount for every new member that you can convince to join, lasting as long as you and that person are both enrolled in the plan. Thus if you can sign up just ten new subscribers, your access to ⑩* will be free; and if you bring in eleven, you've essentially garnered a lifetime income.

My new enterprise operates by monthly subscription, instead of actually selling copies of the software, in part because the software is proprietary, but mainly because ⑩* will change every day, due to constant improvements and upgrades to the system. Once upon a time I took great care in order to ensure that TEX82 would be truly archival, so that the results obtainable today will produce identical output 50 years from now. But that was manifestly foolish. Let's face it: Who's going to care one whit for what I do today, after even 5 years have elapsed, let alone 50? Life is too short to reread anything anymore; in the Internet Age, nothing over 30 months old is trustworthy or interesting. We're best off just enjoying each moment as it happens.

⑩* will benefit the entire world's economy, because it will lead to tens of thousands of new jobs. For example, independent developers will be able to design and sell plugins that are distributed online and available for only a few pennies per week. Any ⑩* user will be able to sell his or her own documents online, without leaving the TEX* system, because TEX* includes facilities for ordering, billing, manufacturing, and shipping. You can, for instance, write a blog, and others can package as many chapters of that blog as they wish into a customized book that is nicely printed and bound. TEX* will collect the appropriate payments from each customer and divide them fairly between you, the printer, the binder, and the shipper; the finished book will then arrive promptly at the customer's residence. The operation will be something like the old Sears and Roebuck catalog, but now each item will be custom-tailored to an extent never before seen.

More importantly, there will be a large network of certified TEX* consultants, at various graded levels of certification. TEX* has no user manual, in the old sense, because the system changes daily. But it does have three varieties of online help: There's online help for dummies, online help for wizards, and personalized online help — in which you get to chat one-on-one with a certified TEX* helper. (Your membership fee entitles you to an hour's worth of one-on-one help each month.) Such helpers can arrange to work part-time for the TEX* consortium, out of their own homes and with flexible hours, in order to supplement their other income.

Let me conclude by describing a few more of TEX*'s features, so that you can begin to get a glimpse of how truly revolutionary it is. I've already told you that dimensions can be specified as arbitrary multiples of standard units; but that's just a tiny part of the story. TEX* actually is able to do arbitrary symbolic calculations, with polynomials and power series and matrices and partial differential equation solvers and convex optimization, etc., all integrated with graphics for automatic curve plotting and statistical charts, together with maps and satellite photographs of the world. When combined with TEX*'s synthesized voice output, you can do things like find a shortest route and navigate your car, all as part of an TEX* hyperdocument. If you're a professor like me, you can write math texts in which the formulas are changeable by each individual reader, who can evaluate them and plot their graphs interactively. (Incidentally I've changed math mode so that formulas must now be specified unambiguously, in such a way that they can be evaluated as well as printed; think MathML. This makes the formulas longer and more difficult to type, but that's a small price to pay for the added functionality.)

The hyperdocuments of TEX* can have any number of users, who can interact with each other and render images of themselves as avatars. This capability goes beyond the traditional kinds of virtual reality that are offered by systems such as Second Life®, not only because of TEX*'s haptics but also because ⊕* uses hyperbolic geometry — in which exponentially many avatars can be within a bounded distance of each other.

Such interactive documents obviously enable videoconferencing as a simple special case. I mentioned earlier that ⊕* can receive input from all kinds of sources: news feeds, webcams, traffic and weather sensors, heart monitors, seismographs, astronomical observations, you name it. All of these can be captured, mixed, and/or converted to other forms, such as audio or video or both. World-class tools are provided for photo retouching and image processing, computer-aided design, character and face recognition, as well as sophisticated filters for all sorts of data — including, for example, audio tracks and email. Output can be automatically formatted for lasercutters, embroidery machines, 3D printers, milling machines, and other CNC devices ... and shipped directly to consumers, as mentioned earlier.

One of our early plugins will feature an interactive cookbook that interfaces directly to your kitchen stove, oven, pantry, and refrigerator, so that you can prepare meals automatically with the ingredients that you already have on hand, and/or replenish your supplies by online ordering.

⊕* naturally incorporates extensive facilities for social networking. You can easily read the hyperdocuments prepared by others, and it's even easier to send and receive "tweets." (Your tweets needn't be limited to 140 characters of Unicode; the actual limit is a parameter. For example, you can set things up so that you receive only tweets of 50 characters or less.) With ⊕* your entire life can be encapsulated into a dynamic hyperdocument, downloadable by anybody you designate.

I had intended to give you a live demonstration of ⊕* today, instead of merely talking about its features. Indeed, ⊕* was supposed to have provided all of my slides for this lecture, because the illustrations for a technical talk are among the simplest of all documents to create. Unfortunately, however, that has turned out to be impossible, because of hardware glitches and breakdowns in communication that I had no way to anticipate. (You can well imagine how difficult it has been to get all the pieces of ⊕* to work together.)

But my coworkers assure me that the system is almost ready for its first major release, and we plan a worldwide press conference when ⊕* is officially launched — hopefully next month.

Well, I've got to stop now: I can't tell you any more until our patent applications have all been filed. But I'm sure that, once you've tried ⊕*, you'll immediately want to become a charter member of iTÙG*.

Addendum

A video of the original presentation, made by Kaveh Bazargan, can be seen at `http://river-valley.tv/an-earthshaking-announcement`.

Some readers will not be surprised to learn that this talk was composed on the first day of April.

I thank my friends Yoichi Hariguchi and Jinmei Tatsuya for setting up and hosting `www.projectmarianne.com`. That website is no longer active; but its historic pages have been preserved at the Internet Archive, thanks to the help of Brewster Kahle. In its heyday, visitors were presented with a login screen, but there was no way to get past that barrier. Helpful admonitions for the supposed users also appeared from time to time on that page, with phrases such as "Remember: Secrecy is key"; "Hard work reaps great rewards"; "Premature optimization is the root of all evil"; "Hush." On 1 April the message was "13 weeks till Demo Day."

Immediately after the lecture, Michael Plass suggested that the version number should be i (imaginary). Barbara Beeton pointed out that ITEX is an anagram of EXIT ...

Index

0-origin indexing, 25.
0^0, 582.
3:4:5 right triangles, 497–498.
3-coloring, 660.
3-dimensional documents, 709,
    710, 714.
3-dimensional dragon curves, 603,
    613.
3-dimensional knight, 489.
3-dimensional leaper graphs, 565,
    569.
3-dimensional printer, 709, 714.
3-dimensional scanner, 681, 709.
3-letter words, 124–125, 464.
4-letter words, 125–126, 250,
    415–420.
5-letter words, 415, 418–420,
    423–428.
    of the Stanford GraphBase,
        216, 404, 419, 422, 429–430,
        433–436.
32 (2^5), 42, 116, 257, 694, 696, 707.
64 (2^6), 9, 14, 69–72, 150, 257,
    691–692, 700.
90° rotation, 177, 492–494, 617.
666 (beast), 140, 151.
12509 (star-chain number), 148.
65536 (2^{16}), 42, 109, 121–123,
    146–148, 708.
$\aleph_0$, 148, 224.
$\aleph_1$, 148.
γ (Euler's constant), 144, 147.

λn ($\lfloor \lg n \rfloor$), 111, 115.
$\lambda^* n$, 111, 115, 117.
π (circle ratio), 2–3, 10, 17–18, 20,
    72, 141–143, 197, 669, 708.
ϕ (golden ratio), 91–92, 100–101,
    144, 197–198, 642–643, 680.
φ (totient function), 69, 152.

A Baby is Promised, 189–191.
AAAS (American Association for
    the Advancement of Science),
    672.
Aarts, Emile Hubertus Leonardus,
    687.
abstention flag, 53.
Academy of Recreational
    Mathematicians, 643.
ace of hearts, 62.
acrostic, ix, 705, *see also* telestich.
actinon, 402.
Adams, Don (= Donald James
    Yarmy), 154.
Adams, Richard George, 131.
Adams, William Wells, 101.
addition, double-double precision,
    47, 55–56.
addition chains, 148.
adjacency matrices, 524, 530.
Adobe Photoshop®, 121, 123.
Adobe Systems, 160, 708.
Advent, 189–191.
Adventure game, xii, 43, 176,
    235–394.

717

Scott, Dana Stewart, 439–442, 447, 449, 450, 453, 467–468.
Scrabble®, 419, 433–434, 436.
Sears, Richard Warren, 713.
second system syndrome, 707–714.
secondary columns, 458, 461, 463, 483.
security, 236, 708, 711.
Sedgewick, Linda Ann née Migneault, 669–670, 672.
Sedgewick, Robert, 669–672, 691–692.
Seeley, Cathy Lynn, 134, 153.
Segers, Lea, 702.
selection of bits, 42.
self-avoiding cycles, 473–481, 484-485, 607.
self-dual states, 525, 528.
self-intersecting paths, 457–459, 477, 490–502, 605.
semidefinite programming, 144.
Serre, Jean-Pierre, 120.
Severin, John Powers, 10, 17.
sewing machine, 676–677, 688, 696–698.
(SEX), 44.
sexist language, 172, 209.
SGB (Stanford GraphBase), 422, 697.
    five-letter words, 216, 404, 419, 422, 429–430, 433–436.
Shahn, Benjamin, 38.
Shallit, Jeffrey Outlaw, 101, 613, 706.
Shannon, Claude Elwood, Jr., 706.
Sharp, Cecil James, 37–38.
Sharp, Richard, 224.
Shatz, Stephen Sidney, 120.
Shaw, Christopher Joseph, 38.
sheep, 400, 419, 436, 633.
shepherds, 639.
Sheppard, Henry Fleetwood, 37.
Sherinyan, William Kerrigan, 124.
shields, 676–677.
shifting right, 43, 57, 92, 605.

shifty poems, 411–414, 635.
Shiokawa, Iekata, 102.
shirt, 677–678.
SHRDLU program, 430.
Shu Shu Chi I (= Shushu Jiyi), 116.
Shubik, Martin, 216.
Sierpiński, Wacław Franciszek, 694–695.
    gasket, 695.
silver bullets, 711.
Silverman, David L., 216.
similar representations, 579, 587.
Simonot, Edmé, 703.
simple cycles and paths, 483.
simple graphs, 145–146.
Simplified Spelling Board, 398.
sink vertex, 516.
skimperlink puzzles, 474–476.
slitherlink puzzles, 474–475.
Sloane, Neil James Alexander, 145–146, 159, 538.
Smale, Stephen, 134.
Smart, Maxwell (= Agent 86), 141.
Smith, Dave, 158.
smoke, black, 361.
    green, 384.
    orange, 370, 375.
Smurdley, Natures, 6, 11, 15, 17, 23.
Snook Walters, Alwilda, 630.
Snow, Charles Percy, 657.
Snyder, Don, 159.
software engineering, 711–712.
Soma cube, 467.
songs, 33–39, 183, 186–191, 645–648.
sorting machine, 200.
space complexity versus time complexity, 33, 39.
space-filling curves, 583, 595, 611.
spanning trees, 644.
SPARCstation 2 computer, 449.
spelling, simplified, 398.
Speziali, Pierre, 664–665.

𝕰𝕽𝕾 , 742.